THE R

MW00964573

MOROCCO

THE REAL GUIDES

REAL GUIDE CREDITS

Series Editor: Mark Ellingham
U.S. Text Editors: Herbie Festov and David Holden
Editorial: Martin Dunford, John Fisher, Jack Holland
Production: Susanne Hillen
Typesetting: Greg Ward and Mark Ellingham
Design: Andrew Oliver

Thanks

This *Real Guide* owes a great deal to those **readers** of previous British editions who took the trouble to write in with news and information, changes and additions. Thanks to all. In particular: Hamish Brown and Dan Eitzen for their contributions towards the hiking sections; Margaret Hubbard for the piece "From a Woman's Perspective," Jonathan Charteris-Black for his article on *moussems*; Andrew Gilchrist for filling in the gaps in the south; Martin Spafford for his efforts on the Figuig map; David Cocovini for the Telouet–Aït Benhaddou walk; Don Grisbrook and Lee Marshall for regular and generous correspondence; Manuel Dominguez and David Muddyman for the section on music; Nicky Lund, Matthew Tostevin, Julie Jones and Peter Obrenshaw, and Mike Easterbrook for their spot-on contributions; and—above all—Natania Jansz.

Thanks also to the many **Moroccan friends**, acquaintances, guides—everyone—who showed us around and shared knowledge and ideas. We hope this guide reflects a shared enthusiasm.

On the **production** front, thanks, as ever, to Susanne Hillen for keeping everything rolling, and to Greg Ward, not just for a fine typesetting job, but also a truly exquisite taste in music.

Small illustrations in Part One and Part Three by Ed Briant.

Grateful **acknowledgments** to Ecco Press and Farrar Straus and Giroux, respectively, for permission to reprint the pieces by Paul Bowles and Elias Canetti in the "Morocco in Literature" section.

Published by Prentice Hall Trade Division, A Division of Simon & Schuster Inc., 15 Columbus Circle, New York, NY 10023.

Typeset in Linotron Univers and Century Old Style.
Printed in the United States by R.R. Donnelley & Sons.

Library of Congress Cataloging-in-Publication Data

Ellingham, Mark
Morocco: The Real Guide / written and researched by Mark Ellingham and Shaun McVeigh; contributors: Andrew Gilchrist, Margaret Hubbard, Peter Morris, Dan Richardson, Hamish Brown, Dan Eitzen, Mañuel Dominguez, and David Muddyman; edited by Mark Ellingham.
432p Includes index.
Rev. ed. of Morocco: The Rough Guide (1985, 1987, 1988).
ISBN 0-13-783697-X : $12.95
1. Morocco—Description and Travel—Guidebooks. I McVeigh, Shaun. II Ellingham, Mark. Rough Guide to Morocco. III. Title.
DT304.E44 1989   89—16218
916.404'5—dc20   CIP

THE REAL GUIDE

MOROCCO

WRITTEN AND RESEARCHED BY

MARK ELLINGHAM and SHAUN McVEIGH

CONTRIBUTORS

Andrew Gilchrist, Margaret Hubbard, Peter Morris, Dan Richardson,
Hamish Brown, Dan Eitzen, Manuel Dominguez, and David Muddyman

Illustrations by Henry Iles

EDITED BY

MARK ELLINGHAM

PRENTICE HALL ■ NEW YORK

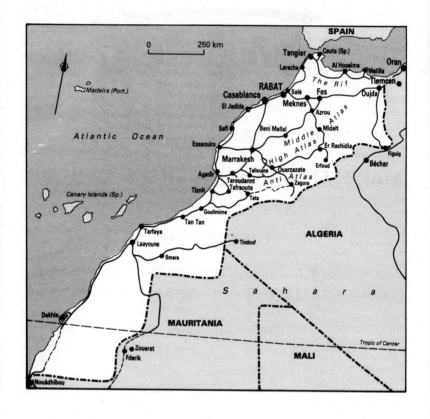

CONTENTS

Introduction viii

PART ONE   BASICS   1

Getting There: From the USA, From Canada (5), Via Britain (6), The Ferries (9) /
Red Tape and Extended Stays (10) / Costs and Money (11) / Health and Insurance (13) /
Information and Maps (15) / Guides—Official and Otherwise (16) / Getting Around (18) /
Driving in Morocco (20) / Sleeping (22) / *Hammams* (23) / Eating and Drinking (23) /
Communications: Mail, Phones, and Media (26) / *Kif* (27) /
Festivals: Ramadan, Holidays, and *Moussems* (28) / *Souks* and Moroccan Crafts (33)/
Mosques and Monuments (34) / From a Woman's Perspective (35) / Directory (38).

PART TWO   THE GUIDE   41

■ 1 TANGIER, TETOUAN, AND THE NORTHWEST 43

■ 2 THE RIF AND THE MEDITERRANEAN COAST 87

■ 3 FES, MEKNES, AND THE MIDDLE ATLAS 109

■ 4 THE WEST COAST; FROM RABAT TO ESSAOUIRA 177

■ 5 MARRAKESH AND THE HIGH ATLAS 224

■ 6 THE GREAT SOUTHERN ROUTES 289

■ 7 AGADIR, THE ANTI-ATLAS, AND THE DEEP SOUTH 322

PART THREE   CONTEXTS   359

The Historical Framework 361
Chronology 376
Islam in Morocco 378
Music 382
Morocco in Literature 388
Onward From Morocco 396
Books 398
Language 402
Moroccan Terms: A Glossary 407

Index 409
Map Index 416

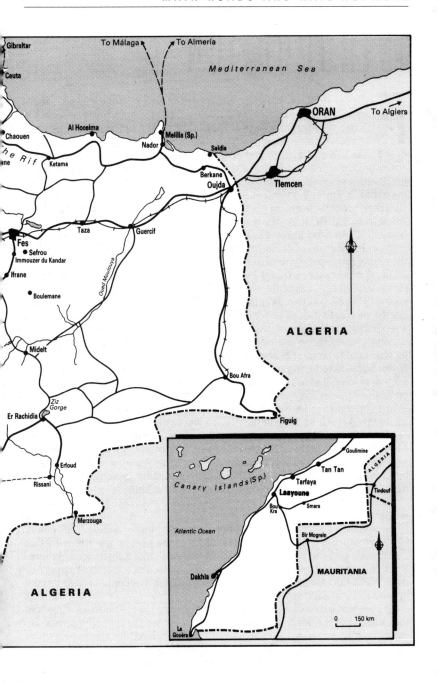

INTRODUCTION

For Westerners, **Morocco** holds an immediate and enduring fascination. Though just an hour's ride on the ferry from Spain, it seems at once very far from Europe, with a culture—Islamic and deeply traditional—that is almost wholly unfamiliar. Throughout the country, despite the years of French and Spanish colonial rule, and with modern and cosmopolitan cities like Rabat or Casablanca, a more distant past constantly makes its presence felt. **Fes**, perhaps the most beautiful of all Arab cities, maintains a life still rooted in medieval times, when a Moroccan empire stretched from Senegal to northern Spain; while in the mountains of the **Atlas** and the **Rif**, it is still possible to draw up tribal maps of the Berber population. As a backdrop to all this, the country's physical makeup is also extraordinary: from a Mediterranean coast, through four mountain ranges, to the empty sand and scrub of the Sahara.

All of which makes **travel** here an intense and rewarding—if not always easy—experience. Certainly, there can be problems in coming to terms with your privileged position as tourist in a nation that, for the most part, would regard such activities as being irrelevant. The northern cities especially have a reputation for hustlers: self-appointed guides whose eagerness to offer their services—and whose attitude to tourists as being a justifiable source of income (and to women as something much worse)—can be hard to deal with. If you find this to be too much of a struggle, then it would probably be better for you to keep just to resorts like Agadir, built very much in the image of its Spanish counterparts, and to packaged sightseeing tours.

But you'd miss a lot that way. Morocco is at its best well away from such trappings. A week's hiking in the Atlas; a journey through the southern oases or into the pre-Sahara; or leisured strolls around Tangier, Fes, or Marrakesh—once you adapt to a different way of life, all your time will be well spent. And it is difficult for any traveler to go for long without running into Morocco's equally powerful tradition of hospitality, generosity, and openness. This is a country people return to again and again.

Regions

Geographically, the country divides into five basic zones: the **coast**, Mediterranean and Atlantic; the great cities of the **plains**; the **Rif** and **Atlas** mountains; and the oases and desert of the **pre-** and fully-fledged **Sahara**. With two or three weeks—even two or three months—you can't expect to cover all of this, though it's easy enough (and highly recommended) to take in something of each aspect.

You are unlikely to miss the **mountains**, in any case. The three ranges of the Atlas, with the Rif a kind of extension in the north, cut right across the interior—physical and historical barriers, and inhabited for the most part by the indigenous Moroccan **Berbers**. Contrary to general preconceptions, it is actually the Berbers who make up most of the population; only around ten percent of Moroccans are "pure" Arabs, although with the shift to the industrialized cities, such distinctions are becoming less and less significant.

A more current distinction, perhaps, is the legacy of Morocco's colonial occupation over the fifty-odd years before it reasserted its independence in 1956. The colonized country was divided into **Spanish** and **French** zones— the former contained Tetouan and the Rif, the Mediterranean and the northern Atlantic coasts, and parts of the (now disputed) Sahara; the latter comprised the plains, the main cities (Fes, Marrakesh, Casablanca, and Rabat), as well as the Atlas. It was the French, who ruled their "protectorate" more closely, who had the most lasting effect on Moroccan culture, Europeanizing the cities to a strong degree and firmly imposing their language, spoken today by all educated Moroccans (after Moroccan Arabic or the local Berber languages).

Highlights

The attractions of the individual regions are discussed in the chapter introductions. Broadly speaking, **the coast** is best enjoyed in the north at **Tangier**, beautiful and still shaped by its old "international" port status; at **Larache**; or at **Saidia**, below the Rif; in the south at **El Jadida**; at **Essaouria**, perhaps the most relaxed resort; or at remote **Sidi Ifni. Agadir**, the main package tour resort, is less worthwhile—but it's still a functional base for exploration inland.

Inland, where the real interest of Morocco lies, the outstanding cities are **Fes** and **Marrakesh**. The great imperial capitals of the country's various dynasties, they are almost unique in the Arab world for the chance they offer to witness some city life that, in many patterns and appearance, remains in large part medieval. Fes, in terms of monuments, is the highlight, though Marrakesh, the "beginning of the south," is for most visitors the more enjoyable and exciting.

Travel in the **south**—roughly beyond a line drawn between Casablanca and Meknes—is, on the whole, more easygoing and relaxing than in the sometimes frenetic north. This is certainly true of the **mountain ranges**. The **Rif**, which can feel disturbingly anarchic, is really for hardened travelers; only **Chaouen**, on its periphery, could be counted a "vacation spot." But the **Atlas ranges** (Middle, High, and Anti-) are beautiful and accessible.

Hiking in the High Atlas, especially around North Africa's highest peak, **Djebel Toubkal**, is in fact something of a growth industry. Even if you are no more than a casual walker, it is worth considering, with summer treks possible at all levels of experience and altitude. And, despite inroads made by commercialization, it remains essentially "undiscovered"—like the Alps must have been in the last century.

Equally exploratory in mood are the great **southern routes** beyond—and across—the Atlas, amid the **oases** of the pre-Sahara. Major routes here can be traveled by bus; minor ones by rented car or local taxi; the really remote

Morocco's **area** of 710,000 sq km is nearly a fifth that of the United States. The **population**, over half of which is under 20 years of age, is around 20 million—a dramatic increase compared with just 8 million at Independence in 1956.

ones by four-wheel-drive vehicles or by getting lifts on local *camions* (trucks), sharing space with the market produce and livestock.

The oases, around **Tinerhir, Zagora,** and **Erfoud**, or, (for the committed) around **Tata** or **Figuig**, are classic images of the Arab world, vast palmeries stretching into desert horizons. Equally memorable is the architecture that they share with the Atlas—bizarre and fabulous mud (or *pisé*) **kasbahs** and **ksour**, with Gothic-looking turrets and multipatterned walls.

Climate

As far as the **climate** goes, it would be better to visit the south—or at least the desert routes—outside **midsummer**, when for most of the day it's far too hot for casual exploration, especially if you're dependent on public transportation. But July and August, the hottest months, can be wonderful on the coast and in the mountains; there are, in fact, no set rules.

Spring, which comes late by European standards (around April–May), is perhaps the best overall time, with a summer climate in the south and in the mountains, and water warm enough to swim in on both the Mediterranean and Atlantic coasts. **Winter** can be perfect by day in the south, though be warned that desert nights can get very cold—a major consideration if you're staying in the cheaper hotels, which rarely have heating. If you're planning to **hike** in the **mountains**, it's best to keep to April–October, unless you have some experience of snow conditions.

Weather conditions apart, the **Islamic religious calendar**, and its related festivals, will have the most seasonal effect on your travel. The most important factor is **Ramadan**, the month of daytime fasting; this can be a problem for transportation, and especially hiking, though the festive evenings do much to compensate. See "Festivals" in the *Basics* section following for details of its timing, as well as that of other festivals.

MOROCCO'S CLIMATE

Average Temperatures (°F)

	JAN	FEB	MAR	APR	MAY	JUN	JUL	AUG	SEP	OCT	NOV	DEC
AGADIR	69	70	72	75	76	78	80	79	79	78	76	69
AL HOCEIMA	61	62	65	67	72	78	83	85	81	74	69	63
CASABLANCA	63	63	66	68	72	75	81	81	80	77	68	64
ESSAOUIRA	64	64	64	66	68	68	72	70	70	70	68	66
FES	61	63	66	72	79	88	97	97	90	81	66	61
MARRAKESH	66	66	73	79	84	91	102	101	91	82	70	66
MEKNES	59	61	64	70	74	84	93	93	86	79	66	61
OUARZAZATE	63	67	73	80	86	96	102	100	91	80	70	62
RABAT	63	64	66	70	73	77	82	82	81	77	68	64
TANGIER	59	61	62	66	72	77	80	82	79	73	64	61
TAROUDANNT	72	73	79	81	86	90	99	100	95	90	77	72
ZAGORA	69	73	78	86	93	102	108	106	97	86	78	70

Note these are all very much average temperatures: Zagora often hits 120° F at midday in midsummer, whilst in the Rif and High Atlas mountains, winters can be literally freezing.

PART ONE

THE
BASICS

EVITEZ LA FATIGUE
ET LES RISQUES
D'UN LONG VOYAGE

Maroc

FAITES VOS CALCULS ET PRENEZ LE TRAIN.

GETTING THERE

Although there are direct flights from New York and Montreal to Casablanca, most North Americans travel to Morocco via Europe. Flights across the Atlantic to London, Paris or Madrid can be purchased with an add-on connection to a number of Moroccan destinations. Alternatively, if budget rather than time is your main concern, you can simply fly to Europe and buy a low-cost flight for yourself or, best of all, travel overland through Spain and cross over to Morocco on the ferry.

DIRECT FROM THE USA

Royal Air Maroc (*RAM*), the Moroccan national airline, operate direct flights to Casablanca from New York and Montreal. These can be bought in conjunction with one or more add-on flights to other Moroccan airports, or, if you are embarking on a trip across North Africa, with flights east to Tunisia or Egypt. Alternatives to the *RAM* routes include flights on **British Airways**, **Air France**, **KLM**, and **Iberia**. These offer a number of Moroccan destinations—Tangier, Casablanca, Marrakesh, and Agadir are the most common—routed through the airlines' respective hubs of London, Paris, Amsterdam, and Madrid. The American carriers **Pan Am** and **TWA** also have flights to Casablanca, transiting via Europe.

Student/youth discount fares are not particularly promising for direct flights, though **STN**, **CIEE**, and **Nouvelles Frontières** (see boxes for addresses) may turn up the occasional

budget fare to Casablanca. All three of these agencies, however, are likely to come up with much better deals on **flights to London, Paris or Madrid**. Given that the cheapest and most frequent flights to Morocco are from France, *Nouvelles Frontières* should probably be your first call if you are planning to vacation purely in Morocco. They should be able to fix up a low cost add-on fare to one or other of the Moroccan airports. Note that although *STA*, *CIEE*, and *Nouvelles Frontières* specialize in the student/youth market, they offer **low cost fares to all travelers**—irrespective of age or student status.

If you decide to make your own way to **Morocco via Britain**, you have a wide range of flights to London to choose from. Contact agents detailed overpage and check the Sunday travel supplements of the major newspapers. Reasonable targets for a return fare to London are around $300–500 from the East Coast, $600–800 from the West Coast or Central USA. Transportation from London to Morocco is covered in the section "Via Britain" following.

EAST COAST

Royal Air Maroc (☎800/344-6726) operates two flights a week from **New York to Casablanca**—the only regular direct flight from the U.S. to Morocco. Departures from New York are on Tuesdays and Saturdays. The high-season fare is $759 on Tuesday and $809 on Saturday. Shoulder period fares are $619 and $669, and low-season fares are $519 and $569. *RAM* offers a discount for persons under 24; the high-season discount fare is $536, making this one of the cheapest ways to get to Morocco direct.

At certain times of year, you may find direct **charter flights** to Morocco from the East Coast. Check the Sunday travel section of the New York Times and phone around. One company always worth a call for charters is *Access International* (☎800/333-7280).

The major European carriers, *British Airways* (☎687-1600), *Air France* (☎800/237-2747), *Iberia* (☎800/772-4642), and *KLM* (☎800/777-5553) have **scheduled flights to Morocco via Europe**. *KLM* flies from New York, Atlanta, and Orlando, via Amsterdam, to both Casablanca and Tangiers. *Iberia* flies from New York and Miami to Casablanca via Madrid. *British Airways* flies

CIEE IN THE U.S.

Head Office: 205 E. 42nd St., New York, NY 10017;
☎800/223-7401

CALIFORNIA
2511 Channing Way, Berkeley, CA 94704; ☎415/
848-8604
UCSD Student Center, B-023, La Jolla, CA 92093;
☎619/452-0630
5500 Atherton St., Suite 212, Long Beach, CA
90815; ☎213/598-3338
1093 Broxton Ave., Los Angeles, CA 90024; ☎213/
208-3551
4429 Cass St., San Diego, CA 92109; ☎619/270-
6401
312 Sutter St., San Francisco, CA 94108; ☎415/
421-3473
919 Irving St., San Francisco, CA 94122; ☎415/
566-6222
14515 Ventura Blvd., Suite 250, Sherman Oaks, CA
91403; ☎818/905-5777

GEORGIA
12 Park Place South, Atlanta, GA 30303; ☎404/
577-1678

ILLINOIS
29 E. Delaware Place, Chicago, IL 60611; ☎312/
951-0585

MASSACHUSETTS
79 South Pleasant St., 2nd Floor, Amherst, MA
01002; ☎413/256-1261

729 Boylston St., Suite 201, Boston, MA 02116;
☎617/266-1926
1384 Massachusetts Ave., Suite 206, Cambridge,
MA 02138; ☎617/497-1497

MINNESOTA
1501 University Ave. SE, Room 300, Minneapolis,
MN 55414; ☎612/379-2323

NEW YORK
35 W. 8th St., New York, NY 10011; ☎212/254-
2525
Student Center, 356 West 34th St., New York, NY
10001; ☎212/661-1450

OREGON
715SW Morrison, Suite 1020, Portland, OR 97205;
☎503/228-1900

RHODE ISLAND
171 Angell St., Suite 212, Providence, RI 02906;
☎401/331-5810

TEXAS
1904 Guadalupe St., Suite 6, Austin, TX 78705;
☎512/472-4931
The Executive Tower, 3300 W. Mockingbird, Suite
101, Dallas,TX 75235; ☎214/350-6166

WASHINGTON
1314 Northeast 43rd St., Suite 210, Seattle, WA
98105; ☎206/632-2448

STA IN THE U.S.

BOSTON
273 Newbury St., Boston, MA 02116; ☎617/266-
6014

HONOLULU
1831 S. King St., Suite 202, Honolulu, HI 96826;
☎808/942-7755

LOS ANGELES
920 Westwood Blvd., Los Angeles, CA 90024;
☎213/824-1574
7204 Melrose Ave., Los Angeles, CA 90046; ☎213/
934-8722

2500 Wilshire Blvd., Los Angeles, CA 90057;
☎213/380-2184

NEW YORK
17 E. 45th St., Suite 805, New York, NY 10017;
☎212/986-9470;☎ 800/777-0112

SAN DIEGO
6447 El Cajon Blvd., San Diego, CA 92115; ☎619/
286-1322

SAN FRANCISCO
166 Geary St., Suite 702, San Francisco, CA 94108;
☎415/391-8407

NOUVELLES FRONTIÈRES

In the United States
NEW YORK 19 W. 44th St., Suite 1702, New York,
NY 10036; ☎212/764-6494

LOS ANGELES 6363 Wilshire Blvd., Suite 200, Los
Angeles, CA 90048; ☎213/658-8955

SAN FRANCISCO 209 Post St., Suite 1121, San
Francisco, CA 94108; ☎415/781-4480

In Canada
MONTREAL 1130 ouest, bd de Maisonneuve,
Montréal, P.Q. H3A 1M8; ☎514/842-1450

QUEBEC 176 Grande Allée Ouest, Québec, P.Q.
G1R 2G9; ☎418/525-5255

via London to Casablanca, Tangier, and Agadir. APEX return fares from New York cost around $750 high season, $650 low season; for Miami or Orlando departures, add around $50.

TWA (☎800/221-2000) and *Pan Am* (☎800/ 221-111) also have scheduled flights to Casablanca, transiting via London.

WEST COAST
Scheduled flights to Morocco via Europe
from L.A. or San Francisco cost around $1000 for high season APEX, $900 low season with the main carriers. *Iberia* (☎800/772-4642) is often a bit cheaper than the opposition. Try phoning them, as well as *British Airways* (☎800/247-9297), *Pan Am* (☎800/211-1111), and *TWA* (☎800/484 9311, or ☎800/864-5731).

Agents worth contacting, in addition to *CIEE*, *STN*, and *Nouvelles Frontières*, include *Airkit* in L.A. (☎213/482-8778) or S.F. (☎415/764-4933). Check also the travel pages in the *L.A. Times* or the *San Francisco Chronicle*—either of which may produce the occasional charter or a good deal to London, Paris, or Madrid.

CENTRAL USA
Once again, it is worth spending a Sunday checking the **travel sections** of major newspapers, which can reveal a range of special offers to

Europe. On the whole, the cheaper flights involve transiting via New York.

For direct **flights to Europe**, with a **connecting flight to Morocco**, the lowest scheduled fares are *Iberia* from Chicago to Casablanca, via Madrid, or *KLM* from Chicago and Houston to Casablanca or Tangier, via Amsterdam. APEX fares on these cost around $950 high season, $850 low season.

DIRECT FROM CANADA

Royal Air Maroc (☎514/285-1435) has weekly scheduled flights **direct from Montreal to Casablanca**. Return *APEX* fares are around CDN $975, low season CDN$800.

For scheduled flights to **Morocco via Europe**, *KLM*, *Iberia*, and *Air France* are the most promising airlines. *KLM* and *Air France* fly from Toronto and Vancouver, *Iberia* from Montreal. APEX fares from Toronto and Montreal are around CDN$1000 high season, CDN$850 low season; from Vancouver, around CDN$1250 and CDN$850.

Shopping around the **travel agencies**, you may be able to get better prices. Good sources include *Travel CUTS* (known as *Voyages CUTS* in Québec) and *Nouvelles Frontières*, which both offer fares in the $700–800 range from Montreal. See boxes for addresses.

TRAVEL CUTS IN CANADA

Head Office: 187 College St., Toronto, Ontario M5T 1P7; ☎416/979-2406

ALBERTA
1708 12th St. NW, Calgary T2M 3M7; ☎403/282-7687. 10424A 118th Ave., Edmonton T6G 0P7; ☎403/471-8054

BRITISH COLUMBIA
Room 326, T.C., Student Rotunda, Simon Fraser University, Burnaby, British Columbia V5A 1S6; ☎604/291-1204. 1516 Duranleau St., Granville Island, Vancouver V6H 3S4; ☎604/689-2887. Student Union Building, University of British Columbia, Vancouver V6T 1W5; ☎604/228-6890 Student Union Building, University of Victoria, Victoria V8W 2Y2; ☎604/721-8352

MANITOBA
University Centre, University of Manitoba, Winnipeg R3T 2N2; ☎204/269-9530

NOVA SCOTIA
Student Union Building, Dalhousie University, Halifax B3H 4J2; ☎902/424-2054. 6139 South St., Halifax B3H 4J2; ☎902/424-7027

ONTARIO
University Centre, University of Guelph, Guelph N1G 2W1; ☎519/763-1660. Fourth Level Unicentre, Carleton University, Ottawa, K1S5B6; ☎613/238-5493. 60 Laurier Ave. E, Ottawa K1N 6N4; ☎613/238-8222. Student Street, Room G27, Laurentian University, Sudbury P3E 2C6; ☎705/673-1401. 96 Gerrard St. E, Toronto M5B 1G7; ☎ (416) 977-0441. University Shops Plaza, 170 University Ave. W, Waterloo N2L 3E9; ☎519/886-0400.

QUÉBEC (Known as *Voyages CUTS*)
Université McGill, 3480 rue McTavish, Montréal H3A 1X9; ☎514/398-0647. 1613 rue St. Denis, Montréal H2X 3K3; ☎514/843-8511. Université Concordia, Edifice Hall, Suite 643, S.G.W. Campus, 1455 bd de Maisonneuve Ouest, Montréal H3G 1M8; ☎514/288-1130. 19 rue Ste. Ursule, Québec G1R 4E1; ☎418/692-3971

SASKATCHEWAN
Place Riel Campus Centre, University of Saskatchewan, Saskatoon S7N 0W0; ☎306/343-1601

VIA BRITAIN

If you decide to transit via Britain, there's quite a wide range of travel routes available. Simplest, of course, is to fly to Morocco direct, either on a regular scheduled or charter flight. Alternatively, you can fly, or travel overland, to France, Spain, or Gibraltar, and pick up one of the ferries from there. Or, no bad option if you pick your company with care, there are several tour operators marketing all-inclusive vacations.

FLIGHTS

Flying to Morocco from Britain, you have the choice between direct flights—scheduled or on charters—or, for the cost-conscious, flying to Spain and making your way on from there (see "Ferries," following). The main problem with charters is time limitation. Most are for just one or two weeks. With a scheduled APEX flight you can normally stay for up to three months.

Scheduled flights are offered by *Royal Air Maroc* (from London Heathrow, Terminal 2) and *British Airways/GB Airways* (from London Gatwick). **Royal Air Maroc** (174 Regent St, London W1; ☎01/439-8854) flies several times a week direct to Tangier, Casablanca, Marrakesh and Agadir. APEX fares, booked two weeks in advance, cost around £150–200 ($240–320) to Tangier or Casablanca, £185–220 ($300–350) for Agadir or Marrakesh; flight times are around three hours to Tangier or Casablanca, five hours to Marrakesh or Agadir. **GB Airways**, part of *British Airways* (75 Regent Street, London W1; ☎01/439-9584), has a Tuesday flight to Casablanca (via Gibraltar) and a Friday flight to Casablanca via Tangier. Return fares are generally a bit cheaper than those of *RAM*. **From Gibraltar**, *GB Airways* have a daily flight to Tangier (Mon.–Fri.; $60 one way, $65 return), and a Tuesday flight to Casablanca. Reservations in Gibraltar through *Bland Ltd*, Cloister Building, Irish Town, Gibraltar 79200.

The main destinations for British **charter flights to Morocco** are **Tangier** in the north and **Agadir** in the south. The cheapest flights are almost always from London. Out of peak season times (July–Aug., Christmas, and Easter), you may find return flights to Tangier or Agadir falling as low as £100–120; in high season periods you should expect to pay £180–200, and you may have problems finding a seat.

Flights to Spain are usually easier to come by, coming down as low as £60–80 return if you strike lucky and are flexible with your plans. **Gibraltar**, with low-season scheduled flights at around £95 (summer and Christmas about £130) return, is also a good standby.

The best **sources for finding a flight** are the classified advertisements in the London weekly magazine *Time Out* or in the travel section of the *Sunday Times* newspaper. Among reliable **agents**, always worth a first call, are STA (74 Old Brompton Rd, London SW7; ☎01/581 8233) and USIT (52 Grosvenor Gardens, London SW1; 01 730 6525), both of which are student/youth travel specialists, but have a range of fares open to all. *Gibraltar Travel Ltd* (24 New Broadway, London W5; ☎01/579-0307) are specialists, as the name suggests, in Gibraltar flights.

Alternatively, contact one of the **Moroccan vacation specialists** in London. *CLM* (☎01/235-2110), *Morocco Bound* (☎01/734-5307), and *Moroccan Travel Bureau* (☎01/373-4411) will all book flights, with or without a vacation package.

BY TRAIN

London to Morocco by **train and ferry** will take the best part of three days travel. It's a great trip if you have the time to stop en route and take in something of France and Spain: Paris, the Pyrenees, Madrid, Córdoba, and Granada all lie pretty much on the route. However, unless you are under 26—the age qualification for discount BIJE tickets or rail passes—you will probably end up paying more than for a flight.

Standard rail tickets to Tangier, inclusive of the ferries en route, cost just under £200 ($320) return. They are available from any *British Rail* travel office, or from *Thomas Cook* and other major travel agents. For schedules contact the **British Railways** International Information Line (☎01/834-2345).

BIJE youth tickets discount standard rail prices by 20–35 percent. They are sold in Britain through **Eurotrain** (main office is *London Student Travel*, 52 Grosvenor Gardens, London SW1; ☎01/730-8111) and available at any youth/student travel agency. Tickets allow any number of stopovers along a pre-specified route and are valid on most European trains (some Express services have a surcharge). BIJE tickets to Europe are valid for two months, but with a Moroccan destination for six months. Return tickets from

HIKING, OVERLAND, AND SPECIALTY TOURS

There are some unusually imaginative **vacation packages** on offer to Morocco, including a range of small group hiking and overland tours, and specialist vacations. These are mostly organized by **British companies**. If you want to make reservations while in North America, most of them will be able to arrange a connecting flight to London, if required, through a North American agent.

Guerba, one of the best of the overland tour operators, are **represented in the USA** by *The Adventure Center* (5540 College Av., Oakland, CA 94618; ☎800/227-8747). *Call Step* (☎212/308-4249) are New York based African specialists, who feature Moroccan tours. Branches of *STN* in the USA (see box for addresses) can retail many of the hiking and overland tours.

HIKING TOURS

Sherpa Expeditions, 131a Heston Rd, Hounslow, Middlesex, TW5 0RD; ☎01/577-2717). Choice of four 15 day tours in the High Atlas (Toubkal area and little explored Mgoun Massif) and Djebel Sahro. Most treks are fine for any fit walker, though there is a strenuous Atlas High Peaks tour.

Exodus Expeditions, 9 Weir Rd, London SW12 0LT; ☎01/675-5550. Fifteen day High Atlas and Djebel Sahro treks.

Explore Worldwide, 7 High St, Aldershot, Hants; ☎0252/319-448. Fifteen day High Atlas treks, Anti-Atlas tour (with trekking), desert truck tours.

Note: High Atlas tours are offered in summer only; operators shift to Djebel Sahro or the Tafraoute region of the Anti-Atlas in winter.

OVERLAND EXPEDITION TOURS

Guerba, 101 Eden Vale Rd, Westbury, Wilts; ☎0373/826-611. Two week tours in customized trucks of the "Moroccan Deserts and Mountains," and "Deep South" (Anti Atlas region).

Encounter Overland (267 Old Brompton Rd, London SW5;☎01/ 370-6845. 15-day tour of Morocco including a trip up the Todra Gorge and on southern pistes, again in customized trucks.

Top Deck, 64-65 Kenway Rd, London SW5 (01 373 5095). General tours of Morocco and southern Spain in converted London double-decker buses. A younger clientèle than the two companies above.

MOROCCAN SPECIALISTS

CLM ("Morocco Made to Measure"), 4a William St, London SW1; ☎01/235-2110. Highly flexible and reliable agency, who will arrange flights (including US-London transfers) and personally planned tours and accommodation. These can include staying in private villas (and visiting the expatriate gardens) in Tangier; and touring the southern kasbahs with accommodation and rental car arranged. Upscale but value-for-money.

Best of Morocco, 100 Week St, Maidstone, Kent ME14 1RG; ☎0622/692-278. A similar service to CLM, with accommodation in quality hotels, and US transfers, arranged. They print a specialty brochure on golfing vacations in Morocco.

Morocco Bound, Suite 603, Triumph House, 189 Regent St, London W1; ☎01/734-5307. *Moroccan Travel Bureau*, 304 Old Brompton Rd, London SW5; 01 373-4411. Two regular package companies, with vacations to suit most wallets.

London, inclusive of ferries, cost £160 ($255) to Tangier, £170 ($270) to Casablanca.

Morocco is also covered on the **InterRail pass**. This costs £145 ($230) and allows one month's unlimited travel on trains in Europe and Morocco, plus half-price reductions on most ferries (including those from Algeciras to Tangier). In the country of purchase you get tickets at half price during the validity of the pass; as with BIJE tickets, express trains normally charge supplements. The problem for North Americans is that officially the pass is only available to those resident in Europe for at least six months. However, travel agencies are not always very strict about the residence condition, and previous entry stamps on your passport may well be judged good enough evidence. The pass

is available through youth/student travel agencies or through any British rail travel office. Hidden costs are occasional supplements, and 50 percent of the fares between the British station you set out at/return to and the channel ports.

Eurail passes are the American equivalent of InterRail. They are sold only in North America and they do not cover travel in Morocco itself—though they will get you down to the ferry at Algeciras in Spain. The under-26 Eurail Youthpass covers one month ($320) or two months ($420) of travel. If you're over 26, the regular Eurail Pass covers first class train travel for 15 days ($298), one month ($470), two months ($650), or three months ($798).

Train departures are from London's **Victoria Railway Station (Victoria tube).**

BY BUS

There are regular bus departures from London to Algeciras, where you can catch the ferry across to Tangier or Ceuta. However, the 48-hour journey is quite an endurance test and recommended only if you can find no alternative means of reaching Morocco.

The bus service is operated jointly by the British and Spanish companies, *Eurolines* and *Iberbus*. Departures are four times a week from April to September, two a week for the rest of the year. London to Algeciras costs £125 return, £70 one way; there is a 10 percent reduction for students or anyone under 26. For details contact **Eurolines** (52 Grosvenor Gardens, Victoria, London SW1; ☎01/730 0202) or any *National Express* office in Britain.

Bus departures are from London's **Victoria Coach Station** (Victoria tube).

DRIVING

If you plan to **drive down to Morocco through Spain and France**, you'll want to set aside at least four days for the journey. The buses detailed above cover the route in 48 hours but they are more or less non stop, with two drivers and just a few short meal breaks.

There are **car ferries** across to Morocco from Spain at Almería and Málaga (to Melilla), and at Algeciras (to Ceuta or Tangier). Ferries also sail to Tangier and (June-Sept. only) Nador from Sète in France, though these departures tend to be booked far in advance. Details from *Continental Shipping & Travel*, 179 Piccadilly, London W1 (☎01/491 4968).

The most direct **route** to drive is:
London–Dover/Folkestone (channel ferry to Calais/Boulogne); Calais/Boulogne–Paris–Tours–Poitiers–Bordeaux–Bayonne; San Sebastian–Madrid–Jaén/Córdoba; then either Jaén–**Almería**, Córdoba–**Málaga**, or Córdoba–**Algeciras**.
However, there is much to be said for getting off at least some of the main routes in France, and exploring the countryside.

Alternatively, if you are not interested in (or don't have the time for) the French section of the route, it is possible to travel by **car ferry from Plymouth** in England to **Santander** in northern Spain. This ferry runs twice weekly most of the year (no sailings in January); for details and prices phone *Brittany Ferries* in Plymouth (☎0752/21321).

If you are taking your own car to Morocco you must take out **Green Card Insurance** (available from insurance companies, or the AA/RAC motoring clubs) for the trip down through Europe. In Morocco you need to take out additional "Frontier Insurance;" see p.20.

Entering Morocco, you will need to present your vehicle registration document, which must be in your name—or accompanied by a letter from the registered owner. Caravans (trailers) need temporary importation documents, which are obtainable at the frontier for no charge. Some visitors choose to tip at the frontier, leaving a note in their passport, or engage the services of a tout to get through quickly. A matter of taste. Entering Morocco through Ceuta or Melilla (the most economic crossings for vehicles, see "The Ferries") try to avoid, if possible, arriving on weekends. If there are any problems, you may well be sent back to Ceuta or Melilla to wait until the Monday to sort them out.

North American **driving licenses** are recognized and valid in Morocco, though for Europe as a whole, an International Driving License ($7 from AAA) is a worthwhile investment. The **minimum age** for driving in Morocco is 21 years.

HITCHING

Hitching down to Morocco **through France and Spain**, it's worth buying a bus ticket to cover the first part of the journey. You will, in any case, have to pay for a channel ferry ticket, and buses from London to French cities such as Rouen or Tours don't add significantly to that cost, at around £50 ($80) round-trip. You could easily spend a lot of time (and money, on food and accommodation) hitching out of London or the French channel ports. Worst place of all to hitch, however, is Paris; people can wait days on the roads out of the city—don't try it!

Once south of Paris, getting rides becomes a little easier, and in Spain the hitching situation is reasonably good. Harassment, however, is more overt in Spain—and hitching there is not recommended for women traveling alone.

Hitching **back from Morocco**, starting at the car ferry in **Ceuta** is by far your best bet. It's quite possible you'll get a lift the whole way back to Britain from there. Other useful points to ask around are the campsites at **Meknes** and **Martil** (near Tetouan), both traditional last stops.

See "Driving" above, for an outline of the routes.

THE FERRIES

Crossing by **ferry to Morocco**—sailing from Europe to Africa—is the most satisfying (and apt) way to arrive in the country. From Spain the trip is not a long one: just a couple of hours by ferry from Algeciras, or as little as half an hour by hydrofoil.

Your main choice is deciding which port to arrive at. Most overland travelers cross to either Ceuta or Tangier. **Ceuta** is a cheaper crossing—considerably so for cars—but time consuming, as it's a Spanish enclave, so you still need to get to the border and cross into Morocco. **Tangier** is more straightforward, as well as better placed, at the beginning of the railroad, for transportation on. The longer crossings from Málaga and Almería to **Melilla** and **Nador** can be useful for drivers, cutting out part of the journey through Spain.

● On all the ferries you must complete a **disembarkation form** and have your passport stamped—*before arrival*—at the purser's office. Announcements to this effect are not always made in English. If you don't have a stamp, you'll have to wait until everyone else has cleared frontier and customs controls, before being attended to.

● The **ferries to Ceuta, Tangier, and Melilla** are booked solid for three to five days from the beginning of August, and **from those ports to Spain** during the last three to five days of August. This is the holiday month for Moroccans working in France, Belgium and Holland, and traveling back to Morocco by car.

● **Hydrofoils** are often block-reserved for tour groups, so at all times of year reservations are advisable.

FERRIES

Algeciras–Tangier 3–4 crossings daily in summer, 1–2 daily in winter. Passenger $22, small car $55; 2 hr. 30 min.
Algeciras–Ceuta 12 crossings daily in summer; 6–8 out. Passenger $10, small car $40; 1 hr. 20 min.
Tickets for Tangier and Ceuta ferries can be bought from any of the agents in Algeciras (there are dozens along the front and the road into the city from Málaga) or from the ferry terminal building.

Málaga–Melilla, Almería–Melilla 1–3 crossings daily, except Sun., from each port in spring/summer; 4–5 a week in winter. Passenger $16, small car $52; 6–7 hr.

*Both ferries are operated by **Transmediterranea**; tickets are available through Spanish travel agencies or at embarkation points. Melilla, like Ceuta a Spanish enclave, is well poised for traveling to Taza and Fes—or Algeria.*

Sète–Tangier 3 crossings a week in summer, 1 a week in winter; 36 hr.
Sète–Nador 1 crossing a week, June–Sept. only; 38 hr.
*Reservations well in advance are essential for Sète ferries—in summer boats are fully booked months ahead. Information and tickets: **SNCM**, 4 Quai d'Alger, Sète (☎67.74.70.55).*

Las Palmas (Canary Islands)–Agadir 1 crossing a week, Jan.–June. Ferry departs 5pm, arriving Thurs. 11am. Passengers $45 per person in a shared 4-bed cabin; small cars (up to 13 ft) $80. Operated by *Comanov*.

HYDROFOILS

Algeciras–Ceuta 4–5 crossings daily, except Sun. (no boats); mid-Mar. to mid-Sept. only. Passenger $16; 30 min.
Algeciras–Tangier 1 crossing daily, except Sun.; mid-Mar. to mid-Sept. only. Passenger $25. 1 hr.
Tarifa–Tangier 3 crossings daily , except Sunday, in season; 1 crossing daily out of season. Passenger $25; 30 min.
*All the hydrofoils are operated by **Transtour** (☎956/665200) and do not run in rough weather. Tickets can be bought either at points of embarkation or in advance from Spanish travel agencies— a good idea, since departures are often block-reserved by tour groups. Tarifa is 40 min. by bus from Algeciras (buses leave regularly, up until around 7pm, from the main bus station, back from the seafront by the Hotel Octavio), and is a pleasant little town to stay the night en route.*

CATAMARANS

Gibraltar–Tangier Daily (except Thurs. and Sat.) in season; 3–4 a week out of season; service usually suspended in February. Passenger $28 one way, $45 round-trip; 2 hr.
Gibraltar–M'diq Every Thursday, mid-Mar. to mid-Sept. Passenger $25; 1 hr. 30 min.
*The Gibraltar catamaran, which has replaced the regular ferry, is notoriously unreliable. It doesn't run in rough weather, and frequently breaks down. It is operated by **Seagle Ltd**, 9b George's Lane, Gibraltar; ☎71415, or 76763.*

RED TAPE AND EXTENDED STAYS

U.S. and Canadian citizens need only a valid passport for entry to Morocco, and can stay for up to 90 days. If transiting via Tunisia and Algeria, or France, however, you will need visas for a stay in those countries.

In theory (though not, it seems, in practice) entry to Morocco is refused to anyone with an **Israeli** or **South African** stamp in their passport. If this applies to you, a replacement passport might be worth obtaining. When entering the country, formalities are fairly straightforward, though you will have to fill in a form stating personal details, purpose of visit, and your **profession**. In recent years, Moroccan authorities have shown an occasional reluctance to allow in those who categorize themselves as "journalist." An alternative profession on the form might be wise. Hippies, too, engender official disfavor. Very long hair is best discreetly tied.

Note: Items such as **electronic equipment and video cameras** are entered on your passport. If you lose them during your visit, they will be assumed "sold" when you come to leave and (unless you have police documentation of theft) you will have to pay 100 percent duty.

VISA EXTENSIONS

To **extend your stay** in Morocco you should—officially—apply to the *Bureau des Etrangers* in the nearest main town for a residents permit (see below). This is, however, a very complicated procedure and it is usually possible to get around the bureaucracy by simply leaving Morocco for a couple of days when your three months is up. If you decide to try this—and it is not foolproof—it is best to at least make a trip of a few days outside Morocco, to Algeria or Spain, and, ideally, to reenter the country at a different port.

OFFICIAL BUSINESS

Extending a stay officially involves opening a bank account in Morocco (a couple of day's procedure in itself), and obtaining an *Attestation de Residence* from your hotel, campground, or landlord. You will need a minimum of 14,000dh ($1550) deposited in your bank account before making an application.

Once you have got through these two stages, you will need to go to the **Bureau des Etrangers** equipped with: your passport; seven passport photos; two copies of the *Attestation de Residence*, two copies of your bank statement (*d'Accompt au Banc*); and a 60dh stamp (available from any Tabac). If the police are not too busy, they'll give you a form to fill out in duplicate, and, some weeks later, you should receive a plastic-coated permit with your photo laminated in.

For anyone contemplating this labyrinthine operation, the *Bureau des Etrangers* in Agadir is perhaps the simplest place to approach, since a number of expatriates live in the city and banking facilities there (try the *Banque Populaire*) are fairly efficient. The *Bureau* is located behind the fire station on the Rue du 18 Novembre.

MOROCCAN CONSULATES ABROAD

New York: 437 Fifth Ave., 39th Floor, New York NY 10016; ☎212/758-2625.

Washington D.C.: 1601 21st Street, NW Washington D.C. 20009; ☎202/462-7979.

Montreal: 1010 Sherbrook W. Montreal PQ 113A 2R7; ☎514/288-8750.

London, England: 40 Queens Gate Gardens, London SW7; ☎01/584-8827.

Málaga, Spain: Av. de Andalucia 63, Málaga; ☎952/329962.

COSTS AND MONEY

Once you've arrived, Morocco is an inexpensive and excellent value destination. Costs for food, accommodation, and travel, are very low by North American standards, and the dollar is at its highest level for some years against the Moroccan dirham. If you stay in the cheaper hotels (or camp out), eat local food, and share expenses and rooms with another person, $75 a week would be enough to survive on. On $120 to $150 you could actually live pretty well, and with $350 to $400 a week between two people, you would be approaching luxury.

SOME BASIC COSTS

Accommodation costs range from little over $2 a night in a basic, unclassified hotel to $200 a night in the country's half dozen luxury palaces. On a limited budget, you can expect to get a decent double room in a one- or two-star hotel for around $10–15. The occasional splurge in a four-star hotel, with a pool, will cost around $40 for a double room.

The price of a **meal** reflects a similar span, but the basic Moroccan staple of soup (usually the bean-based *harira*), brochettes, and dates can be had in a local café for around $1.50–2.50. More substantial Moroccan meals can be had for $4–5 and European-style meals in restaurants from around $8. **Drinks** are really the only things that compare unfavorably with North American (or European) prices: a bottle of Moroccan wine costs upwards of $6 and a small glass of beer at least $1.50—considerably more in the fancy

hotels, sometimes the only places in a city that serve alcohol.

Beyond accommodation and food, your only major outlay will be for **transportation**— expensive if you're renting a car ($300 a week plus gas), but pretty reasonable if you use the local trains, buses, and collective taxis. The 475km trip from Fes to Marrakesh, for instance, costs around $15 by bus, or perhaps $20 if you use the faster collective taxis.

REGIONAL VARIATIONS

To some extent, all of these costs are affected by **where you are and when**. Inevitably, the big **cities** and tourist **regions** (Agadir especially) are going to be more expensive, and bottom-line hotel prices here can get up to around $10 a night for a double. In more **remote parts** of the country, too, where all goods have to be brought in from some distance away and where transportation (often only trucks or Land Rovers) has to be negotiated, prices can be even steeper; this is particularly true of the popular hiking region of Mount Toubkal.

HIDDEN COSTS

Hidden costs in Morocco are twofold. The most obvious, perhaps, is that you'll almost certainly end up buying a few things. Moroccan **crafts** are very much a part of the fabric of the towns and cities, with their labyrinthine areas of *souks* (markets). Rugs, blankets, leather, and jewelry are all outstanding—and few travelers leave without at least one of these items.

A harder aspect to come to terms with is that you'll be confronting real **poverty**. As a tourist, you're not going to solve any great problems, but with a laborer's wages at around 3 dirhams (35c) an hour, and an unemployment rate in excess of 25 percent, even a small tip to a guide can make a lot of difference to individual family life. For Moroccans, giving money and goods is a natural function—and a requirement of Islam. For tourists, rich by definition, local poverty demands at least some response.

CURRENCY

Morocco's basic unit of **currency** is the **dirham** (dh). The curency is not quoted on international money markets, a rate being set instead by the

Moroccan government. At present, a dollar buys just over 9 dirhams—almost 25 percent more than it did three or four years back.

The dirham is divided into 100 **centimes** (5-, 10-, and 20-centime coins are in circulation), and in markets you may well find prices written or expressed in centimes rather than dirhams. Confusingly, centimes may also be referred to as *francs* or, in former Spanish zones of the country, as *pesetas*. And you may also hear prices quoted in **rials**, or *reales*. In most parts of the country a dirham is considered to be 20 *rials*, though in Tangier and the Rif there are just 2 *rials* to the dirham. These are forms of expression only, however. There are no actual physical Moroccan *rials*, *francs*, or *pesetas*.

It is possible to buy a small amount of dirhams at the bank exchange desks in the Algeciras ferry terminal, but the currency is basically **not exchangeable outside Morocco**, and there are, in any case, regulations against taking dirhams out of the country. When you're nearing the end of your stay, it's best to get down to as little Moroccan money as possible.

CARRYING YOUR MONEY

Arriving in Morocco it is useful to have at least two day's survival money in **cash**. U.S. dollars, English pounds, French francs, or Spanish pesetas are easy to exchange. If you are coming from Britain, beware that Scottish currency is not accepted in any Moroccan banks. The rest of your money should, ideally, be spread around various different forms—travelers' checks and plastic—for the sake of security.

Travelers' checks and cash are easily exchanged at most Moroccan banks, and at some hotels, travel agencies, and tourists shops. **VISA** and **MasterCard** can also be used to obtain cash at some banks (see below), as well as in payment at the more upscale hotels, restaurants, and tourist stores, or for car rental. Using credit cards, especially for car rental, you may be asked to pay the card's 6 percent commission. If so, it's always worth bargaining—a compromise can usually be arrived at.

BANKS AND EXCHANGE

For exchange, by far the most useful and efficient chain of banks is the **BMCE** (*Banque Marocaine du Commerce Exterieur*). There is at least one BMCE in all major cities and in some smaller

towns (see listings in the text of the guide) and they stay open every day, including weekends, from 8am to 8pm.. They handle travelers' checks and give cash advances on *VISA* and *MasterCard*, as well as currency exchange.

The **BMCE** and **Banque Credit du Maroc** also handle *VISA*. Other banks don't often have facilities for credit-card transactions, despite the stickers in their windows, though most will exchange cash or travelers' checks. If you are traveling in the south, where often the *Banque Populaire* alone is represented, don't expect to be able to use credit cards outside the few principal cities. **Hours** for banks other than the *BMCE* are normally Monday to Friday, 8:30 to 11:30am and 3 to 4:30pm; during Ramadan (see "Festivals"), 8:30am to 2pm.

Commission is not generally charged on exchange, though some branches of the *Banque Populaire* seem to make a charge of 40dh per transaction (irrespective of the amount exchanged).

Banks tend to take quite a while to exchange money, with customers generally filling in forms at one desk, then joining a second line for the cashier. **Allow an hour** for a transaction in most banks, more if you need to draw cash on a credit card. Cashing travelers' checks, you may be asked to produce the receipts for purchase.

AMERICAN EXPRESS

American Express is represented by the **Voyages Schwarz** agencies in Tangier, Casablanca, Marrakesh, and Agadir. Their agency in Rabat is at present closed, though it is scheduled to reopen in the Hyatt Regency hotel. Not all American Express services are available. Voyages Schwartz can cash and issue *AmEx* travelers' checks, and hold clients' mail, but they cannot cash personal checks or receive wired money.

Addresses are:

TANGIER: *Voyages Schwartz*, 54 Bd. Pasteur; ☎334.59.

CASABLANCA: *Voyages Schwartz*, 112 Av. du Prince Moulay Abdallah; ☎27.80.54.

MARRAKESH: *Voyages Schwartz*, Rue Mauritania; ☎328.31.

AGADIR: *Voyages Schwartz*, Av. Hassan II; ☎228.94.

Most of the offices are open Monday to Friday 8:30am to 12:30 and 3 to 6pm, though banking services are sometimes mornings only.

EMERGENCY CASH

Access to an **emergency source** of money—whether it be a credit card or an arrangement with your bank or family to wire you money after a phone call—is reassuring and may prove invaluable.

Despite the number of travelers' stories, very few people lose (or are conned out of) all their money in Morocco—but it does happen. As a last resort, your **consulate** could lend you the funds to return home or help you get money cabled to you. See Tangier and Casablanca listings for addresses.

HEALTH AND INSURANCE

For most minor health complaints, a visit to a *pharmacie* is likely to be sufficient. Moroccan pharmacists are well trained and dispense a wide range of drugs, including many normally on prescription in North America. If they feel you need a full diagnosis, they can usually recommend a doctor—sometimes working on the premises. A list of English and French speaking doctors in major cities can also be obtained from consulates, large hotels, and the tourist offices.

If you need **hospital treatment**, you should contact your consulate at once and follow their advice. If you are near a major city, reasonable treatment may be available locally. Morocco, however, is no country in which to fall seriously ill.

INOCULATIONS

There are no **inoculations** officially required of travelers, although you should always be up-to-date with polio and tetanus. Typhoid and cholera are widespread, so a shot against these is worthwhile—although some American doctors doubt the effectiveness of the cholera shot. **Malaria**

pills (preferably *Chloroquine* taken weekly) are advisable if you're traveling in the south. **Gamma-globulin** is advised by some doctors as protection against hepatitis.

For up-to-date **health information**, contact the *Center for Disease Control* in Atlanta (☎404/639-3311), stating the area(s) you plan to travel.

WATER AND HEALTH HAZARDS

The **tap water** in northern Morocco is generally safe to drink (in Chaouen it is pumped straight from a well), though in the south it's best to stick to bottled mineral water.

A more serious problem in the south is that most of the **river valleys and oases** are said to be infected with **bilharzia**, so avoidance of all contact with oasis water is a wise precaution. Care should be taken, too, with drinking water from **mountain streams**. In areas where there is livestock upstream, **giardiasis** is prevalent. Use of water purification tablets and boiling any drinking or cooking water are wise precautions.

DIARRHEA

At some stage in your Moroccan travels, it is likely that you will get **diarrhea**. The local cure for this is *Imodium*, available over the counter at pharmacies. You can also counteract diarrhea by adapting your diet. Yoghurt is an effective stomach settler, and cactus fruit (widely available in summer) are good, too.

OTHER HAZARDS

There are few natural hazards in northern Morocco, whose wildlife is not far different to that of Mediterranean Europe. If you venture into the Sahara, however, be aware of the very real dangers of a bite from a **snake, palm rat**, or **scorpion**. Several of the Saharan snakes are deadly, as is the palm rat. Bites should be treated as medical emergencies.

AIDS

Moroccan cities such as Tangier and Marrakesh have a reputation as gay resorts—diminished these days, but still evident. There is very little awareness of AIDS (or *SIDA*, as it is called in French), although the Health Ministry has been represented at recent AIDS conferences. At present, official statistics of AIDS sufferers in Morocco are only just in double figures, but if the European experience is anything to go by, they are likely to rise quickly.

As throughout the world, extreme caution, and safe sex, cannot be overstressed.

INSURANCE

Travel insurance can buy you peace of mind as well as save you money. Before you purchase any insurance, however, check what you have already, whether as part of a family or student policy. You may find yourself covered for medical expenses and loss, and possibly loss of or damage to valuables, while abroad.

For example, **Canadians** are usually covered for medical expenses by their provincial health plans (but may only be reimbursed after the fact). Holders of **ISIC** cards are entitled to $2000 worth of accident coverage and 60 days ($100 per diem) of hospital in--patient benefits for the period during which the card is valid. University **students** will often find that their student health coverage extends for one term beyond the date of last enrollment.

Bank and charge **accounts** (particularly *American Express*) often have certain levels of medical or other insurance included. **Homeowners' or renters'** insurance may cover theft or loss of documents, money, and valuables while overseas, though exact conditions and maximum amounts vary from company to company.

SPECIALIST INSURANCE

Only after exhausting the possibilities above might you want to contact a **specialist travel insurance** company; your travel agent can usually recommend one—*Travelguard* and *The Travelers* are good policies.

Travel insurance offerings are quite comprehensive, anticipating everything from charter companies going bankrupt to delayed (as well as lost) baggage, by way of sundry illnesses and accidents. **Premiums** vary widely—from the very reasonable ones offered primarily through student/youth agencies (though available to anyone), to those so expensive that the cost for two or three months of coverage will probably equal the cost of the worst possible combination of disasters.

A most important thing to keep in mind——and a source of major disappointment to would be claimants—is that *none* of the currently available policies insure against **theft** of anything while overseas. North American travel policies apply only to items lost from, or damaged in, the custody of an identifiable, responsible third party, i.e. hotel porter, airline, luggage consignment, etc. Even in these cases you will still have to contact the local police to have a complete report made out so that your insurer can process the claim.

BRITISH POLICIES

If you are **transiting through Britain**, policies there cost considerably less (under £20/$32 for a month) and include routine cover for theft. You can take out a British policy at almost any travel agency or major bank; check agencies detailed in the "Getting There" section for addresses. ISIS, a "student" policy but open to everyone, is reliable and fairly good value; it is operated by a company called *Endsleigh*, and is available through any student/youth travel agency.

REIMBURSEMENT

All insurance policies—American or British—work by **reimbursing you** once you return home, so be sure to keep all your receipts from doctors and pharmacists. Any thefts should immediately be reported to the nearest police station and a police report obtained; no report, no refund.

If you have had to undergo serious medical treatment, with major hospital bills, contact your consulate. They can normally arrange for an insurance company, or possibly relatives, to cover the fees, pending a claim.

INFORMATION AND MAPS

Besides this book, the most readily available (and obvious) sources of information on Morocco are the country's tourist board (the *ONMT*), its offices and *Syndicats d'Initiatives* located throughout Morocco, and local, often self-appointed, guides (see the section following).

TOURIST OFFICES

The **ONMT** maintains general information offices in several North American cities, where you can pick up various pamphlets and lists. The most useful of these—indeed, the one thing really worth getting there—is the complete **list of offi-**

ONMT OFFICES ABROAD

USA

New York: 20 46th Street, Suite 1201 N.Y. N.Y. 10107; ☎212/557-2520.

Chicago: 6 South Michigan Ave., Chicago, IL 60603; ☎312/782-3413.

Los Angeles: 421 N.Rodeo drive Apt T7, L.A. Ca. 90010; ☎ 213/271-8939

Florida: Epcot Center, P.O. Box 22663. Lake Buena Vista, Orlando, Fla. ☎407/827-5337.

CANADA

Montreal: 114 Place Bonaventure, Post Box 751, Montreal, Quebec; ☎878-9536 or 878-9537.

UK

London: 174 Regent St. W1; ☎01/437-0013 or 437-0074.

---

cially rated hotels, along with an up-to-date sheet listing the maximum hotel rates. We've included numerous small hotels in this book that aren't classified in the *ONMT* book, and many more that are, but there might be times when you'll find it useful to check on facilities.

It is also worth picking up the *ONMT*'s series of **pamphlets** on **Tangier, Rabat-Salé, Casablanca, Fes, Marrakesh,** and **Agadir**. Each has large and colorful maps printed on the reverse; the maps in this guide are generally more functional, but these are bigger and often cover a wider area, so they are useful complements.

In Morocco itself, there's either a **Syndicat** or **ONMT** office in all towns of any size or interest—often both; their addresses are detailed in the relevant sections of the guide. Occasionally, these offices can supply you with particular local information sheets and they can of course try to help you out with specific questions. Their main use, though, is to get you in touch with an officially recognized guide.

MAPS

Maps of Moroccan **cities**, beyond those we've printed and the ones you can get for free from the ONMT, are not particularly worthwhile. The most authoritative series, the **Plan-Guides** published by *Editions Gauthey*, look impressive but are next to useless once you're trying to find your way around the lanes of a Medina.

What you will probably want, though, is a good **road map**. The best are those published by *Michelin* (1:1,000,000; sheet 169; generally the most accurate); *Kummerley & Frey* (1:1,000,000), and *Hildebrand* (1:900,000; new and very clear)

Note that maps (or guidebooks) which do not show the former Spanish Sahara as Moroccan are liable to confiscation. Even maps showing a reduced scale version of the territory can be confiscated. The former British edition of this guide was stopped from sale in Morocco due to its maps—this one should be acceptable—as was the old Michelin guide.

TOPOGRAPHIC MAPS FOR HIKING

The Moroccan government periodically clamps down on distribution of **topographic maps**—which are, of course, invaluable to hikers. At present, the policy is that no such maps are available, even the 1:50,000 sheet covering Djebel Toubkal, the country's major hiking destination.

If you have plans to hike, it is well worth a phone call to **specialist map outlets** in North America before you leave, in case they have old stock. If you are passing through London, check *Stanford's* (12-14 Long Acre, London WC2E 9LP; ☎01/836-1321). In Morocco you may be able to pick up a map of Toubkal on the spot in Imlil, the trailhead for hikes in the area.

In addition to the official Moroccan survey maps, you may be able to find a French satellite-generated 1:100,000 map of *Toubkal/Sirwa* (Editions Astrolabe), and *SMH* (21 Carlin Craig, Kinghorn, Fife, KY3 9RX, Scotland) produce a short map-guide to the Asni-Toubkal area.

Other, more **detailed hiking guides** are also available in both English and French. The most

useful are Michael Peyron's *Grand Atlas Traverse* and Robin Collomb's *Atlas Mountains*, both published in Britain by West Col (Available from specialist travel/hiking stores, or by mail, price £10.95 plus postage, from West Col Productions, Goring, Reading, RG8 9AA, England). A guide to the Atlas Mountains is also forthcoming from another British hiking publisher, Cicerone Press.

If you are **stopping over in London en route**, you might want to consult some of the Expedition Reports at the **Royal Geographical Society** (1 Kensington Gore, London SW7); the RGS's *Expeditionary Advisory Centre* (☎01/581-2057) will help locate relevant material, maps, and reports. The **Alpine Club Library** (74 South Audley Street, London W1Y 5FF; ☎01/499-1542) also has useful reference works; open Tues.–Fri., 9am–5pm.

GUIDES—OFFICIAL AND OTHERWISE

The question of whether to employ a guide will be one of your first (and most frequent) decisions in Morocco. With tourism so important a part of the economy, guiding has become quite a business—especially in the major cities of Fes and Marrakesh. In addition to the guides trained by the government, there are scores of young Moroccans offering their services to show you around the *souks* **(markets) and sights. The "unofficial guides" are not, strictly, legal, and there are occasional crackdowns by the police on offenders. However, they remain very much a factor of tourist life.**

With all guides, it is important to establish what you want to see. You may well find it useful to agree an intinerary in advance—perhaps showing your guide the points you want to visit on the maps in this book. Do not be pushed into a tour of the craft stores—where your guide will be looking for commission on purchases—or you will see nothing else. If you do want to visit stores, make it clear what kind of goods you are interested in seeing, and equally clear that you do not want to purchase on an initial visit.

OFFICIAL GUIDES

Official guides, engaged through tourist offices (or some of the larger hotels), are paid at a fixed rate for either a half or a full day—respectively 30dh ($3.35) and 50dh ($5.50). The rate is for the

guide's time, and can be shared by a group of people—though obviously the latter would be expected to make some additional tip.

Taking an introductory tour of a new city with an official guide can be a useful exercise in orientation—especially in the vast Medinas (old quarters) of Fes and Marrakesh. Your guide may well be an interesting and entertaining presence, too. Some are highly knowledgable. There is an advantage also in that, if you are accompanied by an official guide, you won't be approached or hassled by any of their (sometimes less than reputable) unauthorized equivalents.

Official guides can identify themselves by a large, brass "sheriff's badge" issued by the *ONMT*.

UNOFFICIAL GUIDES AND HUSTLERS

Unofficial guides will approach you in the streets of any sizable town, offering to find you a hotel, show you the sights, or perhaps, if you look a likely customer, sell you some *kif* (hashish). You will need to develop a strategy to deal with these approaches, otherwise you are unlikely to enjoy urban Morocco.

The most important point to realize is that there are good and bad guides. Some are genuine students, who may want to earn a small fee, but may equally be interested (as so many claim) in practicing their English. Others are out-and-out hustlers, preying on first-visit innocence and paranoia. Your task is to distinguish between offers, to accept (perhaps limited) services from those who seem friendly and enjoyable company, and to deal as humanly as possible with approaches you wish to decline. There is rarely any harm in agreeing to let a guide show you to a hotel, though it is best to know which you want to go to—check our listings before arrival.

At other times, when you are approached for a tour of the town, you may well want to avoid the offer. To do so, it is a golden rule to look as if you know where you are going. never admit to this being your first visit to Morocco. If you feel confident enough, say that you have visited the town before and that you are glad to be back. You will be on your way to setting the parameters of discussion. The most exploitative guides will probably drop you to look elsewhere. If you are unsure of a guide, suggest that you take a mint tea together in a café. Don't make any agreement to employ him prior to this, or any suggestion of an agreement. Never allow yourself to be bullied into going with someone with whom you don't feel at ease. There is no shortage of other candidates.

If you do decide to hire an unofficial guide, be sure to fix the rate, as well as the itinerary, in advance. You should make it clear that you know the official rates for guides and should agree on these as a maximum. Many unofficial guides will attempt to charge a rate per person.

Finally, forewarned is forearmed, so a few notes on the most common scams:

● As stressed in the introduction, all guides have an interest in getting you into craft stores. Even if you expressly say you're not interested, they may suggest taking a tea with a cousin or brother who owns a store. Don't be afraid to keep to your agreed itinerary.

● A favorite line is that there is a Berber market taking place—and this is the only day of the week to see it. This is rarely true. You will probably visit everyday stores and souks.

● Some of the more exploitative hustlers will guide you into the Medinas, the, when you have no idea where you are, charge a large fee to take you back out and to your hotel. If this happens to you, don't be afraid to appeal to people in the street; your hustler may not enjoy attention.

● A few tales are told each year of people approaching you with a letter or package to mail to the USA or Europe when you leave Morocco. Never agree to this; you may be entering into a drugs plant.

● Beware of offers to meet "Blue Men" (desert nomads) in the south. They are almost invariably rogues.

● Don't trust anyone who begins their routine with "Where have I seen you before . . ."

DEALING WITH KIDS

In the countryside, and especially along the major southern routes, you will find fewer hustlers and guides, but many more kids, eager for a dirham or a *cadeau* (present). A Dutch correspondent writes:

"Dealing with small children is a lot easier than hustlers. All of us have our own odd tricks, like being able to roll one's eyes, imitate bird calls, or wiggle one's earlobes. Ours is to put one finger in our mouth and produce spectacular plopping noises. As soon as a child had asked for a dirham, we performed our trick and the child was usually flabbergasted. Most of the time we ended up teaching the entire villlage youth the trick. Dirhams were a thing of the past, and giggling the universal language".

ATTITUDES AND BEHAVIOR

If you want to get the most from a trip to Morocco, it is vital not to start assuming anyone who approaches or talks to you is a hustler. Too many tourists do, and end up making little contact with what must be one of the most hospitable peoples in the world.

Behavior and attitude are equally important on your part. If some Moroccans treat tourists with contempt, and exploit them as a simple resource, it has much to do with the way the latter behave.

It is important to be aware of **dress**. Shorts are acceptable only on the beach, in resorts; shirts (for both sexes) should cover your arms. **Photography** needs to be undertaken with care: if you are obviously taking a photograph of someone, ask their permission.

When **invited to a home**, you normally take your shoes off before entering the reception rooms. And at a meal (see "Eating") never use the left hand when in company with Moroccans.

GETTING AROUND

Public transportation in Morocco is, on the whole, pretty good. There is an efficient rail network linking the main towns of the north, the coast, and Marrakesh. Elsewhere you can travel easily enough by bus or collective taxi. In the mountains and over the more remote desert routes, where roads are often just dirt tracks or pistes, locals maintain a network of market-day trucks—uncomfortable but fun. And for hikers, the Atlas mountains, in particular, are crossed by a series of beautiful trails, some easy enough to follow by yourself, others best trekked with a guide and mule.

Renting a car can be a good idea, at least for a part of your trip, opening up routes that are time-consuming or difficult on local transportation. Rental companies generally allow you to hire a car in one city and return it to another.

TRAINS

Trains cover a limited network of routes, but for travel between the major cities they are the best option—comfortable, efficient, and fairly fast.

The communications map at the beginning of this book shows all the train routes in the country, and schedules are listed in the "travel details" at the end of each chapter. These change very little from year to year, but it's wise to check times in advance at stations. If you're lucky, you may be able to obtain the current timetable printed by *ONCF*, the national railroad company.

There are three **classes** of tickets—confusingly, first, second and fourth (economique). It is difficult for foreigners to travel fourth class, which is used only by poorer Moroccans. Some railroad officials won't sell fourth class

tickets to foreigners. **Costs** for a second-class ticket are comparable to what you'd pay for buses, see box below.

Most of the **stations** are located pretty close to the modern city centers, in the French-built quarter, the *Ville Nouvelle*. Major stations generally have luggage consignment lockers.

GRANDS TAXIS

Collective **grands taxis** are one of the best features of Moroccan transportation. They operate on a wide variety of routes, are much quicker than the buses (often quicker than trains, too), and fares are very reasonable. They are also good ways of meeting people and having impromptu Arabic lessons.

The taxis are usually big Peugeot or Mercedes cars that carry six passengers (four in the back, two in the front). Most of their business is along specific routes, and on the most popular routes, there are departures more or less continuously throughout the day. Consequently, you don't have to worry about timetables. You just show up at the terminal (locations are detailed, city by city, in the guide) and ask for a *place* to a specific destination. As soon as six (or, if you're willing to pay extra, four or five) people are assembled, it leaves.

Most of the grands taxis run over a fairly short route, from one large town to the next. If you want to travel farther, you will have to change taxis from time to time. Some routes are covered routinely in stages (e.g. Agadir–Taroudannt, or Agadir–Taliouine) and on others taxi drivers will generally assist you in finding a connecting taxi and in settling the fare with the driver.

Bargaining for *grands taxis* on established routes is not that hard. They keep to fixed prices

FARES

Fares for train, bus and *grand taxi* journeys follow a reasonably consistent pattern.

For **train** or **bus** journeys, reckon on around 1.5dh for each 10km—2–2.5dh for an express service.

Grands taxis charge around 2dh per person for each 10km, if traveling a regular route. Chartering a taxi for yourself or for a group, reckon on 12–15dh per 10km.

for each passenger. Before leaving, ask at your hotel what that price is—or, as a general guideline, consult the "Fares" box below.

If you want to take a non-standard route, or an excursion, it's of course possible to pay for a whole **grand taxi** (*une course*) for yourself or a group. But you'll often have to bargain hard before you get down to a realistic price.

BUSES AND TRUCKS

Bus travel is marginally cheaper than taking a *grand taxi*, and there are far more **regular routes**. Traveling on public transportation for any length of time in Morocco, you are likely to make considerable use of the various networks.

Where you can take a grand taxi rather than a bus, however, do so. The difference in **fare** is small, and is often counteracted by having to pay for your **baggage** to be loaded onto the roof (and taken off). Moroccans pay a small tip for this, but tourists are expected to pay 2–3dh for a rucksack—if you are asked for more, try to resist.

In addition, all except the express buses are very much slower and less comfortable than *grands taxis*. Leg room is extremely limited and long journeys can be painful experiences for anyone approaching six feet or more in height. In summer, it can be worthwhile taking **night buses** on the longer journeys. Though still not very comfortable, many long-distance buses go at night and they are both quicker and cooler.

CTM AND PRIVATE LINES

There are a variety of different bus services and companies. In all sizable towns, you will generally find both *CTM* (the national company) and a number of other companies, privately owned and operated.

The **CTM buses** are usually the more reliable, with numbered seats and fixed departure schedules. Some of the larger **private company** buses, such as *SATAS* (which operates widely in the south) are of a similar standard. However, many other of the private companies are tiny outfits, with a single bus which leaves only when the driver considers it sufficiently full.

In some of the larger cities—Rabat and Marrakesh, for example—*CTM* and the private companies share a single **terminal**, and you can find out the most useful departure times and routes by asking at the various windows. In other cities, there might be two or more separate terminals (you will find these described in the main

section of the guide) and possibly no choice of companies on a particular route.

On the more popular trips, such as those around the oasis valleys in the south, it is worth trying to buy **tickets in advance**; this may not always be possible, but it is always worth asking about. The main problems come with **small towns** along major routes, where buses often arrive and leave already full, and where you might find it difficult to get on at all. It's usually possible to get around this problem by taking a local bus or a *grand taxi* for the next section of the trip (until the bus you want empties a little), or by waiting for a bus that actually starts from the town you're in.

ONCF BUSES

An additional service, on certain major routes, are the express buses run by the train company, *ONCF*. These are fast and very comfortable, connecting Tetouan, Nador, Beni Mellal, Agadir, and Layoune to the main railroad lines leaving, respectively, from Tnine Sidi Lyamani (near Asilah), Taourite, and Marrakesh (Agadir/Layoune). They are, however, fifty percent more expensive than the regular buses, and compare, both in terms of time and cost, with the *grands taxis*.

TRUCKS

In the countryside, where buses may be sporadic or even nonexistent, it is a standard practice for **vans** and **trucks** (*camions*) to charge passengers. You may be asked to pay a little more than the locals, and you may be expected to bargain over this price—but it's straightforward enough.

In parts of the Atlas, the Berbers run more-or-less scheduled **transit-truck** services, generally to coincide with the pattern of local *souks*. If you plan on traversing any of the more ambitious Atlas *pistes*, you'll probably be dependent on these vehicles, or you'll just have to walk. For some general guidelines—above all, about paying at the end—see Dan Richardson's account in Chapter Six.

HITCHING

Hitching is not very big in Morocco. Most people, if they own any form of transportation at all, have mopeds—which are actually said to outnumber cars by something like five *hundred* to one. However, it is often fairly simple to get rides from other **tourists**, particularly if you ask around at the campgrounds, and for **women travelers** this can be an effective and positive option. You won't want to spend all your time driving around in tourists' cars, but they can be a useful respite from the generally male preserves of buses and *grands taxis*.

Out on the road, it's inevitably a different matter—and hitching is definitely not advisable for women traveling alone. For anyone who tries, don't be surprised to be asked to **pay for a ride** if you are picked up by country Moroccans. Local rides can operate in much the same way as trucks, see above.

CAR RENTAL

Car rental is expensive (upwards of $300 a week), but is obviously useful if you don't have much time. A car will allow you to explore unusual routes and take in very much more in a lot less time. This is especially true in the **south**, where getting around and getting to see anything can

DRIVING IN MOROCCO

There are few real problems driving in Morocco, but keep in mind that the experience is often very different from that in North America, or Europe. Accident rates are high—in large part because much of the population is not yet tuned in to looking out for motorized vehicles. You should treat all pedestrians with the suspicion that they will cross in front of you, and all cyclists with the idea that they may well swerve into the middle of the road.

Daytime driving can, with the caveats stated above, be as good as anywhere. Very good road surgfaces, long straight roads, very little traffic, and quite long distances between inhabited areas allow for high average speeds. The official **speed limit** outside towns is 100km per hour, which is difficult to keep down to in desert areas, where concepts of speed change. On certain roads the speed limit can be as low as 40km per hour. There is an on-the-spot fine of 30dh for each offence.

Do not drive **after dark**. It is reputedly legal to drive without lights at up to 20 kilometers per hour. This allows all cyclists and mopeds to wander at will without lights. Donkeys, goats and sheep do not carry lights, either. Obstructions, sand drifts, rocks and pot-holes are additional hazards, and in spring even main roads can ford, when dried-up river beds are flooded with snow streams from the mountains.

PISTE DRIVING

On the **pistes** (rough, unpaved tracks in the mountains or desert), there are special problems. Here you do need a good deal of driving and mechanical confidence—and if you don't feel your car's up to it, don't drive one of these routes. If you're not mechanically minded, make sure to bring a car maintenance manual with you—a useful item, too, for anyone planning to rent.

EQUIPMENT

Whether you rent a car or drive your own, always make sure you're carrying a **spare tire** in good condition (plus a jack and tools). Flat tires occur very frequently, even on fairly major roads, and you can often be in for a long wait until someone drives along with a possible replacement.

Carrying an emergency windshield is also useful, especially if you are driving your own car for a long period of time. There are lots of loose stones on the hard shoulders of single track roads and they can fly all over the place.

GAS AND BREAKDOWNS

Gas stations are plentiful in larger towns but can be few and far between in rural areas. Always fill your tank to the limit. Premium is the standard brand for cars.

If you break down, Moroccan **mechanics** are usually excellent, and all medium-sized towns have garages (most with an extensive range of spare parts for Renaults and other French cars), but if you break down miles from anywhere you'll probably end up paying a fortune to get a truck to tow you back.

If you are driving your own vehicle, there is also the problem of having to reexport any car that you bring into the country (even a wreck). You can't just write off a car: you'll have to take it out of Morocco with you.

VEHICLE INSURANCE

Insurance must by law be sold along with all rental agreements.

Driving your own vehicle, you will need to take out *Assurance Frontière* insurance. (The green card is not accepted, as it is in Algeria, or Spain). *Assurance Frontière* costs around $35 a month, $75 for 90 days. As the name suggests, it can normally be issued at the frontier on your arrival in the country. It is not, however, available at Figuig, the southern entry point from Algeria.

For a renewal, the main office is at 197 Av. Hassan II (opposite the Roxy Cinema), Casablanca; ☎276.142.

turn out to be quite an effort if you have to rely on local buses. Many visitors choose to hire a car in Casablanca, Marrakesh or Agadir, expressly for the southern routes.

Details and addresses of **car rental companies** are given in the text, under the city listings; the cheapest places are mostly in Casablanca and Agadir.

Before making a reservation, be sure to find out if you can pick the car up in one city and return it to another—freeing yourself for the most interesting routes. Most companies will allow this. Check also if you will be charged extra for payment with a credit card; there is often a (negotiable) six percent fee for this.

EXPEDITION ROUTES AND HIKING

Morocco is a country where travel can still feel a bit expeditionary, especially if you take to the *piste* roads or go hiking in the mountains.

Hiking is best in the High Atlas, and most popular around Mount Toubkal. If you haven't had much experience or feel a little daunted by the lack of organized facilities, you might want to try one of the **specialist hiking companies** offering Moroccan trips (see box on p.7). Going your own way is quite feasible, though, with summer trails in the High Atlas and winter ones in the lower and more southerly climes of the Anti Atlas. In recent years, mountain bikers have made an appearance in the Atlas, too. Many of the trails are (more or less) passable by bike, and you can transport cycles around the country on trains and buses.

For practicalities on hiking, see the High Atlas section in Chapter Six. See also p.15 for suggestions on hiking maps and guides.

Piste-driving can take you across the Atlas ranges or along some of the desert tracks between outlying oases in the pre-Sahara. Several of these routes are detailed in the guide, and some of them can be covered also by rides in local trucks—see previous page.

FLIGHTS

Royal Air Maroc (*RAM*) operates **domestic flights** between all the major cities. If you're very pressed for time, you might want to use the service between **Tangier** and **Marrakesh** (via Casa); this would cost around $65, well above the bus and train fares but, at two hours, as opposed to nearly thirteen hours, it'll save you considerable effort. For anyone intrepid enough to explore

POLICE CHECKS ON TRAVEL

Police checks take place on travelers throughout the country. They follow three types. One is on local transport; European cars, or rental cars, are waved through. The second is a routine but simple passport check—usually polite and friendly, with the only delay due to a desire to relieve boredom with a chat.

The third is is more prolonged and involves being stopped by police stationed at more-or-less permanent points on the roads, who will conduct a fairly detailed inquisition into all non-resident travelers. There is considerable form filling and delay. In the Deep South these checks may be conducted by the military rather than by the police.

the **Deep South** of the country, flights can also be worthwhile—returning from the southernmost visitable towns of Ad Dakhla or Laayoune, for example.

Details of other *RAM* flights, and addresses of the company's local offices, are given in the main part of the guide. Remember that you must always confirm flights at a *RAM* office 24 to 48 hours before departure.

Student and under-26 youth **discounts** of 25 percent are available on all *RAM* domestic flights but only if the ticket is bought in advance from one of their offices.

CITY TRANSIT

Most Moroccan towns are small enough to cover on foot, especially if you stay in a hotel in or near the Medina—where you'll want to spend most of your time. In larger cities, however, local buses can be useful, as can *petits taxis*—usually Fiats or Simcas—which take up to three passengers.

Petits taxis, as opposed to *grands taxis*, are limited to trips within city limits. Officially, all of them should have meters, but in practice, you're unlikely to find one that works (at least for tourists) except in Rabat. It is then a matter of bargaining for a price—either before you get in (wise to start off with) or by simply presenting the right sum when you get out. **Fares** vary enormously (in Marrakesh and Agadir, for example, they can often be excessive), though everywhere it depends to a large extent on what you look like, how you act, and where you're going. Don't be afraid to use *petits taxis* or to argue with the driver if you feel you're being unreasonably overcharged.

SLEEPING

Hotels in Morocco are cheap, excellent value, and usually pretty easy to find. The only times you might have a problem getting a room is in the peak seasons (August, Christmas, or Easter), and then only in a handful of main cities and resorts—Fes, Agadir, Tangier, and sometimes Tetouan.

There is a basic distinction between classified hotels (which are given star-ratings by the tourist board and start at around $6 a double) and unclassified hotels (both unrated and unlisted by the ONMT, which start at about $2.50 for a double).

UNCLASSIFIED HOTELS

Unclassified hotels are mainly to be found in the older, Arab-built parts of cities—the **Medinas**—and are obviously the cheapest options. They also offer the advantage of being at the heart of things: where you'll want to spend most of your time, and where all the sights and markets are concentrated.

The disadvantages are that the Medinas can at first be daunting—with their mazes of narrow lanes and blind alleys—and that the hotels themselves can, at worst, be dirty fleatraps with tiny, windowless cells and half-washed sheets. At best, they're far different—and some can be really beautiful, with whitewashed rooms grouped around a central patio.

There is nearly always, however, some problem with **water**. The Medinas remain substantially unmodernized, hot showers are a rarity, and the squat toilets are sometimes pretty disgusting. Nonetheless, a lot of them are fine, and we've included numerous Medina recommendations in the guide.

CLASSIFIED HOTELS

Rated hotels are almost always in a town's **Ville Nouvelle**—the "new" or administrative quarters, originally built by the French and usually set slightly apart from the Medina. The star-ratings are self-explanatory: starting at the bottom with 1*B, 1*A, 2*B, etc., and going up to 4*B, 4*A, finally reaching 5*Luxury. **Prices** are extremely reasonable for all except the 5* categories (which can—and do—set their own rates).

At the **lower end**, there's little difference between 1*B and 1*A places, either of which will offer you a basic double room with a washbasin for $6–7, with a private shower for an additional $1.50. Going up to 2* and 3*, there's a definite progression in comfort, and you can find a few elegant, old hotels in these categories which once used to be very grand but have since slipped in competition with the new tourist complexes that have been built to order.

However, if you want **a bit of luxury**, you'll most likely be looking for a room with access to a **swimming pool**—which means, on the whole, four stars. This will set you back around $20–40 for a double. If you can afford the upper end of this scale (4*A hotels), you'll be moving into real style, with rooms looking out onto palm-shaded pools and gardens, in buildings that have sometimes been converted from old palace residences.

Reservations for the 4- or 5-star hotels are best made through the central reseravations office of the chain owinging the hotel. Details of these are to be found in the *ONMT* hotels guide. Turning up, or phoning ahead, at an individual hotel you may find reluctance to book you in, with staff perhaps claiming the hotel is full. Many rely on tour groups for their business and are not very interested in individual travelers.

A SUGGESTED COURSE . . .

Ideally, the best course in picking your accommodation is to **alternate between the two extremes**, spending most of your time in basic Medina hotels but going for the occasional blast of grandeur.

At any rate don't limit yourself to the middle categories—these are mostly dull, and staying all the time in the Ville Nouvelle will cut you off from the most interesting aspects of traditional Moroccan life.

HAMMAMS

The absence of hot showers in some of the cheaper Medina hotels is not such a disaster. Throughout all Moroccan Medinas, you'll find local **hammams**—steam baths where you can go in and sweat for as long as you like, get scrubbed down and rigorously massaged, and douse yourself with endless buckets of hot and cold water.

Several *hammams* are detailed in the text, but the best way of finding one is always to ask at the hotel where you're staying—you will sometimes need to be led to them, since they are often unmarked and very hard to find.

In some towns, you will find separate *hammams* for women and men; at others there are different hours for each sex—usually 9am–7pm for women, 7pm–1am and sometimes 5–9am for men. Those for women seem particularly welcoming. For men, there's a strange element of modesty: you undress facing the wall, and bathe in your underpants or swimsuit.

As part of the Islamic tradition of cleanliness and ablutions, *hammams* sometimes have a religious element, and you may not be welcome (or allowed in) to those built alongside mosques, particularly on Thursday evenings, before the main weekly service on Friday. On the whole, though, there are no restrictions against *Nisara* ("Nazarenes", or Christians).

YOUTH HOSTELS AND REFUGES

At the lower price levels—though often no cheaper than a shared room in the Medina—there are six **youth hostels**, or *Auberges de Jeunesse*. One, in Asni in the High Atlas, is a hiking base—useful and recommended. The others are all in major cities. Those in Fes and Marrakesh are good fall-backs, close to the train stations; the one in Meknes is all right but a little far from everything; Rabat's and Casablanca's have a reputation for being pretty squalid. Addresses and details are given for all of these in the relevant sections of the guide. One general attraction is their use for meeting other travelers, including Moroccans on vacation who sometimes visit them for just this purpose.

In the High Atlas mountains, you will also find a number of huts, or **refuges**, equipped for hikers. These provide dormitory beds and some-times meals and/or cooking facilities. They are detailed in the relevant sections.

CAMPGROUNDS

Campgrounds, too, are good meeting places, and even if you're staying elsewhere, they can be worth vising in order to find a ride or people to share the cost of gas. Most are extremely cheap, at around 50 cents a person and 50 cents for a tent, but there are also a few fancier "international" places, with major facilities and prices to match. Details and addresses are given in the guide.

Campgrounds don't provide total **security**, and you should never leave valuables unattended. When camping outside official sites, this applies even more; however, if you're hiking in the Atlas, it is usually possible to set up a camp and pay someone to act as a *gardien*.

EATING AND DRINKING

Like accommodation, food in Morocco falls into two basic categories: ordinary Moroccan meals served in the Medina cafés (or bought from stalls), and French-influenced tourist menus in most of the hotels and Ville Nouvelle restaurants. There are exceptions—cheap local cafés in the new cities and occasional "palace"-style places in the Medina—but, in general, this still holds true. Once again, it's best to stick largely to the Medina places (most are cleaner than they look), with an occasional splurge in the best restaurants you can find.

BASIC CAFÉ FOOD

Starting with the basics, the simplest Moroccan meals usually center on a thick, very filling soup—most often the spicy, bean-based **harira** (which is a meal in itself, and eaten as such to break the Ramadan fast). To this you might add a plateful of **kebabs** (either *brochettes*, shish kebabs, or *kefta*, made from chopped meat) and perhaps a **salad** (which is often very finely chopped, and halfway approaches the Spanish *gazpacho*), together with **dates** bought at a market stall. Alternatively, you could go for a **tajine**—essentially a stew, cooked slowly in an earthenware pot over a charcoal fire. Mopped up with bread, it's often unbelievably delicious.

Either alternative will set you back about $1.50 for a hearty meal at one of the hole-in-the-wall places in the Medina, each with about two or three tables. You are not expected to bargain for cooked food, but prices can be lower at café-restaurants without menus if you enquire how much things cost before you start eating.

Vegetarians can get by quite happily on most of the soups (though some use lamb for stock) and usually on the *tajines* (which you can anyway ask to be served without meat).

For **breakfast or a snack**, you can buy a half **baguette**—plus butter and jam, cheese, oreggs, if you want—from many bread or grocery stores, and take it into a café to order a drink.

RESTAURANT MEALS

Slightly more expensive dishes, available in some of the Medina cafés as well as in the more

---

GLOSSARY OF MOROCCAN FOOD

BASICS

Pain	*l-hobs*	Bread	Sel	*l-melha*	Salt
Oeufs	*l-bed*	Eggs	Sauce	*l-merga*	Sauce
Poissons	*l-hout*	Fish	Sucre	zoukar	Sugar
Viande	*l-hem*	Meat		(*Zanida* is granulated sugar;	
Huile	zit	Oil		zoukar, lump sugar)	
Poivre	lebzar	Pepper	Légumes	*l-khoudra*	Vegetables
Salade	shalada	Salad	Vinaigre	*l-khel*	Vinegar

SOUPS, SALADS, AND VEGETABLES

	Harira	Spicy bean soup	Frites	*l'batata*	Potatoes
Potage		Thick soup	Tomates	matecha	Tomatoes
Bouillon		Thin soup	Epinards	salk	Spinach
Salade Marocaine		Mixed salad	Oignons	*l-basla*	Onions

MAIN DISHES

Tajine de viande	*l-hem*	Meat stew
Tajine des poissons	*l-hout*	Fish stew
Couscous (aux sept légumes)		Couscous (with seven vegetables)
Poulet aux olives et citron		Chicken with olives and lemon
	Djaja mahamara	Chicken stuffed with almonds, semolina, and raisins
Boulettes de viande	**kefta**	Meatballs
Bifteck	*l-habra*	Beefsteak
Agneau	Mechoui	Roast lamb
Pastilla	B'stilla	Pigeon pie

MEATS, POULTRY, AND FISH

Poulet	djaj	Chicken	Sardines	sardile	Sardines
Pigeon	lehmama	Pigeon	Merlan	*l-mirla*	Whiting
Lapin	qniya	Rabbit	Crevettes		Shrimp
Mouton	*l-houli*	Mutton	Langouste		Lobster

expensive restaurants, include **fish**, on the coast, and **chicken** *(poulet)*, either spit-roasted *(rôti)* or with lemon and olives *(poulet limon)*.

You will sometimes find **pastilla**, too, a delicious pigeon pie, prepared with phyllo pastry coated with sugar and cinnamon, and a particular specialty of Fes. And, of course, there is **couscous**, the most famous Moroccan dish, based on a huge bowl of steamed semolina piled high with vegetables and mutton, chicken, or occasionally fish. Couscous, however, tends to be disappointing. There is no real tradition of going out to eat in Morocco, and this is a dish that's prepared mostly at home—often for a special occasion (on Friday, the holy day, in richer households; perhaps for a festival in poorer ones). At festivals, which are always good for interesting

food, and at the most expensive tourist restaurants, you may also come across the traditional *mechoui*—a whole sheep roasted on a spit.

To supplement these Moroccan standard offerings, most tourist restaurants add a few **French dishes**—steak, liver, various fish and fowl, etc.—and the ubiquitous *salade marocaine*, actually very different from the Moroccan idea of salad, since it's based on a few tomatoes, cucumbers, and other greens. Together with a dessert consisting either of fruit or pastry, these meals usually come to around $5–8 a head.

CAKES, DESSERTS, AND FRUIT

Cakes and desserts are also available in some Moroccan cafés, though you'll find them more often at pastry shops or street stalls. They can be

SWEETS AND FRUITS

Cornes de gazelles	kab l-ghzal	Sweet pastries	Pêches	l-khoukh	Peaches
Fromage	formage	Cheese	Oranges	limoune	Oranges
Dattes	tmer	Dates	Melon	l-battikh	Melon
Figues	chriha	Figs	Pasteque	dellah	Watermelon
Amandes	louze	Almonds	Raisins	la'anb	Grapes
Bananes	banane	Bananas	Pommes	tufaah	Apples
Fraises	l-fraise	Strawberries	Abricots	mishmash	Apricots
Cerises	hblmluk	Cherries		Kermus d'ensarrah (or	Cactus fruit
				Takanareete)	

DRINKS

Eau (Minerale)	agua, l-**ma** (**maz**dini)	Water (Mineral)	Bière	birra	Beer
Thé (à la menthe)	atay (dial **nez**naz)	Tea (Mint)	Vin	sh-**rab**	Wine
			Café (au lait)	qahwa (bi lahlib)	Coffee (with milk)

SOME ARABIC PHRASES

What do you have . . .	**Ash**noo **kane** . . .
to eat?	. . . f'l-**mak**la?
to drink?	. . . f'l-muchanoubat?
What is this?	Shnoo **had**a?
Can you give me	A**tee**nee . . .
. . . a knife/fork/spoon?	. . . moos/for**shet**a/**mal**ka?
. . . a plate/glass/napkin?	. . . **t'b**-sil/**kess**/l-**fot**a?
Less/without sugar	**Shwee**ya/ble a**zouk**ar
This is not what I asked for!	**Hed**ee **mush**ee **hee**a **lit** lubt!
This is not fresh/clean!	**Hed**ee **mush**ee **tree**a/n'**kee**a!
This is good!	**Hed**ee **mush**ee mu**zyena!**
The check, please.	L'**h'seb** min**fad**lik.
Please write it down.	Min**fad**lik, k'**tib'h**.

NOTE that where food/dishes are commonly available in all kinds of restaurants, both **French** and **Arabic** words are given; where possible it is always a good idea to try to use some Arabic—the letters printed in **bold italics** should be stressed. For further relevant phrases, see the "Language" section in *Contexts*.

excellent. The most common are *cornes de gazelles*, sugar-coated pastries filled with a kind of almond paste, but there are infinite variations.

Yogurt *(yaourt)* is also delicious, and Morocco is surprisingly rich in seasonal **fruits**. In addition to the various kinds of dates—sold all year but at their best fresh from the October harvests—there are grapes, melons, strawberries, peaches, and figs, all advisably washed before eaten. Or for a real thirst quencher (and a good cure for a bad stomach), you can have quantities of **prickly pear**, cactus fruit, peeled for you in the street for a couple of dirhams.

DRINKS

The national drink is **thé à la menthe**—green tea, flavored with sprigs of mint and a minimum of four cubes of sugar per cup. This tastes a little sickly at first, but it's worth getting used to—perfect in the summer heat, the drinking of mint tea is also a ritual if you're invited into anyone's home (you leave after the third glass) or if you're doing any serious bargaining in a shop.

In cafés, it is usually cheaper to ask for a pot (une *théière*) for two or three people. You can also get red or amber tea—more expensive and rarely available, but delicious when you can find it. Also great, and easily found at cafés or street stalls, are fresh-squeezed **juices**: *jus d'orange*, *jus d'amande* (almond), *jus des bananes*, and *jus de pomme* (apple), the last three all milk-based and served chilled. *Leben*—yoghurt and water—is often sold at train and bus stations, and can do wonders for an upset stomach.

Other **soft drinks** inevitably include Coke, along with Fanta and other fizzy lemonades—all pretty cheap and served in large bottles. **Mineral water**, which is a worthwhile investment throughout the country, is usually referred to by brand name, ubiquitously *Sidi Harazem* or *Sidi Ali*, or the naturally sparkling *Oulmes*.

Coffee (*café*) is best in French-style cafés—either *noir* (black), *cassé* (with a drop of milk), or *au lait* (white).

WINE AND BEER

As an Islamic nation, Morocco gives **drinking alcohol** a low profile. It is, in fact, not generally possible to buy any alcohol at all in the Medinas, and for beer or wine, you always have to go to a tourist restaurant or hotel or a bar in the Ville Nouvelle. Moroccan **wines**, however, can often be very good, if a little heavy for drinking without a meal. Among varieties worth trying are the strong reds, *Cabernet* and *Gris de Boulaoune*; the rosés can be tasty, too, though the whites are all a bit insipid. Those Moroccans who drink in **bars**—a growing number in the industrial cities—tend to stick to **beer**, usually the local *Stork*, *Flag Pils*, or, preferably, *Flag Special*.

COMMUNICATIONS—MAIL, PHONES, AND MEDIA

MAIL AND POSTE RESTANTE

Letters between the USA (or Western Europe) and Morocco are totally unpredictable: they arrive, but whether this takes three days or three weeks is very much up to chance. Similarly, receiving letters **poste restante** (general delivery) is like playing the lottery. The main problem here is that Moroccan post office workers don't always file letters under the name you might expect. It is always a good idea to ask for all your initials to be checked (including *M* for Ms., etc.), and if you're half-expecting anything, suggest other letters as well.

To pick up your mail you need your passport. To have mail sent to you, it should be addressed (preferably with your surname underlined) to *Poste Restante* at the *PTT Centrale* of any major city (Marrakesh, though, is notoriously inefficient). **Mailing letters**, always use a drop at a post office; the post boxes found on the streets don't always have regular collections.

Post office hours are Monday to Friday, 8am to noon and 3 to 6pm in winter, 8am to 3pm in summer; Saturday and Sunday closed.

Alternatives to sending *poste restante* to post offices are to pick a big **hotel** (anything with three or more stars should be reliable) or have things sent *c/o American Express*— represented in Morocco by *Voyages Schwartz* in Tangier, Fes, Casablanca, Agadir, and Marrakesh (see p.12 for addresses).

PHONES

The **public telephone section** is usually housed in a city's main post office (*PTT*), though it often has a separate entrance and stays open longer hours—24 hours a day in some of the main cities. Unfortunately, the system can be almost as chaotic as the mail, with calls taking up to two hours to connect. In Rabat, Casablanca, and Fes, however, you can now make **international calls** direct (after standing in line for a while), and this is, hopefully, going to apply to other cities before too long.

In the meantime, you can get around delays to some extent by **placing your call through a hotel**: most of them, even fairly small places, will do this for you, although you should make sure in advance both of possible surcharges and the rate.

Currently it's around 50dh ($5.50) a minute to the U.S. and Canada and 15dh ($1.75) a minute to Britain and Western Europe.

Local calls made from public telephones are pretty straightforward. Each city has its own code (displayed near the phone) and pay phones accept ten-, twenty-, fifty-centime, or one-dirham coins.

FOREIGN MEDIA

As for other means of staying in touch, the *International Herald Tribune* and various British newspapers are available in all the main cities. You can also pick up **Voice of America** and the **BBC World Service**, broadcast on various frequencies throughout the day, from 6am to midnight, local time. The most consistent World Service evening reception is generally on 9.41 and 5.975 mHz (31.88m and 50.21m bands); a full program listing is available from the BBC or from the British Council in Rabat.

THE MOROCCAN PRESS

The **Moroccan press** encompasses a reasonable range of papers, if you can read French or Arabic. The most accessible is the official—and somewhat rigorously pro-government—French language daily, *Le Matin du Sahara*, (70,000 circulation).

In Arabic, there are *Al Alam* (50,000 circulation), which is supportive of the Istiqlal party, and *Al Muharnir* (17,000 circulation), which supports the socialist USFP party. There is also a fundamentalist paper, *Al Djemaa*, though this has a very limited circulation of 3,000 copies.

KIF (HASHISH)

Drug use—almost exclusively kif (hashish, chocolaté, cannabis)—has for a long time been a regular pastime of Moroccans and tourists alike. Indeed, in the 1960s and 1970s (or further back, in the 1930s), its ready availability, good quality, and low cost made *kif* a major tourist attraction. It is, however, illegal, or, as the *ONMT* puts it:

Tourists coming to Morocco are warned that the first article in the Dahir of April 24th 1954 prohibits the POSSESSION, the OFFER, the DISTRIBUTION, the PURCHASE, the SALE and the TRANSPORTATION as well as the EXPORTATION of CANNABIS IN

WHATEVER FORM. The Dahir allows for a penalty of IMPRISONMENT from three months to five years and a fine of 2400 to 240,000 dirhams, or only one of these. Moreover the law court may ordain the SEIZURE of the means of transportation and the things used to cover up the smuggling as well as the toxic products themselves.

What this means in practice is slightly different. There is no real effort to stop Moroccans from smoking or dealing, but as a tourist you are peculiarly vulnerable. Not so much because of the **police**, as because of the **dealers**. Apart from the obvious tricks—selling you camel dung, etc.—many of the dealers have developed meaner, more aggressive tactics. They sell people hash (or, occasionally, even plant it) and then return or send friends to threaten to turn you in to the police; or they themselves may even be actual informers, and turn you in to the police. Either way, it can all become pretty paranoiac and unpleasant.

What can you do to avoid all this? Most obviously, keep well clear—above all, of the kif-growing areas of the **Rif mountains** and the processing center in **Ketama**—and always reply to hustlers by saying you don't smoke ("I prefer drinking," "I have bad lungs. . ."). Or, if you are coming to Morocco to indulge, don't buy anything in the first few days (definitely not in Tangier and Tetouan), and only smoke* where you feel thoroughly confident and in control.

Above all, **do not try to take any out** by air (*Midnight Express* could equally have been about Morocco) and don't even think of taking any into Algeria or over to Spain. Penalties in **Algeria** are amazingly harsh (a life sentence is theoretically possible), and there's nearly always a prison

sentence in **Spain**, too. Apart from which, if you take *kif* over to Spain you're unlikely to save much money: in Malaga and along the Costa del Sol prices are low, and Spanish law is relatively liberal towards those with small quantities for personal use.

If you do find yourself in trouble there are **consulates** for most nationalities in Rabat/Casablanca and, to a lesser extent, in Tangier (see their respective listings for addresses). Consulates are notoriously unsympathetic to drug offenders—the British one in Rabat has an old French poster on the wall, "*Le kif détruit l'esprit*"—but they can help with technical problems and find you legal representation.

Kif is not necessarily smoked in Morocco—a traditional specialty is *majoun*, a kind of fudge made with the pounded flowers and seeds of the plant. As James Jackson wrote in his *An Account of the Empire of Morocco, 1814,* "a piece of this as big as a walnut will for a time entirely deprive a man of all reason and intellect." It is also reputed to be good for settling your stomach.

FESTIVALS: RAMADAN, HOLIDAYS, AND *MOUSSEMS*

If the popular image of Islam is somewhat puritanical and ascetic, Morocco's festivals—the *moussems* and *amouggars*—do their best to contradict it. The country abounds in vacations and festivals of all kinds, both national and local, and coming across one can be the most interesting and enjoyable experience of any travel in

Morocco—with the chance to witness music and dance, as well as special regional foods and market souks.

Perhaps surprisingly, there are rewards, too, in coinciding with one of the major Islamic celebrations—above all, *Ramadan*, when all Muslims (which in effect means all Moroccans) observe a total fast from sunrise to sunset for a month. This can pose some problems for traveling but the celebratory evenings are again good times to hear music and to share in hospitality.

RAMADAN

Ramadan, in a sense, parallels the Christian Lent; the ninth month of the Islamic calendar, it commemorates the time in which the Koran was revealed to Muhammad. In contrast to the Christian West, though, the Muslim world observes the fast extremely rigorously—indeed Moroccans are forbidden by law from "public disrespect" of the fast, and a few are jailed for this each year.

RAMADAN AND ISLAMIC HOLIDAYS

Islamic religious holidays are calculated on the **lunar calendar**, so their dates rotate throughout the seasons (as does Ramadan's). Exact dates in the lunar calendar are impossible to predict—they are set by the Islamic authorities in Fes—but approximate dates for the next three years are:

	1990	**1991**	**1992**
Ramadan	March 29	March 18	March 7
Aïd es Seghir	April 28	April 17	April 6
Aïd el Kebir	July 5	June 26	June 15
Moharem	July 20	July 9	June 29
Mouloud	Oct. 14	Oct. 3	Sept. 23

What the fast involves is abstention from food, drink, and smoking during daylight hours, and abstinence from sex throughout the month. Strict Muslim men will often sit up all night at the cafés, so that everyone knows they have abstained from sex.

With local cafés and restaurants often closing during the day, and people getting on edge toward the month's end, this is in some ways a disastrous time to travel. It is certainly no time to try and hire a guide in the mountains—nobody will undertake the work—and it is probably safer to travel by bus during the month in the mornings, as drivers wil be fasting, too. (Airline pilots are officially forbidden from observing the fast).

But there is a compensation in witnessing and becoming absorbed into the pattern of the fast. At sunset, signaled by the sounding of a siren and the lighting of lamps on the minarets, an amazing calm and sense of well-being fall on the streets, as everyone drinks a bowl of *harira* and, in the cities at least, gets down to a night of celebration and entertainment.

The **entertainment** takes different forms. If you can spend some time in Marrakesh during the month, you'll find the Djemaa el Fna square there at its most active, with troupes of musicians, dancers, and acrobats coming into the city just for the occasion. In Rabat and Fes, there seem to be continuous promenades, with cafés and stalls all open up to 3am. Local cafés will often provide a venue for live music and singing. And in the southern towns and Berber villages, you will often come across the ritualized *ahouaches* and *haidus*—circular, trancelike dances often involving whole communities.

If you are a **non-Muslim** outsider you are not expected to observe Ramadan, but it is good be sensitive about not breaking the fast (and particularly smoking) in public. In fact, the best way to experience Ramadan—and to benefit from its naturally purifying rhythms—is to enter into it. You may not be able to last without an occasional glass of water, and you'll probably have your breakfast slightly later than sunrise, but it is still worth the attempt.

OTHER ISLAMIC HOLIDAYS

At the end of Ramadan comes the feast of **Aïd es Seghir**, a climax to the festivities in Marrakesh, though observed more privately in the villages. Extremely important as well to the Muslim calendar is **Aïd el Kebir**, which celebrates the willingness of Abraham to obey God and to sacrifice Isaac. Both events are traditional family gatherings. At the Aïd el Kebir every household that can afford it will slaughter a sheep. You see them tethered everywhere, often on rooftops, for weeks prior to the event; after the feast, their skins are cured on the streets.

The Aïd el Kebir is followed, about three weeks later, by **Moharem**, the Muslim new year.

The fourth main religious holiday is the **Mouloud**, the Prophet's birthday. This is widely observed, with a large number of *moussems* (see next page) timed to take place in the weeks around it.

PUBLIC HOLIDAYS

Nowadays each of the big **religious feasts** are usually marked by two days off. They are announced or ratified by the king, each time, on TV and radio the preceding day.

On these public holidays, and on the secular *Fêtes Nationales* (see dates on next page), all **banks**, **post offices**, and most **stores** will be closed; **transportation** may be reduced but never stops completely.

MOUSSEMS AND AMMOUGARS

Moussems—or *amouggars*—are held in honor of saints or marabouts. They are basically local, and predominantly rural, affairs. Besides Aid es Seghir and Aid el Kebir, however, they form the main religious and social celebrations of the year for most Moroccans, especially for the country Berbers.

Some of the smaller *moussems* amount to little more than a market day with religious overtones; others are essentially harvest festivals, celebrating a pause in agrictural labor after a crop has been successfully brought in. Quite a number, however, have developed into substantial occasions—similar in some respects to Spanish fiestas—and a few have national significance. If you are lucky enough to coincide with one of the major events, you'll get the chance to witness Moroccan popular culture at its richest, with horseriding, music, singing, and dancing, and of course eating and drinking.

AIMS AND FUNCTIONS

The ostensible aim of the *moussem* is religious—to obtain blessing, or *baraka*, from the saint and/or to thank God for the harvest. But the social and cultural dimensions are equally important. *Moussems* provide an opportunity for country people to escape the monotony of their hard working lives in several days of festivities. They may provide the year's single opportunity for friends or families from different villages to meet. Harvest and farming problems are discussed, as well as family matters—and marriage—as people get the chance to sing, dance, eat, and pray together.

Music and singing are always major components of a moussem, and locals will often bring tape recorders to provide sounds for the rest of the year. The different religious brotherhoods, some of whom may be present at larger moussems, each have their own distinct stuyles of music, dancing, and dress.

Moussems also operate as **fairs**, or markets, with artisans offering their produce to a wider market than is available at the weekly souk. Buyers in turn can inform themselves about new products and regional price differences, as the moussem attracts people from a much wider area than the souk. There is a welcome injection of cash into the local economy, too, with traders and entertainers doing good business, and householders renting out rooms.

At the **spiritual level**, people seek to improve their standing with God through prayer, as well as the less orthodox channels of popular belief. Central to this is *baraka*, good fortune, which can be obtained by intercession of the saint. Financial contributions are made and these are used to buy a gift, or *hedia*, usually a large carpet, which is then taken in procession to the saint's tomb; it is deposited there for the shereefian families, the descendants of the saint, to dispose of as they wish. Country people may seek to obtain baraka by attaching a garment or tissue to the saint's tomb and leaving it overnight to take home after the festival.

The procession which takes the gift to the tomb is the highpoint of the more religious moussems, such as that of Moulay Idriss, where an enormous carpet is carried above the heads of the **religious brotherhoods**. The brotherhoods will each be playing their own music, hypnotic in its rhythms; spectators and participants may go into trance, giving themselves to the music. If you witness such events, it is best to keep a low profile (and certainly don't take photographs); the presence of foreigners or non-Muslims at events is sometimes considered to impede trance.

Release through trance probably has a therapeutic aspect, and indeed some moussems are specifically concerned with cures of physical and psychiatric disorders. The saint's tomb is usually located near a freshwater spring, and the cure can simply be bathing in and drinking the water. Those suffering from physical ailments may also be treated at the moussem with herbal remedies, or by recitation of verses from the Koran. Koranic verses may also be written and placed in tiny receptacles next to the ailment. The whole is reminiscent of the popular remedies found at European pilgrimage centers like Lourdes.

DATES AND PRACTICALITES

There are enormous numbers of *moussems*. An idea of quite how many can be gathered from the frequency that you see *koubbas*, square, white-domed buildings covering a saint's tomb. Each of these is a potential focal point of a moussem, and any one region or town may have twenty to thirty separate annual moussems. Establishing when they take place is, however, not easy for outsiders; most local people find out when they are by word of mouth at the weekly souks.

Many moussems are held around religious occasions such as **Mouloud** , which change date each year according to the lunar calendar (see previous page). Others, concerned with celebrating the **harvest**, have their date decided at a local level according to when the harvest is ready. *Moussems* of this type are actually more difficult to plan to visit than those which occur at points of the Islamic year. **August** and **September** are the most promising months overall, with dozens of *moussems* held after the grain harvest when there is a lull in the agricultural year before sowing starts prior to the first rains in October or November.

The lists over the page give an approximate idea (sometimes an exact one) of when the *moussems* are, but you will generally need to ask at a local level for information. Sometimes tourist offices may be able to help, though often not. Metropolitan Moroccans are not much interested in this aspect of traditional culture and rarely attend *moussems* themselves.

The **accommodation** situation will depend on whether the moussem is in the town or countryside. In the country, the simplest solution is to take a tent and camp—there is no real objection to anyone camping wherever they please during a moussem. In small towns there may be hotels—Moulay Idriss (where non Muslims may not stay) is a special case—and locals will rent out rooms in their houses. **Food** is unlikely to be a problem, with dozens of traders setting up stalls, though it is perhaps best to stick to simple grilled food, as stalls may not have access to running water for cleaning plates and glasses.

MOULOUD *MOUSSEMS*

Meknes: the Ben Aissa Moussem

Probably the largest of all the moussems, this includes a spectacular fantasia (if weather conditions permit) held near Place El Hedim. With the display of charging horsemen and poweder play, the enormous conical tents, and crowds of country people in white djellabahs, beneath the city walls, it has the appearance of a medieval tournament. At least, that is, until you see the adjoining fairground, which is itself fun, with illusionists, and riders of death.

In the past, this moussem was the princioal gathering of the Aissoua brotherhood, and the occasion for them to display their extraordinary powers of endurance under trance—cutting themselves with daggers, swallowing glass, and the like. Their activities today are more subdued, though they still include going into trance, and, of course, music. Their focus is the marabout tomb of ben Aissa, near the road in from Rabat.

Accommodation in Meknes at this time is a big problem unless you arrive a couple of days in advance; alternatively, you could visit from Fes for the day.

Salé: the Wax Candle Moussem

As the name suggests, the festival centers on a procession of wax candles—enormous lantern-like creations, carried from Bab El Rih to the Grand Mosque on the eve of the Mouloud. The candle bearers (a hereditary position) are followed by various brotherhoods, dancing and playing music.

The procession starts about 3pm and goes on for three or four hours; the best place to see it is at Bab Bou Hadja, where the candles are presented to local dignitaries.

OTHER POPULAR *MOUSSEMS*

May	**Moulay Bousselham**. *Moussem of Sidi Ahmed Ben Mansour.*
June	**Goulimine**. Traditionally a camel traders' fair, elements of which remain.
	Tan Tan. *Moussem of Sidi Mohammed Ma el Ainin.* Large-scale religious and commercial moussem. Saharan "Guedra" dance may be seen performed.
July	**Tetouan**. Moussem of Moulay Abdessalem. A very religious and traditional occasion with a large turnout of local tribesmen. Impressive location on a flat mountain top south of the town.
August	**Setti Fatma**. Large and popular moussem in the Ourika valley, southeast of Marrakesh.
	El Jadida. *Moussem of Moulay Abdallah.* Located about 9km west of the city at a village named after the saint. Features displays of horseriding, or *fantasias*.
	Tiznit. *Moussem of Sidi Ahmed ou Noussa.* Primarily religious.
	Chaouen. *Moussem of Sidi Allal Al Hadh.* Located in the hills out of the town.
September	**Moulay Idriss Zerhoun**. *Moussem of Moulay Idriss.* The largest religious moussem, but visitable only for the day as a non-Muslim. Impressive display of brotherhoods, and a highly charged procession of gifts to the saint's tomb. Also a large *fantasia* above the town.
	Imilchil. *Marriage Moussem.* Set in the heart of the Atlas mountains, this is the most celebrated Berber moussem—traditionally the occasion of all marriages in the region. It has lost part of this function, and is now a popular tourist event: in fact there now seem to be two moussems, with one laid on specifically for package tours from Marrakesh and Agadir. Worthwhile nonetheless, if only for the trip, the real event is held in the last week in September or the first in October.
	Fes. *Moussem of Moulay Idriss II.* The largest of the moussems held inside a major city, and involving a long procession to the saint's tomb. The Medina is packed out, however, and you will need to line the route early in order to see anything.

HARVEST *MOUSSEMS*

February	Tafraoute (almonds)
March	Beni Mellal (cotton)
April	Immouzer des Ida Outanane (honey)
May	Berkane (clementines)
	El Kelâa des Mgouna (roses)
June	Sefrou (cherries)
July	Al Hoceima (sea produce)
August	Immouzer du Kandar (apples and pears)
November	Erfoud (dates)
	Rhafsaï (olives)

FOLKLORE AND CULTURE FESTIVALS

Finally, there is a huge folklore festival in Marrakesh during the first and second weeks of June, and an international festival at Asilah (near Tangier) during August.

The **Marrakesh Festival** is essentially a tourist event, with groups of dancers, musicians, and entertainers brought in from all over the country. But apart from the artificiality of the setting it's all very authentic—and always draws large crowds of Moroccans. If you have any interest in traditional music, it is a must.

Events at the **Asilah Festival** are more difficult to generalize about. They include art exhibitions of Moroccan and Arab work, often including murals, and a whole sequence of concerts—from Egyptian or Lebanese singing stars to American college ensembles. Again, a festival worth planning at least a part of your trip around.

SOUKS AND MOROCCAN CRAFTS

Souks—markets—are a major feature of Moroccan life, and one of its great attractions. They are to be found everywhere: every town has its special quarter, large cities like Fes and Marrakesh have labyrinths of individual *souks* (each filling a street or square and devoted to one particular craft), and in the countryside there is a movable network, shifting between the various villages of a region.

Some of the villages, in fact, are named after **their market days**, so it's easy to see when they're held.

The *souk* days are:

Souk el Had —Sunday (literally, "first market").

Souk el Tnine—Monday market

Souk el Tleta— Tuesday market

Souk el Arba—Wednesday market

Souk el Khamees—Thursday market

Souk es Sebt—Saturday market

There are no village markets on Fridays (*el Djemaa*—the "assembly," when the main prayers are held in the mosques), and even in the cities, *souks* are largely closed on Friday mornings and very subdued for the rest of the day.

CRAFT TRADITIONS

Moroccan **craft**, or *artesanie*, traditions are still highly active, and even goods mass-produced for tourists are surprisingly untacky. To find pieces of real quality, however, is not that easy—some crafts have become dulled by centuries of repetition and others have been corrupted by modern techniques and chemical dyes.

In general, if you're planning on buying anything, it's always worth getting as close to the source of the goods as possible, and to steer clear of the main tourist centers. **Fes** might have the richest traditions, but you can often find better work at much cheaper prices elsewhere; **Tangier** and **Agadir**, neither of which have imaginative workshops of their own, are certainly best avoided. As stressed throughout the guide, the best way to get an idea of standards and quality is to visit the various **traditional crafts museums** spread around the country: there are good ones in Fes, Meknes, Tangier, Rabat, and Marrakesh.

CARPETS, RUGS, AND BLANKETS

Moroccan carpets are not cheap—you can pay $1600 and more for Arab designs in Fes or Rabat—but it is possible to find **rugs** at fairly reasonable prices, from $30 to $50, for a strong, well-designed weave.

Most of these will be of Berber origin and the most interesting ones usually come from the High and Middle Atlas; if you're looking seriously, try to get to the town *souk* in **Midelt** or the weekly markets in **Azrou** and other villages around **Marrakesh**.

On a simpler and cheaper level, **Berber blankets** (*foutahs*, or *couvertures*) are imaginative, and often very striking with bands of reds and blacks; for these, **Tetouan** and **Chaouen** on the edge of the Rif, are promising.

WOOD AND POTTERY

Marquetry is one of the few crafts where you'll see genuinely old pieces—inlaid tables and shelves—though the most easily exportable objects are boxes and chess sets, beautifully inlaid in *thuya* and cedar woods in **Essaouira**.

Pottery on the whole is disappointing, but tourist produce though it is, the blue-and-white designs of **Fes** and the multicolored pots of **Chaouen** are highly attractive.

JEWELRY

Silver jewelry went into decline with the loss to Israel of Morocco's Jewish population, the country's traditional workers in precious metals and craftsmen in general; in the **south,** however, you can pick up some fabulous Berber necklaces and bracelets, always very chunky, with bold combinations of semiprecious (and sometimes plastic) stones and beads.

CLOTHING AND LEATHER

There are also specifically **Moroccan clothes**. Westerners—men at least—who try to imitate Moroccan styles by wearing the cotton or wool *djellaba* (a kind of cloak) tend to look a little silly. But some of the cloth is exquisite, and walking down the dyers' *souks* is an inspiration.

Leather is also excellent, and here you can buy and wear goods with confidence. The classic Moroccan shoes are ***babouches***, open at the heel, immensely comfortable, and produced in yellow (the usual color), white, tan, and occasionally gray; a good pair—and quality varies enormously—can cost around $15–20.

BARGAINING

Whatever you buy, and wherever you buy it, you will want (and be expected) to **bargain**. There are no hard and fast rules on this—it is really a question of paying how much something is worth to you—but there are a few general points to keep in mind.

First, **bargaining is entirely natural** in Morocco. If you ask the price in a market, the answer, as likely as not, will come in one breath—"Twenty; how much will you pay?"

Second, don't pay any attention to **initial prices**. These are simply a device to test the limits of a particular deal or situation: don't think, for example, in terms of paying one-third the asking price (as some guides suggest)—it might well turn out to be a tenth or even a twentieth.

Third, **don't ever let a figure pass your lips** that you aren't be prepared to pay—nor start bargaining for something you have *absolutely* no intention of buying—there's no better way to create bad feelings.

Fourth, don't be afraid of **starting too low**, nor of being laughed at or insulted—this is part of the ritual, and your part is to be agreeable,

slightly disinterested (leaving, or having a friend try to get you to leave, will speed things up).

Take your time, if the deal is a serious one (for a rug, say): you'll probably want to sit down over tea with the vendor, and for two cups you'll talk about anything but the rug and the price.

The final and most golden rule of them all is to never go shopping with a **guide** or a hustler, even "just to look"—the pressures will be either too great or it'll be too boring, depending on how long you've been in the country and how you've learned to cope with these people.

In the main city *souks*—and particularly in Marrakesh—you might find **bartering goods** to be more satisfactory than bargaining over a price. This way you know the value of what you're offering better than your partner (though he'll have a pretty good idea, too), and in a sense you're giving a fairer exchange. Items particularly sought after are jogging shoes (even if they're well worn), printed T-shirts (Bob Marley and Prince designs are favorites), brand-name jeans, basic medicines (in country areas), and Western department-store clothes.

An approximate idea of what you should be paying for handicrafts can be gained from checking the **fixed prices** in the state-run *Centres Artisanals*. Even here, though, there is sometimes room for bargaining as prices are set slightly higher than you could expect to pay elsewhere.

MOSQUES AND MONUMENTS

Without a doubt, the major disappointment of traveling in Morocco is not being allowed into its mosques: all non-Muslims are excluded and the rule is strictly observed.

The only "mosques" that you *are* allowed to visit are the ruined Almohad structure of **Tin Mal**, in the High Atlas, the courtyard of the sanctuary-mosque of Moulay Ismail in **Meknes**, and the Bou Inania *medersa* in **Fes**. Elsewhere, you'll have to be content with an occasional glimpse through open doors, and even in this you should be sensitive: people don't seem to mind tourists peering into the Kairaouine Mosque in Fes (the country's most important religious building), but in the country you should never approach a shrine too closely.

This includes the numerous domed and white-washed **koubbas**—the tombs of *marabouts*, or

local saints—and the "monastic" **zaouias** of the various Sufi brotherhoods. It is a good idea to avoid walking through **graveyards**, too, as these are regarded as sacred places.

MONUMENTS ON PUBLIC VIEW

As some compensation, many of the most beautiful and architecturally interesting of Morocco's monuments are open to public view—the imperial gateways, or **babs**, of the main cities, for example, and, of course, the **minarets** (towers from which the call to prayer is made) attached to the mosques.

Of buildings that can be visited, highlights must include the **Berber Kasbahs** (fortified castle residences) of the south; a series of city **palaces** and **mansions**, often converted to use as **crafts museums**, in Fes and Marrakesh; and the intricate **medersas** of Fes, Meknes, Salé, and Marrakesh.

The **medersas**, many of them dating from the thirteenth and fourteenth centuries, are perhaps the most startling—and certainly the most "monumental"—of all Moroccan buildings, each displaying elaborate decoration and designs in stucco (gypsum or plaster), cedar, and tile mosaics (known in Morocco as *zellij*). Originally, these buildings served as religious universities or student residences for a neighboring mosque school, but by the turn of the century they had largely fallen into decay and disuse. Today, they have almost all become secularized. Their role is discussed in the chapter on **Fes**, which has the richest and most varied examples.

ANCIENT REMAINS

Unlike Tunisia and Algeria, Morocco never saw extensive **Roman** colonization—and indeed, the south of the country remained unconquered by any outside force until the French invasion of the 1920s. Ancient sites are, therefore, limited. The most interesting, and really the only one worth going out of your way to visit, is **Volubilis**, close to Meknes.

Prehistoric sites, with well preserved **rock paintings**, are to be found in the south of the country, though most are extremely difficult to gain access to, including the most significant one at Foum El Hassan. The most rewarding ones you can get to without very much difficulty are those around **Oukaimeden**, near Marrakesh.

FROM A WOMAN'S PERSPECTIVE

● **Margaret Hubbard spent one month traveling on her own around Morocco:**

I knew that there were likely to be difficulties in traveling as a woman alone around Morocco. I'd been warned by numerous sources (this book's previous edition included) about hustling and harassment and I was already well aware of the constraints imposed on women travelers within Islamic cultures. But above and beyond this, I knew I'd be fascinated by the country. I had picked up a smattering of Arabic and the impetus to study Islamic religion and culture during trips to Damascus and Amman (both times with a male companion). Also, I already had enough experience of traveling alone to know that I could live

well with myself should I meet up with no one else. So, a little apprehensive, but very much more determined and excited, I arrived in Tangier, took the first train out to Casablanca, and found a room for the night. It was not until I emerged the next morning into the bright daylight of Casablanca that I experienced my first reaction to Morocco.

BEGINNINGS

Nothing could have prepared me for it. Almost instantly, I was assailed by a barrage of: "*Voulez-vous coucher avec moi?*" "*Avez-vous jamais fait l'amour au Maroc?*" "*Venez avec moi, madame.*" "*Viens, m'selle.*" Whatever I had to say was ignored at will, and wherever I went, I felt that I was being constantly scrutinized by men.

Fighting off the panic, I headed for the bus station, where, after a lot of frantic rushing to and fro (I couldn't decipher the Arabic signs), I climbed onto a bus for Marrakesh.

Marrakesh proved to me that I was right in coming to Morocco. It wasn't that the harassment was any less so—in fact, it was almost as constant as in Tangier. But wandering through the Djemaa el Fna (the main square and center of all life in Marrakesh), among the snake charmers, kebab vendors, blanket weavers, water sellers, monkey trainers, and merchants of everything from false teeth to handwoven rugs, I became ensnared to such an extent that my response to the men who approached me was no longer one of fear but rather a feeling of irrelevance.

There was too much to be learned to shut out contact with people, and I heard myself utter, as if it were the most normal reply in the world: "*Non, monsieur, je ne veux pas coucher avec vous, mais pouvez-vous me dire pourquoi ils vendent* false teeth/*combien d'années il faut pour faire des tapis à main/pourquoi les singes* (monkeys). . . ?" That first night, I returned to my room at 2am more alive than I had felt for months.

STRATEGIES

I'd also stumbled upon a possible strategy for preempting, perhaps even preventing, harassment. Moroccan hustlers know a lot about tourists and have reason to expect one of two reactions from them: fear or a sort of resigned acceptance.

What they don't expect is for you to move quickly through the opening gambits and launch into a serious conversation about Moroccan life. Using a mixture of French and Arabic, I developed the persona of a "serious woman," and from Marrakesh to Figuig, discussed the politics of the Maghreb, maternity rights, housing costs, or the Koran with almost anyone who wanted my attention.

It became exhausting, but any attempt at more desultory chat was treated as an open invitation and seemed to make any harassment more determined. That isn't to say that it's impossible to have a more relaxed relationship with Moroccan men—I made good friends on two occasions with Arab men and I'm still corresponding with one of them. But I think this was made easier by my defining the terms of our friendship fairly early on in the conversation. (As a general rule, whenever I arranged to meet up with someone I didn't know very well, I chose well-lit public places. I was also careful about my clothes—I found it really did help to look as inconspicuous as possible, and almost always I wore loose-fitting blouses, longish skirts, and, occasionally, also a head scarf.)

CONTACT: THE *HAMMAM*

After exploring Marrakesh for five days, I took a bus out over the Atlas mountain range to Zagora. The journey took twelve hours and the bus was hot and cramped, but wedged between a group of Moroccan mothers, jostling their babies on my lap and sharing whatever food and drink was going around, I felt reassured, more a participant than an outsider.

This was also one of the few occasions that I'd had any sort of meaningful contact with Moroccan women. For the most part, women tend to have a low profile in public, moving in very separate spheres from the tourists. There are some women's cafés but they're well hidden and not for foreigners.

For me, the most likely meeting place was the *hammam*, or steam bath, which I habitually sought out in each stopping place. Apart from the undoubted pleasures of plentiful hot water, these became a place of refuge for me. It was a relief to be surrounded by women and to be an object of curiosity, without any element of threat. Any ideas about Western status I might have had were lost in the face of explaining in French, Arabic, and sign language to an old Moroccan woman with 24 grandchildren the sexual practices and methods of contraceptions used in the West. "Is it true that women are opened up by machine?" is a question that worries me still.

FESTIVITIES

I arrived in Zagora on the last night of the festival of the king's birthday. It was pure chance. The town was packed with Moroccans who had traveled in from nearby oases. Oddly, though, I met just one other tourist—a German man. We were both swept along, as insignificant as any other single people in the crowd, dancing and singing in time to the echoing African sounds.

At the main event of the night, the crowd was divided by a long rope with women on one side and men on the other, with only the German and I standing side by side. I felt overwhelmed with a feeling of excitement and well-being, simply because I was there.

INTO THE DESERT

From Zagora I headed for Figuig and the desert, stopping overnight en route in Tinerhir. It's possible that I chose a bad hotel for that stop, but it was about the worst night that I had spent in the entire trip. The men in and around the hotel jeered, even spat, at me when I politely refused to accompany them, and throughout the night I had men banging on the door shutters of my room. For twelve hours I stood guard, tense, afraid, and stifled by the locked-in heat of that dismal hotel room. I escaped on the first bus out.

Farther south I met up with a Danish man in a Land Rover and traveled on with him to spend four days in the desert. It was a simple business arrangement—he wanted someone to look after the van while he slept and I wanted someone to look out for me while I slept. I can find no terms that will sufficiently describe the effect the desert had on me. It was awesome and inspiring and it silenced me. I also found that the more recent preoccupations that I had about my life, work, and relationships had entirely slipped from my mind. Yet strangely, I could recall with absolute clarity images from over ten years ago. I remain convinced that the desert, in its simplicity, its expansiveness, and its power changed me in some way.

At Figuig I parted company with the Dane and made it in various stages to Fes. I tended to find myself becoming dissatisfied after traveling for a while with a male companion. This was not because I didn't enjoy the company, which was, more often than not, a luxury for me, but I used to feel cheated that I was no longer at the forefront and that any contact with Moroccans would have to be made through him. This is often the case in Islamic countries, where any approaches or offers of hospitality are proffered man to man, with the woman treated more or less as an appendage. I was prepared to go on alone however uncomfortable it might become, so long as I was treated as a person in my own right.

JOGGING

In Fes I discovered yet another, perhaps even more effective, strategy for changing my status with Moroccan men. I am a runner and compete regularly in marathons, and I'm used to keeping up with my training in almost any conditions. Up until Fes, I'd held back, uncertain as to the effect of dashing out of a hotel in only sweatpants and a T-shirt. My usual outfit, the long skirt and blouse, was hardly suitable for the exercise I had

in mind. After seriously considering confining myself to laps around the hotel bedroom, I recovered my sanity and my sense of adventure, changed my clothes, and set off.

The harassment and the hustling all melted away. I found that the Moroccans have such a high regard for sport that the very men who had hassled me in the morning were looking on with a respectful interest, offering encouragement and advice as I hurtled by in the cool of the evening. From then on, I became known as "the runner" and was left more or less in peace for the rest of my stay.

After this, I made it a rule to train in all the villages and towns I stayed in on my way back to Tangier. Now when I run, I conjure up the image of pacing out of Chaouen toward the shrine on the hillside, keeping time with the chants of the *muezzin* at dawn.

RETURN TO TANGIER

Returning to Tangier, I felt as far removed as it is possible to feel from the apprehensive new arrival of the month before. I felt less intimidated and more stoic about my status as an inferior and an outsider, and I had long since come to accept that I was a source of income to many people whose options for earning money are severely limited.

Walking out of the bus station, I was surrounded by a group of hustlers. I listened in silence and then said, in the fairly decent Arabic that I had picked up along the journey from Figuig to Fes, that I had been in the Sahara and hadn't gotten lost so I didn't think I needed a guide in Tangier, and furthermore, that I had talked with some Touaregs in Zagora who told me that it is a lie that Moroccans buy their women with camels; would they please excuse me, I had arrangements?

I spent the next few days wandering freely around the town, totally immersed in plotting how to return.

Don't be afraid to express outrage. Public harassment of women is never something that would be accepted within the community. If you are harassed in the street, or a public place, a loud expression of outrage, or an attempt to involve passers by, should immediately result in public anger against the man and a very uncomfortable situation for him. This works in Morocco in a way that it wouldn't, for example, in Spain or Italy, where macho male attitudes mean that public harassment is a fact of life for Spanish or Italian women.

DIRECTORY

ADDRESSES Arabic names—*Derb*, *Zankat*, etc.—are gradually replacing French ones. The main street or square of any town, though, is still invariably *Avenue* or *Place* Hassan II (the present king) or Mohammed V (his father). Street signs are usually in French and Arabic lettering.

BAGGAGE can usually be left safely at train station *consignes* (baggage rooms) and at *CTM* bus terminals—for a small charge.

BRING. . . If you want to bargain for handicrafts, bring things to barter with (see "Bargaining"); if you're going hiking in the Atlas, presents are helpful and appreciated (see "Djebel Toubkal"), and salt tablets, insect repellent, water purifying tablets and aspirin are useful. An alarm clock is needed for early-morning—sometimes 5am— buses. Camera film is available but expensive.

CONSULATES AND EMBASSIES are mostly listed under their respective cities—essentially Rabat, but also Tangier and Casablanca, to an extent.

CONTRACEPTIVES Condoms can be bought in most *pharmacies*, and so can the pill (officially by prescription, but this isn't essential). If you're suffering from diarrhea, the pill (or any other drug) may not be in your system long enough to be absorbed, and consequently may become ineffective.

CUSTOMS You're allowed to bring a liter of hard liquor into Morocco, which is well worth doing.

ELECTRICAL VOLTAGE Virtually all the country now runs on 220v, although a few towns (Essaouira, for example) remain on 110v.

GAY ATTITUDES Homosexuality is widespread in Morocco, although in certain parts of the country (the Rif, for example) it is virtually taboo. The days of Tangier—and, to a lesser extent, Marrakesh—as gay resorts are largely over, the Moroccan government having instituted a major crack down (and wholesale closure of brothels) following independence. Gay sex is, of course, still available, and men traveling alone or together will certainly be propositioned—but attitudes are tending increasingly toward hustling and exploitation on all sides. It is, in addition, officially illegal under Moroccan law. Article 489 of the Moroccan penal code prohibits any "shameless or unnatural act" with a person of the same sex and allows for imprisonment of six months to three years, plus a fine. There are also various other provisions in the penal code for more serious offenses, with correspondingly higher penalties in cases involving, for example, corruption of minors.

HOSPITAL EMERGENCIES ☎15 for an ambulance.

LAUNDROMATS in the larger towns will take in clothes and wash them overnight, but you'll usually find it easier to ask at hotels—most will have it done for you (even the really basic places).

POLICE There are two main types: the *Gendarmerie* (who run security, and are the police you meet at checkpoints in the south and in the Rif) and the *Sûreté*. To report any kind of crime, or if you need help, the *Sûreté* are definitely preferable. The police emergency number is ☎19.

RELATIONSHIPS Following clamp downs on "unofficial guides," there are laws in effect that can make relationships with Moroccans problematic. In theory, any Moroccan—without a guide's permit—seen accompanying a tourist can be arrested and imprisoned. In practice this is very rarely enforced. However, friendships, especially in tourist cities like Agadir or Marrakesh, should be discreet.

SKIING The main center is in Oukaimeden, near Marrakesh (Dec.–Apr.); other smaller resorts are in Mischliffen (near Azrou) and Ketama in the Rif. Details are available abroad from the Moroccan Tourist Board, or in Morocco from the *Fédération Royale Marocaine de Ski, Haut Commissariat à la Jeunesse et aux Sports.* Bd. Mohammed V, Rabat.

SWIMMING POOLS Towns of any size tend to have a municipal pool—they're always very cheap and addresses are given in the guide. In the south, you'll be dependent on campground pools or on those at the luxury hotels (who often allow outsiders to swim, either for a charge or for drinks or a meal). On the Atlantic **beaches** always take care—currents and undertows can be very strong.

TAMPONS can be bought at general stores, not *pharmacies*, in most Moroccan cities. Don't expect to find them in country or mountain areas.

TIME Morocco keeps Greenwich Mean Time the whole year. It is therefore one hour (two hours in summertime) behind Spain—something to keep in mind when catching ferries.

WORK Your only chance of paid work in Morocco is teaching English. The *American Language Center* (1 Place de la Fraternité, Casblanca; also in Rabat, Kenitra, Tangier, Tetouan, Meknes, Fes, and Marrakesh), or the *American School* (Rue Al Amir Abdelkader, Agdal, Rabat; also in Casablanca and Tangier). Reasonable spoken French is normally required by all of these.

WORKCAMPS If you are interested in taking part in a workcamp, there are a number of possibilities open. The *United Nations Association* (contact their head office: UN Plaza, New York) recruit international teams to work on manual and community projects for two or three weeks in the summer; applicants pay their own travel costs but are accommodated in Morocco. Alternatively, there are three Moroccan organizations: *Les Amis des Chantiers Internationaux de Meknes* (PO Box 8, Meknes), whose projects generally involve agricultural or construction work in the Meknes area; three weeks in July and August, accommodation and food provided; *Chanteuse Jeunesse Maroc* (PO Box 566, Rabat), with some inspired workcamps—recently, creating green spaces at Asilah, and constructing lanes and alleyways in shanty towns near Mohammedia; or *Pensés et Chantiers* (26 Rue de Pakistan, BP 1423, Rabat), involving community schemes—painting, restoration, and gardening. Most of the workcamps are open to all-comers over 17 years of age; travel costs have to be paid by the participant, but you generally receive free accommodation (take a sleeping bag) and meals.

METRIC WEIGHTS AND MEASURES	
1 ounce = 28.3 grams	1 inch = 2.54 centimeters (cm)
1 pound = 454 grams	1 foot = 0.3 meters (m)
2.2 pounds = 1 kilogram	1 yard = 0.91 meters
1 pint = 0.47 liters	1.09 yards = 1m
1 quart = 0.94 liters	1 mile = 1.61 kilometers (km)
1 gallon = 3.78 liters	0.62 miles = 1km

PART TWO

THE
GUIDE

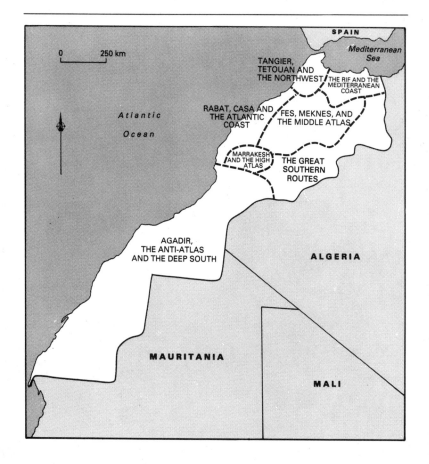

0   250 km

SPAIN

Mediterranean Sea

TANGIER, TETOUAN AND THE NORTHWEST

THE RIF AND THE MEDITERRANEAN COAST

Atlantic

RABAT, CASA AND THE ATLANTIC COAST

FES, MEKNES, AND THE MIDDLE ATLAS

Ocean

MARRAKESH AND THE HIGH ATLAS

THE GREAT SOUTHERN ROUTES

AGADIR, THE ANTI-ATLAS AND THE DEEP SOUTH

ALGERIA

MAURITANIA

MALI

CHAPTER ONE

TANGIER, TETOUAN, AND THE NORTHWEST

Northwest Morocco can be an intense introduction to the country. Its two chief cities, Tangier and Tetouan, are by reputation difficult, with guides and hustlers preying on first-time travelers. However, once you are clear of the points of arrival, and have set your bags down in a hotel, it doesn't take long to get a measure of them—and to enjoy the experience. **Tangier**, hybridized and slightly seedy from its long European contact, has a setting and skyline the equal of any Mediterranean resort, and an immediate fascination in its position as meeting point of Europe and Africa. **Tetouan**, in the shadow of the wild Rif mountains, feels instinctively more Moroccan—its Medina a glorious labyrinth, dotted with squares, souks and buildings from its seventeenth-century foundation by refugees from Spanish Andalusia.

Moving on, the most popular destination is the mountain town of **Chaouen**, a small-scale and laid-back place to come to terms with being in Morocco. It is most easily reached via Tetouan. Heading south from Tangier—the beginning of the railroad lines to Fes, Rabat, Casablanca, and Marrakesh—the easiest places to get acclimatized are the seaside resorts of Asilah and Larache. **Asilah**, a growing tourist center, is maybe a little too exploited, though certainly worth time if you are traveling in August, when it is stage for an **International Festival**—northern Morocco's major cultural event of the year. **Larache** is less well known, though a personal favourite, for its relaxed feel, fine beach, and proximity to the ancient Carthaginian-Roman site of Lixus.

A note is perhaps useful on this region's especially quirky **twentieth-century history**. Prior to Independence, in 1956, northern Morocco was divided into three separate zones of colonial administration. Tetouan was the administrative capital of the Spanish zone, which encompassed Chaouen (and the Rif) and spread south through Asilah and Larache—itself a provincial center. The French zone began at Souk el Arba, the edge of rich agricultural plains sprawling south toward the French Protectorate's capital, Rabat. Tangier, meanwhile, experienced a bizarre period of "International Rule," under a grouping of European embassies. The modern consequences of this

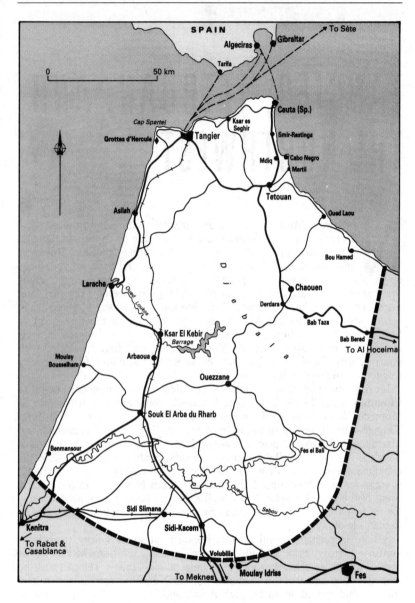

past find expression mainly in **language**. Although French is now the official second language, after Arabic, all but the younger generation of Moroccans are more fluent in Spanish—a basic knowledge of which can prove extremely useful.

TANGIER AND THE COAST

Tangier—in addition to its international airport—has ferry connections with Algeciras and Tarifa in Spain, and (by catamaran) with Gibraltar. Unless you are bringing a car over from Spain (in which case Ceuta is more economic), it's a preferable point of arrival—both in its own right, and for its convenience in moving straight on into Morocco. Asilah is a mere forty minutes' ride on the train; Meknes, Fes, Rabat and Casablanca, are all comfortably reached within the day; while if you are in a hurry to get south, there is a night express train for Marrakesh.

The **coast** detailed in this section is the **Atlantic** stretch, from Tangier south towards Rabat. Asilah, by train, is the easiest destination; Larache can be reached by bus or grand taxi only, either from Tangier or (simpler) from Asilah. The most distinctively Moroccan resort is **Moulay Bousselham**, farther south and accessible by bus from Souk-el-Arba-du-Rharb.

Tangier (Tanger, Tangiers)

For the first five decades of this century, **TANGIER** was one of the most stylish resorts of the Mediterranean—an "International City" with its own laws and administration, plus a bizarre floating community of exiles, expatriates, and refugees. It was home, at various times, to William Burroughs, Jack Kerouac, Allen Ginsberg, and other 1950s beat writers; Spanish and central European refugees; Moroccan nationalists; and—drawn by loose tax laws and free-port status—to over seventy banks and 4000 companies, most of them dealing in currency transactions forbidden in their own countries. It was also the world's first and most famous gay center, and to a small degree remains one.

When Moroccan independence was gained in 1956, Tangier's special status was removed, and almost overnight, the finance and banking businesses shifted their operations to Spain and Switzerland. The expatriate colony dwindled, too, as the new national government imposed bureaucratic controls and instituted a "clean-up" of the city. Brothels—previously numbering almost a hundred—were banned, and in the early 1960s "The Great Scandal" erupted, sparked by a handful of pedophilia convictions and escalating into a wholesale closure of the once outrageous gay bars. These days there's a definite feeling of decline about the city, most evident in the older hotels and bars. What remains has a slightly uneasy identity, halfway toward becoming a mainstream tourist resort—and an increasingly popular one with vacationing Moroccans—but still retaining hints of its dubious past reputation amid the shambling 1930s architecture and style. It is, as already noted, a tricky place for first-time arrivals—and hustler stories here should not be underestimated—but once you get the hang of it, the city can still seem lively and very likable, living in something of a time warp and with an enduring capacity for slight craziness.

POINTS OF ARRIVAL

By Ferry

Embarking at Tangier can be a slow process, with long waits in line for passport control and customs: be prepared. Most importantly, make sure that you have your **passport stamped** (and departure card collected) while *on board the ferry*; announcements to this effect are not always made in English, so make your way to the purser's office during the journey. If you miss out on this, you'll be left until the end of the arrival lines in Tangier.

Once ashore, and through customs, you pass into the **ferry terminal building**. There's a **bureau de change** here which sells dirhams at normal rates for most currencies and travelers' checks (for credit card exchange you need a bank in the city, see *Directory*). Also within the building is an **ONCF Office** for train tickets, worth getting in line for immediately if you're going straight on to Asilah, Rabat, Meknes, or Fes.

The **port train station** (Gare du Port) is almost directly below the terminal; you can't miss it as you come out, and with persistence, you should be able to find a seat, too. For details of connecting trains, see "Leaving Tangier".

By Hydrofoil/Catamaran

Hydrofoils (from Algeciras or Tarifa) and **catamarans** (from Gibraltar) dock close to the ferry terminal. Passport control and customs need to be cleared, though this is usually a quicker operation, as the boats tend to be dominated by groups of day-trippers from the Costa del Sol, accompanied by travel couriers. If you want to change money and have some ready cash, there's no need to subject yourself to the terminal *bureau*—the travel agents along the seafront will take dollars, pesetas, and pounds, and so will most hotels.

By Air

Tangier's **airport** is about 15km outside the city. There is no direct bus, though if you arrive on a package tour, you'll be met by a hotel bus. If you're on your own, you'll either have to bargain with the taxi drivers, who should charge around 100dh for the trip (up to six passengers), or take a two-kilometer walk to the main road, where you can pick up the #17 or #70 buses to the Grand Socco (see *Orientation*, below).

A Note on Taxis

Grands Taxis (mainly large black Mercedes) can be picked up at the port entrance, or at a rank opposite the English church on Rue d'Angleterre; they are permitted to carry up to six passengers. The price for a ride should be fixed in advance—10dh is the regular rate (for foreigners) for any trip within the city, including tip. Small blue/green **petits taxis** (which carry just three passengers) are also often available at the port, and can be flagged down around the town, though there are no longer any ranks. Most of these are metered—standard rate for a city trip is 5dh.

Anywhere in Tangier, you can **flag down a taxi**, whether it has passengers or not. If it is going in your direction it will generally take you. If you join a taxi with passengers, you pay the full fare, as if it were empty.

For details on the bus and taxi terminals for journeys out of Tangier, see "Leaving Tangier," following the Directory.

Orientation and Finding a Place to Stay

After the initial confusion of an unfamiliar, Arab-looking city, Tangier is surprisingly easy to find your way around. As with all the larger Moroccan towns, it's made up of two parts: the **Medina**, the original town, and the **Ville Nouvelle,** built by its European colonizers. Inside the Medina, a classic web of alleyways and stepped passages, is the old fortified quarter of the **Kasbah,** the former Sultanate's palace at its center.

Together with the **beach** and the seafront **Avenue d'Espagne,** there are three other easy reference points in the city's main squares—the Grand Socco, Petit Socco, and Place de France. **Place de France** is a conventional, French-looking square at the heart of the Ville Nouvelle, flanked by elegant cafés and a terrace/belvedere looking out over the ocean. From here, **Boulevard Pasteur** (the main city street) leads off toward the post office and the ONMT tourist office a couple of blocks farther up. In the other direction, **Rue de la Liberté** runs down to the **Grand Socco,** a fairly amorphous open space in front of the Medina. Access to this is through two horseshoe archways; the one on the right opens onto the main Medina street, **Rue es Siaghin,** which culminates in the **Petit Socco**—a tiny square of old cafés and cheap hotels.

Arriving—and "Guides"

Arriving at the port or train station, it's easy enough to walk to a hotel on the seafront or in the Medina; places in the central Ville Nouvelle are a little farther, and you may want to take a cab. For the **seafront** places, simply follow the Avenue d'Espagne/Avenue des FAR. If you want to **stay in the Medina,** there's a choice of routes: either up Rue du Portugal to the Grand Socco, or up the steps behind the port entrance, round to the Grand Mosque and the junction of Rue des Postes/Rue Dar el Baroud. If you're unsure of yourself (and the walk to the Medina can be intimidating if it's your first visit to Morocco), take a taxi at the entrance/exit of the port.

STREET NAMES

Tangier **street-name signs** are the most confusing in the country, with the old French and Spanish colonial names still in use alongside their Arabicized successors. In addition *Rue* and *Calle* are both gradually being replaced by *Zankat, Avenue* and *Boulevard* by *Charih.*

Maps tend to use the new versions, though few streetsigns have been changed. In the text and maps of this guide, we have used new names only when firmly established. Among the main streets, note:

> **Rue de la Plage** — **Zankat Salah Eddine El Ayoubi**
> **Rue Rembrandt** — **Zankat El Jaba El Quatania**
> **Rue Goya** — **Zankat Moulay Al Abdallah**
> **Rue de la Liberté** — **Zankat El Houria**
> **Rue Sanlucar** — **Zankat El Moutanabi**
> **Place de France** — **Place de Faro.**

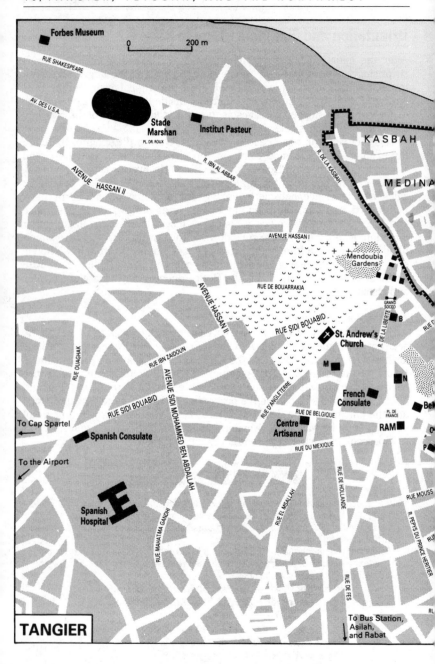

TANGIER

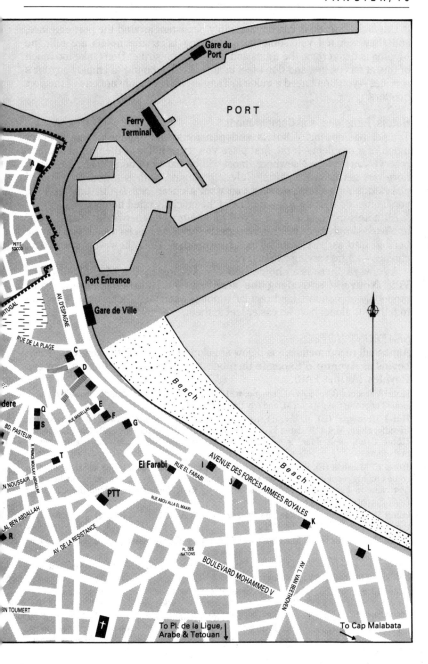

Gare du
Port

PORT

Ferry
Terminal

A

PETIT
SOCCO

AV. D'ESPAGNE

PORTUGAL

RUE DE LA PLAGE

Port Entrance

Gare de Ville

Beach

C

D

dere

E

Q

F

S

RUE MAGELLAN

G

BD. PASTEUR

Beach

R. PRINCE MOULAY ABDALLAH

T

El Farabi

RUE EL FARABI

AVENUE DES FORCES ARMEES ROYALES

N NOUSSAIR

I

PTT

J

RUE ABOU ALLA EL MAARI

LAL BEN ABDALLAH

K

R

AV. DE LA RESISTANCE

PL. DES
NATIONS

L

BOULEVARD MOHAMMED V

AV. L. VAN BEETHOVEN

BN TOUMERT

✝

To Pl. de la Ligue,
Arabe & Tetouan ↓

To Cap Malabata

Unofficial **"guides"** can be incredibly persistent around the port entrance, and they will tell you some fairly amazing tales: the hotels are full, the Medina is dangerous, the trains and buses are on strike. Don't take too much of this at face value, and don't feel in any way dutybound to employ anyone's services—you don't need a guide in Tangier, and certainly not one of the port hustlers.

Hotels, Pensions, and Campgrounds

Tangier has dozens of **hotels and pensions**, and finding a room is never much of a problem—if the first place you try is full, ask them to phone and reserve you a place elsewhere (most will be happy to do so). The city does, however, get crowded during July and August, with some of the unrated places doubling their prices. If you want a cheap bed at this time of year, you'll often do best by going for one of the officially rated hotels.

All hotels listed below are **keyed** on one or the other of our maps. A few are listed simply because they're popular package choices, which you may be booked into as part of an all-inclusive holiday. Most, however, are budget choices—all (to varying extents) recommended.

As always, there is a **choice between staying in the Medina**, or in the **Ville Nouvelle and along the seafront**. The latter areas have a virtual monopoly on comfort (and regular running water), and for women traveling together or alone, have an easier feel to them.

SEAFRONT HOTELS

Almost all recommendations below are along (or just off) the seafront, which begins as **Avenue d'Espagne** then becomes **Avenue des Forces Armeés Royales** (Av. des FAR).

Hôtel Valencia (C), 72 Av. d'Espagne; ☎217.14. Recently renovated and very well situated; almost opposite the port, CTM, and city train station. *2*A*.

Hôtel Bretagne (D), 92 Av. d'Espagne ☎323.39). Once grand, now a bit decayed, but friendly, clean, and 1*B status keeps prices low and fairly standard; *1*B*. The unclassified **Hôtel Cecil**, next door, is similar, though extremely dilapidated—too damp outside midsummer.

Hôtel El Muniria (E), Rue Magellan. Friendly, excellent value and with a late-night bar that comes highly recommended. Burroughs, Kerouac, and Ginsberg all stayed here when they first came to Tangier. (Rue Magellan zigzags up from the seafront behind the crumbling *Hôtel Biarritz*.) *Unclassified–1*A prices*.

Hôtel Ibn Batouta (F), 8 Rue Magellan; 09/371.70. Another good value choice, just across the street from the *El Muniria*. *1*B*.

Hôtel El Djenina (G), 8 Rue Grotius. Dull, though well maintained (hot baths in all rooms, etc.); just off the avenue d'Espagne, one block up. *2*A*.

Hôtel Miramar (J), Av. des FAR; ☎389.48. By far the best budget hotel on the seafront, very 1930s, and big rooms with hot showers. *2*B*.

Hôtel El Farabi (H), 8 Rue Saidia/corner Rue El Farabi; ☎345-66. Excellent alternative to the Miramar, if that's full. Clean, well run and friendly. *Unclassified–2*B prices*.

Hôtel Rif (I), Av. d'Espagne, ☎359.08, *5**; **Hôtel Almohades (K)**, Av. des FAR, ☎403.30, *5**; **Hôtel Solazur (L)**, Av. des FAR, ☎401.64, *4*A*. Three of the main package hotels on the seafront; official rates are high if you book independently, though they sometimes have offers out of season.

OTHER VILLE NOUVELLE HOTELS

Most of these recommendations are within a few blocks of the Place de France and central Boulevard Pasteur. If you've got much baggage, a taxi could be a useful investment.

Hôtel Lutetia (Q), 3 Rue Moulay Abdallah (Goya); ☎318.66. Good for its category and well located—a block below Boulevard Pasteur. *2*A*.

Hôtel Maroc (S), Rue Moulay Abdallah (Goya). A block from the Lutetia—literally falling apart, but a nice place in its own way.

Grand Hôtel Villa de France (H), 143 Rue de Hollande; ☎314.75. This is one of the most elegant hotels in the country (Matisse stayed in, and painted the view from, Room 35), with gardens, swimming pool, and a lively bar. It isn't however, crammed with elevators and luxury fittings, and so remains moderately priced—around $30 for a double room. Reservations essential in midsummer. *4*A*.

Hôtel El Minzah (N), 85 Rue de la Liberté, ☎358.85, *5**; **Hôtel Africa (O)**, 17 Av. Moussa Ibn Noussair, ☎355.11, *4*B*; **Hôtel Chellah (R)**, Rue Allal Ben Abdallah, ☎383.88, *4*A*; **Hôtel Tanjah Flandria (T)**, 6 Bd. Mohammed V, ☎330.00, 4*A. Main package hotels in the centre. If you have unlimited money, the Minzah is Tangier's finest, with a wonderful garden pool overlooking the sea and town.

Rue de la Plage. This street (aka Rue Salah Edddine El Ayoubi) runs up from the town train station to the Grand Socco and is lined with small pensions. Many of them charge outrageous prices to new arrivals sent over by port hustlers. *Pensions Miami* and *Talavera* are probably the best bets.

MEDINA HOTELS

With the exception of the *Continental* and the *Mamora,* these listings are unrated and fairly basic—safe enough, though, and with distinct character if you have the (initial) confidence. See the Medina map for a key to the smaller places.

Hôtel Grand Socco (B on main map), Grand Socco. Very central and extremely easy to find, with some rooms looking out over the square. Good deals on big rooms for three to five people.

Hôtel Mauretania (1), **Pension Becerra (2)**, **Hôtel Fuentes (3)**, all in the Petit Socco, right at the heart of the Medina. *Fuentes,* with a terrace café above the square, is the friendliest, and also the oldest; Camille Saint-Saens was one of its Victorian guests.

Pension Palace (4), **Pension Marhaba (6)**, Rue des Postes. Best of a fairly bad bunch in a real hustler-dive of a street; the *Palace* is quite attractive, though, and *Marhaba,* in an alley to the left (just before reaching the Grand Mosque), has good views of town and sea from some rooms.

Hôtel Mamora (5), 19 Rue des Postes. Overpriced for the facilities (water is as erratic here as in the Socco dives) but offers security and a bit more comfort at the heart of the Medina. *2*B*.

Hôtel Continental (A on main map), Rue Dar el Baroud, ☎310.24. Founded in 1888, and once the most fashionable hotel in Tangier, this is still in class by itself: a grand piano in the hall, a huge parrot cage, and a beautiful terrace overlooking the port. It's just been renovated, but since most mainstream tourists don't want to stay deep in the Medina, prices remain fairly low. To get there, either take a taxi from by the port entrance, or walk up to the Petit Socco and take Rue de la Marine to the left of Rue des Postes. Follow this around past the Grand Mosque and a terrace, and you'll come to the imposing old hotel gates. Reservations recommended—and ask for rooms 108 or 208, which are a treat. *As yet unclassified—2*A prices.*

CAMPGROUNDS

Tangier's campgrounds are sited well outside the city—worth considering mainly if you are traveling in a RV or with a caravan. For those with a tent, security is not great, and costs (especially if you have no transport) the equal of a reasonable budget hotel. Choices are:

Camping Miramonte (☎371.38). The closest and most popular campground, 3km from the center, to the west of the Kasbah; to get there, take local buses #2, # 21, or preferably #1 from the Grand Socco. Grounds are just behind the "Atlantic Beach," fairly pleasant and with a reasonable restaurant.

Camping-Caravaning Tingis (☎401.91). Sited 6km east of the city, over towards Cap Malabata with its Club Mediterannée complex. *Tingis* itself is quite a sizable "vacation village", complete with tennis court, shops and swimming pool. But it's a 2km walk from the beach (which, with the nearby woods, is highly unsafe at night), overpriced, and has a lot of mosquitos.

Robinson Plage Camping, Cap Spartel. A relaxed, beachside campground, 8km east of Tangier by the Caves of Hercules (see "Around Tangier"). No buses; *grand taxi* is pricey, unless you plan to stay a few days.

The City

Tangier's interest and attraction lies essentially in the city itself: its café life, excellent beach, and the tumbling streets of the Medina. The few specific "monuments," with the exception of the Dar el Makhzen palace, are best considered as anchors to your wanderings. The markets, though novel and bright enough, are not on the whole great sources of bargains; Moroccan dealers tend to regard Tangier as a place to sell whatever they can't elsewhere.

The Beach, Grand Socco, and Ville Nouvelle

It was **the beach** and Tangier's mild climate which drew in the first expatriates, the Victorian British, who used to amuse themselves in afternoon rides along the sands and weekends of "pig-sticking" in the wooded hills behind. Today's pleasures come a little more packaged on the **town beach**, with camel rides and a string of semi-clublike beach bars. However, by day the sands are diverting enough, and fun, with Moroccans entertaining themselves in acrobatics and soccer.

It is now compulsory to change in a cabin, so when you arrive you may feel like attaching yourself to one of the **beach bars**, most of which offer showers and deckchairs, as well as food and drink. Some of these are institutions, like *Emma's BBC Bar* (still serving up bacon-and-egg breakfasts to the British), or *The Sun Beach*, where Tennessee Williams reputedly wrote a first draft of *Cat on a Hot Tin Roof* ; some, like *The Windmill*, where Joe (Prick up Your Ears) Orton knocked about, and *The Macumba*, retain a predominantly gay clientèle. Perhaps the most lively and pleasant today is *Miami Beach*, with its gardens to laze around in, but the scenes change with the season, so look around and take your pick.

By day, it more or less goes without saying, don't leave anything on the beach unattended. By night, limit your exploration to the beach bars (a few of which offer evening cabarets—if Arabic Country & Western appeals), as the beach itself becomes a dangerous venue for rough trade.

Rambling around the town, the **Grand Socco** seems like a natural place to start; its name, like so many in Tangier, is a French-Spanish hybrid, stating its origins as the main market square. This is no longer the case; the stalls and entertainers have all been moved to make way for a local bus station. It is still, though, something of a meeting place—everyone wandering through in a Mediterranean evening *paseo*, its cafés an interesting place to sit and view it all.

So, too, are those in **Place de France**, which is where half the people in the Socco are heading. The *Café de Paris* here was a legendary hangout throughout the years of the international zone, above all during World War II, when it was the center of deal making and intrigue between British and American agents and those of Germany, Italy, and Japan. Later, the emphasis shifted to Morocco's own politics: the first Nationalist paper, *La Voix du Maroc*, surfaced at the café, and Allal el Fassi, exiled from the French-occupied zone, set up his Istiqlal headquarters nearby.

The old **markets** of the Grand Socco have been moved partly into Rue de Portugal (running down to the port), partly onto cramped terraces to either side of Rue d'Angleterre. Most interesting of these is a small terrace to the left, near the walls of the *Villa de France* hotel, where Berber women from the villages sell their red-, black-, and white-striped *foutahs*—rough-weave blankets worn sometimes four to the body as skirts, shawl, and head covering. Quality and prices for these are usually better in Tetouan, but the designs are much the same.

On the opposite side of Rue d'Angleterre, a little ways before coming to the former British consulate, is a surprising, still-active **Anglican church**—only slightly bizarre in its fusion of Moorish decoration and English country churchyard. There is generally a caretaker around to show the church, notable for its rendition of the Lord's Prayer in Arabic script above the altar. In the graveyard, among the laments of early deaths from malaria, you come upon the tomb of **Walter Harris** (see *Contexts*), the most brilliant of the chroniclers of "Old Morocco" in the closing decades of the nineteenth century and the beginning of the twentieth. Another eccentric Briton, Emily Keane, is also commemorated. A contemporary of Harris's, she lived a very different life, marrying in 1873 the Shereef of Ouezzane—at the time one of the most holy towns of the country. Her *Life Story*, still to be found in libraries and secondhand bookstores, is one of the minor classics of literature on Morocco, full of contradictions and sympathy.

Further market areas are to be found if you follow Rue de la Liberté toward Place de France, and then turn left, down a series of steps, past the *El Minzah* hotel. The terraces that you come out upon comprise the so-called **Fondouk Market**, a sequence of tiny stalls ranging from pottery to spectacle repairs, from fruit and vegetables to junk.

The **Mendoubia Gardens**, which flank the Grand Socco, are a temptation—and for guests at the Minzah hotel they shelter private tennis courts. However, as the grounds of the city's lawcourts, they are officially out of bounds to the public. On Sundays, the caretaker sometimes gives groups a brief tour; ring if you are interested.

The Medina

The Grand Socco offers the most straightforward aproach to the Medina. The arch on the left of the square leads into Rue d'Italie, which becomes Rue de la Kasbah, the northern entrance to the Kasbah quarter. The smaller gateway, to the left of this, gives onto Rue es Siaghin, off which are most of the *souks* (markets) and at the end of which is the Petit Socco, the Medina's principal landmark and square. An alternative approach to the Medina is from the seafront: follow the steps up, walk round by the Grand Mosque and Rue de la Poste will lead you to the Petit Socco.

Rue es Siaghin (Silversmiths' Street) was Tangier's main street into the 1930s, and remains an active thoroughfare, with a series of fruit, grain, and cloth markets opening off to its sides. Halfway up, locked and decaying, is the old **Spanish Cathedral and Mission**; to the right, just before it, was formerly the **Mellah**, or Jewish quarter, centered around Rue des Synagogues. Moroccan Jews traditionally controlled the silver and jewelry trade—the "Siaghin" of the street name—but few remain in Tangier, having left at independence for Gibraltar, France, and Israel. Siaghin itself, well before that, had been taken over by tourist stalls; needless to say, it's a bad place to buy anything.

The **Petit Socco** (Little Market) seems too small ever to have served such a purpose. Old photographs, in fact, show it almost twice its present size, and it was only at the turn of the century that the Spanish hotels and cafés here were built. These, however, give the place its atmosphere: seedy, slightly conspiratorial, and the location for many of the Moroccan stories of Mohammed Mrabet translated by Paul Bowles (see the "Books" section in *Contexts*). In the heyday of the "international city," with easily exploited Arab and Spanish sexuality a major attraction, it was in the alleys behind the Socco that the straight and boy brothels were concentrated. William Burroughs used to hang out around the square dressed in old suits bought from Moroccans, which had been sent over to them by American charities. "I get averages of ten very attractive propositions a day," he wrote to Alan Ginsberg, ". . . no stasis horrors here." The Socco cafés (the *Centrale* was the prime Beat location) lost much of their allure at independence, when the sale of alcohol was banned in the Medina, but they remain a good place to sit around, talk, and get some measure of the town.

It is beyond the Petit Socco that the Medina proper seems to start, "its topography," to quote Paul Bowles, "rich in prototypal dream scenes: covered streets like corridors with doors opening into rooms on either side, hidden terraces high above the sea, streets consisting only of steps, dark impasses, small squares built on sloping terrain so that they looked like ballet sets designed in false perspective, with alleys leading off in several directions; as well as the classical dream equipment of tunnels, ramparts, ruins, dungeons and cliffs." Walking up from the square, you can follow **Rue des Chrétiens/ Rue Ben Raisouli** through much of this and emerge—with luck—around the lower gate to the Kasbah. Heading past the Socco toward the sea walls are two small streets straddled by the Grand Mosque. If you want to get out and down to the beach, follow **Rue des Postes** and you'll hit a flight of steps. If you feel like wandering, take the other one, **Rue de la Marine**, which curls into **Rue Dar el Baroud** and the entrance to the old *Hôtel Continental*—another excellent place to sit around and drink tea. From here it's relatively simple to find your way across to the square below the Kasbah Gate.

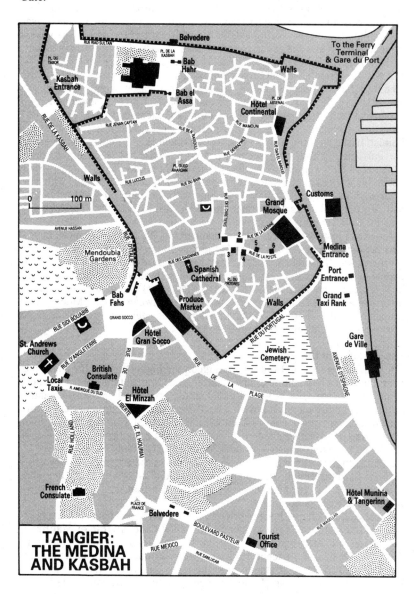

TANGIER:
THE MEDINA
AND KASBAH

The **Grand Mosque** itself, though it spreads across a whole block, is completely screened from public view—and, as throughout Morocco, entrance is strictly forbidden to non-Muslims. Enlarged in the early nineteenth century, the mosque was originally constructed by the great Moulay Ismail in celebration of the return of Tangier to Moroccan control in 1685. Prior to this, the city had seen some two centuries of European rule: it was first conquered by the Portuguese in the aftermath of the Moors' expulsion from Andalusia and the Algarve, and in 1663, it passed to the British as part of the dowry of Catherine of Braganza, bride to Charles II.

It was the British—in just 22 years of occupation—who destroyed the city's medieval fortifications, including a great upper castle which covered the entire site of the Kasbah. Under virtually constant siege, they found it an expensive and unrewarding possession: "an excrescence of the earth," according to Samuel Pepys, "and a nest of papacy where Irish troops and Romish bastards could desport themselves unchecked." Pepys, who oversaw the garrison's withdrawal, seems, in fact, to have had a miserable time, shocked at the women of the town ("generally whores"), at the governor ("with his whores at the little bathing house which he has furnished with jade a-purpose for that use"), and dining alone with the chaplain—with whom he had "a great deal of discourse upon the viciousness of this place and its being time for God Almighty to destroy it."

American history in Tangier is, by comparison, liberal, as evidenced by the **Old American Legation**, just inside the Rue du Portugal wall of the Medina. Morocco was the first overseas power to recognize an independent United States, and this was the first American ambassadorial residence, established in 1777. It is open daily (9am–1pm &4–6.30pm; free) and in addition to a few historical exhibits—notably, correspondence between Sultan Moulay ben Abdallah and George Washington—includes temporary displays of Moroccan-resident American artists.

The Kasbah and Beyond

The **Kasbah**, walled off from the Medina on the highest rise of the coast, has been the palace and administrative quarter since Roman times. It is a strange, somewhat sparse area of walled compounds, occasional colonnades, and a number of luxurious villas built in the 1920s, when this became one of the Mediterranean's most chic residential sites. Richard Hughes, author of *A High Wind in Jamaica* (and of a book of Moroccan tales), was the first European to take a house—his address fabulously titled "Numero Zero, Le Kasbah, Tangier." Among those who followed was the eccentric Woolworth's heiress, Barbara Hutton, whose parties included a ball where thirty Reguibat camel drivers and racing camels were brought a thousand miles from the Sahara to form an honor guard.

Local guides point with some pride to these bizarre locations, but the main point of interest here is the former **Sultanate Palace**, or **Dar el Makhzen**, now converted to an excellent museum of crafts and antiquities (open, in theory at least, daily, except Tuesdays, from around 9:30am to noon, and again from 3 to 6pm). It stands near the main gateway to the Medina, the **Bab el Assa**, to the rear of a formal court, or *mechouar*, where the town's pashas held public audience and gave judgment well into the present century. The entrance to the palace, a modest-looking porch, is in the lefthand corner of the court as you enter from the Medina—scores of children will probably drag you toward it.

The palace—again, built by Moulay Ismail in the seventeenth century—last saw royal use as recently as 1912, with the residence of the Sultan Moulay Hafid, exiled to Tangier after his forced abdication by the French. The extraordinary negotiations which then took place are brilliantly chronicled in Walter Harris' *Morocco That Was*. According to Harris, the ex-Sultan found it "an uncomfortable, out-of-date, and out-of-repair old castle, and it formed by no means a satisfactory place of residence, for it was not easy to install 168 people within its crumbling walls with any comfort or pleasure." Most of the 168 seem to have been members of the royal harem and well able to defend their limited privileges. Moulay Hafid, Harris reported, ended up with "only a couple of very shabby rooms over the entrance," where he apologetically received visitors and played bridge with a small circle of Americans and Europeans.

However out-of-date and uncomfortable the palace may have been, it is by no means a poor example of Moroccan craftsmanship and architecture. The design is classically centered on two interior courtyards, each with rich arabesques, painted wooden ceilings, and marble fountains; some of the flanking columns are of Roman origin, particularly well suited to the small display of **mosaics and finds from Volubilis** (see Chapter Three). The main part of the **museum**, however, is devoted to Moroccan arts, laid out according to region and including an exceptional collection of ceramics from Meknes and Fes.

At the entrance to the main part of the palace is the **Bit el Mal**, the old treasury, and adjoining this is a small private **mosque**, near to which is the entrance to the herb- and shrub-lined **gardens**, shaded by jacaranda trees. If you leave this way, you will come out into a "Moorish" café, the **Café-Restaurant Detroit,** set up in the early 1960s by beat writer Brion Gysin. Gysin created the place partly as a venue for the *Trance Musicians of Jajouka*, drummers and pipe players from a village close to Tangier who achieved cult fame through an LP recorded by Rolling Stone Brian Jones. The café is now an overpriced tourist spot, but worth the price of a mint tea, still, for its views, position, and Andalusian music. Its main entrance is on Rue Riad Sultan, the street running alongside the outer walls of the Kasbah to the main gate and Rue de la Kasbah/Rue d'Italie.

Leaving the Medina by the Kasbah gate, a ten- to fifteen-minute walk will bring you to the **Forbes Museum of Military Miniatures** on Rue Shakespeare. This, the world's largest collection of toy soldiers, is the endowment of millionaire publisher Malcolm Forbes, and exhibited in part of his palace—one of the city's most extravagant. The displays, a series of battle tableaux, are surprisingly imaginative, including a model of Hassan II's 1975 *Marche Verte*, in which 350,000 unarmed Moroccans "reclaimed" the former Spanish Sahara (see *Contexts*). The museum (and part of the palace gardens) are open Monday to Saturday, 9am to 5pm; admission is free.

Consuming Interests: Eating, Drinking, and Shopping

Tangier is more of a daytime than nighttime city. If you're looking for "international resort" nightlife, or the Tangier of sin-city legend, you'll be disappointed. But it does have a scattering of bars and discos, a few good restaurants and some very cheap Medina eateries. Some of the shops and stalls, too, are rewarding—for odds and ends of "antiques" and crafts, books and maps.

Restaurants

As with most Moroccan towns, the **cheapest places to eat** are in the **Medina**. Make your way to the Petit Socco, head off left up Rue de la Marine and you've a choice of several hole-in-the-wall cafés on Rue de Commerce (the first alley to the left) or Rue des Chrétiens. *Restaurant Andaluz* (7 Rue de Commerce) is about as simple as it's possible to be—and excellent, serving impeccably fried swordfish, grilled brochettes, and salad. For a little more variety, the cafés around the Grand Socco are worth a look, too; most stay open all night.

In the **Ville Nouvelle**, there are some inexpensive Spanish seafood restaurants on Rue Sanlucar and its continuation, Rue Méxique, behind Place de France, and reasonable-value set meals along the waterfront. Inexpensive, and highly recommended, is the *Restaurant Africa* at the lower end of Rue de la Plage, a crowded, local place with no-nonsense Moroccan dishes. Also good value are the *L'Marsa*, at the beginning of the seafront Avenue d'Espagne, the *Restaurant Agadir* at 21 Rue Prince Heritier (off Place de France), and the *Chellah Grill*, again on Rue Prince heritier, next to the *Hôtel Chellah*.

Moving **slightly upscale**, *Raihani's* (Rue Ahmed Chaoki, opposite the terrace on Bd. Pasteur) is worth at least one meal; it has superb *harira* (Ramadan soup), *couscous* and *pastilla* (pigeon pie), alongside a good French-based menu. For good Jewish-Moroccan/Spanish cooking, try *El Dorado* (21 Rue Allal ben Abdallah, by the *Hôtel Chellah*); for French food, *La Grenouille* (Rue Rembrandt, just off Bd. Pasteur); for Spanish seafood, served in vast portions, *Romero's* (Av. du Prince Moulay Abdallah, off Bd. Pasteur). *Hammadi's*, on Rue d'Italie (outside the west wall of the Medina), has traditional Moroccan dishes in a rather kitschy salon, not tremendously inspiring but with a good, regular band of Andalusian musicians. If you have a car, the *Sol Beach Restaurant-Bar*, 4km along the coast road towards Cap Spartel, is open year-round, 9am–9pm, for grilled fish and beers. Some of the café-bars on the town beach, too, stay open through the evening—see previous comments.

Note that **alcoholic drinks** are not served in the Medina or Grand Socco restaurants.

Bars, Discos, and Folkloric Shows

Tangier **bars** have been much depleted over the last few years. *The Parade*, the most legendary, died with its owner in 1987, and *Dean's*, once the haunt of people like Tennessee Williams, Francis Bacon, and Ian Fleming, has also finally closed its doors. The longest-running bar in town, now, is the *Tangerinn* (9pm-2am; below *Hôtel Muniria* on Rue Magellan), which does a deadpan imitation of a British seaside pub—quite amusing. Opposite, a new and younger innovation, is the *Club España*, with occasional Berber folk music, beer, and snacks (5dh admission). Other than these, and the recently-opened Carousel *Bar* (a British-run winebar off Rue Prince Heritier), you're down to the hotel bars. Of these, the *Villa de France* is sometimes quite lively; the *Miramar* is seedy; and the *Minzah* is very ritzy and very expensive.

The principal street for **discos** is Rue Sanlucar (aka Zankat Moutanabi), along with the neighboring area around Rue Mexique. They are all expensive, however, with drinks 50dh and up. *Scott's*, traditionally (though not exclusively) a gay disco, on Rue Sanlucar, is the cheapest and generally the liveliest. However, take care leaving late at night, as the street is none too safe; best idea is to tip the doorman 5dh to order you a taxi. Others, good for a night, at least, are *Regine's* (opposite the Roxy Cinema on Rue el Mansour Dahbi), *Borsalino's,* and the attractively seedy *Radio Club* (with the chance of live Moroccan bands), both on Rue Prince Moulay Abdalah.

Of the **folkloric** places, the *Morocco Palace*, on Av. du Prince Moulay Abdallah (off Bd. Pasteur) is a clear winner: a strange, sometimes slightly manic place, with traditional Moroccan music until around 1am, then a Western disco for the Moroccans. Recommended.

For **late-night coffee or snacks**, the *Café Atlas*, by the Hôtel Rembrandt, stays open till 4am, and the cafés in the Grand Socco more or less all night.

Concerts and Movies

Music concerts—traditional and popular—are sporadic events in Tangier. However, the old Spanish bullring, in the Ville Nouvelle, has had a recent major refurbishment as an open air concert hall, so it might be worth asking about events at the tourist office.

There are a dozen or so **movie houses** scattered about the Ville Nouvelle, in the grid around Boulevard Pasteur. Films are frequently shown in their original language, with Arabic subtitles, though some are dubbed into French. The cinema on the Grand Socco shows an exclusive diet of Indian and Kung Fu films.

Stores and Stalls

Many of the Tangier **market stalls and stores** are eminently avoidable, geared to selling tourist goods that wouldn't pass muster elsewhere. But there are a few that are worthwhile, unique, or both.

Ensemble Artisanal (Rue Belgique; left hand side, going up from Place de France). Modern Moroccan crafts are displayed in this government-run store, as in other major cities. They are rarely the best or the cheapest available, but prices are (more or less) fixed, so this is a good first call to get an idea of quality and costs before bargaining elsewhere.

Bazaar Tindouf (64 Rue de la Liberté, opposite the *Hôtel Minzah*). One of the best quality junk-antique shops, with some fine carpet-pillows and a tremendous selection of old postcards. Bargaining difficult but essential.

Unnamed Junk-Antique Store (24 Rue de Hollande). Another good secondhand store for browsing. The **Fes Market**, adjoining, is a lively area for fruit, vegetables, and produce.

Volubilis Boutique (In the Petit Socco, and another branch opposite Romero's restaurant in Rue Moulay Abdallah). Interesting mix of traditional Moroccan and western designer clothes and shoes.

Perfumerie Madini (14 Rue Sebou, in the Medina; from the Petit Socco take the alley between the Tingis and Centrale cafés, which leads into Rue Sebou, and look for the store on your right). Madini makes inspired copies of brand-name perfumes from natural oils, which he sells at a fraction of the "real" price, as well as musk and traditional fragrances. Given a couple of days and a sample, he will reproduce any scent you like. Closed 1–4pm and all day Friday.

Rue Touahin (first right off Rue Saighin, entering the Medina from the Grand Socco). Line of jewelry stalls, which may turn up something appealing. Don't take silver, or gold, or most stones, at face value: judge on aesthetics.

Librairie des Colonnes (54 Bd. Pasteur). Good range of English-language books, including some of Paul Bowles's Moroccan translations.

English-language Newspapers, including the *International Herald Tribune*, are sold outside the post office, in various stores along Bd. Pasteur, and by news dealers around the *Café de France*.

Drugstores/Pharmacies There are several English-speaking pharmacies in the Place de France (try the Paris, opposite the *Café de Paris*) and along Bd. Pasteur.

Beer/Wine Store. The Spanish-run store at 63 Rue Hollande has a good selection of bottles, wrapped discreetly for your travels.

See also the details on markets on p.54.

Directory

Airlines *GBAirways* (83 Rue de La Liberté) operate a 16-seat Trislander to Gibraltar, twice daily for most of the year; their flights to London (direct, or via Gibraltar) are often good value. For domestic flights within Morocco (and some international destinations) contact *Royal Air Maroc* on Place de France. For flights to Spain (cheapest departures are from Melilla) try *Iberia* at 35 Bd. Pasteur. *Air France* (20 Bd. Pasteur) may have good deals, too.

American Express Represented by *Voyages Schwarz*, 54 Bd. Pasteur (☎334.59). Open Mon.–Fri. 9am–noon and 3-7pm; Sat. 9am–12:30pm only.

Banks Most are grouped along Bd. Pasteur/Bd. Mohammed V. The *BMCE bureau de change* on Bd. Pasteur is the most efficient, changing cash and travelers' checks, and handling cash advances on Visa and Mastercard; it stays open 8am–2pm and 4-8pm every day of the week.The *SGM Banque* (opposite the post office on Mohammed V) takes some bank checks backed by credit cards. *Crédit du Maroc* (Bd. Pasteur) also handles *Visa* transactions.

Car Parking The *Hôtel Tanjah Flandria* (keyed "T" on the main plan) has an underground garage: 10dh for 24hr.

Car Rental Most of the big companies have offices along Bd. Pasteur/Bd. Mohammed V— *Avis* at no. 54, *Hertz* at no. 36, *InterRent* at no. 87, among them. Cheaper and fairly reliable are *Leasing Cars* (24 Rue Henri Regnault, and at the airport). Discounts are sometimes available if you arrange car rental through one of the package holiday representatives— contact them at any of the larger hotels (like the *Rif* on the seafront).

Car Repairs and Information Garages can be recommended by the *Royal Automobile Club de Maroc* at 8 Av. Prince Héritier. For Renaults, try *Tanjah-Auto* (2 Av. de Rabat), Citroëns are at 33 Rue Victor Hugo (one block behind the post office).

Consulates *US* (29 Rue el Achouak Chemin des Amoureux, ☎359-04); *Great Britain* (9 Rue Amérique du Sud, ☎358-97).Hours for both are Mon.–Fri. 7am–noon & 1.30-5.30pm.

Hospital Emergency number is ☎342-42; or for the Spanish Hospital (*Hôpital Español*), ☎310-18.

LEAVING TANGIER

Traveling on into Morocco from Tangier is simplest either by train (the lines run to Meknes/Fes, or Rabat/Casablanca/Marrakesh; all trains stop at Asilah en route), or, if you are heading east to Tetouan, by shared grand taxi.

Ferries run to Algeciras, Tarifa (just west of Algeciras), and Gibraltar, and to Sète in France.

Trains

There are two stations: the **Gare du Port** (by the port) and **Gare de Ville** (400 meters along the seafront). At present the **4:10pm** (Rabat/Casablanca/Marrakesh; connection at Sidi Slimane for Meknes/Fes) and **11:15pm*** (Rabat/Casablanca/Marrakesh) trains leave from the Port station, calling at the Ville station ten minutes later. All other departures are from the Ville station only.

If you **arrive in Tangier by ferry and plan to travel straight on**, the 4:15pm train is likely to be the most convenient departure, though if you catch an early ferry you might just make the 2:15pm train to Meknes/Fes (change at Sidi Kacem). The 11:15pm* departure is essentially a night train to Marrakesh, and saves losing a couple of days travel (and a night's hotel bill). If you take it, try to book a couchette, available as a supplement, which gives you a guaranteed reservation and a separate carriage with an attendant—useful for baggage security. You're given a sheet, pillow and blanket; take your own toilet paper. There is a baggage *consigne* at the Ville train station.

*The 11:15pm night train leaves at 9:20pm during the winter months: check departure boards and don't rely on the timetable. For details of other departures, see the Travel Details at the end of this chapter.

Grands Taxis and Buses

There are **grands taxis** leaving through the day to **Tetouan**, from the rank by the entrance to the port. To get a place in a taxi, just announce yourself to the driver at the head of the rank. You will then be crammed (with five other passengers) into the car. The cost is only slightly more than going by bus and journey time is considerably less. Taxis in this rank can be chartered for expeditions further afield, direct to **Chaouen** or Asilah for example, and work out relatively economic shared between a group. On your own, heading to Chaouen, it's a lot cheaper to get a bus on from Tetouan. The cost of a place to Tetouan is a standard tarif (currently 20dh); all other destinations are negotiable.

For destinations in the immediate **vicinity of Tangier**, such as the Caves of Hercules or Cap Malabata, you need to negotiate a *grand taxi* at the rank opposite the English church on Rue d'Angleterre.

Until recently, most of Tangier's **buses** left from down by the port entrance, but a recent shift seems to have moved all departures to a terminal at the end of Rue de Fes. This is some 3km from the centre of town, reached by following Rue de Fes to the Rue de Lisbonne traffic circle where the road to the airport separates from that to Tetouan. Unless you're hooked on bus travel, it is scarcely worth the effort. If you happen to arrive in Tangier by bus, however, it's likely to be here that you'll be set down; try to get a taxi into town—it's a long walk.

Ferry details overpage

LEAVING TANGIER (continued)

Ferries

Tangier–Algeciras ferries: *Transmediterranea* (31 Rue Quevedo, off Bd. Pasteur) and *Limadet* (13 Rue du Prince Moulay Abdallah) operate three to four boats a day in spring and summer, down to two in the winter. You can buy **tickets** direct from the companies or (without commission) from any travel agent along Boulevard Pasteur or the seafront; there is also a ticket office at the entrance to the port. Cars and passengers carried.

Although boats invariably depart an hour or so late, you must **check in** at the port at least one hour before the official departure time. At the ferry terminal, you have to get an embarkation card and departure card from the *Depart* desk of the ferry companies. Take this, along with your passport, to the police *visa de passeport* desk on the same floor (opposite the bar), where you then need to have your passport stamped before going through customs to the boat. Arrive later than an hour before official departure time and you will probably find that the visa police have knocked off—which means you have to wait for the next ferry.

Similar procedures should be observed for *Comanav*'s liner to Sète (times and tickets from *Voyages Comanav*, 149 Av. Mohammed V; ☎304-57).

Tangier–Tarifa/Algeciras hydrofoils: These cost about 30 percent above the regular ferries, and don't run in bad weather, but they are considerably quicker and more efficient. Spring and summer departures are three times daily to Tarifa (30 min.), once to Algeciras (1 hr.); there are no services on Sundays. Again, you can buy tickets directly from the operator (*Transtour*, 54 Bd. Pasteur; ☎340-04) or from most travel agents. Passengers only.

Departures are from a separate dock, just in front of the ferry terminal building, where there's an individual *visa de passeport* office—normally open half an hour before the official (and, more often than not, actual) departure time.

Tangier–Gibraltar catamaran: Operated by *Gibline*, this has replaced the former ferry and hydrofoil services, taking an hour and an half for the crossing. Like the hydrofoils, it doesn't run in bad weather—nor when it breaks down, which is frequent. Otherwise service should be daily (except Thursday and Saturday) in season; three times a week out; no services during the boat's annual overhaul (normally for the month of February). Tickets from *Transtour* (see above) and most agents. Passengers only.

For flights and car rental addresses see the "Directory", above

---

Mail, Phones, General Delivery All at the main PTT, 33 Bd. Mohammed V; open Mon.–Sat. 8:30am–noon & 2.30–6.30pm; phones are available 24 hr.

Motorbike Rental Bikes are available for short-term lease at a garage on Av. Youssef Ibn Tachfine.

Tourist Office There's an *ONMT* office is at 29 Bd. Pasteur, just down from Place de France and open Mon.–Sat. 8am–2pm. English-speaking and helpful; ask for their free maps of Fes, Rabat-Salé, and Marrakesh, each useful supplements to the ones we've printed.

Police Main station is on Rue Ibn Toumert. Emergency ☎ 19.

Tour Companies *Nat Tours* (32068) are a reliable company, who can arrange hotel reservations and most aspects of travel in Tangier and elsewhere in Morocco.

Around Tangier: Capes, Caves, and Ksar Es Seghir

The Bay of Tangier curves around to a pair of capes—Malabata to the east, Spartel to the west. The best beaches are to be found at **Cap Malabata**, where much of the moneyed development of Tangier as a resort has been taking place; if you have transport, better to continue to **Ksar es Seghir**, beyond Malabata on the coast road to Ceuta. The road west to Cap Spartel offers a longer, more exposed beach—Robinson Plage—and the picturesque Caves of Hercules; it's a pleasant route to fill a day waiting for a ferry or flight at Tangier.

West —the Caves of Hercules and the "Atlantic Beach"

If the Tourist Board pushes one image of Tangier it must be the **Caves of Hercules**, whose strange sea window, shaped like a map of Africa, frames the cover of their official brochure. The name, like Hercules' legendary founding of Tangier, is purely fanciful, but the caves, 18km outside the city and above the "Atlantic Beach," make an attractive excursion. They're a good base, too, if you feel like camping for a few days by the sea; even in the middle of August, only stray groups of visitors share the long surf beaches. Take care, though: the currents here can be very dangerous pretty close to the shore.

Heading for the caves you're dependent on *grands taxis* (which charge around 100dh for the 34-kilometer round trip, and can be persuaded to drop you in the morning and pick you up in the late afternoon) or on irregular buses and a 6–7km walk. If you take the **bus** (#17 or #70, from the Grand Socco), ask to be dropped off at the turnoff for "Les Grottes", 5km before the airport. As you approach the coast, a small track leads off left to the ruins of Cotta (see below); the caves themselves are signposted a kilometer or so beyond.

By **taxi or with your own transport**, there's a more interesting route—around and above the coast via La Montagne and Cap Spartel. From Place de France, take Rue Belgique to the beginning of Rue de la Montagne. "**The Mountain**," less imposing than its name suggests, was a rebel base against the British and Portuguese occupations of Tangier, but is now thoroughly tamed; its cork and pine woods shield the city's most exclusive villas. Among them are two vast royal palaces, the first built by Moulay Hafid and now one of King Hassan's roster, the other, heavily guarded, among the numerous retreats of the Saudi sheikhs.

After 11km, you reach a short turnoff to the lighthouse at **Cap Spartel**—a dramatic and fertile point, known to the Greeks and Romans as the "Cape of the Vines"—beyond which begins the vast and wild **Atlantic Beach**, or "Robinson Plage," broken by a rocky spit and then rambling off for as far as you can see. There's a **campground** on each side of the spit, both near reasonably priced **café-restaurants**, as well as two hotels: the expensive 3*A *Hôtel Grottes* and, beyond the caves themselves, the cheaper *Hôtel Robinson*

(2*A). The latter, also known as *Le Mirage*, has a swimming pool, open to anyone having a meal, and a bar.

The **Caves of Hercules** are natural formations, occupied in prehistoric times, but most striking for a manmade addition: thousands of disc-shaped erosions created by centuries of quarrying for millstones. There were still Moors cutting stones here for a living until the 1920s, but by that time, their place was beginning to be taken by professional guides and discreet sex hustlers. It must have made an exotic brothel. Today, there's a standard admission charge (daily 9am–sunset), though you're unlikely to get away without a guide, too, whose descriptive abilities tend to be somewhat dwarfed by the utter obviousness of all there is to see ("wet cave," "dark cave," "sea," etc.).

Ten minutes' walk past the caves, the road turns inland from the beach and a rough farm track leads in 200m to the ruins of **Ancient Cotta**, a small, second- and third-century Roman town based around the production of *garum* (a kind of anchovy paste). Parts of the factory, and of a temple and baths complex, can be made out, but it's not a very inspiring or significant site.

East—Cap Malabata and Ksar es Seghir

There are few quicker contrasts than the bay east of Tangier. As you approach, **Cap Malabata** seems almost a different world to the city, dominated exclusively by a *Club Mediterrané* and a handful of huge modern hotel complexes. But once around the cape (and there is virtually no more development the whole way down the coast to Ceuta), there's a beautiful road winding above some tremendous stretches of beach, which if you're willing to camp for free—there are no organized sites—must be among the best in the north. The only problem is a shortage of **buses**. Tangier and the Ceuta border crossing at FNIDEQ have no connecting service, and the only buses to KSAR ES SEGHIR leave and return early in the morning.

If you can overcome the transport problem, though, **KSAR ES SEGHIR** is as relaxed and picturesque a base as could be imagined, still largely enclosed by twenty-foot-high Portuguese walls. A small fishing port, it attracts a fair number of Moroccan summer campers, but few Europeans. There's a friendly café-restaurant on a terrace above the sea, occasional rooms to rent if you ask around, and, as long as you watch your possessions, infinite scope for camping.

Asilah

The first town beyond Tangier—and the first stop on the railroad—**ASILAH** is very much a resort. Too much so in many ways, with local attitudes shaped by the presence (until its recent closure) of a large *Camp Africa* package complex. Tourists, when it was open, were seen as easy bait, and unfortunately habits die hard. Unattractive, too, is the town's interim state, with the town beach temporarily cordoned off for the construction of a new port and marina complex.

On the positive side, Asilah is one of the most elegant of the old Portuguese Atlantic ports, its square stone ramparts flanked by palms, and its beach outstanding—an immense sweep of sand (beyond the construction site) stretching halfway to Tangier. And it is small and very easy to manage: hustlers limit themselves to souvenir selling and enthusiastic attendance at the tourist discos. If you can visit in August (when the place is packed out) you'll coincide with the annual **International Festival**, a month-long event, encompassing art exhibitions (the town boasts some interesting permanent murals from the festival) and a series of concerts—from Lebanese singers to European jazz, Moroccan folk to American university choirs. Programmes are available in the village, or ask for details at the tourist office in Tangier.

Practicalities

The **train station** is 2km north of the town—an easy enough walk if you miss the connecting shuttle. Arriving by **grand taxi** (1 hr. from Tangier), you're dropped in a small square at the edge of the Medina, about 100m north of the ramparts; buses drop you in an adjacent street to this.

In the square—facing the ramparts and the sea—is the *Hôtel Nasr*, a pretty basic place, but pleasantly run and with the cheapest **accommodation** around. Down toward the ramparts, you come to the slightly more expensive and crazily-decorated *Hôtel Marhaba* (9 Rue Zallakah; ☎71.44) and, to its left, opposite a small town gate, the 1*B *Hôtel Asilah* (79 Av. Hassan II; ☎72.86)— probably the most attractive cheap option, with some rooms on a terrace above the town and walls. One of these places should have space; if not, there are straw-hut rooms on the roof at *Pension al-Karam* (by the beach, just behind the fashionable 2*A *Hôtel Oued el Makhasine*, ☎70.90) or the somewhat decaying *Hôtel Oasis* (2*B; 091/70.69), in a square to the right (facing the sea) of the bus station.

There are a string of **campgrounds**, north of the train station. The closest, about 500m walk, is *Camping Echrigui* (☎71.82), well maintained and adjacent to the old *Camp Africa* .

For **food**, the two most obvious restaurants—in the square just outside the ramparts—are also generally the best. *El Espignon*, with outside tables, does good Spanish-style fried fish. *El Oceano*, opposite, is marginally cheaper.

The Town

As with Tangier, it is the **beach** that's the main focus of life—and by night, too, in season, with its *La Estrella* disco. The **town** itself was just a small fishing port before the tourists came, quietly stagnating after the indifference of Spanish colonial administration. Whitewashed and cleaned up, it now has a prosperous feeling to it—the town mosque, for example, is being rebuilt and doubled in size—and its towers and ramparts are a pleasant place to wander around in. There's a small produce **market** held most days just outside the ramparts, and a bigger Djebali villagers' market, on the far side of the Tangier-Rabat road, every Sunday and Thursday. In the town itself, it's worth asking directions to the small **hammam**, where, unusually, the keeper charges for a group and gives you the place to yourselves; it's in an alley off the second long street inside the Medina walls.

Also, though it doesn't always open without persuasion, there is the town's **palace**, built in 1909 with forced tribal labor by a local bandit, Er-Raisuli—one of the strangest figures to emerge from what was an almost-routinely bizarre period of Moroccan government. He began his career as a cattle rustler, and achieved notoriety with a series of kidnappings and ransoms (including that of the British writer and London *Times* journalist, Walter Harris), and was eventually appointed governor over practically all the tribes of northwest Morocco. Harris described his captivity in *Morocco That Was* as an "anxious time," made more so by being confined in a small room with a headless corpse. Despite this, the two seem to have formed a real friendship, Harris finding Raisuli a "mysterious personage, half-saint, half-blackguard," and often entertaining him later in Tangier.

Another British travel writer, Rosita Forbes, visited Raisuli at his Asilah palace in 1924. The rooms, now mostly bare, were then hung with rugs "of violent colors, embroidered with tinsel," their walls lined with cushions stuffed with small potatoes. The decoration seems logical enough—the palace today still looks more like a glittering Hollywood set than anything real. The great reception room, a long glass terrace above the sea, even has dialogue to match: Raisuli told Forbes that he made murderers walk to their death from its windows—a ninety-foot drop to the rocks. One man, he said, had turned back to him, saying, "Thy justice is great, Sidi, but these stones are more merciful."

Palais de Raisuli, as it is known, overhangs the sea ramparts toward the far end of the Medina (away from the beach). It is used in August for the "International Festival," as is a small fifteenth century **Portuguese fort** just inside the ramparts.

Larache

Much less visited than Asilah, **LARACHE** is a relaxed, easygoing place where Moroccans come on vacation, and it is one of the best towns of the north in which to spend a few days by the sea. Doing as they do is easy: the local beach is a good one, and (for once) it is very mixed, with as many women around as men—a safe feeling for women travelers looking for a low-key spot to bathe. Nearby, too, are the scattered ruins of ancient Lixus, legendary site of the Gardens of the Hesperides.

The town itself is a kind of halfhearted amalgam of Tangier and Tetouan, attractive, if not spectacularly so. It was the main port of the northern Spanish zone and—though the central Plaza de España has become Place de la Libération—still bears much of its former stamp. There are faded old Spanish hotels, Spanish-run restaurants, and Spanish bars, even an active Spanish cathedral for the small colony who still work at the docks. Yet, despite all this, it seems very Moroccan and fairly dignified.

Before the Spanish colonization in 1911, Larache was a small trading port, its activities limited by dangerous offshore sand bars. Without these, it might have rivaled Tangier, for it is better positioned as a trade route to Fes. Instead, it eked out a living by building pirate ships made of wood from the nearby Forest of Mamora for the "Barbary Corsairs" of Salé and Rabat. It was also Spanish for a period in the seventeenth century, and fortified by them before being reclaimed and repopulated by Moulay Ismail. The **Chateau de la Cigogne** (Stork's Castle), a hulking, three-sided fortress-compound, which you pass on the way into town, owes its origin to this first occupation.

From the second, the most striking piece of colonial Spanish architecture is the town's main square, the circular **Place de la Libération**—just back from the sea and a simple 200-meter walk from the (combined) bus station and *grand taxi* stand. There are two **hotels** in the square: the once grand, still elegant *Hôtel España* (1*B; ☎31.95), and the pretty grim *Cervantes*. Cheaper and better than either of them is the unclassified *Pension Amal* (☎27.88), signposted on the street from the bus station to the square, just off to the left in an alleyway. The 3*A *Hôtel Riad* is poor value.

A high archway at the center of the *place* leads into the **Medina**, a surprisingly small wedge of alleys and stairways leading down toward the port. It is now the poorest area of Larache—better off families have moved out to the new parts of town, leaving their houses here to the elderly—but it doesn't seem so bad, artfully shaded and airy in its design. The colonnaded market square, just inside the archway and built by the seventeenth-century Spanish, is a pretty lively spot, while on your left, past the dingy *Hôtel Watan*, there are some reasonable hole-in-the-wall eateries. If you want to stay in the Medina, the *Pension Atlas* is just to the right of the square as you go in, though you probably won't pay much less than in the *Amal*.

Eating, except in the Medina cafés, or the sardine-grills down by the port, is still resolutely Spanish. The cheapest cafés are in the Place de la Libération, around the entrance archway of the Medina. For seafood, try *Restaurant Larache* on Av. Moulay ben Abdallah, the street leading from the *place* to the bus station.

The shore below Larache is wild and rocky, but cross its estuary and there are miles of fine sandy **beach** sheltered by trees and flanked by a handful of café-restaurants. You can go there by bus (# 4 from the port, every 20 min.—sometimes starting from the *place*), a circuitous seven-kilometer route, or you can get straight over from the port in small fishing boats—one dirham per person. From the *place*, the quickest route down to **the port** is along a seafront path, past the crumbling **Fort Kebibat** (Little Domes), built by Portuguese merchants in the sixteenth century.

In summer, an oddity is the amount of foreign languages you hear—yet with few foreigners around. The explanation is the number of migrant families, scattered about Europe, who return to the town for the holiday. As well as communities in Barcelona, Naples, and Paris, Larache accounts for most of the Moroccan community in London, and on the beach you're likely to come upon kids with disarming English accents.

Ancient Lixus

Founded by Phoenician colonists around 1000 B.C., **LIXUS** is thought to have been the first trading post of North Africa and was probably its earliest permanent settlement. It became an important Carthaginian and (later)

Roman city, and was deserted only after the breakup of the empire in the fifth century A.D. As an archaeological site it is significant, and the legendary associations are rich soil for the imagination, but it has to be said that the actual excavated ruins are not especially impressive. In fact, with the single exception of Volubilis (near Meknes), the best surviving monuments of Roman Africa are all to be found in Tunisia and Algeria.

Even so, if you're spending any amount of time at Larache, or passing through by car, the Lixus ruins are well worth an hour or two's exploration. They lie below and upon the summit of a low hill on the far side of the estuary leading from the town, at the crossroads of the main Larache-Tangier road and the narrow lane to Larache beach. It's a four- to five-kilometer walk from either the beach or town, or you can use the bus which runs between the two; alternatively, for about 75dh you could charter one of the boats to row you over from Larache, wait an hour or so, and then row you back to the town or beach. The site is not effectively enclosed, so there are no real opening hours.

The **lower town**, right beside the main road, consists largely of factories for the production of salt—still being panned nearby—and, as at Cotta, anchovy-paste *garum*. They seem to have been developed in the early years of the first century A.D. by the Carthaginians, and they remained in operation until the Roman withdrawal.

A track, some 100m down the road to Tangier, leads up to the *acropolis* (upper town), passing on its way eight rows of the Roman **theater and amphitheater**, unusually combined into a single structure. Its deep, circular arena was adapted for circus games and the gladiatorial slaughter of animals. Morocco, which Herodotus knew as "the wild-beast country," was the major source for these Roman *venationes,* and local colonists must have grown rich from the trade. Amid **baths** built into the side of the theater, a mosaic remains in situ , depicting Neptune and the Oceans.

Climbing above the baths and theater, you pass through ramparts to the main enceinte (fortifications) of the **acropolis**—a somewhat confused network of walls and foundations—and **temple sanctuaries**, an early **Christian basilica**, and a number of **pre-Roman buildings**. The most considerable of the sanctuaries, with their underground cisterns and porticoed priests' quarters, were apparently rebuilt in the first century A.D., but even then retained Phoenician elements in their design.

The **legendary associations** of Lixus—and the site's mystique—center on the Labors of Hercules. For here, on an island in the estuary, Pliny and Strabo record reports of the palace of the "Libyan" (by which they meant African) King Antaeus. Behind stretched the **Garden of the Hesperides**, to which Hercules, as his penultimate labor, was dispatched. In the object of his quest—the Golden Apples—it is not difficult to imagine the tangerines of northern Morocco, raised to mythic status by travelers' tales. And, indeed, the site itself seems to offer reinforcement to conjectures of a mythic pre-Phoenician past. Megalithic stones have been found on the acropolis, and some early form of sun worship seems still to be echoed in the local name—*shamush*, "burned by the sun."

Heading South: Ksar El Kebir, Souk El Arba, and Moulay Bousselham

Heading south from LARACHE, the main road and most of the buses bypass **KSAR EL KEBIR**—and, unless it's a Sunday, when the town has one of the region's largest markets, it seems as well to accept the fact. However, as its name (the Great Enclosure) suggests, this was once a place of some importance. Founded in the eleventh century, it became an early Arab power base, enlarged and endowed by both Almohads and Merenids, and coveted by the Spanish and Portuguese of Asilah and Larache. Here, in 1578, the Portuguese fought the most disastrous battle in their nation's history—a crusading expedition which saw the death or capture of virtually the entire nobility—and the Moroccans saw the fortuitous accession to power of Ahmed el Mansour, the greatest of all Merenid sultans, who went on to conquer Timbuktu.

Ksar el Kebir fell into decline in the seventeenth century, after a local chief incurred the wrath of Moulay Ismail, causing him to destroy the walls. Neglect followed, although its fortunes revived to some extent under the Spanish protectorate. If you stop here a while, the **Sunday market** is held right by the bus and *grand taxi* terminals. On any morning of the week, there are pretty lively **souks** around the main *kissaria* of the old town; this is in the quarter known as *Bab el Oued* (the Gate of the River).

Beyond Ksar el Kebir, a decaying customs post at ARBAOUA marks the old colonial frontier between the Spanish and French zones. **SOUK EL ARBA DU RHARB**, a sprawling roadside town where there are grill-cafés (and hotels, if you get stuck), is the first village of any size, though it is little more than its name suggests (the Wednesday market of the Rharb Plain). However, if you're making for either OUEZZANE or MOULAY BOUSSELHAM, this is the place to go. To Ouezzane there are infrequent buses but pretty routine (and much quicker) *grands taxis*; Moulay Bousselham is well served by both; and it is also a very attractive resort (that is, if you don't mind being more or less the only Westerner).

Moulay Bousselham

Having pledged that buses to **MOULAY BOUSSELHAM** are numerous, it's perhaps worth adding that just because there's one around, this doesn't mean it's about to leave. **The Bousselham bus**—at least when I took it—was one of those classically timeless, Moroccan exercises. It arrived out of nowhere, quarter-full and its engine revving up with urgency; after a flurry of action as everyone piled on, it slammed its doors shut and proceeded fifty meters down the road. There we all stopped, trying to persuade a handful of country women to get on or, if not that, to at least consider the idea. Five eventually did; meanwhile, four other passengers had decided to stay in Souk el Arba. And so it continued, up and down the road to try and fill the bus before an eventual and furious altercation set everything smoothly in motion.

Even after this kind of a morning, though, Moulay Bousselham seems a worthwhile place to arrive in. A smallish village-resort, it's little more than a single street, crowded with grill-cafés and sloping down to the sea at the side of a broad lagoon. The **beach** here is sheltered by cliffs—rare along the Atlantic—and there's an abrupt dropoff, which creates a continual thrash of breaking waves. While lots of fun, the currents are also dangerous and the beach is strictly patrolled by lifeguards. For more realistic swimming, you can wander over to the lagoon, where most people stay at a really beautifully located **campground**. If you're *not* camping, alternatives are distinctly limited: you might get a room above one of the cafés (or even a house if you stay a week or more: ask around), but otherwise there's just one small and expensive **hotel**, the 3*A *Le Lagon* (☎28). The hotel, incidentally, has the only bar in the *place,* along with a surprisingly good movie theater and a somewhat ritzy nightclub.

Moulay Bousselham takes name from the **marabout's tomb** above the village, a tenth-century Egyptian saint, and in July it sees one of the largest **moussems**—or religious festivals—in the region. A further festival, back towards Arboua, is held in early April.

CEUTA, TETOUAN, AND CHAOUEN

The Spanish enclave of **Ceuta** is a slightly frustrating port of entry. Although in Africa, you are not yet in Morocco, and you must make your way to the border at Fnideq, then on from there to **Tetouan**, the first Moroccan town. It can be a time-consuming business. However, if you are making for **Chaouen**, it's the better point of arrival: Tetouan has regular bus connections with Chaouen, as it does, too, with Meknes and Fes.

An alternative, seasonal, port of entry is the village of **Mdiq**, north of Tetouan, which has a weekly (currently Thursdays) catamaran connection with Gibraltar. This could be the gentlest of all introductions to Morocco. Mdiq apart, the **Mediterranean** here has few resorts of note, though **Martil** is pleasant enough, as (in its own, basic way) is the "travelers' resort" of **Oued Laou**, in the shadow of the Rif. All are easily reached from Tetouan.

Ceuta (Sebta)

A Spanish enclave since the sixteenth century, **CEUTA** (or *SEBTA* in Arabic) is a curious political anomaly. It was retained by Spain after Moroccan independence in 1956, but today functions only as a military base, its economy bolstered by limited duty-free status. On a clear day you can almost see Gibraltar, which, in the absence of anything else of interest, seems somehow symbolic.

Entering Morocco: the Border at Fnideq
Since the Algeciras ferries take an hour less than to Tangier (and for cars are significantly economic), Ceuta is a popular **point of entry**. Coming over on a first visit to Morocco, try to arrive early in the day so you have plenty of time

to move on to Tetouan—and possibly beyond. There is no customs/passport check at the port because you don't officially enter Morocco until the border at FNIDEQ: 3km out of town, reached by local bus from the seafront.

As you come off the ferry or hydrofoil, turn left—the bus stop is about 100m down, in the second main square, Plaza de la Constitución. Formalities at the border can be time consuming, especially for car drivers, but you should be clear (in either direction) within an hour. Once across the border, the easiest transportation is a shared *grand taxi* **to Tetouan** (split six ways, that's currently 10dh each); buses are infrequent, though a couple of dirhams cheaper. There are **exchange facilities** (cash only) at the frontier.

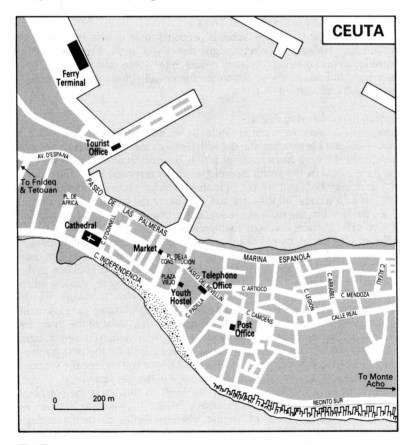

The Town

In Ceuta itself, there isn't a great deal to do. The local authorities are in the midst of creating a town beach, but at present there are no sands to speak of—locals go by bus to *Playa Benzou*, some way out of town. And, though the duty free status draws many of the Tangier expatriates on daytrips to buy cheap spirits, and Spanish daytrippers to buy radios and cameras. Neither are likely to be very compelling pursuits for travelers and tourists; if you do want a cheap bottle, check the *Roma* supermarket on Paseo del Revellin.

Most of the town, which is surprisingly large, is modern, functional, and provincial in the dullest Spanish manner. The **Cathedral** ("Our Lady of Africa") is in the main **Plaza de Africa** opposite the ferry dock, and an oldish quarter rambles up from the end of the long main street, **Paseo del Revellin**. Beyond this, you can walk out and around the peninsula in little over an hour. As the buildings, three to a dozen blocks in width, disappear from view, the land swells into a rounded, pine-covered slope: a geographical echo of the Rock of Gibraltar, with which it forms the so-called **Pillars of Hercules**, gateway to the classical world.

This part of Ceuta, **Monte Acho**, is occupied more or less exclusively by the military. Walking the circuit, signs direct you to the **Ermida de San Antonio**, an old convent completely rebuilt in the 1960s, and dominated by a monument to Franco, whose Nationalist forces sailed from the port to begin the Spanish civil war.

Staying in and Leaving Ceuta

If you **plan to stay** overnight in Ceuta, be warned that it isn't easy to find a room—and not cheap when you do; with its large garrison and cheap consumer goods, the town has a constant flow of Spanish families. The best bet, if you have a card, is the **youth hostel** (*posada de juventud*) at 27 Plaza Viejo, with dormitory beds and low-priced rooms for two to six people. To get there, turn left as you come off the ferry and walk along the seafront to the start of Paseo del Revellin, the main street; just at the beginning of this, by a sign for "Tonyo's Hi-Fi," stairs lead right to the *plaza*.

Besides the hostel, there are a dozen or so **hotels, hostels**, and **pensions**, most of them along Paseo del Revellin or its continuations, Calle Camoens and Calle Real. A complete list (and a map of the town) is available at the **Oficina de Turismo** by the ferry dock, or displayed in its window when closed. Cheaper pensions—and some good **bars** with food—are mostly grouped around Calle Real. The only **campground**, following the closure of the Camping Municipal, is *Camping Marguerita*, 3km west of the town. By car, follow the signs along the road to the west until you see a sign, "Camping: 300m". Don't follow this road! Instead, look for the next turning, concealed between buildings opposite a point where you can see the sea, and follow this uphill, keeping right, until you come to the campground.

Leaving Ceuta for Algeciras, you can normally turn up at the port, buy tickets, and board a ferry within a couple of hours. The one time to avoid, as at Tangier, is the **last week of August**, when the ferries can be full for days on end with Moroccan workers returning from holiday to northern Europe. If you plan to use the quicker **hydrofoil service** to Algeciras, it's best to book a day in advance—though you may strike lucky; details and tickets for the *hidroala* are available from 6 Muelle Caõnero Dato (☎51 60 41). Be aware that on arrival in Algeciras you will need to go through customs—and drug suspects are very thoroughly searched.

Tetouan

For anyone coming from Ceuta, **TETOUAN** is the first experience of a Moroccan city: a disadvantage you'll quickly understand. The Medina here can seem huge and totally unfamiliar, and the hustlers, dealing large quantities of kif, have the worst reputation anywhere in Morocco.

It is, however, an unusually striking town, poised atop the slope of an enormous valley and backed by a dark mass of rock. Its name (pronounced *Tet-tá-wan*) means "open your eyes" in Berber, and this is a possible reference to the town's hasty construction by Andalusian refugees in the fifteenth century. The refugees, both Muslims and Jews, brought with them the most refined sophistication of Moorish Andalusia—an aristocratic tradition that is still reflected in the architecture of the Medina. Their houses, full of extravagant detail, are quite unlike those of other Moroccan towns; indeed, with their tiled lintels and wrought iron balconies, they seem much more akin to the old Arab quarters of Spanish Cordoba and Seville.

Orientation and Practicalities

Despite first impressions (particularly if you arrive at the chaotic bus station), and the number of "guides" and "students" who lay claim to new arrivals, Tetouan is not too hard a city to get your bearings—or to find your own way around.

The **Ville Nouvelle**, built by the Spanish as the capital of their colonial zone, follows a fairly straightforward grid. At its center is **Place Moulay el Mehdi**, with the PTT (post/telephone office) and main banks. From here the grid stretches east toward the Medina, still partially walled, and entered from **Place Hassan II**. This square, sprawling with café tables, is the real heart of the town—a gathering place during the evening, when hash smokers congregate in upper-floor dens and half the town seems to be strolling through it.

By day, at least, the **Medina** is good for just wandering around. It's not as large as it appears and you won't get lost for long without coming to an outer wall or gate, beyond which you can then loop back to the Ville Nouvelle. Specific points of interest are detailed in the section following, and are not too hard to find on your own. If this is your first day in Morocco, however, you might want to consider an easier introduction, arranging an **official guide** at the **tourist office**, a few yards down Bd. Mohammed V from Place el Mehdi. The office (open Mon.–Fri. 8am–2pm and 3–6pm; Sat. and sometimes Sun. 8am–2pm) will also **change money** when the banks are closed.

If you run into trouble, the main **police station** is on Bd. General Franco, opposite the *Hôtel Dersa*.

Points of Arrival

Arriving by bus or *grand taxi*, you'll find yourself on the edge of the Ville Nouvelle—slightly left of center near the bottom of our town map. If you're moving on right away, there are regular **buses** from the station here to Chaouen, Meknes, Fes, and Tangier; ask around at the various windows

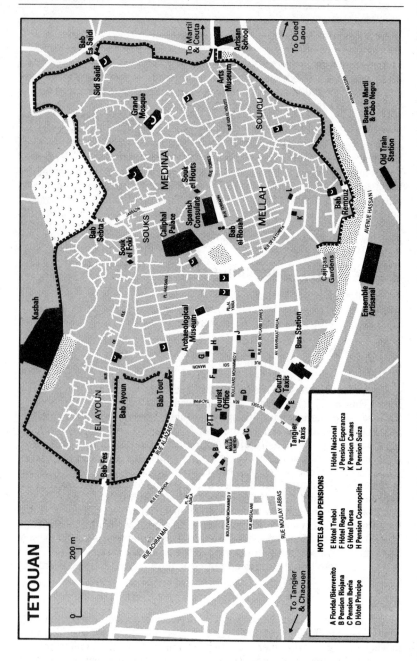

TETOUAN

0 [_____] 200 m

To Tangier & Chaouen

HOTELS AND PENSIONS

A Florida/Bienvenito
B Pension Riojana
C Pension Iberia
D Hôtel Principe

E Hôtel Trebol
F Hôtel Regina
G Hôtel Dersa
H Pension Cosmopolita

I Hôtel Nacional
J Pension Esperanza
K Pension Camas
L Pension Suiza

before buying a ticket because both CTM and private companies operate on each of these routes.

Heading for **Tangier or Ceuta** it's easiest to travel by **grand taxi**; these are routine runs, just go along to the ranks (see map) and get a place (currently 20dh and 12dh, respectively). Ceuta taxis (or buses) will drop you at the border; once there, just walk across and pick up a local Spanish bus for the 3km into town.

For the **beaches** at Martil, Cabo Negro, and Mdiq—each easy daytrips— buses leave frequently through the day in summer from behind the old train station on the road to Ceuta; from the bus station in winter. For **Oued Laou**, there are two buses daily from the main station (8am and 5pm), or— considerably easier—you can share a *grand taxi* (from the Oued Laou road junction).

Finding a Room

Staying in Tetouan, try to ignore all offers from "guides" and head for one of the **hotels or pensions** listed below and keyed on the map. You're likely to get the best deal at the first five—all officially rated—because all the other pensions (including those we've listed) raise their summer prices well above the basic rate. This is partly because newly arrived tourists will pay whatever they're asked, but it also reflects demand. With its excellent local beaches, Tetouan is a popular Moroccan resort and rooms in July/August can take a while to find.

CLASSIFIED HOTELS

Hôtel Trebol (keyed E), 3 Yacoub el Mansour; ☎20.93. Right behind the bus station; safe, a little damp, but more or less adequate. *1*A.*

Hôtel Principe (D), 20 Youssef Tachfine; ☎27.95. Much better in all respects. Halfway up from the bus station to the main *place* of the Ville Nouvelle .*1*A.*

Hôtel Nacional (I), 8 Rue Mohammed Torres; ☎32.90. Reasonable, if dull; sometimes insists on full board in midsummer. *2*A.*

Hôtel Regina (F), 8 Rue Sidi Mandri; ☎21.13. Thoroughly recommended, though often full. Three blocks up from the bus station. *1*A.*

Hôtel Dersa (G), 8 Bd. General Franco; ☎42.15. Expensive, if just slightly the best in town. Opposite the *Regina. 3*B.*

UNCLASSIFIED HOTELS

Pension Riojana (B), **Pension Florida** (A), **Pension Bienvenito** (A), **Pension Iberia** (C). All of these are in—or just off—the central Place Moulay el Mehdi. *Iberia*, above the B.M.C.E. bank, is very small but a definite first choice (☎36.79).

Pension Esperanza (J). Best of many overpriced places along Bd. Mohammed V.

Pension Cosmopolita (H), 5 Bd. General Franco. Slightly expensive but very clean. Opposite the *Regina.*

Pension Camas (K), **Pension Suiza** (L), Rue Luneta. Both very basic—on a narrow street at the edge of the Medina, reached from the corner of Place Hassan II.

Pensions to avoid. There are some thirty or so other pensions, a few of them within the Medina itself—most around its periphery. The highest concentration is in the circular **Place Hassan II**, which separates the new and old towns. These, the favorite choice of bus station hustlers are definitely worth avoiding; if a guide brings you here, he'll have virtual access to your room as long as you stay, and he's *not* going to believe that you don't want to buy kif, or anything else on offer.

CAMPGROUNDS

There are no campgrounds in Tetouan itself. The nearest is 11km out, on the beach, at **Martil**. If you fail to find a hotel, this can be a useful fallback. See "Arrival" for bus details.

Restaurants

As ever, the cheapest food is to be found in the **Medina**, particularly in the stalls inside Bab el Rouah and along Rue Luneta in the Mellah.

For more variety or a more relaxed meal, try one of the many **Ville Nouvelle** places on or around Bd. Mohammed V/Bd. Mohammed Torres. *Restaurant Moderne*, on Pasaje Acharc, is one of the best of these (open 9am–9pm); to get there go through the arcades opposite Cinema Español on Place Hassan II. *Restaurant Zerhoun* (7 Bd. Mohammed Torres) is a little pricier, though with a pleasant "traditional salon".

The Town and Medina

Tetouan has been occupied twice by the Spanish. It was seized, briefly, as a supposed threat to Ceuta, from 1859–1862: a period which saw the Medina converted to a town of almost European appearance, complete with street lighting. Then in 1913 a second occupation began—stretching over five decades of this century. Tetouan served first as a military garrison for the subjugation of the Rif, later as the capital of the **Spanish Protectorate Zone**, and as such almost doubled in size to handle the region's trade and administration. "Native tradition" was respected to the extent of leaving the Medina intact, and even restoring its finer mansions, but in social terms there was more or less negative progress; Spanish administration retained a purely military character, and only a handful of schools were opened throughout the entire zone—a legacy which had effects well beyond independence in 1956.

The town adapted with difficulty to the new French/Moroccan-dominated nation and continues in a slightly uneasy relationship with the central government. This rose to the surface again with the 1984 riots.

The Medina

Looking around Tetouan, you inevitably seem to gravitate toward **Place Hassan II**—the old meeting place and market square, still dominated by the Spanish consulate. The usual approach to the Medina is through the archway beside it, the **Bab el Rouah** (Gate of the Winds). The next lane to the right of this opens onto the main street of the **Mellah**, built as late as 1807, when the Jews were moved from an area around the Grand Mosque. Few of them remain today, although if you ask around, someone will probably point out the old synagogues.

Entering the Medina proper at **Bab el Rouah,** you find yourself on Rue **Terrafin**—a relatively wide lane, which (with its continuations) cuts straight across to the East Gate, Bab el Oqla. To the left of the street, a series of alleys give access to most of the town's food and craft *souks*. The **Souk el Houts**, a small shaded square directly behind the grounds of the Spanish consulate, is one of the most active: devoted to fish in the mornings, meat in the afternoons, and with an all-day smattering of local pottery stalls. At its top end, two lanes wind up through a mass of alleys, *souks* and passageways toward Bab Sebta. Following the one on the left for about 20m you'll see an opening (on the right) to another small square. This is the **Guersa el Kebira**, essentially a cloth and textile *souk,* where a number of stalls sell the town's exceptional *foutahs*—strong and brilliantly striped lengths of ruglike cotton, worn as a cloak and skirt by the Djebali Berber women.

Leaving the Guersa at its top righthand corner, you should emerge more or less on **Place de l'Oussa**, another beautiful little square, easily recognized by an ornate, tiled fountain and trellis of vines. Along one of its sides is an imposing nineteenth-century *xharia*, or almshouse; on another, is an *artesania*, elegantly tiled and with good views over the quarter from its roof. Beyond the square, still heading up toward the Sebta (Ceuta) Gate, are most of the specific **craft souks**—among them copper and brass workers, renowned makers of *babouches* (thick leather slippers), and carpenters specializing in elaborately carved and painted wood. Most of the shops along the central lane here—**Rue el Jarrazin**—focus on the tourist trade, but this goes much less for the *souks* themselves.

So, too, with the *souks* around **Rue de Fes**, off to the left, reached most easily by following the lane up the side of the Caliph's Palace (see below) in Place Hassan II. This is the main thoroughfare of a much more mundane area selling ordinary everyday goods, and the occasional villagers' flea market or *joutia*. At its main intersection—just to the right as you come out onto the lane up from Place Hassan II—is **Souk el Foki**, once the town's main business sector, even though it's little more than a wide alleyway. Following this past a small perfume *souk* and two sizable mosques, you meet up with Rue el Jarrazin about 15m below **Bab Sebta**. Walk out this way, passing (on your left) the superb portal of the **Derkaoua Zaouia** (no admission to non-Muslims), and you enter a huge and very ancient **cemetery,** in use since at least the fifteenth century and containing unusually elaborate Andalusian tombs. Fridays excluded, non-Muslims are tolerated in most Moroccan cemeteries, and walking here you get illuminating views over the Medina and across the valley to the beginning of the Rif.

Had you proceeded along the main drag of Rue Terrafin/Rue Ahmed Torres/Rue Sidi el Yousti, you would have reached the eastern edge of the Medina at **Bab Okla**. The quarter to the north of here, below the Grand Mosque, was the Medina's most exclusive residential area and contains some of its finest mansions. Walking toward the *bab,* you will see signs for one of the best of them, a *palais,* now converted into a (very touristy) carpet and crafts warehouse. Considerably more authentic, and an interesting comparison of real quality, is the **Museum of Moroccan Arts** (*Musée d'Art Marocain*), whose entrance is just on the outside of Bab Okla. A former arms bastion, this has one of the more impressive collections around of traditional crafts and ethnographic objects. Take a look particularly at the *zellij*—enameled tile mosaics—and then cross the road to the **Crafts School** (*Ecole de Métiers*), where you can see craftsmen working at new designs in the old ways, essentially unmodified since the fourteenth century. Perhaps owing to its Andalusian heritage, Tetouan actually has a slightly different *zellij* technique to other Moroccan cities—the tiles are cut before rather than after being fired. A slightly easier process, this is frowned upon by the craftsmen of Fes—whose own pieces are more brittle but brighter in color and closer fitting. Both school and museum are open Mon., Wed., Thur., Fri. 9am–noon and 2:30–5:30pm, Sat. 9am–noon only; closed Tues. and Sun.; note that the school closes down for most of August.

Elsewhere in Tetouan

Outside the Medina there is little of interest. **The Caliphal Palace**, built during the reign of Moulay Ismail, was heavily restored for use by King Hassan's father and predecessor, Mohammed V, and like all of Morocco's royal palaces, is no longer open to visitors. There is a **Centre Artisanal** on the main road below the town, but it's a distinctly unimpressive one, of interest only if you're buying in the *souks* and want to check out prices and quality first. And finally, there is a pleasant, if unmemorable, **Archaeological Museum** (same hours as Arts Museum, above). This was assembled during the Spanish protectorate, so it features exhibits from throughout their zone: prehistoric stones from the Western Sahara among them. Highlights, as so often in North Africa, are the Roman mosaics, mostly gathered from Lixus and the oft-plundered Volubilis.

The Tetouan beaches: from Mdiq to Oued Laou

Despite the numbers of tourists passing through, Tetouan is above all a resort for Moroccans—a character very much in evidence at most of the beaches around. Throughout the summer, and particularly after Ramadan, whole villages of family tents appear at **Martil**, **Mdiq**, and, farther down the coast, around **Restinga-Smir**. At **Oued Laou**, some 40km east of the town, there's a younger and slightly alternative atmosphere—something which is attracting small but growing groups of German, French, and, to a lesser extent, American and British travelers. See Tetouan ("Arriving") for transportation details.

West: Martil, Cabo Negro, and Mdiq

MARTIL, essentially Tetouan's city beach, was its port as well, until the river between the two silted up. Throughout the Middle Ages, it maintained an active corsair fleet, twice prompting Spanish raids to block the harbor. Today it is a small but very active fishing village with a slightly ramshackle appearance, owing to the rows of tourist huts along the seafront. The beach, stretching all the way around to the fashionable villas of Cabo Negro, is excellent, with fine, yellow sand, and long enough to remain uncrowded despite its summer popularity. *Camping Martil*, the official **campground**, is just back from the beach, by the river on the east side of town—friendly and cheap, though not a place to leave bags unattended. Almost opposite it, on Rue Miramar, is the *Hôtel Nuzha*, unrated but charging roughly 1*A prices for standard **pension rooms**. If this is full, they will probably find you a room nearby, or there are two cheapish pensions by the bus station: the *Hôtel Rabat* and, preferable, the clean *Pension Rif*.

Most of the Martil buses go on to **CABO NEGRO**, an attractive alternative for lying around on the sands, but without casual places to stay other than the 3*A *Hôtel Petit Merou* (☎81.10).

To get to Mdiq, or the sprawling complexes and campgrounds of Smir-Restinga, you leave from the same point in Tetouan (see above), but on a separate local bus. **MDIQ** is a lovely coastal village, maintaining an active fishing port. It is becoming a little overdeveloped, but remains a nice enough place to rest up on the beach. If you want a **room**, the one cheap option is *Hôtel Playa* (1*B; ☎85.10); other than this, there are just package tourism complexes—and a large **campground**. Every Thursday (in season) there are **catamarans to and from Gibraltar**.

RESTINGA-SMIR is more a collective name for a length of beach than for an actual place or village: an attractive strip of the Mediterranean, if a little dominated by package hotels; the *Al Fraia* **campground**, by the *Club Mediterrané*, is excellent and secure—a good first or last stop in the country.

East: In the Shadow of the Rif

East of Tetouan the coastline is almost immediately distinct. For a few kilometers, the road follows the sea and the still more or less continuous beach, dotted with communities of tents. But very soon it begins to climb into the foothills of the Rif, a first taste of the crazily zigzagging, Moroccan mountain roads. When you finally emerge at **OUED LAOU**, irrespective of its beach or appeal, you're likely to want to stay.

This, anyway, is a positive option. Oued Laou is not an especially pretty place—Riffian villages tend to look spread out and lacking any core—but it has a terrific, near-deserted beach extending for miles on each side. You can **camp** here down by the river, or there's a small and very relaxed **hotel** right by the sea, the *Hôtel-Café Oued Laou*. If it's full, or if you want to pay less than their one-star prices, they'll find you rooms elsewhere—Oued Laou is a very laid-back, easygoing sort of place. It is also one of the most accessible parts of the Rif, and a good place to meet people and talk: hustlers have nothing to hustle except kif and rooms, and aren't too bothered about either; having come out here, off the tourist track, it is assumed that you're not completely stupid or innocent. There's a Saturday **souk** (held 3km inland), which draws villagers from all over the valley—and produces **bus connections with Chaouen**.

It's possible to continue **along the coast to El Jebha** (see *Chapter Two: The Rif*); the road is now paved the whole way except the last 20km, and there's a daily bus along the route from Tetouan (leaves Tetouan at 7am). **KÂASERAS**, twenty minutes away from Oued Laou, is a relaxed place, geared toward Moroccans camping on the beach, but with a few rooms available.

Chaouen (Chefchaouen, Xaouen)

Shut in by a fold of mountains, **CHAOUEN** becomes visible only once you have arrived—a dramatic approach to a town which, until the arrival of Spanish troops in 1920, had been visited by just four Europeans. Charles de Foucauld, the French missionary explorer, was among them, entering in the disguise of a Jewish rabbi. Another was Walter Harris, whose main impulse, described in his book, *Land of an African Sultan*, was "the very fact that there existed within thirty hours' ride of Tangier a city in which it was considered an utter impossibility for a Christian to enter."

The impossibility—and Harris very nearly lost his life when the town was alerted to the presence of "a Christian dog"—went right back to Chaouen's founding in 1471. The whole region hereabouts is sacred to Muslims due to the presence of the tomb of Moulay Abdessalam ben Mchich—patron saint of the Djebali tribesmen and one of the "four poles of Islam"—and Chaouen was itself established by one of his Shereefian followers, Moulay Rachid, as a secret base from which to attack the Portuguese in Ceuta and Ksar es Seghir. Over the following century, its population grew increasingly anti-European with the arrival of refugees from Moorish Spain, and it became an important center of pilgrimage and *marabouts* ("saints", believed to hold supernatural powers).* But beyond this, the town was extraordinarily isolated. When the Spanish troops began their occupation, they found Jews here speaking, and in some cases writing, medieval Castilian, a language extinct in Spain for nearly four hundred years.

Chaouen is now well established on the excursion routes, and it is becoming a little overconcerned with tourism. There are the inevitable *souks* and stalls for the tour groups, a monstrous hotel that has been allowed to disfigure the twin peaks (*ech-Chaoua*: the horns) from which the town takes its name, and hustlers, sadly, have made an appearance. But local attitudes toward tourists, and to the predominantly backpacking travelers who stop over, remain relaxed; pensions are among the friendliest and cheapest around, and to stay here a few days and walk in the hills remains one of the best possible introductions to Morocco.

Orientation, Rooms, and Practicalities

With a population of around 20,000—a tenth of Tetouan's—Chaouen is more like a large village in size and feel, confusing only on arrival. **Buses** and **grands taxis** drop you at the marketplace, outside the walls of the town in a vague straggle of new buildings grouped about the Mosque of Moulay Rachid. There are a couple of **banks** here for money exchange: the *Banque Marocaine* and *Banque Populaire* (the latter charging 5dh commission).

---

* As the center of so much *maraboutism*, Chaouen and its neighboring villages have a particularly large number of **moussems**. The big events are those in Moulay Abdessalam ben Mchich (40km away: usually in May) and Sidi Allal el Hadj (August 9th), but there are dozens of others—ask around.

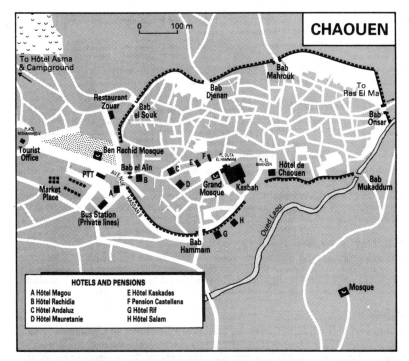

To reach the Medina, walk up across the marketplace to the tiny arched entrance, **Bab el Ain**, just beyond the prominent *Hôtel Magou*. Through the gateway a clearly dominant lane winds all the way up through the town to the main square, **Place Outa el Hammam** (flanked by the gardens and ruined towers of the **Kasbah**), and beyond to a second smaller square, **Place el Makhzen**.

Pensions and Hotels

Either along or just off this main route are a series of small, **unclassified pensions**, converted from private houses in the Medina. If you're young, and you don't have an urge for private bathrooms, these are the places to stay—rooms can be a bit cell-like, but most are exceptionally clean, and all are remarkably inexpensive. For the more conventionally inclined, several of the **classified hotels** are good value, too.

UNCLASSIFIED PENSIONS

Hôtel Rachidia (B). The first you encounter, just inside the Medina walls to the right of Bab el Ain.

Pension Ibn Batouta (C). Possibly the quietest of the pensions—and with less feel of a self-conscious "travelers' hangout"; located in an alley to the left, about 30m along the street from the Bab el Ain.

Hôtel Mauretania (D), ☎61.84. For the participatory—with a communal courtyard and rock music. Down a network of alleys to the right of the street.

Hôtel Andaluz (E), ☎60.34. An excellent, comfortable place, signposted to the left at the near end of the Place Outa el Hammam.

Hôtel Kaskades (F). Just off the square—but not so clean as the rest and not highly recommended.

Pension Castellana (G), ☎62.95. Many travelers return loyally to the Castellana each year, creating a distinctly laid-back and youthful atmosphere.

CLASSIFIED HOTELS

Hôtel Rif (H), on the lower road; ; ☎62.07. More modern and more comfortable, though still mainly youthful clientèle, with a well-stocked sound system. Low rates for long stays, a bar, restaurant, and an exceptionally hospitable manager. *1*A*.

Hôtel Salam (I), again on the lower road; ☎62.39. More mainstream hotel. *1*B*.

Hôtel Magou (A), just outside the Bab el Ain; ☎62.39. Modern, slightly upmarket—and a little bit dull. *2*A*.

Hôtel de Chaouen, Place el Makhzen; ☎61.36. The former Spanish "grand hotel", recently reconstructed for the package trade. Bar and swimming pool goes towards justifying the expense. *3*A*.

CAMPGROUND AND YOUTH HOSTEL

Chaouen's **campground** is on the hill above the town, by the big modern 4* *Hôtel Asma*; follow the signs to the *Asma* by the road, or cut through the cemetery on foot. It is inexpensive but can be crowded in midsummer. The youth hostel (auberge de jeunesse), adjoining, has dormitory beds for 6dh—only really worth considering if all the pensions are full up.

Eating

Compared to the hotels, there's surprisingly little choice in Chaouen's restaurants. In the Place Outa el Hammam a few places serve up regular Moroccan meals—*Restaurant Kasbah* is probably the best of these—and some of the small pensions will arrange communal meals for guests. The *Hôtel Rif* has a regular restaurant, too.

The indisputable best choice, though, so long as you like its music, is *Restaurant Zouar*, outside the Medina (50m uphill, following the walls from the bus station square). Or if you need alcohol served with a meal, there's *Restaurant-Bar Omo Rabi* (again outside the Medina, on Rue Tarik Ibn Zaid), or the significantly more upscale *Hôtel de Chaouen*.

Steambaths and Swimming

The town, a bit unusually, has separate **hammams** (Turkish baths) for men and women. The male one is right next to the *Pension Castellana,* off Place Outa el Hammam; the one for women, which is older and much more elaborate, is in the quarter of the *souks*—ask someone to show you the way because it totally defies written directions.

Over the last couple of years, entrance to non-Muslims has been limited, and sometimes refused unless you have a group and book the hammam together. Ask your pension/hôtel for advice, or for someone to accompany you.

For **swimming**, the *Hôtel Chaouen* has a pool, (sometimes) open to nonresidents for 15dh a day. Locals share a taxi to a **pool in the river**, a few kilometers downstream; an excellent alternative for which any of the pension managers will give full instructions.

Buses and Grands Taxis

Leaving Chaouen by bus can be difficult. Departures to Fes, and to a lesser degree, Meknes, are often full and you should really try to get tickets the day before—an exercise which may need some persistence. Current departure times to Fes are around 6:30am and 10am; to Meknes at noon. If you can't get on any of these, an alternative is to take a *grand taxi* or local bus to Ouezzane and another one from there; or to return to Tetouan (where most of the buses originate). For Tetouan, buses leave at least four times a day—much less of a problem—or you can share a grand taxi.

Daily buses also run to the Ceuta border (11am; 2 hr..) and to Oued Laou (5pm; 1½ hr.). If you like the idea of a dizzying ride through the Rif, and coming to a very small fishing village/beach at the end of it, you might also consider going on to El Jebha (see *Chapter Two: The Rif*), served by two buses a week, leaving around dawn.

For the affluent, or anyone who can get a group of people together, *grands taxis* can be chartered—a stylish way to travel to Tangier or to Fes.

The Town and River

Like Tetouan, Chaouen's architecture has a strong Andalusian character: less elaborate (and less grand), perhaps, but often equally inventive. It is a town of extraordinary light and color, its whitewash tinted with blue and edged by soft, golden, stone walls—and it is a place which, for all its present popularity, still seems redolent of the years of isolation. The roofs of its houses, tiled and with eaves, entailed obvious physical assertion to build, in contrast to the flat ones found everywhere else in Morocco. But this is something you can sense about life in general here, even about the people themselves—something that has been inbred in them over many generations.

Since the **Medina** is so small, it is more than ever a place to explore at random: the things which draw your attention are not so much "sights" as unexpected strands of detail. At some point, though, head for the two main squares, and for the **souks**—just below Place Outa el Hammam. There are basic town *souks* held twice a week (Mon. and Thurs.) in the market square, so these, to some degree, have been set up for, or at least geared to, the tourist industry. But both the quality and variety found here is surprising. When the Spanish arrived—just sixty years ago—Chaouen craftsmen were still working leather in the manner of twelfth-century Cordoba, tanning with bark, and hammering silver to old Andalusian designs. And though you won't see any of this today, the town's carpet and weaving workshops remain active and many of their designs unchanged. Vendors are well used to haggling with travelers, and if you're staying for a few days, prices can fall dramatically.

Interesting, too, is to observe the contrasts in feel between the main, Arab part of Chaouen and the—still modestly populated—Jewish quarter of the **Mellah**. This is to be found behind the jewelers' souk, between the Bab el Ain and the Kasbah.

Place Outa el Hammam, the elongated main square, is where most of the evening life takes place, its cafés overhung by upper rooms—some the preserve of kif smokers. By day, the town's focus is the **Kasbah**, a quiet ruin shaded with gardens, built like so many of northern Morocco by Moulay Ismail. Off to the right, in the first of its compounds, are the old town prison cells, where Abd el Krim (see *Chapter Two: The Rif*) was imprisoned after his surrender in 1926. Five years earlier, he had himself driven the Spanish from the town, a retreat which saw the loss of nearly 20,000 of their troops.

The *place* was once the main market square, and off to its sides are a number of small **fondouks;** one of the more visible is at the beginning of the lane opposite the Kasbah (no. 34). Somewhat bizarrely, the local Djebala tribesmen, who form most of the town's population, have a particular tradition of homosexuality, and there were boy markets held here until as recently as 1937, when they were officially banned by the Spanish administration. Djebali sexual preferences are just one of the characteristics which mark them apart from the notoriously *anti*-homosexual Riffians of the mountains beyond.

Place de Makhzen—the old "government square"—is in some ways a continuation of the marketplace, an elegant clearing with an old fountain and pottery stalls set up for the package tourists. If you leave the Medina at this point, it's possible to follow **the river** around the outside of the walls and up above Bab Onsar. Here, you reach **Ras el Ma** (the water-head), a small cascade in the mountainside with water so clear and cold that, in the local phrase, "it knocks your teeth out to drink it." Long a favorite spot—and, to an extent, a holy one due to the nearby tomb of Sidi Abdallah Habti—there are a couple of cafés close by to while away the midday hours.

Over to the south of the town, an enjoyable walk is to the ruinous "Spanish Mosque." Set on a hilltop, its interior is covered in graffiti, but nevertheless gives a good sense of the layout of a mosque—normally off limits in Morocco. Nobody seems to mind you looking around.

Up into the Hills

Farther along, a good **day's hike** is to head east, up over the mountains behind Chaouen. As you look at the "two horns" from town, there is a path winding along the side of the mountain on your left. A four-hour (or more) hike will take you up to the other side, where a vast valley opens up, and if you walk farther, you'll see the sea. The valley, as even casual exploration will show, is full of small farms cultivating kif—as they have done for years. Walking in the area, you may occasionally be stopped by the military, who are cracking down on foreign involvement in the crop.

For more ambitious hikes—and there are some wonderful trails in the area—ask at the pensions about hiring a **guide**. Someone knowledgeable can usually be found to accompany you, for around 50-100dh a day (the harder the climb, the more it costs!).

Ouezzane (Wazzan)

Midway between Chaouen and the Atlantic coast, **OUEZZANE** lopes down around an outreach of the Djebala mountains—the edge of the Rif and the old traditional border between the *Bled es-Makhzen* (the governed territories) and the *Bled es-Siba* (those of the lawless tribes). As such, it became an important power base during the last two centuries, and its sheikhs were among the most powerful in Morocco.

The sheikhs—the *Ouezzani*—were also the spiritual leaders of the influential **Tabiya brotherhood**. They were *shereefs* (descendants of the Prophet) and came in a direct line from the Idrissids, the first and founding dynasty of Morocco. This, however, seems to have given them little significance until the eighteenth century, when Moulay Abdallah es-Shereef established a *zaouia* (religious cult center) at Ouezzane. It acquired a huge following, becoming one of the great places of pilgrimage and an inviolable sanctuary for all Muslims.

Unlike Chaouen, the town that grew up around this was not itself sacred, but until the turn of this century Jews and Christians were allowed to take only temporary accommodation in one of the *fondouks* set aside for the purpose. Walter Harris, who became a close friend of the Ouezzani *shereefs* in the late nineteenth century, found the town "the most fanatical that Europeans may visit" and the *zaouia* a virtually autonomous religious court. Strange to relate, though, an Englishwoman, Emily Keane, had in 1877 married the principal shereef, and for some decades lived in the town, dispensing medical care to the locals. Her *Life Story*, written after her husband's death, ends with the balanced summing up: "I do not advise anyone to follow in my footsteps, at the same time I have not a single regret."

The **Zaouia**, distinguished by an unusual octagonal minaret, is the most striking building in the town, and though the Tabiya brotherhood now maintain their main base elsewhere, it continues to function and is the site of a lively spring *moussem* (pilgrimage festival). (As in the rest of Morocco, however, entrance to the *zaouia* area is forbidden to non-Muslims.) The older quarters of Ouezzane—many of their buildings tiled, gabled, and sporting elaborate doors—enclose and rise above the building, newer suburbs sprawling into the hills on each side.

It's an attractive enough place, and if of little specific interest, has a definite grandeur in its site. Few tourists stay because it is only a couple of hours out of Chaouen, but there are worse places to be stranded. The bus and *grand taxi* terminal is about 50m below the main square (**Place du Souks**), where you'll find three reasonable, basic **hotels**. The main **souks** climb up from an archway here, behind the *Grand Hôtel*. Ouezzane has a local reputation for its woolen rugs—most evident in the weavers' *souk,* around Place Rouida near the top end of the town.

Ouezzane provides a useful link if you're travelling by public **transportation** (bus or *grand taxi*) between **Chaouen and the Atlantic coast,** or vice versa. There are a fair number of **buses** also to both Meknes and Fes, but if you're stopping or staying, buy onward tickets well in advance; as with Chaouen it's not unusual for them to arrive and leave full.

travel details

Trains

Seven trains a day leave Tangier, all running through either SIDI KACEM or SIDI SLIMANE, where you may need to get a connection to the Fes/Meknes or Rabat/Casablanca/Marrakesh lines. The following timetable is current as of publication, and, though there may be small changes, its pattern should remain very similar

Tangier (12:10am), Asilah (12:57am), Meknes (5:07am), Fes (6:18am). Continues to Taza/Oujda (8:47am/12:39pm).

Tangier (7:22am), Asilah (8:01am), Sidi Slimane (10:26am: change for Meknes/Fes, arriving 11:55am/12:48pm), Rabat (11:49am), Casablanca-Port (12:51pm).

Tangier (8:12am), Asilah (9:01am), Sidi Kacem (11:38am: change for Rabat/Casablanca-Voyageurs/Marrakesh, arriving 2:29pm/3:51pm/9:09pm), Meknes (1:06pm), Fes (1:58pm). Continues to Taza/Oujda (4:47pm/8:12pm).

Tangier (2:15pm), Asilah (3:04pm), Sidi Kacem (5:42pm: change for Meknes/Fes,arriving 7:22pm/8:19pm).

Tangier (Port: 4:10pm; Ville: 4:22pm), Asilah (5:08pm), Sidi Slimane (7:41pm: change for Meknes/Fes, 7:22pm/8:19pm), Rabat (9:09pm), Casablanca-Port (10:12pm: change for Marrakesh, 5:16am).

Tangier (8:50pm) Asilah (9:39pm), Sidi Kacem (12:12am: change for Meknes/Fes, 2:30am/3:34am). Continues to Taza/Oujda (6:07am/9:38am).

Tangier (Port: 11:15pm; Ville: 11:30pm), Asilah (12:14am), Rabat (4:18am), Casablanca Voyageurs (5:25am), Marrakesh (8:54am). *NB: This train leaves at 9.20pm in winter.*

Note: ONCF run connecting bus services to **Tetouan** from Tnine Sidi Lyamani, near Asilah.

Buses

From Tangier Asilah (7 daily; 1 hr.); Larache (6; 1hr. & 40 min.); Tetouan (12; 1½ hr.); Rabat (2; 5 hr.); Meknes (2; 7 hr.); Fes (2; 8 hr.)
From Asilah Larache (5 daily; 1hr.)

From Larache Ksar el Kebir (3 daily; 40 min.); Souk el Arba (5; 1 hr.); Rabat (4; 3½ hr.); Meknes (2; 5½ hr.).
From Souk el Arba Moulay Bousselham (5 daily; 35 min.); Ouezzane (3; 1½ hr.).
From Ouezzane Meknes (2 daily; 4 hr.); Fes (2; 5½ hr.); Chaouen (4; 1 hr. 20 min.).
From Tetouan Tangier (12; 1½ hr.); Chaouen (10; 3 hr.); Fnideq (hourly; 25 min.); Oued Laou (2; 2 hr.).
From Chaouen Tetouan (10 daily; 3 hr.) Ketama/Al Hoceima (2 daily; 5 hr./8 hr.); Meknes (1; 5½ hr.); Fes (2; 7 hr.); El Jebha (2 a week; 7 hr.)
From Chaouen Ketama/Al Hoceima (2 daily; 5 hr./8 hr.); Meknes (1; 5½ hr.); Fes (2; 7 hr.); Tetouan (10; 3 hr.).

Grands Taxis

From Tangier Regularly to Tetouan (1 hr.); less frequently to Larache, Rabat, and occasionally Fes.
From Ouezzane Regularly to Souk el Arba (1 hr.) and Chaouen (1¼ hr.).
From Tetouan Regularly to Tangier (1 hr.), Oued Laou, and Fnideq (Ceuta border).
From Souk el Arba Regularly to Moulay Bousselham (½ hr.) and Larache (50 min.).

Ferries and Hydrofoils

From Tangier: FERRIES to Algeciras (4 daily; 2½ hr.); Gibraltar (3 per week; 2 hr.); and Sète, France (weekly; 18 hr.). HYDROFOILS (in season) to Tarifa (3 daily; ½ hr.), Algeciras (1 daily; 1 hr.), and Gibraltar (1 daily; 1 hr.) See p.62 for details.
From Ceuta: FERRY to Algeciras (12 daily; 1½ hr.). HYDROFOILS (March–September) to Algeciras (½ hr.).
From Mdiq HYDROFOILS daily in season to Algeciras (½ hr.).

Flights

From Tangier Daily flights to Casablanca (and from there to Marrakesh, etc.) International flights most days to London, Madrid, etc., and to Gibraltar (and on to London—fairly cheap on *Gib Air*).

TELEPHONE CODES

ASILAH ☎091	SMIR RESTINGA ☎096
CHAOUEN ☎098	SOUK EL ARBA ☎090
LARACHE ☎091	TANGIER ☎09
MDIQ ☎096	TETOUAN ☎096

CHAPTER TWO

THE RIF AND THE MEDITERRANEAN COAST

> *Goldshot green of the Rif's slant fields here, vapor-blossoms resinous and summery . . . "We've had a windfall of kif. Allah has smiled upon us."*
> Thomas Pynchon: *Gravity's Rainbow*

A nyone who has heard of the **Rif mountains** at all has usually done so in connection with Ketama, and the sale of kif, or hashish. There are towns enough in Morocco where you'll be offered kif for sale, but at Ketama it is simply assumed that this is why you are here. "How many kilos?" they ask. Kif and Ketama are big business.

Talking about the Rif you have to state this first, since it dominates much of the region's character. Even where uncultivated, kif plants grow wild around the stony slopes—and there they seem to stretch forever. The cultivation itself is legal, but "standard" Moroccan rules forbid its sale, purchase, and even possession. Don't be blinded by the local ways: police roadblocks are frequent, informers almost as thick as the smoke.

An additional hazard are the industry's local mafias, cruising around the hills in their black Mercedes and not above a bit of traditional banditry. All through the year you hear stories of tourists driving along the road to Ketama to be stopped by a parked car or fallen tree. For them, "How many kilos?" ceases to be a joke. If you're driving and are reasonably cautious, avoid the whole area around **Ketama**—bounded to the south by Had-Ikauen, to the east and west by Targuist and Bab Berred. If you're cautious and not driving, stay on the bus—it's a tremendous trip.

The **mountain range** itself is a vast, limestone mass, over 300km long, up to 2500m in height, and covered for the most part in dense upland forests. The whole impression is one of enormity, a grandiose place full of faintly outrageous views. You keep feeling it's far too hot for Alpine scenery and there are no happily grazing cattle, just groups of workmen lying back on the pine needles, smoking kif.

Traveling here, too, it's impossible to resist the feeling of nervous excitement—not just that the roads seem designed to terrify, but in the very real

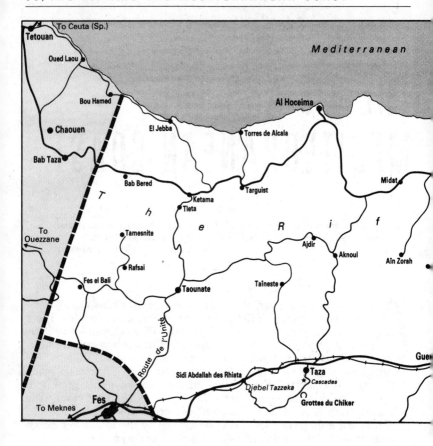

sense of isolation, very unlike the mere remoteness of the Atlas. The Rif is, in fact, the natural boundary between Europe and Africa, and with the Sahara it cuts off central Morocco from Algeria and the rest of the Maghreb. In the past this was a powerful barrier—it took the first European three months to travel from Al Hoceima to Melilla—and it is sustained today by the extraordinary sense of independence and traditional xenophobia among the tribes. There is no other part of Morocco where you feel so completely incidental to ordinary local life.

Things are rather different with the **towns** to the east of the range. **Taza** and **Oujda**, important and historic posts on the "corridor" into Algeria, are among the most easygoing in the country—Oujda, in particular, with its large university population. And there are relaxed times to be had, too, on those few points where the Rif gives way to the **Mediterranean coast**. Contrary to its daunting appearance from the great "backbone" roads, the Rif does have **beaches**—though they're few and far between, and virtually undeveloped east of Tetouan.

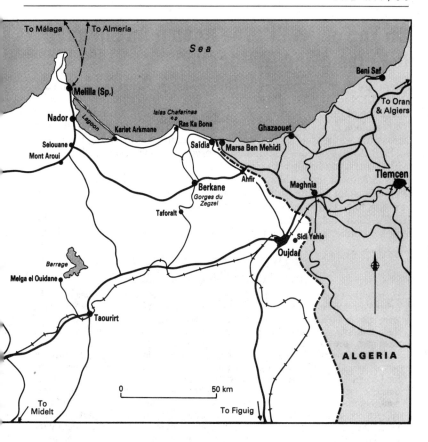

The only actual beach resort is **Al Hoceima,** and even here the hotels spread for less than half a kilometer; elsewhere it's a question of a few sporadic campgrounds, the liveliest being at **Saidia,** on the border with Algeria. These attract quite a number of Moroccan families during July and August and at the end of Ramadan, while fewer come in summer, Few tourists join them, though there's nothing to prevent you; unlike some of the Riffian mountain villages they are easygoing and friendly places—excellent for meeting people, without any tourist hustling.

Lastly, the region has useful **ferry connections** with Spain from **Melilla**—like Ceuta, still a Spanish possession. If you are bringing a car across from Spain, these are well worth considering. Fes is easily reached, either through the Rif, or by cutting down to the Taza road, and from Oujda there is a grand desert route **south to Figuig** and beyond to the oases of the Tafilalt (see *Chapter Seven: The Great Southern Routes*). In past years, travelers wanting to go **on into Algeria** had to enter at Figuig, but with improved Moroccan-Algerian relations, the border at Oujda is now open to all.

On Top of the Rif: The Road from Chaouen to Ketama and Al Hoceima

There are very few journeys in Morocco as spectacular as the one from CHAOUEN to AL HOCEIMA. The road literally (and strangely) follows the backbone of the Western Rif, the highest peaks in the north of the country. You can look down on one side to the Mediterranean coast, and on the other across the whole southern range; "big mountains and more big mountains," as Paul Bowles put it—"mountains covered with olive trees, with oak trees, with bushes, and finally with giant cedars."

Even without the problems of Ketama (see the introduction to this chapter), this is not a route for inexperienced drivers. Though in good condition, it seems to be constructed entirely of zigzags and hairpin turns. Beyond **BAB TAZA**, 23km out of Chaouen, you wind around the tops of ridges, sheer drops on either side to deep and isolated valleys. Going by bus the Riffians

Abd el Krim and the Republic of the Rif

Up until the establishment of the Spanish protectorate in 1912, the tribes of the Rif existed outside government control—a northern heartland of the *Bled es-Siba*. They were subdued temporarily by *harkas*, the burning-raids with which sultans asserted their authority, and for a longer period under Emperor Moulay Ismail; but for the most part, bore out their own name of *Imazighen*, or "Free Ones."

Closed to outside influence, the tribes developed an isolated and self-contained way of life. The Riffian soil, stony and infertile, produced constant problems with food supplies, and it was only through a complex system of alliances (*liffs*) that outright wars were avoided. Blood feuds, however, were endemic, and a major contributor to maintaining a viably small population. Unique in Morocco, the Riffian villages are scattered communities, their houses hedged and set apart, and each family maintained a pillbox tower to spy on and fight off enemies. They were different, too, in their religion: the *Ulema*, the prayer said five times daily—one of the central tenets of Islam—was not observed. *Djinns*, supernatural spirits from pagan nature cults, were widely accredited, and great reliance was placed on the intercession of local *marabouts*, or saints.

It was an unlikely ground for significant and organized rebellion; yet, for over five years (between 1921 and 1927), the tribes forced the Spanish to withdraw from the mountains. Twice they defeated whole armies—bringing down the Madrid monarchy in the process—and it was only through the added intervention of France, and nearly half a million troops, that the Europeans won eventual victory. In the intervening years, the leaders of the revolt, the brothers **Mohammed and M'hamid Abd el Krim**, were able to declare a Republic of the Rif and to establish much of the apparatus of a modern state.

Well-educated, and confident of the Rif's mineral reserves, they manipulated the *liff* system to forge an extraordinary unity among the tribes, negotiated mining rights in return for arms with Germany and South America, and even set up a Riffian State Bank. Still more impressive, they managed to impose a series of social reforms—including the destruction of family pillboxes, and the banning of kif—which allowed the operation of a fairly broad administrative system. In their success, however, was the inevitability of defeat. It was the first nationalist move-

sleep or talk through it—a fact that seems almost as remarkable as the surrounding scenery.

BAB BERRED, a smallish market village and former Spanish administrative center, signals the real beginning of kif country—it is surrounded, in fact, by the plants—and at **KETAMA** you are at the epicenter. Arriving here, even in transit, is an initiation because absolutely everybody (passengers *and* staff) is involved in "Business." If you get off the bus, you will immediately be offered kif—immense, unbelievable quantities of it—and there is nobody who will believe that you are here for any other purpose.

This, really, is fair enough. Nobody does stay in Ketama unless they are doing business, and anywhere in Morocco, if people introduce themselves as being "from Ketama," there is no ambiguity about what they are offering. Dealers here are likely to try and get you to stay at their farms—something not be recommended, even if you've got an insatiable appetite and curiosity for kif production. Tales abound of travelers who have lost everything, often at knifepoint, after taking up one of these offers.

ment in colonial North Africa, and although the Spanish were ready to quit the zone in 1925, it was politically impossible that the French would allow them to do so.

Defeat for the Riffians—and the exile of Abd el Krim—brought a virtual halt to social progress and reform. **The Spanish** took over the administration en bloc, governing through local *caids* (district administrators), but although they exploited some mineral deposits there was no road building program or any of the other "civilizing benefits" introduced in the French zone. There were, however, two important changes: migration of labor (particularly to French Algeria) replaced the blood feud as a form of population control, and the Riffian warriors were recruited into Spain's own armies. The latter had immense consequences, allowing General Franco to build up a power base in Morocco. It was with Riffian troops that he invaded Andalusia in 1936, and it was probably their contribution which ensured the fascist victory in the Spanish civil war.

Abd el Krim was a powerful inspiration to later nationalists, and the Riffians themselves played an important guerrilla role in the 1955-56 **struggle for independence**. When in April 1957, the Spanish finally surrendered their protectorate, however, the Berber/Spanish-speaking tribes found themselves largely excluded from government. Administrators were imposed on them from Fes and Casablanca, and in October 1958, the Rif's most important tribe, the Beni Urriaguel, rose in open rebellion. The mutiny was soon put down, but necessitated the landing at Al Hoceima of then-Crown-Prince Hassan and some two-thirds of the Moroccan army.

A quarter of a century later, the Rif is still perhaps the most unstable part of Morocco, remaining conscious of its under-representation in government and its underdevelopment, despite substantial school building programs, improved road communications, and a large, new, agricultural project in the plains south of Nador and Al Hoceima. Labor **emigration**, too, remains high—with Western Europe replacing Algeria as the main market—and (as in the rest of Morocco) there is widespread resentment at the difficulty of obtaining a passport for this outlet. With the growth of more sophisticated government systems, and a sizable hierarchy of local administration, further tribal dissidence now seems unlikely. It is interesting to note, though, that it was in the Rif—above all in the towns of Nador, Al Hoceima, and Tetouan—that the 1984 Riots began, and it was here that the most serious disturbances were reported.

Some of the tribes in the mountains have always smoked hashish, though it was the Spanish who really encouraged its cultivation—probably to keep them placid. This situation was apparently accepted when Mohammed V came to power, though the reasons for his doing so are obscure. There is a story, probably apocryphal, that when he visited Ketama in 1957, he accepted a bouquet of kif as a symbolic gift; the Riffis add that this was because he feared their power, though this seems to have been swiftly forgotten amid the following year's rebellion. No matter what, Ketama continued to supply the bulk of the country's kif, and in the early 1970s, it became the center of a significant drug industry, exporting to Europe and America. This sudden growth was accounted for by a single factor: the introduction, supposedly by an American dealer, of techniques for producing hash resin. Overnight, the Riffians had an easily exportable product and, inevitably, big business was quick to follow. Large amounts of money are said to change hands between a whole network of officials, and there is a brisk trade among informants denouncing people. In fact, many of the large growers simply tell the police who they're selling to.

The only **hotel** actually in Ketama is the old Spanish *parador* (former government inn), the somewhat implausible four-star *Hôtel* Tidighine (☎10), complete with its own golf course and swimming pool, used by wintering French tourists for the nearby skiing and boar hunting. The Chaouen–Al Hoceima buses let you off right outside, a confusing stop since, apart from the hustlers, there's virtually nothing else in sight. The main village, and the **cheap hotels**, are, in fact, at **TLETA KETAMA**, 8km down the road to Fes.

Continuing east you reach **TARGUIST**, Abd el Krim's last stronghold and the site of his surrender to the French. This is actually outside the dope triangle, and a lot more relaxed if you want to stay up in the mountains, without the all-pervasive *business*. One of the larger villages of the Rif, with a couple of cafés and some **rooms** to rent, Targuist attracts one of the biggest markets around—held every Saturday, and drawing villagers from the dozens of tiny communities in the neighboring hills. If you've got transportation, time, and the urge to see a remote Riffian market, there are also smaller gatherings nearby: on Thursdays in ISAGEN, on Sundays in BENI BAR NSAR.

The Beaches: Torres de Alcala and El Jebha

Scarcely less remote are the **beaches** reached by tracks down from this road; Torres de Alcala/Kalah Iris and El Jebha. **TORRES DE ALCALA** is the most enticing—and the easier to get to, with more or less daily buses from TARGUIST—and soon, it is rumored, from AL HOCEIMA as well. A quiet fishing village, it was the main port for Fes in Saadian times but went into decline after the Turks established themselves on the offshore **Ile de Ghomera**, which they used into the nineteenth century as a base for piracy—and which is now a Spanish territory (like the Chafarinas and Al Hoceima islands). As Al Hoceima continues to expand, Torres is likely to acquire tourist hotels, but for the moment there's just a seasonal **campground**, a small unrated **hotel** and a few further rooms to rent at the cafés. At **KALAH IRIS**, 4km east on a paved road, there's a seasonal **campground**, restaurant, grocery store, and a good beach.

EL JEBHA, accessible by a more or less daily bus from Tetouan (and twice a week from Chaouen), is shabbier—little more than a hamlet, with a group of fishermen's cottages. Few outsiders visit, and, to be honest, there is little to attract, with the beach sporadically polluted. However, the place has its devotees, who can reflect on the contrasts with Spain's Marbella and Torremolinos across the straits. It is accesible either along the potholed and plummeting coast road from OUED LAOU (occasional bus; see *Chapter One*) or, from the mountain road, by turning off at EL KHEMIS (a bus from Tetouan runs more or less daily this way, as does one twice a week from Chaouen).

The Route de L'Unité: Ketama to Fes

At the end of the Spanish protectorate in 1957, there was no north–south route across the Rif, a marked symbol both of its isolation and of the separateness of the old French and Spanish zones. It was in order to counteract this—and to provide working contact between the Riffian tribes and the French-colonized Moroccans—that the great **Route de l'Unité** was planned.

The *route*, completed in 1963, was built with volunteer labor from all over the country—Hassan II himself worked on it at the outset. It was the brainchild of Mehdi Ben Barka, first President of the National Assembly and the most outstanding figure of the nationalist Left before his exile and subsequent "disappearance" in Paris in 1965. Ben Barka's volunteers, 15,000 strong for much of the project, formed a kind of labor university, working through the mornings and attending lectures in the afternoons.

Today the Route de l'Unité sees little traffic—traveling from Fes to Al Hoceima, it's quicker to go via Taza; from Fes to Tetouan, via Ouezzane. Nevertheless, it's an impressive and very beautiful road, certainly as dramatic an approach to Fes as you could hope for. Going by bus, the one village which might tempt you to stop off is **TAOUNATE**, the largest community along the way, set on a dark plateau above the valley of the Oued Sra (soon to be dammed up to form a vast, 35km-long lake). If you can make it for the Friday market here (one of the most important in the Rif), you should be able to get a lift from there out to any number of villages.

There's also a daily bus to FES EL BALI via **RAFSAI**, the last village of the Rif to be overrun by the Spanish and the site of a December **Olive Festival.** If you're into scenic roads and have the transportation, a forty-kilometer dirt road extends out to the Djebel Lalla Outka peak, reputed to offer the best view of the whole Rif range. **FES EL BALI** is a useful connecting point—with buses to the city of Fes and to Ouezzane—though itself only of passing interest. The village takes its name, *el Bali* (the Old), from an eleventh-century Almoravid fort, little of which remains. If you're stuck here, there's a cheap and basic hotel.

Going **east from Taounate,** an attractive though less spectacular route heads through cork and holm oak forests toward the scattered and pretty grim village of **AKNOUL.** From here you can pick up a bus or *grand taxi* down to TAZA, or sporadic buses over to NADOR or AL HOCEIMA.

Taza and the Djebel Tazzeka

TAZA was once a place of great importance; the capital of Morocco during parts of the Almohad, Merenid, and Alaouite dynasties, and controlling the only practicable pass to the east. This, the *Taza Gap*, forms a wide passage between the Rif and Middle Atlas. It was the route taken by Moulay Idriss and the first Moroccan Arabs, and the Almohads and Merenids both successfully invaded Fes from here. Each dynasty fortified and endowed the city but, as a definitive position, it was never, in fact, very effective: the local Zenatta tribe were always willing to join an attack and, in the nineteenth century, they managed to overrun it completely, with centralized control returning only with the French occupation of 1914.

Modern Taza seems little haunted by this past, its monuments sparse and mostly inaccessible to non-Muslims. It is, however, a pleasant market town and its Medina is saved from anonymity by a magnificent hilltop terrace site, flanked by crumbling Almohad walls. In addition, there is a considerable attraction in the surrounding countryside—the national park of **Djebel Tazzeka,** with its circuit of waterfalls, caves, and schist gorges. As a first stop in Morocco, after arriving at Melilla or Oujda, it's as good a choice as any, a friendly and easygoing place to get acclimatized.

Practicalities

Taza splits into two parts, the **Medina** and the French-built **Ville Nouvelle**— separated by nearly 3km of road and, to all intents, completely distinct. A shuttle bus runs between them, and another connects the Ville Nouvelle with the adjacent train station and bus and *grands taxis* terminal, 3km farther away. *Petits taxis* are available, too, for getting between the stations, Ville Nouvelle, and Medina.

The **Ville Nouvelle** was an important military garrison in the Riffian war and retains much of the barrack-grid character. Its center, **Place de l'Indépendence**, actually serves a population of 40,000, but it's so quiet you'd hardly know it. The two most functional **hotels** are both here. The best, if you can afford it, is the *Hôtel du Dauphine* (2*A; ☎35.67), a fairly stylish, Art Deco colonial building, with an excellent café-bar downstairs; more or less opposite it is a cheaper place, unnamed, unrated but adequate. The *campground*, uphill and to the left, is hardly more than scrub land—semifenced and not very inspiring. Just beyond it, a concrete outpost in the middle of nowhere, is the 3*A *Hôtel Friouato* (☎25.93) worth neither the walk nor the money. The cheap and basic *Hôtel de la Gare,* down by the train and bus station, is pretty drab, too—but useful if you have to get the 4:30/5am bus to Nador.

Most of the **restaurants** are grouped around the Place den l'Indépendence, or along Av. de Tetouan. The *Restaurant Majestic* (26 Av. Mohammed V) has reasonable value set meals. There is a small, helpful **tourist office** on Av. de Tetouan.

Transport: Leaving Taza

Moving on from Taza, you have the widest range of options **going to Fes**. *Grands taxis* run throughout the day (just ask and wait for a place), arriving in

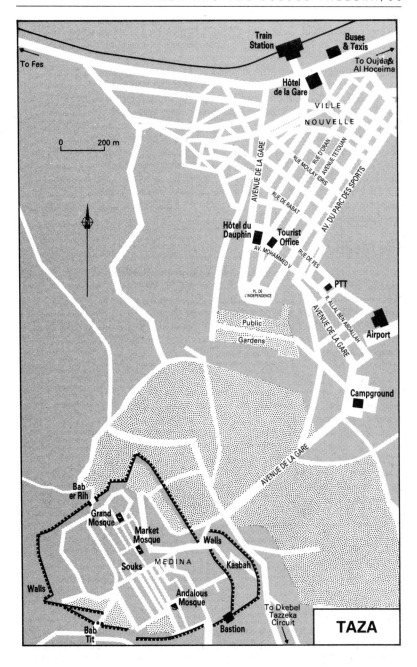

Train Station

Buses & Taxis

To Fes

To Oujda & Al Hoceima

Hôtel de la Gare

VILLE

NOUVELLE

0   200 m

AVENUE DE LA GARE

RUE D'ORAN

RUE MOULAY IDRIS

AVENUE TETOUAN

AV. DU PARC DES SPORTS

RUE DE RABAT

Hôtel du Dauphin

Tourist Office

AV. MOHAMMED V

RUE DE FES

PL. DE L'INDEPENDENCE

PTT

R. ALLAL BEN ABDALLAH

AVENUE DE LA GARE

Airport

Public Gardens

Campground

AVENUE DE LA GARE

Bab er Rih

Grand Mosque

Market Mosque

Walls

Souks

MEDINA

Kasbah

Walls

Andalous Mosque

To Dkebel Tazzeka Circuit

Bab Tit

Bastion

TAZA

the city at Bab Ftouh (where you'll need to pick up a city taxi or bus to get to the hotels at Bab Boujeloud or the Ville Nouvelle). Fes is also served by four daily trains.

In the other direction, the trains run **to Oujda**, by far the easiest and simplest approach. You won't miss much by not stopping off at GUERCIF and TAOURIRT, both dull market towns along the monotonous eastern steppes.

Nearly all the **buses across the Rif** leave very early in the morning. There are currently two to NADOR (at 4:30 and 5am): one going via AKNOUL, the other over a new and more direct road across the Plain of Gharb. There is one (and sometimes two) early bus(es) to AL HOCEIMA; this too goes via AKNOUL, where you can catch sporadic, local buses across the southern slopes of the Rif to TAOUNATE, a much less dramatic route than the Ketama pass. All these buses leave from by the train station— whatever anyone may tell you about buses stopping at Place de l'Indépendence, in the Ville Nouvelle.

The Medina

Buses from Place de l'Indépendence stop at the **Medina** in Place Moulay Hassan. This square lies just below the main street of the quarter, **Mechouar**—a small and modernized area, pretty easy to find your way around in. There are few particular sights, though if you enlist a guide it's possible to visit the former Merenid **medersa of Bou Abul Hassan**, off to the left of the Mechouar, about 20m down from the twelfth-century Andalous Mosque. A somewhat inconspicuous building, usually kept closed, it has a particularly beautiful *mihrab*.

Largely ruined, and to the rear of the well-concealed Andalous Mosque, is an old house which was once the residence of the *Rogui* (Pretender), **Bou Hamra**. There is little to see today, but for some time at the turn of the century, this was a power base controlling much of eastern Morocco. Like most protagonists of the period, Bou Hamra was an extraordinary figure: a sometime forger, conjurer, and saint, who claimed to be the legitimate Shereefian heir and had himself proclaimed Sultan at Taza in 1902. The name *Bou Hamra*—the man on the she-donkey—recalled his bizarre means of travel around the countryside, where he won followers through the performance of miracles. One of these involved talking to the dead, which he perfected by (earlier) burying a disciple, who would then communicate through a concealed straw; the pronouncements over, Bou Hamra flattened the straw with his foot (presumably not part of the original deal) and allowed the amazed villagers to dig up the by-then-dead witness. Captured by Sultan Moulay Hafid, his own death was no less melodramatic. He was brought to Fes in a small cage on the back of a camel, fed to the court lions (who refused to eat him), and was eventually shot and burned. Both Gavin Maxwell and Walter Harris give graphic accounts.

Taza's **souks** branch off to either side of the Mechouar, about halfway down between the Andalous and Grand Mosques. Since there are few and sporadic tourists, the *souks* are very much working and produce markets, free of the artificially produced "craft" goods so often found. In fact, one of the most memorable is a **souk for used European clothing**—a frequent feature of country and provincial markets, the more fortunate dealers having gained access to the supplies of international charities. The **granary** and the covered stalls of the **Kissaria** are also worth a look, in the shadow of the Djemaa es Souk or Market Mosque. The **Grand Mosque** stands at the end of the Mechouar, historically one of the most interesting buildings in the country—but, like that of the Andalous, so discreetly screened that it's difficult to gain any glimpse of the interior. Even the outside is elusive; shielded by a net of buildings, you have to walk up toward Bab er-Rih for a reasonable impression of its ground plan. Founded by the Almohad sultan, Abd el Moumen, it is probably the oldest Almohad structure in existence, predating even the partially-ruined mosque at Tin Mal (see *Chapter Five*), with which it shares most stylistic features.

Above the Medina, at **Bab er-Rih** (Gate of the Winds), it is possible to get some feeling for Taza's historic and strategic significance. You can see up the valley toward the Taza Gap, Djebel Tazzeka and the Middle Atlas on one side, the reddish earth of the Rif behind, on the other.The actual gate now leads nowhere and looks somewhat lost below the road, but it is Almohad in origin and design. So, too, are most of the circuit of walls, which you can follow around by way of a **bastion** (added by Moulay Ismail, in Spanish style) back to Place Moulay Hassan. Off to the left, below the Kasbah, a road leads out toward the Djebel Tazzeka and to the town **swimming pool**.

The Djebel Tazzeka . . . and Beyond

A loop of some 123km around Taza, the **Djebel Tazzeka** is really a car driver's circuit, with views of the mountains to gaze at a while before continuing the trip. It does, however, have particular interest in the transition between Riffian and Middle Atlas scenery, and a specific "sight" in the immense Friouato Caves (*Gouffre du Friouato*). These are only 22km from Taza, a feasible hitch (stand at the turnoff just below the Medina) or a fairly reasonable shared *grand taxi* ride (negotiate at the stand by the train station).

The Tazzeka road curls around below the Medina and climbs to a narrow valley of almond and cherry orchards; around 10km out, are the **Cascades de Ras El Oued**, a series of small waterfalls reduced to a trickle in the dry summer months. Beyond this point, you loop up toward the first pass (at 1198m) and emerge beside the **Chiker Lake**, again pretty dry in midsummer and very strange in appearance.

The **Gouffre du Friouato** lie near the far end of the depression, a short, signposted turning to the right. Explored down to 180m, they are said to be the deepest caves in North Africa, and their entrance (over 30m wide) must certainly be the most impressive. Although unlighted, the caves can be visited. There's a guard around for most of the year who will steer you to some of the more spectacular caverns; you'll need a flashlight—if you don't have one, wait to see if some other tourists might turn up.

For anyone with a car, there are two interesting options beyond this point. Backtracking to the beginning of the Chiker, a fairly reasonable, paved road leads to MEGHRAOUA and a dirt road (very rough) then takes over to

TALZEMT, an adventurous approach **through the Middle Atlas to Midelt**, eventually joining the P20 at ENJIL DES IKHATARN.

Alternatively, and considerably easier, you can **complete the Tazzeka circuit** to rejoin the FES–TAZA road at SIDI ABDALLAH DES RHIATA. The last section of this route runs through the dark schist gorges of the Oued Zireg; but the most dramatic and scenic point is undoubtedly the **ascent of the Djebel** itself. This is passable by car in dry weather but very dangerous at other times: a very rough, seven-kilometer road cuts its way up some 15km beyond Friouato, leading to a TV broadcasting tower near the summit. The view from the top, encased in forests of cedars, stretches to the Rif, to the mountains around Fes, and to much of the eastern Middle Atlas.

Al Hoceima

If you're coming from the somewhat epic existence of the Rif, **AL HOCEIMA** can be a bit of a shock. It is not, in the tourist board's wildly optimistic claim, "Morocco's most exclusive, international resort," but it is Mediterranean, and developed enough to have little in common with the farming villages and tribal markets of the mountains. If you're traveling through the Rif, you will probably want to stop here and rest up a couple of days—maybe for longer. In late Spring, or September, when the beaches are quiet, it's near idyllic. In midsummer, though, be warned that the town can feel cramped, its beaches are overcrowded, and rooms are difficult to find. Nevertheless, even then, it does have a certain charm, and if you're deliberating on staying the night either here or in Nador, this is the infinitely preferable choice.

Orientation and Rooms

The town divides fairly naturally into two parts. Around the **bay**—which saw the Spanish invasion in 1926, and Hassan's forces to quell the Rif revolt in 1958—is a *Maroc-Tourist* complex with two four-star hotels. Everything and everyone else is packed into the old Spanish fishing village of **Villa Sanjura** at the top of the hill. In midsummer this is a lively if slightly characterless place, full of young Moroccans; the rest of the year, it is almost empty, except for a handful of old, misplaced *Spaniolines* who, for one reason or the other, wouldn't or couldn't leave with the rest in 1957.

The town center is up here—**Place du Rif**, enclosed by cafés and cheap places to eat. Most of the **hotels**—the *National* (2*A; 23 Rue du Tetouan, ☎24.31), *Karim* (2*B; 27 Av. Hassan II, ☎21.84), and unclassified *Bilbao* (28 Av. Mohammed V), *Afrique*, *Turismo*, and *Essalam*—are up behind the *place*, along Avenues Hassan II and Abd el Krim, and Rue de Rif. The *Afrique* and *Bilbao* are best of the cheapies.

If none of these have rooms, an alternative are the two **campgrounds**, each situated by a beach and approached along the main road (east) out of town. The nearest, at 2km, is the *Camping Plage el Jamil*, the best place around to swim but geared heavily toward trailers and outrageously expensive for campers with just tents. The main, and much more popular, campground is a little ways down the road at the *Plage Cala Iris*; this is not, incidentally, a wise place to leave anything around.

Beaches and Bars

Swimming—and walking in the olive-groved hills if you want a change—is Al Hoceima's main attraction but if you wake early enough it is worth going down to the bay to watch the *lamparo* fishermen coming in; they work at night using acetylene lamps to attract and dazzle the fish. The town's other minor curiosity is the Spanish offshore islet of Peñon de Alhucemas, a perennial subject of dispute between the Spanish and Moroccans since the seventeenth century.

The best of the **beaches**, as mentioned above, is the Plage El Jamil, east of the town by the campground. There are others, though, to the west, within walking distance. Another, a short ride by *petit taxi*, is just on the Al Hoceima side of the Club Mediterrané. All these strands have teahouses where you can sip mint tea and gaze at the rocks and watch the waves hitting the coast of Africa.

For **nightlife**, you have a choice of the *Jupiter Disco* (at the main beach), discreet bars on the top floors of the smarter hotels (the *Mohammed V, Quemado,* and *El Maghreb el Jadid*), or sitting outside *Café Florido* watching the somewhat illicit parade past the notorious *Hôtel Parador.*

Buses and Taxis

Like in the rest of the Rif, **buses** leave early—to TAZA at 4am; to FES (via the Route de l'Unité), CHAOUEN, and TETOUAN slightly later. If you're going to CHAOUEN, try to take one of the private buses rather than the CTM, which stops at the turnoff 9km out of the village. A small **Tourist Office**, by the prominent *Hôtel Quemado,* can give information and times.

If you need to get anywhere in a hurry, there are plenty of **grands taxis**, negotiable—even for Rabat and Casablanca.

Nador

Entering or leaving Morocco at the Spanish enclave of MELILLA you will have to pass through **NADOR**. But beyond this it is hard to think of any reason for coming here. Landlocked by the shallow—and useless—inland sea of Mar Chica, and rather rashly earmarked as a center for economic development, it is characterized only by an annoying, gritty wind floating down from the cement factory. A depressed as well as a depressing place, this was the site of the first and main troubles in the 1984 riots.

When the Spanish left in 1957, Nador was just an ordinary Riffian village, given work and some impetus by the port of Melilla. Its choice as a Moroccan provincial capital was probably unfortunate—there is little to do for the university students, while the iron foundry proposed to fuel the Rif's mining industry has yet to materialize. Add to this the creation of a population of 45,000 drawn from the mountain villages, and you begin to see some of the problems.

The town is built on a drab and uniform grid, the **bus station** providing its main focal point. There are plenty of **hotels** close by if you need somewhere to stay; the better ones, past a string of real dives, are about 100m down Av. Ibn Tachfine. Moving off from the bus station in the opposite direction (toward the "sea"), you reach the main boulevard with its banks and post office. The nearest campground is at KARIET-ARKMANE, 20km south (reached by *grand taxi*; see below); if you have a car you can also camp at the CAP DES TROIS FORCHES on the Melilla road—this has no campground but Moroccan families descend on it with their tents in the summer. The only **bank** in Nador that will change money or traveler's checks (no plastic transactions) is the *Banque Populaire* (Rue de la Ligue Arabe).

All **transportation** leaves Nador from the bus station, including local buses and *grands taxis* to the MELILLA border. If you're going over the Rif to FES, CHAOUEN, or TETOUAN, it's best to break the trip in AL HOCEIMA (3½ hr.): it is still 8 hr. from there to Fes or Chaouen, even longer to Tetouan. Buses and *grands taxis* to OUJDA are fairly plentiful throughout the day; to get to SAIDIA you can connect at BERKANE. For details on the **Nador-Melilla border**, see Melilla, below. In the summer months, from June to mid-September, there are once- or twice-weekly **ferries from Nador to Sète** in France (37 hr.).

Around Nador

If you're mobile and have the time for it, the region around Nador is a lot more interesting than the town. **KARIET ARKMANE**, to the east (past the airport), gives access to a sand/shell-packed road along the spit of the lagoon. This is a desolate area but picturesque in its own way, and with tangible attractions for bird watchers, as flamingoes and blackwinged stilts are to be seen among the salt marshes. The road follows the edge of the lagoon from Kariet, passing an old Spanish lookout post and—just before it halts at a tiny fishing village, edging past a shell beach—it goes by a popular spot with the Spanish from Melilla, who bring their tents and barbecues on weekends. *Camping Karia Plage* is right on the beach.

The road **east of Kariet** is a pleasant drive, too, twisting into the hills, never far from the sea, and eventually bringing you to **RAZ-KA-BONA (Ras el Ma,** on some maps), another small fishing village with a good beach and a smattering of cafés and street vendors. You can complete a loop back toward Nador from here, following the Moulouya River—or take the road across the river to the beaches around SAIDIA (see below).

SELOUANE, at the junction of the roads to Al Hoceima and Oujda, is worth a couple of hours' visit. There's an interesting Kasbah in the village— now used as a storehouse; a large Saturday *souk;* and—perhaps the main reason for a visit—a Belgian-run restaurant, the *Brabo*. At **MONT ARAOUI**, just to the west along the Al Hoceima road, an even larger **souk** takes place on Sundays: a great occasion, with storytellers, dentists, and a sort of roulette wheel ("spin the live rat in the pail"). The road **south to Guercif** from here, between Mont Aroui and Tiztoutine is narrow and paved; it's an interesting alternative approach to Taza or Oujda, with vistas of palms and scrub, with the occasional wandering camel.

Melilla: A Spanish Possession

There ought to be an eccentric appeal to Spanish-occupied **MELILLA**, but even after Nador it's difficult to muster great enthusiasm. Together with Ceuta, it is the last of Spain's Moroccan enclaves, a former penal colony which saw prosperous days under the protectorate as a port for the Riffian mining industry. Since independence—and its retention as "sovereign Spanish territory"—Melilla's decline has been pretty wholesale. Resented by Morocco, whose claims are a fairly direct parallel to Spain's own on Gibraltar, it survives today on little more than the army, the duty-free tourist trade, and, of course, what's left of the Spanish colonial instinct.

Melilla's streets center on **Plaza de España**, overlooking the port (a five-minute walk), and **Avenida del Juan Carlos I**, leading inland off it. This is the most animated part of town, though not noticeably so until the evening *paseo,* when everyone promenades up and down or strolls through the neighboring Hernandez Park.

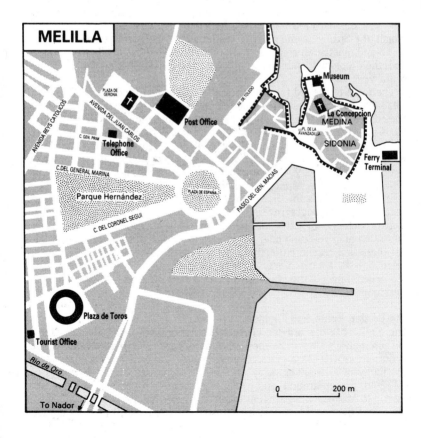

Hotels, as at Ceuta, are hard to come by. Most of the cheaper places are down towards the port, in the sidestreets off the Paseo del Generál Macias. None are worth special recommendation. For a full list, call in at the Tourist Office (Mon.–Fri. 9am–2pm, Sat. 10am–noon) at c/del General Aizpura 20.

Sparser still, it seems, are restaurants. There is scarcely anywhere in the town center to eat. Most places are a fair walk away, down at the beach.

Around the Town

Many of the buildings around the Plaza de España were designed by Enrique Nieto, a *modernista* contemporary of the renowned Catalan architect, Gaudí. Their 1930s tile and stucco facades are a quiet delight of the town, though, sadly, often masked or swamped by the rows of duty-free shops.

Probably more interesting—and certainly more picturesque—are the cramped white streets of the old town of Medina Sidonia, steeped above the port on a superb defensive promontory. At the beginning of the century this was all there was of Melilla: a self-contained little enclave, heavily walled and well able to resist the sporadic years of siege and attack. It was founded in 1497, a kind of epilogue to the expulsion of the Moors from Spain in the year that saw the fall of Granada. Blockaded throughout the reign of Moulay Ismail, the Spanish came close to relinquishing their ownership in the eighteenth and nineteenth centuries, and probably would eventually have done so had their colonial ambitions not been revived at the beginning of this century.

The walls of the old town suggest the Andalusian Medinas of Tetouan or Chaouen, though inside, the design is much more formal, laid out along the lines of a Castilian fort following a major earthquake in the sixteenth century. Steps near the harbor lead up to its main square, Plaza Maestranza, which is flanked by the tiny, Gothic Chapel of Santiago (St. James "the Moor-Slayer"), and beyond that, to an old barracks and armory. If you follow the fortifications around, you'll come to another small fort, now housing a somewhat miscellaneous Museo Municipal (open weekdays 9am–1pm and 3–6pm). Below this is the church of La Concepçion, crowded with baroque decoration, including a revered statue of *Nuestra Señora de Victoria* (Our Lady of Victory), the city's patroness. None of this is especially striking—and there's nothing you can't afford to miss if you've just come over from Spain—but there is a certain curiosity in the markets up here. Although Melilla's population is almost ninety percent Spanish, most markets are run by Moroccans and—in the Mantelat quarter across the moat—by a small Indian community.

The Border, Boats, and Flights

The Nador-Melilla border crossing can take time—and patience. During the summer, it's always crowded, with Moroccans returning from (or to) jobs in Europe, as well as travelers. If you are connecting with a ferry, allow for the possibility of a two-hour delay on the Moroccan side, while passports are collected, passed around, and eventually stamped. If you are planning on a daytrip to Melilla, on no account admit to it—say you are going to Málaga or Almería. Entering Morocco, try to avoid the border in the hours immediately after the ferries arrive, and be prepared to show evidence of 3500dh in foreign currency or checks (about $420); if you have problems, return later in the day for the next shift. To **get to the border** from Nador, there's a bus and numerous *grands taxis;* on the Spanish side there are buses to/from the Plaza de España. The frontier **currency exchange**, on both sides, is for cash only.

The Nador-Melilla border has a smuggling trade, which the police periodically crack down on. Driving to the border at night, keep an eye out for road checks—not always well lit but usually accompanied by tire-puncturing blockades.

In the summer, **ferries** leave Melilla daily for Almería (8 hr.; currently leaves around 11:30am) and daily except Sundays for Málaga (10 hr.; currently leaves around 8:30pm); in winter, ferries go on alternate nights to the two ports. Making advance reservations is critical in August (with possible three-day waits for a boat, if you just turn up), and at any time of year it is important to check departure times—which are highly variable.

Alternatively, for about the same cost, there are **flights** to Málaga; up to five a day in season, two or three daily out of season. Again, reserve ahead of time if possible. Another important thing to remember is that flights don't leave in bad weather.

The Zegzel Gorge, Berkane, and Saïdia

The road between NADOR and OUJDA is fast, efficient, and well served by both buses and *grands taxis*. It is not a tremendously interesting route, but if you've got the time (or ideally a car), there's an attractive detour around BERKANE into the **Zegzel gorge**, a dark limestone fault in the Beni Snassen mountains—the last outcrops of the Rif.

The Zegzel cuts down behind Berkane, a fertile shaft of mountain valleys which for centuries marked the limits of the Shereefian empire. They are very easily accessible today, though still forbiddingly steep: all traffic goes *down*, climbing up again from the main road to TAFORALT and winding from there to Berkane. If you've got transportation, this is the route to follow. If not, stay on the bus to BERKANE, where you can get a seat in a *grand taxi* to TAFORALT and there negotiate another one back, via the gorge road. Neither is an expensive operation because the routes are used locally (and are popular with tourists).

TAFORALT itself is a quiet and very clear mountain village, active (or as active as it ever gets) only for the Wednesday market. It does, though, have a fairly constant supply of taxis, and you should be able to move on fairly rapidly toward the Zegzel. Before agreeing on a price, get the driver to promise he'll stop off for a while at the **Grotte du Chameau** (15km), a cavern of really vast stalactites—one of them remarkably camel-like in shape. The gorge, or rather **gorges**, begin soon after, scrupulously terraced and cultivated with all kinds of citrus and fruit trees. As the road crisscrosses the riverbed, they progressively narrow, drawing your eye to the cedars and dwarf oaks at the summit, until you eventually emerge (28km from Taforalt) onto the plain of Berkane.

Berkane and Saïdia

BERKANE is a strategic little market town, French-built and prosperous, set amid an extensive region of orchards and vineyards. If you stay, you're likely to be the only European in the town—no hustle, and people may even buy *you* a coffee. There are good eating places in the long, unpaved street running uphill from Av. Hassan II, and lots of very dark, tented souks. The best **place to stay** is the *Hôtel Najah*—very inexpensive. **Moving on** is similarly painless. There are frequent buses and *grands taxis* both to Oujda and to the small-scale resort of Saïdia.

Right on the Algerian border, **SAÏDIA** is a good choice to stop over for a few days. A one-street sort of place, it rambles back from the sea in the shadow of an old and still occupied, nineteenth-century Kasbah. The beach is immense and sandy, stretching west toward the tiny Chafarinas islands, and east, across the Oued Kiss, into Algeria. The Moroccans have a saying, that at Saïdia "we swim together with Algerians," which isn't exactly true but not totally false either—there's a very similar resort over on the Algerian side.

In the summer months, Saïdia is very lively and a lot of fun; from mid-September through to May it is nearly deserted, with variable, rather windy weather. There are three smallish **hotels**, the *Al Kalaa* (2*A; ☎51.23), Hannour (2*A; ☎51.15) and *Select* (1*A; ☎51.10)—the latter two closed out of season—and a very expensive bungalow vacation complex. If you want to stay in summer, you'll probably need to camp. In classic, local-resort fashion, Saidia has two **campgrounds**, one for families only (off the main street), another (toward the Kasbah) for single people—pick your category. Liveliest of the cafés are a group by the market, past the Kasbah and looking across into Algeria.

There are regular buses and *grands taxis* between Saïdia and Oujda.

Oujda and the Algerian Border Crossings

Most travelers arrive at **OUJDA** after a lengthy trip, which makes it all the more attractive. Open and easygoing, with a large and active university, it has that rare quality in Moroccan cities of nobody making demands on your instinct for self-preservation. After the Rif, it is a surprise to see women in public again, and to re-enter a French atmosphere—as you move out of what used to be Spanish Morocco into the old French zone.

As Morocco's easternmost town, Oujda became the capital of French *Maroc Orient* and an important trading center. This it remains, even if the "Orient" tag shouldn't be taken too literally: there's nothing more exotic here than the black market trade in Algerian currency* and Melilla whiskey. It is, however, a lively place—and prosperous, too, even strikingly so by Moroccan standards, with a population of over a quarter of a million. Strategically located at the crossroads of eastern and southern routes, the town, like Taza, has always been vulnerable to invasion and has frequently been the focus of territorial claims. The Algerian Ziyanids of Tlemcen occupied Oujda in the

---

*This is not recommended. And beware, if you cross into Morocco from Algeria, of being sold 500-dirham notes—they're no longer legal tender.

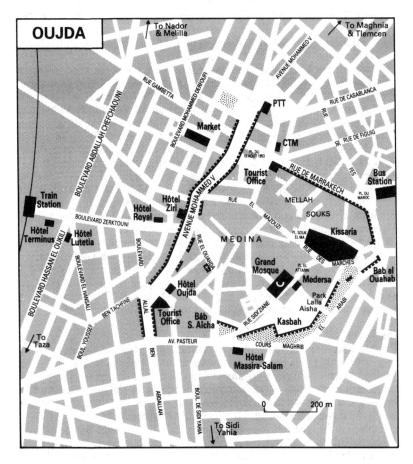

OUJDA

To Nador & Melilla

To Maghnia & Tlemcen

AVENUE MOHAMMED V

RUE GAMBETTA

BOULEVARD MOHAMMED DERKOUR

BOULEVARD ABDALLAH CHEFCHAOUNI

RUE DE CASABLANCA

PTT

RUE

RE. RUE DE FIGUIG

Market

CTM

PL. DU
18 AOÛT 1953

Tourist
Office

RUE DE MARRAKECH

FES

Bus
Station

PL. DU
MAROC

Train
Station

Hôtel
Zirl

RUE

EL

MELLAH

BOULEVARD ZERKTOUNI

Hôtel
Royal

MAZOUZI

SOUKS

BOULEVARD HASSAN EL OUKILI

Hôtel
Terminus

Hôtel
Lutetia

BOULEVARD

PL. SOUK
EL MA

Kissaria

MEDINA

BOULEVARD EL HANSALI

RUE EL OUAHDA

RUE

DES

MARCHES

Grand
Mosque

PL. EL
ATTARIN

Medersa

Bab el
Ouahab

BEN TACHFINE

Hôtel
Oujda

Park
Lalla
Aisha

ALLAL

Tourist
Office

Bâb
S. Aïcha

RUE SIDI ZIANE

EL

ARBI

To
Taza

BEN

AV. PASTEUR

Kasbah

COURS

MAGHRIB

BOUL. YOUSSEF

Hôtel
Massira-Salam

ABDALLAH

BOUL. DE SIDY YAHIA

0   200 m

To Sidi
Yahia

thirteenth and fourteenth centuries, and it was the first place to fall under French control when their forces moved into Morocco in 1907. In recent years, its proximity to the Algerian border and distance from the government in Rabat has led to its being a minor center of dissidence and unrest. This was particularly evident during the Algerian border war in the early 1960s, and again, over the last couple of years, in a series of student strikes.

Orientation and Practicalities

Oujda consists of the usual **Medina** and **Ville Nouvelle**, the latter highly linear in its layout, after starting out as a military camp.

The Medina, more or less walled, lies right in the heart of town—the main square of the Ville Nouvelle, **Place du 16 Août 1953**, at its northwest corner. Around this square you'll find all the main facilities, including the **post office**, **banks**, and **tourist office** (open daily 8am–noon & 2:30-

6:30pm). The **train and bus stations** are in easy walking distance; CTM buses run from Rue Sidi Brahim (just off the square), private lines from the Gare Routière in Place du Maroc. There is an **RAM** office (flights to Casablanca most days) inside the *Hôtel Oujda.*

Hotels in the Medina are poor value, but there are some good, **inexpensive** places just outside the walls. In Rue de Marrakech (between the main square and Place du Maroc) pick from the *Hôtel du 16 Aout, Hôtel Zegreg* and *Hôtel Marrakesh* ; or try the *Hôtel Royal (2*A)* on Bd. Zerktouni. A little more expensive are the classified *Hôtel Ziri* (1*A; Av. Mohammed V, ☎43.05), *Hôtel Royal* (1*A; 13 Bd. Zerktouni, ☎22.84), and *Hôtel Lutetia* (2*B; 44 Bd. Hassan Loukili, ☎33.65). If you want to get rid of your dirhams, the *Hôtel Terminus* (4*A ; ☎40.93) is the best **upscale** choice, right by the train station; it has a **swimming pool,** as do the more modern, less characterful *Hôtel Massira-Salam* (4*A; Bd. maghreb Al Arabi, ☎53.00) and *Hôtel Oujda* (4*B; Bd. Mohammed V, ☎40.93). The closest **campgrounds** are in Saïdia (see above). **Booking ahead** is a good idea for any class of hotel, as they're often full with Algerians on shopping sprees, taking advantage of the exchange rate.

The focus of evening activity—and the best source of cheap eateries—is around **Bab el Ouahab**, a prominent gate just below the **Gare Routière,** where you can get all kinds of grilled food. In the old days, more or less up until the French occupation, this was the gate where the heads of criminals were displayed. It is still a square where storytellers and musicians come to entertain, an increasing rarity in post-independence Morocco.

The Town

The **Medina** is largely a French reconstruction—revealingly obvious by the ease with which you can find your way around. Unusually, though, it has retained much of the city's commercial functions and has an enjoyably active air. Entering from Bab el Ouahab, you'll be struck by the amazing variety of food—and it's well worth a look for that alone. Olives are Oujda specialities—wonderful if you are about after the September harvest.

Exploring the quarter, a good route to follow is straight down the main street toward **Place d'Attarine**, flanked by a *kissaria* and a particularly grand *fondouk*. At the far end of the *souks* you come upon **Souk el Ma**, the irrigation *souk,* where the supply of water used to be regulated and sold by the hour. Walking on from here, you'll arrive back at Place du 16 Août 1953.

Outside of the Medina, the old **French Cathedral** is an evocative place. The present congregation numbers about ten, and the fonts are dry, the statue niches empty, but there is a beautiful chapel. It is kept locked; for admission, ring at the door of the presbytery at the back.

Sidi Yahia: An Oasis Marabout

SIDI YAHIA, 6km outside Oujda, is an unexpected little oasis, with immense palms and ancient baobab trees breaking the wide empty plain. It's best in spring, when streams water the grass and flowers; in summer they can be down to a trickle.

The oasis has been a holy place since pre-Islamic times, the main object of veneration being the tomb of **Sidi Yahia**—a shadowy *marabout,* identified by local tradition with John the Baptist. Oujda's patron saint, he seems to have had a broad ecumenical appeal—Jews and even Christians pay homage in their pilgrimage to the tomb over the centuries. Nobody is quite sure where he is buried (several of the cafés stake an optimistic claim), but there is a lot of reverence toward one of the great wells, said to be his water supply before the springs rose up after his death. On Fridays—and above all at the great *moussems* held here in August-September—this spot, together with almost every shrub and tree in the oasis, is festooned with little pieces of cloth, a ritual as lavish and extraordinary as anything in the Mediterranean church.

Scattered around the oasis are other lesser shrines—the tombs, *koubbas* (small domes), and hermitages of numerous saints who followed Sidi Yahia to live within the grove. Among them is a former hermitage of **Sidi Bel Abbes**, one of the **Seven Saints of Houriyat** (or *Cave of the Houris)*—the obliquely sensual handmaidens of Paradise promised to good Muslims in the Koran.

Regular **buses** run to Sidi Yahia from Oujda (from near to Bab el Ouahab), or, if you have the energy, it is only a little over an hour's walk down a broad (signposted) avenue.

Crossing into Algeria

The state of Moroccan-Algerian relations, and their common border, changes so frequently that it is impossible to give any definitive instructions. At present, however, and for the foreseeable future, the **Rabat-Algiers trains** (the *Trans-Maghreb Express*) do not cross the border. Instead, the line terminates at OUJDA and restarts inside Algeria at MAGHNIA. For the remaining 27km (15km in Morocco, 12km in Algeria), you're dependent on hitching, taxis, or the somewhat sporadic local buses.

The good news, however, following Hassan II's rapprochement with Algeria at the June 1988 Maghreb Summit, is that **the border is now routinely open**. Until then, only car passengers could cross, all "pedestrians" having to detour via Figuig. Hopefully, this will prove to be a permanent move, but before making hard and fast plans, it would be wise to ask fellow travelers and the tourist office in Oujda's main square (whose staff are usually well briefed and helpful).

Heading for the Oujda-Maghnia border, there are frequent *grands taxis* from the fountain at the end of Rue Marrakech (5dh a place), and buses (no fixed timetable) nearby. Better still, try and hitch a ride with other travelers—you can usually arrange this the night before by going around the better hotels (the *Terminus, Al Massira*, and *Oujda*), and it should take you through to TLEMCEN, the first Algerian town of any size and a place well worth spending some time in.

Crossing over at FIGUIG (see *Chapter Six*) is by no means a bad option, though an unbelievably hot one in the midsummer months. Despite its uncertain appearance on some maps, there's a fast new road down from Oujda—a 369km trek, but no more than seven hours by bus. Try and get the early morning departure (currently at 6am); there are two later on, but by noon things can be pretty stifling. All of these buses leave from the *Gare Routière* in Place du Maroc.

Visas and Currency Exchange

Americans and Australasians (though not Britons) must obtain a **visa in advance** to enter Algeria. You can get one at any overseas Algerian consulate, including **Rabat** (where they are issued on the same day; see *Chapter Four*). The Algerian consulate in Oujda (11 Bd. de Taza) can issue visas, too, but they take about a week to do so, having to send all details to Rabat. If you are in Oujda without a visa, and in a hurry to cross into Algeria, it's easier and quicker to get the night train up to Rabat and back.

Formalities at the border are relatively quick and straightforward on the Algerian side, at least for pedetrians. Cardrivers should allow three to four hours for registration. While in Algeria, you must **change US$150** at the official rate (currently, $1 = 7 dinar). This can be at any time during your stay—you don't have to do it at the border, though the sum should last for a good week or so of traveling. Staying beyond that, many travelers pay for items in foreign currency or use the thriving black market (about three times the official exchange rate).

travel details

Trains

From Taza Four trains daily to Oujda (3½ hr.), and in the other direction to Fes (2 hr.).

From Oujda Four trains daily to Taza (3½ hr.) and Fes (5½–6 hr.). Also a night train (mainly for freight) to Bouarfa (8 hr.).

Note: *ONCF* run connecting bus services to Nador from Taourite.

Buses

From Chaouen Ketama/Al Hoceima (2 daily; 5 hr./8 hr.); El Jebha (2; 7 hr.).

From Ketama Fes (2 daily; 3½ hr.).

From Fes el Bali (village) Daily to Taounate and Aknoul.

From Taza Fes (3 daily; 2½ hr.); Al Hoceima (2; 4½ hr.); Nador (2; 5–5½ hr.).

From Al Hoceima Nador (2 daily; 3½ hr.); Fes (1; 1½ hr.).

From Nador Berkane/Oujda (5 daily; 2 hr./3 hr.); Melilla (local buses to the border).

From Berkane Oujda (6 daily; 1 hr.); Saidia (4; 1 hr.).

From Oujda Saidia (4 daily, 1 hr. 20 min.); Figuig (3; 7 hr.), Midelt (1; 13 hr.).

Grands Taxis

From Taza Regularly to Fes (1½ hr.) and Oujda (2½ hr.) Occasionally to Al Hoceima.

From Al Hoceima Regularly to Nador (3 hr.). Infrequently to Fes and Taza.

From Nador Regularly to Oujda (2½ hr.) and Al Hoceima (3 hr.).

From Oujda Regularly to Saidia (50 min.) and Taza (2½ hr.). Negotiable for the Algerian border.

Flights

From Oujda Casablanca (most days; **RAM** office at *Hôtel Oujda*).

From Melilla Malaga (4-6 daily; 35–40 min.); Almeria (most days; ½ hr.).

Ferries

From Melilla Daily except Sundays to Malaga (10 hr.) and Almeria (6½ hr.). Drops to 3 times a week out of season.

From Nador Summer-only ferry to Sète (France). Once or twice weekly from June to September.

TELEPHONE CODES

AL HOCEIMA ☎093	OUJDA ☎068
MELILLA ☎52	SAÏDIA ☎061
NADOR ☎060	TAZA ☎067

CHAPTER THREE

FES, MEKNES, AND THE MIDDLE ATLAS

T he imperial capital of the Merenid, Wattasid, and Alouite dynasties, **Fes** has for ten centuries been at the heart of Moroccan history—and for five of them it was one of the major intellectual and cultural centers of the West. It is today unique in the Arab world, preserving the appearance and much of the life of a medieval Islamic city. In terms of monuments, above all the university *medersas*, you can find as much here as in all the other capitals combined. The *souks,* extending for over a mile, maintain the whole tradition of urban crafts, and you won't easily forget their sounds and smells.

In all of this—and equally in the most mundane everyday aspects—there is a lot to be fascinated by and, as an outsider, you get a strong feeling of being privileged to be here. But inevitably, this has come at a cost. Declared a historical monument by the French, and deprived of its political and cultural significance, Fes retains its beauty but is now in drastic and evident decline. Its university is today overshadowed by the one in Rabat and its business elite have left for Casa. For survival, the city depends increasingly on the tourist trade.

Fes's attractions are well known, and after Tangier, it is by far the most touristed city of the north. **Meknes**, in contrast, sees comparatively few visitors, despite being an easy and convenient stopover en route by train from Tangier or Rabat, or by bus from Chaouen. The megalomaniacal creation of Moulay Ismail, the most tyrannical of all Moroccan sultans, it is once again a city of lost ages, its enduring impression being that of an endless series of walls. But Meknes is also an important market center and its *souks*, though smaller and less secretive than the ones in Fes, are almost as varied as them and generally more authentic. There are, too, the local attractions of **Volubilis**, the best preserved of the country's Roman sites, and the sacred, hilltop town of **Moulay Idriss,** forbidden to non-Muslims and unseen by Europeans until 1916.

Beyond the two imperial cities stretch the cedar-covered slopes of the **Middle Atlas**, which in turn give way to the High Atlas and eventually the sub-Sahara. Across and around this region, often beautiful and for the most part remote, there are three main routes. The most popular, a day's journey by bus, skirts the range beyond Azrou to emerge via **Beni Mellal** at Marrakesh. A second one climbs southeastward from Azrou toward **Midelt**, an excellent carpet center, before passing through great gorges to Er

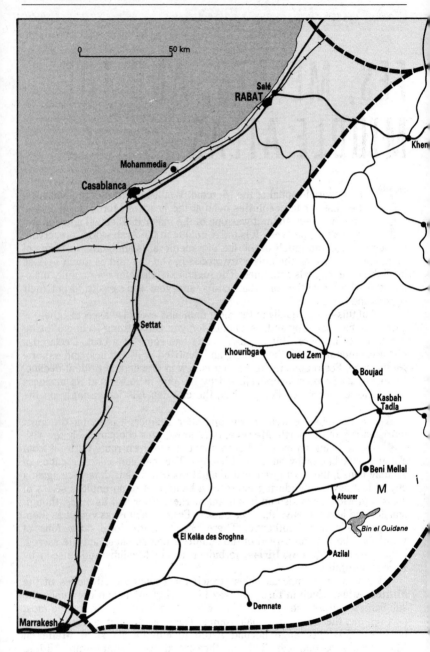

Rachidia and the vast date palm oasis of Tafilalt—the beginning of a tremendous southern circuit (see *Chapter Six*). The last route, running between the other two, is much more adventurous and is described (in reverse order) in the High Atlas section (see *Chapter Five*). Leaving the main Azrou–Marrakesh highway at **El Ksiba**, it follows a series of *pistes* (dirt roads) which are best negotiated by local Berber trucks, and which lead directly across the High Atlas to Tinerhir.

If you're traveling one of the main highways, and you've got the time, the Middle Atlas has attractions of its own. Close to Fes, **Immouzer** and **Ifrane** have each been developed as summer resorts, their air and waters a cool escape. Then, there is the Berber market town of **Azrou**, and beyond that, just off the Marrakesh road, the **Cascades d'Ouzoud**—waterfalls which crash down from the mountains even in midsummer, beside which you can swim, camp, hike, and rest up completely.

Meknes

Cut in two by the wide, river valley of the Oued Boufekrane, **MEKNES** is a sprawling, prosperous provincial city. Its past—dominated by the extraordinary creations of Moulay Ismail (of whom more below)—rewards a day's rambling exploration, as do the varied and busy souks of its Medina. To get the most out of it all, visit before heading to Fes. Getting a grasp for Meknes prepares you a little for the drama of Fes, and certainly helps give an idea of quality (and prices) for crafts shopping. As a predominantly Berber, rather than Arab, city—in so much as these distinctions continue to apply in Morocco—it has, too, a somewhat gentler feel.

Orientation and Practicalities

Meknes is considerably simpler than it looks on the map. Its **Ville Nouvelle** stretches along a slope above the east bank of the river. The **Medina** flanked by its former Mellah, occupies the west bank, with the walls of Moulay Ismail's **Ville Imperial** edging away, seemingly forever, to its south. Focal point of the Medina is **Place el Hedim**, and it would be a good idea to adopt this to get your bearings; from here, there are *petits taxis* and regular bus shuttles (#5, #7, and #9) up toward the main Ville Nouvelle avenues.

There are two **train stations**, both in the Ville Nouvelle on the east bank. The main one is a kilometer away from the downtown area; a smaller, more convenient one (**Gare El Amir**) is a couple of blocks from the center (behind the *Hôtel Majestic*); trains stop at both.

Arriving by **bus** you will probably find yourself dropped at the terminal by **Place el Hedim** (actually just outside of the Bab Zein el Abidin), which seems to have taken over from the CTM station on Av. des Forces Armées Royales in the Ville Nouvelle (another possible setting down point). **Grands taxis** (regular connections with Fes and Moulay Idriss) run from the Place el Hedim. Buses from Chaouen (and some other private line services) may drop you on the Medina side of the bridge.

Leaving Meknes for Fes, you have the choice of either taking a bus (8 *CTM* departures per day), train, or, quickest of all, *grand taxi*; the latter arrive in Fes el Djedid at Place des Alaouites. *CTM* have at least daily departures, too, for Azrou, Midelt, Rabat, and Marrakesh. Heading for Chaouen, check the schedule with the tourist office, and try to buy a ticket ahead of time—preferably the night before.

Accommodation

Hotels, including a very reasonable youth hostel, are mainly in the Ville Nouvelle. But comfort aside, this is a dull place to stay and if you're happy with a fairly basic room, it would be better to head for the *Maroc Hôtel* (103 Av. Benbrahim; ☎307.05; keyed **H** on the main map), opposite the Apollo Movie Theater on Rue Rouamazin. This is by far the cleanest and quietest of the **Medina** hotels. The others, at the corner of Rue Rouamazin/Rue Dar Semen, are drab and stifling. See the Medina map for exact locations.

In the **Ville Nouvelle** most good value possibilities are grouped in an area around the bus station and main avenues. Recommendations below, all keyed on the main map, are in ascending order:

Youth Hostel (*Auberge des Jeunesses*), Av. Okba Ibn Nafi; ☎217.43. A bit out of the way, but well maintained, with rooms around a courtyard. No curfew; reception closed 10am–noon & 4–7pm. YHA card necessary. Getting there, follow signs to the luxury *Hôtel Transatlantique*.

Hôtel Moderne (C), 54 Bd. Allal Ben Abdallah; ☎217.43. Clean, balconied rooms—and the best cheap Ville Nouvelle choice. *Unclassified*.

Hôtel Excelsior (G), 57 Av. des Forces Armées Royales; ☎219.00. Recently renovated—but retaining lowish prices. *1*A*.

Hôtel Continental (E), 92 Av. des Forces Armées Royales. Tucked behind the restaurant of the same name. *2*B*.

Hôtel Majestic (B), 19 Av. Mohammed V; ☎220.35. Handy for the El Amir train station. Friendly. *2*A*.

Hôtel Palace (A), 11 Rue du Ghana; ☎223.88. Respectable enough, if nothing special. *2*A*.

Hôtel Panorama (D), 9 Av. des Forces Armées Royales; ☎227.37. Best of the 2* places, if you want a bit of comfort. *2*A*.

Hôtel Volubilis (F), 45 Av. des Forces Armées Royales; ☎201.02. Reasonably priced for its class, and with one of the town's few bars. *3*B*.

Alternatively, there's a pleasant, if slightly distant, **campground**, (20-min. walk from Place el Hedim, or an 8–10dh taxi ride) opposite the Heri as-Souani. There are **bungalow rooms** for rent here, too, at around 2*B prices—or at least there were until recently, when the caretakers disappeared with all the fittings! These might have been replaced by now, so check first.

Restaurants and Bars

Eating in Meknes tends to be a functional affair; there's nothing very exciting and, apart from the Ramadan period, the town pretty much closes up around ten at night.

For straight Moroccan food pick from any of the café-grills along Rue Dar Semen, toward Place el Hedim, **in the Medina**. One place to avoid, despite the enthusiastic handbills given out at the *Maroc Hôtel*, is the *Rôtisserie Oumnia*. The *Café Bab Mansour*, near the gate of the same name, is among the best of the basic choices—and stays open late.

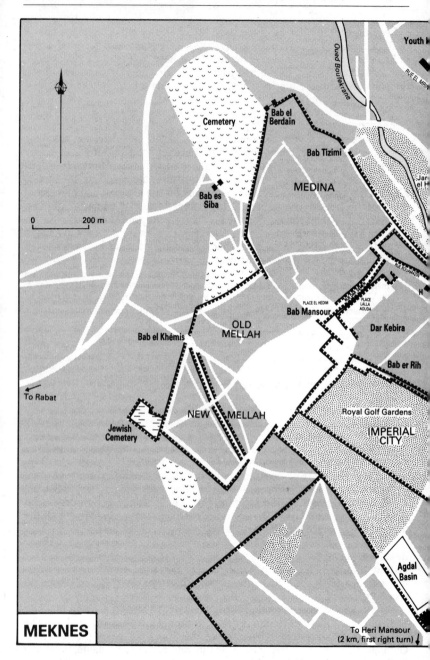

Youth M

RUE EL MRIN

Ouad Boufekrane

Bab el
Berdain

Bab Tizimi

Cemetery

MEDINA

Jar
el H

Bab es
Siba

0   200 m

RUE ROUAMZIN

PLACE EL HEDIM

PLACE
LALLA
AOUDA

Bab Mansour

Dar Kebira

Bab el Khémis

OLD
MELLAH

Bab er Rih

To Rabat

NEW   MELLAH

Royal Golf Gardens

IMPERIAL
CITY

Jewish
Cemetery

Agdal
Basin

MEKNES

To Heri Mansour
(2 km, first right turn)

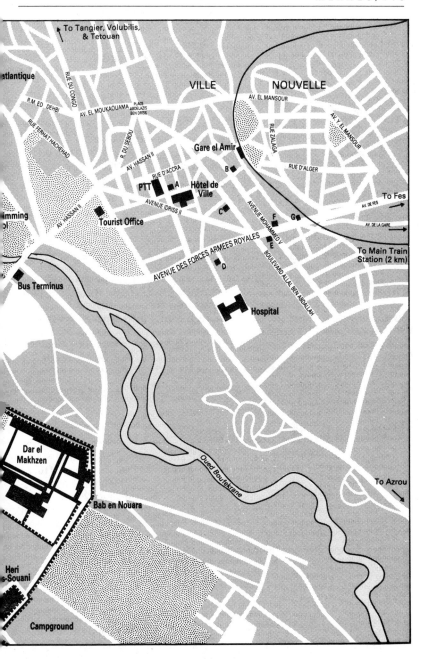

In the Ville Nouvelle, there are a handful of fair French restaurants in and around Place de France. Rue du Ghana, which leads off from here past the PTT, has a couple of cheap places (*La Coupole*, toward the intersection with Av. Hassan II is a good bet); so, too, does Av. Hassan II itself—the unnamed restaurant at no. 12 in particular. *Restaurant Marhaba* (Ave. Mohammed V; past the cinema, coming from the CTM station) is perhaps the best of the lot.

There are a surprising number of **bars**. Pick from the *Roi de la Bière*, Av. Mohammed V (but often closed in summer); the *Bar Continental* (corner of Av. des FAR/Av. Hassan II); the Club de Nuit (more or less opposite, on Av. Hassan II), the *Cabaret Oriental* (again Av. Hassan II), with bands sometimes playing till the early hours; or the *Novelty Bar-Restaurant* at 12 Rue de Marseille. There are also bars in the *Volubilis*, *Rif* and *Nice* hotels.

Directory

Banks are concentrated on Av. Mohammed V (the *Crédit du Maroc* is at no. 33) and Av. des Forces Armées Royales (*BMCE* at no. 98). Another *BMCE* branch is in the Medina, near the *Maroc Hôtel* at 66 Rue Rouamazin. When banks are closed, you can change cash at the *Hôtel Rif.*

Hammam. If you're staying in the Medina, the *Maroc Hôtel* should be able to steer you toward a *hammam*; in the Ville Nouvelle, you'll find a good one off Av. Hassan II, at 4 Rue Patrice Lumumba, with separate sections for women and men (both 7am–9pm).

Post Office. The PTT, just off Place de France, is open Monday–Saturday 8am–2pm; its **phone** section stays open until 9pm.

Swimming Pools. There are two public pools down by the river, reached along a lane from Bd. El Haboul or from the intersection of Av. Hassan II and Av. Moulay Ismail. The first you encounter is very cheap; a little farther down there's another—classier, less crowded, and three or four times the price.

Tourist Office. A *Syndicat d'Initiative* (☎201.91) is located inside the gates at the iintersection of Av. Hassan II and Av. Moulay Ismail.

Moulay Ismail and the Imperial City

More than any other Moroccan town, Meknes is associated with a single figure—the **Sultan Moulay Ismail**, in whose fifty-five year reign (1672–1727) the city was built up from a provincial center to an immense and spectacular capital with twenty gates, over fifty palaces, and some 25km of exterior walls. "The Sultan," wrote his chronicler, Ezziani, "loved Mequinez, and he would have liked never to leave it." But leave it he did, ceaselessly campaigning against the rebel Berber chiefs of the south until the entire country, for the first time in five centuries, lay completely under government control. Each time he returned, with his "Black Guard" composed of dark-skinned troops assembled from throughout Morocco, the obsessive building program would be redoubled, the sultan acting as the architect and sometimes even working alongside the slaves and laborers.

A tyrant even by the standards of his own times (and remember that Europe was then actively burning and torturing its enemies and putting them on the rack), Ismail was almost unbelievably violent and sadistic. His reign began with the display at Fes of 700 heads, most of them of captured chiefs, and over the next three decades, apart from battles, it is estimated that he was responsible for over 30,000 deaths. Many of these killings were quite arbitrary. Mounting a horse, Ismail might slash the head off the eunuch holding his stirrup; inspecting the work on his buildings, he would carry a weighted lance, with which to batter skulls in order to "encourage" the others. "My subjects are like rats in a basket," he used to say, "and if I do not keep shaking the basket they will gnaw their way through."

The passing of time has not been easy on Moulay Ismail's constructions. Built mainly of *tabia*, a mixture of earth and lime, they were severly damaged by a hurricane even in his lifetime, and since then, with subsequent Alaouite sultans shifting their capitals back to Fes and Marrakesh, they have been left to crumble and decay. Walter Harris, writing only 150 years after Ismail's death, found Meknes "a city of the dead . . . strewn with marble columns, and surrounded by great masses of ruin." And even with its Ville Nouvelle across the river, built as military headquarters by the French, there is still this feeling of emptiness.

The principal remains of Ismail's creation—the **imperial city** of palaces and gardens, barracks, granaries, and stables—sprawl below the Medina amid a confusingly manic array of walled enclosures. It's a long morning's walk if you intend to take in everything but also a fairly straightforward one. From the Ville Nouvelle, just make your way down to the main street at the edge of the Medina (**Rue Rouamazin/Rue Dar Semen**), and along to **Place el Hedim** and its immense gateway, **Bab Mansour**. There are usually **guides** hanging around here if you want to use one; you don't need to, but if you can find someone entertaining, he'll probably elaborate on the story of the walls with some superbly convoluted local legend.

Bab Mansour and Around

Place el Hedim (Square of Destruction) immediately recalls Moulay Ismail; originally, it formed the western corner of the Medina, but the houses here were demolished in order to form a grand approach to the palace quarter, or *Dar Kebira*. The centerpiece of this ensemble of walls and gateways is the great **Bab Mansour**, startlingly rich in its ceremonial intent, and almost perfectly preserved. Its name comes from its architect—one of a number of Christian renegades who converted to Islam and rose to high position at Ismail's court; there is a tale that when the sultan inspected the gate, he asked El Mansour whether he could do better, a classic Catch 22, whose response ("yes") led to immediate and enraged execution. It is probably apocryphal, however, for the gate was actually completed under Ismail's son, the almost equally perverse Moulay Abdallah.*

Nevertheless, the gate is the finest in Meknes and an interesting adaptation of the classic Almohad design, flanked by unusually inset and fairly squat bastions, which are purely decorative, their marble columns having been brought here from Volubilis. The decorative patterns on both

---

* Moulay Abdallah was said to have "a predilection for standing slaves in a row beside a wall he was about to demolish, and letting it fall about them." He once had a European slave exucuted for refusing to serve as a footstool for him to fornicate with a mare.

gate and bastions are basically elaborations of the *darj w ktarf* (a cheek-and-shoulder pattern, begun by the Almohads), the space between each motif filled out with a brilliant array of *zellij* created by a layer of cut away black tiles, just like the ornamental inscription above, which extols the triumph of Ismail and, even more, that of Abdallah, adding that there is no gate in Damascus or Alexandria which is its equal.

To the left of Bab Mansour is a smaller gateway in the same style, **Bab Djemaa en Nouar**. Through Bab Mansour, and straight ahead through a **second gate**, you will find yourself in a large open square, on the right of which is a domed **koubba**—once a reception hall for ambassadors to the imperial court. Below it, a stairway (small entrance fee to the guide) descends into a vast series of subterranean vaults, known in popular tradition as the **Prison of Christian Slaves**. It was, in fact, probably a storehouse or granary, although there were certainly several thousand Christian captives at Ismail's court. Most were captured by the Sallee Rovers (see Rabat) and brought here as slave laborers on the interminable construction projects; reputedly any of them who died while at work were simply buried in the walls they were building.

Ahead of the *koubba*, set within the long wall and at right angles to it (see Medina map), are two very modest **gates**. The one on the right is generally closed and is at all times flanked by soldiers from the royal guard; inside it, landscaped across a lake and the sunken garden of Ismail's last and finest palace, are the **Royal Golf Gardens**—private and *interdit*. The gate on the left opens onto an apparently endless corridor of walls and, a few meters down, the entrance to the **Mausoleum of Moulay Ismail**.

The Mausoleum

Together with the tomb of Mohammed V in Rabat, **Moulay Ismail's Mausoleum** is the only active Moroccan shrine that non-Muslims may visit. It is generally open from around 9am to noon and 3 to 6pm, but even then admission is occasionally refused; women especially must dress with total modesty.

The fact that Ismail's mausoleum, completed within his lifetime, has remained a shrine is itself perhaps puzzling. Yet, as Walter Harris wrote a century ago, this "deceased Sultan who, having killed more men, Christians and Moors, than any of his predecessors, having wasted more money on impossible palaces and such-like than could ever be counted, and, when tiring of a wife, having her for amusement tortured and killed before his very eyes, is reverenced as one of the greatest saints of the Moorish religious calendar." So it was, too, in Ismail's lifetime. His absolute tyranny of control, his success in driving out the Spanish from Larache and the British from Tangier, and his extreme observance of Islamic form and ritual all conferred a kind of magic on him.

Entering the mausoleum, you are allowed to approach the sanctuary in which the sultan is buried—though you cannot go beyond the annex. Decorated in bright *zellij* and spiraling stuccowork, it is a fine if unspectacular series of courts and chambers. But what is most interesting, perhaps, is that the shrine was thoroughly renovated in the 1950s at the expense of

Mohammed V, and also that the sarcophagus is still the object of prayer. You will almost invariably see country people here, especially women, seeking *baraka* (charismatic blessing) and intercession.

The Old Palaces

Past the mausoleum, a gate to your left gives access to the dilapidated quarter of **Dar el Kebira**, Ismail's great palace complex. The imperial structures—the legendary fifty palaces—can still be made out between and above the houses here: ogrelike creations, whose scale is hard to believe. They were completed in 1677 and dedicated at an astonishing midnight celebration, when the sultan personally slaughtered a wolf so that its head might be displayed at the center of the gateway. In the grandeur of the plan there is sometimes claimed a conscious echo of Versailles—its contemporary rival—though, in fact, it was another decade until the first reports of the French building reached the imperial court. When they did, Ismail was certainly interested, and in 1699 he even sent an ambassador to Paris with the task of negotiating the addition of Louis XIV's daughter, Princess Conti, to his harem.

On the opposite side of the long-walled corridor, beyond the Royal Golf Gardens, more immense buildings are spread out, making up Ismail's last great palace, the **Dar el Makhzen**. Unlike the Kebira, which was broken up by Moulay Abdallah in 1733, this has remained in use as a minor royal residence (Hassan II rarely, if ever, visits Meknes). The most you can get are a few brief glimpses over the heads of the bored guards posted by occasional gates in the crumbling, twenty-foot-high wall. The corridor itself, which eventually turns a corner to bring you out by the **campground** and the **Heri as-Souani,** may perhaps be the **"strangee"** which all the eighteenth-century travelers recorded. A mile-long terrace wall, shaded with vines, it was a favorite drive of the emperor, who, according to several sources, was driven around in a bizarre type of chariot drawn by his women or eunuchs.

At its end, and the principal "sight" of the imperial city, is the **Heri as-Souani**—often introduced by local guides as "Ismail's stables." The stables, in fact, are farther down (see below), and the startling series of high vaulted chambers to be seen here were again a series of storerooms and granaries, filled with abundant provisions for either a siege or a drought. A twenty-minute walk from Bab Mansour, they are certainly worth seeing and give a powerful impression of the complexity of seventeenth-century Moroccan engineering. Ismail's palaces had underground plumbing (well in advance of Europe), and here you find a remarkable system, with chain-bucket wells built between each of the storerooms. One on the left, near the back, has been restored; there are lights you can switch on for a closer look.

Equally worthwhile is the view from the **roof of the as-Souani**, approached through the second entrance on the right. From the roof garden, beautifully maintained and with a good **café**, you can gaze out across much of the **Dar el Makhzen** and the wonderfully still Agdal Basin—built both as an irrigation reservoir and a pleasure lake for boating parties. Over to the southwest, in the distance, you can make out another seventeenth-century royal palace, the **Dar al-Baida** (the "White House"), now a military academy, and beyond it (to the right), the Rouah, or stables.

The Rouah

Known locally as **Heri Mansour** (Mansour's Granary), **the Rouah** are a further twenty- to thirty-minute walk. They are officially closed to visitors, though if you hang around for a while you will probably find the local guide turning up to show you around. To get out here, follow the road which runs diagonally behind the campground and Heri as-Souani for about half a kilometer; when you reach a junction, turn right and you should come out at **Djemaa Rouah** (Stable Mosque), a large and heavily restored building preceded by a well-kept gravel courtyard. Walk around behind the mosque and you will see the stables off to your right—a massive complex perhaps twice as large as the as-Souani.

In contemporary accounts the Rouah was often singled out as the greatest feature of all Ismail's building projects: some three miles in length, traversed by a long canal, with flooring built over vaults used for storing grain, and space for over twelve thousand horses. Today, the province of a few scrambling goats, it's a more or less complete ruin—piles of rubble and *zellij* tiles lining the walls and high arched aisles of crumbling *pisé* extending out in each direction. As such, it perhaps recalls more than anything else in Meknes the scale and madness of Moulay Ismail's vision. The emperor once decreed that a wall should be built from here all the way to Marrakesh—a convenient access for his carriage and a useful guide for the blind beggars to find their way.

The Medina

The Medina, although taking much of its present form and size under Moulay Ismail, bears less of his stamp. Its main sights—in addition to the **souks**—are a Merenid *medersa,* the **Bou Inania**, and a nineteenth-century palace museum, the **Dar Jamai**.

Dar Jamai

The **Dar Jamai** stands directly in Place el Hedim and is open daily from 9am to noon and 3 to 6pm. Built by the same family of viziers (high government officials) who put up the Palais Jamai in Fes (see p.155), it is an interesting example of domestic architecture and craftsmanship—the best the late nineteenth century could offer.

The exhibits, some of which have been incorporated to recreate reception rooms of the period, are predominantly of the same age, though there are pieces of **Fes and Meknes pottery** which date back more or less to Ismail's reign. These ceramics, elaborate polychrome designs from Meknes and strong blue and white patterns from Fes, make for an interesting comparison, and the superiority of Fes's handicrafts tradition during the last two centuries is immediately apparent. The best display here, however, is of **Middle Atlas carpets,** particularly from the Beni Mguild tribe. If at any time you're planning to buy a rug—and Meknes itself can be good place— take a long hard look at each of these; you won't find anything approaching their quality but you'll get a sound idea of what to look for.

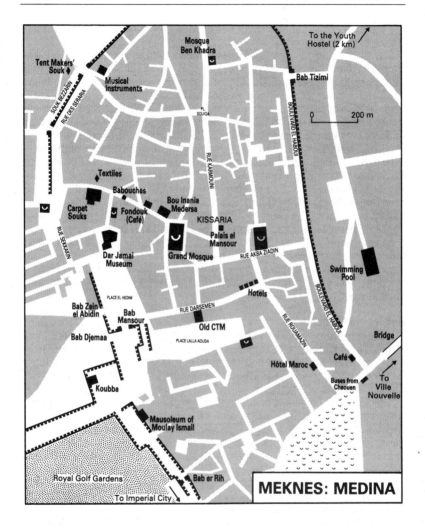

MEKNES: MEDINA

The Souks

To reach the souks from Place el Hedim, follow the lane immediately behind the Dar Jamai. You will come out in the middle of the Medina's major market street; on your right, leading to the Grand Mosque and *medersa,* is **Souk es Sebbat**; on your left is **Souk en Nejjarin**. Turning first to the left, you'll enter an area mainly of textile stalls, though they later give way to the carpenters' (*nejjarin*) workshops from which the *souk* takes its name. Shortly after this, you pass a mosque on your left, beyond which is an entrance to a parallel arcade. The **carpet market**, or **Souk Joutiya as-Zerabi,** is just off of here to the left. Quality can be very high (and prices, too), though without the constant stream of tourists of Fes or Marrakesh, dealers are much more willing to bargain. Don't be afraid to start too low.

Out at the end of Souk en Najjarin you come out on another *souk,* the **Bezzarin,** which runs up at right angles to it, on either side of the city wall. This looks like a pretty ramshackle, rundown neighborhood, but if you follow the outer side of the wall, you'll come across an interesting assortment of craftsmen, grouped together in their own trading guilds and often with an old *fondouk* or warehouse to the front of them. As you proceed, there are **basket-makers, ironsmiths and saddlers,** while near **Bab el Djedid**, at the top, you'll find **tent makers** and a couple of **musical instrument workshops.**

Had you turned right beyond the Dar Jamai, onto **Souk es Sebbat,** you would have entered a classier section of the market—starting off with the *babouche* vendors, and then moving on to the ritzier goods aimed at tourists near the *medersa,* finally exiting into the covered **kissaria**, dominated here mostly by caftans. The place to head for is inevitably the Bou Inania, whose imposing portal is very easy to spot on the lefthand side of the street.

If you want a break before doing that, there's a nineteenth-century **fondouk** a short ways back which now doubles as a café and carpet/crafts emporium—look for its open courtyard. Meknes mint, incidentally, is reputed to be the best in Morocco and exported all around the north for the making of quality tea.

Bou Inania Medersa

The **Bou Inania Medersa** was built around 1340–50, and is therefore more or less contemporary with the great *medersas* of Fes. It takes its name from the somewhat notorious Abou Inan (see p.143), though it was actually founded by his predecessor, Abou el Hassan, the great Merenid builder of Chellah in Rabat.

A modest and functional building, it follows the plan of Hassan's other principal works, the Chellah *zaouia* and Salé *medersa,* in that it has a single **courtyard** opening onto a narrow **prayer hall** and encircled on each floor by the students' **cells,** with exquisite screens in carved cedar. It has a much lighter feel to it than the Salé *medersa,* and in its balance of wood, stucco, and *zellij* achieves a remarkable combination of intricacy (no area is left uncovered) and restraint. Architecturally, the most unusual feature is a ribbed dome over the **entrance hall,** an impressive piece of craftsmanship which extends right out into the *souk.*

From **the roof,** to which there's usually access, you can look out (and feel as if you could climb across) to the tiled pyramids of the Grand Mosque. The *souk* is mainly obscured from view, but you can get a good, general sense of the town and the individual mosques of each quarter. Inlaid with bands of green tiles, the minarets of these mosques are distinctive of Meknes; those of Fes or Marrakesh tend to be more elaborate and multicolored.

North from Bou Inania

Beyond the Medersa and the Grand Mosque, the Medina is for the most part residential, dotted with the occasional produce market, or (up past the mosque of Ben Khadra) a carpenters' *souk,* for the supply of wood. If you continue this way, you'll eventually come out in a long, open *place,* which culminates in the monumental **Bab el Berdain** (The Gate of the Saddlers). This was another of Ismail's creations, and echoes, in a much more rugged and genuinely defensive structure, the central section of Bab Mansour.

Outside of it, the city walls continue to extend up along the main road to Rabat and past (1500m out) **Bab el Khemis** (or Bab Lakhmis), another very fine gate with a frieze containing a monumental inscription etched in black tiles on the brickwork. Between the two gates, inside of the wall on your left, you will catch occasional glimpses of an enormous **cemetery**—almost half the size of the Medina in extent. Non-Muslims are not permitted to enter this enclosure, near the center of which lies the shrine of one of the country's most famous and curious saints, **Sidi Ben Aissa**.

Reputedly a contemporary of Moulay Ismail, Ben Aissa conferred on his followers the power to eat anything, even poison or broken glass, without suffering any ill effects. His cult, the *Aissaoua*, became one of the most important in Morocco, and certainly the most violent and fanatical. Until prohibited by the French, some 50,000 devotees regularly attended the saint's annual *moussem* on the eve of *Mouloud*. Entering into a trance, they sometimes pierced their tongues and cheeks with daggers, ate serpents and scorpions, or devoured live sheep and goats. The only other confraternity to approach such frenzy was the *Hamacha* of Moulay Idriss, whose favorite rites included cutting off each other's heads with hatchets and tossing heavy stones or cannonballs into the air, allowing them to fall down on their skulls. Both cults continue to hold *moussems,* though successive Moroccan governments have effectively outlawed their more extreme activities.

Volubilis and Moulay Idriss

The classic excursion from Meknes, **Volubilis** and **Moulay Idriss** embody much of Morocco's early history—Volubilis as its Roman provincial capital, Moulay Idriss in the creation of the country's first Arab dynasty. They stand 4km apart, at either side of a deep and very fertile valley.

Unless you're driving—in which case you might want to continue on to Fes or Ouezzane—Volubilis and Moulay Idriss are most easily visited by setting out from and returning to Meknes. You can take in both on a leisurely day's circuit, and at **Bab Mansour** you have the choice of either a **grand taxi** (6dh a place to Idriss; very frequent) or a **private bus** (4dh; on the hour; last one returning at 5pm). Whichever way you go, ask to be let off at the turnoff for Volubilis, on the left side of the road a couple of kilometers before you reach Moulay Idriss (or negotiate with the driver to drop you off right at the ruins). One and a half kilometers from the main road turnoff, you'll come to a fork signposted "Aïn El Jamaa/Col du Zegotta": either road will bring you to the ruins in about 2km. From Volubilis you'll probably be able to get a lift into Moulay Idriss, where you can later pick up one of the taxis or buses back to Meknes. Moulay Idriss taxis do not as a rule run to Fes, unless you're willing to pay for a *course* (a white taxi), though from Volubilis hitchers may well strike lucky with a lift.

Non-Muslims are still not permitted to stay overnight in Moulay Idriss, but there is a good shaded **campground** (no facilities, the bar has closed down) midway along the "outer road" to Volubilis. Roads here are slightly confusing, and it's a good idea to ask directions to *le refuge Zerhoun*.

Volubilis

A striking site, visible for a few miles from bends in the approach road, **VOLUBILIS** occupies the ledge of a long, high plateau. Below its walls, toward Moulay Idriss, stretches a rich river valley; beyond lie the dark, outlying ridges of the Zerhoun mountains. The drama of this scene—and the scope of the ruins—may well seem familiar. It was the key location for Martin Scorcese's film, *The Last Temptation of Christ*.

Except for a small trading post on the island off Essaouira, Volubilis was the Roman Empire's most remote and far-flung base. The roads stopped here, having reached across France and Spain and then down from Tangier, and despite successive emperors' dreams of "penetrating the Atlas," the southern Berber tribes were never effectively subdued.

Direct Roman rule here, in fact, lasted little over two centuries—the garrison withdrew early, in A.D. 285, to ease pressure elsewhere. But the town must have taken much of its present form well before the official annexation of North African *Mauretania* by Emperor Claudius in A.D. 45. Tablets found on the site, inscribed in Punic, show a significant Carthaginian trading presence in the third century B.C., and prior to colonization it was the western capital of a heavily Romanized but semiautonomous Berber kingdom, which reached into northern Algeria and Tunisia. After the Romans also left, Volubilis saw very gradual change. Latin was still spoken in the seventh century by the population of Berbers, Greeks, Syrians, and Jews; Christian churches survived until the coming of Islam; and the city itself remained alive and active well into the eighteenth century, when its marble was carried away by slaves for the building of Moulay Ismail's Meknes.

What you see today, well excavated and maintained, are largely the ruins of second- and third-century A.D. buildings—impressive and affluent creations from its period as a colonial provincial capital. The land around here is some of the most fertile in North Africa, and the city exported wheat and olives in considerable quantities to Rome, as it did wild animals from the surrounding hills. Roman games, memorable for the sheer scale of their slaughter (9000 beasts were killed for the dedication of Rome's Colosseum alone), could not have happened without the African provinces, and Volubilis was a chief source of their lions. Within just two hundred years, along with Barbary bears and elephants, they became virtually extinct.

The Site

The entrance to the site is through a minor gate in the city wall, built with a number of outer camps in A.D. 168, following a prolonged series of Berber insurrections. Just inside are the *ticket office* (the ruins are open daily, sunrise–sunset; 15dh admission), a shaded *café-bar*, and a small, open air **museum** of sculpture and other fragments. The best of the finds made here—which

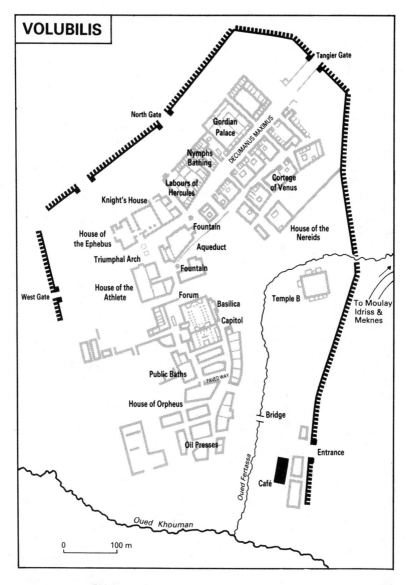

VOLUBILIS

Tangier Gate

North Gate

Gordian Palace

DECUMANUS MAXIMUS

Nymphs Bathing

Labours of Hercules

Cortege of Venus

Knight's House

House of the Ephebus

Fountain

House of the Nereids

Aqueduct

Triumphal Arch

Fountain

House of the Athlete

Forum

Temple B

Basilica

To Moulay Idriss & Meknes

West Gate

Capitol

Public Baths

PAVED WAY

House of Orpheus

Bridge

Oil Presses

Entrance

Oued Fertassa

Café

Oued Khouman

0   100 m

include a superb collection of bronzes—have all been taken to the Rabat museum. Volubilis, however, has retained in situ the great majority of its **mosaics**, some thirty or so in a good state of preservation. You leave with a real sense of Roman city life and its provincial prosperity, while in the layout of the site, it is not hard to recognize the essentials of a medieval Arab town.

Following the path up from the museum and across a bridge over the Fertassa stream, you come out on a mixed area of housing and industry, each of its buildings containing the clear remains of at least one **olive press**. The extent and number of these presses, built into even the grandest mansions, reflect the olive's absolute importance to the city and indicate perhaps why Volubilis remained unchanged for so long after the Romans' departure. A significant proportion of its 20,000 population must have been involved in some capacity in the oil's production and export.

Somewhat isolated in this suburban quarter is the **House of Orpheus,** an enormous complex of rooms which begin just beside the start of a paved way. Although now substantially in ruins, it still offers a strong impression of its former luxury—an opulent mansion for perhaps one of the town's richest merchants. It is divided into two main sections—public and private—each with its separate entrance and interior court. The private rooms, which you come to first, are grouped around a small patio containing a more or less intact *dolphin mosaic*. You can also make out the furnace and heating system (just by the entrance), the kitchen with its niche for the household gods, and the *baths*—an extensive system of hot, cold, and steam rooms. The public apartments, a bit farther inside, are dominated by a large *atrium*, half reception hall, half central court, and again preserving a very fine mosaic (*the chariot of Amphitrite drawn by a seahorse*). The best example here, however, and the mosaic from which the house takes its name, is that of the *Orpheus myth*, located to the south in a room which was probably the *tablinium*, or archives.

Above the Orpheus House, a broad, paved street leads up toward the main group of public buildings—the *capitol* and *basilica*, whose stork-topped, sand-colored ruins dominate the site. Taking the approach on the left, you will first pass through the remains of the city's main **public baths**. Restored by Emperor Gallienus in the second century A.D., these are clearly monumental in their intent, though sadly the mosaics are only fragmentary. The arrangement of the **forum** is typical of a major Roman town: built on the highest rise of the city and flanked by a triumphal arch, market, capitol and basilica. The **capitol**, the smaller and lower of the two main buildings, is dated from inscriptions to A.D. 217—a time at which this whole public nucleus seems to have been rebuilt by the African-born Severian emperors. Adjoined by small *forum baths*, it is an essentially a simple building, a porticoed court giving access to a small temple and altar. Its dedication—standard throughout the Roman world—was to the official state cult of Capitoline Jove, Juno, and Minerva. The large five-aisled **basilica** to its side served as the courthouse, while immediately across the forum were the small court and stalls of the central **market**.

The **triumphal arch**, right in the middle of the town, had no particular purpose other than creating a ceremonial function for the principal street, the Decumanus Maximus—on whose side it is more substantially ornamented. Erected in honor of the Severian emperor, Caracalla, its inscription records that it was orginally surmounted by a great, bronze chariot. This, and the nymphs which once shot water into its basins below, are now gone, though with its tall Corinthian columns (of imported marble) and unashamed pointlessness, it is still an impressive monument. The medallions on either side, heavily eroded, presumably depict Caracalla and his mother, Julia Donna, who is also named in the inscription.

The finest of Volubilis's mansions—and its mosaics—line the **Decumanus Maximus**, fronted in traditional Roman and Italian fashion by the shops built in tiny cubicles. Before you reach this point, however, take a look at the remains of an **aqueduct** and **fountains** across from the triumphal arch; these once supplied yet another complex of public baths. Opposite them are a small group of **houses**, predominantly ruined but retaining an impressive *mosaic of an athlete* or "chariot jumper"—he is depicted receiving the winner's cup for a *desultor* race, a display of great skill which entailed leaping on and off a horse in full gallop.

First of the Decumanus Maximus mansions, the **House of the Ephebus** takes its name from the bronze of a youth found in its ruins (and today displayed in Rabat). In general plan it is very similar to the House of Orpheus, once again containing an olive press in its rear section, though this building is on a far grander scale—almost twice the size of the other—with pictorial mosaics in most of its public rooms and an ornamental pool in its central court. Finest of the mosaics is a representation of *Bacchus Being Drawn in a Chariot by Panthers*—a suitable scene for the *cenacula,* or banquet hall, in which it is placed. Separated from the Ephebus House by a narrow lane is a mosaic-less mansion, known after its facade as the **House of Columns**, and adjoining this, the **Knight's House** with an incomplete mosaic of *Dionysos Discovering Ariadne* asleep on the beach at Naxos; both houses are themselves largely ruined. More illuminating is the large mansion which begins the next block, similar again in its plan, but featuring a very complete mosaic of the **Labors of Hercules**. Almost comic caricatures, these give a good idea of typical provincial Roman mosaics—immediate contrasts to the stylish Orpheus and Bacchus, and to the excellent **Nymphs Bathing** of the second house down.

Beyond this area, approaching the partially reconstructed *Tangier Gate*, stands the **Palace of the Gordians**, former residence of the procurators who administered the city and the province. Despite its size, however, even with a huge *bath house* and pooled courtyards, it is an unmemorable ruin. Stripped of most of its columns, and lacking any mosaics, its grandeur and scale may have made an all-too-obvious target for Ismail's building mania. Indeed, how much of Volubilis remained standing before his reign began is an open question; Walter Harris, writing at the turn of the twentieth century, found the road between here and Meknes littered with ancient marbles, left as they fell following the announcement of the sultan's death.

Back on the Decumanus, cross to the other side of the road and walk down a block to a smaller lane below the street. Here, in the third house you come to, is the most exceptional ensemble of mosaics of the entire site—the **Cortege of Venus**. Zealously guarded by the custodians, not all of these are easily seen from the officially designated vantage points. But you can walk into the main section of the house, a central court preceded by a paved vestibule and opening onto another, smaller patio, around which are grouped the main reception halls (and mosaics). As you enter, the *baths* are off to your left, flanked by the private quarters, while immediately around the central court are a small group of mosaics, including an odd, very worn representation of a *chariot race* with birds instead of horses.

But the outstanding examples lie beyond, in the "public" sections of the villa. On the left, in the corner, is a geometrical design, with medallions of *Bacchus Surrounded by the Four Seasons*; off to the right are *Diana Bathing* (and surprised by the huntsman Actaeon) and the *Abduction of Hylas by Nymphs*. Each of these scenes—especially the last two—is superbly handled in stylized but very fluid animation. They date, like that of the **Nereids** (two houses farther down), from either the late second or early third century A.D., and were obviously a very serious commission. It is not known for whom this house was built, but its owner must have been among the city's most success-ful patrons; here were found the bronze busts of Cato and Juba II which are now the centerpiece of Rabat's museum.

Leaving the site by a path below the forum, you pass close by the ruins of a **temple** on the opposite side of the stream. This was dedicated by the Romans to Saturn, but had probably previously been involved with the worship of a Carthaginian god; in its excavation several hundred votive offer-ings were discovered.

Moulay Idriss

MOULAY IDRISS takes its name from its founder, Morocco's most vener-ated saint and the creator of its first Arab dynasty. His tomb and *zaouia* lie right at the heart of the town, the reason for its sacred status and the object of constant pilgrimage—and an important September *moussem*. Even today, while open to non-Muslims for almost seventy years, it is still a place which feels closed and introspective, continuing with some dignity the business of religion; for the infidel, barred from the shrines, there is little specific that can be seen, and nothing that may be visited. But coming here from Volubilis, the site in itself is enough—a girdle of hills with no European build-ing of any kind.

Moulay Idriss el Akhbar (The Elder) was a great-grandson of the Prophet Muhammad through the marriage of his daughter, Fatima, to his cousin and first follower, Ali. Heir to the Caliphate in Damascus, he fled to Morocco around 787, following the Ommayad victory in the great civil war which split the Muslim world into Shia and Sunni sects. In Volubilis, then still the main center of the north, he seems to have been welcomed as an *Imam* (a spiritual and political leader), and within five years had succeeded in carving out a considerable kingdom. This town, more easily defended than Volubilis, he built as his capital, and he also began the construction of Fes, later contin-ued and considerably extended by his son Idriss II, that city's patron saint. News of his growing power, however, filtered back to the East, and in 792, the Ommayads had Idriss poisoned, doubtless assuming that his kingdom would likewise disappear. In this they were mistaken. Idriss had instilled with the faith of Islam the region's previously pagan (and sometimes Christian or Jewish) Berber tribes and had been joined in this prototypical Moroccan state by increasing numbers of Arab Shiites* loyal to the succession of his *Alid* line. After his assassination, Rashid, the servant who had traveled with

Idriss to Morocco, took over as regent until 807, when Idriss II was old enough to assume the throne.

The Town

Arriving in Moulay Idriss, you find yourself just below an enlongated *place* near the base of the town; above you, almost directly ahead, stand the green-tiled pyramids of the shrine and *zaouia,* on either side of which rise the two conical quarters of *Khiber* and *Tasga.* The **souks,** such as they are, line the streets of the Khiber (the taller hill) above the *zaouia,* but apart from the excellent local nougat, made and sold here in great quantities, they're not of great interest.

Moulay Idriss's shrine and zaouia, rebuilt by Moulay Ismail, stands cordoned off from the street by a low, wooden bar placed to keep out Christians and beasts of burden. To get a true sense of it, you have to climb up toward one of the vantage points near the pinnacle of each quarter—ideally, the **Terrasse Sidi Abdallah el Hajjam** right above the Khiber. It's not easy to find your way up through the winding streets (most end in abrupt blind alleys), and, unless you're into the challenge of it all, you'd do better to enlist the help of a young guide down in the *place.*

Fes

> *The history of Fes is composed of wars and murders, triumphs of arts and sciences, and a good deal of imagination.*
>
> Walter Harris: *Land of an African Sultan*

The most ancient of the imperial capitals, and the most complete medieval city of the Arab world, **FES** is, for the moment, at least unique. It is a place that stimulates your senses—with haunting and beautiful sounds, infinite visual details, and unfiltered odors—and it seems to exist suspended in time somewhere between the Middle Ages and the modern world. As is usually the case, there is a French-built Ville Nouvelle, but some 200,000 of the city's approximately half-million inhabitants continue to live in an extraordinary Medina/city—**Fes el Bali**—which owes absolutely nothing to the West besides its electricity and its tourists.

As a spectacle, this is an entirely satisfying experience, and it's difficult to imagine a city whose external forms (all you can really hope to penetrate) could be so constant and enduring a source of interest. But stay in Fes a few days and it's equally hard to avoid the paradox of the place. Like much of "traditional" Morocco, Fes was "saved" and then recreated by the French—mostly under the auspices of General Lyautey, the protectorate's first resident-general. Lyautey took the philanthropic and startling move of declaring the city a historical monument; philanthropic because he was certainly saving Fes el Bali from destruction (albeit from less benevolent Frenchmen), and

---

* Although of Shiite origin, the Moroccan tribes soon adopted the Sunni (or Malekite) system, in line with the powerful Andalusian Caliphate of Cordoba. Present day Morocco remains orthodox Sunni.

startling because until then many Moroccans were under the impression that Fes was still a living city—the imperial capital of the Moroccan empire rather than a preservable part of the nation's heritage. In fact, this paternalistic protection conveniently helped to disguise the dismantlement of the old culture. By building a new European city nearby (the Ville Nouvelle), and then transferring Fes's economic and political functions to Rabat and the west coast, Lyautey successfully ensured the city's eclipse along with its preservation.

To appreciate the significance of this demise, you only have to look at the Arab chronicles or old histories of Morocco, every one of which takes Fes as its central focus. The city had dominated Moroccan trade, culture, and religious life—and usually its politics, too—since the end of the tenth century. It was closely and symbolically linked with the birth of an "Arabic" Moroccan state due to their mutual foundation by Moulay Idriss I, and was regarded, after Mecca and Medina, as one of the holiest cities of the Islamic world. Early European travelers wrote of it with a mixture of awe and respect—as a "citadel of fanaticism" and yet the most advanced seat of learning in mathematics, philosophy, and medicine.

The decline of the city notwithstanding, **Fassis**—the people of Fes—have a reputation throughout Morocco as being successful and sophisticated. Just as the city is situated at the centre of the country, so are its inhabitants placed at the heart of government, and most government ministries are headed by *Fassis*. What is undeniable is that they have the most developed Moroccan city culture, with an intellectual tradition, and their own cuisine (sadly absent in the modern city restaurants), dress, and way of life.

Some History

When the city's founder, Moulay Idriss I, died in 792, Fes seems to have been little more than a village on the east bank of the river. It was his son, **Idriss II**, who really began the city's development at the beginning of the ninth century, by making it his capital and allowing in refugees from Andalusian Cordoba and from Kairouan in Tunisia—at the time, the two most important cities of western Islam. The impact on Fes of these refugees was immediate and lasting; they established separate, walled towns (still distinct quarters today) on either riverbank, and provided the superior craftsmanship and mercantile experience for Fes's industrial and commercial growth. It was at this time, too, that the city gained its intellectual reputation. The tenth-century Pope Silvester II studied here at the Kairouine University, and from this source he is said to have introduced Arabic mathematics to Europe.

The seat of government—and impetus of patronage—shifted south to Marrakesh under the Berber dynasties of the **Almoravides** (1068–1145) and **Almohads** (1145–1250). But with the conquest of Fes by the **Merenids** in 1248, and their subsequent consolidation of power across Morocco, the city regained its preeminence and moved into something of a "golden age." Alongside the old Medina, the Merenids began the construction of a massive royal city—Fes el Djedid, literally "Fes the New"—which reflected both the wealth and confidence of their rule. They enlarged and decorated the great Kairaouine Mosque, added a network of *fondouks* for the burgeoning commercial activity, and, above all, were responsible for the meteoric rise of the university—building the series of magnificent **medersas**, or colleges, to accommodate its students. Once again this was an expansion based on an influx of refugees, this time from the Spanish reconquest of Andalusia, and it helped to establish the city's reputation as a haven of Islamic Moorish culture—"the Baghdad of the West."

It is essentially Merenid Fes which you witness today in the form of the city and its monuments. From the fall of the dynasty in the mid-sixteenth century, there was decline as both Fes and Morocco itself became isolated from the main currents of Western culture. The new rulers—the **Saadians**—in any case preferred Marrakesh, and although Fes reemerged once again as the capital under the **Alaouites,** it had lost its international stature. Moulay Ismail, whose hatred of the Fassis was legendary, almost managed to tax the city out of existence, and the principle building concerns of his successors lay in restoring and enlarging the vast domains of the royal palace. Under **French colonial rule,** there was certainly the preservation of the old city and the relative prosperity of the Ville Nouvelle, but little progress; as a thoroughly conservative and bourgeois city, Fes became merely provincial. Even so, it remained a symbol of Moroccan pride and aspirations, playing a crucial role in the **struggle for independence**—events marvellously brought to life in Paul Bowles's novel, *The Spider's House*, the best possible companion for a visit.

Since **independence**, the city's position has been less than happy. The first sultan, Mohammed V, retained the French capital of Rabat, and with this signaled the final decline of the Fassi political and financial elites. In 1956, too, the city lost most of its Jewish community to France and Israel. In their place, the Medina population now has a predominance of first-generation, rural migrants, poorly housed in mansions designed for single families but now accommodating four or five of them, who are increasingly dependent on handicrafts and the tourist trade. If UNESCO had not moved in over the last decades with its Cultural Heritage plan for the city's preservation, it seems likely that its physical collapse would have become endemic and much more obvious than it appears today.

Orientation and a Place to Stay

Even if you'd felt you were getting used to Moroccan cities, Fes can still seem bewildering. The basic layout is simple enough, with a Moroccan **Medina** and French-built **Ville Nouvelle**, but here the Medina is actually two physically separate cities—**Fes el Bali**, the oldest part, in the main stretch of the Sebou valley, and **Fes el Djedid**, the "New Fes" established on the edge of the valley in the thirteenth century. The latter, dominated by a vast enclosure of royal palaces and gardens, is pretty easy to find your way around in; Fes el Bali, however, where you'll want to spend most of your time, is an incredibly intricate web of lanes, blind alleys, and *souks,* and it takes two or three days before you even start to feel confident in where you're going.

For this reason—and because there is such a concentration of interest—you may find it worthwhile to have a **guide** for your first encounter with Fes

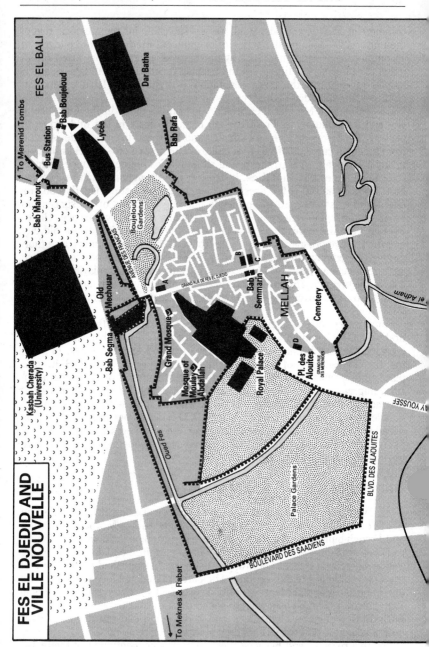

FES EL DJEDID AND VILLE NOUVELLE

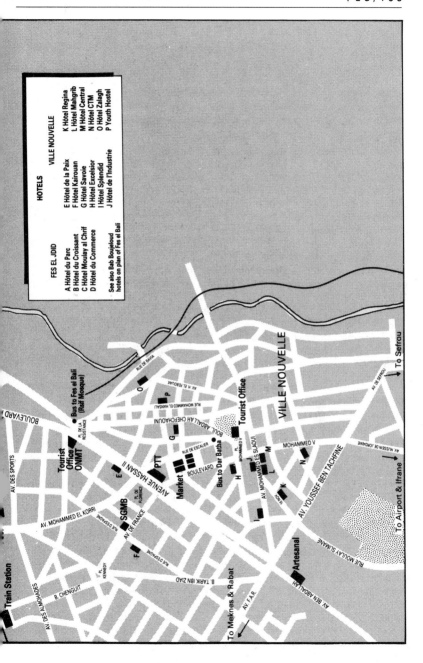

HOTELS

FES EL JDID

A Hôtel du Parc
B Hôtel du Croissant
C Hôtel Moulay al Chrif
D Hôtel du Commerce

See also Bab Boujeloud
hotels on plan of Fes el Bali

VILLE NOUVELLE

E Hôtel de la Paix
F Hôtel Kairouan
G Hôtel Savoie
H Hôtel Excelsior
I Hôtel Splendid
J Hôtel de l'Industrie

K Hôtel Regina
L Hôtel Mahgrib
M Hôtel Central
N Hôtel CTM
O Hôtel Zalagh
P Youth Hostel

el Bali. A half-day tour from an official guide (who can identify himself with a round gold medallion) is probably the best option, and you'll be charged only 30dh (50dh for a full day) no matter how many people are in your group. Official guides can be hired at the **Syndicats d'Initiatives** at Bab Boujeloud (the main entrance to Fes el Bali) or in the Ville Nouvelle (Place Mohammed V; open Mon.–Sat. 8am–7pm), or outside the more upscale hotels (such as the *Palais Jamai* or the *Merenides* above the Medina).

Anywhere else, guides who tout their services are likely to be **unofficial** and technically illegal. This doesn't necessarily mean that they're any worse—and some who might be genuine students (as they all claim to be) can be excellent. You'll have to choose carefully, though, ideally by drinking a tea together before settling a rate (or even declaring real interest). An unpleasant little trick, employed by the more disreputable, is to take you into Fes el Bali and, once you're disorientated (and maybe dusk descending) demand rather more than the agreed upon fee to take you back to your hotel. Don't allow yourself to feel intimidated.

Whether you get an official or unofficial guide, it's essential to work out the main points you want to see in advance, making it absolutely clear that you're not interested in **shopping**—even "just to look." This you can do quite easily, and much more effectively, later on your own. See "Handicrafts" in the Directory for some ideas on this.

You should find the **maps** we've printed as functional as any available. The free *ONMT map* (on the back of their Fes pamphlet) is a useful complement, folding out to show how each of the three cities (*el Bali, Djedid,* and *Ville Nouvelle*) relate. The main ONMT **tourist office** is on Place de la Résistance, in the Ville Nouvelle; open Mon.–Fri., 8am–noon and 2–6pm, Sat. 8am–noon only.

Points of Arrival and Getting Around

The most straightforward way **to arrive** in Fes is by train. The **train station** is in the Ville Nouvelle and only a ten-minute walk from the main concentration of cheap hotels around Place Mohammed V. If you prefer to stay in the Boujeloud hotels (see the following section), walk down to Av. Hassan II, where you can pick up the #9 bus to Dar Batha/Place de l'Istiqlal. Beware of unofficial taxi drivers who wait at the train station and charge very unofficial rates for the trip into town; the standard fare for Boujeloud should be no more than 5dh. Be prepared, too, for hustlers: Fes is possibly the worst city in Morocco in this respect, and the station is a key locale.

Coming in by **bus** can be confusing, since Fes has terminals dotted all over the city, in the Ville Nouvelle and by the gates to the Medina. However, they have recently been reorganized, so you will more than likely now arrive at the main **bus station** (or more accurately, "bus yard") by **Bab Boujeloud**, the main gate to Fes el Bali. It's here—unless given firm directions otherwise—that you should come in order to leave Fes by bus, too. The main exception is if you're coming from, or departing for, Taza and the east, in which case the buses use a terminal by the Medina's southeast gate, **Bab Ftouh**. Note that there are convenient **night buses for the south**, to Marrakesh and Rissani, for example.

Grands taxis, like buses, also tend to operate in and out of Boujeloud, though they're tucked around the corner in Place el Baghdadi (just downhill from the gate). Exceptions are those from/for Azrou/Sefrou, which use Rue de Normandes (between Place de l'Atlas and Bd. Mohammed V).

Petits taxis in Fes on the whole use their meters, so they're very good value. Useful stands include Place Mohammed V and the post office (in the Ville Nouvelle); Place des Alouites (Fes el Djedid); Place Baghdadi (by Boujeloud), Dar Batha, Bab Guissa, Mosque er Rsif Square, and Bab Ftouh (all in Fes el Bali). After 9:30pm, there's a fifty percent surcharge on top of the meter price.

Useful **city bus routes** are detailed in the text but as a general guide these are the ones you're most likely to want to use:

#1: Place des Alaouites–Dar Batha (by Bab Boujeloud).
#2: Rue Escalier (below the post office)–Dar Batha.
#3: Place des Alaouites–Place de la Résistance (Ville Nouvelle).
#9: Place de la Résistance–Dar Batha.
#10: Bab Guissa–Place des Alaouites.
#18: Place de la Résistance–Bab Ftouh (via Rsif Mosque square).
#19: Train station–Place des Alaouites.

Note that these numbers are marked on the side of the buses, not on the back.

Finding a Place to Stay

Staying in Fes, you have the usual choice between comfort (and water) out in the **Ville Nouvelle** or a number of much more basic places on the edge of the **Medina**. Neither option is perfect; the city can get very full in mid-summer and the Medina places raise their prices to 2* rates, while most of those in the Ville Nouvelle, stuck out on the plains, do little to cope with the heat. However, given these limitations, there's quite a range of rooms available.

Note that the **Fes campground**, still noted on most maps in the Ville Nouvelle, is 5km west of the city at Aïn Chkeff. It is pleasantly situated, in a forest, and there is plenty of space—but you really need your own transport for it to be of much use.

AROUND BAB BOUJELOUD

If you want to be at the heart of things—to be able to walk out at night straight into the great main *souk*—the half a dozen hotels around **Bab Boujeloud** are the obvious choice. You're very well positioned here for exploring Fes el Bali, since the *Bab* (or Gate) is the main approach from Fes el Djedid and the Ville Nouvelle. The gate—multicolored on each of its sides, with an elaborate bright blue and gold floral pattern—is an easy and very obvious landmark.

All six of the Boujeloud hotels are marked on the plan overpage. Apart from the friendly and noticeably cleaner **Hôtel Jardin Publique** (☎330.86)—signposted down a short lane by the Boujeloud Mosque—there's not a lot to choose between them. A second choice is probably the **Hôtel**

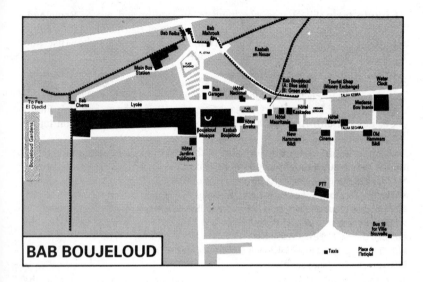

BAB BOUJELOUD

National—noisy but clean, and with no hustlers. In summer, however, don't expect anyone to rent you a "single room," and at all times, if you can possibly join up with two or three other people, do so—you'll get a much better deal.

The problem of water (or lack of it) in many of the Boujeloud hotels is easiest overcome by taking a **hammam** (steam bath). Just through the gate, following the Talaa Seghira around to the left, you come to the new *Hammam Bildi*. This is open to foreigners, though it is best (especially for women) to ask somene at the hotel to escort you. Hours are 1pm to midnight for women, midnight to 1pm for men; bring a towel and a swimsuit.

The **Boujeloud cinema**, incidentally, if you need more entertainment than the city itself, shows an Indian and a Kung Fu film each day.

FES EL DJEDID

As an alternative to the Boujeloud hotels—but remaining within a ten- to fifteen-minute walk of Fes el Bali—you might want to try one of the places in **Fes el Djedid**. Less well known, these are generally cheaper, and even in midseason you've got a fair chance of finding an ordinarily priced single.

By far the best—and run like a small provincial French hotel—is the **Hôtel du Commerce**, right opposite the royal palace in Place des Alaouites. If this is full, it's worth returning every day, until you get a room: it's a gem. The other alternatives are less enticing. **Hôtel du Parc**, at the beginning of Fes el Djedid's main street, Grand Rue des Merenides, is the closest and the best value, but gets very mixed reports on cleanliness. The other two, the **Hôtel du Croissant** and **Hôtel Moulay al Chrif**, wouldn't win any health or safety awards either, but they've (just) enough character to save them from the squalor category. They, too, are found easily enough, on either side of Bab Semmarin at the far end of Grand Rue des Merenides.

THE VILLE NOUVELLE
The **Ville Nouvelle** has by far the highest concentration of hotels, and if you arrive in the afternoon or evening, you might as well settle for a room around here. Well outside from the life of the old city, you will miss the real atmosphere of Fes—and the amazing sound of dawn breaking there as the *muezzins'* calls are preceded by the chanting of other holy men, "the companions of the sick." But even though you lose out on style, you'll have the bars and restaurants—and a couple of swimming pools—close at hand. Below, listed roughly in an ascending order of price, are most of the options; during July or August don't expect too much choice. All are keyed on the main Ville Nouvelle/Fes el Djedid map.

Youth Hostel (*Auberge de Jeunesse*), 18 Bd. Mohammed el Hansale (☎240.85). An easygoing, friendly hostel, which rents out space on the roof if the dormitories are full. Traveling on your own, you won't get a cheaper bed. Closes 10pm.

Hôtel Savoie (G), just off Bd. Chefchaouni. Tends to be the cheapest of the unclassified hotels—if nothing else. However, avoid the *Volubilis* next door like the plague.

Hôtel Rex, Place de l'Atlas. Another very basic, but very cheap, unclassified hotel. Cold showers only but very clean rooms.

Hôtel Regina (K), **Hôtel Maghreb** (L), both on Av. Mohammed es Slaoui. Still unstarred but considerably better than the *Savoie*, with cool, spacious rooms. Both raise their prices a lot in the summer.

Hôtel l'Industrie (J), Bd. Mohammed V. Similar to the above. *Unclassified.*

Hôtel Central (M), Rue Nador, off Bd. Mohammed V; ☎.223.33. The cheapest classified hotel—and for that reason very popular and often full. A good choice, nonetheless. *1*B.*

Hôtel Excelsior (H), Bd. Mohammed V; ☎256.02.. Standard for its class— fairly clean and with functional showers. *1*A.*

Hôtel CTM (N), Rue Ksar el Kbir/Av. Mohammed V; ☎228.11. A little pricier, but worth the difference. *1*A.*

Hôtel Royal (F), 36 Rue d'Espagne, ☎246.56. Usefully situated for the train station—just off Av. de France—and tends to have space, perhaps due to its total lack of distinction. *2*B.*

Hôtel de la Paix (E), 44 Av. Hassan II; ☎250.72. Straightforward and very reasonable tourist hotel, considerably more comfortable than any of the above. *2*A.*

Hôtel Splendid (I), 9 Rue Abdelkrim; ☎221.48. Excellent and friendly new hotel—with a swimming pool.

Hôtel Zalagh (O), Rue Mohammed Diouri; ☎228.10. With fine views over Fes el Djedid and a swimming pool of its own, this is the place to head for if you've got the money (but not enough for the *Palais Jamai*, see below). It is also a favorite hangout for successful young Moroccans. *4*B.*

TOTAL LUXURY/DIFFERENT WORLDS
Hôtel Palais Jamai, Bab Guissa; ☎343.31. A principal setting for Paul Bowles's novel, *The Spider's House*, and one of the three most luxurious hotels in Morocco (the others are the *Mamounia* in Marrakesh and the *Gazelle d'Or* in Taroudannt), the **Palais Jamai**, poised above Fes el Bali, is an experience in itself: twenty-four hours spent here leave you feeling like you've spent a week on a presidential junket. On the other hand, you do have to pay for this privilege—the cheapest double rooms start at around $100 a night. If you *really* have money, ask for a room in the old part of the hotel, originally a nineteenth-century vizier's palace, and something genuinely spectacular. See Fes el Bali map for location.

Fes el Bali

With its mosques, *medersas*, and *fondouks*, combined with a mile-long network of *souks*, there are enough "sights" in **Fes El Bali** to fill three or four days just trying to locate them. And even then, you'd still be unlikely to stumble across some of them except by chance or through the whim of a guide. In this—the apparently willful secretiveness—lies part of the fascination, and there is much to be said for Paul Bowles's somewhat lofty advice to "lose oneself in the crowd—to be pulled along by it—not knowing where to and for how long . . . to see beauty where it is least likely to appear." If you do the same, be prepared to really get lost; however, despite what the hustlers tell you, the Medina is not a dangerous place, and you can always ask a boy to lead you out toward one of its landmarks like **Bab Boujeloud, Talaa Kebira, the Kairaouine Mosque,** or **Bab Ftouh**.

Making your own way in purposeful quest for the *souks* and monuments, you should be able to find everything detailed in the following pages—with a little patience. As a prelude it's not a bad idea to head up to the **Merenid tombs** on the rim of the valley (see box below), where you can get a spectacular overview of the city and try to make out its shape. For a break or escape from the intensity of the Medina, head to the **Boujeloud Gardens**—a real haven, just east of the Bab Boujeoud (see "Fes el Djedid").

The Merenid Tombs and a View Of Fes

A crumbling and fairly obscure group of ruins, the **Merenid tombs** are not of great interest in themselves. Nobody knows any longer which of the dynasty's sultans had them erected and there is not a trace remaining of the "beautiful white marbles' vividly colored epitaphs" which so struck Leo Africanus in his sixteenth-century description of Fes. Poised at the city's skyline, however, they are a picturesque focus and a superb vantage point. All around you are spread the Muslim cemeteries which ring the hills on each side of the city, while looking down you can delineate the more prominent among Fes's reputed 365 mosque minarets.

Getting up to the tombs is no problem. You can walk it in about twenty minutes from Bab Boujeloud, or take a taxi (around 10dh from the Ville Nouvelle). From the Boujeloud area, leave by **Bab el Mahrouk**, above the bus terminal, and once outside the walls, turn immediately to the right. After a while you come to a network of paths, climbing up toward the stolid fortress of **Borj Nord**. Despite its French garrison-like appearance, this and its southern counterpart across the valley were actually built in the seventeenth century by the Saadians. The dynasty's only endowment to the city, they were used to *control* the Fassis rather than to *defend* them. Carefully maintained, the Borj now houses the country's **arms museum**—an interminable display of row upon row of muskets, most of them confiscated from the Riffians in the 1958 rebellion.

Clambering across the hillside from Borj Nord—or following (by road) Route du Tour du Fes past the imposing and controversially located *Hôtel des Merenides*—you soon emerge at **the tombs** and an expectant cluster of guides. Wandering around here, you will probably be standing on the city's original foundations, before its rapid expansion under Moulay Idriss II. But it is **the view** across the deep bowl

Down below, there are four principal entrances and exits—by far the easiest at which to gather your bearings is **Bab Boujeloud**. The others are: an open square by the **Mosque er Rsif**, a few blocks below the Kairaouine Mosque and connected by bus #19 to the Ville Nouvelle; **Bab Ftouh** at the bottom of the Andalous quarter (bus #18 goes from here to Dar Batha, near to Boujeloud); and **Bab Guissa**, an alternative approach to the Merenid tombs, up at the top of the city by the *Palais Jamai Hotel*.

Into the Medina: Bab Boujeloud and Dar Batha

The area around **Bab Boujeloud** is today the main entrance to Fes el Bali: a place where people come to talk and stare, and a great concentration of cafés, stalls, and activity. Provincial buses leave throughout the day from a square (**Place Baghdadi**) just behind the gate, while in the early evening there are occasional entertainers and sort of a flea market spreading out toward **Bab el Mahrouk**.

This focus and importance is all comparatively recent, since it was only at the end of the last century that the walls were joined up between Fes el Bali and Fes el Djedid and the subsequently enclosed area was developed. Nearly all the buildings here date from this period, including those of the elegant **Dar Batha** palace, designed for the reception of foreign ambassadors and now a very fine **museum of Moroccan arts and crafts**. Open daily except

of the valley below which holds everyone's attention—Fes el Bali neatly wedged within it, white and diamond shaped, and buzzing with activity.

Immediately below is Adourat el-Kairaouine, or the Kairaouine quarter: the main stretch of the Medina, where Idriss settled the first Tunisian refugees. At its heart, toward the river, stands the green-tiled courtyard of the **Kairaouine Mosque**, the country's most important religious building, preceded and partially screened by its two minarets. The main one has a dome on top and is whitewashed, which is an unusual Moroccan (though characteristically Tunisian) design; the slightly lower one to its right (square, with a narrower upper floor) is *Borj en Naffara* (The Trumpeter's Tower), from which the beginning and end of Ramadan are proclaimed. Over to the right of this, and very easily recognized, are the tall pyramid-shaped roof and slender, decoratively faced minaret of the city's second great religious building, the **Zaouia of Moulay Idriss II**.

The **Andalous quarter**, the other area settled by ninth-century refugees, lies some ways over to the left of this trio of minarets—divided from the Kairaouine by the appropriately named **Bou Khareb** (The River Carrying Garbage), whose path is marked out by a series of minarets. **Djemaa el-Andalous**, the principal mosque of this quarter, is distinguished by a massive, tile-porched, monumental gateway, behind which you can make out the roofs enclosing its great courtyard.

Orientation aside, there is a definite sense of magic if you're up here in the early evening or, best of all, at dawn. The sounds of the city, the stillness, and the contained disorder below; all seem to make manifest the mystical significance which Islam places on urban life as the most perfect expression of culture and society.

From the tombs you can enter Fes el Bali either through **Bab Guissa** (which brings you out at the Souk el Attarin), or by returning to **Bab Boujeloud**. There is a *petit taxi* stand by Bab Guissa.

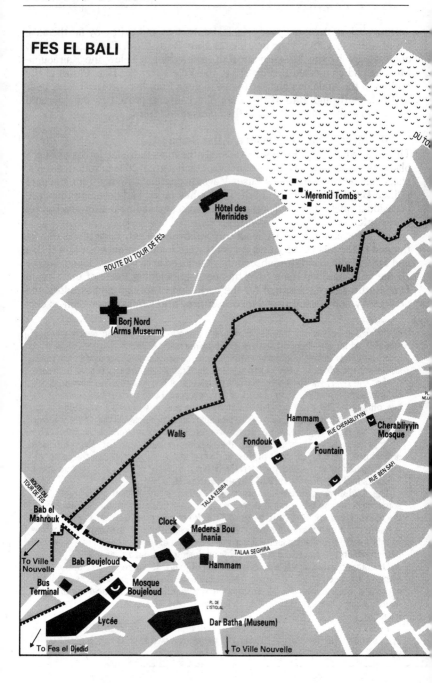

FES EL BALI

Merenid Tombs

Hôtel des Merinides

DU TOUR

ROUTE DU TOUR DE FÈS

Walls

Borj Nord
(Arms Museum)

Hammam

RUE CHERABLIYYIN

Cherabliyyin
Mosque

Fondouk

Fountain

Walls

RUE BEN SAFI

PL.
NEJJ

TALAA KEBIRA

ROUTE DU
TOUR DE FÈS

Bab el
Mahrouk

Clock

Medersa Bou
Inania

To Ville
Nouvelle

Bab Boujeloud

TALAA SEGHIRA

Hammam

Bus
Terminal

Mosque
Boujeloud

PL. DE
L'ISTIQLAL

Lycée

Dar Batha (Museum)

To Fes el Djedid

To Ville Nouvelle

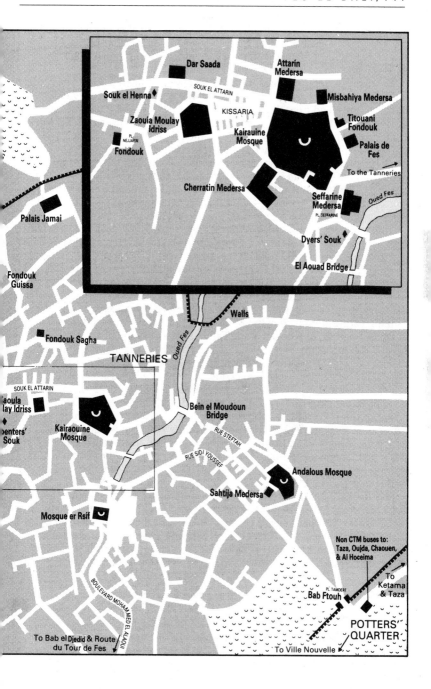

Tuesdays from 9 to 11:30am and 3 to 6pm, this is well worth a visit and its gardens offer a useful respite from the general exhaustion of the Medina. Admission is now a standard 3dh and the entrance is through a small door on its lower side, about 30m down from Place de l'Istiqlal.

The displays here are probably the finest anywhere in Morocco, concentrating on local traditional crafts. There are stunning collections of **carved wood,** much of it rescued from the Misbahiya and other *medersas;* another magnificent room of **Middle Atlas carpets;** and excellent examples of **zellij-work, calligraphy** and **embroidery.** Above all, though, it is the *pottery* rooms which stand out—the pieces, gathered from the sixteenth century to the 1930s, show remarkably the preservation of technique long after the end of any form of innovation. This in its own way is impressive and creates a kind of timeless quality which keeps being asserted as you wander around Fes. There is no concept here of the "antique"—something is either new or it is old, and if the latter, its age could be anything from thirty years to three centuries.

Until you get a certain grasp of Fes el Bali, you'd find it useful to stick with **Bab Boujeloud** as a **point of entry and reference.** Decorated with blue and gold tiles (green and gold on the inside face) it is a pretty unmistakable landmark, and once inside, things are initially straightforward. You will find yourself in a small square, flanked by the *Hôtel Kaskades* (on your right) and with a couple of minarets almost directly ahead. Just beyond the *Kaskades,* the square splits into two main lanes, traversed by dozens of alleys but running parallel for much of the Medina's length. The lower (righthand) fork is **Talaa Seghira,** or **Rue du Petit Talaa,** a street which begins with a handful of small foodstalls, where you can buy chunks of *pastilla,* the great Fassi delicacy of pigeon-pie; farther down, it has little of specific interest until it rejoins the upper lane, Talaa Debira, just before Place Nejjarin.

Talaa Kebira, or **Rue du Grand Talaa,** is really the fork to take—bending around and off to the left of the two visible minarets. The major artery of the Medina, this, with its continuations, runs right through to the Kairaouine Mosque, and for virtually the whole stretch it is lined with shops and stalls. About 100m down, too, it is host to the most brilliant of all the city's monuments—**Medersa Bou Inania**. You can see the entrance to it, down a step on your right, just before you come to a whitewashed arch-bridge over the road.

Just to the south of Place Boujeloud is an area of shops known as the **Kasbah Boujeloud**. Although most of these are tourist-oriented, there are some worthwhile stalls scattered about. One such is no. 85, where Abdillah Alami sells *bildi* (country/homemade) **ceramic drums**. Drums are ubiquitous in Moroccan craft stores, but most are poor quality, with not enough thongs for colder climates. These, which are exported to Europe, are the real thing.

Bus #18 from the Ville Nouvelle will let you off more or less outside Dar Batha in Place de l'Istiqlal, two minutes' walk below Bab Boujeloud. Here, and around the gate, you'll be pestered with offers of a **guide**. If you don't want one, be firm but unaggressive and explain you're only going down to Bou Inania—which will probably be your first move anyway. Most hustlers give up chasing after your business after about 50m or so. If you do want a guide, arrange an official one at the tourist post by Bab Boujeloud. To get a **petit taxi** around Boujeloud, walk up to Place Baghdad by the Boujeloud bus terminal.

The Bou Inania Medersa and Clock

If there is just one building you should actively seek out in Fes—or, frankly, in Morocco—it is this one. The most elaborate, extravagant, and beautiful of all Merenid monuments, **Bou Inania Medersa** comes close to perfection in every aspect of its construction—its dark cedar is fabulously carved, the *zellij* tilework classic, and the stucco a revelation. In addition, it is the city's only building still in religious use which you are allowed to enter, so it's the nearest you'll come to sharing a mosque with Moroccans. You cannot, of course, enter the prayer hall—which is divided from the main body of the *medersa* by a small canal—but you can sit in a corner of the marble courtyard and gaze across to it. The **admission hours** are daily from around 8am until 5pm, with the exception of Friday mornings (closed) and times of prayer (when you might be made to leave); as with all the *medersas* in Fes, there is now a standard 3dh admission fee.

The **medersas**—student colleges and residence halls—were by no means unique to Fes and, in fact, originated in Khorassan in Iran, gradually spreading west through Baghdad and Cairo. They seem to have reached Morocco under the Almohads, though the earliest ones still surviving in Fes are fourteenth-century Merenid—possibly the last flowering of the system. The word *medersa* means "place of study," and there may have been lectures delivered in some of the prayer halls. In general, however, the *medersas* acted as little more than dormitories, providing room and board to poor (male) students from the countryside, allowing them to attend lessons at the mosques. In Fes, where students might attend the Kairaouine university for ten years or more, rooms were always in great demand and "key money" was often paid by the new occupant. Although they had largely disappeared from the Islamic world by the late Middle Ages, most of these Fassi *medersas* remained in use right up to the 1950s, and a few still remain occupied today.

Set somewhat apart from the other *medersas* of Fes, the Bou Inania was the last and grandest built by a Merenid sultan. It shares its name with the one in Meknes, which was completed (though not designed) by the same patron, **Sultan Abou Inan** (1351–58). But it is infinitely grander. Its cost alone was legendary, and Abou Inan is said to have thrown the accounts into the river on its completion, claiming (though perhaps not originally) that a thing of beauty is beyond reckoning.

At first glance, Abou Inan doesn't seem the kind of sultan to have wanted a *medersa*—his mania for building aside, he was most noted for having 325 sons in ten years, deposing his father, and committing unusually atrocious murders. The *Ulema*, the religious leaders of the Kairaouine Mosque, certainly thought him an unlikely candidate and advised him to build his *medersa* on the city's garbage dump, on the basis that piety and good works can cure anything. Whether it was this, or merely the desire for a lasting monument, which inspired him, he set up the *medersa* as a rival to the Kairaouine itself, and for a while it became the most important religious building in the city. A long campaign to have the announcement of the time of prayer transferred here failed in the face of the Kairaouine's powerful opposition; but the *medersa* was granted the status of a Grand Mosque—unique in Morocco—and retains the right to say the Friday *khotbeh* prayer.

The basic **layout of the building** is really quite simple: a single large court-yard flanked by two sizable halls and opening onto an oratory—essentially the same design as the wealthier Fassi mansions. For its effect it relies on the mass of decoration and the light and space held within it. You enter the **court-yard**—the *medersa's* outstanding feature—through a stalactite-domed entrance chamber, a feature adapted by the Merenids from Andalusia. Off to each side here are stairs to the upper floor, lined with student cells, and to the roof. Depending on the progress of restoration work, you may or may not be able to go up; if you can, head straight for the roof to get an excellent (and very useful) view across this part of the city. The cells, as usual, are bare and monkish except for their windows and decorated ceilings.

In the courtyard, the **decoration** covers every possible surface and is start-lingly well preserved. Perhaps most striking in terms of craftsmanship is the wood carving and joinery, an almost unrivaled example of the Moorish art of *laceria*, "the carpentry of knots." For the rest, the elegant, black Kufic script that rings three sides of the courtyard and divides the *zellij* (ceramic tile-work) from the stucco is largely a list of the properties whose incomes were given as an endowment to the *medersa,* rather than the usual Koranic inscriptions. Abou Inan, too, is bountifully praised amid the inscriptions, and on the foundation stone he is credited with the title *caliph,* an emotive claim to leadership of the Islamic world followed by none of his successors.

More or less opposite the *medersa,* just across Talaa Kebira, Bou Inania's property continues with an extraordinary **water clock** built above the stalls in the road. An enduring curiosity, this consists of a row of thirteen windows and platforms, seven of which retain their original brass bowls. Nobody has been able to discover exactly how it functioned, though a contemporary account detailed how at every hour one of its windows would open, dropping a weight down into the respective bowl. Clocks had great religious signifi-cance during the Middle Ages in establishing the time of prayer, and it seems probable that this one was bought by Abou Inan as part of his campaign to assert the *medersa's* preeminence; there are accounts of similar constructions in Tlemcen, just across the border in Algeria. As to its destruction, Fassi conspiracy tales are classically involved—most of them revolve around the miscarriage of a Jewess passing below at the time of its striking and a Jewish sorcerer casting the evil eye on the whole device. The building to which the clock is fixed, which was, in fact, once owned by a rabbi, is popularly known as "The House of the Magician."

Completing the *medersa* complex, and immediately adjacent to the clock, are the original **public latrines** built for Friday worshipers. These have recently been closed down, though it is possible that this will only be tempo-rary. Predating their use in the West by some four centuries, the "Turkish-style" toilets here are still very functional, flushed by vast quantities of running water. If they look open—and you're male—take a look inside at the large central patio with its ablutions pool and unexpectedly rich stucco ceiling.

Farther Down Talaa Kebira

Making your way down **Talaa Kebira**—a street that is very easy to follow—you will eventually emerge at the labryrinth of lanes around the Kairaouine

Mosque and Zaouia Moulay Idriss II. It's an interesting route, though less for any specific "sights" than for the general accumulated stimuli for your senses. The diarist Anaïs Nin expressed her reaction in terms of odor: ". . . the smell of excrement, saffron, leather being cured, sandalwood, olive oil being fried, nut oil so strong at first that you cannot swallow." To which might be added sound— the shouts of muleteers (*balak!* means "look out!"), mantric cries from the beggars, the bells of water vendors—and above all, the sight of the people, seen in shafts of light filtered through the rushes which cover much of the Talaa's length.

Along the first (upward) stretch watch out for a very large **fondouk**—on your left, just after a row of blacksmiths' shops, about 300m beyond Bou Inania. This was originally a **Merenid prison**, fitted out with suitably solid colonnades and arches; it is now home to people selling butter and honey out of large vats. Before the advent in Morocco of French-style cafés, at the beginning of this century, the *fondouks* (or *caravanserais* as they're called in the East) formed the heart of social life outside the home. They provided rooms for traders and richer students, and frequently became centers of vice, intrigue, and entertainment. There were once some two hundred in Fes el Bali, but although many still survive, often with beautiful fourteenth- and fifteenth-century decorations, they tend now to serve as small factories or warehouses. Another **fondouk**, about 100m farther down, is today used for curing animal skins (and smells awful).

A little ways down, the street changes name—to **Rue ech Cherabliyin**— and, passing the oldest **hammam** still in use in Fes, you find yourself in a district of **leather stalls and shoemakers**. The Fassi *babouches*, thick leather slippers, are reputed to be the best in the country, and here, unusually, you'll find fairly sophisticated gray ones in addition to the classic yellow and white. If you want to buy a good pair, you'll have to spend some time examining the different qualities; for the best, be prepared to bargain hard until you're down to around 100dh. The **Cherabliyin** (Slippermakers) **mosque**, in the midst of the quarter, was endowed by the Merenid sultan, Abou el Hassan, builder of Rabat's Chellah. It has been substantially restored, though the minaret, its decoration inspired by the Koutoubia in Marrakesh, is original. If you've gazed at the Koutoubia, or the great Almohad monuments of Rabat, you'll recognize the familiar *darj w ktarf* motifs.

Continuing on, the lane is flanked by a drab series of "typical" handicraft shops before reaching, at the bottom of the hill, an arched gateway marked quite undramatically, **Souk el Attarin**. The "Souk of the Spice Vendors," this is the formal heart of the city, and its richest and most sophisticated shopping district. It is around the grand mosque of a city that the most expensive commodities are traditionally sold and kept, and approaching the Kairaouine, this pattern is more or less maintained. Spices themselves are still sold here, as well as Egyptian and Japanese imports, while in the web of little squares off to the left, you'll find all kinds of manufactured goods. There are a few small cafés inside the *souk*, while returning to the Attarin you'll find **Dar Saada**, a large, nineteenth-century mansion now housing an expensive carpet shop and restaurant—you can look in or drink a cup of tea feeling only moderate pressure to buy something. Just beyond, this time on the right of the street, is the principal **kissaria**, or covered market, again dominated by textiles and modern goods; it had to be totally rebuilt after a fire in the 1950s, and so lacks any particular character.

Reaching the end of Souk el Attarin you come to a **crossroads of lanes** lying slightly askew from the direction of the street. On your right (and ahead of you) are the walls of the **Kairaouine Mosque;** to your left, and entered a few yards up the lane, is the magnificent **Attarin medersa** (see below). First, however, it seems logical to take a look at the area below the Souk el Attarin—dominated, as it has been for five centuries, by the **shrine and zaouia of Moulay Idriss II,** the city's patron saint.

Below Souk el Attarin: the Zaouia of Moulay Idriss II, Place Nejjarin, and Souk el Henna

Although enclosed by a highly confusing web of lanes, **Zaouia Moulay Idriss II** is not itself difficult to find. Take the first lane to the right—Rue Mjadliyin—as soon as you have passed through the arch into the Attarin and you will find yourself in front of a wooden bar which marks the beginning of its *horm,* or sanctuary precinct. Until the French occupation of the city in 1911, this was as far as Christians, Jews, or mules, could go, and beyond it any Muslim had the right to claim asylum from prosecution or arrest. These days non-Muslims are allowed to walk around the outside of the *zaouia* and, although you are not permitted to enter, it is possible to get a glimpse inside the shrine and even see the saint's tomb.

Passing to the right of the bar, make your way around a narrow alleyway, emerging on the far side of the *zaouia* at the **women's entrance.** Looking in from the doorway you'll see the tomb over on the left, with a scene of intense and apparently high-baroque devotion all around it. The women, who are Idriss's principal devotees, burn candles and incense here and then proceed around the corner of the precinct to touch, or make offerings at, a round brass grille which opens directly onto the tomb. A curious feature, common to many *zaouias* but rarely within view, are the numerous European clocks—prestigious gifts, and very popular in the last century, when many Fassi merchant families had them shipped over from Manchester, England (their main export base for the cotton trade).

There is no particular evidence that **Moulay Idriss II** was a very saintly *marabout,* but as the effective founder of Fes and the son of the founder of the Moroccan state, he obviously has considerable *baraka,* the magical blessing which Moroccans invoke. Originally, in fact, it was assumed that Idriss, like his father, had been buried near Volubilis. But in 1308, an undecomposed body was found on this spot and the cult was launched. Presumably, it was an immediate success, since in addition to his role as the city's patron saint, Idriss has an impressive roster of supplicants. This is the place to visit for poor strangers arriving in the city, for boys before being circumcised, and for women wanting to facilitate childbirth, while for some unexplained reason, Idriss is also a national protector of sweetmeat vendors. The shrine itself was rebuilt in the eighteenth century by Sultan Moulay Ismail—his only act of pious endowment in this city.

Standing at the women's entrance to the *zaouia,* you'll see a lane off to the left—**Bab Moulay Ismail**—full of candle and nickelware stalls for devotional offerings. If you follow this lane to the wooden bar, go under the bar (turning to the right), and then, keeping to your left, you should come out in the picturesque square of **Place Nejjarin** (Carpenters' Square). There is a very imposing *fondouk* here, built in the early eighteenth century, and a beautiful canopied fountain, which is probably its contemporary. The *fondouk*, crumbling all around its courtyard, is generally closed, though it was in use up until a few years ago as a hostel for Kairaouine students. In the alleys off this square, you'll find the **Nejjarin souk**, the carpenters chiseling away at sweet-smelling cedar wood. The carpenters here make mainly stools and tables—three-legged so they don't wobble on uneven ground—along with various implements for winding yarn, wooden boxes for storage, and coffins. If there's a wedding coming up, you may see them making special ornamented tables, with edges, used for parading the bride and groom at shoulder level—a Fassi custom. Parallel to this lane is a **metalworkers' souk**, where the men hammer patterns onto large iron tubs and implements. To return to the Souk el Attarin, turn left at the point where you entered the square.

A similar arrangement of buildings characterizes **Souk el Henna**, a quiet, tree-shaded square adjoining what was once the largest madhouse in the Merenid empire (and is now a modern storehouse). It is not such an inappropriate setting, since apart from the henna and the usual cosmetics (kohl, antimony, etc.) sold here, people still come to the *souk's* stalls to buy the more esoteric ingredients required for aphrodisiacs and other magical spells. Notice on one side of the square a huge pair of scales used for weighing the larger deliveries. On the others, **pottery stalls** are gradually encroaching on the traditional business. Cheap but often striking in design, the pieces include Fassi pots (blue and white, or very simple black on earthenware) and others from Safi (heavy green glazed) and Salé (elaborate modern designs on a white glaze). To get down to the square, take the lane to the right immediately *in front of* the entrance arch to Souk el Attarin.

The Kairaouine Mosque

The largest mosque in Morocco*, and one of the oldest universities anywhere in the world, **el-Kairaouine** remains the fountainhead of the country's religious life. It was founded in 857 by a Tunisian woman, a wealthy refugee from the city of Kairouan. The present dimensions, with sixteen aisles and room for 20,000 worshippers, are essentially the product of tenth- and twelfth-century reconstructions: first by the great Caliph of Cordoba, Abd er Rahman III, and later under the Almoravids.

Even if all the roads in Fes el Bali *do* lead to the Kairaouine—an ancient claim with still some truth to it—the mosque remains a thoroughly elusive place to non-Muslims. The building is so enmeshed in the surrounding houses and shops that it is impossible to get any clear sense of its shape, and at most you can only get partial views of it from the adjoining rooftops (especially from the Attarin *medersa*) or through the four great entrances to its courtyard. Surprisingly, for such an important religious building, nobody

---

*The new **Hassan II mosque at Casablanca** will, when completed in 1990, remove this distinction from Fes.

objects (publicly, at least) to tourists gaping through the gates to look inside; inevitably, however, the centerpieces that would give order to all the separate parts—the main aisle and the *mihrab*—remain hidden from view.

The overall effect of this obscurity is compounded by the considerable amount of time you no doubt will spend getting lost around here—forever returning to familiar places you've been lost in before, in bewildered pilgrimage. The best **point of reference** around the Kairaouine—and the building most worth visiting in its own right—is the Attarin Medersa, whose entrance (a bronze door) is just to the left at the end of Souk el Attarin. From here you can make your way around the mosque to a succession of other *medersas* and *fondouks*, picking up glimpses of the Kairaouine's interior as you go.

The Attarin Medersa

Open daily, except Friday mornings, from 9am to noon and 2 to 6pm (3dh admission), the **Attarin Medersa** is, after the Bou Inania, the finest of the city's medieval colleges. It has an incredible profusion and variety of patterning—equally startling in the *zellij,* wood, and stucco. Each aspect of the decoration is handled with an apparent ease, the building's proportions never under any threat of being overwhelmed. The *medersa* was completed in 1325 by the Merenid sultan, Abou Said, and so is one of the earliest in Fes. Interestingly, its general lightness of feel is achieved by the relatively simple device of using pairs of symmetrical arches to join the pillars to a single weight-bearing lintel—a design repeated in the upper floors and mirrored in the courtyard basin. The later Merenid design, as employed in the Bou Inania, was to have much heavier lintels (the timbers above the doors and windows) supported by shorter projecting beams; this produces a more solid, steplike effect, losing the Attarin's fluid movement.

The basic ground plan, however, is more or less standard: an entrance hall opening onto a courtyard with a fountain, off of which to the left are the latrines, and directly ahead the prayer hall. On your way in, stop a while in the **entrance hall,** whose *zellij* decoration is perhaps the most complex in Fes. A circular pattern, based on an interlace of pentagons and five-pointed stars, this perfectly demonstrates the intricate science—and the philosophy—employed by the craftsmen. As Titus Burckhardt explains (in his *Moorish Art in Spain*), this lies in direct opposition to the Western arts of pictorial representation:

> . . . *with its rhythmic repetitions, [it] does not seek to capture the eye to lead it into an imagined world, but, on the contrary, liberates it from all the pre-occupations of the mind. It does not transmit specific ideas, but a state of being, which is at once repose and inner rhythm.*

Burckhardt adds that the way the patterns radiate from a single point serves as a pure simile for the belief in the oneness of God, manifested as the center of every form or being.

In the **courtyard** you'll notice a change in the *zellij* base to a combination of eight- and ten-pointed stars. This probably signifies the hand of a different *maallem* (master craftsman), most of whom had a single mathematical base which they worked and reworked with infinite variation on all commissions.

In comparison with these outer rooms, the actual **prayer hall** is very bare and meditative, focusing on its *mihrab* (or prayer niche) flanked by marble pillars and lit by a series of small *zellij*-glass windows.

If you are allowed to go up the stairs in the entrance hall, do so. Around the second floor are **cells** for over sixty students, and these operated as an annex to the Kairaouine University until the 1950s. Budgett Meakin (in 1899) estimated that there were some 1500 students in the city's various *medersas*—a figure which may have been overestimated since it was based not on an actual count of the students themselves but on how many loaves of bread were prepared for them each day. Non-Muslims were not allowed into the *medersas* until the French undertook their repair at the beginning of the protectorate, and were banned again (this time by the colonial authorities) when the Kairaouine students became active in the struggle for independence.

From **the roof** of the *medersa,* not always open to visitors, you can get one of the most complete views possible of the **Kairaouine Mosque**. Looking out across the green tiles of its roof there are three minarets visible. On the left, tall and square, is that of Zaouia Moulay Idriss; to its right, Burj an-Naffara (The Trumpeter's Tower), and finally, the Kairaouine's original **minaret**. Slightly thinner in its silhouette than usual—most minarets are built to an exact 5:1 (width:height) ratio—this is the oldest Islamic monument in the city, built in 956. Below it, you can also make out a considerable section of the central courtyard of the mosque—**the sahn**. For a closer glimpse at ground level, the best vantage point is the Bab el Wad gate: 20m down from the Attarin entrance (turn left as you step out, then immediately left again). At the end of the courtyard, a pair of magnificent pavilions are visible—the last additions to the structure of the mosque, added by the Saadians in the sixteenth century. They are modeled on the Court of the Lions in Granada's Alhambra palace, and were perhaps constructed by Spanish Muslim craftsmen.

Around the Kairaouine: Place Seffarine

There is another different angle onto the *sahn* of the Kairaouine from a gate farther down—**Bab Medersa**, near the end of this first stretch of the mosque wall. Opposite, as you'd expect, is another college—the semiderelict (but occasionally open) **Misbahiya medersa**. If you can get in, this has some fine details, though much of its wood carving is now displayed at the Dar Batha museum. The elegant central basin was brought over by the Saadians from Almeria in Spain; the marble floor in which it is set level came from Italy. Surprisingly large, with courtyards (and two latrines) at each corner, it was built a couple of years before Bou Inania, again by the Merenid sultan, Abou el Hassan.

Moving on around the corner of the Kairaouine, you pass the **Tetouani** (or *Istroihani*) **fondouk**, a well-preserved Merenid building where the traders from Tetouan—even then known for their dishonesty—used to stay. Now partially occupied by a carpet store, you can look inside without any obligation and you'll probably be shown the huge, ancient door lock which draws across its gateway. A few doors down, past another, much smaller *fondouk,* is the so-called **Palais de Fes**, a grand nineteenth-century mansion now converted to a fashionable restaurant and rug shop. Again you can walk in, and if you ask you'll be allowed up to the roof to get a different view of the Kairaouine and an interesting exercise in orientation concerning the immediate area. There is a restaurant on the roof, which will serve tea and pastries outside of meal times.

Another gate to the Kairaouine, essentially of Almoravid construction, stands right opposite the Palais de Fes; it is one of the ten which are opened only for Friday prayers. Alongside, notice the cedar paneling, placed to guide the blind toward the mosque. If you follow this around, through a tight-wedged alley, you soon emerge into a very distinctive open square, metal-workers hammering away on each of its sides, surrounded by immense iron and copper cauldrons and pans for weddings and festivals. This is **Place Seffarine**—almost willfully picturesque, with its faience fountain and gnarled, old fig trees. On the near side, a tall and very simple entrance in the white-washed walls leads into the **Kairaouine Library**, one of the most frustrating buildings denied to non-Muslims. Established by the Kairouan refugees in the ninth century, and bolstered by virtually the entire contents of Cordoba's medieval library, this was once the greatest collection of Islamic, mathematical, and scholarly books outside of Baghdad. Amazingly, and somewhat pointedly marking Fes's decline, much of the library was lost or dissipated in the seventeenth century, but now restored and in use, it remains one of the most important in the Arab world.

The **university** here has had its function largely usurped by the modern departments established around Fes el Djedid and the Ville Nouvelle, though until recent decades it was the only source of Moroccan higher education. Entirely traditional in character, studies comprised courses on Koranic law, astrology, mathematics, logic, rhetoric, and poetry—very much as the medieval universities of Europe. Teaching was informal, with professors gathering a group of students around them in a corner of the mosque, the students contriving to absorb and memorize the body of the professors' knowledge. It was, of course, an entirely male preserve.

A major point with which to get your bearings, Place Seffarine offers a number of possible routes. You can continue around the mosque by taking the first lane to the right as you enter the square—**Sma't el Adoul** (The Street of the Notaries). The notaries, professional scribes, are sadly out of business, but before looping back to reach the Attarin *medersa*, you will be able to peek through a number of gates revealing the Kairaouine's rush-matted and round-arched interior. If you don't take this turnoff but continue straight ahead, you enter an area of *souks* specializing in **gold and silver jewelry** and used metal goods—a magnificent range of **pewter teapots** among them. As this road begins to veer left down the hill, a right turn will lead you up to the **Cherratin medersa** (and eventually to Zaouia Moulay Idriss).

First though, right on the square, is the earliest of Fes's Merenid *medersas*—**the Seffarine.** Its entrance is fairly inconspicuous, and you might need it pointed out to you: leaving the Seffarine square at the bottom lefthand corner you follow a short lane down to the left and then briefly to the right—the door (studded and with an overhanging portico) is on your left. Built around 1285—twenty years before the Attarin, forty-two before the Bou Inania—the Seffarine is unlike all the other *medersas* in that it takes the exact form of a traditional Fassi house, with an arched balcony above its courtyard. It is heavily decayed, though still with suggestions of former grandeur in the lofty prayer hall. Elsewhere, the wandering vine and delicate ablutions pool give it a rather domestic air; in the far left hand corner are wash basins and latrines. Once again there is a 3dh entrance fee. For a small tip, the custodian will unlock the door to the roof, an atmospheric place where you can look down on the Seffarine square and listen to the individual rhythms of the metalworkers. Next to the building are two newer *medersas*, still used for housing groups of students from the Lycée.

Very different from the Seffarin, and indeed all the previous *medersas*, **the Cherratin** (see directions from Place Seffarine, above) dates from 1670 and the reign of Moulay er Rachid, founder of the Alaouite dynasty. The whole design represents a shift in scope and wealth—to an essentially functional style, with student cells grouped around three corner courtyards and a latrine around the fourth. Comprising some 120 rooms (each with space for two students), it was in use until very recently and the cells are still partitioned and occasionally provided with electric light. The craftsmanship here represents a significant decline, though there is still some impressive woodwork around the individual courtyards. It is interesting, too, in a general way as a rare surviving building from this period.

Continuing down the lane **beyond the entrance to the Seffarine Medersa**, swinging off down the hill to the right, you reach **Rue des Teinturiers** (The Dyers' Souk: see the following section) and a **bridge** over the Oued Fes, below which you can leave the Medina by the *place* beside the **Mosque er Rsif**.

South of the Kairaouine: The Dyers' Souk and Tanneries

If you're beginning to find the medieval prettiness of the central *souks* and *medersas* slightly unreal then this region, just below the Kairaouine, should provide the antidote. That's because the dyers' and tanners' *souks*—basis of the city's commercial wealth from the tenth to the nineteenth century—represent the nauseating underside of everything you've seen until now.

The **dyers' street—Souk Sabbighin**—is directly below the Seffarine *medersa*. Continue down past the *medersa* to your left, and then turn right immediately before the bridge ahead. Short and very weird, the *souk* is draped with fantastically colored yarn and cloth drying in the heat. Below, workers in gray, chimney-sweep-looking clothes toil over ancient cauldrons of multicolored dyes. The atmosphere is thick and mysterious, and not a little disconcerting so close to one of the city's main entrances.

At the end of the Souk Sabbighin you come to a second bridge, the hump-backed **Qantrat Sidi el Aouad**—almost disguised by the shops built on and around it. Walking across, you'll find yourself in the **Andalous quarter** (see below), and if you follow the main lane up to the left, Rue Sidi Youssef, you'll come out at the Andalous Mosque. Staying on the Kairaouine side of the river and taking the lane down to your right at the end of the *souk,* you should emerge at the open **square by the Rsif Mosque**; from here, if you want to return to the Ville Nouvelle, you can get a #19 bus, or a *petit taxi*.

For the **tanneries quarter**—the **Dabbaghin**—return to Place Seffarine and take the righthand lane at the top of the square (the second lane on your left if you're coming from the Palais de Fes). This street is known as **Darb Mechattine** (The Combmakers Road), and it runs more or less parallel to the river for 150m or so, eventually reaching a fork. The righthand branch of this goes down to the river and the **Bein el Moudoun Bridge**—another fairly direct approach to the Andalous Mosque. The left branch winds up amid a maze of eighteenth-century streets for another 150 to 200m until you see the tanneries on your right; it sounds like a ridiculously convoluted route but, in fact, it's a well-trodden one. The most physically striking sight in Fes, the tanneries are constantly being visited by groups of tourists, with whom you can tag along for a while if you get lost. Otherwise, follow your nose or accept a guide up from the Seffarine. The best time to visit is in the morning, when there is most activity.

Inside **the tanneries**, there is a compulsive fascination about everything. Gigantic streams of water pour through holes that were once the windows of houses; hundreds of skins lie spread out to dry on the rooftops; while amid the vats of dye and pigeon dung (used to to treat the leather) an unbelievably gothic fantasy is enacted. The rotation of colors in the enormous honeycombed vats still follows the traditional sequence—yellow (saffron), red (poppy), blue (indigo), green (mint), and black (antimony)—though most of the vegetable dyes have now been replaced by chemicals. This innovation and the occasional rinsing machine aside, there must have been little change here since the sixteenth century, when Fes took over from Spanish Cordoba as the preeminent city of leather production. As befits such an ancient system, the ownership is also pretty feudal: the foremen run a hereditary cooperative and the workers pass down their specific jobs from generation to generation.

All of this can best be seen from one of the surrounding terrace rooftops, where you'll be directed along with the other tourists. There is, oddly enough, a kind of sensuous beauty about it—for all the stench and voyeurism involved—though sniffing the mint that you are handed as you enter (to alleviate the nausea), and looking across at the others doing the same, there could hardly be more pointed exercises in the nature of comparative wealth. Like it or not, this is tourism at its most extreme.

North to Bab Guissa and the Palais Jamai

This region—**north from Souk el Attarin** toward Bab Guissa and the Palais Jamai Hôtel—is something of a tailpiece to the Kairaouine quarter of Fes el Bali. It is not a route which many tourists take, scattered as it is with curiosities rather than monuments, but in this alone there's a distinct attraction. Additionally, leaving the city at Bab Guissa you can walk out and around to the **Merenid tombs**, a beautiful walk as the sun is going down on the city.

From **Souk el Attarin,** there are dozens of lanes climbing up in the general direction of Bab Guissa, very many of them blind alleys which send you scuttling back to retrace your steps. For one of the more interesting and unproblematic approaches, take the first lane to your left just inside the entrance arch to the *souk* (that is, about 15m before you come to the *Dar Saada* palace restaurant). Following this as directly as you can, you will soon emerge at the **Joutia**, the ancient fish and salt market. Spreading out above here is the **Sagha**—the *jewelers' quarter*—which curves around to the right into a small square flanked by an eighteenth-century **fondouk** and fountain. The *fondouk* is now used as a wool storehouse, though you can wander in to take a look at the elegant cedar woodwork and (heavily restored) stucco.

Back at the main lane—Place Sagha and its *fondouk* are about 20m off to the right—you pass a series of small café-restaurants and a movie theater near **Place Achabin**, "the herbalists' square," where remedies and charms are still sold. The **café-restaurants** here are among the best value in Fes el Bali, serving good solid meals, and many double as *pâtisseries*, good for a cup of tea or some fresh orange while rambling around the Attarin/Kairaouine area. The official name of the lane in which most of them are located is Rue Hormis.

Beyond Place Achabin, the road continues uphill, through an area filled with carpenters' workshops, toward Bab Guissa. On your way, look out for the **Fondouk Guissa**—or *Fondouk el Ihoudi* (The Jews' Fondouk)—on the lefthand side of the road. This dates back to the thirteenth century and was at the center of the city's Jewish community until their removal to the Mellah in Fes el Djedid. It is used today for the sorting and storing of skins brought up from the tanneries.

The **Bab Guissa and Mosque**, at the top of the hill, are of little interest, rebuilt in the nineteenth century to replace a string of predecessors which have occupied this site for 800 years. A quick right just before the gate, however, takes you up to the **Hôtel Palais Jamai**—Fes's finest, and quite some shock after a day's rambling through the Medina below. It was built toward the end of the last century by the Jamai brothers, viziers to Sultan Moulay Hassan and, in effect, the most powerful men in the country. Fabulously rapacious, even by the standards of their age, the brothers eventually fell from power amid spectacular intrigues at the accession of Abdul Aziz in 1894. Walter Harris records the full story in *Morocco That Was*, dwelling in great detail on the brothers' ignominious fate—"perhaps the blackest page of Moulay Abdul Aziz's reign."

> *They were sent in fetters to Tetouan, and confined, chained and fettered, in a dungeon. In the course of time—and how long those ten years must have been— Hadj Amaati (The Elder) died. The governor of Tetouan was afraid to bury the body, lest he should be accused of having allowed his prisoner to escape. He wrote to the court for instructions. It was summer, and even the dungeon was hot. The answer did not come for eleven days, and all that time Si Mohammed remained chained to his brother's corpse! The brother survived. In 1908 he was released after fourteen years of incarceration, a hopeless, broken, ruined man. Everything he had possessed had been confiscated, his wives and children had died; the result of want and persecution. He emerged from his dark dungeon nearly blind, and lame from the cruel fetters he had worn. In his days of power he had been cruel, it is said—but what a price he paid!*

In overt and dramatic contrast to this tale, you can, with a bit of confidence and a fistful of dirhams to spare, wander in to the hotel for a drink. Ask to do so on the terrace beside the old palace, now dwarfed by a huge modern extension. An hour in the gardens here, with their box-hedge courtyards and fountains, really does merit the bar prices. The palace quarters themselves are still used as special suites and conference rooms, but if they're unoccupied you may be able to look around one or two—and they are sumptuous in the extreme. Ask at reception if one of the porters can show you the "Royal Suites"; a tip will be expected.

From **Bab Guissa** you can take a shortcut across through the hill cemetery to the Merenid tombs, or you can follow the road up and around. At **Bab Ferdaous,** just outside the *Palais Jamai,* there's a *petit taxi* stand, and from here **bus #10** runs to Place des Alaouites in Fes el Djedid.

The Andalous Quarter

Coming across the **Bou Khareb** river from the Kairaouine to the **Andalous bank** is not quite the adventure it once was. For the first three centuries of their existence, the two quarters were entirely separate, walled cities and the intense rivalry between them often resulted in factional strife. The rivalry still lingers enough to give each a distinct identity, though since the thirteenth century this has been a somewhat one-sided affair: as the Fassis tell it, the Andalusians are known for the beauty of their women and the bravery of their soldiers, while the Kairaouinis have always had the money.

Whatever the reasons, the most famous Andalusian scholars and craftsmen have nearly all lived and worked on the other side of the river and as a result the atmosphere here has a somewhat provincial character. Monuments are few and comparatively modest, and the streets are quieter and predominantly residential. As such, it can be a pleasant quarter to spend the early evening—and to get caught up in the ordinary, daily life of Fes el Bali. Street trading here (and in the southern quarters of the Kairouine side, too) tends to revolve around daily necessities, providing a strong link between the "medieval" town and continuing urban life. And your relationship with the city changes alongside, as you cease for a while to be a consuming tourist—a factor reflected also in the near total absence of "guides" and hustlers.

There are four principal approaches to the quarter, all providing more or less direct access to the area around the Andalous Mosque.

•**Cross the river at the El Aouad Bridge**. From here, take **Rue Sidi Youssef** up the hill to the right, and keep going straight to the top, where you'll come into line with the minaret of the Andalous Mosque. At this point, veer left, and you will see (on your right) the elaborate facade of the **Sahrija medersa**.

•**Cross the river to the north, near the tanneries, on the Bein el Moudoun Bridge** (The Bridge Between the Cities). Then follow the main street, **Rue Seftah,** all the way up the hill as it winds around to the Andalous Mosque.

•**Start at the square by Mosque er Rsif**. From here you can get onto **Rue Sidi Youssef** by going through the gate opposite the mosque entrance, then taking a first left by the first mosque (Sidi Lemlili) you come to, followed by a right turn up the hill. The square can be reached (somewhat circuitously) from the area around the Kairaouine mosque, or you can get a **bus** to it (#19) from the Ville Nouvelle.

•**Start at Bab Ftouh, at the bottom of the quarter, and head north to the Andalous mosque.** Bab Ftouh is connected by **bus #18** to the Place de l'Istiqlal, by the Dar Batha; a handy point from which to leave Fes el Bali.

If you are seeking direction for your wanderings in the quarter, the **Sahrija** (or *es-Sihrij*) **medersa** is by far the quarter's most interesting monument and is generally rated third in the city after the Attarin and Bou Inania. Anywhere else but Fes it would be a major sight, though here, perhaps because of its state of dilapidation, it fails to stand out as much as it should. Still, it is currently undergoing restoration, and there's a considerable range and variety of original decoration. The *zellij* is among the oldest in the country, while the wood carving harkens back to Almohad and Almoravid motifs with its palmettes and pine cones. Built around 1321 by Sultan Abou el Hassan, it is slightly earlier than the Attarin and a more or less exact contemporary of the *medersa* in Meknes—which it in many ways resembles.

Once again, it is worth going up to the roof of the *medersa* for a view across the city, though there's frustratingly little to be seen of the **Andalous Mosque**. Down below, however, you see almost nothing of the building other than its monumental entrance gates because it's built right at the highest point of the valley. Like the Kairaouine, it was founded in the late ninth century and saw considerable enlargements under the Almoravids and Merenids. The Sahrija and the adjoining Sebbayin medersa (which is currently in use for Lycée students) both served as dormitory annexes for those studying at the mosque's library and under its individual professors.

South from the mosque—out toward **Bab Ftouh**—you emerge in a kind of flea market: clothes sellers at first, then all variety of household and general goods and odds and ends. At the top of the hill, on the edge of a cemetery area, there are often entertainers—clowns, storytellers, the occasional musician, all performing to large audiences. This region of the city, a strange no-man's land of **cemeteries** and rundown houses, was once a leper colony, and traditionally a quarter of necromancers, thieves, madmen, and saints. At its heart, close by Bab Ftouh, is the whitewashed **koubba of Sidi Harazem**, a twelfth-century mystic who has been adopted as the patron saint of students and the mentally ill. The saint's *moussem*, held in the spring, is one of the city's most colorful and was in the past a frequent spark for rioting.

About 1500m out beyond Bab Ftouh, and easily distinguished by the smoke from its kilns, is the **Potters' quarter** (*quartier des potiers*). If you're interested in the techniques—the molding, drying, and decorating of the pots and tiles—follow the road and wander up to some of the workshops. The quarter itself is actually quite new, the potters having been moved out of an enclosure by Bab Ftouh only a few years back, though the designs and work-manship remain traditional.

At **Bab Ftouh** you can pick up a *petit taxi* to any part of town (the route up to the Merenid tombs is good for its views), or you can catch bus #18 back to the Ville Nouvelle.

Fes el Djedid

Unlike Fes el Bali, whose development and growth seem almost organic, **FES EL Djedid**, "Fes the New," was an entirely planned city, built by the Merenids at the beginning of their rule as both a practical and symbolic seat of government. It was begun around 1273 by the dynasty's second ruling sultan, Abou Youssef, and in a manic feat of building was completed within three years. The capital for much of its construction came from the Meknes olive presses; the Jews were taxed to build a new grand mosque; and the labor, at least in part, was supplied by Spanish Christian slaves.

The site which the Merenids chose for el Djedid lies some distance from Fes el Bali. In the chronicles this is presented as a strategic move for the defense of the city, though it is hard to escape the conclusion that its main function was a defense of the new dynasty against the Fassis themselves. It was not an extension for the people in any real sense, being occupied largely by the **Dar el Makhzen,** a vast royal palace, and by a series of army garrisons. With the addition of the **Mellah**—the Jewish ghetto—at the beginning of the fourteenth century, this process was continued. Forced out of Fes el Bali following one of the periodic pogroms, the Jews could provide an extra barrier (and scapegoat) between the sultan and his Muslim faithful, as well as a useful source of income close to hand.

Over the centuries, Fes el Djedid's fortunes have generally followed those of the city as a whole. It was extremely prosperous under the Merenids and Wattasids, fell into decline under the Saadians, lapsed into virtual ruin during Moulay Ismail's long reign in Meknes, but revived with the commercial expansion of the nineteenth century (at which point the walls between the old and new cities were finally joined). Events this century, largely generated by the French Protectorate, have left Fes el Djedid greatly changed and somewhat moribund. As a "government city," it had no obvious role after the transfer of power to Rabat—a vacuum which the French filled by establishing a huge *quartier reservé* (red-light district) in the area around the Grand Mosque. This can have done little for the city's identity, but it was not so radical or disastrous as the immediate aftermath of independence in 1956. Concerned about their future status, and with their position made untenable by the Arab-Israeli war, virtually all of the Mellah's 17,000 Jews left for Israel, Paris, or Casablanca; today only a few families remain in the Mellah, and a small community in the Ville Nouvelle.

You can reach Fes el Djedid in a ten-minute walk from **Bab Boujeloud** (the route outlined below), or from the Ville Nouvelle by walking up or taking a **bus** (#3 from Place de la Résistance) to **Place des Alaouites** beside the Mellah.

Down from Boujeloud

Walking down to Fes el Djedid from **Bab Boujeloud** involves a shift in scale. Gone are the labyrinthine alleyways and *souks* of the Medina, to be replaced by a massive expanse of walls. Within them, to your left, are a series of gardens: the private **Jardins Beida**, behind the Lycée, and then the public **Jardins de Boujeloud** with their pools diverted from the Oued Fes. The latter have an entrance toward the end of the long Av. des Français, and are a vital lung for the old city. If everything gets too much, wander in, lounge about on the grass, and spend an hour or two at the tranquil **café**, by an old waterwheel, at their west corner.

Moving on, near the end of the gardens, you pass through twin arches to reach a kind of square, the **Petit Mechouar**, which was once the focus of city life and still sees the occcasional juggler or storyteller during Ramadan evenings. To its left, entered through another double archway, begins the main street of Fes el Djedid proper—**Grande Rue.** Up to the right is the monumental **Bab Dekakine** (Gate of the Benches), a tremendous Merenid structure which served until a decade ago* as the main approach to the royal palace and to Fes itself. It was on this gate that the Infante Ferdinand of Portugal was hanged, upside down, for four days in 1437; he had been captured in an unsuccessful raid on Tangier and his country had failed to raise the ransom required—as a further, salutary warning, when his corpse was taken down from the Bab, it was stuffed and displayed for the next 29 years.

Through the three great arches you will find yourself in another, much larger **Mechouar** (the *Vieux Mechouar*). Laid out in the eighteenth century, this is flanked along the whole of one side by an old arms factory—the Italian-built *Makina*—which is today partially occupied by a rug factory and various local clubs. A smaller gate, the nineteenth-century **Bab as Smen**, stands at the far end of the court, forcing you into an immediate turn as you leave the city through the Merenid outer gateway of **Bab Segma** (whose twin octagonal towers slightly resemble the contemporary Chellah in Rabat).

If you are making your way up to the **Merenid tombs** from here, turn sharp right. Directly ahead, and closed to the public, is the huge **Kasbah Cherrada**, a fort built by Sultan Moulay Rashid in 1670 to house—and keep at a distance—the Berber tribes of his garrison. It is now the site of a hospital, school, and annex of Kairaouine University.

Back at the Petit Mechouar—and before turning through the double arch onto the Grande Rue of Fes Djedid—a smaller gateway leads off to the right at the bottom of the square. This is the entrance to the old *quartier reservé* of **Moulay Abdallah**, where the French built cafés, dance halls, and brothels; the prostitutes were mostly young Berber girls, drawn by a rare chance of quick money, and usually returning to their villages when they had earned enough to marry or keep their families. The quarter today has a slightly solemn feel about it, with the main streeet twisting down to Fes el Djedid's **Great Mosque**.

Within the main gateway, the **Grand Rue** zigzags slightly before leading straight down to the Mellah. There are **souks**, mainly for textiles and produce, along the way but nothing very much to keep you. Just by the entrance, though, immediately to the left after you go through the arch, a narrow **lane** curves off into an attractive little area on the periphery of the Boujeloud gardens. There's an old water wheel here which used to supply the gardens, and the small café (mentioned above in the gardens) nearby. On the way down, you pass a handful of stalls; among them are, traditionally, the *kif* and *sebsi* (kif pipe) vendors.

The Mellah and Royal Palace

With fewer than a dozen Jewish families still remaining, **the Mellah** is a somewhat melancholic place—resettled by poor Muslim emigrants from the countryside. The quarter's name—*mellah*, "salt" in Arabic—came to be used for Jewish ghettos throughout Morocco, though it was originally applied only to this one in Fes. In derivation it seems to be a reference to the job given to the Fassi Jews of salting the heads of criminals before they were hung on the gates.

---

* In 1967-71 Hassan II reoriented the royal palace and the city, developing **Place des Alaouites** (which faces the Ville Nouvelle) as the principal approach.

The enclosed and partly protected position of the Mellah fairly accurately represents the Moroccan Jews' historically ambivalent position. Arriving for the most part together with compatriot Muslim refugees from Spain and Portugal, they were never fully accepted into the nation's life. Nor, however, were they quite the rejected people of other Arab countries. Inside the Mellah they were under the direct protection of the sultan (or the local *caid*) and maintained their own laws and governors. Whether the creation of a ghetto ensured the actual need for one is, of course, debatable. Certainly, it was greatly to the benefit of the reigning sultan, who could both depend on Jewish loyalties and manipulate the international trade and finance which came increasingly to be dominated by them in the nineteenth century. For all this importance to the sultan, however, even the richest Jews had to lead incredibly circumscribed lives. In Fes before the French Protectorate, no Jew was allowed to ride or even to wear shoes outside the Mellah, and they were severely restricted in their travels elsewhere.

Since the end of the protectorate, when many of the poorer Jews here left to take up an equally ambivalent place at the bottom of Israeli society (though this time above the Arabs), memories of their presence have faded rapidly. What still remain are their eighteenth- and nineteenth-century **houses**—immediately and conspicuously un-Arabic, with their tiny windows and elaborate ironwork. Cramped even closer together than the houses in Fes el Bali, they are interestingly designed if you are offered a look inside. It is worth weaving your way down toward the **Hebrew cemetery**, too, with its neat, white, rounded gravestones restored to pristine condition as part of the UNESCO plan. There are two surviving **synagogues**: the *Fassiyin* (which is now a carpet workshop) and the *Serfati*, slightly grander but currently occupied by a Muslim family. If you hire a guide, offer him a few dirhams and you may be able to see them both.

At the far end of the Mellah's main street—Grand Rue des Merenides (or Grand Rue de Mellah)—you come into **Place des Alaouites**, fronted by the new ceremonial gateway to the **Royal Palace**. The palace is one of the most sumptuous complexes in Morocco, set amid vast gardens, with numerous pavilions and guest wings. In the 1970s, it was sometimes possible to gain a permit to visit part of the palace grounds—described in Christopher Kininmonth's guide as "the finest single sight Morocco has to offer . . . , many acres in size and of a beauty to take the breath away." Today, strictly off limits to all except official guests, it is reputedly little used by Hassan II, the present king, who divides most of his time between his palaces in Ifrane, Rabat, and Marrakesh.

Practicalities—and the Ville Nouvelle

By day at least, there's absolutely nothing to keep you in the **Ville Nouvelle**, the new city established by Lyautey at the beginning of the protectorate. Unlike Casa or Rabat, where the French adapted Moroccan forms to create their own showplaces, this is a straightforward and pretty dull European grid. It is, however, home to most of the faculties of the city's university, and is very much the city's business and commercial center. If you want to talk with Fassis on a basis other than that of guide to tourist, you'll stand the most chance in the cafés here. It's more likely, too, that the *students* you meet are exactly that—rather than the "friends" who want to walk with you, fare-meters rolling, in the Medina.

Fes el Bali and **Fes el Djedid** are quieter at night, except during Ramadan (when stores stay open till 2 or 3am). They have, of course, no bars, and with the exception of a scattering of touristic "Palace-Restaurants", fairly basic eateries.

Cafés and Bars

Cafés are plentiful throughout the Ville Nouvelle, with some of the most popular around Place Mohammed V and, in particular, along Av. Mohammed es Slaoui and Bd. Mohammed V (both of which run between the *place* and the main Av. Hassan II).

For **bars**, you have to look a little harder. There are a couple along the Av. Slaoui (the *Es Saada* here is usually lively); a somewhat more expensive outdoor one at the *Hôtel Zalagh* swimming pool; and the pretty seedy, but cheap, *Dalila* at 17 Bd. Mohammed V, its upstairs bar a place for serious Moroccan drinking.

Restaurants

Eating, too, is generally better in the **Ville Nouvelle**, though there are few restaurants which go any way toward justifying the city's reputation as the home of the country's most exotic cooking. Most places here serve fairly standard French-Moroccan food, and you have to pay pretty heavily (see below) if you want the works.

For a **cheap, solid option**, try one of the handful of café-restaurants near the municipal market—on the lefthand side of Bd. Mohammed V as you walk down from the post office. Rue Kaid Ahmed, here, has two of the best: *Restaurant Chamonix* (at no. 5) and *Casse-Croute Balkhaiat* (at no. 41); good, too, and with copious portions, is the *Restaurant du Centre* (105 Bd. Mohammed V). *Chawarma Sandwich* (42 Rue Normandie, off Place de l'Atlas) is modern and unatmospheric, but very friendly, and serves good fish and Moroccan dishes at low prices. Moving **a little upscale**, there is the once-famous (but now unlicensed) *Tour d'Argent* (40 Av. Slaoui), where you still get considerable style and massive portions of food. For a break from Moroccan food, *Chez Vittorio's* pizza (opposite the *Hôtel Central* on Rue Nador) is a good standby.

If you're **eating in Fes el Bali** there are two main areas for **budget eating**: around Boujeloud, and along Rue Hormis (which runs up from Souk el Attarin toward Bab Guissa: see "North from the Attarin"). The places around Boujeloud have seen too many tourists to remain particularly good or cheap, though there is always plenty going on. *Restaurant Bouayad*, next to the *Hôtel Kaskades,* is about the best one there, with a decent *tajine;* it's also open pretty much through the night. If your money doesn't allow a full meal, you can get a range of snacks around Boujeloud, including chunks of *pastilla* from the stalls near the beginning of Talaa Seghira; ask the prices before you're served and they'll probably work out lower. In **Fes el Djedid** there are fewer—but much less touristy—places, most of them concentrated around Bab Semmarine. The unnamed restaurant opposite the *Hôtel Moulay al Chrif* is basic but pretty wholesome.

For a real **Fassi banquet**, in an appropriate palace setting, you'll have to reckon on spending at least 80dh a head. If you're interested try the *Dar Saada* (21 Souk el Attarin: see the Fes el Bali map), where you can get a wonderful *pastilla*, or (ordered in advance) *mechoui*; all their portions are vast, and two people can do well by ordering one main dish and a plate of vegetables. The *Hôtel Palais Jamai* (up by Bab Guissa) also has a distinguished restaurant, and with its terrace outside overlooking the Medina, there are few more stylish ways to spend an evening. Count on at least 100dh each, though; and considerably more if you get the full courses. Less ethereal, but with music and belly dancing, is the nearby *Restaurant Firadaous* (just below the gate); 45dh buys admission and a drink here, 90dh a full meal.

Directory

Banks Most are grouped along Bd. Mohammed V. As always, the *BMCE* (on Place Mohammed V) is best for exchange and handles *VISA/Mastercard* transactions, as well as traveler's checks. Others include: *Banque Populaire* (Av. Mohammed V; quick service for currency and travelrs' checks), *Crédit du Maroc* (Av. Mohammed V; also handles *VISA*), and the *SGMB* (at the intersection of Av. de France and Rue d'Espagne). *Crédit du Maroc* also has a branch in Fes el Bali (currency exchange only), in the street above the Cherratin *medersa*.

Birdlife Fes is home to a great colony of Alpine swifts, who make their nests in the old walls of Fes el Bali and Fes el Djedid. Best sightings as they return at dusk.

Books The *English Bookshop* (68 Av. Hassan II; by Place de la Résistance) has a great selection of English novels stocked for the Fes students, and carries a fair number of Islamic/ African writers—including books and translations by Paul Bowles. *Librairie du Centre* (60 Bd. Mohammed V; near the post office) and the boutique inside the *Hôtel de Fes* (Av. des F.A.R.) can also be worth trying.

Car Rental Fes has quite a number of rental companies, though none are as cheap as the best deals in Casa. Call the following, which all allow return delivery to a different center: *Zeit* (35 Av. Slaoui; ☎236-81/☎255-10); *Transcar* (21 Rue Edouard Escalier; ☎217-76); *Avis* (23 Rue de la Liberté; ☎227-90); *Tourist Cars* (Grand Hôtel, Bd. Mohammed V; ☎229-58); *Hertz* (Hôtel de Fes, Av. des F.A.R.; ☎228-12); or *Caravan Maroc* (21 Rue de la Liberté).

Car Repairs *Mécanique Générale* (22 Av. Cameroun, Ville Nouvelle) is highly recommended: excellent mechanics and fair prices. Try also *Source Pièce Auto* (50 Rue Zambia, Labeta, Ville Nouvelle) for car parts and advice.

Cultural Events are relatively frequent, both Moroccan and French sponsored. Go in and ask for details at one of the tourist offices.

Festivals The city's two big events are the *students' moussem of Sidi Harazem* (Spring) and the *Moulay Idriss II moussem* (September). There are others locally—ask at the tourist office for details..

Handicrafts Fes has a rightful reputation as the center of Moroccan traditional crafts—but if you're buying rather than looking, bear in mind that it also sees more tourists than any of its rivals. Rugs and carpets, however much you bargain, will probably be cheaper in Meknes, Midelt, or Azrou; and although the brass, leather, and cloth here is the best you'll find, you will need plenty of energy, a good sense of humor, and a lot of patience to get them at a reasonable price. Fassi dealers are experts in intimidation techniques—making you feel like an idiot for suggesting such a low price, jumping up out of their seats and pushing you out of the shop, or lulling you with mint tea and elaborate displays. All of this can be fun but you do need to develop a certain confidence and have some idea of what you're buying and how much to pay for it. As a preliminary check on quality (which may put you off buying anything new at all), take a look around the *Dar Batha* museum; to check on official prices (which are themselves on the high side), visit the state-run *Centre Artesanal* in the Ville Nouvelle (on Bd. Allal Ben Abdallah: bottom lefthand corner of our map).

Newspapers The *International Herald Tribune*, and British papers, are sold at the *Hôtel de Fes bookstore* and at some of the stands around Bd. Mohammed V.

Pharmacy Among numerous ones throughout the Ville Nouvelle, there's an all-night *Pharmacie du Municipalité* just up from Place de la Résistance, on Bd. Moulay Youssef.

Police *Commissariat Central* is on Av. Mohammed V; ☎19.

Post Office The main *PTT* is on the corner of Bd. Mohammed V/Av. Hassan II in the Ville Nouvelle (open summers 8am–2pm; winters 8:30am–noon and 2:30–6pm). *General delivery* is next door to the main building; the *phones section* (open until 9pm) has a separate side entrance when the rest is closed.

Swimming Pools Cheapest is the *Municipal Pool* (on Av. des Sports, just west of the train station; open mid-June until mid-September). For more space you can pay a bit more to use the pool at the *Hôtel Zalagh* (close by the Youth Hostel).

THE MIDDLE ATLAS

Heading south from Fes, most people take a bus straight to **Marrakesh** or to **Er Rachidia**, the start of the great desert and *ksour* routes. Both, however, involve at least ten to twelve hours of continuous travel, which, in the summer at least, is reason enough to stop off along the way. The additional attraction, if you have the time (or, ideally, a car), is to get off the main routes and up into the mountains. Covered in forests of oak, cork, and giant cedar, the **Middle Atlas** is a part of the country few tourists get to explore. The brown-black tents of nomadic Berber encampments immediately establish a shift from the European north, the plateaus are pockmarked by dark volcanic lakes, and, at **Ouzoud** and **Oum er Rbia,** there are some magnificent waterfalls.

You'll probably hear that it's difficult to stop en route to Marrakesh, since many of the **buses** arrive and depart full. But even though this is true to an extent, by taking the occasional *grand taxi* or stopping over a night to catch a dawn bus, you shouldn't find yourself stuck for long. Along the Fes-Azrou-Midelt-Er Rachidia route, buses are no problem.

Around Fes: Sidi Harazem and Sefrou

You need a definite sense of purpose to break out from the all-enveloping atmosphere of Fes's Medina. The surrounding countryside—the foothills of the Middle Atlas—is pleasant but is explored most easily by car; local bus services can be tiresome and day trips are something of an effort. The spa villages of **Sidi Harazem** and **Moulay Yacoub**, however, are easy enough escapes from the summer heat. While, further to the south, **Sefrou** is an enjoyable market center—and, again, considerably cooler than Fes, up in the hills.

Sidi Harazem and Moulay Yacoub

The eucalyptus-covered shrine of **SIDI HARAZEM** was established by Sultan Moulay er-Rachid in the seventeenth century, though the center owes its current fame to being the home of Morocco's best selling mineral water. Fifteen kilometers from Fes, it is served by frequent **buses** from the CTM station in the Ville Nouvelle and from Bab Boujeloud, and by private ones (and *grands taxis*) from Bab Ftouh.

The oasis is today rather overorientated towards its health industry. The old thermal baths have an appeal, still, but in summer they can be very crowded indeed. Hotels are modern and functional affairs, too. If you visit from Fes, it's best to plan to return the same day.

MOULAY YACOUB, 20km to the northwest of Fes, is, like Sidi Harazem, a spa. However, it is more of a real village—albeit dependent on the waters—and an attractive, colourful place for a daytrip. The easiest access is by grand taxi—negotiable at the stands by Boujeloud or in the Ville Nouvelle.

Sefrou

SEFROU, 28km (and an hour by bus) to the south, is an altogether more interesting proposition. A very ancient, walled town, this was the first stop on the caravan routes from Fes to the Tafilalt, and, up until the protectorate, marked the mountain limits of **Bled el Makhzen**—the governed lands. Into the 1950s, it was also a predominantly Jewish town; there was an indigenous Jewish-Berber population here long before the coming of Islam and, although subsequently converted, a large number of Jews from the south again settled in the town under the Merenids.

All of this made Sefrou a classic case study for postwar French anthropologists—who found a convenient contrast 8km to the north in BHALIL, a small village claiming pre-Islamic Christian origins and, more visibly, a number of troglodyte (cave) dwellings. If you have a car, this is worth a brief detour on your way from Fes; the village is signposted to the right 5km before Sefrou and the cave dwellings are to the rear, reached by a dirt road.

Although Sefrou itself is not a large place (pop. 40,000), its general layout is confusing. If you are coming in by bus the first stop is usually in **Place Moulay Hassan**—the main entrance to the Medina, whose walls (and two gates) you see below. Beyond, the road and most of the buses continue around a loop above the town and valley, crossing the river and straightening out onto **Bd. Mohammed V**. This, as you'd expect, is the principal street of the Ville Nouvelle and contains all the usual facilities. On the right, about 300m along, is the **post office**, next door to which is the *Hôtel des Cerises*, the only cheap and central **place to stay**. Ask to be let off here, if possible—it'll save the kilometer's walk from the *place*. If you can afford it, there's an alternative choice, halfway between the two, in the 3* *Hôtel Sidi Lahcen Lyoussi* (☎604.97); this has an alpine chalet feel, with its wooden 1950s fixtures, and a good restaurant, though don't count on its swimming pool being full. Back by the bridge, you'll find a sporadically open **Syndicat d'Initiative** in the isolated, white building.

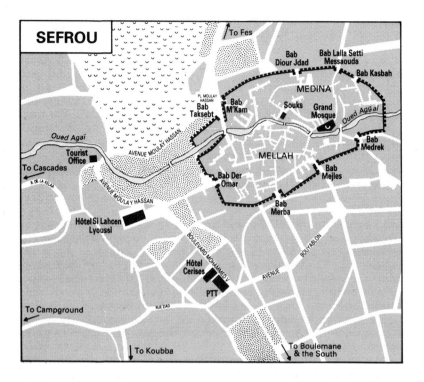

The Medina and Mellah

In many ways it's a pity that Sefrou's **Medina** is so close to Fes el Bali—in comparison with which it inevitably suffers. It is, though, on its own modest scale, equally well preserved, and the untouristy atmosphere (despite a straggle of hasslers) makes it a much more believable place to be in. The **Thursday souk**, for example, remains very much a local affair, drawing Berbers from the neighboring villages to sell their garden produce and buy basic goods. The one time the town draws crowds is for the annual **Fête des Cerises**—the cherry festival, usually held in June and accompanied by various music and folklore events.

Enclosed by its nineteenth-century ramparts and split in two by the river, the **Medina** isn't difficult to find your way around. Coming from the post office/Bd. Mohammed V, you can take a shortcut down on the right of the road straight into the Mellah (or, if you turn up to the left, this will eventually lead you to Place Moulay Hassan). The most straightforward approach, though, is through **Bab M'Kam** in Place Moulay Hassan—on your left as you face the walls. Entering here, you are on the main street of the old Arab city, which winds down to the river, passing through a region of **souks**, to emerge at the **Grand Mosque**. The *souks* include some impressive ironwork stalls and, reflecting the traditional Jewish heritage, a number of silversmiths.

The Mellah, a dark and cramped conglomeration of tall, heavily shuttered houses and tunnel-like streets, lies across the river from the Grand Mosque. It is today largely occupied by Muslims, though many of Sefrou's Jews only left for Israel after the June 1967 Six-Day War, and the quarter still seems very distinct. Over the years of the French Protectorate, the Jews had become quite well off, owning good agricultural land in the environs. But when most of the houses were built, in the mid-nineteenth century, the people's living conditions must have been pretty miserable. Edith Wharton, visiting in 1917, found "ragged figures . . . in black gabardines and skull-caps" living one family to a room in most of the mansions, and the alleys were lit even at midday by oil lamps. "No wonder," she concluded, "[that] the babies of the Moroccan ghettoes are nursed on date-brandy, and their elders doze away to death under its consoling spell."

Into the Hills
High enough into the Middle Atlas to avoid the dry summer heat of Fes, Sefrou is a place where you might actually want to do some walking. There are dozens of springs in the hills above the town and, for at least part of the year, there are active waterfalls. For a relatively easy target, take the road up behind the post office, which will divide into a fork after about a kilometer. The right branch goes up to a semi-maintained **campground** (which is sign-posted); the left one leads to a small, French-built fort (known as the *Prioux*) and the **Koubba of Sidi Boualserghin**. At the *koubba,* a strange annual *moussem* takes place, involving the ritual sacrifice of a black hen and a white cock.

Close by, with cool air and a tremendous view of the valley, is the *Hôtel-Café Boualserghin*—a cheap, attractive but somewhat remote option. Another possible walk is to go up in the hills above the river, a path followed by **Rue de la Kelaa** (just before the bridge, coming from the post office). There are gorges, coves and waterfalls in this direction (for which the *Syndicat* may be able to give more detailed directions or suggest a guide).

South from Sefrou
Going **south from Sefrou** can be frustrating. There is a daily bus to Midelt, but no regular connection onto the Fes-Marrakesh road. If you want to cross over to the Marrakesh route, either take the Midelt bus, or a grand taxi to the garrison town of BOULEMANE. Connections are possible from there.

Alternatively, if you can afford it, or can muster a group of people, you might be able to persuade a taxi driver to take you over to IMMOUZER DU KANDAR (see below), over the mountainous **Massif du Kandar** (*piste* 4620; 34km). This, if you have a car, is definitely a tempting option, though check out the state of the road before setting out—in winter it can be impassable. The **P4620** turns off from the Midelt road 12km after Sefrou, climbing up into the hills around the Djebel Abad (1768m) before descending to Immouzer. If you reckon your car can make it—or you feel like walking— there's a rocky road almost to the summit of the mountain (4km each way), on the right of the road, 10km down the P4620.

Immouzer du Kandar, Ifrane, and the Mischliffen

The first hills you see of the Middle Atlas, heading directly south from the plains around Fes, seem perversely un-Moroccan. In **Ifrane** the king has a summer palace; in **Mischliffen** there's a ski center; and the road up to both of them is almost ceremonial. Immouzer du Kandar, en route, is a little more approachable and mundane.

Immouzer du Kandar

Just under an hour by bus from Fes, **IMMOUZER DU KANDAR** is a one-road, one-square kind of place, where the Fassis come up to swim, picnic, and spend a few days. There are a handful of cheap **hotels,** if you feel like doing the same: the 1*A *Hôtel des Truites* (☎630.02), near the beginning of town, is probably the best, with a bar and restaurant; slightly cheaper is the unclassified *Hôtel du Centre* right beside the bus stop.

Other description of Immouzer comes down to facilities, too. The municipal **swimming pool**, near the center, is open from mid-June to mid-September and filled, like everything here, with natural spa water. There's a famous **restaurant**, the *Auberge de Chambotte*; a small Monday **souk**; and a July **festival**, the *Fête des Pommes*, which takes in a number of music and dance events.

Otherwise, the main thing to do is to get a lift (or the Ifrane bus) up to **Dayet Aouwa**—a beautiful freshwater lake just to the left of the Ifrane road, 9km to the south. You can camp around the lakeside here, and ride around in pedal boats run by the 2*A *Chalet du Lac*—the one source of rooms, meals, and drinks. Like other lakes in the Ifrane area, Aouwa is a good **birdlife habitat**, attracting breeding birds, ducks in passage, waders, and terns. Species to sight include Crested Coot, Ruddy Shelduck, and Marbled Teal.

On to Ifrane and the Mischliffen

With a car it's possible to reach Ifrane by following the *piste* (P4628) up behind the Dayet Aouwa, looping to the right, past another lake (Dayet Ifrah), before joining the last section of the road in from Boulemane. By bus the approach is simpler, the main road climbing through more and more dense shafts of forest before emerging in a bizarre clearing of pseudo-Alpine chalets and broad, suburban streets.

Created in 1929, this is **IFRANE**, a deliberate *"poche de France,"* whose affluent villas have now been taken over by the Moroccan government ministries and the wealthier bourgeoisie. For the average traveler, there's not a lot of interest here besides the possibility of gaining a certain ironic insight into the way these people have fun, as well as getting a glimpse of the royal hunting lodge across the valley. If you're into **skiing**, though, and are here between January and March, this is the main base for the slopes of the Mischliffen; there are taxis up to the **refuge/club** (food and drink; no accommodation) and **ski lifts,** and you can rent equipment in town from the *Café-Restaurant Chamonix*.

The rest of the year, Ifrane's cool air and excellent **swimming pool** are the main attractions. If you find yourself stranded here—which, with four buses daily to Azrou and Fes, is unlikely—finding a room can be a problem. Besides the **youth hostel** (which may or may not be open: ask at the *Syndicat* in the center of town), the only cheap **hotel** is the unclassified *Hôtel Tilleuls,* which in midsummer (and in the ski season) is frequently full. Other than this there are only resort hotels—least expensive, the 3*A *Hôtel Perce Neige* (☎63.50). A summer alternative, though again somewhat classy, is the **campground,** signposted just off the principal street through the town. There is nowhere to stay, or to eat, in the "Medina quarter" of Ifrane, a drab, modern complex built some distance away from the villas to house the resort's servants and workers.

Skiing aside, **MISCHLIFFEN** has little of interest—it is merely a shallow bowl in the mountains, the crater of an extinct volcano, enclosed on all sides by more cedar forests. There's no village and few buildings, though there is said to be a brothel. French *Michelin* readers somewhat manically head up here as an excursion: if they offer you a lift, try to dissuade them.

Azrou

AZROU, the first real town of the Middle Atlas, stands at a major junction of routes—north to Meknes and Fes, south to Khenifra and Midelt. As might be expected, it's an important market center (the main *souk* is held on Tuesdays), and it has long held a strategic role in controlling the mountain Berbers. Moulay Ismail built a Kasbah here, the remains of which still survive, while more recently the French established a prestigious prep school—the *Collège Berbère*—as part of their attempt to split the country's Berbers from the urban Arabs. The *collège*, still a dominant building in the town, provided many of the protectorate's interpreters, local administrators, and military officers, but in spite of its ban on using Arabic and any manifestation of Islam, the policy proved to be a failure. Azrou graduates played a significant role in the nationalist movement—and were uniquely placed to do so, as a new French-created elite. Since independence, however, their influence has been slight outside of the army; many of the Berber student activists followed Mehdi Ben Barka's ill-fated, socialist UNEP party (see *Contexts*).

Practicalities

Arriving in the town, the feature you immediately notice is a massive outcrop of rock—the *Azrou,* from which the town takes its name. The bus drops you off just in front of it, at the end of the main square, **Place Mohammed V.** The best cheap **hotel,** the *Hôtel des Cèdres* is here; or you can walk around the corner into a smaller, adjacent square, to find the more basic *Hôtel Ziz* and *Hôtel Beausejour.* An alternative place to stay, quiet but slightly out of town, is the **Youth Hostel** (*Auberge de Jeunesse*; ☎83.82); to get there, walk back out toward the crossroads to Fes and Midelt—it's about 1km uphill on the left.

There are cheap **food stalls** around the bus station, an erratic **restaurant** in the *Cèdres* and a bar/restaurant right next door—*Le Relais Forestier* (whose meals can be expensive). The Café-Patisserie on the corner of the main square, near the CTM office, is plush by Moroccan standards, but prices are normal and the coffeee and croissants superb.

Azrou has two **bus stations**, both of them in Place Mohammed V. Between them, you can choose from five buses per day to Midelt, Er Rachidia, and Rissani, and it's not usually a problem to get a bus to Fes (or, less frequently, to Meknes). For Marrakesh, you should ask around and try to buy tickets the night before you plan to leave; several of the buses tend to arrive full, though there is one (currently departing at 4am, arriving in Marrakesh at 10:30–11am) which starts at Azrou. Around the other side of the rock, there is a **grand taxi stand,** with regular departures for Ifrane and Fes, sporadic (but still possible) ones for Khenifra.

The Souk and the Town

If you can manage it, by far the best time to be in Azrou is for the **Tuesday souk,** which draws Berbers from all the surrounding mountain villages. It's held a little above the main part of town—just follow the crowds up to a separate quarter across the valley. The produce stands sprinkled all over the main area seem at first to be all there is; look further, though, and you'll see a stretch of wasteland (usually filled with musicians and storytellers), beyond which is a smaller section for carpets, textiles, and general goods. The carpet stalls, not particularly geared toward tourists, can turn up some beautiful items, reasonably priced (if not exactly bargains).

For a more modern selection—including high-quality, heavy woolen rugs—take a look, too, at the **Cooperative artesanale** (open daily 8:30am–noon and 2:30–6pm) back in Place Mohammed V, to the left of the rock. This is one of the best crafts cooperatives in the country, and quite a contrast to the usual junk in the tourist shops. In addition to the rugs, containing bright, geometric designs based on the traditional patterns of the Beni M'Guild tribe, there is impressive cedar and stone carving.

There is little else to do in the town, though you can spend most of the day climbing around the hills (which again have seasonal springs) or wandering down to the river, reputedly well stocked with trout. Local guides tout the cedar forest and, above all, a very ancient tree known as the **Cèdre Gouraud;** if this appeals to you, it's a fourteen-kilometer hike or taxi ride—8km up the Midelt road and then down a signposted track to the left. Stopping off for a rest from the Fes-Marrakesh/Midelt journey, you might find the **swimming pool** (behind the rock and main square) equally tempting.

Aïn Leuh and the Waterfalls of Oum er Rbia

South of Azrou lies some of the most remote and beautiful country of the Middle Atlas—dotted with cedar forests and home to numerous groups of monkeys (even close to Azrou). At the heart of the region are the magnificent waterfalls of **Oum er Rbia,** the source of Morocco's largest river. There's a daily bus from Azrou to Aïn Leuh, 30km along the route to the falls, or you can get a taxi the whole way. The road, all the way to Khenifra, has recently been paved but can still become waterlogged and impassable in winter.

AÏN LEUH (17km down the main Khenifra road, then left along the S303) is a large Berber village, typical of the Middle Atlas, with its flat-roofed houses tiered above the valley. As in Azrou, there are ruins of a Kasbah built by Moulay Ismail and there are **springs** (with a more or less year-round waterfall) in the hill to the rear. Market day here is basically Wednesday (a good day to hitch), though it can extend a day in either direction. It is the weekly gathering point of the Beni M'Guild tribe—still semi-nomadic in this region, and to be seen camping out beside their flocks in heavy, dark tents. As a colonial *zone d'insécurité*, this part of the Atlas was relatively undisturbed by French settlers and the traditional balance between pasture and forest has remained largely intact.

The road to the **Sources de l'Oum er Rbia** begins just before you reach Aïn Leuh and is signposted "Aguelmane Azigza/Khenifra." It runs mostly through mountain forest, where you're almost certain to come across Middle Atlas monkeys. About 20km from Aïn Leuh, to the left of the road, there's a small lake—**Lac Ouiouane**—with scope for camping in blissful isolation.

Thirteen kilometers from here, you come to a sizable **bridge** over the Oum er Rbia; stay on the road until you reach a second, concrete bridge, with a small parking area by the river; the footpath on the far side of the bridge leads in after a fifteen-minute walk to the **sources**. These are truly spectacular—forty or more cascades, shooting out from an enormous limestone cliff. The basin below, sculpted by the adjacent rocks, seems like a tempting place to have a swim, though be warned that the currents here are extremely strong; there are smaller, natural pools nearby. The water, full of salt sediments, is not drinkable.

On past the bridges, the main road heads off to the west, crossed by a confusing array of *pistes*. After 18km, a turnoff on the left leads to the **Aguelmane Azigza**, a dark and very deep lake, where again you can camp — and swim, as many Moroccans do. If you stay, you'll have to bring along your own food, because there are no supplies nearer than Khenifra.

From the Azigza turnoff, it's a further 24km to Khenifra. Alternatively, for the exploring minded, there's a *piste* (3km past the Azigza turnoff) which leads into the mountains to emerge eventually near the junction of the Azrou and Khenifra roads to Midelt; this, however, is a very rough road and suitable only for vehicles with four-wheel drive.

Midelt and the Route to Er Rachidia

If you're traveling the southern circuits of the *ksour* and *kasbahs* of the sub-Sahara, you're almost certain to take this route in one direction or the other. It's 125km from Azrou to Midelt and a further 154km to Er Rachidia—quite possible distances for a single bus trip or a day's driving, but much more satisfying when taken in a couple of stages. You cross passes over both the Middle and High Atlas ranges, catch a first glimpse of the south's extraordinary *pisé* architecture and end up in the desert.

The Road to Midelt

Climbing up from Azrou, the Midelt road follows a magnificent stretch of the Middle Atlas, winding through the pine and cedar forests around the town to emerge at the river **valley of the Oued Gigou**, the view ahead taking in some of the range's highest peaks.

By bus you have little alternative but to head straight to Midelt, reached in around two hours. With a car, though, there are two very brief and worthwhile detours. Fifty-two kilometers from Azrou, as the road levels out on a strange volcanic plateau littered with dark pumice rock, there's a turnoff on the left marked **Aguelmane Sidi Ali**. This is a mountain lake, the largest of many formed in the extinct craters of this region. It's only a kilometer from the road—long, still and eerily beautiful. Besides a *marabout's* tomb on the far shore (from which the lake takes its name) and perhaps a shepherd's tent and flock, there is unlikely to be anything or anyone in sight; if you can improvise a fishing rod, there are reputed to be plenty of trout, pike, and perch.

The other point where you might want to leave the road is 24km farther down, just before the junction with the old road (and caravan route) from Sefrou and Boulemane. Six kilometers off to the right here is the small village of **ITZER**, whose **market** remains one of the most important in the region. Held on Mondays and Thursdays, it (like Midelt) can be a good source of local Berber rugs and carpets.

Midelt

At **MIDELT**, approached through a bleak plain of scrub and desert, you have left the Middle Atlas behind. Suddenly, through the haze, appear the much greater peaks of the High Atlas rising sheer behind the town to a massive range, the **Djebel Ayachi**, at over 3700m.

The drama of this site, tremendous in the clear, cool evenings, is the most compelling reason to stop over, for the town itself initially looks very drab, one street with a couple of cafés and hotels and a small *souk*. Actually, it's a very pleasant place to stay—partly because so few people do, partly because it's the first place where you become aware of the much more relaxed (and largely Berber) atmosphere of the south. The best time to be here is for the huge **Sunday souk**, which spreads back along the road toward Fes.

There are food stalls and a cheap unnamed **hotel** by the bus station (midway through the town); another, *El Aghouar*, further into town; and—the preferable options—the *Roi de la Bière* and the *Occidentale* (clean and with a café—highly recommended), near the **campground** (cheap but lacking facilities), 2km out on the road to Er Rachidia. The only classified hotel is the 3*A Hôtel Ayachi (☎21.61). For food, choose between *Restaurant Fes* (with a massive *menu du jour*), on Rue des Essayaghane, and *Brasserie Chez Aziz*, on the Er Rachidia road. The town has separate **hammams** for women and men—ask directions at your hotel.

The most interesting section of town, worth at least a stop between buses, is the old *souk*—**Souk Djedid**—behind the stalls opposite the bus station. This is exclusively a **carpet market**, the wares slung out in rotation in the sunlight (for natural bleaching) and piled up in bewildering layers of pattern and color in the various shops to the rear. It's a relaxed place for shopping and the rugs are superb—mostly local, geometric designs from tribes of the Middle Atlas. Ask to see the "antique" ones—few will be more than ten or twenty years old, but they are usually the most idiosyncratic and inventive.

More carpets—and traditional-styled blankets and textiles—can be seen or bought at the **Atelier de Tissage** run by a group of French Franciscan nuns in a convent just off to the left on the road to **Tattiouine** (signposted "Cirque Jaffar;" first right after the bus station). Many of the nuns have been living here for years, and they will happily talk about Morocco for hours, if you can speak French or Italian.

If you follow this road a bit more—two or three kilometers is enough—you find yourself in countryside very different from that around Midelt, with eagles soaring above the hills and mule tracks leading down to the valleys and an occasional *kasbah*. There are more ambitious hikes up into the **Djebel Ayachi**, if you can get a taxi to take you up to the village of Tattiouine.

The Cirque Jaffar

The most adventurous possibility from Midelt is to take the **Cirque Jaffar** road—a very poor *piste*, practicable only in dry weather, which leaves the Tattiouine road to edge its way through a kind of hollow in the foothills of the Ayachi. If you have a car, there's a classic route around the Cirque, which loops back to the Midelt-Azrou road after 34km (turn right, onto the 3426, near the *maison forestière de Mitkane*); it is only 79km in all back to Midelt, though it'll take you at least half a day to get around it. Alternatively—and highly recommended for the more intrepid—you can continue along the *Cirque* road right **over the backbone of the Atlas**, eventually reaching ARHBALA and EL KSIBA , or IMILCHIL (see *Chapter Six*).

Along this route, you don't necessarily need a car; as long as you have the time, it's possible to ride in Berber trucks (for which you pay as if they were buses) going over the various stages. Bear in mind, though, that you'll be largely dependent on the patterns of local markets, and reckon on three, perhaps four days up to Imilchil, and a similar number from there down to the fabulous TODRHA GORGE and TINERHIR (again, see *Chapter Six*). It will help, too, if you decide that, for at least part of the way, you'll walk.

If, incidentally, you set out to walk the whole way, you might want to acquire one of the two French *CAF hiking guides* which detail the whole zone between Midelt and the Toukbal *massif*, and you'll certainly want to get some of the *Carte de Maroc* national grid sheets.

South to Er Rachidia

There's less adventure in continuing the trip **south from Midelt to Er Rachidia,** though it is still a memorable route, marking as it does the transition to the south and the sub-Sahara.

You cross one of the lower passes of the High Atlas, **Tizi n'Talrhmeht** (Pass of the She-Camel) some 30km beyond Midelt, descending to what is essentially a desert plain. At AÏT MESSAOUD, just beyond the pass, there's an old, thoroughly Beau Geste-like military fort, and a few kilometers farther down, you come across the first southern *ksar*, AÏT KHERROU, a river oasis at the entrance to a small gorge. After this, the *ksour* (plural form for these high-walled, fortified villages) begin to dot the landscape as the road follows the path of the great Ziz River.

En route there is the possible, if distinctly quixotic, prospect of a stopover in **RICH**: a small (and inappropriately named) market town, which is approached from the main road by a vast and bizarre red-washed esplanade. Utterly desolate, with mountains stretching off into the distance, this seems a perfect stage for some fatalistic gesture. Staying here would probably be enough. On a more prosaic level, the *piste* behind the town (trailing the last section of the Ziz) offers an alternative approach to IMILCHIL—less dramatic than that from Midelt but said to be passable for most of the year.

One last highlight: 25km from the Rich turnoff, and 54km before Er Rachidia, begins the **Ziz gorge**—a tremendous, gothic piece of erosion that cuts its way through a final stretch of the Atlas. Impressive at any time of day, it's unbelievably majestic in the late afternoon, with great shafts of sunlight shining through the valleys. ER RACHIDIA (see *Chapter Six*) sprawls out ahead of you as you emerge, past a huge dammed reservoir. Unless you arrive late in the day, you'll probably want to press straight on from here to MESKI or ERFOUD (again, see *Chapter Six*).

Toward Marrakesh: the Routes from Azrou and the Cascades d'Ouzoud

The **main route from Azrou to Marrakesh**, the P24, skirts well clear of the mountains, its interest lying in the subtle changes of land, cultivation, and architecture on the plains, as you move into the south. The towns along the way—hot, dusty, functional market centers—are unlikely to tempt you to linger. However, once again, contact with the Middle Atlas is close at hand, if you leave the main road and take to the *pistes*. A great network of them spreads out behind the small town of **El Ksiba**, itself 8km off the P24 but easily hitched to from the turnoff or reached by bus from Kasba Tadla.

Khenifra—and a Side Trip to Oulmes

It's unlikely that you'll get stranded in **KHENIFRA** and it's equally difficult to imagine any other reason to stay there. A small town, for all its prominence on the maps, it springs into occasional life with the weekly **souks** (Wednesdays and Sundays); otherwise, there's not much going for it. If you're following this chapter in reverse (from Marrakesh) note that you can approach the Cascades of Oum er Rbia (see p.167) from here. If you've just done this, or plan to do so, there's a particularly gloomy **hotel** by the CTM station at the end of town, or a couple of somewhat more enticing ones (each with a restaurant) down by the river—the *Voyageurs* and the *France*. All are unclassified, the only starred hotel being the luxury Hôtel Hamou (4*B; ☎60.20).

Northwest of Khenifra, a road leads through forested outcrops of the Middle Atlas, the Djebel Mouchchene, **towards Rabat**. This is an attractive route, the countryside cut by mountain rivers and ravines, and with wild boar in the hills. Midway is the small, spa town of **OULMES**, home of Morocco's most popular sparkling water. It's a good stop, if you can afford 3*A **hotel** prices at the *Hôtel les Thermes* (☎901). Below the town you can walk down to a spot known as Lalla Haya, where Oulmes water cascades out from the rocks.

El Ksiba and Beyond

EL KSIBA, a sizable and busy Berber village (with a Sunday *souk*), is again no great shakes in itself—though the approach up here, hemmed in by dense woods, gives a hint of the countryside beyond. There's a pleasant, small **hotel**, the 2*B *Hostelerie Henri IV* (☎2), on a kind of miniature beltway which bypasses the main part of the village. But if you arrive here in the morning, you should be able to get a bus straight to the market village of Arhbala, in the mountains proper.

En route to Arhbala, the road passes a series of **campgrounds** hidden in the wooded Atlas slopes (and with good hiking opportunities). **ARHBALA** itself is at the beginning of the **piste to Midelt**, and if you are heading for IMILCHIL and the PLATEAU DES LACS (see *Chapter Six*), you can either try and get a lift from a truck here (most likely on a Wednesday, when Arhbala has its *souk,* or Fridays for Imilchil), or take a chance by getting out at the Imilchil turnoff—50km from El Ksiba and 13km before Arhbala. The usual route from the turnoff to Imilchil—see the map in *Chapter Six*—goes via the villages of CHERKET and TASSENT; there's a Berber truck/bus along each stage at least every other day.

Kasba Tadla and Beni Mellal

KASBA TADLA was created by Moulay Ismail, and takes its name from a fortress he built here. It is not really worth a special detour; however, if you have a car or are between buses, take some time to look around. The **Kasbah** is only a few blocks from the bus station—a massive, crumbling quarter, whose palace and even mosque have lapsed into dereliction, their shells now occupied by small farmholdings and cottages. The town owed its original importance (as did Khenifra) to its being beside the Oum er Rbia River. Ismail, the first sultan since the Almoravids to impose order on the whole country, billeted a large garrison of Sudanese troops here. There are two cheap and very basic **hotels** right by the bus station, and another, the *Hôtel des Alliés*, just around the corner.

BENI MELLAL, market town for the broad, prosperous flatlands to the south, is the base for setting out to the Cascades d'Ouzoud (see below), and it has a sizable **Tuesday souk** (good for blankets, sold here with unusual designs). It's a more attractive place to stay, too, with a couple of cheapish **hotels** just up the road from the bus station in the "New Medina"—the unrated *Hôtel Afrique* and (with a lively and pretty seedy bar) and the 1*A *Hôtel de* Paris (☎22.45). The town's Kasbah, again built by Moulay Ismail, has been often restored and is of no great interest; time would be better spent by walking up to the smaller, ruined **Kasbah de Ras el Aïn**, set above the gardens, and to the spring of **Aïn Asserdoun**, to the south of town.

If you're in Beni Mellal on a Saturday, the Middle Atlas's largest weekly **market** is at SOUK SEBT DES OULAD NEMÂA (35km; regular buses).

The Cascades d'Ouzoud

The **Cascades d'Ouzoud** are off a fairly long detour from the Beni Mellal-Marrakesh road—at least half a day's journey if you're going by local bus and taxi. But there are few places in Morocco so enjoyable and easygoing, and in midsummer it's incredible to encounter the cool air here, the falls crashing down onto a great drop of dark red rocks and thickets of lush green trees and vegetation, flocks of birds wheeling above.

Getting There

Getting to Ouzoud is simplest by bus from Beni Mellal. There's a regular service to Azilal (a winding 63km), where you can generally pick up a taxi to the springs, after a little bargaining. There is also a bus twice a day from MARRAKESH along the old S508 road, which passes by Azilal.

On the way from Beni Mellal to Azilal, the road climbs almost straight up from the plain, zigzagging through the hills and crossing an immense dammed lake at **BIN EL OUIDANE**, where there's a small **1*A hotel**, the *Auberge du Lac* (no phone), with a bar, a good restaurant, and river fishing/swimming; beware that in winter it's cold, with hot water but no room heating. There's also a **campground**. One of the earliest (1948-55) and most ambitious of the country's irrigation schemes, the barrage has changed much of the land around Beni Mellal—formerly as dry and barren as the phosphate plains to the west—and provides much of central Morocco's electricity.

AZILAL is just a small village, with transportation links. If you find yourself stranded, there's a single **2*A hotel**, the *Tanout*, on the Beni Mellal road out.

The Cascades

OUZOUD is a popular place to camp in the summer, the air cooled by the falls and altitude, and it is refreshingly uncommercialized. At the roadside, there is a small **café-hotel**, but to get the most from the location you really need to camp. Two or three seasonal and makeshift **campgrounds** (open March–September) are poised on trellis-covered terraces right above the springs. Both sell drinks and hot food, and, with a predominantly young Moroccan/European clientèle, are very relaxed.

From the campgrounds, a series of signposted trails wind down to the valley and the great basins below the **cascades**. You can swim in one of these—a fabulous natural pool, and if you don't mind the occasional monkey (still a fairly common sight in this stretch of hills), you could pitch a tent under the oak and pomegranate trees.

The most memorable hike, however, is to go beyond the lower pools to the so-called **"Mexican Village"**—a fascinating place connected by semi-underground passages. To get there, follow the path down to the lower pools and you will see a path climbing up on the left, past a farmhouse and up to the top of the plain. Follow this path west. The village is sited on the slopes of the wooded hills, about 1km along the path (which drops to a small stream before climbing up to the houses). Tourists are very much a novelty.

On from Ouzoud—and into the High Atlas

Without your own vehicle, it's easiest to backtrack to Azilal, picking up a bus there to Beni Mellal or (if you time it right) Marrakesh. Continuing **north, past Ouzoud**, a very poor *piste*—with no buses and occasional tourist traffic—cuts through to join up with the main P24 Marrakesh-Beni Mellal road.

If you're into a spot of High Atlas exploration, and especially if you've read Ernst Gellner's anthropological study, *Saints of the Atlas*, you might be tempted by one of the **pistes south from the S508**. These lead into the **Irhil M'Goun** mountains, a remote region, populated in part by transhumant shepherds who bring their flocks up here in summer from the oases beyond the Atlas ranges. Center of the region (and Gellner's study) is ZAOUIA AHANESAL.

There are two possible approaches. The first is at Bin el Ouidane, where a small road turns off to OUAOUIZARNT, crosses to the south of the lake and then turns into an extremely rough road, practicable only by jeep or truck. This winds through the mountains for some 70km before reaching Ahanesal, passing ZAOUIA TEMGAL (after 40km), above which are some strange rock formations shaped like a Gothic cathedral and known as such: **La Cathédrale Des Rochers.**

Alternatively—and much easier—there's a dirt track southeast of AZILAL leading to the village of AÏT MEHAMMED and on to TAMDA, which joins the *piste* running south from Ahanesal. Continuing up into the Central Atlas from Aït Mehammed, a difficult *piste* leads to the **Bou Goumez valley**—a possible hiking/climbing base for the 4000m peaks of the **Irhil M'Goun**, the highest in Morocco outside the Toubkal *massif.* If you're interested, Mohammed Achari (address: Imelghas, Aït Bou Goumez, Azilal) is a **mountain guide** and has mules for rent.

South to Marrakesh: Demnate

Having come as far as Azilal and the cascades, it is easier to continue along this secondary road to Marrakesh—in any case it's the more interesting one—rather than try and cut back onto the main route from Beni Mellal.

You'll probably have to change buses along the way at **DEMNATE**, a walled market town whose **Sunday souk** is by far the largest in the region and an interesting, unaffected event you should try to attend, if possible. It is held just outside the ramparts, the stalls spreading out into the town streets with their used clothes and other goods, together with enormous stacks of fresh produce. There is a small **hotel** here, close by the bus station, and if you have the time and the transportation, a road up above the town climbs after 6½km to a curious-looking natural bridge—**Imi n'Ifri**. Close to a series of springs, which account for the Demnate Valley's prosperous and intense cultivation, this is the site of a large *moussem* held two weeks after the Aid el Kebir.

The land between Demnate and Marrakesh is generally poor and rocky, distinguished only by sporadic clusters of farmhouses or shepherds' huts. If you take the bus, it might follow either of the routes to Marrakesh—via Tamelelt (where you rejoin the P24) or a perfectly well paved road via Tazzerte and Sidi Rahhal.

Given the choice, go for the latter. An old Glaoui village, **TAZZERTE** is fronted by four crumbling Kasbahs, from which the clan (see *The High Atlas* for its history) used to control the region and the caravan routes to the north. There is a small Monday market held here, and a larger one on Fridays at **SIDI RAHHAL**, 7km farther down. Sidi Rahhal, named after its *marabout,* is also a point of significant local pilgrimage and host to an important, week-long *moussem* (flexible date in the summer). The saint, in whose honor the festivities take place, has an unusual Judeo-Muslim tradition. He seems to have lived in the fifteenth century, but the stories told about him are all time-less in their evocations of magic and legend. The most popular ones recount how he had the power to conduct himself and other creatures through the air—a "talent" which led to a minor incident involving the Koutoubia minaret in Marrakesh, whose upper floor one of his followers supposedly knocked down with his knee.

Coming into Marrakesh from either Demnate or Beni Mellal, you skirt part of the huge **palmery** which encloses the northern walls of the city. Arriving by bus, you will almost certainly find yourself at the main **bus station** by Bab Doukkala—a ten-minute walk from the center of Gueliz (or the Ville Nouvelle), or twenty minutes (or an 8–10dh taxi ride) from Place Djemaa el Fna and the Medina.

travel details

Trains

Fes–Meknes Seven daily in each direction (around 45 min.).

Fes–Rabat/Casablanca Six daily (around 4½–5 hr./6 hr.); all via Meknes, Sidi Kacem (2½ hr.), Kenitra (3½ hr.) and Salé (4 hr.).

Fes–Taza/Oujda Four daily (2–2¼ hr./5¾–6 hr.).

Fes–Tangier Three daily (around 6 hr.); all via Meknes, Sidi Kacem (3½ hr.), and Asilah (5 hr.).

Fes/Marrakesh Three daily via Marrakesh (around 11½ hr.).

Meknes–Marrakesh No direct bus.

Buses

From Meknes Fes (hourly; 50 min.); Larache/Tangier (2 daily; 5½ hr./7 hr.); Rabat (3; 4 hr.); Ouezzane (2; 4 hr.); Chaouen (1; 5½ hr.); Azrou (4; 3½ hr.); Midelt (1; 5½ hr.); Beni Mellal/Marrakesh (1; 6 hr./9 hr.).

From Fes Chaouen (2; 5 hr.); Mdiq (1; 5 hr.); Larache/Tangier (2; 4½ hr./6 hr.); Rabat (6; 5½ hr.); Casa (8; 7 hr.); Taza (3; 2½ hr.); Al Hoceima (1; 11½ hr.); Sefrou (3; 1½ hr.); Immouzer/Ifrane (5; 1 hr./1½hr.); Azrou (5; 2½ hr.); Midelt/Er

Rachidia (3; 5½ hr./8½ hr.); Beni Mellal/Marrakesh (3; 8½ hr./11 hr.).

From Sefrou Boulemane/Midelt (2 hr./5 hr.).

From Azrou Ifrane/Immouzer (4 daily; 1 hr./1½ hr.); Midelt/Er Rachidia (5; 2 hr./5 hr.); Khenifra/Kasba Tadla/Beni Mellal/Marrakesh (3; 3 hr./4 hr./4½ hr./7 hr.).

From Midelt Er Rachidia (2; 3 hr.), Oujda (1; 13hr.).

From Kasbah Tadla El Ksiba (3 daily; 20 min.); Beni Mella (4; 1 hr.).

From Beni Mellal Demnate (4 daily; 3 hr.); Marrakesh (6; 6 hr.).

Grands Taxis

From Meknes Regularly to Fes (40 min.) and Volubilis/Moulay Idriss (35 min.).

From Fes Regularly to Meknes, Sefrou (1 hr.), Immouzer/Ifrane (1 hr. 20 min./1 hr. 40 min.) and Taza (1 hr. 40 min.).

Other **local and Middle Atlas** routes are specified in the text.

Flights

From Fes Daily to Casablanca (and on from there to Marrakesh, etc.).

TELEPHONE CODES

AZROU ☎056	KHENIFRA ☎058
BENI MELLAL ☎048	MEKNES ☎05
FES ☎06	MIDELT ☎058
IFRANE ☎056	SEFROU ☎06

CHAPTER FOUR

THE WEST COAST: FROM RABAT TO ESSAOUIRA

This chapter takes in almost 500km of Morocco's **Atlantic Coast**, from Kenitra in the north, down to Essaouira in the south. It is, inevitably, a mix of influences, characters and landscapes. The central region, around **Rabat and Casablanca**, is the power base of the nation—the seat of its government and heartland of its industry and commerce. The two cities, together with the neighbouring towns of **Salé**, **Kenitra**, and **Mohammedia**, have a combined population of over 4 million, a fifth of the country's total. It is an urban escalation that has come almost wholly in this century. In 1900, Rabat was a straggling port with a population of 30,000 (today it is 518,000); Casablanca, today the largest Moroccan city (2,140,000) was a minor harbor town of 20,000 inhabitants.

Inevitably, given this rapid and immense development, it is French and postcolonial influences here which are dominant. Don't go to "Casa" (as it's popularly known) expecting it to "look Moroccan"—it doesn't; it looks much like Marseille. And likewise Rabat, which the French developed as a new capital to replace the old imperial centers of Fes and Marrakesh, and whose cafés and broad avenues are recognizably European. Neither of them may seem very compelling options; yet, if you want to get any real idea of what Morocco is all about—and of how most Moroccans now actually live—these, at some stage, are both places to stop. **Casa** is perhaps best visited after spending some time in the country—when you'll find its beach clubs and bars a novelty, and appreciate both its differences and its fundamentally Moroccan character. **Rabat**, on the other hand, is one of the best places to make for as soon as you arrive in the country: well connected by train with Tangier, Fes, and Marrakesh, and an easy cultural shift in which to gain some initial confidence. With the old port of **Salé**, facing Rabat across a river estuary, it also has some of Morocco's finest and oldest monuments, dating from the Almohad and Merenid dynasties.

As you move **south along the coast**, populations and towns thin out, as the road skirts a series of beaches and dunes, with the odd detour inland when (particularly between Safi and Essaouria) cliffs take hold. **Essaouira**, easily accessible from Marrakesh, is a long-established "travelers' resort," and remains the coastal highlight for most visitors to Morocco, blending as it does a slightly alternative feel with the air of a traditional provincial town. **El Jadida**, established as a beach resort by the French, is more the preserve of

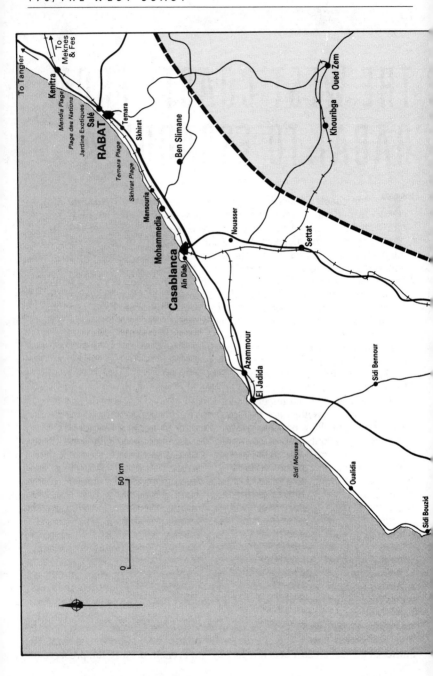

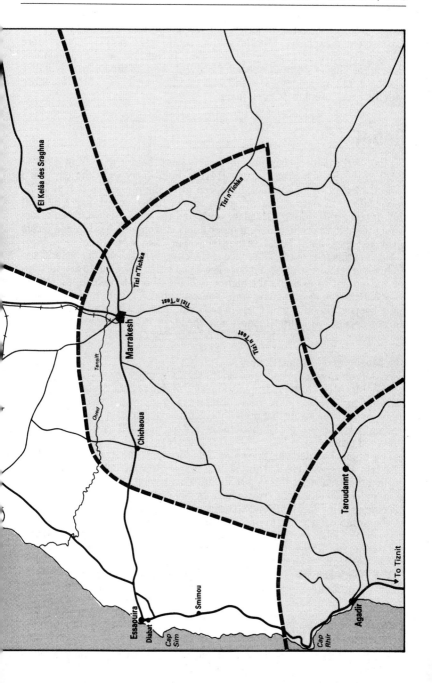

people from Casablanca; it sees fewer foreign visitors and, oddly, is more expensive and exclusive. **Oualidia**, to its south, has a similar, though more relaxed and small-scale, style. Finally, there is **Safi**, between El Jadida and Essaouira. This is a quirkier choice for a visit, with its predominantly industrial base, but a friendly place, and with excellent beaches nearby for those with the transportation to reach them.

Rabat

Capital of the nation since independence—and, before that, from 1912 to 1956, of the French Protectorate—**RABAT** is in many ways the city you'd expect: elegant in its spacious European grid, slightly self-conscious in its very civilized modern ways, and, as an administrative center, just a little bit dull. If you arrive during Ramadan, you'll find the main boulevards an astonishing night-long promenade—at other times, it would be hard to find a café open past ten at night. Rabat, as they tell you in Casa, is *provincial*.

None of this makes any difference to the city's very substantial historic and architectural interest, though it does leave you little choice but to act the tourist and go out to examine the sights; unlike Fes or Marrakesh, there's no involved city life to drift along with. You can, however, get around the place quite happily without a guide; talk in cafés with people who, for the most part, do not depend on tourist money; and spend an easy few days seeing the monuments and lying on the excellent neighboring beaches.

The Monuments—Some History

Rabat's **monuments**—more so than those of any other town—punctuate the span of Moroccan history. The inland plains of this region, designated *Maroc Utile* by the French, have been occupied and cultivated since Paleolithic times, and it is probable that both Phoenicians and Carthaginians established trading posts on the site of modern-day Rabat, endowed as it is with a low, sheltered estuary.

The original settlement, known as *Sala*, occupies the site of what is now **Chellah**. Here was created the southernmost **Roman** colony, lasting well beyond the breakup of the empire in Africa, and eventually forming the basis of an independent Berber state, which, by the eighth century, seems to have become of some local influence. Developing a code of government inspired by the Koran but adapted to Berber customs and needs, it represented a challenge to the Islamic orthodoxy of the **Arab** rulers of the interior. To stamp out the heresy, a *ribat* (the fortified monastery from which the city takes its name) was founded on the site of the present Kasbah.

The *ribat's* activities, a sort of Knights-Templar-style persecution, led to Chellah's decline—a process hastened in the eleventh century by the founding of a new town, **Salé**, across the estuary. With the arrival of the **Almohads** in the twelfth century, however, the Rabat Kasbah was rebuilt and a city again took form around it. The fort, renamed **Ribat el Fathi** (Stronghold of Victory), served as a launching point for the Almohads' Spanish campaigns, which by 1170, had brought virtually all of Andalusia back under Muslim rule. Under the Caliph **Yacoub el Mansour,** a new imperial capital was begun. The greatest of Almohad builders, el Mansour was responsible for the superb **Oudaia Gate** of the Kasbah, for **Bab er Rouah** at the southwest edge of town, and for initiating the construction of the **Hassan Mosque.** The largest ever undertaken in Morocco, its minaret, standing high above the river, is still the city's great landmark. Mansour also erected a vast enclave of walls, stretching over 5000m in length—but neither his vision nor his success in maintaining a Spanish empire were to be lasting. He left the Hassan Mosque unfinished, and only in the last sixty years has the city expanded to fill its dark circuit of *pisé* walls.

Its significance dwarfed after Mansour's death by the imperial cities of Fes, Meknes, and Marrakesh, Rabat fell into neglect. Sacked by the Portuguese, it was little more than a village when, as New Salé, it was resettled by seventeenth-century Andalusian refugees. In this revived form, however, it entered into an extraordinary period of international piracy and local autonomy. Its corsair fleets, **the Sallee Rovers,** specialized in the plunder of merchant ships returning to Europe from West Africa and the Spanish Americas, but on occasion also raided as far afield as Plymouth, England and the Irish coast— where they took captive whole village communities. Defoe's Robinson Crusoe began his captivity "carry'd prisoner into Sallee, a Moorish port," and it is estimated than in a single decade (1620–30), over a thousand ships were seized. The Andalusians, owing no loyalty to the Moorish sultans and practically impregnable within their Kasbah perched high on a rocky bluff above the river, established their own pirate state, the **Republic of the Bou Regreg**. They rebuilt the Medina below the Kasbah in a style reminiscent of their homes in Spanish Badajoz, dealt in arms with the English and French, and even accepted European consuls.

With the accession of Moulay Rashid, and of his successor, Moulay Ismail, the town reverted to official government control, but the nature of its activity was little changed. As late as 1829, an Austrian ship is recorded as having been forced into the port and sacked.

Arriving, Orientation, and Hotels

With its **Medina** and French-built **Ville Nouvelle** bounded by the river and old Almohad walls, central Rabat never feels like a big city. It's an easy place in which to find your way around, too, with its points of interest all within walking distance.

Arriving by train—by far the simplest approach—you're at once in the heart of the Ville Nouvelle: the two main thoroughfares (**Avenue Mohammed V** and **Avenue Allal Ben Abdallah**) lead up from the station to **Bd. Hassan II** and, walled off beyond, the **Medina**.

The main **bus terminal**, and the **grands taxis** leaving for Casa, are now located some ways out of town, in Place Zerktouni—by the road junction for Casa and Beni Mellal. To get to the middle of town from here (or vice versa), you'll have to take a local bus (#30 and others stop along Bd. Hassan II by the *Hôtel Majestic*) or a *petit taxi* (5dh or so—usually metered—for up to three people). **Grands taxis** for Casa cost only a couple of dirhams more than the

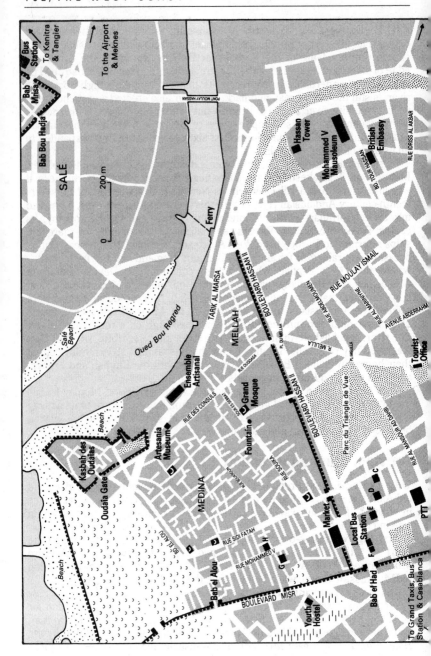

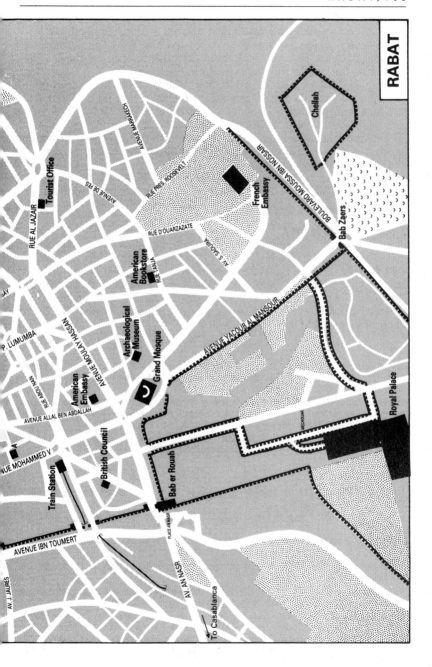

RABAT

Chellah

AVENUE MARRAKECH

Tourist Office

RUE AL JAZAIR

RUE PRES. ROOSEVELT

RUE DE FES

AVENUE DE FES

French
Embassy

RUE D'OUARZAZATE

BOULEVARD MOUSSA IBN NOSSAIR

Bab Zaers

AV. S SOUIRA

American
Bookstore

RUE TANJA

JAY

P. LUMUMBA

AVENUE MOULAY HASSAN

Archaeological
Museum

Grand Mosque

AVENUE YACOUB AL MANSOUR

RUE ABOU NAN

American
Embassy

AVENUE ALLAL BEN ABDALLAH

NUE MOHAMMED V

A

British Council

Bab er Rouah

Royal Palace

Train Station

AVENUE IBN TOUMERT

AV. J. JAURES

PLACE ANNASR

AV. AN NASR

To Casablanca

bus, and are considerably faster; just turn up at the stand and ask for a place—more or less continously through the day. Other *grands taxis*—to Tangier, Meknes, Fes, and local destinations like Skhirat and Bouknadel—leave from the lengthy and chaotic stand on Bd. Hassan II.

From the **Mohammed V Airport** (out towards Casablanca), buses run to the square outside the *Hôtel Terminus* (by the Rabat Ville train station); journey time is approximately 90 minutes. Departures **to the airport** from Rabat are (currently) at 5am, 6:30am, 8:30am, 10am, 12:30pm, 3:30pm, 6:30pm. Tickets are sold at the kiosk by the departure point, immediately before the bus leaves. *Grands taxis* are a very expensive alternative, unless you can split the fare between several people.

Local bus services leave from Bd. Hassan II. Buses #1, #2, and #4 run from here (via Allal Ben Abdallah) to Bab Zaer, by way of Chellah; #6 and #12 cross the bridge to Salé; and #17 heads south to Temara Beach.

Finding a Place to Stay

Accommodation can be a slight problem in midsummer and especially in July. Good rooms in the budget hotels tend to go early in the day, and by midafternoon many of the Medina places have inflated their prices to almost as high as those of a 2* hotel in the Ville Nouvelle. At these times, take the first place you're offered, and concentrate on the officially rated options.

Recommendations below are in roughly ascending price order. The better choices are keyed by letter on the main map.

MEDINA

Hôtel France, Hôtel Algers, Hôtel du Marche. These three are all on the second turnoff to the left on Rue Mohammed V, the extension of Avenue Mohammed V; continue on a bit and there are several more. None are especially inviting.

Hôtel el Alam (H), Hôtel Marrakech, Hôtel Regina. One street beyond the previous group and off to the right, these are on Rue Gebbali. *El Alam,* outrageously decorated, is usually very cheap; *Marrakech* is good but overpriced.

Hôtel Darna (I), 24 Bd. el Alou; ☎224.56. Just inside Bab el Alou at the far side of the Medina. By far the best in another small cluster of hotels. *2*A*.

VILLE NOUVELLE

Hôtel Majestic (F), 121 Bd. Hassan II; ☎229.97. Probably the best, cheap choice—when they have room. *1*A*.

Hôtel Central (B), 2 Rue el Basra; ☎221.31. Basic choice, nicely located by the *Hôtel Balima*. *1*A*.

Hôtel de la Paix (C), 2 Rue Ghazza; ☎229.26. Fair for its class and useful for single rooms. *2*A*.

Hôtel Splendide (D), 24 Rue Ghazza (formerly Rue du 18 Juin); ☎232.83. Large rooms—ask for one looking onto the garden. *2*A*.

Hôtel Gauloise (E), 1 Zankat Hims; ☎230.22. This, and the two hotels above, are the best value of a cluster of eight 2* hotels at the top of Av. Mohammed V. *2*B*.

Hôtel Balima (A), Rue Jakarta, just behind Av. Mohammed V; ☎216.71. This was Rabat's top hotel into the 1960s. Today, it is faded and superseded, but still has a deco grandeur—as well as absurdly cheap *suites*! Thami el Glaoui, Pasha of Marrakesh, stayed in one on his visits to the city in the 1950s. If you have the money, do the same; or just hang out in the hotel café—still the focus of the evening promenade. *3*B*.

Hôtel d'Orsay, 11 Av. Moulay Youssef/Place de la Gare; ☎613.19. Conveniently located behind the station. A bit pricey but a good alternative if the Balima is full. *3*B.*

YOUTH HOSTEL AND CAMPING

The **youth hostel** (*Auberge de Jeunesse*; 34 Bd. Misr; ☎257.69) is well-sited—just outside the Medina walls, a block to the north of Bd. Hassan II. However, standards of cleanliness generally leave a lot to be desired.

The nearest **campground** is across the river at Salé (see section on that town, following). An alternative is the campground 15km south at Temara Plage.

The Medina and Souks

Rabat's **Medina**—all that there was of the city until the French arrived in 1912—is a compact quarter, wedged on two sides by the sea and the river, on the others by the Almohad and Andalusian walls. It is not among the country's most interesting—open and orderly in comparison to those of Fes or Marrakesh—but coming here from the adjacent avenues of the modern capital is always a surprise. In appearance, it is still essentially the town created and settled in the seventeenth century by Muslim refugees from Spanish Badajoz; and with these external features intact, its way of life seems at once traditional and un-Western.

That this is possible—here and throughout the old cities of Morocco—is largely due to **Marshal Lyautey**, the first, and certainly the most sympathetic to the indigenous culture, of France's resident generals. Colonizing Algeria over the previous century, the French had destroyed most of the Arab towns, replacing their traditional structures (evolved through the needs of Islamic customs) with completely European plans. In Rabat, Lyautey found this system already in operation, the builders tearing down parts of the Medina for the construction of a new town and administrative quarters. Realizing the aesthetic loss—and perhaps, too, the arrogance of "Europeanization"—he ordered work to be halted and the Ville Nouvelle built outside the walls. It was a precedent accepted throughout the French and Spanish zones of the colony, a policy which inevitably created "native quarters," but one which also preserved continuity, maintained the nation's past, and, at least as Lyautey believed, showed the special relationship of the protectorate.

Into the Medina

The basic grid-like regularity of the Medina, cut by a number of long main streets, makes this a good place to get to grips with the feel of a Moroccan city. In plan it is largely traditional, with a main market street (**Rue Souika/ Souk es Sebbat**) running beside the Grand Mosque, and behind it a residential area scattered with smaller *souks* and "parish" mosques. The buildings, characteristically Andalusian in the style of Tetouan or Chaouen, are part stone and part whitewash, with splashes of yellow and turquoise and great, dark-wood, studded doors.

From **Bd. Hassan II,** a series of streets give access to the Medina, all of them leading more or less directly through the quarter, to emerge near the Kasbah and the old, hillside cemetery. The two on the left—**Rue**

Mohammed V and **Rue Sidi Fatah**—are really continuations of the main **Ville Nouvelle** avenues; flanked by working-class café-restaurants and cell-like hotels, though, their character is immediately different. Entering here, past a modern food market and a handful of stalls selling fruit, orange juice, and snacks, you can turn very shortly to the right and come out onto the cubicle shops of **Rue Souika**. Dominated by textiles and silverware along their first stretch, these give way to a concentration of *babouche* and other shoe stalls as you approach the Grand Mosque. They are all fairly everyday shops, not for the most part geared to tourists, though they are generally a bit on the expensive side; the cheaper goods, and the *joutia* (flea market) are off toward the river, around the old Jewish quarter of the Mellah. Along the way are few buildings of any particular interest, most of the medieval city (which predated that of the Andalusians on this site) having been destroyed by Portuguese raids in the sixteenth century. The **Grand Mosque**, founded by the Merenids in the fourteenth century, is a partial exception but has been considerably rebuilt—its minaret, for example, was only completed in 1939. Opposite, however, there is a small example of Merenid decoration in the stone facade of a public **fountain**, now forming the front of an Arabic bookstore.

The Mellah and Joutia

The most direct approach from Bd. Hassan II to the Grand Mosque is a broad, tree-lined, pedestrian way, about halfway up. Alternatively, continuing a couple of blocks (past the *Hôtel Rex*), you can go in by the Mellah, alongside Rue Ouqqasa. The poorest and most rundown area of the city, the **Mellah** no longer has a significant Jewish population, though some of its seventeen synagogues still survive in various forms. The only one active today is in a modern building, a block away in the Ville Nouvelle. The quarter itself, where all of the city's Jews were once required to live, was created only in 1808; the Jews previously owned several of the mansions along Rue des Consuls, a bit farther up. With its meat and produce markets, it looks a particularly impenetrable area, but it is worth walking through toward the river.

The **joutia**, or **flea market**, spreads out here along the streets below Souk es Sebbat, down to Bab el Bahr. There are clothes, pieces of machinery whose parts can no longer be replaced, and (something you don't see too often) a number of vendors hawking wonderful 1950s and 1960s movie posters, garishly illustrating titles like *Police Militaire* and *La Fille du Désert*.

Towards the Kasbah: Rue des Consuls

Beyond the Mellah, **heading toward the Kasbah**, you can walk out by **Bab el Bahr** and follow an avenue near the riverside up to the Oudaia Gate; to the left of this road is a small **crafts museum** (usually closed), to the right a pretty dull **Centre Artesanal.**

Rue des Consuls, a block inland, is a more interesting approach; like the Mellah, this, too, used to be a reserved quarter—the only street of the nineteenth-century city where European consulates were permitted. Many of the residency buildings survive, and there are also a few, impressive, old, merchants' *fondouks* in the alleys off to the left. The street, particularly at its upper end, is today largely a center for **rug and carpet shops** and on

Tuesday and Thursday mornings becomes a **souk,** with local people bringing carpets—new and old—to sell.

Rabat carpets, woven with very bright dyes (which, if vegetable-based, will fade with time), are traditionally a cottage industry in the Medina, though they're now usually produced in factories, one of which you can take a quick look at on the Kasbah's *platforme.*

The Kasbah des Oudaias

Site of the original *ribat,* and citadel of the Almohad, Merenid, and Andalusian towns, the **Kasbah des Oudaias** is a striking and evocative quarter. Its principal gateway, the Bab el Kasbah (or Oudaia Gate), is the most beautiful surviving in the Moorish world, and within its walls are one of the country's best craft museums and a perfect Andalusian garden. Even if you've just a few hours in Rabat between trains, you should at least make it here.

The Oudaia Gate

The **Oudaia Gate**, like all the great external monuments of Morocco, is of Almohad foundation. Built around 1195, concurrently with the Hassan Tower, it was inserted by Yacoub el Mansour within a line of walls already built by his grandfather, Abd el Moumen. The walls in fact extended well to its west, leading down to the sea at the edge of the Medina, and the gate cannot have been designed for any genuine defensive purpose—its function and importance must have been purely ceremonial. It was to be the heart of the Kasbah, its chambers acting as a courthouse and staterooms, with everything of importance taking place within its immediate confines. The **Souk el Ghezel**—the main commercial center of the medieval town with its wool and slave markets—was located just outside, while the original sultanate's palace stood immediately inside it.

The effect of the gate is startling. It doesn't impress so much by its size, which is not unusual for an Almohad structure, as by the visual strength and simplicity of its decoration. This is based on a typically Islamic rhythm, establishing a tension between the exuberant, outward expansion of the arches and the heavy, enclosing rectangle of the gate itself. Looking at the two for a few minutes, you begin to sense a kind of optical illusion—the shapes appear suspended by the great rush of movement from the center of the arch. The basic feature is, of course, the arch, which here is actually a sequence of three, progressively more elaborate ones: first, the basic horseshoe; then, two "filled" or decorated ones, the latter with the distinctive Almohad *darj w ktarf* patterning, a cheek-and-shoulder design somewhat like a fleur-de-lis. At the top, framing the design, is a band of geometric ornamentation, cut off in what seems to be an arbitrary manner but which again creates the impression of movement and continuation outside the gate.

The dominant motifs—scallop-shell-looking palm fronds—are also characteristically Almohad, though without any symbolic importance; in fact, there's very little that's symbolic in the European sense in any Islamic decoration, the object being merely to distract the eye sufficiently in order to allow (hopefully religious) contemplation.

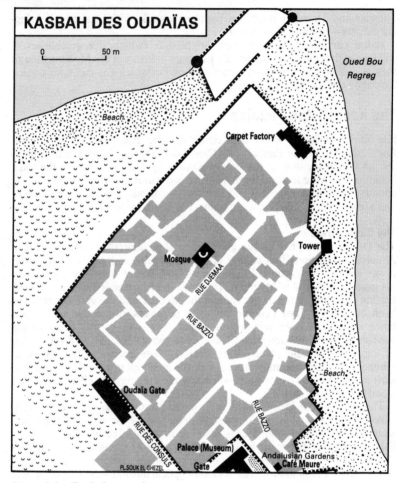

KASBAH DES OUDAÏAS

0 50 m

Oued Bou Regreg

Beach

Carpet Factory

Mosque

RUE DJEMAA

Tower

RUE BAZZO

Beach

Oudaïa Gate

RUE BAZZO

RUE DES CONSULS

Palace (Museum)

Andalusian Gardens

Café Maure'

PL.SOUK EL GHEZEL   Gate

Around the Kasbah

You can enter the **Kasbah** proper through the Oudaia Gate (or, if it's closed, the small gateway on the right), or by a lower, horseshoe arch at the base of the ceremonial stairway. This latter approach leads directly to the **Andalusian gardens** and **palace museum,** but you can also reach these fairly easily after a brief loop through the Kasbah.

An airy, village-like part of the city, the Kasbah is a pleasant quarter in which to wander—and not remotely dangerous or "closed to visitors," as the hustlers around the gate may try to suggest. Hardly more than 150m from one end to the other, it's not a place where you really need a guide; but if you're approached, talk to the hustlers, be easygoing, and explain you're only wandering down to *le platforme*. Hustling business isn't a lot of fun, and tourist arrogance can seem a just provocation.

Once inside the Oudaia Gate, it would actually be hard not to find the way down to the *platforme* since there's just one main street, **Rue Djemaa** (Street of the Mosque) which runs straight down to a broad belvedere/terrace commanding views of the river and sea. Along the way, you pass by the minaret of the **Kasbah Mosque**, the city's oldest mosque, founded in 1050, though considerably rebuilt in the eighteenth century by an English renegade known as Ahmed el Inglize—one of a number of European pirates who joined up with the Sallee Rovers.

El Inglizi was responsible, too, for several of the forts built below and around the **platforme**, their gun positions echoed across the estuary by those in Salé. The Bou Regreg (literally, Father of Reflection) is quite open at this point and it would appear to have left the corsair fleets vulnerable, harbored a little downstream, where the fishing boats today ferry people across to Salé beach. In fact, a long sandbank stretches submerged across the mouth of the estuary—a feature much exploited by the low-keeled pirate ships, which would draw the merchant ships in pursuit, only to leave them stranded within the sights of the city's cannon. This is action which you can still imagine, up here amid the low-lying alleys and the sea towers, though, as so often in Morocco, it is hard to come to terms with just how recent this past was.

From the *platforme* of the Kasbah, it is possible to climb down toward the **ocean beach**, crowded with local people throughout the summer, like the Salé beach across the water. Neither, however, is particularly inviting, and if you're more interested in swimming than in keeping your head above the water, you'd be better off going to the more relaxed sands at Bouknadel or Temara; in addition, the Rabat and Salé beaches are (unlike those of the resorts) almost exclusively used by men.

The Palace Museum and Gardens

Getting down to the **palace museum** and **gardens** is fairly straightforward: from the main Kasbah street just follow Rue Gazzo, which zigzags down toward them.

Depending on which fork you take, you'll either come out by the entrance to the palace or at the **Café Mauré**—beside the gardens. Oddly enough, the café is not at all "Moorish," but it's a wonderful place in which to retreat: high on a terrace overlooking the river, serving excellent mint tea, Turkish coffee, and great trays of traditional pastries. It is used as much by Moroccans as tourists, and it's ordinarily priced.

The Palace itself is seventeenth-century, one of many built for the notorious Moulay Ismail, the first sultan since Almohad times to force a unified control over the country. Ismail, whose base was at Meknes, gave Rabat—or New Salé, as it was then known—a relatively high priority. Having subdued the pirates' republic, he took over the Kasbah as a garrison for the Oudaias—Saharan tribesmen who had accepted military service in return for tax exemption, and who formed an important part of his mercenary army. This move was in part because they proved uncontrollable in Fes or Meknes, but it also was an effective way of ensuring that the pirates using the port below kept up their tribute in a constant supply of slaves and booty.

Elegantly converted to a **Museum of Moroccan Arts** (open 8am–noon and 4–6pm; closed Tues.), the palace is an interesting building in its own right. Its design is classic: a series of reception rooms grouped around a central court, giving access to the private quarters where you can take a look at the small *hammam*—a feature of all noble mansions. The displays within the main building include collections of Berber and Arab jewelry from most of the regions of Morocco, while the main reception hall has been furnished in the styles of nineteenth-century Rabat and Fes. All of this is well labeled and fairly obvious, though there is a room just on your left as you're leaving which is often kept shut except by request; once the palace mosque, it houses a very fine display of local carpets.

The collections—including groups of traditional costumes, which again reveal the startling closeness of a medieval past—are continued in a series of rooms bordering on the beautiful "**Andalusian garden**." Occupying the old palace grounds, this was actually constructed by the French in the present century—though its form is entirely in the Spanish-Andalusian tradition, with deep, sunken beds of shrubs and flowering annuals. If you've come here from Granada, it is illuminating to compare this (the authentic Moorish concept) with the neat box hedges with which the Alhambra has been restored. But such historical authenticity aside, this is really a delightful place, full of the scent of datura, bougainvillea, and a multitude of herbs and flowers. It has a definite role, too, in modern Rabat, as a meeting place for women, who gather here in dozens of small groups on a Friday or Sunday afternoon.

The Hassan Mosque and Mohammed V Mausoleum

The most ambitious of all Almohad buildings, the **Hassan Mosque and Tower** dominates almost every view of the capital—a majestic sight from the Kasbah, from Salé, or glimpsed as you arrive across the river by train. If it had been completed, this would (in its time) have been the second largest mosque in the Islamic world, outflanked only by the one in Smarra, Iraq. Even today its size seems a novelty.

The tower, or minaret, was begun by Yacoub el Mansour in 1195—at the same time as the Koutoubia in Marrakesh and the Giralda in Seville—and it is one of the few Moroccan buildings which approach the European idea of monumentality. This is due in part to its site, on a level above the river and most of the city, but perhaps equally to its unfinished solidity. The other great Moroccan minarets, perfectly balanced by their platform decoration and lanterns, are left "hanging" as if with no particular weight or height. The Hassan Tower, with no such movement, stands firmly rooted in the ground.

There is also the poignancy of its ruin. Designed by el Mansour as the centerpiece of the new capital and as a celebration of his great victory over the Spanish kings at Alarcos, its construction seems to have been more or less abandoned at his death in 1199. The tower was probably left much as it appears today. The **mosque**, roofed in cedar, was actually used for some years, though its extent must always have seemed an elaborate folly. Morocco's most important mosque, the Kairaouine in Fes, is less than half its size but has long served a much greater population, with adequate space for

20,000 worshipers. Bearing in mind that it is only men who gather for the weekly Friday prayer—when a town traditionally comes together in its Grand Mosque—Rabat would have needed a population of well over 100,000 to make adequate use of the Hassan's capacity. As it was, the city never really took off under the later Almohads and Merenids, and when Leo Africanus came here in 1600, he found no more than a hundred households, gathered for security within the Kasbah.

The **minaret** is unusually positioned at the center rather than the northern corner of the rear of the mosque. Some 50m tall in its present state, it would probably have been around 80m if finished to normal proportions—a third again the height of Marrakesh's Koutoubia. Despite its apparent simplicity, it is perhaps the most complex of all Almohad structures. Each facade is different, with a distinct combination of patterning, yet the whole intricacy of blind arcades and interlacing curves is based on just two formal designs. On the south and west faces these are the *darj w ktarf* of the Oudaia Gate; on the north and east are the *shabka* (net) motif, an extremely popular form adapted by the Almohads from the lobed arches of the Cordoba Grand Mosque—and still in modern use. Although both are austere in comparison to some of the earlier exterior decoration of the Almoravids, it is hard to reconcile their exuberant and technically exacting display with the history and culture of a "fanatical" puritan movement.

The Mohammed V Mausoleum

Facing the tower—in an assertion of Morocco's historical independence and continuity—are the **Mosque and Mausoleum of Mohammed V**, begun on the sultan's death in 1961, and dedicated six years later. The **mosque**, extending between a pair of stark white pavillions, gives a somewhat foreshortened idea of how the whole site must once have appeared, roofed in its traditional green tiles.

The **mausoleum**, designed, oddly, by a Korean architect, was one of the great prestige projects of modern Morocco. Its brilliantly surfaced marbles and spiraling designs, however, seem to pay homage to traditional Moroccan techniques, while failing to capture their rhythms and unity. It is, nevertheless, an important shrine for Moroccans, and one which non-Muslims are permitted to visit. You file past the magnificently costumed royal guards to an interior balcony; the tomb lies below, groups of old men squatting beside it, reading constantly from the Koran.

Around the Ville Nouvelle—and Chellah

French in construction, style and feel, the **Ville Nouvelle** provides the main focus of Rabat's life, above all in the cafés and promenades of the broad, tree-lined Avenue Mohammed V. There's a certain grandeur in some of the old, *Mauresque* public buildings here, built with as much attention toward impressing as any earlier epoch, but it is the Almohad walls and gates, Chellah (see the following section), and the excellent archaeological museum which hold the most interest.

The Walls and Gates

More-or-less complete sections of the **Almohad walls** run right down from the Kasbah to the royal palace and beyond—an extraordinary monument to Yacoub el Mansour's vision.

Along its course four of the original **gates** survive. Three—**Bab el Alou, Bab Zaer** and **Bab el Had**—are very modest. **Bab er Rouah** (Gate of the Wind), however, is on a totally differrent level, recalling and in many ways rivaling the Oudaia. Contained within a massive stone bastion, it again achieves the tension of movement (the sunlike arches contained within a square of Koranic inscription) and a similar balance between simplicity and ornament. The east side, which you approach from outside the walls, is the main facade, and must have been designed as a monumental approach to the city; the shallow-cut, floral relief between arch and square is reputed to be the finest anywhere in Morocco. Inside, you can appreciate the gate's archetypal defensive structure—the three domed chambers aligned to force a sharp double turn. Generally locked, they are used for occasional exhibitions.

From Bab er Rouah, it's about a fifteen-minute walk down toward the last Aomohad gate, the much-restored **Bab Zaer**, and the entrance to the **Necropolis of Chellah.** On the way, you pass a series of modern gates leading off to the vast enclosures of the **royal palace**—which is really more a collection of palaces, built mainly in the nineteenth century—and, off to the left (opposite the *Hôtel Chellah*), the Archaeological Museum.

The Archaeological Museum

Rabat's Archaeological Museum (open daily except Tues. 8:30am–noon and 2:30–6pm) is by far the most important in Morocco—small (surprisingly so in a country which saw substantial Phoenician and Carthaginian settlement and three centuries of Roman rule) but with one exceptionally beautiful collection.

This is a series of **Roman bronzes** from the first and second centuries AD, found mainly at the provincial capital of Volubilis (see p.124) but including a few from Chellah and the small coastal colonies of Banasa and Thamusidia. They are actually displayed in an annex to the main part of the museum, and you may have to ask for it to be opened and lit. Highlights include superb figures of a guard dog and a rider, and two magnificent portrait heads, reputedly those of Cato the Younger (Caton d'Utique) and Juba II—the last significant ruler of the Romanized Berber kingdoms of Mauretania and Numidia before the assertion of direct, imperial rule.

The Chellah Necropolis

The most beautiful of Moroccan ruins, **Chellah** is a startling sight as you emerge from the long avenues of the Ville Nouvelle. Walled and towered, it is a much larger enclosure than the map suggests, and it seems for a moment as if you've come upon a second Medina. It is, in fact, long uninhabited—since 1154, when it was abandoned in favor of Salé across the Bou Regreg. But for almost a thousand years prior to that, Chellah (or *Sala Colonia*, as it was known) had been a thriving city and port, one of the last to sever links with the Roman Empire, and the first to proclaim Moulay Idriss founder of

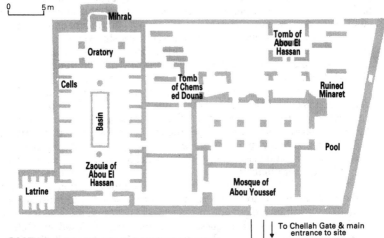

0 5m

Mihrab

Oratory

Cells

Basin

Tomb of
Chems
ed Douna

Tomb of
Abou El
Hassan

Ruined
Minaret

Pool

Zaouia of
Abou El
Hassan

Latrine

Mosque of
Abou Youssef

To Chellah Gate & main
entrance to site

CHELLAH: THE SANCTUARY

Morocco's original Arab dynasty. An apocryphal local tradition maintains that the Prophet himself prayed at a shrine here.

Under the Almohads, the site was already a royal burial ground, but most of what you see today, including the gates and enclosing wall, is the legacy of the Merenid sultan, **Abou el Hassan** (1331–51). The greatest of Merenid rulers, conquering and controlling the Maghreb as far east as Tunis, Abou el Hassan, "The Black Sultan," was also their most prolific builder. In addition to Chellah, he was responsible for important mosques in Fes and Tlemcen, as well as the beautiful *medersas* of Salé and Meknes.

The **main gate** here is the most surprising of his monuments, its turreted bastions almost Gothic in appearance. The base is still recognizably Almohad, but each element has become inflated, and the combination of simplicity and solidity has gone. In its original state, with bright-colored marble and tile decoration, the effect must have been incredibly gaudy—a bit like the nineteenth-century palaces you see today in Fes and Marrakesh. An interesting technical innovation, however, are the stalactite (or "honeycomb") corbels which form the transition from the bastion's semioctagonal towers to their square platforms; this was later to become a feature of Merenid building. The Kufic inscription above the gate is from the Koran and begins with the invocation: "I take refuge in Allah, against Satan, the stoned one. . . ."

There are usually a number of guides hanging around the gate, but once again hiring them is not mandatory. Admission charge is the standard 3dh, and once inside, things are clear enough. Off to your left, in a state of long-suspended excavation, are the main **Roman ruins,** including the visible outlines of a forum, temple, and craftsmen's quarter. The **Islamic ruins** are down to the right, within a second inner sanctuary approached along a broad path through half-wild gardens of banana, orange, and ancient fig trees, sunflowers, dahlias, and datura plants. Their most prominent and picturesque feature is a tall stone-and-tile minaret, a ludicrously oversized stork's nest perched invariably on its summit. Storks, along with swallows and crows, have a certain sanctity in Morocco, and their presence on minarets is a sign of good fortune.

The **Sanctuary** itself seems to be a slightly confusing cluster of tombs and ruins, but it is essentially just two buildings: the **mosque,** built on the site by the second Merenid sultan, Abou Youssef (1258–86), and a **zaouia,** or mosque-monastery, added along with the enclosure walls by Abou el Hassan.

You enter directly into the *sahn,* or courtyard, of **Abou Youssef's Mosque,** a small and presumably private structure built as a funerary dedica-tion. It is now very much in ruins, though you can make out the colonnades of the inner prayer hall with its *mihrab* to indicate the direction of prayer. Off to the right is its minaret, now reduced to the level of the mosque's roof. Behind, both within and outside the sanctuary enclosure, are a series of scat-tered **royal tombs**—each aligned so that the dead, dressed in white and lying on their right hand sides, may face Mecca to await the Call of Judgment. Abou Youssef's tomb has not been identified, but you can find those of both **Abou el Hassan** and his wife **Shams ed Douna.** Hassan's is contained within a kind of pavillion whose external wall retains its decoration, the *darj w ktarf* motif set above three small arches in a design very similar to that of the Hassan Tower. Shams ed Douna, (Morning Sun) has only a tomb-stone—a long, pointed rectangle covered in a mass of verses from the Koran. A convert from Christianity, Shams was the mother of Abou el Hassan's rebel son, Abou Inan, whose uprising led to the sultan's death as a fugitive in the High Atlas during the winter of 1352.

The **Zaouia** is in a much better state of preservation, its structure, like Abou el Hassan's *medersas,* that of a long, central court enclosed by cells, with a smaller oratory or prayer hall at the end. Each of these features are quite recognizable, along with those of the latrine, preceding the main court, for the worshipers' purification. There are fragments of *zellij* (mosaic tile-work) on some of the colonnades and on the minaret, which again give an idea of its original brightness, and there are traces too of the *mihrab's* elabo-rate stucco decoration. Five-sided, the **mihrab** has a narrow passageway (now blocked with brambles) leading to the rear—built so that pilgrims might make seven circuits around it. This was once believed to give the equivalent merit of the *hadj,* the trip to Mecca: a tradition, with that of Muhammad's visit, most likely invented and propagated by the *zaouia's* keep-ers to increase their revenue.

Off to the right and above the sanctuary enclosure are a group of **koub-bas**—the domed tombs of local saints or *marabouts*—and beyond them a **spring pool,** enclosed by low, vaulted buildings. This is held sacred, along with the eels which lurk in its waters, and women bring hard-boiled eggs to invoke assistance in fertility and childbirth.

Practicalities

For a capital city, Rabat's potential for fun—and even for eating well—is not very impressive. The city's practical attractions rest mainly in its **cafés** (the *Hôtel Balima's*, in particular) and in its **access to beaches** (see the sections following). As the capital, though, it does have embassy and **consulate** facilities, for visas and official business, and a reasonable range of **bookstores** (see the "Directory").

Restaurants, Cafés, and Nightlife

As ever, the cheapest restaurants are to be found **in the Medina**. Just on the edge of the quarter, down Rue Mohammed V, and along Rue Souika, there are a string of good everyday café-restaurants—clean enough, and serving regular Moroccan fare. They are excellent value at lunchtime, when many have fixed price meals for the office and shop workers. Alternatively, for only a few dirhams, you can pick up a range of snacks and juices just inside the Medina walls (by the **market** on our map).

In the **Ville Nouvelle** most of the better-value places are around the train station and Avenue Moulay Youssef (the diagonal street behind it). *Restaurant l'Oasis* (7 Rue Al Osquofiah, close to the train station) serves well-prepared and inexpensive Moroccan food. *Le Clef*, just off Av. Moulay Youssef, is slightly classier, but recommended. So too (in the 30–40dh range), are *Restaurant Saadi* (87 Av. Allal Ben Abdallah), *Les Fouquets* (285 Av. Mohammed V) and the *Balima restaurant* (on Av. Mohammed V). Except during Ramadan, all tend to stop serving around 9:30–10pm. If you want a break from Moroccan food, there's an excellent Lebanese restaurant, the *Saïdoune*, set back in a mall off Av. Mohammed V, opposite the *Hôtel Terminus*, and a number of Chinese places (try *Le Pagode*, 5 Rue de Baghdad, or *Le Mandarin*, 44 Av. Abdel Krim El Khattabi).

Both Mohammed V and Allal Ben Abdallah avenues have some excellent **cafés**, though **bars** (outside of the main hotels) are few and far between. The *Hôtel Balima* is as good a place as any. It tends to stay open late, if there is clientele, and it is popular with Moroccans—many of whom come to watch Sky Channel on its TV. When the *Balima* is closed, about your only **late-night options** are the European-style **disco-bars** around Place de Melilla (to the right of the main park, below Bd. Hassan II). The *Baghdad Bar* (Zankat Tanto) might also fill the odd hour.

Directory

Airlines *Royal Air Maroc* is just down from the train station on Av. Mohammed V; *Air France* is on the same avenue at no. 281; *Iberia* at no. 104 (2nd floor). See p.184 for details of transportation to/from the airport.

American Express had an office in the *Rabat Hilton*, but the hotel is currently closed for refurbishment and *AmEx* temporarily unrepresented. Check with the tourist office (see below) for any change. Otherwise, Casablanca has the nearest office.

Banks Most are concentrated along Av. Allal Ben Abdallah and Av. Mohammed V. The BMCE (daily 10am–2pm and 4–8pm) have offices at 241 Av. Mohammed V and at the port train station; they handle *VISA/Mastercard*, travelers' checks, and cash.

Beaches Nearest are the Kasbah and Salé beaches, with the latter best reached by the ferry leaving from below the Mellah. For clearer waters, head by bus to either Plage des Nations or Temara, detailed in the section following Salé.

Books The *American Bookstore* (Rue Tanja: see map) has a good selection of Penguin novels, etc., along with an enterprising shelf on Moroccan architecture, Islam, and some of Paul Bowles's translations of Moroccan fiction. You can get Moroccan Arabic-French phrasebooks from several of the bookstores along Av. Mohammed V.

Car rental *Leasing Cars*, usually the cheapest option, have an office in Casa (see p.211) but not in Rabat. Here, you're dependent on the usual standards: *Hertz* (467 Av. Mohammed V; ☎344.75),*Avis* (7 Rue Abou Faris Al Mairini; ☎697.59), and *Marloc/InterRent* (inside the *Hôtel Tour Hassan*, Av. Annegai; ☎223.228). *Tourist Cars* (inside the *Hôtel Rex*, 1 Rue de Nador; ☎241.10) may be able to offer slightly better rates.

Car repairs Try *Concorde* (6 Av. Allal Ben Abdallah) or, particularly for Renaults, the garage at 14 Av. Misr.

Embassies and Consulates *U.S.* (2 Av. de Marrakesh—near the far end of Allal Ben Abdallah; ☎62.265); *Canada* (13 Zankat Joafar Essadik; ☎71.375); *Great Britain* (17 Bd. Tour Hassan; ☎20.905); *Ireland* (representation c/o Britain); *Australia* (representation c/o Canada). Most of these are open from around 8:30–11:30am, Mon.–Fri., though you can phone at any time in an emergency. For **Algerian visas**, you'll need to go to the *Special Mission for Algerian Affairs* (8 Zankat Azrou, just off Av. de Fes; open Mon.–Fri. 9:30am–2:30pm). This is straightforward enough, and if you turn up at 8:30am, you should be able to collect your visa the same day: take along four passport photographs and the 60dh fee. **Tunisian visas** are issued on the spot at the Tunisian Consulate (Av. de Fes); 26dh for a week, 34dh a month.

Galleries Unusual for Morocco, Rabat has a number of worthwhile art galleries, showing works by contemporary artists. *L'Atelier* (16 Rue Annaba) is the major dealer; try also *Galerie Marsam* (6 Rue Oskofiah) and *Galerie Le Mamoir* (7 Rue Baitlahm).

Libraries Both the *American Embassy* (Annex on Av. Allal Ben Abdallah) and the *British Council* (6 Av. Moulay Youssef) have library rooms where you can walk in and read newspapers and magazines. They can also put you in touch with people if you want to take **lessons in Moroccan Arabic**.

Hiking maps Topographic maps used to be sold, on production of a passport, at the *Division de la Cartographie*, Ministère de l'Agriculture et de la Réforme Agraire (MARA), 31 Av. Moulay Hassan. At present all sales of survey maps are suspended—but this may change. If you are planning to hike in the Atlas, the office may still be worth a call.

Police Central office in Rue Soekarno, a couple of blocks from Av. Mohammed V. ☎19.

Post office The *PTT Centrale*—24 hr. a day for phones—is halfway down Av. Mohammed V. The *poste restante* section is across the road from the main building. The PTT also maintains a small **philatelic museum**, with displays and sales of Moroccan stamps.

Public baths Beside the *Hôtel Rex*, just off Bd. Hassan II.

Tourist offices *ONMT* (22 Av. Al Jazair); *Syndicat d'Initiative* (Rue Patrice Lumumba); both are open Mon.–Sat. 8am–noon, with the *Syndicat* open on weekday afternoons as well. The *ONMT Dépôt* in Av. Moulay Ismail (next to a branch of the Banque Populaire, a short walk from Place Melilla) has a "cave" full of the whole range of Moroccan tourist posters, and will give you as many as you can carry away.

Salé

Although it is now essentially a suburb of Rabat, **SALÉ** was the preeminent of the two right through the Middle Ages, from the decline of the Almohads to the town's uneasy alliance in the pirate republic of Bou Regreg. Today, largely neglected since the French creation of a capital in Rabat, it looks and feels very distinct. The spread of a Ville Nouvelle outside its walls has been restricted to a small area around the bus station and the north gates, and the *souks* and life within its medieval limits remain surprisingly traditional.

From Rabat you can cross the river by **boat** (see the map), or take a **bus** (#6 or #12) from Bd. Hassan II. The boats charge one dirham per person and drop you close to the Salé beach, a lively stretch, though less enticing at close quarters; from here it's a steep walk up to **Bab Bou Haja**, one of the main town gates. Both buses drop you at an open terminal just below the train station, opposite another major gate, **Bab Fes**, which leads straight toward the *souks*.

Salé has a basic and somewhat shadeless **campground**, *Camping de Salé*, at its beach, and a small **hotel**, the *Saadiens*, by the bus station. But unless you want to use the campground as a base for Rabat, there seems little reason to stay. It is an interesting town to wander through for an afternoon, and you can eat at one of the many workers' **cafés** along Rue Kechachin, but, if anything, its streets empty even earlier than Rabat's.

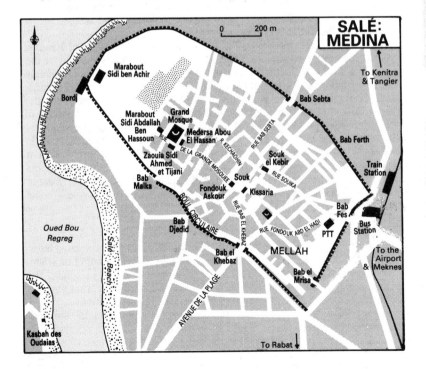

Into the Medina: the *Souks*

The most interesting point to enter Salé's Medina is through **Bab Mrisa**, just south of the bus terminal. The gate's name—"of the small harbor"—recalls the marine arsenal which used to be sited within the walls, and explains the gate's unusual height. A channel running here from the Bou Regreg has long silted up, but in medieval times it allowed merchant ships to sail right into town. The device must have been a useful defense during the years of the pirate republic, though in fact Salé was much less of a corsair base than the Rabat Kasbah and its trading traditions went back some centuries before the arrival of the Andalusians; in 1600, Leo Africanus reported the presence here of ships from Genoa, Flanders, Venice, and England. Bab Mrisa itself is a very early Merenid structure of the 1270s, its design and motifs (palmettes enclosed by floral decoration; bands of Kufic inscription and *darj w ktarf*, etc.) still inherently Almohad in tone.

Inside the gate you'll find yourself in a small square at the bottom of the old Mellah quarter. Turning to the left, and continuing close to the walls, you come out after around 350m at another gate, **Bab Bou Haja**, beside a part of a small park. If you want to explore the *souks*—the route outlined below— take the road along the left hand side of the park. If not, continue on just inside the walls to a long open area; as this starts to narrow into a lane (about 40m farther down) veer to your right into the town. This should bring you out more or less at the **Grand Mosque,** opposite which (see below) is the **Medersa of Abou el Hassan.**

The park-side street from Bab Bou Haja is known as **Rue Bab el Khabaz** (Street of the Bakers Gate), a busy little lane which emerges right at the heart of the **souks** by a small *kissaria*—or covered market—devoted mainly to textiles. Most of the surrounding alleys are grouped around specific crafts, a particular specialty here being the pattern-weave mats produced for the sides and floors of Moroccan mosques. From the *kissaria,* the main street of the Medina, **Rue de la Grande Mosque**, leads uphill through the middle of town to the Grand Mosque. This is the simplest approach, but you can take in more of the *souks* by following **Rue Kechachin**, parallel but slightly above it (away from the river walls). Along Kechachin are located the carpenters and stone-carvers, as well as other craftsmen. In **Rue Haddadin**, a fairly major intersection which leads off to its right up toward Bab Sebta, you'll come upon gold- and coppersmiths.

The Grand Mosque and Medersa

As far as buildings go, the **Grand Mosque** signals very much the most interesting part of town, its surrounding lanes fronting a concentration of aristocratic mansions and religious *zaouia* foundations. Almohad in origin, the mosque is one of the largest and earliest in Morocco, though what you can see as a non-Muslim (the gateway and minaret) are recent additions.

You can, however, visit its **Medersa** (opposite the monumental, stepped, main entrance), Salé's main monument and recently restored; admission is the standard 3dh. Founded in 1341 by Sultan Abou el Hassan (see Chellah, in Rabat), the building is more or less contemporary with the Bou Inania *medersas* in Meknes and Fes. Like them, it follows the basic Merenid plan of a central courtyard opening onto a prayer hall, with a series of cells for the students—for whom these "university halls" were endowed—around its upper floors. If this is the first one you've seen, it will come as a surprise after the sparse Almohad economy of the monuments in Rabat. The great Merenid *medersas* are all intensely decorated—in carved wood, stucco, and *zellij*—and this is no exception. As you stand within the entrance gate (itself highly elaborate with its stucco surround and painted and carved portal), there is hardly an inch of space which doesn't draw the eye away into a web of intricacy. Even the pillars, here unusually rounded, are completely encased in *zellij* mosaic.

What is remarkable, though, despite a certain heaviness which the great Merenid *medersas* manage to avoid, is the way in which each aspect of the workmanship succeeds in forging a unity with the others, echoing and repeating the standard patterns in endless variations. The patterns, for the most part, derive from Almohad models, with their stylized geometric and floral motifs, but in the latter there is a much more naturalistic, less abstracted approach. There is also a new stress on calligraphy, with monumental inscriptions carved in great bands on the dark cedarwood and incorporated within the stucco and *zellij*. Almost invariably these are in the elaborate cursive script, and they are generally passages from the Koran. There are occasional poems, however, such as the beautiful foundation inscription, set in marble against a green background, on the rear wall of the court, which begins:

> *Look at my admirable portal!*
> *Rejoice in my chosen company,*
> *In the remarkable style of my construction*
> *And my marvelous interior!*
> *The workers here have accomplished an artful*
> *Creation with the beauty of youth. . . .**

Only sporadically visited, you'll probably have the *medersa* to yourself (except for the sparrows and the caretaker)—it's a quiet, meditative place. Close to its entrance there is a stairway up to the old, windowless cells of the students and to the roof, where, looking out across the river to Rabat, you can really sense the enormity of the Hassan Tower.

Marabouts and Moussems

Out beyond the *medersa,* a street runs down the near side of the Grand Mosque to emerge amid a vast and very ancient **cemetery**, at the far end of which you can see (though you should not approach) the white *koubba* and associated buildings of the **marabout of Sidi ben Achir**. Sometimes known as "Al Tabir" (The Doctor), ben Achir was a fourteenth-century ascetic from Andalusia. His shrine, said to have the ability to attract shipwrecks and quiet storms—good pirate virtues—is also a reputed cure for blindness, paralysis, and madness. Enclosed by nineteenth-century pilgrim lodgings, it still has its devotees and is the scene of a considerable annual *moussem*, or pilgrimage festival.

The most important of Salé's *moussems,* however, is that of its patron saint, **Sidi Abdallah ben Hassoun**, whose **zaouia** stands just to the right of the road, a few steps before you came out at the cemetery. The saint, who, for Muslim travelers, plays a role similar to St. Christopher's, lived in Salé during

---

* Quoted in translation from a French book by Charles Terrasse in Richard B. Parker's *Islamic Monuments in Morocco* (Baraka Press, Virginia).

the sixteenth century, though the origins and significance of his *moussem* are unclear. Taking place each year on the eve of *Mouloud*—the Prophet's birthday—it involves a spectacular procession through the streets of the town with local boatmen, dressed in corsair costumes, carrying huge and elaborate wax lanterns mounted on giant poles.

North of Rabat: the Jardins Exotiques, Plage des Nations, and Kenitra

Respectively 12km and 18km from Rabat, the **Jardins Exotiques** and **Plages des Nations** provide the capital's most enjoyable excursions. The first, as its name suggests, is a French colonial creation of botanical extravagance; the second, an immense stretch of fine shore, which, together with Temara (see the next section), is *the* sophisticated local beach to hang out on. Both gardens and beach can be reached by bus #28 from the **Salé terminal** (about every 20 min.). The bus stops and turns around a few kilometers before it reaches the turnoff for the **Plage** (which is where everyone will be heading); for the **Jardins** you'll have to ask the driver to let you off—the entrance is just to the left of the road and there's a bus stop 20m beyond it. Alternatively, there are regular *grands taxis* direct to the beach from Salé.

The Jardins Exotiques

The **Jardins**, laid out by one M. François, in what the French guidebooks call *"une manière remarquable,"* have obviously seen better days—a fact which adds considerably to their charm. Full of precarious bamboo bridges and bizarre, dot-directed routes, you wander through a sequence of brilliant regional creations. There is a Brazilian rain forest, dense with water and orchids; a formal Japanese garden; and then suddenly a great shaft of French Polynesia, with rickety summerhouses set amid long pools, turtles paddling past you, palm trees all around, and terrific flashes of bright-red flowers. On a more local level, there is also a superbly maintained Andalusian garden, but the appeal of this place really has little to do with Morocco.

The gardens are open daily from sunrise to sunset for a nominal (currently 5dh) admission fee.

On to Plage des Nations

There is a good modern road right down to the Plage des Nations, but the #28 bus (which you can hail outside the Jardins) stops some way before this turnoff—just after the village of BOUKNADEL, by a café in what seems to be the middle of nowhere. Everybody gets out here and takes the diagonal path off toward the sea and a cape past a couple of farms, around some woods, and then joining the tail end of the asphalt road down to the beach itself.

After this approach, you imagine a rather wild beach, with battered cliffs and a few picnic groups. **PLAGE DES NATIONS**, or SIDI BOUKNADEL as it's also known, is nothing of the kind. Flanked by the 4*A *Hôtel Firdaous* (☎451.86), a slick, new complex with a freshwater pool (open to all for a small charge), it seems more westernized than Rabat itself. Certainly, unlike the Kasbah or Salé beaches, it's a resort where young Rabat women feel able to come out for the day, rather than suffer the uncontestedly male domination of the city's beaches. And with everyone here to take a day's vacation, it's a very relaxed and friendly sort of place. The beach itself is excellent, with big, exciting waves—but dangerous currents, so it is patrolled by lifeguards along the central strip. There are also a couple of reasonably priced cafés.

North to Kenitra

If you're planning to go farther north by bus or train, you'll have to return to Salé or Rabat. Hitching from BOUKNADEL may be feasible.

It is probably just as well to bypass **KENITRA** itself, unless you have friends or relations to visit. A major port established by the French, the town is nowadays a formidable U.S. and Moroccan military base, established in the 1970s in return for American military aid for the war with Polisario. It is a drab-looking place, with a self-conscious garrison-town prosperity reflected in an unusual number of bars, hotels, pizza joints, and half-hearted discos.

If you want or need to stay—and it's not somewhere you'd want to get stuck in for long—most of the cheaper **hotels** are along the main Av. Mohammed V from the bus station, or just off of it (like the 2*B *Hôtel La Rotonde* at 60 Av. Mohammed Diouri).

MEHDIYA PLAGE, Kenitra's local beach, is a dull, grayish strip with a few houses and plenty of summer crowds. There is a **campground** and one (invariably full) hotel. A couple of kilometers north are the crumbling ruins of a **Kasbah**, built during the reign of Moulay Ismail (see Meknes). **Grands taxis** run frequently in season between the beach and Kenitra.

South Toward Casa: Temara, Skhirat, and Mohammedia

It's a little over an hour by *grand taxi* from Rabat to Casa (an hour and a half if you go by train) and there's little en route to delay your progress. The landscape, wooded in parts, is a low, flat plain, punctuated only by the resort center and industrial port of Mohammedia, and the turnoffs for a few, local beach resorts. These are popular weekend escapes from Rabat and Casablanca, and as such, have an attraction. In summer, especially, they can be lively—and remain so well into the night.

Temara Plage

TEMARA PLAGE, 16km southwest of Rabat, is probably the best of the bunch—just twenty minutes by *grand taxi* (from the main stand on Bd. Hassan II) and flanked by a number of discos, a summer alternative to the lack of action in Rabat. Few people stay here overnight, though if you want to, there should be no problem: there's a **campgound** and two **hotels**, the 3*A *La Felouque* and unrated *Hôtel* Casino. The *Felouque* has an excellent French-style restaurant.

Bus #17 leaves Rabat from Av. Hassan II for TEMARA VILLE, a small village with ruins of a Kasbah. From here it's a four-kilometer walk to the beach.

Ech Chiana and Skhirat Plage

ECH CHIANA, 9km south from Temara, is in a smaller but similar vein; again with a luxury **hotel** (the 4*B *Kasbah Club*, ☎416.33), cheap **auberge** (the unclassified*Gambusia*), and **campgound**.

Moving south from here, there is a distinctly classier shift as you approach **SKHIRAT PLAGE** and the summer royal palace, site of the notorious coup attempt by senior Moroccan generals during the king's birthday celebrations in July 1971. Mounted by a force of Berber cadets, who took over the palace, imprisoned King Hassan, and massacred a number of his guests, this came within hours of being successful—until it was thwarted, ironically, by the accidental shooting of the cadets' leader, General Mohammed Medbuh. The palace today still forms the centerpiece of a somewhat exclusive resort.

If you want to stop over for a swim, there are two **hotels**—the unclassified *Auberge Potinière* and 3*B *Amphitrite* (☎422.36). Easiest access is by train—from Rabat or Casa—to the town of SKHIRAT, only a couple of kilometers from the beach.

Mohammedia

Finally, before you move into the industrialized outskirts of Casablanca, there is **MOHAMMEDIA,** an industrial and commercial port now conclusively dominated by the refineries of its petrochemical developments. A town with a population of some 70,000, it has also been a popular and somewhat elitist resort over the last few decades—a pleasure dome for Casa, with its excellent five-kilometer-long beach, plus a racecourse, 18-hole golf course, casino, and yacht marina. The recent industrial growth has dampened enthusiasm, but only to an extent.

There are a number of big luxury hotels along the beach, together with dozens of restaurants and discos. Cheaper **hotels** are scattered around the old, eighteenth-century Kasbah, close behind the **train station**. Try the *Hôtel Ennasr*, or, as fallback choices, the *Hôtel des Voyageurs* or *Hôtel Castel*. The best restaurant in the town, if you are willing to pay high prices for well-cooked fish, is *Chez Irene*, by the port.

Casablanca (Casa, Dar El Baida)

Principal city of Morocco, and capital in all but administration, **CASABLANCA** (*Dar el Baida* in its literal Arabic form) is now the largest port of the Maghreb—busier even than Marseilles, the city on which it was modeled by the French. Its development, from a town of 20,000 in 1906, has been astonishingly rapid, and quite ruthlessly deliberate. When the French landed their forces here in 1907 (and established their protectorate five years later), it was Fes which was Morocco's commercial center, and Tangier was its main port. Had Tangier not been in international hands, this most likely would have remained the case. Instead, the demands of an independent colonial administration forced the French to seek an entirely new base. Casa, at the heart of *Maroc Utile*, the country's most fertile zone and center of its mineral deposits, was a natural choice.

Superficially, Casa is much like any other large Western city—a familiarity which makes it fairly easy to get your bearings, and a revelation as you begin to understand something of its life. It is a genuinely dynamic city, still growing at a rate of 50,000 people a year; arriving here from the south, or even from Fes or Tangier, most of the preconceptions you've been traveling around with will be happily shattered.

Casa's Western image—with the almost total absence of women wearing veils, and its fancy beach clubs—shields, however, what is still substantially a "first-generation" city, and one which has an inevitably large number of problems. Alongside its wealth and a handful of showpiece developments—it recently hosted the Mediterranean Games—it has had since its formation a reputation for extreme poverty, prostitution, *bidonville* shantytowns, and social unrest. The *bidonville* problem resulted partly from the sheer extent of population increases (over 1 million in the 1960s), partly because few of the earlier migrants intended to stay permanently—sending back most of their earnings to their families in the country.

The pattern is now much more toward permanent settlement, and this, together with a strict control of migration and a limited number of self-help programs, have eased and cleared many of the worst slums. The problem of a concentrated urban poor, however, is more enduring and represents, as it did for the French, an intermittent threat to government stability. Casa, through the 1940s and 1950s, was the main center of anti-French rioting, and it was the city's working class, too, which formed the base of Ben Barka's Socialist Party. There have been strikes here sporadically since independence, and on several occasions, most violently in the food strikes of 1982, they have precipitated rioting. Whether Casa's development can be sustained, and the lot of its new migrants improved, must decide much of Morocco's future.

Arrival, Orientation, and Hotels

A large city by any standards, Casa can be a confusing place in which to arrive—particularly if you're on one of the trains that stop at the main **Gare des Voyageurs** (2km from the center) rather than continuing on to the better-situated **Gare du Port.**

Once you're in the city, though, things are pretty simple. There are two main squares—**Place Mohammed V** and **Place des Nations Unies**—and most of the places to stay, to eat, or (in a rather limited way) see, are located in and around the avenues off to their sides. The **Old Medina,** *the* town of Casablanca until around 1907, remains largely within its walls behind Place Mohammed V (which was formerly the site of its weekly *souk*). The **New Medina**, a slightly bizarre, French creation, lies a couple of kilometers to the south—reached most easily by following Rue Hadj Amar Riffi. And beyond this, it is only the beach suburb of **Aïn Diab**, west of the port, which you're likely to want to explore.

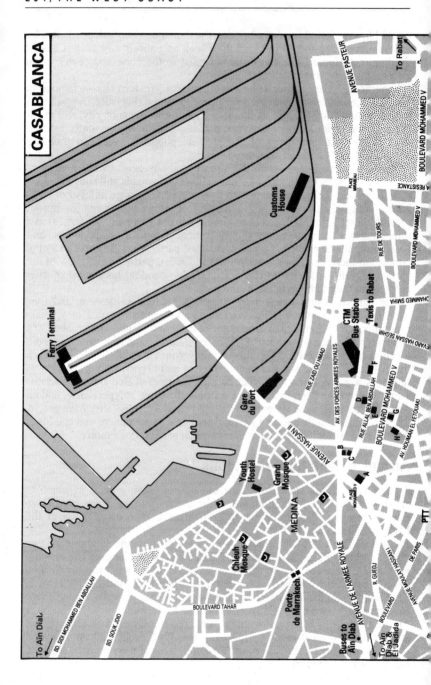

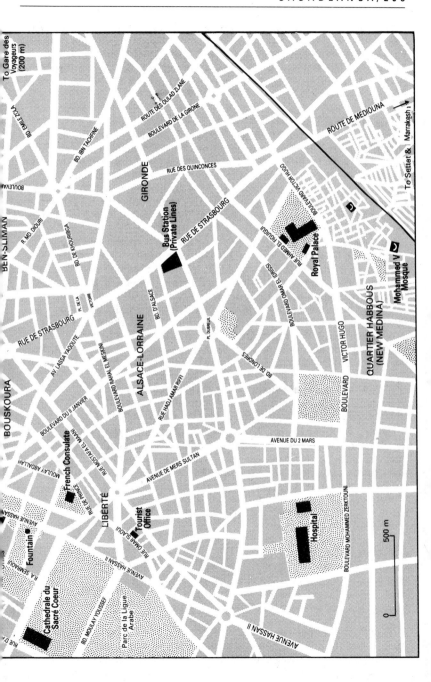

The Casablanca Tourist Pamphlet prints a fairly clear map of the city, covering a much larger area than ours and detailing Aïn Diab, the Gare des Voyageurs and the New Medina (labeled *Habbous*, its local name). You can pick this up in advance from any Moroccan tourist office, or here from the **ONMT** (55 Rue Omar Slaoui) or **Syndicat d'Initiative** (98 Bd. Mohammed V), both marked on our map.

Points of Arrival/Departure

Most of the **trains** from Marrakesh go to both stations, allowing you to stay on until the **Gare du Port,** just 150m from Place Mohammed V. From Rabat (and Fes/Tangier), however, trains sometimes terminate at the **Gare des Voyageurs**, at the far end of Bd. Mohammed V. If you're quick, bus #30 runs downtown from the square in front of the station; otherwise, reckon on a twenty-minute walk. Bd. Mohammed V runs straight ahead from the square in front of the station, curving slightly to the left as you come to the next main square (Place Albert 1er).

Bus stations and **grand taxi stands** are more central and straightforward. All the **CTM buses** arrive at the **Gare Routière** on Rue Léon l'Africain (off Rue Colbert, center-right on our map) and the *grands taxis* for Rabat usually stop just across the street to the rear. Non-CTM buses use the **private-bus station** below Place de la Victoire at the bottom of our map.

Coming from the **Aeroport Mohammed V**, used by all international and most domestic flights, there is a shuttle bus to the Gare Routière. For flights at odd hours, or if you can share costs, a **grand taxi** can be a reassurance, especially if you are catching a flight out of the country. In Casa, negotiate at the main stand for Rabat taxis (see above). Note that, when leaving Morocco, there is no exchange facility in the departure area.

Within the city, **petits taxis** can be tricky to find; try the corner of Place Mohammed V/Av. des F.A.R. Very few are metered, so establish a price in advance for Aïn Diab (about 17dh) or the Gare des Voyageurs (12dh).

Moving on from Casa, *CTM* run **buses** to just about everywhere, including El Jadida, Agadir, Tiznit, and various European destinations; tickets and times from the terminal on Rue Léon l'Africain (see map). For Rabat you'll find **grands taxis** are the most efficient service—they leave regularly from the block behind the *CTM*. For Tangier, Meknes, Fes, or Marrakesh, you'll probably want to go **by train**. Check times in advance at the *Gare du Port*, above Place Mohammed V, and try to find one that's leaving from this station rather than from the *Voyageurs*.

Accommodation

Hotels in Casa are easy enough to find—though beware that they operate at near capacity for much of the year. If at all possible, it's a good idea to phone ahead for a room, or at least to arrive fairly early in the day. On the plus side, many of the cheaper one- and two-star places are quite stylish in a faded, art deco sort of way.

All of the recommendations below are for hotels in the main, **central area**. As in Rabat the Medina hotels are comparatively expensive, with most of them charging the equivalent of 1*A prices for fairly miserable rooms.

HOTELS

Hôtel Les Negociants (E), **Hôtel Bon Reve (F)**, Rue Allal Ben Abdallah. The two best options in a promising area for cheap, more or less reasonable, hotels. A third choice, the Hôtel Kon Tiki, is farther down the same street at no. 89. *All unclassified.*

Hôtel du Perigord (B), 56 Rue de Foucauld. Arguably the best of the unstarred hotels. *Unclassified.*

Hôtel Foucauld (C), 52 Rue de Foucauld; ☎22.26.66. Next door to the Perigord. *1*A.*

Hôtel Touring (D), 87 Rue Allal Ben Abdallah; ☎31.02.16. Art Deco touches and a popular choice. Best try this before its unclassified neighbors in the street—whose prices are very much the same. *1*A.*

Hôtel Colbert, 30 Rue Colbert; ☎31.42.41. Useful location if you arrive by bus—right next to the CTM. A bit gloomy and ramshackle, but more or less clean rooms. *1*A.*

Hôtel Rialto (G), 9 Rue Claude; ☎27.51.22. A good, safe bet, with a *hammam* next door. *1*A.* (The unclassified *Hôtel de France*, opposite, is tolerable).

Hôtel du Louvre (I), 36 Rue Nationale; $27.37.47. Regular prices for its class, but not much to be said for the rooms. *1*A.*

Hôtel Guynemer, 2 Rue Pégoud; ☎27.57.64. Pleasant, clean rooms in an attractive, "seen-better-days" hotel.

Hôtel Excelsior (A), 2 Rue Nolly, on Place Mohammed V; ☎26.22.81. Strongly recommended if you can afford it; this (like the *Balima* in Rabat) used to be the city's "Grand Hotel" until the big chains moved in. Pleasant café, too. *2*A.*

Hôtel Georges V, 1 Rue Sidi Belyout/corner Av. des FAR; ☎31.24.48. Across the road from the *Excelsior*, if you strike unlucky. Very reasonable. *2*A.*

Hôtel Windsor, 93 Place Oued El Makhazine; ☎27.88.74. Large rooms with showers/bathrooms. A bit pricey, but good. *3*B.*

Hôtel Plaza, 18 Bd. Mohammed El Hansali; ☎22.02.26. Again, good rooms and facilities, and fairly priced for its class. *3*A.*

YOUTH HOSTEL AND CAMPGROUND

Youth Hostel (*Auberge de Jeunesse*), 6 Place Admiral Philbert; ☎22.05.51. A friendly enough place, nicely sited just inside the Medina, but poorly maintained (pretty disgusting on our last visit!). To reach it from the Gare du Port or Place Mohammed V, walk up to the corner of the Medina walls and follow them down to the first entrance off the boulevard—the hostel's on your right at the near side of the square.

Camping Oasis, Av. Mermoz. The nearest campground to Casa is miles out on the road to El Jadida. If you're using it as a last resort, and dependent on public transportation, take bus #31 from the *CTM* terminal.

Around the City

It used to be said, with some amazement, that Casa had not a single "real" monument. And indeed, with the exception of a sad-looking aquarium, flanked by penguinless penguin pools, out on the way to Aïn Diab, the statement was true. However, with the construction of the Hassan II Mosque, on a platform overlooking the sea towards Aïn Diab, all that has well and truly changed.

The **Hassan II Mosque** represents the present monarch's most ambitious-ever building project—and will surely be his great legacy to Moroccan architecture. It is startling project. The minaret has a height of 172 meters—the tallest building in the country, and the world record of any mosque in the world. At its summit, a laser projects its beams towards Mecca. The mosque itself has space for 80,000 worshippers, and is the center of a cultural complex that includes a major library and (as yet uncompleted) museum.

Equally extraordinary is the fact that its cost—an estimated $500m—was raised entirely by public subscription. Press-reports outside Morocco have indicated some resentment toward an over enthusiastic sponsoring operation, which generated donations from virtually every citizen both at home and overseas, with collectors approaching expatriate workers from Germany to Saudi Arabia. However, in Morocco there is certainly a genuine pride in the project, and pictures of the mosque are displayed in homes and cafés throughout the nation.

At the time of writing, in mid-1989, the mosque is almost complete, with 2500 workers laboring in night and day shifts, and a further 80,000 artisans employed on the decorative marble and wood decoration, so that the building can be officially opened on King Hassan's 60th birthday. That the mosque bears his name has inspired rumors that it is designed in part as his mausoleum, along the lines of that of his father, Mohammed V, in Rabat. But it is important to add that in addition to his secular positon, Hassan is also "Commander of the Faithful", the spiritual leader of Moroccan Muslims. And the building's site, in addition to reflecting Hassan's intent to "give the city a heart," is designed to illustrate the Koranic saying, "Allah has his throne on the water".

Around the City Center and the Medinas

The French city center and its formal colonial buildings already seem to belong to a different and distant age. Grouped around **Place des Nations Unies**, these have served as models for administrative architecture throughout Morocco, and to an extent still do; their style, heavily influenced by art deco, is known as *Mauresque*—a French idealization and "improvement" on Moorish design. The effect, orchestrated on a *son et lumière* fountain three nights a week, is actually very impressive, the only intrusively French feature being a clocktower in the *préfecture*. More European in style, though again adopting traditional Moroccan forms, is the old **Cathedral of Sacre Cœur** at the far end of the **Parc de la Ligne Arabe**. Now used as a school, it is perhaps the one building in Casa worth seeing in itself—a wonderfully balanced and airy design very much out of character with the repressive colonialism of its age.

If you have time to spare, visit the **New Medina** (or **Quartier Habbous**), which displays a somewhat bizarre extension of this French-*Mauresque* interest. Built in the 1930s as a response to the first *bidonville* crisis, it is an odd recreation of what the French felt domestic Moroccan architecture should be like. The streets, laid out in neat little rows, now have a somewhat folksy, shopping-center feel to them—not at all Moroccan even with the years. What's actually unreal, however, is the neighborhood mosque, flanked by a tidy stretch of green as though it were a provincial French church.

The **Old Medina**, lapsing into dilapidation above the port, is largely the product of the late nineteenth century, when Casa began its modest growth as a commercial center. Before that, it was little more than a group of village huts, half-heartedly settled by local tribes after the site was abandoned by the Portuguese in 1755. *Casa Branca*, the city the Portuguese founded here in the fifteenth century, had been virtually leveled by the great earthquake of that year (which also destroyed Lisbon). Only its name ("The White House", or *Casablanca* in Spanish, *Dar el Baida* in Arabic) survives.

Now relatively underpopulated, the Medina has a slightly disreputable, if also fairly affluent, air. It is said to be the place to go to look for any stolen goods you might want to buy back—a character well in keeping with many of the stalls. There's nothing sinister though, and it can be a good source for cheap snacks and general goods. A single main street, Rue Djemaa ech Chleuh, edges its way right through the quarter, past most of the market stalls and the principal mosque from which it takes its name.

Aïn Diab: the Beach

You can get out to Aïn Diab by bus (#9 from Bd. de Paris; see our map), by *petit taxi* (wait around Place Mohammed V), or by foot. The beach starts around 3km out from the port and Old Medina, past the Hassan II mosque, and continues for about the same distance.

A beach right within Casa may not sound exactly alluring, and it's certainly not the cleanest and clearest of the country's waters. But the big attraction of Aïn Diab is not so much the sea (in whose shallow waters Moroccans gather in phalanx formations, wary of the currents), as the "beach clubs" along its front. Each of these has one or more pools (usually with filtered seawater), a restaurant, and a couple of snack bars; in the fancier ones there'll also be additional sports facilities like tennis or volleyball, and perhaps even a disco. On paper this must sound very ordinary and average, but its novelty in a Moroccan city is quite amazing. Country people and recent immigrants must think so as well, and it's a strange sight to see women veiled from head to toe looking down onto the cosmopolitan intensity unfolding beneath them.

Prices and quality of the **beach clubs** vary enormously, and it's worth wandering around a while to check out what's available. Most locals have annual membership, and for outsiders a day or weekend ticket can work out surprisingly expensive ($6–15). But there's quite often one place which has thrown its doors open for free in an attempt to boost its café business. *Piscine Eden Roc,* the first you encounter coming from the port, is usually among the cheapest, though it's a little dull and away from the center of things. If you're taking a *petit taxi*, ask to be let off a kilometer or so farther down, at one of the group of clubs near *Le Lido* or *Kon Tiki.*

And finally, an oddity. If you feel like practicing your English with Moroccans, in the premises of a British "club," call in at the **Churchill Club** in Rue Pessac, Aïn Diab. Established in 1922, this was formerly the "British Bank Club." Its major condituon of membership is that "the English language only should be spoken on the premises." All English-speaking visitors are welcomed.

Eating and Nightlife

Casa has the reputation of being the best **place to eat** in Morocco, and if you can afford the fancier restaurant prices, this is certainly true. There are some excellent seafood restaurants along the *corniche* (coast) road at Aïn Diab, and some very stylish, old French colonial ones around the central boulevards.

Restaurants and Cafés

For anyone keeping to a **budget**, some of the best restaurant possibilities lie in the smaller streets off Bd. Mohammed V. Rue Mohammed el Quori, by the *Café de France* (no. 9 on our map), has a couple of cheap café-restaurants including *Brasserie el Sphinx* and, signposted off of it, *Restaurant Ouarzazale*. The area around the *Syndicat*, and especially Rue Colbert, is also a good area. For rock-bottom Moroccan standbys, there are the **Medina cafés** near the beginning of Rue Djemaa ech Chleuh and (farther down) on Rue Centrale.

Slightly **more expensive**, *Las Delicias* (18 Bd. Mohammed V) is a good Spanish place, with big salads and huge plates of fried fish. Or, if you want a real chunk of Casablanca style, dressed up like a 1920s Parisian *salon* (which is really what it is), there's the *Petit Poucet* at 8 Bd. Mohammed V. The *Poucet*, one of those classic French restaurants offering infinite portions and service, also has a (much cheaper) snack bar next door—one of the best places around for some serious drinking. It was in *Le Petit Poucet* that the French aviator and writer Sainte–Exupery used to recuperate between his flights south to the Sahara. In Aïn Diab, there are some good-value places, though the best are most active at lunchtime. Good Moroccan restaurants include *L'Etoile Marocaine* (107 Rue Allal Ben Abdallah) and the more upscale *Al Mounia* (95 Rue du Prince Moulay Abdallah).

Casa also has a reputation for its **ice cream parlors** and **pâtisseries**. The finest of the former is *Oliveri's* on Av. Hassan II; of the latter it's *Gâteaux Bennis*, 2 Rue Fkih El Gabbas, in Habbous.

Nightlife

For a city with such a glamorous film image, Casa has a surprisingly elusive **nightlife**—at least downtown. Here, apart from the Mohammed V bars—try the *Sphinx* (see above) or the *Rich Bar*—it's pretty much limited to a few seedy strip joints out toward the harbor. *La Fontaine*, on Bd. Mohammed el Hansali, is one of the more conspicuous, if you're curious—belly dancing, live music, and obligatory drinks for the barwomen. Others include *Don Quichote* (44 Place Mohammed V), the *Embassy* (2 Bd. Mohammed V), and the *Negresco* (Rue Poincaré).

In **Aïn Diab** there's usually more happening, but for the most part its a question of western-style discos, like *Le Balcon* or *Zoom Zoom*.

And lastly, if you cannot leave Casa without a visit to **Rick's Bar**, some salutary news. The bar has never in reality existed. For a session of postcard-writing, your only option is a very contrived bar, touting the legendary monicker, in the *Hôtel Hyatt Regency* on Place Mohammed V. It is a little safe, to say the least.

Directory

Airlines *Royal Air Maroc*, 44 Av. des F.A.R.; *Air France*, Av. des F.A.R.; *British Airways*, 57 Place Zellaqa (in the *Tour Atlas* building, 6th floor).

American Express *Voyages Schwarz*, 112 Av. Moulay Abdallah (☎743.33); open Mon.–Sat. 8:30am–Noon and 2:30–6:30pm.

Banks *SGMB*, 84 Bd. Mohammed V; *Crédit du Maroc*, 48–58 Bd. Mohammed V; others along the same boulevard.

Books and Newspapers For English-language **books**, try *English Forum* (27 Rue Clémenceau) or the *American Language Center Bookstore* (Bd. Moulay Youssef), both of which have a good range of paperbacks and fair sections on Morocco. *Librairie Farairie* (near Place Mohammed V, between Bd. Mohammed V and Av. des F.A.R.) and *Librairie Nationale* (Av. de Mers Sultan) are also good for a browse. The *International Herald Tribune*, and some British **newspapers**, are available from stands around Place Mohammed V.

Car Rental Cheapest is *Leasing Cars*, 100 Bd. Zerktouni (☎265-331; you'll have to go out there by *petit taxi*). Others are concentrated along Av. des F.A.R.

Car Repairs Garages include *Renault-Maroc* on Place de Bandoeng (just off our map, below Place Paquet). For information and addresses, contact the *Touring Club du Maroc* (3 Av. des F.A.R.) or *R.A.C. du Maroc* (3 Rue Lemercier).

Consulates *U.S.* (8 Bd. Moulay Youssef; ☎22.41.49);*Great Britain* (60 Bd. d'Anfa; ☎22.16.53 or 22.17.41).

Department Stores *Alpha 55* (Av. de Mers Sultan; with a good, 7th-floor restaurant) and *Centre 2000* (near the Gare du Port) can be useful for stocking up on supplies before heading south.

Hammams Every neighborhood has several; the best is reputed to be *Hay Ali* in the Maarif area—ask a *petit taxi* to take you there.

Medical Aid Dial ☎15 for emergency services. Addresses of doctors from the larger hotels, or from the *Croissant Rouge* (Cité Djemaa, 44 Av. E.; ☎340.914). Nightlong *pharmacie* is open in Place des Nations Unies.

Police Phone ☎19. Main station is on Bd. Brahim Roudani.

Post Office The main *PTT* (for phones/*poste restante*) is in Place des Nations Unies. Open Mon.–Thur. 8:30am–12:15pm, Fri. 8:30–11:30am.

Soccer Casa's about the best place in Morocco to see some: at the Marcel Cédan stadium. Check the local press.

Tourist Offices *ONMT*, 55 Rue Omar Slaoui (Mon.–Thurs. 8:30am–noon and 2:30–6:30pm, Fri. 8:30–11am and 3–6:30pm; *Syndicat d'Initiative*, 98 Bd. Mohammed V (Mon.–Sat. 9am–noon and 3–6:30pm, Sun. 9am–noon).

El Jadida

By far the most popular of the "central" Atlantic resorts, **EL JADIDA** is also a stylish and beautiful town, retaining the lanes and ramparts of an old Portuguese Medina. Known as Mazagan under the Portuguese and by the French, it was renamed—*El Jadida* means "The New"—after independence in 1956, a signal of its proposed resort development.

It's the beach, today, that's undeniably the focal point. Moroccans from Casablanca and Marrakesh, even from Tangier or Fes, come here in droves, and, alongside this cosmopolitan mix, there's an unusual feeling of openness. The bars are crowded (an unusual feature in itself), there's an almost frenetic evening promenade, and—as at Casa—women are for once visible and active.

Some Details: Arrival and Hotels

Orientation is straightforward, with the old **Portuguese Medina**, walled and looking out over the port, and the **Ville Nouvelle** spreading to its south along the seafront. By public transportation, you will almost certainly arrive at the **main bus station** at the southern end of town (bottom-center on our map). From here it's a ten-minute walk to the Medina or to most hotels.

In summer, you'd be well advised to make a **hotel** reservation—rooms can be very hard to find in July and August—and at all times you may prefer to make some phone calls before pacing the streets. The town extends for some distance along the oceanfront. Since the closure of the *Hôtel Marhaba*, there is a distinct lack of reasonable upscale hotels.

Remaining options, in ascending order of price, are:

Hôtel d'El Jadida (A), Av. Zerktouni. **Hôtel Maghreb (C)**, **Hôtel du Port (D)**, Bd. de Suez. Three unclassified hotels, which are often the last to fill. The *El Jadida* is basic but reasonable; the others, basic and a bit seedy—not recommended for women travelers.

Hôtel de la Plage (H), Av. Al Jamia al Arabi; ☎26.48. Formerly a 1*B hotel, this has just slipped to become unclassified. It's clean enough, and again a good fallback.

Hôtel Provence (F), 42 Av. Fqih Mohammed Errafi; ☎23.47. British-run hotel: clean and central, with a good restaurant, and covered parking nearby (10dh for 24 hr.). The best budget choice—phone in advance. *1*B.*

Hôtel Bruxelles (E), 40 Rue Ibn Khaldoun; ☎20.72. Pleasant, balconied rooms at the front. *1*B.*

Hôtel Royal (G), 108 Av. Mohammed V; ☎28.39. A bit pricier but large rooms and generally functional showers. 1*A.

Hôtel Suisse (B), 145 Bd. Zerktouni; ☎28.16. Similar to the above, in a useful central location. *1*A.*

Camping International, Av. des Nations Unies; ☎25.47. Well-equipped, if a bit expensive. It is signposted—a five-minute walk south from the bus station.

For a largish resort, it's surprisingly hard to find anywhere good **to eat**; try around Place el Hansali (the real center of town), or by the fairly mundane town *souks,* just off Av. Zerktouni. The Safari Pub (Av. Mohammed Er Riffi) has a reasonable *prix fixé* meal, and a full license. **Bars** are mainly in the hotels; the liveliest are at the *de la Plage*. Since El Jadida is very much a resort, prices at most establishments tend to the high side, even for standard café drinks.

And lastly, a few other details. The **PTT** is in Place Mohammed V. **Bus tickets** for Casa or Marrakesh should be bought in advance (from the main station). There's a **Wednesday souk**, held out by the lighthouse southwest of town. And there's no tourist office.

The Cité Portugaise

El Jadida's Medina is the most European-looking in Morocco: a quiet, walled, and bastioned seaside village, with a handful of churches scattered on its lanes.

It was founded by the Portuguese in 1513—and retained by them until 1769—and it is still popularly known as the **Cité Portugaise**. The Moors who settled here after the Portuguese withdrawal tended to live outside the walls.

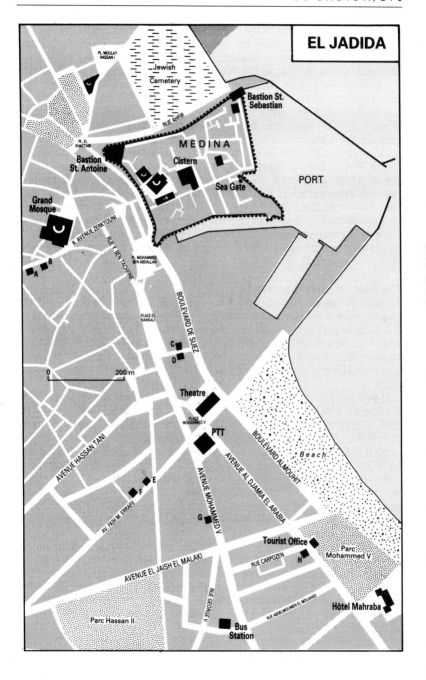

EL JADIDA

PL. MOULAY HASSAN I

Jewish Cemetery

Bastion St. Sebastian

RUE AHFIR

PL. EL KHATTABI

M E D I N A

Cistern

Bastion St. Antoine

Sea Gate

PORT

Grand Mosque

R. AVENUE ZERKTOUNI

RUE Y BEN TACHFINE

PL. MOHAMMED BEN ABDALLAH

B

A

PLACE EL HANSALI

BOULEVARD DE SUEZ

C

D

0   200 m

Theatre

PLACE MOHAMMED V

PTT

BOULEVARD ALMOUHIT

Beach

AVENUE HASSAN TANI

E

F

AVENUE AL DJAMIA EL ARABIA

AVENUE MOHAMMED V

AV. FKIH M. ERRAFI

G

Tourist Office

Parc Mohammed V

RUE CARPOZEN

H

AVENUE EL JAISH EL MALAKI

RUE GEORGE V

RUE ABDELMOUMEN EL MOUAHDI

Hôtel Mahraba

Parc Hassan II

Bus Station

Budgett Meakin, writing in the 1890s, found an "extensive native settlement of beehive huts, or *nouallahs*" spreading back from the harbor, while European merchants had reestablished themselves in the "clean, prosperous and well-lighted streets" of the Medina. As in all the "open ports" on this coast, there was also an important Jewish community handling the trade with Marrakesh; uniquely, Mazagan had no separate Jewish quarter, or *Mellah*.

The *cité* today—decaying and insignificant—is not of enormous interest, though it does have one distinct and very beautiful sight. This is the **Portuguese Cistern**, a dramatic subterranean vault that mirrors its roof and pillars in a shallow film of water covering the floor—a startling effect that Orson Welles used in his *Othello*, staging a riot here and filming it from above. These days you'll see it on virtually all the town's postcards. It is normally open weekdays from around 9:30am until 6:30 or 7pm; the entrance is midway down the main street, on the left opposite a small souvenir shop.

Walk farther up this street and you'll come to the old **Porte de la Mer**, a sea gate opening onto the port. The churches and chapels, long converted to secular use, are generally closed; the **grand mosque** here was once a lighthouse—and looks it.

The Beaches—and South to Tit

El Jadida's **beach** spreads north from the *cité* and port, well beyond the length of the town. It's a popular strip, though from time to time polluted by the ships in port. If it doesn't look too good, or you feel like a change, take a *petit taxi* 3km south along the coastal road to **PLAGE SIDI OUAFI**, a broader strip of sand where dozens of Moroccan families set up tents for the summer. There is good swimming to be had here, and cheap temporary food stalls.

If you want to head on from Sidi Ouafi, you can usually find *grands taxis* leaving for Sidi Bouzid and Moulay Abdallah (5km and 11km respectively from El Jadida). **SIDI BOUZID** is another beach, but much more developed than Sidi Ouafi, with fancy villa-bungalows and a chic bar-restaurant.

MOULAY ABDALLAH, in contrast, is a tiny fishing village—dominated, to its left, by a large *zaouia* complex and partially enclosed by a circuit of walls in ruins. These span the site of a twelfth-century *ribat,* or fortified monastery, known as **Tit** ("eyes" or "spring" in the local Berber dialect), and built, so it is thought, in preparation for a Norman invasion: a real threat at the time—the Normans had already launched attacks on Tunisia—but one which never materialized.

Today, there is little to see, though the minaret of the modern *zaouia* (prominent and whitewashed) is Almohad in origin; behind it, up through the graveyard, you can walk to a second, isolated minaret, which might be from even earlier. If it is, then it is perhaps the only one surviving from the Almoravid era—a claim considerably more impressive than its simple, block-like appearance might suggest. At the *zaouia* an important *moussem* is held toward the end of August.

To **reach Sidi Bouzid** direct from El Jadida, catch the local #2 bus from Place Mohammed Ben Abdullah.

Azzemour

Sixteen kilometers north of El Jadida, **AZZEMOUR** has an altogether different feel and appearance to it—oddly remote, considering its strategic site on
the great Oum er Rbia River. It has long been outside the mainstream of
events. When the Portuguese controlled El Jadida, Safi, and Essaouira, they
stayed in Azzemour for under thirty years; later, when the European traders
moved in on this coast, the town remained a "closed" port. Today, it sees
possibly fewer tourists than any other Moroccan coastal town.

The Portuguese stayed long enough to build its walls, stacked directly
above the banks of the river, and these were dramatically extended by the
white, cubical line of the **Medina**. The best view of all this—and it is impressive—is from across the river, on the way out of town toward Casablanca. To
look around the town, however, make your way down from the bus station to
the main (landward) side of the ramparts. At the far corner are the former
Kasbah and **Mellah** quarters, now largely in ruins, but safe enough to visit.
If you wait around, the local *gardien* will probably arrive, open things up and
show you around; if he doesn't turn up, you can find him by asking at the
tourist office (141 Av. Mohammed V, near the bus station). Once inside the
ruins, you can follow the parapet wall around the ramparts, with views of the
river and the gardens, including henna orchards, along its edge. You'll also
be shown **Dar el Baroud** (The House of Powder), with its ruined Gothic
window, and the old town **synagogue**.

It might not sound like much, and you'll have to negotiate the final tip, but
all in all it's an interesting and enjoyable break from El Jadida, and easily
combined with a swim. The river is notoriously dangerous, but there's a fabulous stretch of **beach** half an hour's walk through the eucalyptus trees above
the town. If you go by road, it's signposted *"Balneaire du Haouzia,"* a small
complex of cafés and cabins occupying part of the sands. For **birdwatchers**
(see also the section following), the scrub dunes around the mouth of the
river are rewarding territory—with the possibility of sighting the rare slen-
der-billed curlew in fall or winter.

If you want **to stay** in Azzemour, you'd probably be better off camping;
there are, however, a couple of small, basic **hotels**—one close by the bus
station on Av. Mohammed V.

South to Oualidia and Safi

For one reason or another, few tourists take **the road between El Jadida
and Essaouira**. Even though El Jadida is an attractive, lively resort, few
people want to spend time both there *and* in Essaouira.

Enthusiastic birdwatchers, however, may find the route itself an attraction.
For the 70km of coast between SIDI MOUSSA (36km south of El Jadida) and
CAP BEDDOUZA (34km south of Oualidia) are among the richest **birdlife
habitats** in the country. The coast is backed almost continuously by huge
dunes, which have cut off a long expanse of salt marshland north of Oualidia.
These wetlands, and the lagoons at Sidi Moussa and Oualidia, shelter a huge

range of species—storks, waders, terns, egrets, warblers—and there are sometimes flocks of shearwaters to be seen not far offshore. The best watching locations are the lagoons, and the rocky headland at Cap Beddouza.

Oualidia

OUALIDIA, 78km from El Jadida (regular buses), is a picturesque little resort—a fishing port and bay, flanked by an old Kasbah and recent royal villa. Most of the people who come here are Moroccan families and they settle into summer colonies in the two sizable **campgrounds**: a standard *Camping Municipal* and, nearer the beach and a bit fancier, the *International Camping Tourist Center*. The latter, with cabins and rooms, is fairly staid— and Oualidia on the whole does have a middle-of-the-road feel to it. However, the beach is good, and it's all pretty laid back. If you want a room, there are two **hotels**, both of which have enticing (though expensive) seafood restaurants: the 1*A *Auberge de la Lagune* (☎105) and 2*A Hôtel Hippocampe (☎111). The latter is cleaner and not much more expensive, with a terrace overlooking the lagoon. There is a seasonal **campground** on the edge of town.

Twelve kilometers farther south, just before you reach Cap Beddouza, there's another **campground**, and an unclassified roadside **auberge**, by the little village of **SIDI BOUCHTA**. The beach itself is more exposed: long stretches of weed-strewn sands, flanked by parched wasteland.

Safi and its Beaches

Flanked by a long stretch of sulfur-spewing chimneys and vast sardine-canning factories, **SAFI** is not the prettiest of Moroccan towns. It does, however, provide a glimpse of an active, modern and working community— even if a predominantly poor one—and the old Medina in its center, walled and turreted by the Portuguese, holds a certain interest. In the Medina, too, there is an industrial tradition, with a whole neighborhood above the walls still devoted to the town's pottery workshops, which have a virtual monopoly on the green, heavily-glazed roof tiles used on palaces and mosques.

Arriving by **bus**, you'll find yourself at one of the terminals in **Place Ibnou Sina**, a busy traffic square some 300m outside the Medina. To reach the Medina, or find somewhere to stay; follow any of the streets leading down toward the sea and bear to the right.

You'll soon come to the old port, with its waterfront **Dar el Bahar** fortress, the main remnant of the town's brief Portuguese occupation (1508–41) and still well maintained following long use as a fortress and prison. It is sporadically open. From here on back, the old walls continue up, enclosing the Medina, to another and larger fortress known as **Kechla**—again, Portuguese in origin, but this time housing the town's modern prison. The **quartier des potiers** sprawls above it to the left and is impossible to miss, with its dozens of whitewashed kilns and chimneys. The processes here, certainly for tile production, remain traditional and are worth at least the time it takes to wander up. The color dyes, however, and the actual pottery designs are mostly pretty drab—hardly comparable to the beautiful old pieces you see around the country's crafts museums.

The potteries apart, there's little particular to say about Safi's Medina—or about the extensive suburbs of the new city. The **souks**, ordinary food and domestic-goods markets, are grouped around the Medina's one main street—**Rue du Socco**, which runs up from a small square by Dar el Bahar to the old city gate of Bab Chaaba and the potteries.

Most of the cheap **hotels** are either around Rue du Socco or on the one to the right of it (almost directly opposite the Bahar). All are fairly basic, though the *Hôtel de Paris* and the *Hôtel Majestic* (both unrated) are clean enough. The classified alternatives are both upscale: the 3*B *Hôtel Les Mimosas* (Rue Ibn Zaidoun; ☎32.08) and 4*B *Hôtel Atlantide* (Rue Chawki; ☎21.60). If you want to **camp**, there's a year-round grounds near the beach of Sidi Bouzid, 3km north of town.

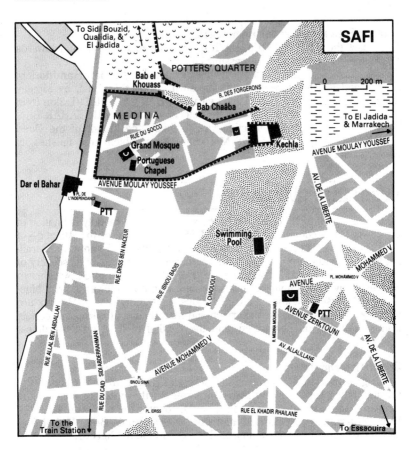

For **meals**, try *Restaurant Calypso*, in a courtyard just off Place de l'Independance, or the (fairly good value) restaurant in the *Hôtel Les Mimosas*.

Beaches around Cap Safi
The coast immediately south of Safi is heavily polluted and industrialized, and for a beach escape you'll want to head north.

Here, **SIDI BOUZID** is the main local beach (regular buses and *grands taxis*), but, a couple of pleasant restaurants notwithstanding, there are better targets just around Cap Safi.

Fifteen kilometers from Safi is a superb, cliff-sheltered beach known as **LALLA FATMA**—totally undeveloped, with nothing more than a *koubba* (and a few Moroccan campers) in sight. If you try it, you'll have to take food and drink along; ideally, you should have your own transportation, too, though it would be possible to survive by just hitching and using the Safi–Oualidia bus.

South to Essaouria: Kasbah Hamidouch
Once past the industrial strip, south of Safi, the road runs inland towards Essaouira—the coast is all inaccessible cliff.

If you have a car, there is a worthwhile excursion to **Kasbah Hamidouch**, a large and isolated fortress built, like so many on this coast, by Moulay Ismail. It is situated near the fishing village of DAR CAID HADJI, 2km from the main road and signposted to the left as you pass DAR TAHAR BEN ABBOU. The fort's main function was to guard the mouth of the Oued Tensift, one of the most active Moroccan rivers, which here finishes its course from Marrakesh.

Essaouira (Mogador)

Apart from the immediate impact of the sea air and the friendly animation of the town, the predominant images of **ESSAOUIRA** are of the Atlantic—of the rugged coast and offshore islands, the vast expanse of empty sands trailing back along the promontory to the south, and the almost Gothic scenery of the eighteenth-century fortifications. It is an atmospheric place, windblown and distinctly melancholic out of season but, with its whitewashed and blue-shuttered houses and lines of arcaded shops, thoroughly likable. The mixture of Berber villagers, sardine fishermen and Marrakchi and European tourists seems easy and uncomplicated, and the handful of local hustlers almost apologetic.

Orientation and Hotels
Getting around the town couldn't be easier. Buses (both *CTM* and the private companies) arrive at **Bab Doukkala**, at the northern edge of the ramparts, and once inside the gates, you encounter the two main streets—**Rue Mohammed Zerktouni** and **Av. Mohammed Ben Abdallah**—parallel to each other and running all the way down to the **harbor**.

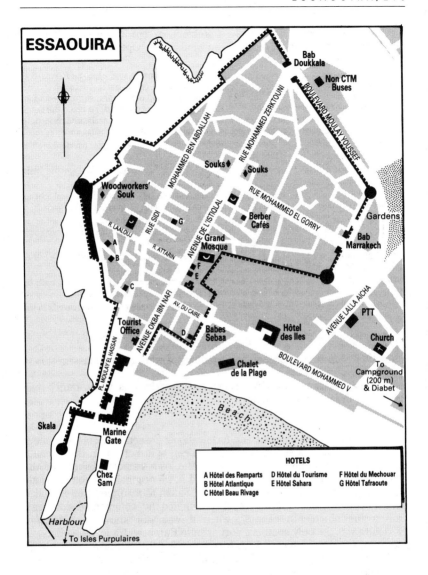

At the far end of these streets, flanking the small **tourist office**, is a long, open square, **Place Moulay El Hassan**, around which are located most of the cafés, restaurants, and hotels. Walk down here when you first arrive and you'll get a pretty good sense of the layout. If you're driving, there is a **parking lot**, manned around the clock, at the south end of the town (5dh for 24 hr.).

Accommodation is not usually a problem, except in the fall, when the town attracts a fair number of European windsurfers. Options include:

Hôtel des Remparts (A), 18 Rue Ibn Rochd; 22.82. As the name suggests, the *Remparts* is built right into the walls overlooking the sea. It was once quite grand, but has decayed and is a bit seedy. But it does have good, big rooms—a bit too damp outside the summer—and an added bonus in a rooftop terrace where you can sunbathe out of the wind. To reach the hotel, leave Place Moulay Hassan along the road opposite the Grand Mosque; at the end, turn right and then immediately left onto Rue Ibn Rochd—the hotel is on the left at the far end. *1 *B.*

Pension Smara, almost opposite the *Remparts*. Similarly priced and again overlooking the sea. Useful fallback choice. *Unclassified.*

Hôtel Beau Rivage (C), Place Moulay Hassan. Another inexpensive hotel, in the main square. *Unclassified.*

Hôtel du Tourisme (D), Rue Mohammed Ben Messaoud; ☎20.75. Clean and cheap. Located at the corner of the ramparts to the right of Place Moulay Hassan. *Unclassified.*

Hôtel Mechouar (F); ☎20.18. **Hôtel Sahara**; ☎23.79. These are next door to each other on Rue Okba Ibn Nafia, just off Avenue de l'Istiqlal. They're a bit more upscale with rather glitzy decor—but clean and pleasant enough. Respectively, *1 *A, 2 *B.*

Hôtel Tafraout (G), 7 Rue Marrakech; ☎21.20. In the heart of the Medina, with some rather cell-like rooms. A women's *hammam* is right next door. *1 *A.*

Hôtel Tafoukt, ☎25.04. **Hôtel des Iles**, ☎23.29. The two more expensive hotels, both on Boulevard Mohammed V. The latter has a swimming pool. Respectively, *3 *A, 4 *A.*

If all of these are full—which is unlikely—there are half a dozen other **basic hotels** in the alleyways between the two main streets.

Camping Municipal, 600m east along the seafront. Cheap and reasonably secure.

Another **hammam** (for men and women), offering robust massages, is to be found just behind the bus station.

Note that, for some obscure reason, the **electricity** is 110 v, rather than 220 v as in the rest of the country.

Around the Town

With its dramatic sea bastions and fortifications, Essaouira seems a lot older than it is. Although a series of forts had been built here from the fifteenth century on, it was only in the 1760s that the town was established and the present circuit of walls constructed around it. Its original function was military—Agadir was in revolt at the time and Sultan Mohammed Ben Abdallah needed a base—but this was soon preempted by commercial concerns. During the nineteenth century, when it was still known as *Mogador*, Essaouira was the only southern port open to European trade: its harbor was free from customs duties, British merchants lived in the town, and a large Jewish community settled. With the coming of the French Protectorate, and the emergence of Casablanca, decline set in; when it came to an end, and the Jews left, it declined even more. Now a fishing port and market town, it has lapsed into a somewhat genteel obscurity, boosted a little by its growing popularity as a resort.

Just recently opened, the **Musée Sidi Mohammed Ben Abdallah** (8:30am–noon and 2:30–6pm; closed Tues.) is worth visiting. Featuring excellent displays on marquetry, as well as standard handicrafts collections, it is housed in a nineteenth-century mansion on the road running down from the ramparts to Av. de l'Istiqlal. Next door is the **Ensemble Artisanal**, exhibiting local crafts. Besides these, there are few formal "sights" in the town: it's more a place just to walk around in, exploring the *souks* and ramparts or wandering along the immense beach.

At some point, though, make your way down to the **harbor,** where fresh sardines are cooked on the landings, and climb up to the **Skala**, the great sea bastion which runs back from it along the northern cliffs. Orson Welles filmed much of his *Othello* here, staging a bizarre (but very Moroccan) "punishment" of Iago, suspended above the sea and rocks in a cramped metal cage. Along the top of the Skala are a collection of European cannon, most of them presented to the sultan by ambitious nineteenth-century merchants.

Underneath the Skala, toward the "angle" of the ramparts, are a group of cedar and *thuya* **craftsmen,** who have been long established in Essaouira and produce some amazingly painstaking and beautiful marquetry work. Quite justifiably, they claim this is the best in the country, and if you see good examples elsewhere they've probably come from here. If you're thinking of buying—boxes and chess sets are for sale, as well as traditional furniture—this is the best place to do it, after checking out the *Ensemble Artisanal* (see above). The town's **other souks** spread around two arcades, on either side of Rue Mohammed Zerktouni, and up toward the old Mellah—an interesting area and a good place to start thinking about food (see below).

Out across the bay lie the **Isles Purpuraires**: two rocky islets, the larger dominated by a fortress-like building which saw intermittent use as a state prison and a quarantine station for pilgrims returning from Mecca. The islands are semiprotected as a nature reserve, since they are the only non-Mediterranean breeding site of Eleonora's falcon—clearly visible, with binoculars, from the town. If you want to visit the isles (and this should be strongly discouraged, in summer), you'll have to get a *permet d'autorisation* from the tourist office (50dh) before beginning to negotiate for the boat ride. Don't pay for the ride until you're collected and returned to the town!

Restaurants and Bars

Off to the right (if you're walking up from the harbor) of the Rue Zerktouni *souks* are a series of **"Berber Cafés,"** a unique Essaouira institution amounting to little more than a street of tiny rooms covered with matting. All of them serve soup, tea, and a variety of *tajines*. In a way they're a bit of a tourist trap, and travelers here have been badly ripped off (and not just for *tajines*), but local fishermen and workers also frequent them—and they are by far the liveliest places around.

Among the mainstream tourist **restaurants,** *Café-Restaurant Essalam* (Place Moulay Hassan) offers the cheapest meals; *Restaurant El Khaima*, is worth a meal, too, though it's a bit pricier. A little more upmarket, but recommended, are *Restaurant-Bar Bab Lachouar* (Place Moulay Hassan), for fine seafood, and *Restaurant Riad* (18 Rue Zayane, off Av. Allal Ben Abdallah), which serves imaginative French-Moroccan dishes in beautiful, traditionally decorated rooms, with rare antiques. A bit more unpredictable—but good when it's good—is *Chez Sam*, down at the end of the harbor: a seafood restaurant and bar, serving huge portions of fish and (at a price) lobster.

Beyond *Sam's* and the *Bab Lachouar*, places to have a **drink** are limited. There is a restaruant-bar, the *Chalet de la Place*, just off the beach, opposite the imposing *Hôtel des Iles*; another attached to the *Iles* itself, where Moroccans gather to drink beer and play chess and checkers; and a cheaper one at the *Hôtel Sahara*.

The Beach, Diabat, and Cap Sim

Essaouira's **beach** extends for miles south of the town, toward Cap Sim. The sands are fine, and safe, though at times (especially in early summer) the wind can be pretty relentless—making sunbathing, at least, impossible. But windiness is a complaint that could be levelled generally against most of the Atlantic coast, and the flip side is that it does keep temperatures cool (70° F is about average).

Only the area of a hundred meters or so near the town ever even remotely gets crowded. The rest, beyond the ruins of an old fort and royal summer pavilion half buried in the sand, is yours for the walking. The riverbed, just south of Diabat, is well reputed for its **birdlife**, with a variety of waders and egrets, and numerous warblers in the scrub behind.

Diabat

In the direction of Cap Sim, an hour's walk along the beach and then a kilometer's climb, over a trail through some thorny scrub, is the village of **DIABAT**. This was one of the legendary hippie hangouts, popularized by Jimi Hendrix, who spent a while in the colony here. These days, it has reverted back to an ordinary Berber farming village, a ragged sort of place which (since a police crackdown in the early 1970s) is no longer permitted to rent rooms.

Three kilometers south of the village, however, there are some attractive **accommodation** possibilities. The French-owned and distinctly chic *Auberge Tangaro* is a tempting alternative to staying in Essaouira, especially if you have transportation of your own. A small and wonderful place, little used except on weekends, when groups of French and German windsurfers come down from Casablanca and Marrakesh, the *auberge* has a number of chalet **rooms**, and it serves excellent meals throughout the day. Next door is a small, rather primitive **campground**. To get there by car, take the Agadir road for about 6km out of Essaouira and then turn off to the right; the "direct" approach from Essaouira is no longer possible after the collapse of a bridge just below Diabat. There is a good **beach** a half-hour hike from the campground and *auberge*.

Cap Sim

There is no road or track access to **Cap Sim** from Diabat. To get there, drive south for 12km along the Agadir road, and then take a right fork, signposted SIDI KAOUKI—a *marabout* near the cape. There is no public transportation on this route, though you could negotiate for a taxi in Essaouira.

At the cape, there are usually a couple of **camels** and their drivers, who hire out the beasts to tourists. The trip that's touted is actually quite fun—a four-hour return ride to (otherwise hard of access) **dunes**.

travel details

Trains

Rabat–Casablanca More or less hourly departures (50 min.–1½ hr.). Most run to/from *Casa-Port*, though a few exclusively to/from *Voyageurs*.

Casablanca–Tangier Four daily, via Rabat, Mohammedia, Salé, Kenitra, Asilah, and Tangier.

7:15am Casa–Port, arrives Rabat (8:15am), Asilah (12:13pm), and Tangier (1:15pm).

12:45pm Casa-Voyageurs, arrives Rabat (2:03pm), Sidi Slimane (4:18pm: change for Asilah/Tangier, 6:59pm/7:55pm).

3:15pm Casa-Voyageurs, arrives Rabat (6:12pm: change for Asilah/Tangier, 10:42pm/11:26pm).

11:10pm Casa-Voyageurs, arrives Rabat (12:08am), Asilah (4:43am), Tangier (5:37am).

Casablanca–Fes/Meknes Five daily, via Rabat, Salé, and Kenitra; all from **Casa-Voyageurs**:

6am, arrives Rabat (7:18am), Meknes (10:36am), and Fes (11:33am).

12:45pm, arrives Rabat (2:03pm), Meknes (5:38pm), and Fes (6:40pm).

5:15pm, arrives Rabat (6:12pm), Meknes (4:09pm), and Fes (5:16pm).

10:05pm, arrives Rabat (11:17pm), Meknes (2:30am), Fes (3:34am).

Rabat/Casablanca–Marrakesh Seven daily in 4–6 hr. (from Rabat), 5–7½ hr. (from Casablanca). Departures from Rabat/Casablanca-Voyageurs are: 4:18am/5:25am (arrives Marrakesh 8:54am), 5:18am/7:54am (11:31am), 8:45am/9:39am (12:43pm), 11:03am/12:08pm (3:13pm), 2:34pm/17:16pm (9:09pm), 6:19pm/7:13pm (10:17pm), and 10:52pm/1:23am (changing at Casa, 5:16am).

Casablanca–El Jadida Three daily (8:52am from Port, arrives Azzemour 10:13am, El Jadida 10:25am; 6:20pm from Port, arrives Azzemour 7:47pm, El Jadida 8pm; 8:05pm from Casa-Voyageurs, arrives Azzemour 9:02pm, El Jadida 9:12pm).

Buses

From Rabat: Tangier (2 daily; 5 hr.); Larache (4: 3½ hr.); Salé (frequent; 15 min.); Casablanca (10; 1hr. & 40 min.); Meknes (3; 4 hr.); Fes (6; 5½ hr.)

From Casa Dozens of destinations, including Tangier (2 daily; 6½ hr.); Rabat (10; 1hr. & 40 min.); El Jadida (3; 2· hr.); Essaouira (3; 5–7 hr.; best is the *SATAS*); Agadir (1; 10 hr.); Marrakesh (3; 4 hr.)

From El Jadida Casablanca (3 daily; 2½ hr.); Rabat (2; 4 hr.); Oualidia (daily; 1½ hr.)

From Safi Oualidia/El Jadida (3 daily; 1¼ /2½ hr.)

From Essaouira Agadir (6 daily; 3½ hr.); Safi (2; 6 hr.); El Jadida (2; 8 hr.); Casablanca (4; 5–9 hr.); Tiznit (1; 7 hr.) **Note**: Most of the Essaouira–Marrakesh services (6 daily; 3 hr.) are non-*CTM* buses.

Grands Taxis

Rabat–Casablanca: Regular route, 1 hr. 20 min.

From El Jadia Negotiable to Casablanca.

Flights

Rabat/Casa Mohammed V Airport: International flights to London, Paris, and most major destinations. Domestic flights to all major cities in Morocco.

TELEPHONE CODES

CASABLANCA ☎0	SAFI ☎046
ESSAOUIRA ☎047	SALÉ ☎07
KENITRA ☎016	SKHIRAT ☎07
MOHAMMEDIA ☎032	TÉMARA ☎07
RABAT ☎07	

CHAPTER FIVE

MARRAKESH AND THE HIGH ATLAS

Marrakesh—'Morocco City,' as the early travelers called it—has always been something of a pleasure city, a marketplace where the southern tribesmen and Berber villagers bring in their goods, spend their money, and find entertainment. For tourists it's an enduring fantasy—a city of immense beauty, low, pink, and tent like before a

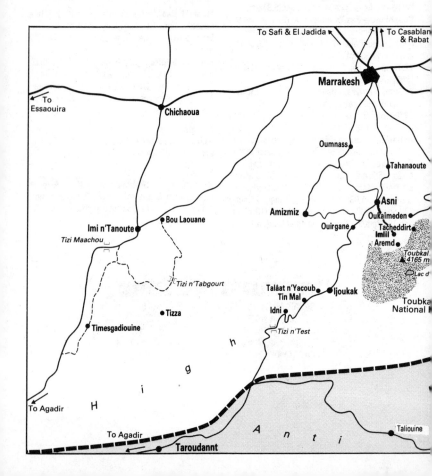

great shaft of mountains, and immediately exciting. At the heart of it all is a square, **Djemaa el Fna**, really no more than an open space in the center of the city, but the stage for a long established ritual in which shifting circles of onlookers gather around groups of acrobats, drummers, pipe musicians, dancers, storytellers, and comedians. However many times you return there, it remains compelling. So, too, do the city's architectural attractions: the immense, still basins of the **Agdal** and **Menara** parks, the delicate Granadine carving of the **Saadian Tombs**, and, above all, the **Koutoubia Minaret**, the most perfect Islamic monument in North Africa.

Some 50km south of Marrakesh rise the **High Atlas**, the grandest and most rewarding Moroccan mountain range. Its foothills and the lush summer pleasureground of **Ourika Valley** can be reached in just an hour by bus or *grand taxi*. Or, within the space of a morning, you can leave the city and get up to the village and hiking center of **Imlil**, where trails begin for **Djebel Toubkal**—at 4165m the tallest Atlas peak and one of the highest in Africa. To

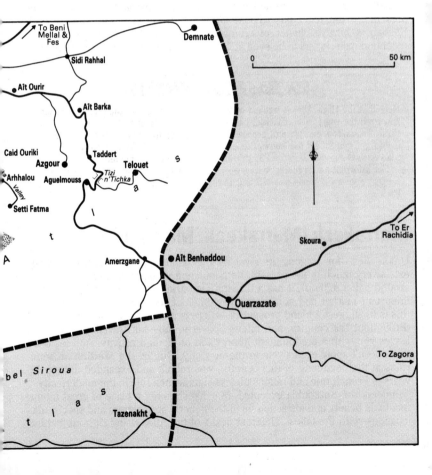

explore the *massif*, you don't have to be a serious climber; there are well-established hiking trails to refuge huts. This, and the High Atlas as a whole, is also a surprisingly populated region—the slopes drop to valleys and streams, with small Berber villages (where you can usually stay) terraced into their sides.

The remoteness of these mountain villages—easily maintained despite the growing popularity of trekking—is also reflected in the two High Atlas passes, the n'Test and n'Tichka *tizis*. **Tizi n'Test**, the pass beyond Toubkal over to Taroudannt, is the steepest: a crazy, adrenalin-plugged switchback of almost continuous hairpin curves. If you drive along this road, beware of what's in store for you— it's pretty alarming even by bus. Stopping over at Ijoukak, toward the summit, you can walk up to the dramatic valley and ruins of the twelfth-century mosque of **Tin Mal**, the base from which the Almohads swept down to take Marrakesh and, ultimately, to reconquer Spain.

Tizi n'Tichka, which today bears most of the traffic, has a more recent but equally evocative history. It was built to replace the old caravan route to Tafilalt, which was controlled over the last century and for much of the present by the legendary Glaoui family, "the Lords of the Atlas." Their Kasbah, a bizarre cluster of crumbling towers and kitschy-looking 1930s reception halls, is still to be seen at **Telouet**, just an hour from the main road.

WINTER TRAVELING

Note that the High Atlas is subject to snow from November to the end of February, and even the major Tizi n'Tichka pass can be closed for periods of a day or more. Flash floods, too, can present problems, when the snows melt in February–March. If you get caught by the snow, the easiest route from Marrakesh to the south is road 6543 to Agadir, then the P32 through Taroudannt and Taliouine.

For information on hiking seasons—and winter treks above the snow line are a serious endeavor here—see "Hiking Practicalities" box, under "Toubkal National Park".

Marrakesh (Marrakech, Marrakch)

Unlike Fes—for so long its rival as the nation's capital—**MARRAKESH** exists very much in the present. Its population is rising (and stands today at around half a million), it has a thriving industrial area and remains the most important market and administrative center of southern Morocco. None of this is to suggest a bland prosperity—there is heavy unemployment here, as throughout the country, and intense poverty, too—but traveling through it leaves you with a predominant impression of life and activity. And for once this doesn't apply exclusively to the new city, **Gueliz**; the **Medina**, in semi-ruins at the beginning of this century, was rebuilt and expanded during the years of French rule and retains no less significant a role in the modern city.

Indeed, the Koutoubia excepted, Marrakesh is not a place of great monuments. Is beauty and attraction lie in the general atmosphere and spectacular location—with the tallest, sheerest peaks of the Atlas rising right up behind the city, towering through the haze. The feel, as much as anything, is a product of this. Marrakesh is a **Berber** rather than an Arab city: the traditional metropolis of Atlas tribes, Mahgrebis from the plains, Saharan nomads, and former slaves from Africa beyond the desert—Sudan, Senegal, and the ancient kingdom of Timbuktu. All of these strands have shaped the city's *souks* and its way of life, and in the crowds and performers in Djemaa el Fna, they can still occasionally seem distinct.

For most travelers, Marrakesh is the first experience of the south and its generally more relaxed atmosphere and attitudes. **Marrakchis** themselves are renowned for their warmth and sociabililty, their humor and directness—all qualities that (superficially, at least) can seem absent among the Fassis. Certainly, the city has a more relaxed and laid-back feel than anywhere in the north, with women, for example, having a greater degree of freedom—and public presence, often riding mopeds around on the streets. Another notable difference with Fes is that Marrakesh is much less homogenous and cohesive. The city is more a conglomeration of villages than an urban community, with quarters formed and maintained by successive generations of migrants from the countryside.

Some History

The original date of Marrakesh's **foundation** is disputed, though it was certainly close to the onset of **Almoravid** rule—around 1062–70—and must have taken the initial form of a camp and market, a *ksour*, or fortified town gradually developing around it.

Its founder (as that of the Almoravid dynasty) was **Youssef bin Tachfine**, a restless military leader who conquered northern Morocco within two years and then, turning his attention toward Spain, defeated the Christian kings, to bring Andalusia under Moroccan rule. Tachfine maintained as bases for his empire both Fes and Marrakesh, but under his son, the pious **Ali Ben Youssef**, Marrakesh became very much the dominant center. Craftsmen and architects from Cordoba worked on the new city: palaces, baths, and mosques were built; a subterranean system of channels was constructed to provide water for the growing palmery; and, in 1126–27, the first, seven-kilometer **circuit of walls** was raised, replacing an earlier stockade of thorn bushes. These, many times rebuilt, are essentially the city's present walls—made of *tabia*, the red mud of the plains, mixed and strengthened with the addition of lime.

Of the rest of the Almoravid's building works, there remains hardly a trace. The dynasty that replaced them—the orthodox and reforming **Almohads**—sacked the city for three days after taking possession of it in 1147. Once again, though, Marrakesh was adopted as the empire's preeminent capital, its domain this time stretching as far as Tripolitania (modern Libya) in the wake of phenomenal early conquests. With the accession to the throne in 1184 of **Yacoub el Mansour**, the third Almohad sultan, the city entered its greatest period. Under this massively prolific builder, *kissarias* were constructed for the sale and storage of Italian and oriental cloth, a new Kasbah was begun, housing twelve separate palaces, mosques, and gardens, and a succession of poets and scholars arrived at the court—among them Averroes, the most

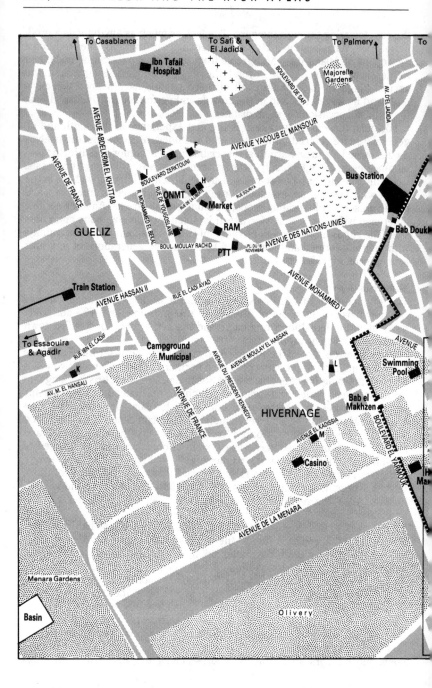

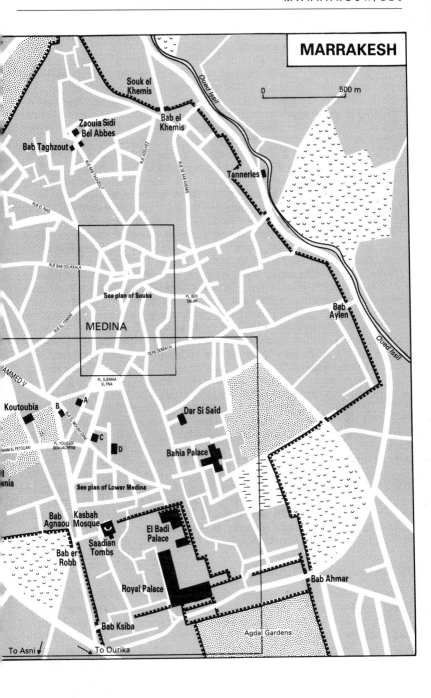

MARRAKESH

0   500 m

Oued Issil

Souk el Khemis

Bab el Khemis

Zaouia Sidi Bel Abbes

Bab Taghzout

RUE DE BAB AGUOLL

RUE DE BAB EL KHEMIS

RUE ASSOUKEF

Tanneries

RUE EL RIAD

RUE BAB DOUKKALA

See plan of Souks

PL. BEN SALAH

RUE EL YAMAN

MEDINA

Bab Aylen

Oued Issil

DERB DEBBACHI

…AMMED V

PL. DJEMAA EL FNA

A

B

Koutoubia

RUE EL MOUASSINE

C

D

Dar Si Said

…AM EL FETOUAKI

PL. YOUSSEF BEN TACHFINE

Bahia Palace

…nia

See plan of Lower Medina

Bab Agnaou

Kasbah Mosque

Saadian Tombs

El Badi Palace

Bab er Robb

Royal Palace

Bab Ahmar

Bab Ksiba

Agdal Gardens

To Asni

To Ourika

distinguished Arabic medieval philosopher. Mansour's reign, too, saw the construction of the **Koutoubia Mosque** and minaret.

It is astonishing, though, to think that this whole period of Almoravid and Almohad rule—so crucial to the rise of both the city and the nation—lasted barely two centuries. By the 1220s, the empire was beginning to fragment amid a series of factional civil wars, and Marrakesh fell into the familiar pattern of pillage, ruination, and rebuilding. It revived for a time to form the basis of an independent **Merenid** kingdom (1374–86) but overall it gave way to Fes until the emergence of the Saadians in the early sixteenth century.

Taking Marrakesh, then devastated by famine, in 1521, and Fes in 1546, the **Saadians** provided a last burst of imperial splendor. Their first sultans regained the Atlantic coast, which had been extensively colonized by the Portuguese; **Ahmed el Mansour**, the great figure of the dynasty, led a conquest of Timbuktu, seizing control of the most lucrative caravan routes in Africa. The **El Badi Palace**—Marrakesh's largest and greatest building project—was constructed from the proceeds of this new wealth, though it again fell victim to dynastic rivalry and, aside from its mausoleum (the **Saadian Tombs**), was reduced to ruins by Moulay Ismail.

Subsequent history under the **Alaouites**—the dynasty perpetuated today by King Hassan—is for the most part less distinguished. Marrakesh remained an imperial capital, and the need to maintain a southern base against the tribes ensured the regular, alternating residence of its sultans. But from the seventeenth to the nineteenth century, it shrank back from its medieval walls and lost much of its former trade. A British traveler's description of the city at the turn of the century as "a squalid, straggling mazy kind of open cesspool about the size of Paris" is probably not inaccurate, though for the last decades prior to the protectorate, it enjoyed a return to favor with the Shereefian court. **Moulay Hasan** (1873–1894) and **Moulay Abd el Aziz** (1894–1908) both ran their governments from here in a bizarre closing epoch of the old ways, accompanied by a final bout of frantic palace building.

On the arrival of **the French**, Marrakesh gave rise to a short-lived pretender, the religious leader el Hiba. For the remainder of the colonial period, the city was a virtual fief of its pasha, **T'hami el Glaoui**—the most powerful, autocratic, and extraordinary character of his age (see Telouet). Then, and especially since **independence**, the city has undergone considerable change, with rural emigration from the Atlas and sub-Sahara, new methods of cultivation in the plains, and the development of a sizable tourist industry combining to make it today the country's largest modern trading center outside Casablanca.

Orientation and Hotels

Despite its size—and the tortuous maze of its *souks*—Marrakesh is not too difficult to find your way around. The broad, open space of **Djemaa el Fna** (or "big square," as the guides call it) lies right at the heart of the Medina, and almost everything of interest is concentrated in the web of alleyways above and below it—the two areas detailed on our individual maps. Only in the *souks* (see section following) might you want to consider taking a guide.

Just to the west of the Djemaa, and an unmistakable landmark, is the minaret of the **Koutoubia**—in the shadow of which begins **Avenue Mohammed V**, leading out of the Medina and up the length of the new city, **Gueliz**.

Going from the Djemaa to Gueliz is a fairly long walk, but there are plenty of **petits taxis** (from the post office in Gueliz, and from the Djemaa—about 15dh) and a regular **bus** (#1: between the Koutoubia/Place de Foucauld and the main squares in Gueliz along Av. Mohammed V). In addition, there are **calèches**, horse-drawn cabs which line up near the Koutoubia, the Badi Palace, and some of the fancier hotels. These can take up to five people and are often no more expensive than *petits taxis*—though again bargain and fix the price before setting out.

Points of arrival are fairly straightforward.

By bus. There is now a single **bus terminal** (both for *CTM* and private companies), located just outside the walls of the Medina by Bab Doukkala. You can **walk** into the center of Gueliz from here in around ten minutes by following Av. des Nations Unies; to the Djemaa it's around twenty to twenty-five minutes, most easily accomplished by walking down beside the Medina walls to Place de la Liberté, and then following Av. Mohammed V toward the Koutoubia. Alternatively, catch the #3 or #8 **bus**, which run in one direction to the Koutoubia, and in the other to the center of Gueliz and the train station; or save a lot of sweat by taking a *petit taxi* (about 15dh to the Djemaa, for up to three people).

By Train. Getting into the Djemaa from the **train station** you'll certainly want transportation (the #3 or #8 **bus**, or again about 15dh for a **petit taxi**). However, the station is only ten minutes' walk from the center of Gueliz, and within easy reach of the campground and youth hostel.

From the Airport. The city's **airport** is 5km to the southwest. The #11 **bus** is supposed to run every half hour to the Djemaa. In reality, you might want to opt for a **petit taxi**, in which case you're basically at the mercy of the going rate that day: anything above 50dh is beginning to get unreasonable, but, whatever you do, agree on a price beforehand. Arriving on a Friday afternoon, or after about 6pm any day of the week, you'll find the **bureau de change** closed. Taxis will accept dollars or pounds, though they will charge significantly more than the equivalent dirham rate.

For details on transportation out of Marrakesh, see "Leaving Marrakesh", under "Practicalities."

Hotels

Virtually all the **cheap hotels** in Marrakesh are grouped in a triangular grid of streets below Djemaa el Fna: the area (see the "Lower Medina" map) bounded by Rue de Bab Agnaou, Rue Zitoun el Qedim, and Av. El Mouahidina. A few of them are miserable and overpriced but most are quite pleasant—small, family-run places, with eight or ten rooms grouped around a cool, central courtyard—and their location keeps you close to the Medina and its life.

With only four or five exceptions, all the regular, **classified hotels** are in Gueliz, the Ville Nouvelle, or in the upscale "hotel quarter" of **Hivernage**. These have the advantage of convenience if you are arriving late at night, particularly at the train station—but if you stay for any time, taxi fares to the Medina can soon eat away at budgets.

For anyone with the money for a few **luxury nights** in Morocco, Marrakesh is one of the best places to do so—particularly in summer, when temperatures hover around 100°F, with midday bursts of 120-130°F. Your main criterion will be a swimming pool. The most affordable option is the *Hôtel Yasmine*, on the edge of the Medina, which charges around $20 a double. At the top of the range, for anyone with serious money to burn, the country's most famous hotel, *La Mamounia*, charges from $150 a night.

MEDINA HOTELS: UNCLASSIFIED

Hôtel du Café de France, and **Hôtel Oukaïmeden**. These are actually in the Djemaa el Fna and have some rooms overlooking the square. The *Café de France* has one of the most famous roof terraces, from which to view the scene below, and clean but rather stuffy rooms. The *Oukaïmeden* is over on the far side of the square, beside the huge, strictly guarded *Club Med* complex.

Hôtel de France, 197 Rue Zitoun el Kedim, ☎430.67; **Hôtel Chellah**, ☎419.77; **Hôtel Medina**. Facing the *Hôtel CTM*, turn down the arched lane to its left, Rue Zitoun el Kedim. The *Hôtel de France* (not to be confused with the *Hôtel Café de France* listed above) is near the beginning of this street: one of the best of the cheapies, recently modernized, and secure. Fifty meters down, the *Chellah* is signposted on an alley to the left: it can be a bit hustley, but is again cheap, and a nice building. The *Hôtel Medina* , in the first alley to the right, heading down Rue Zitoun el Kedim, is a real gem—small, clean, family-run, and friendly; good value, too, with hot showers included.

Hôtel de la Jeunesse, ☎436.31; **Hôtel Afriquia**; **Hôtel Nouzah** and **Hôtel Eddakla**; all in Rue de la Recette. The best in a zigzagging lane of small, cheap hotels entered (coming from the Djemaa) through the first alley on your left off Rue Bab Agnaou. Rue Bab Agnaou itself doesn't have a very prominent street sign, but it's on our map of the Lower Medina—look out for the Crédit du Maroc bank, near its beginning. The hotels offer similar, clean but basic, facilities. The *Afriquia* has a pleasant courtyard, with orange trees; the *Nouzah* is youth-oriented, with a taste for 1970s rock on its tape system.

Hôtel Souria; **Hôtel Hillal**; **Hôtel El Farah**, and **Hôtel El Al-lal**; These are scattered along the next lane down off Rue Bab Agnaou—reached through a smaller, arched entrance opposite the *Hôtel du Tourisme* (and just before you come to the Banque Populaire). Of the cheap places, the *Souria* is by far the best, though correspondingly popular.

MEDINA HOTELS: CLASSIFIED

Hôtel CTM, Place Djemaa el Fna, ☎223.25. Located above the old bus station. Good-sized rooms, clean, and as cheap as many unclassified places. *1*A.*

Hôtel Gallia, Rue de la Recette; ☎259.13. (2*B). Follow directions as for the Souria, etc, above; the Gallia is on the left at the end of the lane. Pleasant building and worth the extra money over its neighbors if you are offered one of the larger, better rooms. *2*B.*

Hôtel de Foucauld (B, on main plan), Rue El Mouahidine; ☎254.99. Good location and a (sometimes good) restaurant attached. Rooms are on the small side, though, and there are frequent problems with the water supply. *2*B.*

Grand Hôtel Tazi (C, on main plan), Rue Bab Agnaou/corner of Av. Hoummam el Ftouaki; ☎221.52/421.55. Same management as the Foucauld, and only a fraction more expensive—for larger rooms, with hot showers, heating in winter, a garage to the rear, and a rooftop bar. When busy, they may insist on you taking half-board. *2*A.*

Note. At most times of year, the city has a shortage of space in the classified hotels (the Medina places are less of a problem), so **advance reservations** are a wise idea, especialy if you want to stay in one of the classified Medina hotels. Worst time is around the Easter vacation period, when you may arrive and find virtually every hotel full to capacity.

Hôtel Ali (A, on main plan), 10 Rue Dispensaire/Place de Foucauld; ☎449.79. A fairly new and very popular, small hotel; well run and with reliable showers. Does excellent Moroccan food in its restaurant, and next door is an excellent pâtisserie The hotel is used as a pick-up point for various hiking tours to the High Atlas, which could be useful for independent travelers. *2*A.*

Hôtel Minaret, 10 Rue du Dispensaire. Another new—and recommended—hotel, in the street behind the *Tazi. 2*A.*

Hôtel Yasmine, 8 Bd. de la Madeleine, south of Place de la Liberté; ☎461.42. Only 400m from the Djemaa, and with a swimming pool.*As yet unclassified: 3*A prices.*

Hôtel Mamounia, Av. Bab Jdid; ☎323.81. Something of a legend, set within its own palace grounds, this is the most beautiful and also the most expensive hotel in Morocco (doubles from 2500dh). Room prices drop a bit during the low season, or if you book as part of a vacation package—but they are still pretty astronomical. For the merely curious, tea in the gardens comes a lot cheaper, if the staff deign to let you in; no jeans, shorts, or sneakers allowed.

GUELIZ HOTELS

Keyed letters refer to main map.

Hôtel du Haouz, 66 Av. Hassan II. Close by the train station. *Unclassified.*

Hôtel Franco-Belge, 62 Bd. Zerktouni, ☎303.72; **Hôtel des Voyageurs**, 40 Bd. Zerktouni, ☎40 Bd. Zerktouni, 312.72. Unexciting but cheap; on a main thoroughfare. *Both 1*B.*

Hôtel Oasis (E), 50 Av. Mohammed V; ☎311.35. Similar to the above—but with a bar. *1*A.*

Hôtel la Palmeraie, 8 Rue Souraya (parrallel to Bd. Zerktouni, two blocks below); ☎310.07. Good value basic rooms, and a few more expensive ones with showers. *1*A.*

Hôtel Excelsior, Tarik Ibn Zaid/Ibn Aicha (parallel to Av. Mohammed V, a block above; and a block above Bd. Zerktouni); ☎317.33. Popular French-run hotel with slightly kitsch, Moorish decor. *2*A.*

Hôtel Koutoubia (J), 51 Av. El Mansour Eddahbi; ☎309.21. Vaguely stylish and set amid gardens, though sadly, its pool always seems empty; prices are a little high. *2*A.*

Hôtel Imilchil, Av. Echouhada; ☎314.53. One of the least expensive hotels with a (reliably full) swimming pool.

Hôtel Siaha Safir, Av. Kennedy, Hivernage; ☎342.52. A good hotel, with its own hammam, as well as a fine pool— and not that expensive for its classification. *4*A.*

Hôtel Es Saadi (M), Av. Qadissia, Hivernage; ☎320.11. The most elegant in Hivernage, with prices a fair bit below the Mamounia, despite luxury classification. *5*.*

YOUTH HOSTEL AND CAMPGROUND

Youth Hostel (Auberge de Jeunesse), Rue el Jahid; ☎328.31. Quiet, clean, and a useful first-night standby if you arrive late by train. Located five minutes' walk and three blocks from the train station: take any of the roads opposite it to Rue Ibn el Qadi, turning left a block before you reach the park behind the campground. Closes 10pm in the winter, around midnight in the summer. To get to the Djemaa from here, take the # 3 or #8 bus near the station. Those with hostel cards only.

Camping Municipal, Av. de France. Nothing special, though, located close by the youth hostel, useful for the same reasons as above—and for meeting people for information and possible lifts. There's a café-restaurant and small pool (not always full). Again, bus #3 or #8 to the Djemaa.

Djemaa el Fna and the Koutoubia

There's nowhere in North Africa like **Djemaa el Fna**—no place that so effortlessly involves you, blows aside travel cynicism, and keeps you returning for as long as you stay. By day it's basically a market, with a few snake charmers and an occasional troupe of acrobats. In the evening it becomes a whole carnival of musicians, clowns, and street entertainers. When you arrive in Marrakesh, and after you've found a room, come out here and you'll get straight into the ritual: wandering around, squatting amid the circles of onlookers, giving a dirham or two as your contribution. If you get tired, or if things slow down, you can move over to the rooftop terraces of the *Café de France* or the *Restaurant Argana* to gaze at it all and admire the frame of the Koutoubia Minaret.

What you are part of is a strange process. Tourism is probably now vital to the Djemaa's survival, yet apart from the snake charmers, water vendors (who live by posing for photographs), and the hustlers (who have more subtle ways), there's little that has compromised itself for the West. In many ways it actually seems the opposite. Most of the people gathered into circles around the performers are Moroccans—Berbers from the villages and lots of kids. There is no way that any tourist is going to have a tooth pulled by one of the dentists here, no matter how neat the piles of molars displayed on their square of carpet. Nor are you likely to use the scribes or street barbers or understand the convoluted tales* of the storytellers, around whom are gathered perhaps the most animated crowds in the square.

Nothing of this, though, matters very much. There is a fascination in the remedies of the herb doctors, with their bizarre concoctions spread out before them. There are **performers,** too, whose appeal is universal. The acrobats, itinerants from the Tazeroualt, have for years supplied the European circuses—though they are probably never so spectacular as here, thrust forward into multiple somersaults and contortions in the late afternoon heat. There are child boxers and sad-looking trained monkeys, clowns, and Chleuh boy dancers—their routines, to the climactic jarring of cymbals, totally sexual (and a traditional invitation to clients). And finally, the Djemaa's enduring sound—the dozens of **musicians** playing all kinds of instruments. Late into the night, when only a few people are left in the coffee stands at the center of the square, you can encounter individual players, plucking away at their *ginbris,* the skin-covered, two- or three-string guitars. Earlier in the evening, there are full groups: the *Aissaoua,* playing oboe-like *ghaitahs* next to the snake charmers; the Andalusian-influenced groups, with their *aouds* and crude violins; and the predominantly black *Gnaoua,* trance-healers who beat out hour-long hypnotic rhythms with iron clanging hammers and pound tall drums with long curved sticks.

---

* According to the novelist/translator Paul Bowles, these repertoires tend to be "rather grandiose stories about the sultan and his daughter and the rich Jew who tries to get her . . . very full of plot . . . with lots of magic and transportation."

DJEMAA EL FNA: SECURITY

As a foreigner in the Djemaa el Fna, you can feel something of an interloper—your presence accepted, though not wholly welcomed.

Entering into the spectacle down below, go denuded of the usual tourist trappings—cameras, money belts, etc. **Pickpockets** do very well out of the square. Beware, also, of being duped into the various board games, whose operators have perfected their systems many, many years ago.

If you get interested in the music there's a small section in the Djemaa, near the entrance to the *souks,* where stalls sell recorded **cassettes.** Most of these are actually Egyptian, the pop music that dominates Moroccan radio, but if you ask they'll play you Berber music from the Atlas, classic Fassi pieces, or even Gnaoua music—which sounds even stranger on tape, cut off only by the end of the one side and starting off almost identically on the other. These stalls apart, and those of the nut roasters, whose massive braziers line the immediate entrance to the potters' *souk,* the **market** activities of the Djemaa are mostly pretty mundane.

Not to be missed, however, even if you lack the stomach to eat at any of them, are the rows of makeshift **restaurants** that come into their own toward early evening. Lit by enormous lanterns, their tables piled high with massive bowls of cooked food, each vendor extols his own range of specialties. Sitting at a bench along one of their sides, you can eat for next to nothing, though even if you stick to vegetables, you may not escape the effects. If you're wary, head for the orange and lime juice vendors opposite the Café de France, or go for a handful of cactus fruit, peeled in a couple of seconds at the stalls nearby. For details on more substantial eating in the Djemaa and elsewhere, see "Practicalities."

Nobody is entirely sure when or how Djemaa el Fna came into being—nor even what its name means. The usual translation is "assembly of the dead," a suitably epic title that seems to refer to the public display here of the heads of rebels and criminals. This is certainly possible, since the Djemaa was a place of execution well into the last century; the phrase, though, might only mean "the mosque of nothing" (*djemaa* means both "mosque" and "assembly"— interchangeable terms in Islamic society), recalling an abandoned Saadian plan to build a new grand mosque on this site. Whichever is the case, as an open area between the original Kasbah and the *souks,* the *place* has probably played its present role since the city's earliest days. It has often been the focal point for rioting—even within the last decade—and every few years there are plans to close it down and to move its activities outside the city walls. This, in fact, happened after independence in 1956, when the new "modernist" government built a corn market (which still stands) on part of the square and tried to turn the rest into a parking lot. The plan, however, lasted for only a year. Tourism was falling off and it was clearly an unpopular move—it took away one of the people's basic psychological needs, as well as eliminating a possible necessary expression of the past.

The Koutoubia

The absence of any architectural feature in the Djemaa—which even today seems like a haphazard clearing—serves to emphasize the drama of the **Koutoubia Minaret**, the focus of any approach to the city. Nearly seventy meters high and visible for miles on a clear morning, this is the oldest of the three great Almohad towers (the others being in Rabat and Seville) and the most complete. Its proportions—a 1:5 ratio of width to height—established the classic Moroccan design. Its scale, rising from the low city buildings and the plains to the north, is extraordinary, and the more so the longer you stay and the more familiar its sight becomes.

Completed by Sultan Yacoub el Mansour (1184–99), work on the minaret probably began shortly after the Almohad conquest of the city, around 1150. It displays many of the features that were to become widespread in Moroccan architecture—the wide band of ceramic inlay near the top, the pyramid-shaped, castellated *merlons* rising above it, the use of *darj w ktarf* (fleur-de-lis), and other motifs—and it also established the alternation of patterning on different faces. Here, the top floor is similar on each of the sides but the lower two are almost eccentric in their variety; the most interesting is perhaps the middle niche on the southeast face, a semicircle of small lobed arches, which was to become the dominant decorative feature of Almohad gates.

If you look hard, you will notice that at around this point, the stones of the main body of the tower become slightly smaller. This seems odd today but originally the whole minaret would have been covered with plaster and its tiers of decoration painted. To see just how much this can change the whole effect—and, to most tastes, lessen much of its beauty—take a look at the Kasbah mosque (by the Saadian Tombs) which has been carefully but completely restored in this manner; there have been plans over the years to do the same with the Koutoubia, though for the present they have been indefinitely shelved. The only part of the structure that has really been renovated are the three gilt balls made of copper at the summit. The subject of numerous legends—mostly of supernatural interventions to keep away the thieves—these are thought originally to have been made of gold, the gift of the wife of Yacoub el Mansour, and presented as a penance for breaking her fast for three hours during Ramadan.

The Souks and Northern Medina

It is spicy in the souks, and cool and colorful. The smell, always pleasant, changes gradually with the nature of the merchandise. There are no names or signs; there is no glass . . . . You find everything—but you always find it many times over.
                    Elias Canetti: *The Voices of Marrakesh*

The **souks** of Marrakesh sprawl immediately north of Djemaa el Fna. They seem vast the first time you venture in, and almost impossible to navigate, though, in fact, the area that they cover is pretty compact. A long, covered street, **Rue Souk Smarine**, runs for half their length and then splits in two—becoming **Souk el Attarin** and **Souk el Kebir**. Off of these are virtually all the individual *souks:* alleys and small squares devoted to specific crafts, where you can often watch part of the production process. At the top of the main area of *souks*, too, you can visit the Saadian **Ben Youssef Medersa**—the most important monument in the northern half of the Medina and arguably the finest building in the city after the Koutoubia Minaret.

If you are staying for some days, you'll probably return often to the *souks*—and this is a good way of taking them in, singling out a couple of specific crafts or products to see, rather than being swamped by the whole. To come to grips with the general layout, though, you might find it useful to walk around the whole area once with a **guide**. Despite the pressure of offers in the Djemaa, don't feel that one is essential, but until the hustlers begin to recognize you (seeing that you've been in the *souks* before), they'll probably follow you in; if and when this happens, try to be easygoing, polite, and confident—the qualities that force most hustlers to look elsewhere. The most interesting **times** to visit are in the very early morning (between 5 and 8am if you can make it) and in the late afternoon, at around 4 to 5pm, when some of the *souks* auction off goods to local traders. Later in the evening, most of the stalls are closed, but you can wander unharassed to take a look at the elaborate decoration of their doorways and arches; those stalls that stay open, until 7 or 8pm, are often more open to bargaining at the end of the day.

Toward Ben Youssef: The Main Souks

On the corner of Djemaa el Fna itself there is a small potters' *souk*, but the main body of the market begins a little further beyond this. Its **entrance**, usually lined with hustlers, is initially confusing. Standing at the *Café de France* (and facing the mosque opposite), look across the street and you'll see the *Café el Fath* and, beside it, a building with the sign "Tailleur de la Place"—the lane sandwiched in between them will bring you out at the beginning of Rue Souk Smarine.

Busy and crowded, **Souk Smarine** is an important thoroughfare, traditionally dominated by the sale of textiles. Today, classier tourist "bazaars" are moving in, with *American Express* signs displayed in the windows for the

---

CRAFTS, "GUIDES," AND THE SOUKS

Like Fes, Marrakesh can be an expensive place to **buy craft goods**—though if you have anything to barter (designer T-shirts, sneakers, rock music cassettes, etc.), you'll find people eager enough to arrange an exchange. Before setting out into the souks in search of rugs, blankets, or whatever, check out the classic designs in the **Dar Si Said** museum (see "The Lower Medina") and take a look at the (higher than reasonable) prices in the official state-run **Centre Artesenal**—just inside the ramparts beside Av. Mohammed V.

Official **guides** can be arranged at the *ONMT* or *S.I.* tourist offices (see "Directory"), unofficial ones in Djemaa el Fna and almost anywhere you're seen looking perplexed. Some of the latter can be fine, others a struggle, as you are escorted into shop after shop. A favorite recommendation of the Djemaa and *souk* hustlers is the so-called Berber market—"only today," they'll tell you, with great urgency. In fact, all the main **souks** are open every day, though they're quiet on Friday mornings. Even the big Souk el Khemis (The Thursday Market, held outside Bab Debbagh) now operates most days of the week.

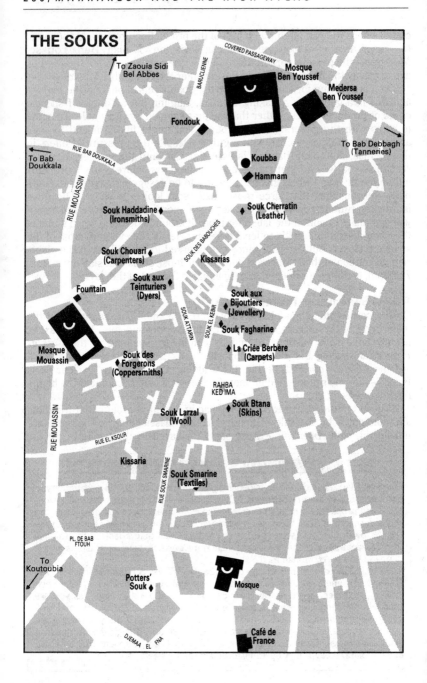

THE SOUKS

COVERED PASSAGEWAY

BARUCLIENNE

To Zaouïa Sidi
Bel Abbes

Mosque
Ben Youssef

Medersa
Ben Youssef

Fondouk

To Bab Debbagh
(Tanneries)

RUE BAB DOUKKALA

To Bab
Doukkala

Koubba

Hammam

RUE MOUASSIN

Souk Haddadine
(Ironsmiths)

Souk Cherratin
(Leather)

SOUK DES BABOUCHES

Souk Chouari
(Carpenters)

Kissarias

Souk aux
Teinturiers
(Dyers)

Souk aux
Bijoutiers
(Jewellery)

SOUK ATTARIN

SOUK EL KEBIR

Souk Fagharine

Fountain

La Criée Berbère
(Carpets)

Mosque
Mouassin

Souk des
Forgerons
(Coppersmiths)

RAHBA
KED IMA

RUE MOUASSIN

Souk Larzal
(Wool)

Souk Btana
(Skins)

RUE EL KSOUR

Kissaria

RUE SOUK SMARINE

Souk Smarine
(Textiles)

PL. DE BAB
FTOUH

To
Koutoubia

Potters'
Souk

Mosque

DJEMAA EL FNA

Café de
France

guided hordes, but there are still dozens of shops in the arcades selling and tailoring shirts and caftans. Along its whole course, the street is covered by a broad, iron trellis that restricts the sun to shafts of light; it replaces the old rush (*smar*) roofing, which along with many of the *souks'* more beautiful features was destroyed by a fire in the 1960s.

Just before the fork at its end, Souk Smarine narrows and you can get a glimpse through the passageways to its right of the **Rahba Kedima**, a small and fairly ramshackle square with a few vegetable stalls set up in the middle of it. Immediately to the right, as you go in, is **Souk Larzal**, a wool market feverishly active in the dawn hours, but closed for most of the rest of the day. Alongside it, easily distinguished by smell alone, is **Souk Btana,** which deals with whole sheepskins—the pelts laid out to dry and be displayed on the roof. You can walk up here and take a look at how the skins are treated. But the most interesting aspect of Rahba Kedima are the **apothecary stalls** grouped around the near corner of the square. These sell all the standard traditional cosmetics—earthenware saucers of cochineal (*kashiniah*) for rouge, powdered *kohl* or antimony for darkening the edges of the eyes, *henna* (the only cosmetic unmarried women are supposed to use), and the sticks of *suak* (walnut root or bark) with which you see Moroccans cleaning their teeth. But, in addition to such essentials, the stalls also sell the herbal and animal ingredients that are still in widespread use for manipulation, or spell-binding. There are roots and tablets used as aphrodisiacs, and there are stranger and more specialized goods—dried pieces of lizard and stork, fragments of beaks, talons, and gazelle horns. Magic, white and black, has always been very much a part of Moroccan life, and there are dozens of stories relating to its effects, nearly always carried out by a wife on her husband.

At the end of Rahba Kedima, a passageway to the left that gives access to another, smaller square—a bustling, carpet-draped area known as la **Criée Berbère**. It was here that the old **slave auctions** were held, just before sunset every Wednesday, Thursday, and Friday, until the French occupied the city in 1912. They were conducted, according to Budgett Meakin's account in 1900, "precisely as those of cows and mules, often on the same spot by the same men . . . with the human chattels being personally examined in the most disgusting manner, and paraded in lots by the auctioneers, who shout their attractions and the bids." Most had been kidnapped and brought in by the caravans from Guinea and Sudan; Meakin saw two small boys sold for £5 apiece, an eight-year-old girl for £3 and 10 shillings, and a "stalwart negro" went for £14; a beauty, he was told, might exceptionally fetch £130 to £150.

These days, **rugs and carpets** are about the only things sold in the square, and if you have a good deal of time and willpower you could spend a lot of it here while endless (and often identical) stacks are unfolded and displayed before you. Some of the most interesting items on offer are the Berber rugs from the High Atlas—bright, geometric designs that look very different after being laid out on the roof and bleached by the sun. The dark, often black, backgrounds usually signify rugs from the Glaoua country, up toward Telouet; the reddish-backed carpets are from Chichaoua, a small village on the way to Essaouira, and are also pretty common. There is usually a small **auction** in the *criée* at around 4pm—an interesting sight with the auctioneers wandering around the square shouting out the latest bids, but it's not the best place to buy a rug—it's devoted mainly to heavy, brown woolen *djellabas*.

Cutting back to **Souk el Kebir**, which by now has taken over from the Smarine, you emerge at the **kissarias**, the covered markets at the heart of the *souks*. The goods here, apart from the numerous and sometimes imaginative *couvertures* (blankets), aren't especially interesting; the *kissarias* traditionally sell the more expensive products, which today means a sad predominance of Western designs and imports. Off to the right, near the beginning, is **Souk des Bijoutiers**, a modest jewelers' lane, which is much less varied than the one established in the Mellah (see "The Lower Medina") by Jewish craftsmen. At the top end of the *kissarias* is a convoluted web of alleys that comprise the **Souk Cherratin**, essentially a leather workers' *souk* (with dozens of purse makers and sandal cobblers), though it's also interspersed with smaller alleys and *souks* of carpenters, sieve makers, and even a few tourist shops. If you bear left through this area and then turn right, you should arrive at the open space in front of the Mosque Ben Youssef; the *medersa* (see the section below) is off to its right.

Had you earlier taken the left fork along **Souk el Attarin**—the spice and perfume *souk*—you would have come out on the other side of the **kissarias** and the long lane of the **Souk des Babouches** (slipper makers). The main attraction in this area, and by far the most colorful sight in the city, is the *souk* of the dyers, or **Teinturiers**. To reach it, turn left a couple of steps before you come to Souk des Babouches. Working your way down this lane (which comes out in a square by the Mouassin Mosque), look to your left and you'll see the entrance to the *souk* about halfway down—its lanes rhythmically flash with bright skeins of wool, hung from above. If you have trouble finding it, just follow the first tour group you see, or ask one of the kids to lead you.

There is a reasonably straightforward alternative route back to Djemaa el Fna from here, following the main street down to the **Mouassin Mosque** (which is almost entirely concealed from public view, built at an angle to the square next to it) and then turning left onto Rue Mouassin. As you approach the mosque, the street widens very slightly opposite an elaborate triple-bayed **fountain**. Built in the mid-sixteenth century by the prolific Saadian builder, Abdallah el-Ghalib, this is one of many such fountains in Marrakesh with a basin for humans set next to two larger troughs for animals; its installation was a pious act, directly sanctioned by the Koran in its charitable provision of water for men and beasts.

Below the Mouassin Mosque is an area of coppersmiths, **Souk des Forgerons**. Above it sprawls the main section of **carpenters'** workshops—with their beautiful smell of cedar—and beyond them a small *souk* for **oils** (**Souk des Huivres**) and the **Souk Haddadine** of blacksmiths and metalworkers—whose sounds you'll hear long before arriving.

The Ben Youssef Medersa

One of the largest buildings in the Medina, and preceded by a rare open space, the **Ben Youssef Mosque** is quite easy to locate. Its **medersa**—the old school annex for students taking courses in the mosque—stands off a side street just to the east, distinguishable by a series of small, grilled windows. The entrance porch is a short ways down the side street, covering the whole lane at this point. Recently restored, it is open from around 8am to noon and 2:30 to 6pm, except on Mondays and Friday mornings. Admission is the standard 3dh.

Like most of the Fes *medersas* (see Chapter Three for a description of their development and function), the Ben Youssef was a Merenid foundation, established by Sultan Abou el Hassan in the fourteenth century. It was, however, almost completely rebuilt under the Saadians, and it is this dynasty's intricate, Andalusian-influenced art that has left its mark. As with the slightly later Saadian Tombs, no surface of the architecture is left undecorated, and the overall quality of its craftsmanship, whether in carved wood, stuccowork, or *zellij,* is startlingly rich. That this was possible in sixteenth-century Marrakesh, after a period in which the city was reduced to near ruin and the country to tribal anarchy, is remarkable. Revealingly, parts of it have exact parallels in the Alhambra Palace in Granada, and it seems likely that Muslim Spanish architects were employed here.

Once admitted to the *medersa,* you reach the main court by means of a long outer **corridor** (an unusual feature in a college, though fairly common in palace architecture) and a small entry **vestibule**. To the side of this are stairs to the **student cells** arranged around smaller internal courtyards on the upper floors, an **ablutions hall**, and **latrine**. At the corner of the vestibule is a very rare marble **basin**, rectangular in shape and decorated along one side with what seem to be heraldic eagles and griffins; an inscription amid the floral decorations records its origin in tenth-century Cordoba, then the center of the western Muslim world. The Ommayad caliphs, for whom it was constructed, had few reservations about representational art. What is surprising is that it was brought over to Morocco by the Almoravid sultan Ali Ben Youssef and, placed in his mosque, was left untouched by the Almohads before finally being moved to the *medersa* in the course of the Saadian rebuilding.

The **central courtyard**, weathered almost flat on its most exposed side, is much larger than usual. Along two sides run wide, sturdy, columned arcades, which were probably used to supplement the space for teaching in the neighboring mosque. Above them are some of the windows of the student quarters, from which, if you are allowed up, you can get an interesting perspective—and attempt to fathom how over eight hundred students were once housed in the building.

At its far end the court opens onto a **prayer hall,** where the decoration, mellowed on the outside with the city's familiar pink tone, is at its best preserved and most elaborate. You notice here, as in the court's cedar carving, a predominance of pinecone and palm motifs, and around the *mihrab* (the horseshoe-arched prayer niche) they've been applied so as to give the frieze a highly three-dimensional appearance. This is unusual in Moorish stuccowork, though the inscriptions themselves, picked out in the curling, vegetative arabesques, are from familiar Koranic texts. The most common, in as in all Moroccan stucco and *zellij* decoration, is the ceremonial *bismillah* invocation: "In the name of Allah, the Tenderhearted, the Merciful . . . ."

The Almoravid Koubba

After the *medersa* or the *souks*, the **Almoravid Koubba** is easy to pass by —a small, two-story kiosk, which at first seems little more than a gray dome and a handful of variously shaped doors and windows. Look closer, though, and you will begin to understand its significance and even fascination. For this, the only intact Almoravid building, is at the root of all Moroccan architecture. The motifs you've just seen in the *medersa*—the pinecones, palms, and acanthus leaves—were all carved here for the first time. The windows on each of the different sides became the classic shapes of Almohad and Merenid design—as did the *merlons*, the Christmas tree–like battlements; the complex "ribs" on the outside of the dome; and the dome's interior support, a sophisticated device of a square and star-shaped octagon, which is itself repeated at each of its corners. Once you see all this, you're only a step away from the eulogies of Islamic art historians who sense in this building, which was probably a small ablutions annex to the original Ben Youssef Mosque, a powerful and novel expression of form.

Excavated only in 1952—having been covered over amid the many rebuildings of the Ben Youssef—the *koubba* lies just to the south of the present (mainly nineteenth-century) mosque. It lies mostly below today's ground level, though standing with your back to the mosque you can make out the top of its dome (probably covered by scaffolding) behind the long, low brick wall. There is an entrance gate down a few steps, opposite the Ben Youssef mosque, where a *gardien* will emerge to escort you around what little there is to be seen; if this is closed, you can get almost as good a view from the roof of a very ancient (but still active) *hammam* down to the right. Either way, you'll be expected to tip.

The Tanneries and Northern Gates

The main *souks*—and the tourist route—stop abruptly at the Ben Youssef *medersa*. Above them, in all directions, you'll find yourself in the ordinary **residential quarters** of the Medina. There are few particular "sights" to be found here, but if you've got the time, there's an interest of its own in following the crowds, and a relief in getting away from the central shopping district of Marrakesh, where you are (very legitimately) expected to come in, look around, and buy.

Probably the most interesting targets are **Bab Debbagh** (The Tanners' Gate) and **Souk el Khemis** (The Thursday Market). From Ben Youssef you can reach these quite easily: it's about a fifteen-minute walk to the first, another fifteen to twenty minutes around the ramparts to the second. As you pass the entrance porch to the *medersa,* you'll quickly reach a fork in the side street. To the left, a covered passageway leads around behind the mosque to join Rue Amesfah (see below). Head instead to your right, and then keep going as straight as possible until you emerge at the ramparts by Bab Debbagh; on the way you'll cross a small square and intersection, **Place el Moukef**, where a busy and sizable lane goes off to the left—a more direct approach to (and alternative route back from) Bab el Khemis.

Bab Debbagh is supposedly Almoravid in design, though over the years it must have been almost totally rebuilt. Passing through it, you become aware of its very real defensive purpose: three internal rooms are placed in such a manner as to force anyone attempting to storm it to make several turns. To the left of the first chamber, there's a stairway that (for a small fee) you can use to climb up to the roof. Looking down, you have an excellent view over the **tanneries**, built out here at the edge of the city for access to water (the summer-dry Oued Issil runs just outside the walls) and for the obvious reason of smell. If you want to take a closer look at the processes, come in the morning, when the cooperatives are at work. Any of the kids standing around will take you in.

Following the road from Bab Debbagh, outside the ramparts, is the simplest approach to **Bab el Khemis** (Gate of the Thursday Market) another reconstructed Almoravid gate, built at an angle in the walls. The **Thursday market** now seems to take place more or less daily, around 400m to the north, above a cemetery and *marabout's* tomb. It is really a local produce market, though odd handicraft items do occasionally surface.

North of the Ben Youssef Mosque

The area immediately **north of the Ben Youssef Mosque** is cut by two main streets: Rue Assouel (which leads up to Bab el Khemis) and Rue Bab Taghzout, which runs up to the gate of the same name and to the Zaouia of Sidi Bel Abbes. These were, with Bab Doukkala, the principal approaches to the city until the present century and along them you find many of the old **fondouks** used for storage and lodging by merchants visiting the *souks*. There is one just below the mosque and a whole series along Rue Amesfah—the continuation of Baroudienne—above and to the left. Most are still used in some commercial capacity, as workshops or warehouses, and the doors to their courtyards often stand open. Some date from Saadian times and there are often fine details of wood carving or stuccowork. If you are interested, nobody seems to mind if you wander in.

Rue Amesfah runs for around 150m above the intersection with Baroudienne before reaching the junction of Rue Assouel (to the right) and **Rue Bab Taghzout** (to the left). Following the latter, you pass another *fondouk*, opposite a small recessed fountain known as **Chrob ou Chouf** ("drink and admire"), and, around 500m farther down, the old city gate of **Bab Taghzout**. This marked the limits of the original Almoravid Medina, and continued to do so into the eighteenth century, when Sultan Mohammed Abdallah extended the walls to enclose the quarter and the **Zaouia of Sidi Bel Abbes**.

Sidi Bel Abbes, a twelfth-century *marabout* and a prolific performer of miracles, is the most important of Marrakesh's seven saints, and his **zaouia**, a kind of monastic cult center, has traditionally wielded very great influence and power, often at odds with that of the sultan, and provided a traditional refuge for political dissidents. The present buildings, which are strictly forbidden to non-Muslims, date largely from a reconstruction by Moulay Ismail—an act that was probably inspired more by political manipulation than piety. You can see something of the complex and its activities from outside the official boundary—do not, however, try to pass through the long central corridor. The *zaouia* still owns much of the quarter to the north and continues its educational and charitable work, distributing food each evening to the blind.

There is a smaller, though again significant, *zaouia* dedicated to **Sidi Slimane**, a Saadian *marabout,* a couple of blocks to the southwest.

West to Bab Doukkala: the Dar el Glaoui

A third alternative from Ben Youssef is to head west **toward Bab Doukkala.** This route, once you've found your way down through Souk Haddadine to **Rue Bab Doukkala,** is a sizable thoroughfare, very straightforward to follow.

Midway, you pass the **Dar el Glaoui**, the old palace of the pasha of Marrakesh and a source of legendary exoticism throughout the first half of this century. El Glaoui, cruel and magnificent in equal measure, was the last of the great southern tribal leaders, an active and shrewd supporter of French rule, and a personal friend of Winston Churchill. He was also one of the most spectacular partygivers around—in an age where rivals were not lacking. At the extraordinary *difas* held at Dar el Glaoui, "Nothing," as Gavin Maxwell wrote, "was impossible"—hashish and opium were freely available for the Europeans and Americans to experiment with, and "to his guests T'hami gave, literally, whatever they wanted, whether it might be a diamond ring, a present of money in gold, or a Berber girl or boy from the High Atlas."

Not surprisingly, there has been little enthusiasm for showing off the palace since el Glaoui's death in 1956, but there are said to be plans to open it as a museum of some sort. You might ask at the tourist office in Gueliz— by all accounts, the combination here of traditional Moroccan architecture and 1920s chic is unique and pretty wonderful.

The Lower Medina: The Palaces, Saadian Tombs, and Mellah

Staying in Marrakesh even for a few days, you begin to sense the different appearance and life of its various Medina quarters, and nowhere more so than in the shift from north to south, from the area above Djemaa el Fna to the area below it. At the base here (a kind of stem to the mushroom shape of the city walls) is **Dar el Makhzen**, the royal palace. To its west stretches the old inner citadel of the **Kasbah**; to the east, the **Mellah**, once the largest Jewish ghetto in Morocco; while rambling above it are a series of mansions and palaces built for the nineteenth-century elite.

All in all, it's an interesting area to wander around in, especially the Mellah, though you inevitably spend time trying to figure out what seem to be the sudden and apparently arbitrary appearance of ramparts and enclosures. And there are two obvious focal points, not to be missed: the **Saadian Tombs**, preserved in the shadow of the Kasbah mosque, and the ruined palace of Ahmed el Mansour—**El Badi**, "The Incomparable."

The Saadian Tombs and El Badi

Sealed up by Moulay Ismail after he had destroyed the adjoining Badi Palace, the **Saadian Tombs** lay half-ruined and half-forgotten at the beginning of this century. In 1917, however, they were rediscovered on a French aerial

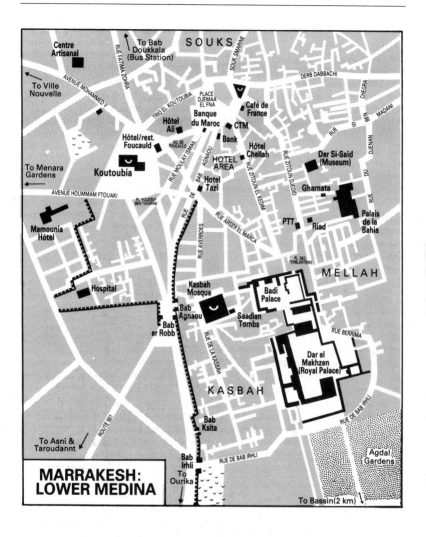

map and a passageway was built to give access from the side of the Kasbah mosque. Restored, they are today the city's main "sight"—overlavish, maybe, in their exhaustive decoration, but dazzling nonetheless. Friday mornings excepted, they are open daily from around 8am to 7pm (sometimes closed at lunchtime); go either early or late, if possible. As a national monument, admission is the usual 3dh. There is no longer a compulsory guided tour — you are left to look around on your own or even just to sit and gaze. A quiet, high-walled enclosure, shaded with shrubs and palms and dotted with bright *zellij*-covered tombs, it seems as much a pleasure garden as a cemetery.

Some form of burial ground behind the royal palace probably predated the Saadian period, though the earliest of the tombs here dates from 1557, and all the principal structures were built by Sultan Ahmed el Mansour. This makes them virtual contemporaries of the Ben Youssef *medersa*—with which there are obvious parallels—and allows a revealing insight into just how rich and extravagant the El Badi must once have been. Their escape from Moulay Ismail's systematic plundering was probably due to superstition—Ismail had to content himself with blocking all but an obscure entrance from the Kasbah mosque. Despite this, a few prominent *Marrakchis* continued to be buried in the mausoleums; the last, in 1792, was the "mad sultan," Moulay Yazid, whose brief, 22-month reign was probably the most violent, vicious, and sadistic in the nation's history.

There are two main **mausoleums** in the enclosure. The finest is on the left as you come in—a beautiful group of three rooms, built to house El Mansour's own tomb and completed within his lifetime. Continuing around from the courtyard entrance, the first hall is a **prayer oratory,** a room probably not intended for burial, though now almost littered with the thin marble stones of Saadian princes. It is here that Moulay Yazid was laid out, perhaps in purposeful obscurity, certainly in ironic contrast to the cursive inscription around the band of black and white *zellij:* "And the works of peace they have accomplished," it reads amid the interlocking circles, "will make them enter the holy gardens."

Architecturally, the most important feature of this mausoleum is the *mihrab*, its pointed horseshoe arch supported by an incredibly delicate arrangement of columns. Opposite this is another elaborate arch, leading to the domed **central chamber** and El Mansour's own tomb, which you can glimpse through the next door in the court. The tomb, slightly larger than those surrounding it, lies right in the middle, flanked on either side by those of the sultan's sons and successors. The room itself is spectacular, faint light filtering onto the tombs from an interior lantern in a tremendous vaulted roof, the *zellij* full of color and motion, and the undefined richness of a third chamber almost hidden from view. Throughout, there are echoes of the Alhambra in Granada, from which its style is clearly derived; oddly, though, it was completed nearly two centuries later and, except in detail and exuberance, seems hardly to show any development.

The **other mausoleum,** older and less impressive, was built by Ahmed in place of an existing pavilion above the tombs of his mother, Lalla Messaouda, and of Mohammed esh Sheikh, the founder of the Saadian dynasty. It is again a series of three rooms, though two are hardly more than loggias. Lalla's tomb is the niche below the dome in the outer chamber. Mohammed is buried in the inner one—or at least his body is, since he was murdered in the Atlas by Turkish mercenaries, who salted his head and took it back for public display on the walls in Istanbul.

Outside, around the garden and courtyard, are scattered the tombs of over a hunded more Saadian princes and members of the royal household. Like the privileged sixty-six given space within the mausoleums, their gravestones are brilliantly tiled and often elaborately inscribed. The most usual inscription reads quite simply:

There is no God but God. Muhammad is God's envoy.
Praise Be to God.
The occupant of this tomb died on . . . .

But there are others (epitaphs and extracts from the Koran) that seem to express of the turbulence of the age to a greater degree—which, with Ahmed's death in 1603, was to disintegrate into nearly seventy years of constant civil war. "Every soul shall know death," reads one tombstone; "Death will find you wherever you are, even in fortified towers," another. And, carved in gypsum on the walls, there is a poem:

O mausoleum, built out of mercy, thou whose
walls are the shadow of heaven.
The breath of asceticism is wafted from thy tombs
like a fragrance.
Through thy death
the light of faith has been dimmed,
the seven spheres are fraught with darkness
and the columns of glory
broken with pain.

Getting to the Saadian Tombs, the simplest route from Djemaa el Fna is to follow **Rue Bab Agnaou** outside the ramparts. At its end you come to a small square flanked by two gates. Directly ahead is **Bab er Robb**—behind which the *grands taxis* and private-line buses leave for Ourika and other local destinations. To the left, somewhat battered and eroded, is the city's only survivng Almohad gateway, **Bab Agnaou** (Gate of the Gnaoua [the blacks]). This is an impressive structure, smaller than the monumental gates of Rabat, but sharing much of their force and apparent simplicity. Notice how the semi-circular frieze above its arch creates a strong, three-dimensional effect without any actual depth of carving. At the time of its construction, it was the only stone building in Marrakesh apart from the Koutoubia Minaret. Passing through the gate, the **Kasbah mosque*** is in front of you; the narrow passageway to the Saadian Tombs is well signposted, at the near righthand corner.

El Badi Palace

To reach the ruins of the **El Badi Palace**—which seems originally to have sprawled across the whole area east of the Kasbah mosque—you have to backtrack slightly from the Saadian Tombs. At Bab Agnaou, follow the ramparts up again, this time taking the road just inside them, until you come to a reasonably sized street on your right (just before the walls temporarily give out). Turn into this street, keep more or less straight, and in about 550m, you'll emerge at **Place des Ferblantiers**—a major intersection. On the south side of the *place* is a gate known as **Bab Berrima**, which opens onto a long rectangular enclosure, flanked on either side by walls; go through it, and on your right you'll come to the Badi's entrance. Hours are generally 9am to

---

* The mosque's minaret looks gaudy and modern but is, in fact, contemporary with both the Koutoubia and Hassan towers. It was restored to its exact original state in the 1960s.

noon and 2:30 to 5:30pm; admission, once again, is 3dh; a guided tour is touted but far from essential.

Though substantially in ruins, and reduced throughout to its red *pisé* walls, enough remains of **El Badi** to suggest that its name—"The Incomparable"— was not immodest. It took Moulay Ismail over ten years of systematic work to strip the palace of everything movable or of value, and even so, there's a lingering sense of luxury and grandeur. The scale, with its sunken gardens and vast, ninety-meter-long pool, is certainly unrivaled, and the odd traces of *zellij* and plaster still left evoke a decor that was probably as rich as that of the Saadian Tombs.

Begun shortly after Ahmed el Mansour's accession, the palace's initial financing came from the enormous ransom paid out by the Portuguese after the Battle of the Three Kings at Ksar el Kabir. Fought in the summer of 1578, this was one of the most disastrous battles in Christian medieval history; ostensibly in support of a rival Saadian claimant, but to all intents a Portuguese crusade, it was led by King Sebastião, and supported by almost his entire nobility. Few escaped death or Moorish capture. Sebastião himself was killed, as were both the Saadian claimant and the ruling sultan. As a result, Ahmed—dubbed *El Mansour* (The Victorious)—came to the throne, undisputed and commanding immediate wealth. He reigned for twenty-five years, trading in sugar and slaves with Britain, Spain, and Italy; seizing the gold route across the Sahara with the capture of Timbuktu, which earned him the additional epithet *El Dhahibi* (The Golden); and maintaining peace in Morocco through a loose confederation of tribes. It was the most prosperous era in the country's history since the Almohad—a cultural and political renaissance reflected in the coining of a new title, the Shereefian Empire, which was to remain the country's official name until independence in 1956.

What you see today is essentially the ceremonial part of **the palace complex**, planned on a grand scale for the reception of ambassadors, and not meant for everyday living. It seems likely that El Mansour and the multiple members of his court each had private palaces—smaller, though built to a similar ground plan—to the west and south, covering much of the area occupied today by the Dar el Makhzen.

The **entrance** in current use was probably not the main approach. Going through, you find yourself at the side of a **mosque**, like everything else within this complex, of enormous height. To the rear extends the great **central court,** over 130m long and nearly as wide, and entirely constructed on a substructure of vaults in order to allow the circulation of water through the pools and gardens. When the pools are filled—as during the June folklore festival which takes place here —they are an incredibly majestic sight, above all the main one, with an island that was originally surmounted by an elaborate double fountain. On each side there were once summer pavilions, traces of which survive. The most prominent of them is at the far end, a monumental hall that was used by the sultan on occasions of state and known as the *Koubba el Hamsiniya* (The Fifty Pavilion), for the number of its columns. Strangely enough, the size and splendor of them is documented by a completely separate source from the Arab chroniclers who extolled their beauty. The French philosopher Montaigne, while traveling through Italy, saw craftsmen preparing the columns—"each of an extreme height . . . for the king of Fes and Barbary."

North of the courtyard are ruins of the palace **stables,** and beyond them, leading toward the intriguing walls of the present royal palace, a series of **dungeons,** used into the present century as a state prison. You can explore part of these and could easily spend a whole afternoon wandering around the various inner courts above, with their fragments of marble and *zellij* and their water conduits for the fountains and *hammams.* Like the Saadian Tombs, the Badi inspired contemporary poets, and there is an account, too, by the chronicler El-Ifrani, of its construction:

El Mansour made workmen come from all the different countries . . . .He paid for the marble sent from Italy in sugar, pound for pound awarded his workers very generously . . . and paid attention even to the entertainment of their children, so that the artisans might devote themselves entirely to their work without being distracted by any other preoccupation.

If this is even half true, there could be no greater contrast with the next great Moroccan builder, and dismantler of the palace, Moulay Ismail, whose workmen were instead beaten up, starved, and abused, and then buried in the walls where they fell. But sixteenth-century crèches aside, the most enduring account of the palace concerns its state opening, a fabulous occasion attended by ambassadors from several European powers and by all the sheikhs and *caids* of the kingdom. Surveying the effect, Ahmed turned to his court jester for an opinion on the new palace. "Sidi," the man replied, "this will make a magnificent ruin."

The Mellah

It was in 1558—five years before Ahmed's accession—that the city's **Mellah,** the separate Jewish quarter, was created. There is no exact record of why this was done at this particular time. Possibly it was the result of a pogrom, with the sultan moving the Jews to his protected Kasbah—and they, in turn, forming a useful buffer zone (and scapegoat) between his palace and the populace in times of social unrest. But, as likely as not, it was simply brought about to make taxation easier. The Jews of Marrakesh were an important financial resource—they controlled most of the Saadian sugar trade, and comprised practically all of the city's bankers, metalworkers, jewelers, and tailors. In the sixteenth century, at least, their quarter was almost a town in itself, supervised by rabbis, and with its own *souks,* gardens, fountains, and synagogues.

The present Mellah, much smaller in extent, is now almost entirely Muslim—most of the *Marrakchi* Jews left long ago for Casablanca (where some 6000 still live) or emigrated to France or Israel. The few who remain, outwardly distinguishable only by the men's small black skullcaps, are mostly poor or old or both. Their quarter, however, is immediately distinct: its houses are taller than elsewhere, the streets are more enclosed, and even the shop cubicles are smaller. Until the protectorate, Jews were not permitted to own land or property—nor even to ride or walk, except barefoot—outside the Mellah; a situation that was greatly exploited by their landlords, who resisted all attempts to expand the walls. Today its air of neglect and poverty—since this is not a prized neighborhood in which to live—is probably less than at any time during the past three centuries.

The main entrance, in what is still a largely walled district, is at **Place des Ferblantiers**. This square, formerly called Place du Mellah, was itself part of the old Jewish *souk,* and an archway (to your right, standing at Bab Berrima) leads into it. Near the upper end is a jewelers' *souk,* one of the traditional Jewish trades now more or less taken over by Muslim craftsmen; farther down are some good spice and textile *souks.* Right at the center—and situated very much as the goal of a maze—is a small square with a fountain in the middle, **Place Souweka**. You will almost certainly find yourself back here if you wander around for a short while and manage to avoid the blind alleys.

To the east, some 200m away, is the old Jewish **cemetery**, the *Mihaara.* Closer by (and you'll need to enlist a guide to find them) are a number of **synagogues** (*s'noga*). Even when they were in active use, many were as much private houses as they were temples—" . . . serving also as places in which to eat, sleep, and to kill chickens," according to Budgett Meakin— and most of them today remain lived in. One of the larger ones, attached to a kind of hostel financed by some American Jews, can usually be visited, as (depending on who your guide knows) can a couple of other ones.

El Bahia Palace

Heading north from the Mellah—back toward Djemaa el Fna—there are three direct and fairly simple routes. To the left of Place des Ferblantiers, **Avenue Hoummam el Ftouaki** will bring you out by the Koutoubia. Above the *place,* two parallel streets, **Rue Zitoun el Kedim** and **Zitoun el Jdid** lead up to the Djemma itself. El Kedim is basically a shopping street, lined with general stores, barbershops, and at the upper end, a couple of *hammams* (open all day; one each for men and women). El Jdid is more residential, and it is here that you find the major concentration of **palaces and mansions** built in those strange, closing decades of the last century, and the first few years of our own, when the sultans Moulay Hassan and Moulay Abd el Aziz held court in the city.

By far the most ambitious and costly of these was the **Palais El Bahia**, residence of the grand vizier, Si Ahmed Ben Moussa. Shrewd, willful, and cruel, as was the tradition of his age, Bou Ahmed (as he was better known) was a black slave who rose to hold massive power in the Shereefian kingdom and, for the last six years of his life, exercised virtually autocratic control. He was first chamberlain to Moulay Hassan, whose death while returning home from a *harka* he was able to conceal until the proclamation of Abd el Aziz in Rabat (see "Writers on Morocco," in *Contexts,* for the dramatic account). Under Abd el Aziz (who was just twelve when he acceded to the throne), Bou Ahmed usurped the position of vizier from the ill-fated Jamai brothers (see Fes), and then proceeded to rule.

He began building the Bahia in 1894, later enlarging it by acquiring the surrounding land and property. He died in 1900. The name of the building means "The Effulgence" or "Brilliance," but after a **guided tour** around various sections of the rambling palace courts and apartments you might feel this to be a somewhat tall claim. There is reasonable craftsmanship in the main

reception halls, and a pleasant arrangement of rooms in the **harem quarter,** but for the most part it is all fabulously vulgar and hasn't aged too well. Perhaps this is the main reason for a visit: you come away realizing just how much mastery and sophistication went into the Saadian *medersa* and tombs, and how corrupted and dull these traditions had become.

But there is also a certain pathos to the empty, echoing chambers—and the inevitable passing of Bou Ahmed's influence and glory. Walter Harris, who knew the vizier, described his demise and the clearing of his palace in *Morocco That Was*, published just twenty years later, by which time his name had already become "only a memory of the past:"

For several days as the Vizier lay expiring, guards were stationed outside his palace waiting in silence for the end. And then one morning the wail of the women within the house told that death had come. Every gateway of the great building was seized, and no one was allowed to enter or come out, while within there was pandemonium. His slaves pillaged wherever they could lay their hands. His women fought and stole to get possesion of the jewels. Safes were broken open, documents and title-deeds were extracted, precious stones were torn from their settings, the more easily to be concealed, and even murder took place . . . . A few days later nothing remained but the great building—all the rest had disappeared into space. His family were driven out to starvation and ruin, and his vast properties passed into the possession of the State. It was the custom of the country.

For some years during the protectorate, the palace was used to house the resident-general, and it is still called into use when the royal family is in the city. This is usually from January through March, at which times there is no public admission. Its normal **opening hours** are from 9:30am to noon and 2:30 to 5:30pm, closed Tuesdays; 3dh charge.

Finding your way to the palace is easy enough: from Rue Zitoun follow the signs to *Palais Gharnata*, keeping straight when they suddenly direct you to the right under an arch. The **Gharnata**, and the nearby **Riad**, "palaces" are among a number of mansions in this part of the city that have been converted into "Tourist Spectacle" restaurants. All of them are expensive—and the shows hideously unauthentic—but it's worth looking into one or two of them during the day, just to see the turn-of-the-century decor.

Dar Si Said Museum

Also worth your while on this route is **Dar Si Said**, a smaller version of the Bahia built by a brother of Bou Ahmed. The brother, something of a simpleton, nonetheless gained the post of royal chamberlain.

The palace is today a **museum of Moroccan arts**, particularly strong on its collections of southern **Berber jewelry and weapons**—large, boldly designed objects of real beauty. There are also excellent displays of eighteenth- and nineteenth-century **wood carving** from the Glaoui Kasbahs, **modern Berber rugs,** and a curious group of traditional **wedding chairs**—once widely used for carrying the bride, veiled and hidden, to her new home—and **fairground swings,** used at *moussems* until the 1940s.

There's pleasure, too, in the palace itself, with its beautiful pooled courtyards, cool and scented with lemon trees, palms, and flowers. Dar Si Said is just a block to the west of Rue Zitoun el Jdid (turn right opposite a mosque, around halfway down); admission hours are as for the Bahia; 3dh charge.

The Gardens

With summer temperatures reaching 90 to 100°F—and peaks well above that—it seems best to devote at least the middle of a Marrakesh day to total inactivity; and, if you want to do this in style, it means finding your way to a garden. There are two—**Agdal** and **Menara**—designed for this exact purpose. Each begins near the edge of the Medina, rambles through acres of orchards and olive groves, and has, near its center, an immense, lake-size pool of water. This is all—they are not flower gardens, but, cool and completely still, they seem both satisfying and luxurious, and in perfect contrast to the close city streets. For a more conventional, European-style garden, try also the **Jardin Majorelle**, created by the French nineteenth century painter.

You will want **transportation** to get to any of these gardens—either a *petit taxi* or *calèche*. If you are considering a *calèche* trip at any stage, this is as perfect a destination as any. Alternatively, to take in both gardens and tour the ramparts and palmery, you could rent a **bike** for the day: there are several places to do this along Av. Mohammed V (try *Peugeot* at no. 225) and it'll set you back less than the price of returning to the Agdal by *petit taxi*.

Jardin Agdal

The **Agdal** is a confusingly large expanse— some 3km in extent and with half a dozen smaller irrigation pools in addition to its *grand bassin*. Beginning just south of the Mellah and royal palace, it is watered by an incredible system of wells and underground channels that go as far as the base of the Atlas in the Ourika Valley and that date, in part, from the earliest founding of the city. Over the centuries, they have often fallen into disrepair and the gardens have been abandoned, but the present (nineteenth-century) layout probably differs little from any of its predecessors. It is surrounded by walls, with gates at each of the near corners, while inside, the orange, fig, lemon, apricot, and pomegranate orchards are divided into square, irrigated plots by an endless series of raised walkways and broad avenues of olive trees.

If you walk out here, the perimeter is around 4km from Djemaa el Fna—but it's a further 2km of unsignposted paths before you reach the main series of pools at its heart. The big one to ask for is the **Sahraj el Hana** (Tank of Health), which was probably dug by the Almohads and is flanked by a ramshackle old *menzeh*, or summer pavilion, where the last few precolonial sultans held picnics and boating parties. You can climb up on the roof for a fabulous view over the park and across to the Koutoubia and Atlas, and if the caretaker's around, you'll be shown the steam-powered launch which capsized in 1873, bringing Sultan Sidi Mohammed to his death— or, as his epitaph put it, he "departed this life, in a water tank, in the hope of something better to come."

These days, probably the most dangerous thing you could do here would be to swim in the algae-ridden waters, though the kids do it and it does look unbelievably tempting. It's perhaps better just to pick up some food beforehand—and perhaps a bottle of wine from the Gueliz—and spread out a picnic in local fashion on the paved, shaded pathway around the water's edge.

To **get to the Agdal**, take the road outside the ramparts below Bab Agnaou/Bab er Robb, and then turn left as you are about to leave the city at Bab Irhli; this route will take you through a *mechouar* (parade ground) by the royal palace and to the corner gate of the garden.

Jardin Menara

The **Menara** is in a similar vein to the Agdal, though it has only a single tank and, being much closer to the city, is much more visited. If you just want to gaze upon one of these still sheets of water, then come out here; it's a lot easier to get to than the Agdal (and a cheaper ride, too).

Like the Agdal, the Menara was restored and its pavilions rebuilt by Sultan Abd er Rahman (1822–59). The famous poolside *menzeh* is said to have replaced an original Saadian structure.

The Menara couldn't be simpler to find: just follow Av. de la Menara from Bab Jdid (see the "Lower Medina" map).

The Palmery and Jardin Majorelle

The best section of the **palmery** is signposted ("Route de Palmeraie"), around 2km out on Av. el Jadida after the intersection with Av. Yacoub el Mansour. It is impressive as a first experience of southern landscape, though perhaps not a great priority if you are planning to cross the Atlas to the desert oases of the Drâa or Dades.

On the way, however, you can stop and take a look at the subtropical **Jardin Majorelle**, or *Bou Saf Saf* as it's now officially known. This small botanical garden was created in the 1920s by the minor French painter, Louis Majorelle, and is now owned by Yves St Laurent. It is open daily for visits.

A sobering contrast to this luxuriance, as you pass **Bab Doukkala** en route, is the shantytown just outside the walls above the bus station—a quarter with its own industry, scrap, and general goods *souks,* that is located in the city's old leper colony. Even in the early years of the protectorate, lepers from here used to beg at the gates of the Medina, which they were forbidden to enter.

The Hôtel Mamounia

Finally—and much closer—you might consider spending an hour or two looking around the gardens of the famed **Hôtel Mamounia**. Walled from the outside world, yet only five minutes' walk from the Djemaa, these were once royal grounds, laid out by the Saadians with a succession of pavilions. They are today slightly Europeanized in style, but have retained the traditional elements of shrubs and walkways.

For the cost of a drink or some tea on the terrace—neither exactly cheap options—you can sit down and admire the surroundings. Be prepared, though, to resist the swimming pool, since it is strictly reserved for residents.

If you ask at the desk, and the staff aren't too busy, someone may be prepared to give you a quick tour of the old part of the hotel—where the **Winston Churchill suite** is preserved as visited by its namesake. There are editions of Churchill's books on the shelves, a truly sultan-like bed (and smaller sleeping quarters for his manservant), and photographs of him painting in the gardens. Churchill was a frequent visitor to Marrakesh from the 1930s to the 1950s, and the Mamounia, so it is said, was his favorite hotel in the world. Even though it's been rebuilt and enlarged since his day, it's not hard to understand the lasting appeal.

Practicalities—and Gueliz

As stressed earlier, it's distinctly preferable to stay in or near the Medina, rather than out in the Ville Nouvelle—the French-created **Gueliz** quarter. However, Gueliz is not completely without charms. In addition to the various restaurants, cafés and bars, detailed below, an evening in the new town offfers the opportunity to start up conversations with Moroccans other than hustlers. There are, also, a number of exceptional **antique crafts shops**, where for a not too inflated price, you can secure some original, elegant objects—spired scent bottles, velvet-covered wooden water flasks, wooden Koranic tablets, and the like.

Eating in the Medina

You might decide against eating at one of them—as even the hustlers caution—but at some stage you should at least wander down the makeshift lane of **food stalls** near the top of **Djemaa el Fna**. They tend to specialize in a few main dishes (though with often a larger range on display), and it's worth watching the crowds for a while to check out what is best to eat where. If you do decide to throw caution to the winds, take a seat on one of the benches, ask the price of a plate of food, and order all you like; if you want to wash it down with a soft drink or some mineral water, the owners will send a boy off to get it for you. (Opinions differ widely on the health risks of these stalls: a lot of travelers eat there regularly and with no ill effect; others are convinced that the stalls acounted for three days laid out with upset stomachs).

No more expensive and generally healthier are some of the **café-restaurants** on the side of the Djemaa. The best of these is an unnamed place with a small terrace next to the *Café Montréal* (about 10m past the *Café de France* in the direction of the *souks*); this serves excellent kefta and brochettes, a fine chicken and lemon *tajine*, harira, salad, and fresh yogurt, and all at very low prices. Good too, at the north end of the square, is the *Café el Fath*, with an excellent value set meal. Or, just off the square to the south, try one of the places in the street running between Rue Moulay Ismail and Rue de Bab Agnaou; many of these stay open late.

Slightly **more expensive options**, for a variation on the usual fare, include:

Restaurant Argana, Place Djemaa el Fna. Possibly the best Djemaa el Fna vantage point—and it's worth waiting in line for a table for this reason alone. Regular French-Moroccan food. Sited opposite the Banque de Maroc/*Hôtel CTM*.

Restaurant Marrakech, Place Djemaa el Fna (on the corner of the road just north of the *Café de France*). A sumptuous new restaurant high up above the Djemaa. Imperial but intimate decor, impeccable service, and indescribably delicious *pastilla*. Around $16–25 a head for a 3–5 course, blowout meal.

Hôtel-Restaurant Foucauld, Place de Foucauld. Quality can be patchy, but on good days the Foucauld is worth the prices (about $10 a head), with its palace-type salon, low-key musicians, and massive portions of *pastilla* (pigeon/chicken/vegetable pie), soups, pâté, and vegetables.

Grand Hôtel Tazi, Rue Bab Agnaou. The Foucauld's sister hotel, the *Tazi*, just down the road, has a couple of restaurants, too—one on the roof in summer—and similar menus. As a lot of Moroccan businessmen stay in the hotel, the cooking is generally better. The Tazi also has a **bar**—the only one near the Djemaa el Fna.

Restaurant Iceberg, Rue Bab Agnaou (between the *Foucauld* and the *Tazi*).Good, solid, French cuisine.

Gueliz Restaurants

Café Chaabia, Bd. Moulay Rachid; **Café de l'Union**, Rue Ibn Aicha (at the end of Av. Yacoub el Mansour/beginning of Bd. Zerktouni). Two of the cheapest Gueliz café-restaurants. the former is very close to the youth hostel and campground.

Café Toubkal, 153 Rue el Beqal. Another very cheap, very reasonable café-restaurant.

Café La Mama, Rue Souraya (opposite the *Hôtel Palmeraie*), Open twenty-four hours a day, seven days a week, for diner-style food.

Le Petit Poucet, 56 Av. Mohammed V. Stylish, though overpriced, old established French restaurant.

Restaurant Chinois, 134 Av. Mohammed V; **La Trattoria**, Rue Mohammed Beqal; **La Pizza**, 63 Av. Mohammed V. For those in need of a break from French-Moroccan food: Chinese and Italian options, as the names suggest.

The **food market**, in the arcade off the middle section of Av. Mohammed V, is a convenient place for stocking up on supplies before heading off to the High Atlas.

Bars and Nightlife

The only bars in easy reach of the Medina are in the hotels, Tazi, Foucauld, and Yasmine, or for those on expense accounts, the Mamounia. See hotel listings for addresses.

In **Gueliz**, there's more variety, and you are more likely to have Moroccans for company—though be aware that most of the bars are very much male preserve. The liveliest places are generally the *Renaissance* (by the hotel of the same name on Av. Mohammed V) and the *Petit Poucet* (56 Av. Mohammed V); neither, however, keep especially late hours. The *Bar-Café Oasis* (50 Av. Mohammed V) is good value for beer and snacks; other bars on the same street incude the *Ambassadeurs* (6), *Regent* (34) and *Negociants* (108). On Rue Yougoslavie there are the *Fiarée* (33) and *Bagatelle* (101). An alternative and fairly late night option, open to 2am, is the *Café Oued el Had* (100 Av. Casablanca, a taxi ride out on the Casa road). This is in fact a complex of three bars—the best upstairs.

Entertainment and **nightlife** in the Medina revolve around Djemaa el Fna and its cafés. Sometimes, though, there might be a **music group** playing in an enclosure behind the Koutoubia on Av. Mohammed.

In Gueliz, there are also half a dozen or so **discos**. These include the *Pub Laurent,* on Rue Ibn Aicha (see above for directions), and *L'Atlas* and *Le Flash* on Av. Mohammed V. Also—and recorded largely because they are unique in Morocco—there are **casinos**: the main one in Hivernage, and a smaller one (winter only) in the *Hôtel Mamounia*.

The Marrakesh Festival, Moussems, and Local Markets

The annual two-week **Folklore Festival**, held in the Badi Palace around the end of May/beginning of June, is almost worth planning your trip to Morocco around. Despite its touristy name, it is in fact a series of authentic and unusual performances, with groups of musicians and dancers coming in from all over the country. A typical programme will span the whole range of Moroccan music—from the Gnaoua drummers and the panpipers of Jajouka, to Berber *ahouaches* from the Atlas and southern oases, to classical Andalusian music from Fes. The shows are held each evening; before they start, toward sunset, there is a **fantasia** at Bab el Jdid—a spectacle by any standard, with dozens of Berber horsemen firing their guns in the air at full gallop.

Outside of Marrakesh, local **moussems** include: Setti Fatma (Ourika; August), Sidi Bouatmane (Amizmiz; September) and Moulay Brahim (Asni; over the Mouloud). Major **weekly markets** in the area around the city include: Amizmiz (Tuesdays; see section following), Dar Caid Ouriki (Monday; see Ourika Valley), Aït Ourir (on the road to Ouarzazate; Monday), Asni (Saturday), and Tamasloht (on the road to Amizmiz; Tuesday).

Directory

American Express c/o *Voyages Schwarz*, Rue Mauritania (off Av. Mohammed V: second left after Place de la Liberté if you're coming from the Medina). Business hours Mon.–Fri. 9am–12:30pm and 3–4:30pm, but stays open until 7pm for mail.

Banks As in other Moroccan cities, the *BMCE* is the best bet for exchange—accepting VISA/Mastercard, travelers' checks, and most currencies. It has branches in both the Medina (Place Foucauld) and Gueliz (144 Bd. Mohammed V), open from 8am to 8pm every-day. *Crédit du Maroc, Banque Populaire* and the *SGMB* all have branches on Rue Bab Agnaou—just off Djemaa el Fna—and in Gueliz.

Bikes can be rented from the *Toubkal, Sigha,* and *Andalous* hotels in the new city. Call 439-06 for details.

Car Rental Marrakesh is the city where you're most likely to want to rent a car—and rates here are generally the most competitive after Casablanca. One of the cheapest places to arrange rental is *Menara Tours* (59 Bd. Mansour el Eddabhi). Alternatively, call around the individual companies, which include:*LVS*, 41 Rue Yougoslavie (☎332-14); *Budget Cars*, 213 Bd. Mohammed V (☎334-24); *Europ-Car*, 189 Bd. Mohammed V (☎303-68); *Sud Cars*, 213 Av. Mohammed V (☎309-97); *Transcar*, 10 Bd. Zerktouni (☎316-47); *Tourist Cars*, 64 Bd. Zerktouni (☎315-30); and *Hertz*, 154 Bd. Mohammed V (☎346-80).

Car Repairs The garage beside the *Hôtel Tazi* in Rue Bab Agnaou fixes Renaults—and should be able to direct you elsewhere for spare parts of the makes they don't stock.

Dentist Dr. E. Gailleres (112 Av. Mohammed V, opposite the *ONMT* office) is recommended; he speaks some English.

Doctor Dr. Perez (169 Av. Mohammed V; ☎310-30) is English speaking and reliable. Also see Pharmacies, below.

Newspapers The *International Herald Tribune, Time, Newsweek,* etc., plus occasional British newspapers, are available from the newsstands along Av. Mohammed V in Gueliz, and in the fancy hotels.

Pharmacies There are several along Av. Mohammed V, including a good one just off Place de la Liberté, which has a doctor on call.

Post Office The main *PTT*, which receives all **Poste Restante** mail, is on Place 16 Novembre, midway down Av. Mohammed V; service hours are Mon.–Sat. 8am–2pm. The **telephone** section, with its own entrance, stays open until 9pm, and operators will (eventually) place a call for you. The Medina *PTT* in Place Djemaa el Fna stays open until 7pm; here you can phone direct, though it takes as long as in Gueliz.

Swimming Pools There's a large, very popular municipal pool on Rue Abou el Abbes Sebti—the first main road to the left off Av. Mohammed V as you walk past the Koutoubia toward Gueliz. In the low season, you might try asking at one of the 4* hotels if they'll let you in for a fee.

Tourist Offices Both the *ONMT* and *Syndicat d'Initiative* are on Av. Mohammed V—the first is in Place Abd el Moumen Benali, the second is a little ways up toward the Medina, at no. 170. Both open daily 8:30am–noon and 3–6pm (S.I. is closed Sat. afternoons and Sun.).

LEAVING MARRAKESH

Trains are the quickest and most comfortable way of getting to Casa and Rabat. If you're heading back to Tangier it's possible to do the trip in one go, most easily by booking (in advance) a *couchette* on the night train (depart 7:40pm, arrive Tangier 5:50am in theory, around 7am in practise). The train company, *ONCF*, also run **express buses**, from the train station, to Agadir (12:58pm, 10:37pm), and Laayoune (10:37pm).

Buses to all except local destinations leave from the main terminal at **Bab Doukkala**. Buy tickets in advance for the more popular destinations such as Fes, Essaouira, and El Jadida, or you could find yourself waiting for the second or third bus that's leaving. And be sure to turn up at least half an hour early if you're heading for Taroudannt over the Tizi n'Test route (the *SATAS* bus currently leaves at 5am), or for Zagora (7am; arrives 4:30pm). Bear in mind, too, that *CTM* and all the private companies have their own individual ticket windows—choices can be more extensive than at first appears.

The **local exceptions** are buses to **Ourika, Asni** (trailhead for Djebel Toubkal), and **Moulay Brahim**, which leave from just outside Bab er Robb. Some buses also run to Asni from the Bab Doukkala bus station, from 10am–7pm.

Grands Taxis can also be useful for getting to Ourika or to Asni—negotiate for these by Bab er Robb (about 15dh a place to Asni). Other destinations are less frequent, but you can try asking some of the drivers at the stands in Djemaa el Fna and by Bab er Raha (between Av. Mohammed V and Bab Doukkala).

Flights *Royal Air Maroc* operates domestic flights to Casa (with onward connections to Tangier and Fes), and to Ouarzazate (25 min.!). They are currently rebuilding their office and have a temporary stand inside the Hôtel Atlas Asni in Gueliz. International tickets should be reconfirmed there. The **airport** is 5km out, off Av. de Menara: bargain hard with the *petit taxi* drivers, but don't expect "normal" fares.

Hitching As always, the campground can be a good place to arrange lifts, or find people to share the cost of renting a car or buying gas. There are always people setting out for Ouarzazate and the southern Kasbah/oasis routes.

THE HIGH ATLAS

The High Atlas, the greatest mountain range of North Africa, is perhaps the most beautiful and intriguing part of Morocco. A historical (and physical) barrier between the northern plains and the pre-Sahara, it has maintained a remoteness that until recent decades was virtually complete. When the French began their "pacification" in the 1920s, the Atlas way of life was essentially feudal, based upon the control of the three main passes (the Tichka, n'Test, and Imi n'Tanaout) by three "clan" families, "the Lords of the Atlas." And even with the cooperation of these warrior chiefs, it was not until 1933 (twenty-one years after the establishment of the protectorate) that the colonial power was able to subdue them and conquer their tribal lands. Today, the region is under official government control through a system of local *caids*, but in many villages the role of the state is still largely irrelevant—the Atlas Berbers generally are not taxed and do not receive any national benefits or services.

If you go hiking in the Toubkal region—or even just stop for a day or two in one of the Tizi n'Test or Tichka villages—you soon become aware of the distinct **culture and traditions** of the mountains. Longest established inhabitants of Morocco, the **Atlas Berbers** here never adopted a totally orthodox version of Islam (see *Contexts*) and the Arabic language has, even today, made little impression on their indigenous Tachelhait dialects. Their music and the *ahouache* dances (in which women and men join together in broad circles) are unique, as is the village **architecture**, with stone or clay houses tiered on the rocky slopes; craggy fortified *agadirs* (collective granaries); and Kasbahs, which continued to serve as feudal castles of sorts for the community's defense right into the present century.

Berber **women** in the Atlas are unveiled and have a much higher profile than their rural counterparts in the plains and the north. They perform virtually all the heavy labor—working in the fields, herding and grazing cattle and goats, and carrying vast loads of brushwood and provisions. Whether they have any greater status or power within the family and village, however, is questionable. The men, who often seem totally inactive by day, retain the "important" tasks of buying and selling goods and the evening/nighttime irrigation of the crops.

As an outsider in the mountains, you'll be constantly surprised by the friendliness and openness of the Berbers, and by their amazing capacity for languages—there's scarcely a village where you won't find someone who speaks French or English, or both. In the areas where tourism has become important, particularly around Toubkal, there is now some exploitation of foreign visitors, but given the struggle of life up here it is hardly surprising.

Out Of Marrakesh: Ourika, Oukaïmeden, and Amizmiz

If you spend a few days in Marrakesh you're bound to hear about **Ourika,** a long and beautiful valley where young *Marakchis* ride out on their mopeds to escape the city heat and lie around beside the streams and waterfalls. It is not a particularly dramatic "sight," nor (with the exception of the ski resort of Oukaïmeden) is it on the mainstream tourist circuit. But for a day or two's summer break, it's pretty much ideal. If you plan to stay in Ourika during the winter, beware that the valley's steep sides means that the sun leaves early, and nights can be very cool.

Access by public transportation is simple. *Grands taxis*, buses, and a fast minibus service all leave Marrakesh's Bab er Robb fairly regularly, from around 6am–noon, returning in the late afternoon/early evening. The best place to head for is **Setti Fatma**, at the end of the road (67km from Marrakesh): the trip takes a little under two hours (more by bus) and taxi fares work out at about 20–25dh one way. Keep in mind that some of the Ourika taxis only run as far as Dar Caid Ouriki (33km) or Arhbalou (50km), and unless it's market day (Monday, when rides are easy), wait until you get one going the whole way or at least to Asgaour (63km), the last village before Setti Fatma. Returning to Marrakesh, you might have to walk up to Asgaour to pick up the bus.

Ourika's main **market** takes place on Mondays at Nike Ourika, 10km back toward Arhbalou, so that's a good day to come out. Even better, if you can time it right, is Setti Fatma's annual **mousseum**, which takes place for four days (around the middle of August); it's as much a fair and market as it is a religious festival.

The Valley: Setti Fatma

The Ourika Valley took a terrific beating from freak storms in spring 1987—dozens of houses, bridges, fields, and roads were washed away. The effects are still to be seen, with many of the smaller trails now hardly defined; the roads, though, have been more or less patched up. In spring, nonetheless, expect to have some trouble toward the end of the valley road. The road is often impasable at IRHEF, where a tributary of the Ourika regularly washes away the bridge/ford.

Dar Caid Ouriki and Arhbalou
The valley really begins at **DAR CAID OURIKI**, a small roadside village with a mosque and *zaouia* set in the rocks to the left. Beyond it, scattered at intervals over the next 40km, are a series of very small villages, a few summer homes, and café-restaurants (many more disappeared in the storms).

The one sizable settlement is **ARHBALOU**, where most of the local people on the bus or in taxis will get off. It wouldn't be a bad idea to join them. There is a new, rather upscale (at least for meals) **hotel-restaurant**, *Le Lion de l'Ourika* (☎453.22), as well as rooms for rent in the village; good walking in the surrounding hills; and the possibility of some serious hiking in Djebel Yagour (see below). Farther on, between Arhbalou and Setti Fatma is the *Hôtel Amnougar* (☎28), pleasant but charging 3*-plus prices.

Setti Fatma
SETTI FATMA is the most compelling Ourika destination. Here, a little over a kilometer before you arrive, the road comes to an end and taxis drop off their passengers by the side of a stream of clear, icy water—it runs across the trail even in August. On the far side is a **café**, the village focus, and below it an incredible flank of grassy terrace. People camp for weeks on end in the summer—a real oasis as you arrive from the dry plains around Marrakesh—and in the rocky foothills in the distance are a series of six (at times, seven) waterfalls.

The first couple of **waterfalls** are a not too strenuous clamber over the rocks, but the higher ones are a bit trickier. On your first visit, it's worth hiring a guide. From the falls, you can double back to Setti Fatma via the village's twin, ZAOUIA MOHAMMED, a few hundred meters farther down the valley.

Setti Fatma has several **accommodation** options, besides camping. The *Hôtel Azro* has rooms overlooking the river (cold in winter!), the main café rents out a few rooms, the *Café Atlas*, at the north end of the village, has roof space; or you can ask around for space in a village house. A second hotel, *La Chaumière*, is 2km back toward Arhbala—once quite chic, now rundown and a bit squalid (and closed in winter). Best meals are at the *Azro*.

Hiking from Setti Fatma

Ourika cuts right into the **High Atlas**, whose peaks begin to dominate as soon as you leave Marrakesh. At Setti Fatma they rise on three sides to 3658m: a startling backdrop which, to the southwest, takes in the main **hiking/climbing zone of Toubkal**. The usual approach to this is from Asni—described in the following pages—but it is possible to set out from Setti Fatma, or from Oukaïmeden (see below).

If you are thinking of approaching from Setti Fatma, the best route is the two to three day **trek to Tachedirrt**. It's possible to hire mules and a guide (the initial section of the route is tricky to find); ask at the café. The trek, however, is a lot easier covered in the opposite direction—and is described as such in the Toubkal section. An alternative and slightly easier approach to Toubkal is to hike, via Timichi, to Oukaïmeden, and take the trail from there (see following).

If you're feeling ambitious, you could alternatively head up **into Djebel Yagour**, with its numerous prehistoric rock carvings; explore the Djebel Tougledn (4064m; involving a night's camp); try a longer excursion to **Miltsen**, via Ambougi and Turcht; or cut **through the Zat Valley** to emerge just beneath **Taddert on the Tizi n'Tichka**. This latter route takes three days to hike—carry all food for the journey. The trailhead is a few kilometers north of Setti Fatma.

For all of these trips, a **guide** would be useful.

Oukaïmeden

The village and ski center of **OUKAÏMEDEN** is a much more regular hiking base from which to set out toward Toubkal—and a good target in its own right, even if you don't have anything that ambitious in mind. Ouka, as it's known, is reached via a good, modern road which veers off from Ourika just before Arhbalou. There are regular **grands taxis** going up from Marrakesh in the winter for the skiers; at other times, you might have to charter a taxi for *la course*. The resort has a 5dh entrance fee.

Finding a place to stay is easy. There are numerous **hotels**, including the excellent *Chalet-Hôtel Chez Ju Ju*, which has rooms and dormitory accommodation, as well as solid French food. An alternative for hikers is the *Club*

Alpine Chalet. Though this is officially for *CAF* members only, it is generally open to others of similar mind—at least for a night. It is well equipped, with a bar and restaurant, and the manager and fellow hikers are good sources of hiking information.

Even if you don't stay at the chalet, you might still want to drop in and check the *CAF* diagram describing the whereabouts of the many **prehistoric rock carvings** cut into the sides of the mountain and plateau. Some of the drawings, depicting animals, weapons, and geometric designs, are within a twenty-minute walk from the chalet.

Skiing
Ouka has the best skiing in Morocco—on the slopes of Djebel Oukaïmeden—and up until the war it could boast the highest ski lift in the world, still impressive at 3273m. This gives access to good *piste* and *off-piste* skiing, with several nursery and intermediate runs on the lower slopes.

Snowfall and snow cover can be erratic, but February to April is fairly reliable. Slopes are icy early and wet by afternoon, but not having to wait in line in the mornings lets you get in plenty of sport. Several other summits are accessible for ski-mountaineering sorties from here as well, and cross-country enthusiasts often ski across to Tachedirrt (not for the casual).

Hiking to Tachedirrt
For **hikers**, the trails from Oukaïmeden are strictly summer only: routes can be heavily snow covered even fairly late in spring. However, weather conditions allowing, the **trail to Tachedirrt** (and from there to Imlil) is pretty clear and easygoing.

It begins a short distance beyond the *teleski* (ski lift), veering off to the right of the dirt road that continues for a while beyond this point. The *col,* or pass, is reached in about two hours; on the descent, the trail divides in two, either of which will lead you down into Tachedirrt.

For more details, see "Toubkal National Park," following.

Amizmiz

An easy day trip from Marrakesh, **AMIZMIZ**, to the west of the Tizi n'Test, is the site of a long established **Tuesday souk**. One of the largest Berber markets south of the Atlas, this attracts few tourists—although it is an event worth catching. It takes place in the morning, stopping around midday.

The town in itself is interesting in a modest sort of way, its clusters of distinct quarters—including a *zaouia,* Kasbah, and former Mellah—separated by a small ravine. There are regular bus and *grand taxi* connections to Marrakesh (both operate in and out of Bab er Robb); taxis are recommended, taking about 1 hr. (as opposed to 2–3 hr. on the bus). At Amizmiz there is basic **accommodation** at the *Hôtel du France*.

Amizmiz is another possible entrance to, or exit from, the High Atlas. There is a trail leading in about 7 hr. to **Ouirgane** (see "Tizi n'Test").

Hiking in the Atlas: Toubkal National Park

Hiking in the Atlas is one of the best possible experiences in Morocco, and in summer, at least, it's completely accessible for anyone reasonably fit. The mule trails around the mountain valleys are well contoured and kept in excellent condition, the main ridges of the range are usually quite broad, and there's a surprising density of villages and refuge huts. The villages look amazing, their houses stacked one on top of another in apparently organic growth from the rocks. And, corny as it might sound before you arrive, absolutely nothing rivals the costumes of the Berber women, which seem to be routinely composed of ten or twenty different and brilliant-colored strips of material.

The **Toubkal National Park**, a more or less roadless area enclosing the Atlas's tallest peaks, is the goal of 95 percent of people who hike in Morocco.

HIKING PRACTICALITIES

Seasons Toubkal is usually under snow from November until mid-June. If you have some experience of winter hiking and conditions, it is feasible to hike the low-level routes, and Djebel Toubkal itself, at these times of the year, though you will need to use crampons (sometimes available for hire in Imlil or Aremd), and for Toubkal you may need to wait around a couple of days for a clear day. For beginners, hiking is better limited to late spring/summer. And only those with winter climbing experience should try anything more ambitious than Toubkal, or going much beyond hut level, from November to May; ice ax, crampons, good rain gear, and winter competence are required, as several fatalities have recently shown. Full rivers and flash floods in February–March can pose additional problems to the snow.

Guides and Hire of Mules Guides can be engaged at Imlil and at a number of the larger villages in Toubkal; mules, too, can be hired, usually in association with a guide or porter. Rates are around 120–150dh a day for a guide, 70dh for a mule. One mule can usually be shared among several people—and if you're setting out from Imlil, say, for Lac d'Ifni, Lepiney, or Neltner, it can be a worthwhile investment. Two extras are to be added to the price—a fee to the supervisor in Imlil and a tip to the porter at the end. Guides aren't necessary for the trek up Toubkal (which is a fairly clear and very well-trodden trail) but can be invaluable for a group trying more ambitious routes. Note that guides are very reluctant—and reasonably so—to work during the month of **Ramadan** (see Basics).

Hiking Books There are almost limitless Atlas hiking routes, only a mere selection of which are detailed in these pages. For further information ask the guides at Imlil, or invest in Robin Collomb's *Atlas Mountains Guide* and/or Michael Peyron's *Grand Atlas Traverse* (both sometimes available at Imlil). Peyron's book is also available in a fuller French edition, with brief summaries of routes in English. Hamish Brown's Great Walking Adventure (Oxford Illustrated Press) has an extensive chapter written for those visiting the Toubkal area, and an appendix on the splendid day-long walk from Oukaïmeden to Asni.

Accommodation At most Atlas villages, it is possible to arrange a room in a local house. At some of the villages on more established routes, there are regular homes to which you'll find yourself directed for the night. A preparedness to camp, however, is essential if you are doing anything remotely ambitious.

It's easy to get to from Marrakesh (Asni, the "first base," is just two hours by bus or, simpler, by *grand taxi*: both from Bab er Robb), and is reasonably well charted. It has not, however, been turned into an African version of the Alps: walking even fairly short distances, you still get a sense of excitement and remoteness—and you feel very much a visitor in a rigidly individual world.

Djebel Toubkal, the highest peak in North Africa, is walkable right up to the summit; if you're pushed for time, you could hike it, and be back in Marrakesh, in three days. Farther away, and much less visited, is the high plateau of **Lac d'Ifni**, while infinite variations on **longer treks** could lead you into the mountains for a week, two weeks, or more. For anyone really low on time, or who feels unable to tackle an ascent of Toubkal, it's possible to get a genuine taste of the mountains by exploring the beautiful valley between **Imlil and Aremd**, or between **Asni and Tachedirrt**. The former is a just feasible day trip from Asni.

Altitude Toubkal is 4167m above sea level and much of the surrounding region is above 3000m, so it's possible that you might get altitude sickness and/or headaches. Aspirins can help, but just sucking on some candy or swallowing often is as good as anything. If you experience more than slight breathlessness and really feel like vomiting, go down straight away.

Water There is *Giardia* bacteria in many of the streams and rivers downriver from human habitation—including Imlil. Purification tablets are advisable, as, of course, is boiling the water.

Clothes Even in the summer months you'll need a warm sweater or jacket and preferably a windbreaker, but tents at this time aren't necessary if you have a good sleeping bag and bivibag/groundcloth. Hiking boots are ideal—you can get by with a decent pair of sneakers or jogging shoes, but certainly not sandals. Some kind of hat is essential and sunglasses are helpful.

Other Things Worth Bringing You can buy food in Asni, Imlil, and some of the other villages—or negotiate meals—though it gets increasingly expensive the higher and the more remote you get. Taking along a variety of canned food, plus tea or coffee, from Marrakesh is a good idea. A quart bottle of water is enough because you can refill it regularly; water purification tablets are worthwhile on longer trips, as are stomach pills and insect repellent. Children are constantly asking you for *cigarettes, bon-bons,* and *cadeaux*—but it's perhaps better for everyone if you don't give in, and limit gifts to those who offer genuine assistance. A worthwhile contribution hikers can make to the local economy is to trade or give away some of your gear—always welcomed by the guides, who need it.

Maps Survey-type maps are tricky to obtain in Morocco, and if you can possibly get a map of Toubkal in advance, do so. The best is a French satellite map, "Jebel Toubkal, 1:100,000." Moroccan government-produced *IGN* survey maps of Toubkal (1: 50,000) and, covering a wider area, the 1: 100,000 Toubkal-Oukaïmeden (NH-29-XXIII-1), are sporadically available at Imlil, and can be consulted in some refuges.

Skiing The Toubkal Massif is popular with ski-mountaineering groups from February to April. Most of the *tizis* (cols), including Djebel Toubkal, can be ascended, and a *Haute Route* linking the huts is possible. The Neltner refuge can get pretty crowded at these times, and the Tachedirrt refuge (or, for a serious approach in winter, Lepiney refuge) can make better bases.

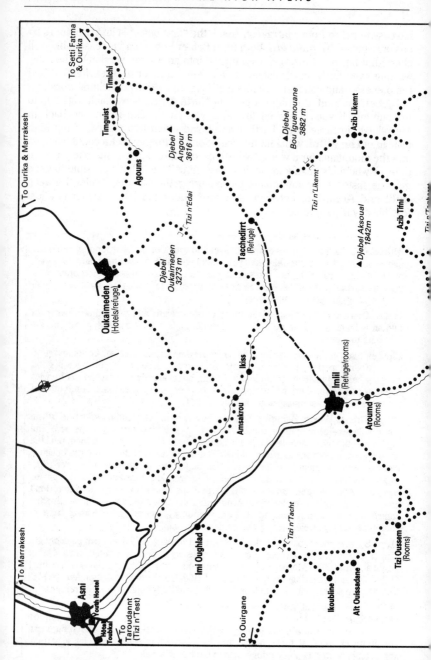

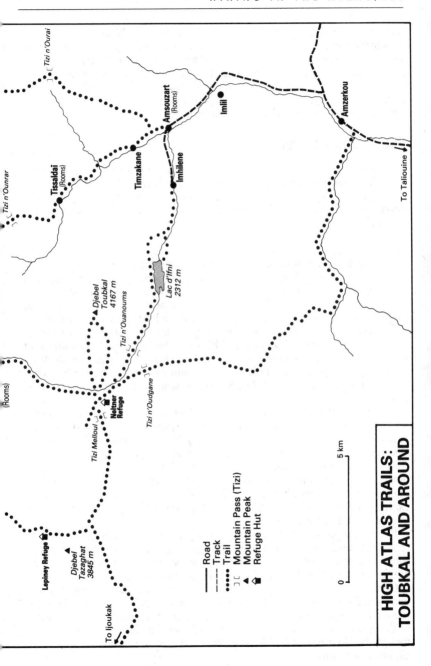

HIGH ATLAS TRAILS: TOUBKAL AND AROUND

Tizi n'Ourai

Amsouzart
(Rooms)

Imlil

Amzerkou

To Taliouine

Tissaldai
(Rooms)

Timzakane

Imhilene

Tizi n'Ounrar

Djebel
Toubkal
4167 m

Lac d'Ifni
2312 m

Tizi n'Ouanoums

Tizi n'Oudgane

(Rooms)

Tizi Melloul

Neltner
Refuge

Tizi n'Oudgane

Lepiney Refuge

Djebel
Tazaghat
3845 m

To Ijoukak

Road
Track
Trail
Mountain Pass (Tizi)
Mountain Peak
Refuge Hut

0   5 km

Unless you're undertaking a particularly long or ambitious hike—or are here in **winter conditions** (see "Hiking Practicalities" box) —you don't need any special equipment, nor will you need to do any actual climbing. The only physical problems are the high altitudes (from 3000–3700m throughout the Toubkal region), the midday heat, and the tiring process of walking over long sections of loose *scree*—the mass of small volcanic chippings and stones which cover much of the mountains' surface.

The Trailheads: Asni and Imlil

The end of the line for the Toubkal bus and Marrakesh *grands taxis*, **Asni** is really little more than a roadside village and marketplace—and a place many hikers pass straight through to get right up into the mountains. If you're in a hurry, this is good reasoning, though it's no disaster if you have to stay overnight.

Asni
ASNI can feel a bit overcommercialized on arrival, as you are greeted with offers of meals and jewelry. But this hawking doesn't last for long, and between buses the village drifts back to its usual farming existence. Its big event—and the most interesting time to be here before heading on to Toubkal—is the **Saturday market,** when the whole enclosure behind the row of shop cubicles is filled with produce and livestock stalls, an occasional storyteller, and a pretty bizarre assembly of Berber barbers. An advantage of arriving on a Saturday morning (or Friday night) is that you can stock up with good, cheap supplies, before heading into the mountains. With time to spare, there are plenty of local walks round Asni, in the fruit growing areas around.

The village has two accommodation options. At the far end of the settlement is a very pleasant, shaded **youth hostel** (*Auberge de Jeunesse*); open all year and to all comers, with slightly higher charges for non-IYHF members. Blankets are available here, and necessary in winter, since the location by the river can be very cold. Just beyond the hostel, a last taste of **hotel** luxury before the mountains is offered by the 3*A *Grand Hôtel du Toubkal* (no phone), complete with bar, swimming pool, and excellent French cooking. Both the hostel and hotel will store baggage for you, if you want to carry a minimum load into the mountains.

For **meals**, most of the café-stalls will fix a *tajine* or *harira*. The offers of "couscous meals" are an alternative, though bargaining to get down to a half-way reasonable price can be a tedious business. Staying at the hostel, there are cooking facilities. Provisions are available at the village stores.

Getting to Imlil is pretty straightforward, with trucks (*camionettes*) and taxis shuttling back and forth along the 17km of road from Asni. The most regular departures from Imlil are in the morning, from Asni in the afternoon. Both trucks and taxis normally wait until they fill their passenger quota, though the latter can be individually chartered; a place in a taxi is about 15dh, slightly less in a truck.

If you want to get straight into hiking, there is a beautiful route **up the n'Imenane valley to Tachedirrt**. This is described, in reverse, under "Tachedirrt."

Imlil

The trip from Asni to **IMLIL** is a beautiful and a startling transition. Almost as soon as it leaves Asni, the road begins to climb, while below it the brilliant and fertile valley of the Oued Rhirhaia unfolds before you, and small villages crowd into the rocky slopes above. At Imlil the air feels quite different—silent and rarefied at 1740m—and trails and streams head off in all directions.

The village itself is a small cluster of houses, along with many provisions shops, a prominent CAF refuge, and several cafés. If you want to make an early start for the Neltner hut and the ascent of Toubkal, it's a better "first base" than Asni. Most hikers choose to stay at the **CAF refuge**, which is open all year round and provides bunk beds, camping mattresses, and blankets, as well as kitchen and washing facilities, and luggage storage; rates are 20dh for a dormitory bed. In addition, Imlil now has a small hotel (pretty basic), and several houses offer **village accommodation**. The guide Aït Idir Mohammed (contact at shop behind the concrete route indicator) has a fantastic view (and a toilet!) at his house in a village overlooking Imlil.

Two other **guides**, in particular, should also be recommended. The first is Lahcen Esquary, who runs the "Shopping Center", *Ribat Tours*, in Imlil. He speaks English well and has years of experience in organizing things from Imlil. The second is Aziam Brahim, who owns the *Café Soleil*, and who works for part of the year for a French trekking company. Both men, along with Aït Idir Mohammed, are among the qualified guides listed on the noticeboard in the square, all of whom can arrange treks, ascents, mules, camping, guides, *gardiens* for your baggage, and food. Standard prices are 100dh a day for a guide, 60dh a day for mules (allow one for every two walkers); rates displayed on the noticeboard are long out of date. Group rates, or rates for longer trips, are however always negotiable. The other source of **information** in Imlil, apart from the steady flow of hikers passing through, is the *CAF* refuge, its noticeboard and book, and its *gardiens* (wardens).

Imlil to Neltner—and the Ascent of Djebel Toubkal

In winter the **ascent of Toubkal** is a serious business, requiring skill, ice ax, and crampons. But in summer, it's pretty straightforward; there's no climbing involved anywhere along the line, though some of the stonier stretches are a pretty energetic scramble. From Imlil the refuge at **Neltner** is about 12km, a hike that should take you about five and a half hours if you set out early enough to benefit from the morning cool and shade. If you're starting later in the day, **Aremd**, just 4km walk from Imlil, makes a good first stop.

Once at Neltner most people stay the night, setting out at first light for **Toubkal** to get the clearest possible panorama from its heights. And since this *is* the highest peak in North Africa, it seems a shame to rush it any more than this.

Imlil to Aremd

AREMD (or AROUND; 1840m, 6040ft) is a walk of 1–1½ hours from Imlil—the first stage on the trail to Neltner and Toubkal, and the largest village of the Mizane Valley. It's an extraordinary looking place, built on a spur of loose rock above the valley—a site that resembles nothing so much as a landslide but also commands one of the most fertile stretches of the Atlas. Terraced fields of corn, potatoes, onions, barley, and various kinds of fruit, line the valley sides, and there is some grazing, too; the village streets are often blocked by goats or cattle—and permanently covered in animal excrement and flies.

This notwithstanding, Aremd is very much on the hiking circuit. A British trekking company maintains a base in the village, and there is a now a café and guesthouse by the river, and quite a number of **rooms** rented out in the village houses. Alternatively, it's possible to **camp** slightly upstream: you should ask permission first, and, as is usual, pay a small fee—a compensation for nonproduction of crops, since all possible land in this valley is cultivated. There is as yet only one store in Aremd—despite a population of some 500—so if you lack the energy to arrange a meal, you'd better take along food from Asni or Imlil. The local **organizer for guides and mules** is Brahim Aït el Kadi, who arranges treks for the British company. He rents out rooms (and will prepare meals) in his house, and can often loan crampons in winter.

To **get to Aremd from Imlil**, you basically follow the course of the Mizane River. On the west side (i.e., the right bank, coming from Imlil) there's a well-defined mule trail that zigzags above the river for about 2km before dropping to the floor of the valley, just before a crossing point to Aremd; over on the east bank, there's a much rougher path—around the same distance but slightly harder to follow.

Aremd to Neltner

From Aremd, the **Neltner trail** follows the east (i.e. the Aremd) side of the Mizane valley, climbing and zigzagging around the hard, gray rocks, high above the river. At intervals some of the larger rocks have been marked with red dots to reassure you that you're on the right track. If you have been following the main mule trail on the west side of the valley from Imlil to Aremd, you can join the Neltner trail without going into Aremd—it crosses over and merges with the section from Aremd a short distance after you pass the village to your left.

The river is crossed once more 1½–2 hours farther down, just before you arrive at the village of **SIDI CHAMHAROUCH**, set beside a small waterfall—a perfect rest stop. The village is an anarchic cluster of houses, all built one into another, whose seasonal population of ten or twelve people run softdrinks/grocery stores for tourist hikers and Moroccan pilgrims, who come to the village's **marabout** shrine. This lies across the gorge from the village, reached by a modern concrete bridge, which non-Muslims are strictly forbidden to cross. It is probably a survival of a very ancient nature cult—which in these parts are often thinly veiled in the trappings of Islam. (On the approach to the village you might have noticed a tree, sacred to local tradition, where the Berbers hang strips of cloth and make piles of stones). **Camping** below the village, beside the stream, is possible. **Rooms** are also available.

Beyond Sidi Chamharouch, the Neltner trail climbs steeply in zigzags and then traverses the flank of the valley well above the Mizane. The water from the river is not safe to drink untreated until you get above the Neltner hut, though the smaller streams and springs by the path are said to be safe.

The trail itself is pretty clear the whole way to the **Neltner Refuge**, which, at 3207m, marks the spring snow line. Even in mid-August it gets pretty cold up here after the sun has disappeared behind the ridge, and you'll probably want to take advantage of its shelter (open all year: around 35dh to non-Alpine Club members). The *gardien* is usually prepared to cook meat or vegetable tajine for guests, though beware that the hut can be very busy—and crowded. It is badly in need of extension.

Another reason for staying at the refuge is that the area around is covered in rubbish (human waste, too), so if you plan on camping, you'll want to go some way up toward the summit, where vegetation (but also rubbish) is sparse.

Climbing Toubkal

At Neltner you're almost bound to meet people who have just come down from **Djebel Toubkal**—and you should certainly take advantage of them (and/or the Neltner *gardien*) for a description on the routes and on the state of the vaguely defined South Cirque trail to the summit. The initial trail from the refuge, especially, can be easy to miss.

The **South Cirque** (*Ikkibi Sud*) is the most popular and straightforward ascent and, depending on your fitness, should take between 2½ and 3½ hours (2–2½ hr. coming down). With reasonable instructions on the spot, it's easy enough to follow without hiring a guide, though there are confusing paths going off all over the place and you need to be careful in finding the right track down. The trail actually begins just below the Neltner hut, dropping down to cross the stream and then climbing over a short stretch of grass and rock to reach the first of Toubkal's innumerable fields of boulders and scree. These—often needing three steps to gain one—are the most tiring (and memorable) feature of the hike up, and pretty grueling for inexperienced walkers. The summit, a triangular plateau of stones marked by a tripod, is eventually reached after a lot of zigzagging through a gap in the ridge. It should be reiterated that in winter the ascent is a snow climb; not for walkers.

Robin Collomb, in his *Atlas Mountains* guide, recommends the **North Cirque** (*Ikkibi Nord*) as an alternative—though longer (4½ hr.) and more ambitious—ascent. It's a bad way down, however, vitually guaranteeing periods of sliding and scraping down the scree. The **southwest/west cirque**, a third possible approach, is only for experienced rock climbers.

Lac d'Ifni: The Route from Neltner

One of the largest mountain lakes in the Atlas—and the only one of any size in the Toubkal region—**Lac d'Ifni** is an impressive and satisfying destination. From Neltner it's a four- to four-and-a-half-hour hike, easy enough to do, though again involving long, tedious stretches over loose rock and scree. On the way back, this is even more pronounced. To make the trip worthwhile, it's worth taking along enough food for a couple of days' camping; there are no facilities, or villages, en route.

Neltner to Ifni

The **Ifni trail** begins immediately behind the Neltner hut, climbing up a rough, stony slope and then winding around to the head of the Mizane valley toward the imposing *tizi* (or col) of **Tizi n'Ouanoums**. The col is reached in about an hour and the path is reasonably easy to follow. There is just one vague division, a little before the ascent of the pass, where a path veers off to the right along the final stretch of the Mizane. The trail up the col itself is a good, gravel path, zigzagging continually until you reach the summit (3664m), a narrow platform between two shafts of rock.

The views from the summit here are superb, taking in the whole route that you've covered and, in the distance to the south, the hazy green outline of the lake. At this point the hard work seems over—but this is a totally false impression! The path down the valley to Lac d'Ifni is slow, steep progress, the scree slopes are apparently endless, and the lake often fades completely out of sight. It is, in fact, virtually enclosed by the mountains, and by what seem to be demolished hills—great heaps of rubble and boulders.

The only human habitation at **Lac d'Ifni** are a few shepherds' huts, and the only sound, that of water idly lapping on the shore. You can camp on vague, scrubby terraces, somewhat fly-ridden by day, or up at the huts. If you have some tackle (and, officially, a permit) you can also fish—there are apparently plentiful trout. Be warned, however, that the lake is exceptionally deep—50m over much of its area—and some of the sides are a sheer drop.

On from Ifni

Most people return from Ifni to Neltner by the route they came. But it's feasible to make a longer, counterclockwise, loop toward Imlil or Tachedirrt.

From the lake, you can reach AMSOUZERTE (eat/sleep at Omar's house) in around 3 hr., then strike north to TISSALDAI (another 4 hr.; eat/sleep at Dilh Ahmed's) and SIDI CHAMHAROUCH (6 hr. minimum of strenuous hiking over Tizi n'Ounrar and Tizi n'Tagharat). Over this last stage, AZIB TIFNI, east of Tizi n'Tagharat is a possible overnight stop (*azib* is a goat shelter, usually, like here, with primitive huts) to break up the trip.

Another alternative is to cross the first *tizi* and descend to AZIB LIKEMT, stay there overnight, then cross the high **Tizi n'Likemt to Tachedirrt**. The country down from Azib Likemt is wild to an extreme (too hard even for mules!), so don't try to reach the Ourika Valley that way.

Note. All this area behind Toubkal needs to be treated as a proper expedition, and hiring a **local guide** is strongly recommended.

Tachedirrt and Beyond

TACHEDIRRT (3000m), to the east of Imlil, is an alternative and in many ways more attractive base for trekking expeditions. As at Imlil, there is a **CAF**

refuge, and there is a fine range of local hikes and onward routes. But despite its comparatively easy access—a pleasant mule trail up the valley over Tizi n'Tamatert (more direct than the recently blasted-out *piste*)—the village sees only a handful of the trekkers who make it up to Toubkal.

You can walk the mulepath from Imlil in three to four hours, or on Saturdays there's a Berber truck (for the Asni *souk*) along the *piste*. There are as yet no stores in the village (though soft drinks are sold), so take along your own food. The CAF refuge (20dh a bed; cooking facilities and some suplies available through the *gardien*) is just above the trail on the lefthand side as you enter the village; it's kept locked, but the *gardien* should soon appear. He can arrange a guide, and mules, if you are looking to do a long walk, like that over to Ourika.

Tachedirrt to Setti Fatma

This is one of the more obvious routes for anyone contemplating more than a day or two's trip into the hills. Taken at a reasonably human pace, the route can be accomplished in three days' walking from Tachedirrt—two if you're fit. There is a well defined trail all the way, used by locals (who take mules along the whole length), so no particular skills are demanded beyond general fitness. However, several sections are quite exposed—and there are points where a fall from the path would be fatal. You need a reasonable head for heights.

You'll probably want to carry some food supplies with you. However, meals are offered at the refuge at Timichi, so cooking gear and major provisions are not essential. If you are carrying all your gear along, you might want to consider hiring mules at Tachedirrt.

Tachedirrt to Timichi is a superb day's walk. The first three hours or so is spent climbing up to the col, at 3616m, and with ever more spectacular views. The character of the valley changes abruptly after the col, green terraced fields giving way to rough and craggy mountain slopes. The path down is one of the more exposed sections of the route. As you approach Timichi the valley again becomes more green and vegetated.

There are six villages in the valley and this can be a little confusing. Local children, however, will soon show you the correct path to **TIMICHI** and its **refuge**. The refuge is a welcoming place, with a very helpful *gardien*, who offers a tempting range of meals. If you arrive reasonably early in the day, you can make a loop around the hill, exploring all six valley villages, in around three to four hours.

Timichi to Setti Fatma is another beautiful hike. The path becomes steadily wider and more used as you approach Setti Fatma, but it is clear enough along the whole course. At first you follow the river fairly closely but, at a very impressive village perched on a huge rock buttress, you climb upward, to about 1000–1500ft above the riverbed. There is little water available on the path for several miles, and potential campsites are limited to small, flat bivvying sites. The path is good but appears perched on the side of the extremely steep valley: care must be taken, as you would only bounce a few times before arriving at the river far below, if you fell. The path finally zigzags down into the Ourika valley about 2km north of Setti Fatma.

Tachedirrt to Oukaïmeden

This is a fairly straightforward route—a three- to four-hour walk over a reasonable mule trail by way of the 2960m Tizi n'Ou Addi; the Angour ridge lies off to the east along the first part of the trek.

For details of Oukaïmeden itself, see the preceding section.

The Angour Ridge

Hiking along the ridge of Angour is pretty demanding, taking a full day from Tachedirrt and (if the weather turns on you) demanding a night's bivouac.

From Tachedirrt, the trail zigzags up the lefthand side of the **Imenane valley** up toward **Tizi n'Tachedirrt** (which remains visible the whole way). At the col (a three-and-a-half-hour steep walk, taking you up to 3616m), a path climbs due north up a rough, grassy slope, to break through crags onto the sloping **plateau**, which can be followed to the **summit of Angour**. This plateau is an unusual feature on a peak with such dramatic cliffs. It is split by a valley.

With care, experienced hikers can follow a ridge down from here to **Tizi n'Ou Addi** (to pick up the Oukaïmeden trail), or break away straight down to Tachedirrt. A guide would be useful.

Tachedirrt to Imlil via Tizi n'Aguensioual

Less ambitious, but still demanding a lot of care on the loose, steep scree paths, is an alternative route back from **Tachedirrt to Imlil** by way of **Tizi n'Aguensioual**.

This takes you first by a tricky-surfaced path to the hamlets of TINERHOURHINE (1 hr.) and IKISS (15 min. farther down; soft drinks/rooms). From Ikiss a good path (ask someone to point it out) leads up to the Aguensioual pass; over the other side, it's another stony scramble down to the village of AGUENSIOUAL, from where you can follow the road to Asni back up to Imlil.

Tachedirrt to Asni

There is a long but straightforward trail from Tachedirrt downvalley to Asni, taking around seven to nine hours. It's an enjoyable route, through a fine valley with no road or electricity—a good exit from the mountains, which is covered by few hikers.

If you are approaching from Imlil, there is a short cut to the trail at the Tizi n'Tamatert (1hr. from Imlil), dropping down to the bottom of the valley at TINHOURINE. Beyond Tinhourine, the valley trail leads to IKISS and ARG, with a few possible campsites below the former, and many below the latter. There are rooms and soft drinks available at IKISS and AMSAKROUTE (or AMSEKROU; half an hour north of Ikiss).

Approximate **walking times**: IMLIL/TACHEDIRRT–TINHOURINE (1 hr.); TINHOURINE–IKISS (40 min.); IKISS–ARG (2 hr.); ARG–IMESKER (1½–2 hr.); IMESKER–TANSGHART (1½hr.); TANSGHART–ASNI (1 hr.).

West of Imlil: Tizi Oussem and Lepiney

The area west of Imlil and the Djebel Toubkal trail offers a good acclimatization hike to **Tizi Oussem**, harder treks to the south to the **Lepiney refuge** (accessible also, from Neltner), and the possibility of one- or two-day hikes **out to Ouirgane or Ijoukak** on the Tizi n'Test road, or back to the Asni-Imlil road at **Tamadout**.

Tizi Oussem and on to Ouirgane

The village of **TIZI OUSSEM** is in the next valley west of Imlil and is reached in about four hours over the Tizi Mzic. The most interesting section is the path straight down from the col to the village; if you are heading for Lepiney, another path from the col follows around the hillside to Azib Tamsoult, and then to the gorge for the Lepiney hut.

The valley itself offers a long day's hike **down to Ouirgane** on the Tizi n'Test road. At its foot it becomes a road, but this wanders off to the right and you should abandon it in order to go left and, with luck, arrive at the *Au Sanglier Qui Fume* (see Ouirgane). Experienced walkers can make a two-day expedition to reach **Ijoukak**, with one camp/bivouac en route.

The route to Ouirgane keeps to the west side of the valley. Perhaps even more spectacular is to keep to the east side, crossing, eventually, the Tizi n'Tacht, angle down on a piste, then on by mule tracks to the Asni-Imlil road at **Tamadout**. This hike, in spring, is hard to equal, with green fields, blossoms, and snow mountains beyond.

Lepiney and Around

Some 6½ to 7½ hours from Imlil, the **Lepiney refuge** is essentially a rock-climbing base, above all for the barren cliffs of **Tazaghârt**, with its year-round snow. A porter or someone would have to go down to the village to get the hut *gardien*, Omar Abdallah, who can also rent you a room in the village. Details of a number of climbs are given in the Collomb guide.

Tizi Melloul (3–4 hr. from Lepiney) allows hiking access to Tazarghârt (3843m), an extraordinary plateau and fine vantage point. You can also cross Tizi Melloul and, with one camp or bivouac, walk **down the Agoundis Valley to Ijoukak**. This walk is described in *Travels* by Hamish Brown (Scotsmen Publications, 1986).

Tizi n'Test: Ijoukak, Some Hikes, and the Mosque of Tin Mal

The **Tizi n'Test**, the road that extends beyond Asni to Taroudannt and Taliouine, is unbelievably impressive. Cutting right through the heart of the Atlas, it was blasted out of the mountains by the French in the first years of their "pacification"—the first modern route to link Marrakesh with the Souss plain and the desert, and an extraordinary feat of pioneer-spirit engineering.

Until then, it had been considered impracticable without local protection and knowledge: an important pass for trade and for the control and subjugation of the south, but one that few sultans were able to make their own.

Through much of the last century—and the beginning of the twentieth—the pass was the personal fief of the **Goundafi** clan, whose huge Kasbahs still dominate many of the crags and strategic turns along the way. Much further into the past it had served as the refuge and power base of the Almohads, and it was from the holy city of **Tin Mal**, up toward the col, that they launched their attack on the Almoravid dynasty. As remote and evocative a mountain stronghold as could be imagined, Tin Mal is an excursion well worth making in its own right for the chance to see the ruins of the twelfth-century mosque, a building close in spirit to the Koutoubia, and for once accessible to non-Muslims.

First, **some practicalities**. If you are setting out by **bus from Marrakesh,** you should have four choices, leaving at either 5am (sometimes 6am), 2pm, or 6pm. The 5am/6am bus is the only direct one to Taroudannt (7½ hr.), but the others go as far as Ijoukak (4 hr.); the 2pm bus stops there, and the 6pm one goes on to Taliouine (arriving, after a scary night descent, at around 1–2am). It's important to turn up at least half an hour early if you want tickets on the morning bus. If you're **coming from Asni**, you can pick up any of these buses a little over an hour after they leave Marrakesh.

For anyone **driving**, some experience of mountain roads is essential. The route is well contoured and now completely paved, but between the col (the summit of the pass) and the intersection with P32, the Taliouine-Taroudannt road, it is extremely narrow (1½ times a car's width) with almost continuous hairpin curves and blind corners. Since you can actually see for some distance ahead, this isn't as dangerous as it sounds—but you still need a lot of confidence and have to watch out for suicidal local drivers bearing down on you without any intention of stopping or slowing down. Bus and truck drivers are, fortunately, more considerate. If you are driving a hire car, which is liable to overheat, try to avoid driving the route at midday in the summer months.

From November to the end of April, the pass can occasionally be **blocked with snow**. When this occurs, a sign is put up on the roadside at the point where the Asni-Test road leaves Marrakesh and also on the roadside past Tahanoute.

The Road to the Pass and Beyond

Heading out on the dawn bus from Marrakesh, you have the least interesting part of the Taroudannt journey to catch up on lost sleep. The landscape over the first couple of hours—before you come to the village of Ouirgane and the beginning of the **Oued Nfis gorges**—is fairly monotonous.

Ouirgane and the Nfis Gorges
OUIRGANE is a tiny place, long touted by French guidebooks as a beautiful valley and *étape gastronomique*. In the early hours of an Atlas morning, this might not be much of an attraction, but if you have some money to spend

after hiking around Toubkal, you could do a lot worse than come up here to lie around and recover.

There are two **hotels**, both with swimming pools. The big one, *Résidence la Roseraie* (☎04), is a grand 4*A place, with prices to match (sauna, tennis, and equestrian options). A lot cheaper, and equally pleasant, is the idiosyncratic *Au Sanglier Qui Fume* ("the smoking wild boar"; ☎09). Run by a Frenchwoman of considerable character, this has a series of cool chalet-type rooms, scattered around a colorful garden setting. Its cooking these days is erratic, though you may strike a good day—if possible, avoid Tuesdays, when tour groups come out from Marrakesh.

From Ouirgane, a 7 hr. walk by the **Nfis gorges** leads to **Amizmiz** (bus/taxis to Marrakesh: see "Out of Marrakesh"). A route can also be made to the **Tizi Ouzla** and the "lost world" of the **Kik plateau**—the plateau edge being the crags seen above the route from Asni to Ouirgane, descending from Tizi Ouadou to Asni on or along the scarp, part marble quarries, to MOULAY BRAHIM (small hotel; bus/taxi to Marrakesh). These places can equally well be visited from Asni. The spring flowers on the limestone plateau are interesting and the views to the High Atlas cannot be matched.

On to Ijoukak

Moving on, the best base for a stay in the Tizi n'Test area is **IJOUKAK**. The village has a few basic shops and a couple of small **cafés**, both of which rent out rooms. The one nearest the bend in the road serves excellent *tajines*, and its rooms are actually part of the large, rambling house that extends down the hill behind the café. There's no electricity—candles are provided when asked for—and there are no sheets, only blankets. It's also possible to camp, though the riverbed is pretty rocky and wouldn't be very suitable. *Guide Collomb* indicates a *CAF*-supervised hut at Ijoukak, but it is actually the state forestry house and does not welcome guests.

Walking out from Ijoukak, you can easily explore Tin Mal and Talaat n'Yacoub (see below) or try some more prolonged **hiking in the Nfis and Agoundis valleys**—see the box overpage. The Agoundis can be enjoyable just as a day's wandering, if you have nothing ambitious in mind. In Talaat an interesting mountain *souk* takes place on Wednesdays.

Idni and the Col du Tizi n'Test

Until the death of its *patronne*, Mme. Giplou, in 1985, the *Hôtel Alpina* made **IDNI**, just below the mountain pass, an even better place in which to stay over. Sadly, the hotel seems shut for good now; a loss to the whole neighborhood and to the buses, which used to break the journey here. Due to the *Alpina's* reputation, however, a number of travelers do still turn up in Idni (many, alas, guided by previous British editions of this guide) and the **café** across the road from the hotel has started renting out very basic rooms (with bed mats), as well as preparing hot meals and tea. It can get very cold up here at night (there's no electricity), but it's not a disastrous option.

The **Col du Tizi n'Test** (2100m) lies 18km south of Idni. There's a **café-restaurant**, the *Cassecroute*, just to the south of the pass, where you can normally get buses either to drop you off or pick you up. Walk back along the

HIKES AROUND IJOUKAK

Ijoukak gives access to some of the most enjoyable hiking in the High Atlas—much less developed than the main Toubkal area. Starting from the village, you can hike east up the **Agoundis valley toward Toubkal**, or west up the long **Ogdemt valley**. The region to the **west of the Tizi n'Test road** is wilder still; for details—in reverse—of the hike to Afensou and Imi n'Tanoute (on the Marrakesh-Agadir road), see the "Western High Atlas" section at the end of this chapter.

The **survey map** for the area (if you can get hold of it) is *Tizi n'Test* (1:100,000).

Agoundis Valley

East from Ijoukak winds the **Agoundis River valley**. It offers alternative access to Toubkal, but is seldom used. To reach the Neltner refuge below Toubkal would take two days of serious hiking. However, if "peak bagging" is not part of your plan, you could still enjoy a day's hike or an overnight trip up this way.

From Ijoukak walk back down the road toward Marrakesh until you cross the river (200m). A dirt road leads off to your right. A small sign there warns you not to fish for trout in the river. This road continues along the valley for about 10km. It's used by trucks hauling ore from the mines. If you're in a hurry, you could hitch a ride; otherwise, the walk is a pleasant one. There are several villages strung out along the valley making use of the year-round water to farm small patches in the river bottom and on the terraced hillsides.

About 2km down the road there is a small square hut below the road on the right. It's a water powered **millstone** which is fascinating to watch if you happen to catch someone inside. Another 2km farther and you'll pass an abandoned **rock crushing factory**, its huge tin and timber structure half falling down. Just beyond it is the village of **TAGHBART**. The road splits after 8km, the right fork descending to the river, crossing and continuing on into the mountains to the south. Take the left fork (get off the truck if you've hitched this far) and follow it as it curves around to the left, to the northeast. At the curve is another village, **EL MAKHZEN**. The road has now been extended a couple of kilometers to **TIJRHICHT**. Along this last section is an ingeniously constructed irrigation ditch hugging the cliffside beneath the road. Here the road ends and a mule trail begins. If you've hitched up here, it probably will have taken you no more than half an hour; on foot it's about two to three hours.

The **trail towards Neltner** begins to climb into a narrowing limestone gorge with the river a great distance below. Tiny Berber villages are perched on rocky outcrops every 2–3km. Good views in both directions. Toubkal finally appears, rising above the upper reaches of the valley.

road a kilometer from here and you'll find a track leading straight up to the col—which itself is dark and restricted—toward a platform mounted by a TV relay station. The views down to the Souss Valley and back toward Toubkal can be stunning.

Over the col, the **descent toward Taroudannt/Taliouine** is hideously dramatic: a drop of some 1600m in little over 30km. Throughout, there are stark, fabulous vistas of the peaks, and occasionally, hundreds of feet below, a mountain valley and cluster of villages. Taroudannt is reached in around 2½ to 3 hours on the descent, Taliouine in a little more; coming up, needless to say, it all takes a good deal longer. For details on Taroudannt and Taliouine, see *Chapter Seven*.

At **AÏT YOUB** (8km from the end of the road), you will have reached the last and highest cultivated areas (1900m). *Guide Collomb* estimates 3½ hours to arrive this far, with the help of the occasional lift. Figure on six to eight hours' walking, depending on your fitness.

Neltner hut and Djebel Toubkal are another long day's hike from here. It's possible to rent a mule and hire a muleteer, who acts as a guide simply because he knows the way. However, this is not as straightforward and organized as in more frequented places like Imlil. This far into the mountains it is unlikely that you will find anyone who speaks English, but with simple French or Arabic phrases you should be understood.

If you wish to continue on foot alone, *Guide Collomb* is helpful from here. Keep in mind that snow can impede your crossing the pass until midsummer. In any case, you'll need to stay overnight in Aït Youb. Camping should be no problem. It's usually best to ask permission for politeness' sake. When you ask, be prepared for an offer of hospitality and a night's stay in the village. You're in no way imposing by accepting it, but it is understood in all but a few cases that you'll offer something in return when you leave. It will customarily be turned down at least once but usually accepted with persistence on your part.

Ougdemt Valley

West from Ijoukak and the Agoundis valley lies **the Ougdemt**, a long, pleasant valley filled with Berber villages surrounded by walnut groves.

A dirt road for trucks now stretches for several kilometers up the valley from **MZOUZITE** (3km beyond Tin Mal and 8km from Ijoukak). Beyond this, a trail continues winding up along the river to **ARG** at the head of the valley (6–7 hr. walking). From Arg you could go for **Djebel Erdouz** (3579m) to the north of Tizi n'Tighfist (2895m), or the higher **Djebel Igdat** (3616m) to the south, by way of Tizi n'Oumslama. Both are fairly straightforward when following the mule paths to the passes and can be reached in five to six hours from Arg. Be sure to take your own water in summer as the lower elevations can be dry.

For the very adventurous, a further expedition could be undertaken **all the way to the Tichka plateau**—summer grazing pastures at the headwaters of the Nfis River—and across the other side to the Marrakesh-Agadir road. This would take at least six days from the Tizi n'Test road and require you to carry provisions (and water in summer) for several days at a time. For a detailed route description, see M. Peyron's *Great Atlas Traverse*. A brief summary of this trail, taken from the opposite direction, follows in the "Western High Atlas" section.

Tin Mal Mosque

The **Tin Mal Mosque**, quite apart from its historic and architectural importance, is an extraordinarily beautiful ruin—isolated above a sudden flash of river valley, with stack upon stack of pink Atlas peaks towering beyond its roofless arches. It's an easy eight-kilometer walk from Ijoukak, passing en route the old Goundafi Kasbah in Talaat n' Yacoub (see below).

The mosque is set a little ways above the modern village of TIN MAL (or IFOURIREN), reached by wandering uphill, across the stream. A massive, square, Kasbah-like building, it is kept locked, but the *gardien* will soon spot you, open it up, and let you look around undisturbed.

Some History

Tin Mal's site seems now so remote, and the land around here so unpromising, that it is difficult to imagine a town ever existing in this valley. In some form, though, it did. It was here that **Ibn Toumert** and his lieutenant, **Abd el Moumen**, preached to the Berber tribes and welded them into the **Almohad** (or "unitarian") movement; here that they set out on the campaigns which culminated in the conquest of all Morocco and of southern Spain; and here, too, a century and a half later, that they made their last stand against the incoming Merenid dynasty.

This history—so decisive in the development of the medieval Shereefian empire—is outlined in "The Historical Framework" in *Contexts*. More particular to Tin Mal are the circumstances of Ibn Toumert's arrival and the appeal of his puritan, reforming teaching to the local tribes.

Known to his followers as the *Mahdi*—"The Sinless One," whose coming is prophesied in the Koran—Toumert was himself born in the High Atlas, a member of the Berber-speaking Masmouda tribe (who held the desert-born Almoravids, the ruling dynasty, in traditional contempt). He was an accomplished theologian and studied throughout the centers of eastern Islam—a period in which he formulated the strict Almohad doctrines, based on the assertion of the unity of God and on a verse of the Koran in which Muhammad set out the role of religious reform: "to reprove what is disapproved and enjoy what is good." For Toumert, Almoravid Morocco contained much to disapprove of and, returning from the East with a small group of disciples, he began to preach against all manifestations of luxury (above all, the use of wine and performance of music), and against women mixing to any degree in male society.

In 1121, Toumert and his group arrived in Marrakesh, the Almoravid capital, where they immediately began to provoke the sultan. Ironically, this was not an easy task—Ali Ben Youssef, one of the most pious rulers in Moroccan history, accepted many of Toumert's charges and forgave his insults. It was only in 1124, when the reformer struck Ali's sister from her horse for riding unveiled (as was desert tradition), that the Almohads were finally banished from the city and took refuge in the mountain stronghold of Tin Mal.

From the beginning in this exiled residence, Ibn Toumert and Abd el Moumen set out to mold the Atlas Berbers into a religious and military force. They taught prayers in Arabic by giving each follower as his name a word from the Koran and then lining them all up to recite it. They also stressed the significance of the "second coming" and Toumert's role as *Mahdi*. But more significant, perhaps, was the savage military emphasis of the new order. Hesitant tribes were branded "hypocrites" and were massacred—most notoriously in the Forty-Day Purge of the mountains—and within eight years none remained outside Almohad control. In the 1130s, after Ibn Toumert had died, Abd el Moumen began to attack and "convert" the plains. In 1145, he was able to take Fes and, in 1149, just twenty-five years after the march of exile, his armies entered and sacked Marrakesh.

The Mosque

The **Tin Mal Mosque** was built by Abd el Moumen around 1153–54; partly as a memorial and cult center for Ibn Toumert, and partly as his own family mausoleum. Obviously fortified, it probably served also as a section of the town's defenses, since in the early period of Almohad rule, Tin Mal was entrusted with the state treasury.

Today, it is the only part of the fortifications—indeed, of the entire Almohad city—that you can make out with any clarity. The rest was sacked and largely destroyed in the Merenid conquest of 1276—a curiously late event, since all of the main Moroccan cities had already been in the new dynasty's hands for some thirty years. That Tin Mal remained standing for that long, and that its mosque was maintained, says a lot about the power Toumert's teaching must have continued to hold over the local Berbers. Even two centuries later the historian Ibn Khaldun found Koranic readers employed at the tombs, and when the French began the work of restoration in the 1930s they found the site littered with the shrines of *marabouts*.

Architecturally, Tin Mal presents a unique opportunity for non-Muslims to take a look at the interior of a traditional Almohad mosque. It is roofless, for the most part, and two of the corner pavilion towers have disappeared, but the *mihrab* (or prayer niche) and the complex pattern of internal arches are substantially intact.

The arrangement is in a classic Almohad design—the T-shaped plan with a central aisle leading toward the *mihrab*—and is virtually identical to that of the Koutoubia in Marrakesh, more or less its contemporary. The one element of eccentricity is in the placing of the **minaret** (which you can climb for a view of the general layout) over the *mihrab:* a weakness of engineering design that meant it could never have been much taller than it is today.

In terms of decoration, the most striking feature is the variety and intricacy of the **arches**—above all those leading in to the *mihrab,* which have been sculpted with a stalactite vaulting. In the **corner domes** and the **mihrabvault,** this technique is extended with impressive effect, despite their crumbling state. Elsewhere, and on the face of the *mihrab,* it is the slightly austere geometric patterns and familiar motifs (the palmette, rosette, etc.), of Almohad decorative gates that are predominant.

The Goundafi Kasbahs

The **Goundafi Kasbahs** don't really compare with Tin Mal—nor with the Glaoui Kasbah in Telouet (detailed in the following Tizi n'Tichka section). But, as so often in Morocco, they provide an extraordinary assertion of just how recent is the country's feudal past. Despite their medieval appearance, the buildings are all nineteenth or even twentieth century creations.

Talâat n'Yacoub

The most important of the Kasbahs is the former Goundafi stronghold and headquarters in the village of **TALÂAT N'YACOUB**. Coming from Ijoukak, this is reached off to the right of the main road, down a very French looking, tree-lined country lane; it is 6km south of Ijoukak, 3km north of Tin Mal.

The **Kasbah**, decaying, partially ruined and probably pretty unsafe, lies at the far end of the village. Nobody seems to mind if you take a look inside, though you need to avoid the dogs near its entrance. The inner part of the palace-fortress, though blackened from a fire, is reasonably complete and retains traces of its decoration.

It is difficult to establish the exact facts with these old tribal Kasbahs, but it seems that it was constructed late in the nineteenth century for the next-to-last Goundafi chieftain. A feudal warrior in the old tradition, he was constantly at war with the sultan during the 1860s and 1870s, and a bitter rival of the neighboring Glaoui clan. His son, Tayeb el Goundafi, also spent most of his life in tribal campaigning, though he finally threw in his lot with Sultan Moulay Hassan, and later with the French. At the turn of the century, he could still raise some 5,000 armed tribesmen within a day or two's notice, but his power and fief eventually collapsed in 1924—the result of El Glaoui's maneuvering—and he died three years later. The Kasbah here in Talaat must have already been in decay then; today, it seems no more linked to the village than any castle in Europe.

Tagoundaft

Another dramatic looking Goundafi Kasbah is to be seen to the left of the road, a couple of kilometers south of Tin Mal. This one, **Tagoundaft**, is set on a hilltop, and is now privately owned. It is well preserved—as indeed it should be, having been constructed only in 1907.

Telouet and Tizi n'Tichka

The **Tizi n'Tichka**—the direct route from Marrakesh to Ouarzazate—is less remote and less spectacular than the Test pass. As it is an important military (and tourist) approach to the south, the road is modern, well constructed, and comparatively fast.

At Telouet, however, only a short distance off the modern highway, such mundane current roles are underpinned by an earlier political history, scarcely three decades old and unimaginably bizarre. For this pass and the mountains to the east of it were the stamping ground of the extraordinary Glaoui brothers, the greatest and the most ambitious of all the Berber tribal leaders. Their Kasbah-headquarters, a vast complex of buildings abandoned only in 1956, are a rewarding detour (44km from the main road).

For **hikers**, Telouet has an additional and powerful attraction, offering an alternative and superb approach to the south, following the old tribal **pass over the Atlas to Aït Benhaddou**.

Telouet: the Glaoui Kasbah

The **Glaoui Kasbah** at **TELOUET** is one of the most extraordinary sights of the Atlas—fast crumbling into the dark red earth, but visitable, and offering a peculiar glimpse of the style and melodrama of recent Moroccan government and power.

The Glaoui: Some Background

The extent and speed of **Madani** (1866–1918) **and T'Hami** (1879–1956) **el Glaoui's rise to power** is remarkable enough. In the mid-nineteenth century, their family were simply local clan leaders, controlling an important Atlas pass—a long established trade route from Marrakesh to the Drâa and Dades valleys—but lacking much influence outside of it. Their entrance into national politics began dramatically in 1893. In that year's terrible winter, **Sultan Moulay Hassan**, on returning from a disastrous *harka* (subjugation/ burning raid) of the Tafilalt region, found himself at the mercy of the brothers for food, shelter, and safe passage. With shrewd political judgment, they rode out to meet the sultan, feting him with every detail of protocol and, miraculously, producing enough food to feed the entire 3000-strong force for the duration of their stay.

The extravagance was well rewarded. By the time Moulay Hassan began his return to Marrakesh, he had given *caid*-ship of all the lands between the High Atlas and the Sahara to the Glaouis and, most important of all, saw fit to abandon vast amounts of the royal armory (including the first cannon to be seen in the Atlas) in Telouet. By 1901, the brothers had eliminated all opposition in the region, and when **the French** arrived in Morocco in 1912, the Glaouis were able to dictate the form of government for virtually all the south, putting down the attempted nationalist rebellion of El Hiba, pledging loyalty throughout World War I, and having themselves appointed **pashas of Marrakesh**, with their family becoming *caids* in all the main Atlas and desert cities. The French were content to concur, arming them, as Gavin Maxwell wrote, "to rule as despots, [and] perpetuating the corruption and oppression that the Europeans had nominally come to purge."

The strange events of this age—and the legendary personal style of T'Hami el Glaoui—are beautifully evoked in Gavin Maxwell's *Lords of the Atlas*, the brooding romanticism of which almost compels a visit to Telouet:

At an altitude of more than 8,000 feet in the High Atlas, [the castle] and its scattered predecessors occupy the corner of a desert plateau, circled by the giant peaks of the Central Massif.... When in the spring the snows begin to thaw and the river below the castle, the Oued Mellah, becomes a torrent of ice-gray and white, the mountains reveal their fantastic colors, each distinct and contrasting with its neighbor. The hues are for the most part the range of colors to be found upon fan shells—reds, vivid pinks, violets, yellows, but among these are peaks of cold mineral green or of dull blue. Nearer at hand, where the Oued Mellah turns to flow though the Valley of Salt, a cluster of ghostly spires, hundreds of feet high and needle-pointed at their summits, cluster below the face of a precipice; vultures wheel and turn upon the air currents between them ....

Even in this setting the castle does not seem insignificant. It is neither beautiful nor gracious, but its sheer size, as if in competition with the scale of the mountains, compels attention as much as the fact that its pretension somehow falls short of the ridiculous. The castle, or Kasbah, of Telouet is a tower of tragedy that leaves no room for laughter.

And that's about how it is. If you've read the book, or if you've just picked up on the fascination, it's certainly a journey worth making, though it has to be said that there's little of aesthetic value, many of the rooms have fallen into complete ruin (restoration is "planned"), and without a car, it can be a tricky and time-consuming trip. Nevertheless, even after thirty years of decay, there's still vast drama in this weird and remote eyrie, and in the painted salon walls, often roofless and open to the wind.

The Kasbah

Once at Telouet, make your way to the second **Kasbah** on the hillside—beyond a desolate and total ruin which is all that remains of the original castle built by Madani and his father in the mid-nineteenth century. The castle-palace above is almost entirely T'Hami's creation, and it is here that the road stops, before massive double doors and a rubble strewn courtyard.

Wait a while and you'll be joined by a caretaker-guide, necessary in this case since the building is an unbelievable labyrinth of locked doors and connecting passages, which, so it is said, no single person ever completely knew their way around. Sadly, these days, you're shown only the main halls and reception rooms. You can ask to see more—the harem, the kitchens—but the usual reply is *"dangereux,"* and so it most likely is: if you climb up to the roof (this is generally allowed) you can look down upon some of the courts and chambers, the bright *zellij* and stucco enclosing great gaping holes in the stone and plaster.

The **reception rooms**—"the outward and visible signs of ultimate physical ambition," in Maxwell's phrase—at least give a sense of the quantity and style of the decoration, still in progress when the Glaouis died and the old regime came to a sudden halt. They have delicate, iron window grilles and fine carved ceilings, though the overall result is once again the late nineteenth-and early twentieth-century combination of sensitive imitation of the past and out-and-out vulgarity. There is a tremendous scale of affectation, too, perfectly demonstrated by the use of green Salé tiles for the roof—usually reserved for mosques and royal palaces.

The really enduring impression, though, is the wonder of how and why it ever came to be built at all, since, wrote Gavin Maxwell :

It was not a medieval survival, as are the few European castles still occupied by the descendants of feudal barons, but a deliberate recreation of the Middle Ages, with all their blatant extremes of beauty and ugliness, good and evil, elegance and violence, power and fear—by those who had full access to the inventions of contemporary science. No part of the Kasbah is more than a hundred years old; no part of its ruined predecessors goes back further than another fifty. Part of the castle is built of stone, distinguishing it sharply from the other Kasbahs that are made of pisé or sun-dried mud, for no matter to what heights of beauty or fantasy these might aspire, they are all, in the final analysis, soluble in water.

Getting to Telouet: Irherm and Taddert

Getting to Telouet **by public transportation**, there are several options open to you. From Marrakesh you'll have to take the Ouarzazate bus as far as either Irherm or Taddert. At **IRHERM**, 10km beyond the Tichka mountain pass, there are shared *grands taxis* out to Telouet, and a small basic **hotel** and bar, if you need to stay the night.

TADDERT, on the Marrakesh side of the pass, is in fact a more interesting place to stay: a terraced roadside hamlet, with beautiful walks nearby (for example, to the village of TAMGUEMEMT, half an hour away, above a mountain stream), and a good, cheap **auberge**, *Le Noyer*, run by an old French expatriate. The problem here, though, is that you'll have to hitch onward to Telouet: there's no bus or taxi, and many of the buses going toward the pass and turnoff are often full.

Getting back from Telouet should be less of a problem. There is usually some traffic—and a handful of tourists—and most people find it hard to turn down a lift.

By car you can easily set out from Marrakesh in the morning, take in Telouet and perhaps also the Kasbahs of Aït Benhaddou (see Ouarzazate), and reach Ouarzazate in the early evening.

Telouet to Aït Benhaddou

An alternative possiblity, for hikers, is to continue **south beyond Telouet to Aït Benhaddou**. This is a great route, through some of the most beautiful and tranquil countryside in the High Atlas. Before the construction of the Tichka road, it was in fact the main pass over the Atlas. It was only the presence in the Telouet Kasbah of T'Hami's xenophobic and intransigent cousin, Hammou ("The Vulture") that caused the French to construct a road along the more difficult route to the west.

Today there is a *piste* south from Telouet as far as **ANEMITER**, a large village (much larger than Telouet), with a welcoming **café-hotel**. This is run by one Elyazid Mohammed, who is a mountain guide and will take groups (or, at a price, individuals) on five day hiking tours into the Atlas. He speaks excellent French and a spattering of English.

South of Anemiter the trails and dirt roads take over for the 35km to Aït Benhaddou. The trail is just about negotiable—at least in summer—by sturdy vehicle—and a couple of correspondents have got through with few problems on mountain bikes (8 hours' leisurely ride from Anemiter to Aït Benhaddou). It is perhaps best of all for walkers, though, offering tranquility and unparalleled views of green valleys, a river that splashes down the whole course, and remarkable turquoise scree slopes amid the high, parched hillsides.

Despite the absence of settlements on most of the maps, much of the **valley's northern reaches** are scattered liberally with communities, all making abundant use of the narrow but fertile valley plain. This unveils a wealth of dark red and crumbling Kasbahs, collections of homes grouped among patchworks of wheatfields and hay, terraced orchards, olive trees, date palms, and figs—and everywhere children calling to each other from the fields, the river, or the roadside.

As you walk, all these are to be seen down below you in the valley. The main mule track clings to the valley side, alternately climbing and descending, but with a general downhill trend as you make your way south. Some 8km south of Anemiter you encounter the first of three **fords** (probably impassable for cars outside the summer months). Here the track forks: take the **lefthand trail** that mounts the hillside on the opposite bank of the river.

Moving toward Aït Benhaddou, the nature of the trail begins to change, as settlements become sparser and the track strays away from the river for some kilometers at a time. The countryside is dusty, the valley wider, and in summer dry and very hot. If you want to stay along the way, **TOURHAT**

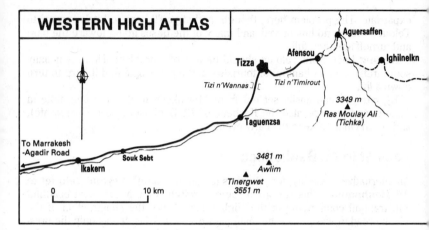

makes a good base—either for camping, or, as is likely to be offered, for a night in a village home. The village is about 6–7 hr. walking from Anemiter.

A few miles south of Tourhat, the trail takes you past **TAMDAGHT** (about 3 hr.), a scattered collection of buildings with a classic **Kasbah**. This was used in as a filmset for an *MGM* epic, and retains some of its authentic Hollywood decor, along with ancient and rickety storks' nests on the battlements.

From **Tamdaght to Aït Benhaddou** the road is again paved. At the village (see Ouazarzate in *Chapter Six*), you can get drinks at a café, and pick up a taxi to Ouazarzate.

Marrakesh To Agadir: the Tizi Maachou and Hiking in the The Western High Atlas

The direct route from **Marrakesh to Agadir**—the **Imi n'Tanoute**, or **Tizi Maachou**, pass—is, in itself, the least spectacular of the Atlas roads. If you are in a hurry, it is a reasonably fast (4 hr.) trip and when the Text and Tichka are closed through snow, it normally remains open.

Convenience aside, **hikers** have the most reason for taking this road, with access from Chichaou, midway along the road, to the **Western High Atlas**. Exploring this region of the Atlas, you move well away from the usual tourist routes, miles from any organized refuge, and pass through Berber villages which see scarcely a tourist from one year to the next. You'll need to pack your own provisions, carry water supplies, and be prepared to camp or possibly stay in a Berber village home if you get the invitation, as you probably will. Sanitation is poor in the villages and it's not a bad idea to bring water purification tablets if you plan to take water from mountain streams—unless you're higher than all habitation. Both eating and drinking in a village home have given many a foreigner an upset stomach.

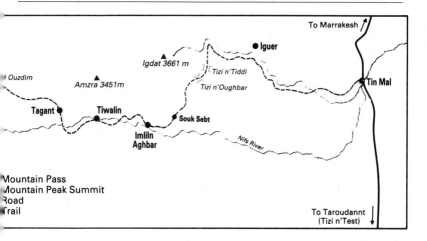

Getting into the mountains, there are two main access points—**Imi n'Tanoute** and **Tinesgadiouine**, both on the Marrakesh-Agadir bus route. From these, it's usually possible to get rides to the trailheads from trucks bound for mines or markets. The (elusive) IGN survey **maps** for the area are *Tizi n'Test* and *Igli* (1:100,000).

The Pass and Chichaoua

Leaving Marrakesh, the buses* normally follow the Essaouira road as far as **CHICHAOUA**, a small village and administrative center, with several cafés and **hotels**. It is set at the entrance to the mountains, and is famed in a small way for its carpets. These—brightly colored and often using stylized animal forms—are sold at the *Centre Coopératif* and also at the **Sunday market**. The village is the most pleasant stop along the road to break your journey.

Beyond Chichaoua, the road to Essaouira continues efficiently across the drab **Chiadma plains**. For Agadir, you begin a slow climb toward **IMI N'TANOUTE**, another administrative center (with a Monday *souk*), and then cut through the last outlying peaks of the High Atlas. Imi n'Tanoute is of little interest, though if you need to stay before setting out on a hike (see below), there are rooms at a couple of the cafés, and provisions. In the hillside above the town, the phrase "Allah—Country—King" is laid out (in Arabic) in white painted stones, in letters over 50ft high.

The pass, **Tizi Maachou**, is at 1700m. Beyond it, there are occasional gorges and a handful of difficult paths up into the mountains. The buses usually take a break at one of the villages on the way. If you are planning to hike into the Atlas from TIMESGADIOUINE, make sure you get dropped at the turnoff, 50km south of Imi n'Tanoute. Hiking aside, there's nowhere very compelling or interesting to stop.

---

*Only one *CTM* bus runs direct from Marrakesh to Agadir. Others stop at Inezgane, which has regular local bus connections on to Agadir.

Imi n'Tanoute to the Tizi n'Test

A dirt road leads up into the mountains from **Imi n'Tanoute to Afensou**. There's a Thursday market about 17km along the road, at SOUK EL KHEMIS, and so your best chance is to hitch up on a Wednesday with one of the trucks. This trip takes several hours, so don't arrive late in Imi n'Tanoute or you might get stranded. The road (possible for ordinary passenger cars) crosses the **Tizi n'Tabghourt** pass at 2666m, from where you have an excellent panorama of the entire area, which includes some peaks reaching 3350m.

At **AFENSOU** you are as close as you'll get by road to the center of the Western High Atlas region. From here you can hike in either direction—east toward Ijoukak or west toward the Marrakesh-Agadir road at Timesgadiouine. Or perhaps just wander around the valleys and peaks at random. It's a somewhat complex system of intervening ridges, so you'll probably need the survey map.

Afensou to Ijoukak

To reach **Ijoukak** and the Tizi n'Test road, hike north from Afensou 4km up the Sembal River to AGUERSAFFEN. Here you turn east–southeast to follow the long **Gourioun River valley** to the **Tichka Plateau**, via the **Tizi 'n Asdim** pass (2842m), a trek requiring a whole day.

Cross the plateau—where you'll see shepherds, sheep, and their shelters (*azib* on the map) in summer—following the **Nfis River** (see Ijoukak) as it winds through gorges which might detour you occasionally. Continue east down the river valley through villages and the shade of walnut trees which reappear after the Tichka Plateau. At the village of IMLIL (not to be confused with the Toubkal Imlil) is a shrine to Ibn Toumert, the founder of the Almohad dynasty.

A day's hike from the plateau should bring you to **SOUK SEBT TANAMMERT**. From this Saturday market, a truck road climbs up to the Test road, not far from the pass itself. You can hitch out here or continue hiking for two more days to MZOUZITE, near Tin Mal: one day north to ARG via Tizi n'Aghbar (2653m) and Tizi n'Tiddi (2744m), and the second day east along the long Ogdemt Valley to MZOUZITE, as described in the Tizi n'Test section.

West and a little south from Afensou lie two parallel valleys which culminate at Souk Sebt Talmakent. The more scenic of the two, Assif n'Aït Driss, is described below.

Timesgadiouine and the Aït Driss

The second access point along the Marrakesh-Agadir road is **TIMESGADIOUINE**, about 50km south of Imi n'Tanoute. Argana looks more plausible on the map, but the road is no longer used. A small sign around 15km north of Argana indicates Timesgadiouine. Get off the bus here, where you'll see a dirt road, a small building and perhaps a few people who, like yourself, are waiting for rides. Nothing else signifies this as an entrance to the mountains. The actual village is 3–4km along the dirt road.

EAST OF THE TIZI N'TICHKA

Some of the wildest *pistes* and countryside in the High Atlas are to be found east of the Tizi n'Tichka—dirt roads climbing up above KASBA TADLA and BENI MELLAL (see "Middle Atlas") to the high plateaus around IMILCHIL, eventually emerging in the fabulous gorges of the Drâa and Todrha.

These are really exciting—well off the standard routes of the country and taken, for the most part, by organized landrover expeditions. But, despite this, they are actually quite feasible for independent travel, and with the patience to fit in with the local market patterns, you can go all the way across by Berber or transit truck. Details of some of these routes, and an account of what it's like to try them, can be found in the following chapter (see "Todra Gorge").

Souk Sebt and into the Mountains

Your hitching destination is **SOUK SEBT TALMAKENT**. Trucks will be driving up on Friday afternoon for the Saturday *souk*, but others go up during the week to a mine above AFENSOU and they all pass through Souk Sebt. Be prepared for a wait and a long dusty ride. If you ride up on Friday afternoon, you can camp overnight. Basic food items can be bought here. There are no cafés and no rooms, although the government workers posted to this nowhere place might offer you a room in their offices.

The **Aït Driss River** winds its way just below Souk Sebt. It's a pretty valley that narrows to a gorge for a kilometer or two before spreading out and filling up with walnut trees and Berber villages. As you hike up, several other tributaries come down on your right from the main ridge. The two most conspicuous peaks, **Tinerghwet** (3551m) and **Awlim** (3482m) are the same two you can see from Taroudannt, which lies in the Souss plain on their far side. Turn up any of these tributaries for an interesting day's hike. For camping, you're better off in the Aït Driss valley, where the ground is flatter.

In August you'll see entire families out for the **walnut harvest**. The men climb high into the trees to beat the branches with long poles. Underneath, the women and children gather the nuts, staining their hands black for weeks from the outer shells. In this part of the Atlas, the women often wear their hair in pigtails that hang down the sides of their faces.

To the Head of the Aït Driss

You can reach the **head of the Aït Driss** at TAMJLOCHT in a day's hiking from Souk Sebt. From there a steep climb over the **Tizi n'Wannas** pass (2367m) takes you to TIZZA, a small village at the head of the parallel valley, the Warguiwn. Tizza is not a big market town nor does any road reach it, yet it interestingly merits a place on most Moroccan road maps.

From Tizza hike east up a small valley 2–3km, then climb up **Tizi n'Timirout** (2280m)—not named on the survey map. There's a dramatic view of the main ridge from this pass, its rugged peaks stretching to the northeast. The most prominent one is Moulay Ali at 3349m. **AFENSOU** (see account above) awaits you after a long descent, from where you can hitch back out to Souk Sebt or Imi n'Tanoute or continue on across to the Tizi n'Test road.

Note. An alternative, little-explored approach to, or exit from, the Tichka plateau leads **from Taroudannt,** to the south. Some very wild *pistes* run into the Atlas from Taroudannt, to valley head bases such as IMOULAS, MEDLAWA, and SOUK TNINE TIGOUGA. See Taroudannt for details of guide and mule hire from that end.

travel details

Trains
Marrakesh–Casablanca (4 daily; currently at 1:20am, 7:25am, 9:00am, and 5:27pm; 4 hr.).
Marrakesh–Fes/Meknes via Casablanca) (3 daily; 10 hr. 45 min.).
Marrakesh–Tangier (2 daily; currently 1:20am and 5:25pm; 15 hr. 30 min.).
Marrakesh–Safi (1 daily; 3 hr. 40 min.; but this is essentially a phosphate/freight train).

Buses
From Marrakesh Asni (8 daily; 1½ hr.); Taroudannt (2 at dawn; 8½ hr.);
Taliouine (1; 7–8 hr.); Ouarzazate (4; 4–5 hr.)*; Zagora (2; 9–11 hr.)*; Agadir (1; 3 hr. 45 min.); Inezgane (4; 3 hr. 30 min.—change for Agadir); Essaouira (6; 3 hr.–4 hr. 30 min.); Safi (4; 3 hr. 30 min.); El Jadida (9; 3 hr. 30 min.); Casablanca (hourly; 4 hr.); Rabat (8 daily; 5 hr. 30 min.); Fes (3; 11 hr.); Beni Mellal (9; 3 hr.); Azrou (4; 5 hr. 30 min.) Demnate (4; 3 hr.).
The most comfortable is the 10am bus operated by Ligne du Zagora.

Grands Taxis
From Marrakesh Frequent and useful services to the Ourika Valley, Asni, and Amizmiz; negotiable elsewhere, though no particular standard runs.

Flights
From Marrakesh Daily (except Tuesdays) to Casablanca with connections on to Tangier. International flights via Tangier or Casablanca.

TELEPHONE CODE

MARRAKESH ☎04

THE GREAT SOUTHERN OASIS ROUTES

Immediately when you arrive in the Sahara, for the first or the tenth time, you notice the stillness. An incredible, absolute silence prevails outside the towns; and within, even in busy places like the markets, there is a hushed quality in the air, as if the quiet were a constant force which, resenting the intrusion of sound, minimizes and disperses it straightaway. Then there is the sky, compared to which all other skies seem faint-hearted efforts. Solid and luminous, it is always the focal point of the landscape. At sunset, the precise, curved shadow of the earth rises into it swiftly from the horizon, cutting it into light section and dark section. When all daylight has gone, and the space is thick with stars, it is still of an intense and burning blue, darkest directly overhead and paling toward the earth, so that the night never really grows dark.

Paul Bowles: *The Baptism of Solitude*

The **Moroccan Pre-Sahara** begins as soon as you cross the Atlas to the south. It is not sand for the most part—more a wasteland of rock and scrub—but it is powerfully impressive. The quote from Paul Bowles may sound like romantic exaggeration or quasi-mysticism, but staying at Figuig or Merzouga, or just stopping in the desert between towns, somehow has this effect. There is, too, an irresistible sense of wonder as you catch a first glimpse of the great river valleys—the **Drâa**, **Dades**, **Todra**, and **Tafilalt**. Long belts of date palm oases, scattered with the fabulous mud architecture of kasbahs and fortified *ksour* villages, these are the old caravan routes that reached back to Marrakesh and Fes and out across the Sahara to Timbuktu, Niger, and the Sudan. They are beautiful routes—even today, tamed by modern roads and with the oases in decline—and if you're traveling in Morocco for any length of time, this is the part to head for. The simplest circuit (**Marrakesh–Zagora–Marrakesh**, or **Marrakesh–Tinerhir–Midelt**) takes a minimum of five days; to do them any degree of justice, or merely to see the highlights, takes a lot longer.

Although the old trading routes are now no longer in use, and date production is not what it once was, the **southern oases** were long a mainstay of the precolonial economy. Their wealth, and the arrival of tribes from the desert, allowed three of the royal dynasties to rise to power, including, in the seventeenth century, the present ruling family of the Alaouites. By the nine-

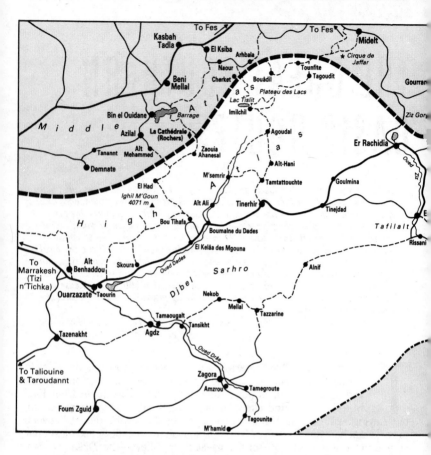

teenth century, however, the advance of the Sahara and the uncertain upkeep of the water channels had led to a bare subsistence even in the most fertile strips. Under the French, with the creation of modern industry in the north and the exploitation of phosphates and minerals, they became less and less significant, and subject to massive emigration to the cities.

Today, there are a few urban centers in the south—**Erfoud, Ouarzazate,** and **Er Rachidia** are the largest—but these seem only to underline the end of an age. Although the date harvests in late October can still give employment to the *ksour* communities, and tourism itself brings in a little money, the rest of the year sees only the modest production of a handful of crops—henna, some cereal grains, citrus fruits, and roses (introduced by the French to produce *attar*, or rose water, in the spring). To make the situation even more critical, in recent years the seasonal rains have failed, and perhaps as much as half the male population of the *ksour* now seeks work in the north for at least part of the year.

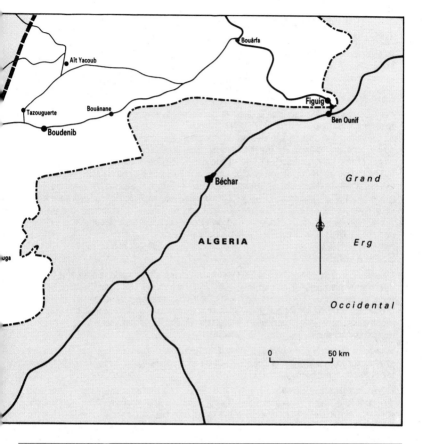

OUARZAZATE AND THE DRÂA

Ouarzazate—easily reached from Marrakesh (6 hr. by bus) or Taroudannt (6½ hr.—via Taliouine)—is the standard starting point for the south. East of here stretches the Dades River, the "Valley of the Kasbahs," as the *ONMT* promotes it. South of it, on the other side of a tremendous ridge of the Anti-Atlas, begins the **Drâa**, 125km of date palm oases, eventually merging into the Sahara near the village of M'hamid.

Although it is possible to make a circuit on along the *pistes* to Rissani, for most people (and anyone relying on buses alone), exploring **the Drâa** means going down to **Zagora** and then returning to Ouarzazate by the same route. If you're in a hurry, this might sound somewhat gratuitous, but it is a route that really shouldn't be missed, taking you well south of anywhere in the Tafilalt and flanked by an amazing series of turreted and cream-pink-colored *ksour*.

SOUTHERN PRACTICALITIES

All the main routes in this chapter are covered by ordinary **local buses,** and often *grands taxis,* too. On many of the others, there are regular **Berber trucks** or **land-rover taxis** (detailed in the text). There are, however, a few really adventurous desert *pistes*—such as the direct desert route from Zagora to Rissani—which are only practicable by car. If you plan to drive on these, or on the very rough roads over the Atlas behind the Dades or Todra gorges (which can be covered also by rides in Berber trucks), you'll need to be decently equipped and able to do basic mechanical repairs.

Traveling by **bus** in the desert, in summer, the only real disadvantage is the sheer physical exhaustion involved: most trips tend to begin at dawn to avoid the worst of the heat, and for the rest of the day it can be difficult to summon up the energy to do anything. If you **rent a car** you'll lose out by cutting yourself off from everyday life in the country, but you'll gain by being in the position to take in a lot more, with a lot less frustration, in a reasonably short period of time. There are a couple of rental outlets in Ouarzazate and one in Tinerhir; otherwise the nearest rental agencies are in Marrakesh and Agadir. Most allow you to complete a circuit and return the car to Marrakesch, Casablanca or Fes.

Some details

Gasoline/car repairs Gas stations can found along all the main routes, but they're not exactly plentiful. Fill the tank whenever and wherever you have the opportunity; carry water in case of overheating; and, above all, be sure you've got a good spare tire—flats tend to be frequent on all southern roads. As throughout the country, mechanics here are excellent (particularly in Er Rachidia), however, and most minor problems can be quickly dealt with.

Rivers in the south are reputed to contain bilharzia, a parasite that can enter your system through the soles of your feet. Even when walking by streams in the oases, take care to avoid contact.

Temperatures can climb well above 120° F (50° C) in mid-summer and you'll find the middle of the day is best spent being totally inactive. If you have the option, spring is by far the most enjoyable time to travel—particularly if you're heading for Zagora (reckoned to be the hottest town in the country), Rissani-Merzouga, or Figuig. Fall, with the date harvests, is also good. In winter, the days remain hot, though it can get pretty cool at night, and farther south into the desert, it can actually freeze. Some kind of hat or cap, and sunglasses, are pretty much essential.

Spring Floods The Drâa, in particular, is subject to spring floods, as the snow melts in the Atlas and forges the river currents. Passes across the Atlas at this time, and even trips such as Ouarzazate to Aït Benhaddou, can be difficult or impossible.

These—**ksour** is the plural, **ksar** the singular—are to be found throughout the southern valleys and, to an extent, in the Atlas. They are essentially fortified tribal villages, massive but temporary structures, built in the absence of other available materials out of the mud-clay *pisé* of the riverbanks and lasting only as long as the seasonal rains allow. A unique and probably indigenous development of the Berber populations, they are often monumental in design and fabulously decorated, with bold geometric patterns incised or painted on the exterior walls, and slanted towers. The **kasbah,** in its southern form, is similar to the *ksar*, though instead of sheltering a mixed village community, it is traditionally the domain of a single family and its dependents. **Agadirs** and **tighremts**, also variants of the *ksar* structure, used to serve as a combination of tribal fortress and communal granary or storehouse in the villages.

Ouarzazate and Aït Benhaddou

At some stage, you're almost bound to spend a night in **OUARZAZATE** and it can be a useful base from which to visit the *ksour* and kasbahs of Aït Benhaddou or Skoura. It is not exactly compelling in itself, however. Like most of the new Saharan towns, it was created as a garrison and administrative center by the French and remains pretty much the same today: a deliberate line of functional buildings, set along the main highway and lent an odd sort of permanence by the use of concrete in place of the *pisé* of the *ksour*.

What attraction it does have is due to the fact that it's a bit of a boomtown at present. The tourist industry has moved in with half a dozen luxury hotels, recognizing Ouarzazate's marketability as a staging point for the "Saharan Adventure." And the town has had an additional boost from the attentions of Hollywood. The region first came to prominence in the film world twenty years ago, when David Lean shot *Lawrence of Arabia* at nearby Aït Benhaddou (see below). In the last few years, scarcely a month has gone by without a director and crew in residence. There is even a permanent sound stage and processing plant—*Atlas Studios*—on the outskirts.

Practicalities

Orientation is simply a matter of getting your bearings along the highway and main strip, Av. Mohammed V. The **CTM bus station** more or less marks the center, with a **PTT** (with a direct dial international phone section; Mon.–Sat. 8:30am–noon and 2:30–6pm) alongside, and an ONMT **tourist office** across the road. The **private-company buses** use a station a block to the west of the *CTM*. There are regular departures to Marrakesh, Zagora, and east along the Dades; also two daily buses (8am and 3:30pm) for the marathon run to Taliouine, Taroudannt, and Inezgane (connection for Agadir).

Grands taxis operate in and out of Place Mouhadine, again near the center of town. They make regular runs along the Dades to Boumalne, and can be negotiated for Marrakesh or Zagora. **Car rental** is available through *Hertz* (near the center of town on Av. Mohammed V) and *Budget*, by the *Hôtel Gazelle*, 1km west on the road to Taliouine.

Most of the **cheap hotels** are grouped in the center, near the bus stations. Pick from the recently modernized *Royal* (24 Av. Mohammed V; ☎22.58) or the *Es* Salam (no phone), just across the road; the *Atlas* (13 Rue du Marché; ☎23.07), on a street parallel, a block north. The best **upscale alternatives** are the 2*B *Hôtel Gazelle* (Av. Mohammed V—1km toward Taliouine; ☎21.51), a comfortable, if overpriced, place with a (usually full) swimming pool, or the 3*A *Hôtel Tichka* (Av. Mohammed V; ☎22.06), midway between the center of town and the Kasbah Taorirt. To be sure of a room, it's wise to phone ahead: the town can get surprisingly full.

The municipal **campground** is 4km east of the center, on the right of the Tinerhir road, a short ways past the Kasbah Taorirt (see below). It has a tent restaurant (order meals in advance) and washing facilities (often pretty filthy); there's a pool (sometimes open to campers) at the adjoining tourist complex. The site backs onto the Ouarzazate "lake," whose banks support a large pack of howling dogs.

The best of the **café-restaurants** are on Rue du Marché, by the private company bus station—try the *Essalen*; off the same street is a small food *souk*. A little bit pricier, but good, is the restaurant at the *Hôtel Royal*. If you want a **drink**, head for *Chez Dimitri*, a Foreign Legion era café-bar, in the middle of Av. Mohammed V. It serves inexpensive *Flag* Specials. Stocking up with your own supplies of alcohol, there's a grocery store across the street from *Dimitri's* that sells discreet, newspaper-wrapped bottles of wine. For anyone interested in **buying rugs or carpets**, the *Maison Berbère* is a must—one of a chain of three stores (others are at Tinerhir and Rissani) offering good quality goods at very reasonable prices.

Kasbah Taorirt

Ouarzazate's one sight is the Glaoui-built **Kasbah Taorirt**, to the right of the highway at the east (Tinerhir direction) end of town—a dusty, twenty-minute walk from the bus station. The kasbah was never an actual residence of the Glaoui chiefs—as were Telouet or Marrakesh—but, located at this strategic junction of the southern trading routes, was always controlled by a close relative. In the 1930s, when the Glaouis were the undisputed masters of the south, it was perhaps the largest of all Moroccan kasbahs—an enormous family domain housing numerous sons and cousins of the dynasty, along with several hundred of their servants and laborers, builders, and craftsmen, even semi-itinerant Jewish tailors and money lenders.

Since then, and especially after it was taken over by the government at the time of independence, the kasbah has fallen into drastic decline. Parts of the structure have simply disappeared, washed away by heavy rains; others are completely unsafe; and it is only a small section of the original, a kind of village within the kasbah, that remains occupied today. That part is toward the rear of the rambling complex of rooms, courtyards, and alleyways. What you are shown (admission daily, except Sundays, 9am to noon and 3 to 6pm) is just the main reception courtyard and a handful of principal rooms, very lavishly decorated but not especially significant or representative of the old order of things. With an eye to tourist demands and fantasies, they have become known as "the harem."

Opposite the kasbah a *Centre Artesanal* is under construction. At present, the town's **crafts co-op** (*Coopérative des Tisseuses*) is located at the crossroads on the route out to Zagora. There is no true local craft tradition, but stone carving, pottery, and the geometrically patterned, silky, woolen carpets of the region's Ouzguita Berbers are all displayed and sold here. Hours are Mon. to Fri. 8:30am to noon and 1 to 6pm, Sat. 8:30am to noon.

Tifoultoutte

There is little else in—or to—Ouarzazate, and really the most interesting option is to get out for the day, either to Aït Benhaddou (see below) or a little along the Dades to Skoura—a beautiful and rambling oasis (see "The Dades"), easily accessible as a daytrip using the Boumalne/Tinerhir buses.

The kasbah in **Tifoultoutte**, which the tourist office might recommend, is nicely situated but unless you have a car and a strange sense of humor, it's hardly worth the time. Nine kilometers outside Ouarzazate, on the P31, which bypasses the town en route to Zagora, it was again a former Glaoui kasbah, though much smaller than the one in Taorirt, and built (or at least rebuilt) only this century. In the 1960s, it was converted to a hotel, and it was used—claim of all claims in this region—by the cast of *Lawrence of Arabia.* Today, with various luxury hotels (and a huge Club Med) in Ouarzazate itself, it has been reduced to the role of "traditional-entertainment annex" for the various hotel tour groups. It is all fabulously inauthentic—mock banquets and German belly dancing—and just a bit gross.

Aït Benhaddou

The first thing you hear from the guides on arrival at **AÏT BENHADDOU** is a list of its movie credits. This is a feature of much of the Moroccan south, where landscapes are routinely fantastic, and cheap, exotic-looking extras are in plentiful supply; but, even so, the Benhaddou kasbahs have a definite edge over the competition. *Lawrence* was here, of course, and for *Jesus of Nazareth,* the whole lower part of the village was rebuilt.

If this puts you off—and Aït Benhaddou is not really the place to catch a glimpse of fading kasbah life—don't dismiss it too easily. Piled upon a dark shaft of rock above a shallow, reed-strewn river, the village is one of the most spectacular in the Atlas and its kasbahs among the most elaborately decorated and best preserved. They are less fortified than is usually the case along the Drâa or the Dades, but, towered and crenellated and with high, sheer walls of dark red *pisé,* they must have been near impregnable in this remote, hillside site.

As ever, it's impossible to determine how old the kasbahs actually are, though there seem to have been buildings here since at least the sixteenth century. The importance of the site, which commands the area for miles around, was its position on the route from Marrakesh through Telouet to Ouarzazate and the south: a significance that disappeared with the creation of the new French road over the Tichka pass, and which has led to severe depopulation over the last thirty years. There are now only half a dozen families living in the kasbahs, earning a sparse living from the valley's agriculture and from the steady trickle of tourists.

When you reach the village the road comes to an end at a newly built café, where you'll be "adopted" by the one of the village **guides** and led up through the incredibly confusing web of streets. If you ask, it's usually possible to see the interior of one or two of the **kasbahs**. At the top of the hill, there are the ruins of a vast and imposing **agadir**, into which the villagers once must have been able to retreat.

To get to **Aït Benhaddou** is simple enough by car. Leaving Ouarzazate on the P31 (Tichka: Marrakesh) road, you turn right after 22km—along a rough, but signposted, 9km road.. Without a car, the best solution is to get together with others and charter a *grand taxi*. Otherwise, you're dependent on hitching along the turnoff road (which isn't easy) and, if you don't get a ride back from fellow visitors, later picking up one of the buses going back into Ouarzazate (not all of which are inclined to stop). As is often the case in the south, the best solution is probably to negotiate a ride with other tourists: if you ask around in the evening at the Ouarzazate campground (or at *La Gazelle*), someone can usually be persuaded to go.

If you're into **hiking**, or very rough driving, the jeep track beyond Aït Benhaddou continues to TAMDAGHT, and from there mule paths go up to the old pass to TELOUET (see pages 282–283 for a description of this journey).

South To Zagora: The Drâa Oases

The road from Ouarzazate to Zagora is wide and well maintained, though it does seem to take its toll of tires. As in the rest of the south, if you're driving make sure you have a good spare and the tools to change it with: there is regular traffic, but you can easily go half an hour to an hour without seeing or passing a thing.

Across the Djebel Sahro

The route begins unpromisingly: the course of the Drâa is some ways to the east, and the road goes across bleak, stony flatlands of semidesert. However, at AÏT SAOUN, one of the few roadside villages along this initial stretch, a dramatic change takes place. Leaving the plains behind, you begin a truly monumental ascent up **Djebel Sarhro,** the steepest of all the Anti-Atlas ranges, full of grandeur and desolation with its brown-gray, heat-hazed ridge of peaks.

The main pass through the Djebel, 1660m **Tizi n'Tinififft,** comes just 4km beyond Aït Saoun, but it is not for another 20km or so that you emerge from the mountains to catch a first glimpse of the valley and the oases—a thick line of palms reaching out into the haze, and the first sign of the Drâa kasbahs, rising as if from the land where the green gives way to desert.

Although Zagora is the ostensible goal of this trip along the Drâa, the valley is the real attraction. If you've got a car, try to resist the impulse to burn down to the desert, and take the opportunity to walk out to one or another of the *ksour* or kasbahs.

Agdz

You descend into the valley at **AGDZ** (68km from Ouarzazate), a stopping point for many of the buses and a minor administrative center for the region. It has a couple of unclassified hotels, and if you want a low-key introduction to the valley, you could do a lot worse than stay here for a first night; the hotel on the corner is good value.

THE DRÂA KSOUR

Ksour line the route more or less continously from Agdz to Zagora; most of the larger and older ones are grouped a little ways from the road, up above the terraces of date palms. Few that are still in use can be more than a hundred years old, though you frequently see the ruins and walls or earlier *ksour* abandoned just a short ways from their modern counterparts.

Most are populated by **Berbers**, but there are also Arab villages here, and even a few scattered communities of **Jews**, still living in their *Mellahs*. All of the southern valleys, too, have groups of **Haratin**, black people descended from the Sudanese slaves brought into Morocco along these caravan routes. Inevitably, these populations have mixed to some extent—and the Jews here are almost certainly converted Berbers—though it is interesting to see just how distinct many of the *ksour* still appear, both in their architecture and customs. There is, for example, a great difference from one village to the next as regards women's costumes, above all in the wearing and extent of veils.

Visiting the ksour, bear in mind that all of the Drâa *ksour* and kasbahs tend to be farther from the road than they look: it's possible to walk for several hours without reaching the edge of the oasis and the upper terraced levels.

From Agdz, there is access to a beautiful **palmery**, a short walk from where the bus stops, and if the river is low enough, you can get across (take care to avoid the bilharzia-laden water) to view a few kasbahs on the far side. If you're interested in the valley's rugs and carpets this is also about the best place to see them: **carpet stores** line the road, and in the few minutes before the bus leaves, prices can drop surprisingly.

Tamnougalt, Timiderte, and Tinzouline

The *ksour* at **TAMNOUGALT**—off to the left of the road, about 4km past Agdz—are perhaps the most dramatic and extravagant of any in the Drâa. A wild cluster of buildings, each is fabulously decorated with pockmarked walls and tapering towers. The village was once the capital of the region, and its assembly of families (the *djemaa*) administered what was virtually an independent republic.It is populated by a Berber tribe, the Mezguita. A farther 8km south is the more palace-like Glaoui kasbah of **TIMIDERTE**, built by the eldest son of the one time Pasha of Marrakesh, T'hami El Glaoui (see "Telouet").

Another striking group of *ksour,* dominated by a beautiful and imposing caidal kasbah, is at **TINZOULINE**, 57km farther on (30km north of Zagora). There is a large and very worthwhile Monday *souk* held here and, if you're traveling by bus, the village is one of the more realistic places to break the journey for a while.

Zagora and Beyond

ZAGORA at first sight seems like a rerun of Ouarzazate: the same grouping of modern administrative buildings and hotels, the same single street and highway. Two things, however, set it apart. The first is its location: this is the most productive stretch of the Drâa (indeed, of all the southern valleys) and you only have to walk a mile or so out of town to find yourself amid the palms and oasis cultivation. The second is its distinct air of unreality. Directly behind the town rises a bizarre Hollywood-sunset mountain, at the end of the main street is a mock-serious roadsign to Timbuktu ("*52 jours*"—by camel), and in summer the heat and dryness of the air is totally staggering.

Accommodation

Though it can seem a bit hustley on arrival, Zagora is a pretty easy place to get oriented—and it has some good accommodation to set you up for a couple of day's visit and daytrips. (See also the box on Tinfou).

Along the main drag, Av. Mohammed V, are four **hotels**:

Hôtel Café-Restaurant des Amis, on the left in the middle of town. The cheapest in Zagora; in summer it rents (slightly cooler) space on its *terrasse*.

Café-Hôtel Vallée du Drâa, next door to the above. Very welcoming and clean, and serving meals. Formerly 1*A, now unclassified.

Hôtel de la Palmeraie (☎8), at the far (south) end of the street. Opinions differ on the Palmeraie, which, admittedly, looks a bit dilapidated on first acquaintance. But once resident, it's an enjoyable place, with a Berber tent out the back serving generous meals—and a lively bar. The *Palmeraie* also runs tours into the desert "on the backs of camels, with nights under the stars or in tents, eating bread cooked by nomads on the sand" for a half day, a day, or a week. As yet untried by the editor . . .

Hôtel La Tinsouline (☎22), at the near end of Av. Mohammed V. Zagora's "grand hotel," this has recently dropped a star to 3*A—making it a pretty tempting option. Its **swimming pool** is open to nonresidents for 30dh a day.

An attractive alternative to the hot, Mohammed V places, are the camp-grounds and hotel in the **oasis at Amazrou**—which in many ways is where you want to be in Zagora. To reach these, follow the signposts from town to the hotel, *La Fibule*, which is located just by the river, 2km from the center of Zagora. Off to the left (a further 1km) is Camping Montagne; to the right (600m), Camping d'Amazrou.

Hôtel-Restaurant La Fibule du Drâa. A choice of rooms (spacious) or tented accommoda-tion, set amid a beautiful garden. The Moroccan **restaurant**, reasonably priced for set meals, is worth a trip out in itself. The hotel, like the *Palmeraie*, offers camel rides.

Camping d'Amazrou. Lowish prices and a good, grassy area for tents.

Camping Montagne. A beautiful site in the shadow of the sugarloaf Djebel Zagora moun-tain. Running water, cold drinks (sometimes food), a swimming pool (quite often filled), and very friendly people in charge. Camel rides are also offered here—expensive, at around 180dh a person per day, but genuinely worthwhile.

The best **place to eat** in Zagora is, as hinted above, *La Fibule*—under 50dh for a memorable meal. The restaurant at *La Tinsouline* is good, too, though more expensive. Cheapest food is at the hotels *Palmeraie* and *des Amis* hotels, both of which are reasonable. For a drink, try the *Palmeraie* bar; the one at the *Tinsouline* is very overpriced.

Amazrou

The closest village in the Zagora palmery, **Amazrou** is a wonderful place to spend the afternoon, wandering amid the shade of its gardens and *ksour*. It is, inevitably, wise to the ways of tourism (the children try to drag you in for some mint tea), but the oasis life and cultivation are still pretty unaffected.

The **Auberge** at **TINFOU**, 27km south of Zagora (7km beyond Tamegroute), is one of the most enjoyable small hotels in Morocco. It is run by a family of artists, who produce some intriguing naïve paintings and sculpture. The *auberge* itself is an ancient kasbah building, with a medieval room key system, art for sale on every inch of the wall, and a wonderfully ramshackle pool. At nights, you can move your mattress into the courtyard, for the cool and the stars.

In addition, if further encouragement is needed, a **camel** driver is among the many permanent residents. He is a bit crazy, but don't be put off: a camel trip out with him to the sand dunes is a lot of fun.

Getting to Tinfou, without your own vehicle, it's possible to charter a *grand taxi*, though even with haggling it'll be expensive—try to get together a group.

The **dates** here are some of the finest in Morocco and if you meet up with a guide, he'll probably explain a few of the infinite varieties: the sweet *boufeggou,* which will last for up to four years if stored properly; the small, black *bousthami*; and the light, olive-colored *bouzekri*.

The local sight, which any of the kids will lead you toward, is the old Jewish Kasbah, **La Kasbah des Juifs**.

Djebel Zagora

If you have the energy or can find a means of transportation, the other sight in Zagora, and the real focus of the oasis, is the mountain, **Djebel Zagora**. There is a narrow, somewhat hair-raising trail up to the summit. It begins about 2.5km from the Tamegroute road; take the same turning as for *Camping La Montagne*—left just after crossing the river.

Up on the mountain top, if you can make it in the early morning or the last few hours before sunset, the views are nearly startling—you look out across the palmery to further *ksour* and even a stretch of sand dunes to the south. On the spur itself there are ruins of two enclosures built by the Almoravids in the eleventh century as a fortress outpost against the powerful rulers of Tafilalt.

M'hamid and Tamegroute

The Zagora oasis reaches some 30km south of the town, when the Drâa disappears for a while, to resurface in a final fertile belt before the desert— **M'hamid el Ghouzlane** (Plain of the Gazelles). You can follow this route all the way down—the road is paved as far as M'hamid (90km from Zagora)— and with a car, it's an enticing option. It is no longer necessary to get authorization or to take a guide, as it was in the past, since the region no longer has any military significance, with Polisario contained way to the south.

If you don't have a car, there are buses to both M'hamid and Tamegroute, though times (evening departure to Tamegroute) are a bit inconvenient. It's worth asking around at the campgrounds and hotels to get a ride; negotiating for a *grand taxi* tends to work out expensive unless you can find a group to share costs—and perhaps more trouble than it's worth. If you try, it's more economic to limit your sights to **Tamegroute** and its *zaouia*, and the **sand dunes** en route.

Note that there are no gas stations in M'hamid or Tamegroute, or on the routes, so fill your tank in Zagora before setting out.

M'hamid

The route down to **M'HAMID** is the main attraction. The village itself is just a small administrative center, with a not very memorable **Monday Souk** (no sign of any Blue Men, as the tourist literature suggests). There are sand dunes about 4km away from the village—not an easy route to follow, so it's best to take a guide from the village. If you want to **stay**, the *Hôtel Sahara* is functional, and its proprietor, Abderahman Naamani, claims to organize camel rides.

Tamegroute and Tinfou

Tamegroute is reached by a straightforward road down the **left bank of the Drâa**. Leave Zagora by the left fork and continue straight past the turnoff to the *djebel;* Tamegroute lies about 3km away from the edge of the oasis belt. The **dunes of Tinfou** (see box for accommodation possibilities) rise to the left of the Tamegroute road, about 13km out of Zagora. The best formations in the region, they should be enough to satisfy most people's movie fantasies.

TAMEGROUTE, 16km from Zagora, is an interesting and unusual village. It is essentially a group of *ksour* and kasbahs, wedged tightly together and divided by low, covered passageways. But at its heart is a very ancient and once highly prestigious **zaouia**. This, the base of the Naciri Brotherhood, exercised great influence over the Drâaoui tribes from the seventeenth century up until the last few decades. Its sheikhs, (or holy leaders) were known as the "peacemakers of the desert," and it was they who settled disputes among the *ksour* and among the caravan traders converging on Zagora from the Sudan. They were missionaries, too, and even as late as the seventeenth and eighteenth centuries they sent envoys to preach and convert the wilder tribes of the Rif, Middle Atlas, and Anti-Atlas.

When you arrive in the village, you'll be "adopted" by a guide and taken off to see the **zaouia's outer sanctuary**, even today a refuge for the sick and the insane, and its **library**—once the richest in Morocco and still preserving a number of very early editions of the Koran printed on gazelle hide. The village also has a small *souk* of **potters' workshops**.

On from Zagora: The Pistes

Almost all travelers return from Zagora back to Ouarzazate, the only route possible by bus and in some ways the most interesting—this allows you to continue along the Dades and reach Tinerhir and the Todra gorge. For the desert-minded, however, there are adventurous *piste* road alternatives **east to Rissani** or **west to Foum Zguid** (and beyond to Tata).

The Rissani route is possible by landrover taxi, and the Foum Zguid route by truck, if you coincide with the markets. With your own transportation, you'll need a fair amount of confidence in desert driving and orientation skills over the uncertain and rough tracks.

Zagora to Rissani

The long route east from Zagora to Rissani, in the Tafilalt, is covered by **landrover** each Wednesday. Departure is normally at some point between noon and 2pm, from Zagora's regular produce market.. Ask your hotel to try and reserve a seat for you (around 120dh). It's a rough ride (take along food and water), but you should be left off outside the Rissani hotel (see the Tafilalt section) in around ten hours. Rissani's market takes place on Thursdays, and the landrover then makes the return trip.

The route is taken by some cars as well as trucks, though unless you have a really good sense of direction (and comprehensive spares and supplies), it might be wiser to drive back along the Drâa to TANSIKHT for the first part of the trip to TAZZARINE: the unpaved road marked on the *Kummerley & Frey* map as being direct from Zagora to Tazzarine has partially disappeared and you have to negotiate a tricky (and difficult to follow) track around by Aït MENAD and AJMOU N'AÏT ALI OU HASSO. If in doubt, follow the telegraph poles. If you start at first light, it's possible to complete the journey in a (long) day.

Along the way, **TAZZARINE**, which sees an occasional bus or *grand taxi* from Tansikht, has a fairly large **café-hotel** that serves cold drinks. Travelers driving their own vehicles (and the occasional "expedition tour" group, in 4-wheel drive trucks) tend to stop for a night either here or in **ALNIF** (67km farther), a very small oasis with a café, where you can **camp** and get fresh water. Rissani is 100km beyond Alnif, along a fair track over flattish valleys framed by the mountains of the Djebel Ougnat.

West to Foum Zguid

West from Zagora the maps indicate a road direct to FOUM ZGUID: a route which extends beyond to TATA and from there on toward Tiznit or Taroudannt. It has recently become possible for tourists to take this route, and most hire cars should be able to withstand the road surface.

On market days (Sunday/Wednesday), a **truck** leaves the marketplace in Zagora, again around noon to 2pm, arriving in Foum Zguid toward nightfall. Like the Rissani run, it's a bumpy, crowded ride and you should take along food and drink; it costs about 40dh. In FOUM ZGUID, you can pick up transportation the following day to TATA (see *Chapter Seven*).

Agdz to the Taliouine Road

Finally, and again to the west, there is a *piste* from **AGDZ** to **TAZENAKHT**, on the road to TALIOUINE. This dirt road is fairly practicable for cars but at times very difficult to follow—at least until you reach the paved section from the cobalt mines in ARHBAR. It *might* be possible to approach Foum Zguid from this direction—but, again, ask first.

THE DADES AND TODRA

The **Dades**, rambling east from Ouarzazate, is the harshest and most desolate of the southern valleys. Along much of its length, the river is barely visible aboveground, and the road and plain are hemmed in between the parallel ranges of the High Atlas and Anti-Atlas, broken, black-red volcanic rock and dismal limestone peaks. This makes the oases, when they appear, all the more astonishing, and there are two here—**Skoura** and **Tinerhir**—that are among the richest and most beautiful in the country. Each lies along the main bus route from Ouarzazate to Er Rachidia, offering an easy and excellent opportunity for a close look at a working oasis and, in Skoura, a startling range of kasbahs.

Impressive though they are, however, it is the two **gorges** that cut out from the valley **into the High Atlas** that realy steal the points. The **Dades** itself forms the first gorge, carving up a final fertile strip of land behind Boumalne. The second—a classic, narrowing gorge of high walls of rock—is the **Todra**, which you can follow by car or transit truck from Tinerhir right into the heart of the Atlas. If you're happy with the isolation and uncertainties of the **pistes beyond**, it is possible, too, to continue across the mountains—emerging finally near Beni Mellal on the road from Marrakesh to Fes. This needs a good four of five days, if you're relying on local Berber trucks, and a certain craziness or wanderlust, but it's as exciting and rewarding a trip as you can make this side of the Sahara.

Skoura

The **Skoura Oasis** begins quite suddenly, a little over 30km out from Ouarzazate. It is an extraordinary sight even from the road, which for the most part follows along its edge—a very extensive, very dense palmery, with an incredibly confusing network of tracks winding across fords and through the trees to scattered groups of *ksour* and kasbahs.

Arriving by bus in **SKOURA** village—just a market square and a small cluster of administrative buildings—you'll probably want to accept a guide to explore some of the kasbahs, and possibly visit one or two that are still inhabited. If you plan to stay, there is now a basic **hotel**, which enjoys a monopoly (bargain for rates) and has intermittent running water. Food is available at a couple of café-restaurants dotted about the oasis.

Kasbah Amerhidl

If you have a car, the best point to stop and explore is some 4km before you arrive at Skoura village proper (38km from Ouarzazate). Here, after 600m, on the left of the road, is the kasbah of **Amerhidl**, the grandest and most extravagantly decorated in the oasis. As soon as you stop, you'll be surrounded by any number of boys, and you really have no option but to pay one to watch your car and another to be your guide.

Other Kasbahs

Among the finest kasbahs elsewhere in Skoura are those of **Dan Aït Sidi el Mati, Dar Aït Haddou,** and two former Glaoui residences, **Dar Toundout** and **Dar Lahsoune.**

Most of these are, at least in part, nineteenth-century, though the majority of the Skoura and Dades kasbahs are much more modern. Dozens of the older fortifications were destroyed in a severe tribal war in 1893, and many that survived were pulled down in the French "pacification" of the 1930s.

The kasbah walls in the Dades—higher and flatter than in the Drâa—often seem unscalable, but in the course of a siege or war, there were always other methods of conquest. A favorite means of attack in the 1890s, according to Walter Harris, who journeyed through the region in disguise, was to divert the water channels of the oasis around a kasbah and simply wait for its foundations to dissolve.

El Kelâa des Mgouna and Boumalne

Traveling through the Dades in spring, you'll find Skoura's fields delineated by the bloom of thousands of pink Persian roses—cultivated as hedgerows dividing the plots. At **EL KELÂA DES MGOUNA,** 50km east across another shaft of semidesert plateau, there are still more, along with an immense kasbah-like **rose water factory,** *Capp et Floral,* where the *attar* is distilled. Here, in late May (or sometimes early June), a **rose festival** is held to celebrate the new year's crops: a good time to be here by all accounts, with villagers coming down from the mountains for the market, music, and dancing. The factory can be visited, too, for a look at (and an overpowering smell of) the distillation process.

The rest of the year, El Kelaa's single, rambling street is less impressive. There's a **Wednesday souk,** worth a break in the bus ride, but little else of interest beyond the site—above and back from the river—or the locked and deserted ruins of a **Glaoui Kasbah,** on a spur above it. The only **hotel** of any kind is the luxury 4*A *Les Roses du Dades* (☎18), next door to the kasbah: if you have a car and the money for a drink, it should be possible to stop here and use their pool.

Boumalne

It would perhaps be a better idea to head straight for Boumalne and the Dades gorge or, if you're strapped for time, Tinerhir.

BOUMALNE, once again, is nothing much in itself: a garrison town with an elongated market square, a "Grand Hôtel du Sud" (the 4*B *El Madayeq,* with a pool and a bar; ☎31), a new **auberge** (by the hotel), and a garage that fixes flats. The *Café Atlas,* above the taxi stand, does excellent *tajine blehem* (without meat).

In addition to the town's regular **grands taxis** (arranged through a blue-coated *gardien*), there are unofficial Peugeot taxis and also transit vans and Berber trucks leaving intermittently from the market square. You can sometimes negotiate one of these (or maybe a landrover taxi) **up the Dades gorge**, to which the approach road veers off to the left a couple of kilometers before you reach the town. The trip as far as MSEMRIR (60km; 2 hr.) is a fairly standard, local transportation route and you should be able to get a place for around 20dh.

The Dades Gorge

The **Dades Gorge**—high cliffs of limestone and weirdly shaped erosions—begins almost as soon as you leave the main road north of Boumalne. Most travelers cover the first 25km or so by car, then turn back. If you're equipped for an expedition route, however, you can continue up into (and across) the Atlas, or loop over to the Todra gorge. Alternatively, a couple of days walking from Boumalen will take you over the most interesting section of the gorge, with plenty of mud architecture (and fine landscapes) to keep your interest, and a number of rooms, or infinite camping sites, along the way.

For **the first 15–20km**, the gorge is pretty wide and the valley carved out of it is green and well populated. There are *ksour* and kasbahs clustered all along this stretch, many of them flanked now by more modern looking houses, but retaining the decorative imagination of the traditional architecture.

Just 2km from Boumalne, you pass an old **Glaoui Kasbah**—strategically sited as always to control all passage. Three kilometers farther down, where the road turns more and more into a hairpin corniche, there is another dramatic group, the **ksour** of AÏT ARBI, built against a fabulous volcanic twist of the rocks. These, like all the kasbahs of the Dades and the Todra, seem like natural extensions of their setting: tinged with the color of the earth and fabulously varied, ranging from bleak lime-white to dark reds and greenish blacks.

The rocks in the valley around **TAMNALT**, just beyond Aït Arbi (15km down the road), are known by the locals as the "Hills of Human Bodies," after their strange formations (in fact they look more like feet). The village itself is a good place to stop, though you'll need to haggle to get a reasonable price from the *Hôtel-Restaurant* **Kasbah**, whose management lays on "Berber Weddings" for tour groups. Cheaper, 2km south (towards Boulemane), is a friendly, unnamed **Café-Hôtel**, with double rooms at around 20dh.

The **bridge over the Dades**, where the road turns into a very poor and difficult track, is about a 45-minute (24km) drive from Boumalne at AÏT OUDINAR. There is a **café** here where you can eat, rent a **room**, and, if you're driving, ask about the state of the road beyond—with a hire car, you may decide to go no further. Within walking distance of the café is one of the most spectacular sections of the gorge.

About 6km north of the bridge, there are several café-restaurants, offering **rooms**, at one of the most spectacular sections of the gorge—a very narrow section, full of hairpin bends. At AÏT HAMMOU, 5km farther on, there is also the basic (no electricity, outside toilet) *Café-Hôtel Taghea*, with numerous **rooms** and a terrace.

Msemrir and Over the Atlas

The roads get worse beyond Aït Hammou, and in spring are likely to be impassable due to flooding. At other times of year, however, you can drive to MSEMRIR, and from there over the Atlas to Imilchil and Arhbala (see Middle Atlas), or across to TAMTATOUCHTE or AÏT HANI (see map over-page), where you can loop around to Tinerhir through the Todra.

It must be stressed, though, that these are really routes for trucks or land-rovers. A Renault 4 *can* make it around to Todra between mid-June and late September, but it is a bit of a struggle. In either case, you'll need to be a confident driver (hairpin curves are routine) and an even more confident mechanic: rented cars are uninsured for trips like this and anyway they're usually not in very good condition.

If you're really intent on **crossing between the Dades and Todra gorges**, you'll find it considerably easier to go in the other direction; this way, it's a long, uphill trek, and the approximately one hundred kilometers of *piste* can easily take a full day. The approach to AGOUDAZ and IMILCHIL, too, is better from the Todra side.

There is a café with basic rooms in **MSEMRIR**. See the "Todra Gorge" for details beyond.

Tinerhir (Tineghir)

While **TINERHIR** again is preeminently a base—this time for the trip up into the **Todra Gorge**—it is also a much more interesting town than the other administrative centers along this route. Only a couple of kilometers east of the modern section is the beginning of the oasis, really a world apart, with its groups of tribal *ksour* built at intervals into the rocky hills above. When passing through, don't be in too much of a hurry to catch the first truck out to Todra or the next bus: this spot by itself offers rewarding exploration for the day, and, what's more, it's completely ignored by most tourists.

Practicalities

Arriving, things are again pretty straightforward. The **buses** stop at the arcaded Place Principal, and here you will also find all the other **facilities**—hotels, a couple of cafés, a post office, a bank, and a **car rental agency**.

The best value of the cheap **hotels** is the unrated *Oasis*, a good place to eat as well, and with cooler rooms than the *Salam*, over on the far side of the square. The other option, the *Hôtel Todra* (☎09), is officially 1*A, though apart from its spectacularly kitsch decor, it doesn't seem a lot different. Once more, the only **swimming pool** belongs to the big luxury hotel, the 3*A *Hôtel Sargho* (☎01; left of the main road as you come in from Skoura/ Ouarzazate); the pool is open to non-residents for 20dh a day. Beware that there is no **campground** in (or near) the town. The "Camping" signposted near the center is in fact 8km up the Todra gorge.

If you're interested in buying rugs or carpets, Tinerhir has a new branch of the *Maison Berbère* (run by the same family as the stores in Zagora and Rissani), good for picking up quality **rugs and carpets**.

Buses and **grands taxis** make standard runs west to Boumalne (change for Ouarzazate if you're going by taxi) and east to Er Rachidia.

Around the Town and Oasis

Dominating the town and with a tremendous view over the Todra, is yet another **Glaoui Kasbah**—one of the grandest and most ornamental after Telouet and Ouarzazate, though now substantially in ruins.

To reach **the oasis,** walk out—or hitch a ride—along one of the tracks behind the town. When you arrive, it is possible to rent a mule (and a guide) in the main village, the former Jewish quarter, now essentially Berber, but still known as the **Mellah.** The finest of the kasbahs is that of **Aït Amitane,** with its extraordinarily complex patterns incised on the walls. This is just one of many *ksour* and kasbahs here, however, and it's a very satisfying experience to just wander around.

The oasis follows the usual pattern in these valleys: date palms at the edge, terraces of olive, pomegranate, almond, and fruit trees farther in, with grain and vegetable crops planted beneath them. The *ksour* each originally controlled one section of the oasis, and there were frequent disputes over territory and, above all, over access to the mountain streams for each *ksour's* network of water channels. Even in this century, the fortifications were built for real, and, as Walter Harris wrote (melodramatically, but probably with little exaggeration): "The whole life was one of warfare and gloom. Every tribe had its enemies, every family had its blood feuds, and every man his would-be murderer."

The Todra Gorge and a Route over the Atlas

Whatever else you do in the south, at least spend a night at the **Todra Gorge.** You don't need your own transportation, nor any great expeditionary zeal, to get up there, and yet it seems totally remote from the routes through the main valleys—very still, very quiet, and magnificent in the fading evening light. The highest, narrowest, and most spectacular part is only 15km from Tinerhir, and there are three small hotels at its mouth where you can get a room or sleep up on the roof. Beyond it, the road turns into a *piste* and you're into true isolation: this is a route you can take all the way over the Atlas, if you can time your visit to fit in with schedules of the Berber trucks, or, if driving yourself, you have considerable confidence and a very reliable and sturdy car.

From Tinerhir, the mouth of the gorge (where the *Hôtel el Mansour* is located) can be reached either by Peugeot **grand taxi** or (considerably cheaper) by **Berber truck:** both leave regularly throughout the day from Place Principal.

Into the Gorge

En route to the gorge proper, the road climbs along a last, fertile shaft of land—narrowing at points to a ribbonlike line of palms between the cliffs. There are villages more or less continuously along this part, all of them the

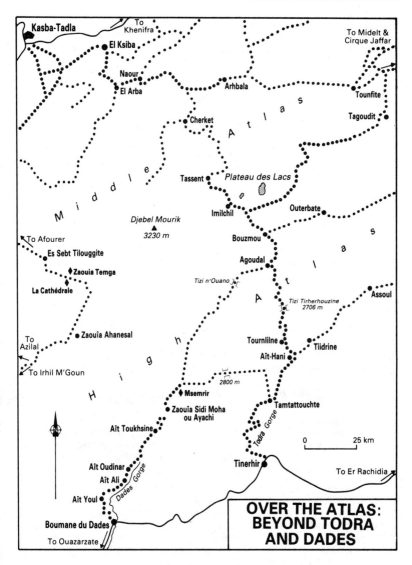

**OVER THE ATLAS:
BEYOND TODRA
AND DADES**

pink-gray color of the local rock, and there are the ruins of kasbahs and *ksour* up above or on the other side.

To the right of the road, 9km from Tinerhir (and *past* the first signposted campground), there is a freshwater pool, somewhat fancifully named "**The Source of the Sacred Fish**" and flanking a particularly luxuriant palmery. It is a beautiful spot, with a small **café-hotel** opposite it and a couple of **campgrounds** in the clearing. Anywhere else, this would be worth a major recommendation—here, though, it seems almost churlish not to continue to the beginning of the gorge. If the heat is not too much for you, there's a lot to be said for getting the truck to let you off here and walking the final 6km.

The really enclosed section of **the gorge**, where the cliff walls rise sheer to 3000m on either side, runs for only a few hundred meters—its mouth a short walk from the group of hotels at the end of the surfaced road. The main attraction of this site is lost unless you stay the night: the evening skies here are really incredible, and, if you're remotely interested in bird watching, this is one of the best locations in the south. Possible sightings include Pale Crag Martins, Rock Doves, and Grey Wagtails, and, higher up the gorge, Tristram's Warblers, Bonelli's Eagles, and Lanners.

The first **hotel** you see at the mouth of the "real" gorge, the *El Mansour*, is generally the cheapest: a very easygoing place, with a pair of palm trees growing out through the roof, reasonable food, and a choice of sleeping on the roof (easily the best option) or on couches downstairs. If you feel like having your own room, walk a couple of hundred meters around the corner to either the *Hôtel des Roches* or the the *Yasmina*: they're slightly more expensive and fancier, with restaurants catering for the half-dozen tour groups shuttled up each day. The *Yasmina* has the best food; the *Roches*, like the *El Mansour*, allows you to sleep out on the terrace.

Over the Atlas

If you want to continue beyond the gorge to TAMTATOUCHTE, and from there **across the High Atlas** to IMILCHIL and ARHBALA, it is possible to do so by catching a succession of **Berber trucks**. Hire **cars** will have problems, though French travelers seem to make it through in their Renaults and

---

BOUZMOU AND BEYOND

Dan Richardson and Jill Denton set out from the *Hôtel El Mansour* with a Belgian traveler they met there; he had a useful spattering of Arabic phrases, they themselves had reasonable French. Both these factors, they felt, made some difference in the way they were received. They traveled the route in midsummer.

As we clambered into the back of the truck the hotel owner tried to dissuade us. "You don't want to go there . . . This truck's only going to Aït Hani, a horrible place . . . ," But after fourteen hours waiting on the porch for a lift we weren't going to be deterred. Whatever was up there in the dry wastes of the High Atlas—the maps were enticingly vague—we meant to find out. The truck bumped and strained along the unpaved track, swathed in choking dust, and climbed steadily up out of the Gorge of Todra. As the sun fell, the stars gradually emerged until the bowl of the sky sparkled with dozens of constellations and shooting stars.

After four hours, we reached a vast plateau and the gates of **Aït Hani**, incongruously manned by an armed soldier. Inside the village—a jumbled blur of mud huts and towers—there was a lengthy discussion on what to do with the *Nazarenes* (Christians). Finally, a man offered us his stable, outside the village. Despite our misgivings, he did us proud, bringing rugs for the floor and reappearing the next morning with mint tea, bread, and his wife, who was entranced by our foreign appearance. We found *her* looks fascinating, too—a tatooed chin, luminous eyes, and a bizarre dress resembling a huge tinfoil doily shot with pale blue threads.

Citröens. It is possible, too, to cover the route by **bike**—mountain models a distinct advantage.

The arrival of ongoing **trucks**, or *camions*, as they're known, is inevitably hard to predict, though the people at the hotels usually have some idea of when the next ones will be going as far as AÏT HANI. The most promising days to set out are generally Wednesday (for Aït Hani's souk) or Friday (for Imilchil's Saturday souk). But it is all a bit pot luck, and you should certainly be prepared for the odd day's wait in a village for a ride, or, better, to walk one or other of the stages of the route. Eventually, however, everyone seems to get across to ARHBALA or NAOUR, where there is an asphalt road again and regular buses down to EL KSIBA and KASBA TADLA or KHENIFRA.

There is, of course, no **bank** between Tinerhir and Khenifra/Kasba Tadla. Don't underestimate the expense of buying **food** in the mountains (30–100 percent above normal rates), nor the prices charged for rides in the **Berber trucks**; as a very general guideline, reckon on about 15dh for every 50km.

The Route

A personal account of the route, getting rides from the trucks, is printed below. Everyone's experience (and exact route) is bound to differ a fair amount, but the pattern of travel should be pretty similar.

The first place to head for is **TAMTATOUCHTE** (17km from the *Hôtel El Mansour*), quite a sizable village, with several basic **hotels** and café-restaurants. If you're driving, this section of the route is the worst part; here the track is little more than the stones of the river path. Beyond that point, the road improves considerably, though it is still unsurfaced and slow, difficult mountain driving—and practicable for cars only from June until September. (It's at Tamtatouchte that anyone intent on crossing over to the

It was only in the daylight that we understood the previous day's warnings. The mountain, plateau, and buildings were uniformly barren and colorless, except for a few tiny plots of withered vegetables. People peered at us from courtyards and from behind grilled windows, ignoring our tentative greetings, and our host of the night before led us to a low, mud building bearing (in English) the name of "The Modern Coffee House." This title, we later learned, had been bestowed by a lone Englishman who had been marooned for four days in the village. We guess we were luckier—we only had to wait for two.

Once the sun was up, swarms of flies would lift off from piles of dung and come to crawl all over us. There was virtually nothing to see—the heat kept everyone indoors—and little to do but drink mint tea and gaze glumly at the decor of the coffee house; sooty mud walls, pastel colors, and a collage of sardine cans, postcards, and Koranic inscriptions. The proprietor was a diminutive, dessicated ancient who vastly enjoyed our plight and told us that the next truck out wasn't due "for some time, if Allah wills it," and in the meantime, wouldn't we like some food, which he could procure with great difficulty? Naturally, the price was astronomical, while the eggs smelt sulfurous and their yolks were flecked with blood. We couldn't really blame him, though, for in a village where there had been no rain for four *years*, where agriculture had almost collapsed, and most of the young men had fled, we represented a veritable goldmine.

When we eventually left, it was in a subdued state—obvious enough to the truck driver, too, for he demanded an enormous price (40dh each to Imilchil) which, stupidly, we paid. A cardinal rule of this kind of travel is to pay only on arrival at your destination, as the Berbers do themselves, and it

/continues overpage

Dades gorge should turn off to the west, toward MSEMRIR; rides are most unlikely, so it's basically an option for drivers).

Continuing north, into the High Atlas, you need to head towards **AÏT HANI**, another large village, almost the size of Tamtatouchte. It's just off the main route, and if you're driving you can keep going, turning after the town, rather than into it. On the outskirts as you approach from the south, there is a military post, café, and store; there's no regular accommodation (but see the boxed account). This region is generally high and barren landscape—the locals travel amazing distances each day to collect wood for fuel.

After Aït Hani there is a stiff climb up to 2,700m at **Tizi Tirherhouzine**, then down to **AGOUDAL**. This is a friendly village, and though there is no official hotel, you'll probably be offered a room. It is in a less harsh setting, too, better irrigated, and people seem more relaxed than at Aït Hani.

IMILCHIL is only 45km further on from Agoudal, on a fast road through a very fertile and highly populated region. A beautiful village, with a fine caidal kasbah, this is for most people the highlight of the route. It is famed in guides about Morocco for its **September moussem**—the so-called *Marriage Market of Aït Haddidou*. The *moussem*, once a genuine tribal function, is now considerably corrupted by tourism (landrover parties are shuttled up from Marrakesh for the day), but it's a lively, extravagant occasion all the same. Imilchil has a couple of small **hotels**, or you can camp out on the nearby **Plateau des Lacs**—beside one of the twin mountain lakes, **Isli** and **Tislit**.

---

was all too predictable when, five hours later, the driver pulled into a village some 50km short of our destination and announced he was going no further. Our protests were useless—the man shrugged, pretended to speak no French, and smirked at the other passengers. Then, inspired, the Belgian we were traveling with quoted a Koranic phrase equivalent to "by their deeds shall ye know them,"* adding, for good measure, that the driver's behavior was "not beautiful" (*hyrba*) in the sight of Allah. The effect was miraculous. The driver shriveled with humiliation, and returned half the money to us. In a more cheerful mood, we surveyed the village of Bouzmou, found an excellent teahouse on the roadside, and a cheerful lad to show us around.

Bouzmou was delightful: domed, honey-colored houses, lofty trees, a gushing spring, and a soccer match with fifty participants stirring up the dust in the *place*. Enchanting little girls with hennaed hair and huge earrings, torn between fear and the desire to touch us, scurried back and forth, clinging to each other and shrieking with laughter. The women were straightforward and curious to talk to us, a rarity in Morocco—even in the more "open" communities of Berber villages. Jill was swiftly "adopted," lent a shawl, and her eyebrows and cheeks hennaed. It was proposed that the women tattoo her as well, though the needle was like a cobbler's awl and caked with grime. Later, we were all directed to a small square where a rain dance was just beginning. Villagers formed circles around the dancers, beating tom-toms and uttering shrill cries. Once we were discovered, they demanded that we join in. Despite the clouds of dust, the noise, and the heat, we gave a good ten-minute performance, hoping foolishly that the rain would fall and make us village heroes (it didn't).

Next morning—a Monday—nomads came in for the *souk* with their sheep herds roped neck to neck, to buy clothing, salt, and tinware. Among the curiosities on sale were white rocks, which if burned "would reveal in the fire the face of your secret enemy," and smooth, sweet-smelling stones to be used as an "aftershave."

---

* The phrase, which literally means, "you can tell by the traces on his forehead how a man prays," can be rendered phonetically as: *Si-ma-HOM-fi-hiJOO-hi-HEEM.*

The next stage is a long slog to Arhbala, through spectacular scenery; with steep drops off the road side, constant climbs and descents, and a slow move into forestation. This section has few settlements—nowhere the size of Imilchil—and locals are curious about travelers passing through. A paved road starts a few miles after **CHERKET**. At ARHBALA, there is a very basic hotel near the marketplace (Wednesday souk), and a daily bus on to El Ksiba (see the Middle Atlas).

Tinerhir to Er Rachidia and Erfoud

Going east from Tinerhir, you can get buses or *grands taxis* direct to Er Rachidia, via Goulmina. Alternatively, there is a daily bus leaving TINEJDAD (private company) along the minor 3451 road to Erfoud and Rissani; it leaves at 9:30am from the square used by the *grands taxis*, on the main road, arriving at Rissani about four hours later. To make the connection, it's best to get a grand taxi from Tinerhir to Tinejdad.

Er Rachidia via Goulmina

This is a straightforward and largely barren route, broken only by the oases of Tinejdad (see below) and Goulmina.

GOULMINA, a long straggling palmery, is made up of some twenty or so scattered *ksour,* whose towers, it is said, are unusual in their height and forti-

---

We had to leave Bouzmou that afternoon, for our money was low and all the trucks were departing, laden with sheep and people. Our own—and we counted—held some thirty sheep on the upper deck, an unknown number on the lower, and 28 Berbers balanced on the rails and luggage racks. In the scorching heat, at an average speed of 20km an hour, we spent the next six hours ascending tortuous roads, circumventing precipices, and seemed to *accelerate* as we approached blind corners. At every bend, the sheep bleated with fear and pissed and crapped over everyone's feet and luggage, while above them a Berber periodically unwrapped from the folds of his *djellabah* a hunk of fresh mutton, which he prodded appreciatively.

At some point in the journey, we passed through **Imilchil**, and skirted one of the azure, salt-rimmed lakes on the **Plateau des Lacs**. We saw black nomad tents pegged in the wilderness, the occasional camel, and dozens of donkeys laden down with firewood from the distant forests. At a crossroads, around 15km from Arhbala, we got down from the sheep truck and picked up another—this time comparatively luxurious with its freight of rough-cut stones.

Arhbala, a small town surrounded by soft mountains and oak and cedar forests, seemed almost metropolitan with its semi-paved streets, electric lighting, and double row of shops and cafés. There was no bus to Khenifra, where we hoped to change money, until 3am but, as is common in Morocco, we were "adopted" and taken home to be fed. The meal—couscous specially prepared in our honor—was delicious and our host and two older, male companions were hospitable. It left a sour taste, though, as the light bulb in the kitchen was brought out to give us extra light, leaving the man's wife and daughters (who had prepared the meal but not appeared) to crouch over the remains of the meal in the dark.

Around one o'clock, we left for the bus, crawled onto the seats and tried to sleep. Arguments—always so intense that you imagined they were about to escalate to killing—blew around us, but the journey was straightforward and, after the mountains, dull, routine, and enormously anticlimactic. At **Khenifra** we were back on the main road to Fes and could sample all that civilization had to offer: croissants, squat toilets, and banks.

fication. Without transportation, though, and without the time to work out the complex network of tracks, you'll see little of it. The modern, one-road town beside the highway is about as drab as any in Morocco—the only sign of life is in the sentry boxes next to the "triumphal" entrance and exit arches. (These arches, which you find all over the south, were introduced by the French—presumably as a kind of militaristic flourish; it's a tradition that's been carried on by the Moroccans since independence.)

Tinejdad to Erfoud

The alternative route—**direct to Erfoud**—is more interesting, and, in parts, eerily impressive. It is covered by just the one daily bus, but any kind of transportation along it is sparse: if you're driving, stock up on water, since any breakdown could let you in for a long wait (probably half a day).

The road branches off from the main route to Rachidia at **TINEJDAD** and follows much of the course of this oasis—an extremely lush strip populated by the Aït Atta tribe, traditional warriors of the south who used to control land and exact tribute as far afield as the Drâa.

Once you leave the oasis, at MELLAB, there is desert *hammada* more or less continuously until the beginning of the **Djorf Palmery** outside ERFOUD. Beside the road, over much of this distance, the land is pockmarked by strange, volcanic-looking humps—actually manmade repair points for the underground **irrigation channels** that brought water to the Tafilalt almost 100km from the Todra and Ferkla rivers. Another curiosity that you notice here, and elsewhere along the oasis routes, are the bizarre Berber **cemeteries** walled off from the desert at the edge of the *ksour*. These consist of long fields of pointed stones, thrust into the ground but otherwise unidentified—a wholly practical measure to prevent jackals from unearthing bodies (and in so doing, blocking their entrance to paradise).

Although paved all the way to Erfoud, sections of this **road** are sometimes covered over with sand: this is the result of small, spiraling sandstorms that can suddenly blow across the region and, for twenty or thirty seconds, block out all visibility. It's a simple road to drive, though, and shouldn't be any problem to follow.

ER RACHIDIA
AND THE TAFILALT

The great date palm growing regions of **the Tafilalt** come as near as anywhere in Morocco to fulfilling all the Western fantasies about the Sahara. They do so by occupying the last desert stretches of the Ziz River valley: a route shot through with lush and amazingly cinematic scenes, from its beginnings at the *Source Bleu* (springwater pool) and oasis meeting point of **Meski,** to an eventual climax amid the rolling sand dunes of **Merzouga**. Along the way, once again, are an impressive succession of *ksour,* and an extraordinarily rich palmery—traditionally the most important territory this side of the Atlas.

As a terminus of the strategic caravan routes across the desert, Tafilalt has a **history** of giving rise to religious dissent and separatist movements. It formed an independent kingdom in the eighth and ninth centuries, and was at the center of the *Kharijisite heresy* (a movement which used a Berber version of the Koran—orthodox Islam forbids any translation of God's direct Arabic revelation to Muhammad); later it was to become a stronghold of Shi'ite Muslims; and in the fifteenth century again emerged as a source of trouble, fostering the Marabout uprising that toppled the Saadian dynasty.

It is with the rise of Moualy er Rachid, however, and the establishment of the **Alaouite** (or, after their birthplace, *Filali*) dynasty that the region is most closely associated. Launched from a *zaouia* in Rissani, this is the dynasty which still holds power in Morocco, through Hassan II, the fourteenth sultan in the line. The Alaouites are also the secret of the wealth and influence behind many of the old kasbahs and *ksour;* from the time of Moualy Ismail, right through to this century, the sultans exiled princes and disenchanted relatives out here in the desert.

Er Rachidia

ER RACHIDIA, established by the French as a regional capital, represents more than anywhere else the new face of the Moroccan south: a shift away from the old desert markets and trading routes, and, alongside it, increasing militarization. During the protectorate, this militarization was directed against the tribal uncertainty of the region; since independence, the perceived threat has turned to the Polisario and to vague territorial claims from Algeria. Neither of these, however, have any direct bearing on the town—which is basically an administrative center and garrison for troops who might be needed elsewhere.

Unless you need to use the town's facilities—or await an early morning bus out—you're unlikely to want to stay. However, Er Rachidia has quite a relaxed, pleasant (and distinctly untouristed) feel, especially in the evenings, when the streets and cafés are packed out. The layout is pretty functional, with a sprawl of buildings lining the highway for some 3–4km before climaxing, inevitably, in a pretentious ceremonial arch. The one sight—worth the walk if you really have time to kill—is a large nineteenth-century **ksar**, visible from the bridge leading to Erfoud.

Practicalities

From the **bus station,** just about everything you might want to make use of is along the main street/highway (**Av. Mohammed V**) to your right. About 250m down is a **tourist office**, and opposite it the *Banque Populaire* (the only **bank** that operates substantially in the south). The **post office** is down a side street behind the bank—turn left just before you reach it. Note that Er Rachidia and Erfoud have the only banks in the Tafilalt—there's nowhere official to change money in either Meski or Rissani, and if you're going on to Figuig and Algeria you'll need to change travelers' checks here. Er Rachidia is useful, too, if you want **car repairs** or spare parts: the *Elf* garage on the main square carries a large supply of standard parts and will order others efficiently from Fes.

For **cheap hotels**, cut up to the left of Av. Mohammed V after you pass the municipal market and you'll find yourself—in the square with the garage—facing a choice between the *Hôtel Mahraba* and the preferable *Hôtel Renaissance* (19 Rue Mountay Youssef). Alternatives, a bit **more expensive**, are the 2*A *Hôtel Oasis* (Rue Abou Abdellah; ☎25.26) and the 2*B *Hôtel Meski* (Av. Moulay Ali Cherif; ☎20.65), both of which have pools and bars. There is a **campground**, 2km from the bus station, beside the road to Erfoud; this, too, has a pool, though not much in the way of security. **Eating** is cheapest at the food stalls around the bus station; otherwise, there are quite a number of restaurants along Av. Mohammed V.

Buses leave Er Rachidia at least four times a day for Erfoud/Rissani, and a similar number head north to Midelt and Fes or Meknes. If you miss out on these, it is usually no problem to get a seat in a **grand taxi** to Erfoud or, if you gather together a group of people, to Meski. All of these leave from opposite the bus station. Note that the only bus to **Figuig** leaves at 5am, passing the turnoff for Meski about 25 minutes later.

Meski: The Source Bleu

The small palm grove of **MESKI** centers on a natural springwater pool—the famous *source bleu*, long a postcard image of the south and a favorite camping site for travelers. It's set in the shadows of a ruined *ksar* beside a riverbank, surrounded by wheat and barley fields, and in the past was a picturesque and enjoyable stop.

Recently, however, the **campground**, seems to have gone into terminal decline—it's certainly not the relaxed, cosmopolitan place it used to be. The problem is partly one of overcrowding: Meski is firmly on the overland tour circuit, and in the summer Er Rachidia's (male) youth also arrive in force. But there are effects, too, from the drought that has struck over the last few years; showers no longer function and flies have become a major problem.

The oasis is somewhat insignificantly signposted, to the right of the Erfoud road, 17km south of Er Rachidia. Coming by bus, ask to get out by the turnoff: from here it's only 400m down to the pool and campground. **Going on** to Erfoud or back to Er Rachidia can be a slight problem, since most of the buses pass by full and don't stop. However, this is one of the easiest places around to hitch a ride and you should never be stranded for long.

South from Er Rachidia to Erfoud, Rissani, and Merzouga

Make sure you travel this last section of **the Ziz** in daylight. It's one of the most pleasing of all the southern routes: a dry, red belt of desert just beyond Meski, and then, suddenly, a drop into the valley and the great palmery and grain fields of central Tafilalt.

Away from the road, **ksour** are almost continuous—glimpsed through the trees and the high walls enclosing gardens and plots of farming land. If you want to stop and take a closer look, AOUFOUSS, midway to Erfoud and the site of a Thursday market, is perhaps the most accessible. MAADID, too, off to the left of the road as you approach Erfoud, is interesting—a really massive *ksour* and, like many in the Tafilalt (but few elsewhere in the south), with an entirely Arabic population.

Erfoud

ERFOUD is a modern administrative center, with a rather desultory, frontier-town atmosphere. Arriving from Er Rachidia, you get a first, powerful sense of closeness to the desert, with frequent sandblasts ripping through the streets. If you have the energy, climb up to **Borj Est**, the military hill-fort 3km across the river (leave by the back of the main square), and you can glimpse the sands to the south—if things are clear you can look back, too, right across the Tafilalt oasis to the beginnings of the Atlas.

Views apart, for most travelers Erfoud functions very much as a staging post for continuing on to Rissani and the sand dunes near Merzouga. It has a **bank** and a **post office** in the center of town by the intersection of the two main roads—Mohammed V and Moulay Ismail. Unless you have to wait until they open, there's no great reason to stay—four buses a day go on to Rissani, as well as innumerable *grands taxis* (about 5dh a seat).

If you need a bed, there are three cheap **hotels** around Mohammed V/ Moulay Ismail (walk down to the right as you come out of the bus station); again, there's nothing much to distinguish them, and nothing much to be said for any of them either. More upscale choices are between the 2*A *Hôtel Tafilalet* (Av. Moulay Ismail; ☎30), or the 4*A "Grand Hotel", *Hôtel Sijilmassa* (☎80); both have bars, and the latter has a pool.

The town's **campground**, a ten-minute, signposted walk, is fairly basic, but on the whole it's slightly more congenial than the cheap hotels: if you don't have a tent, you can rent a small, very inexpensive **cabin** for the night. Don't however, expect the swimming pool to be filled—water is heavily rationed in Erfoud.

Moving on from Erfoud

Continuing on from Erfoud, the most popular trip is to **the dunes at Merzouga, via Rissani** (see below). There are landrover tours from Erfoud along this route, or you can go by bus to Rissani and then on by truck or land-rover to Merzouga. Alternatively, if you have the money or enough people to share expenses, it's possible to rent a landrover yourself in Erfoud (for around 1000dh per day).

This—or using your own car—would enable you to take the 57km **direct route from Erfoud to Merzouga**, which, although unpaved, is reasonably easy to follow and takes a little over 45 minutes; en route (about 35km from Eroud) there is even a small café, with a gesture of a swimming pool.

The **route from Erfoud to Tinejdad** is covered in reverse order: see "Tinerhir to Erfoud."

Rissani

RISSANI stands at the last visible point of the Ziz River; beyond it, steadily encroaching on the village and its ancient *ksour* ruins, begins the desert. The former capital of Tafilalt, this was for eleven centuries the final stop on the great caravan routes south, and site of the first Arab kingdom of the south—the semilegendary Sijilmassa, founded in 707. Later, from the *zaouia* here (still an important national shrine), the Alaouite dynasty launched its bid for power, conquering first the oases of the south, then the vital Taza Gap, triumphing finally in Fes and Marrakesh.

The **modern village** musters scarcely enough houses to merit the name. Most of the people live in a single, large and decaying **ksar**, and, in addition to this, there is just a single administrative street with a couple of **cafés**, a **bank**, a (men's) **hammam**, and a **hotel**. If you plan to stay here rather than continue on to Merzouga, the best—and the cheapest—place to sleep is up on the hotel roof. The rooms themselves are invariably dirty, the water sulfurous. The cafés are not much better. A rare bright spot is the *Maison Berbère*, part of the chain of **rug and carpet** stores (see also Zagora and Tinerhir) and well worth an hour or two's browsing.

In fact, Rissani's only discernible life—the one time you might want to linger in the village—comes with the **market** held three times a week, though even then it's a pretty quiet place if compared to the old days when the caravans passed through. They still remained active into the 1890s, when the English journalist Walter Harris reported seeing thriving gold and slave auctions. Predictably enough, today's money making goods are all tourist oriented, with prices generally pretty high to boot. However, there's often a good selection of local Berber jewelry—including the crude, almost iconographic designs of the desert Touaregs—and some of the basic products (dried fruits, farming implements, and so on) are interestingly distinct from those of the richer north. Don't expect camels, though—apart from the caravans, these were never very common in Tafilalt, the Berbers preferring (as they still do) more economical donkeys.

Sijilmassa, the Zaouia, and Nearby Ksour

Rissani's older monuments are well into the process of erosion—both through crumbling material and the slow progress of the sands. **Sijilmassa**, whose ruins were clearly visible at the beginning of this century, has more or less vanished, though you can just about make out a few ruins along the course of the river west of the village. The various kasbahs and reminders of the Alaouite presence, too, are mostly in some stage of decay, but there is just enough remaining to warrant a battle with the morning heat.

The **ksar** that is still occupied by the Rissani market square is itself seventeenth century in origin, though much restored since. From here you can cut across diagonally from the bus terminal toward another collection of *ksour*.

The first one you encounter, about 2–3km southeast, is the **Zaouia of Moulay Ali Shereef**, the original Alaouite stronghold and the mausoleum of the dynasty's founder. Many times rebuilt—the last following the 1955 floods—the shrine is forbidden to non-Muslims, though you are allowed to look in from the outside.

Beside it, dominating this group of buildings, is the **Ksar d'Abbar**, an awesomely grandiose ruin which was once a kind of palace exile, housing the unwanted members of the Alaouite family and the wives of the dead sultans. Most of the structure, which still bears considerable traces of its former decoration, dates from the beginning of the nineteenth century.

A third royal *ksar*, the **Oualad Abd el-Halim**, stands about 1km farther down. Notable for its huge ramparts and the elaborate decorative effects of its blind arches and unplastered brick patterning, this is one of the few really impressive imperial buildings completed in this century. It was constructed around 1900 for Sultan Moulay Hassan's elder brother, the appointed governor of the Tafilalt.

Transportation On

The trip from **Rissani to Merzouga** can be covered in a variety of ways. Simplest is if you have your own vehicle—the route is not that clear (sand often covers sections) but the destination, Merzouga's huge golden sand dune, the Erg Cherbi, is hard to mistake.

Without a vehicle, you've got a choice between **market day trucks**, laden to the hilt, which leave three times a week from the market square, or local landrovers (they park opposite the cafés where the buses arriving in town stop). The trip takes about two hours and costs about 10dh. Getting **back to Rissani** can be more difficult, so try if possible to arrange a ride back, or ask around among car-driving fellow tourists when you arrive.

An alternative **route out from Rissani** is the **piste west to Zagora**. This is detailed in reverse (see Zagora). It's a possible route with your own car, or if you can coincide with the market days, by a local landrover taxi. This leaves every Thursday after the Rissani market, arriving in Zagora around ten hours later; a seat can be arranged through the Rissani hotel.

Merzouga

MERZOUGA is not the only, nor the least commercial, way to see the sun rise or set over the desert sands—but it must certainly be the most impressive. Above the village, and stretching for some 15km or so into the haze, is **Erg Chebbi** (The Small *Erg*), Morocco's largest sand dune. It is now very much part of the tourist circuit, but it would be foolish to let this put you off. Just getting out from Rissani is an adventure in itself—and the *piste* is really a more appropriate approach than the road from Erfoud as you blaze your way across the desert.

If you're in no hurry, it's good to stay a night at Merzouga, experiencing the isolation and silence of the desert. There are several **café-hotels** below the dunes. The most obvious of these is about 1km from the main village—well run and with good dinners, though a bit on the pricey side for accommodation, charging 50dh for a double room, 20dh a person for sleeping on its *terrasse*. A good alternative, *Café-Restaurant de Palmeraie*, offers couch space at 10dh a person; it is signposted from Merzouga'a triumphal arch, and within easy walking distance.If you've got the equipment, sleeping out on the dunes is perhaps the best option of all.

The area near Merzouga, incidentally, is used for the **North African Rally** every June–July, and it's the Erg Chebbi that appears in the famous Renault 5 advertisement, with the car driving down the dune. Rally drivers' stickers on the Merzouga café windows add a rather surreal touch to the place. The Erg itself can be walked across in about an hour.

Birdwatchers may also find the area around Merzouga—and the route down from Rissani—of interest. More unusual sightings, if you strike lucky, might include the Desert Sparrow, Desert Warbler, Egyptian Nightjar, and Arabian Bustard. Numerous migrants should also be in evidence.

OUT EAST TO FIGUIG
AND THE ALGERIAN BORDER

The ten-hour desert journey from **Er Rachidia to Figuig** is one of the most exhilarating and spectacular that you can make—certainly among those accessible to travelers without landrovers and proper expeditionary planning. It is startlingly isolated—almost throughout its entire 393km length—and physically extraordinary: the real outlands of Morocco, dominated by huge, empty landscapes and blank, red mountains.

What you have in the way of human presence is a series of struggling mining villages and military outposts, ranging from the desolate, tiny mudhut-type constructions of MENGOUB to the prosperous administrative and garrison center of BOUARFA (where you'll probably have to change buses). The real focus of the region, though, is **Figuig** itself—a great medieval datepalm oasis, in the bowl of the mountains and right on the border with Algeria.

If you want to continue on **into Algeria**, the border crossing here is open and functional. Staying in Morocco, you can head north from **Figuig to Oujda** (7 hr. by bus) and the Mediterranean coast.

The Figuig Oasis

The southern oases are traditionally measured by the number of their palms, rather than in terms of area or population. **FIGUIG**, with something like 200,000 trees, has always been one of the largest—an importance further enhanced by its strategic border position. At least twice it has been lost—in the seventeenth-century wars, and again at the end of Moulay Ismail's reign—and as recently as 1963, there was fighting in the streets between Moroccan and Algerian troops.

Orientation and Hotels
The oasis has even less of an administrative town than usual, still basically consisting of seven distinct *ksour* villages—which in the past were often fighting among themselves. Getting some orientation is relatively simple. The road from the **bus station** leads to an open *place* and the **administrative buildings**, passing the town's three (unclasssified) hotels on the way.

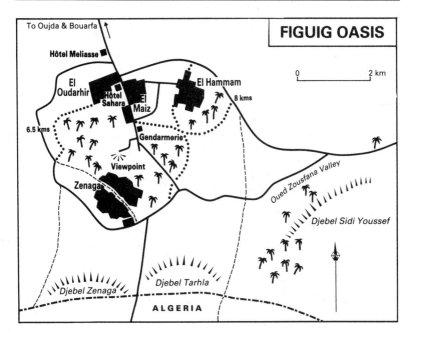

The *Hôtel Meliasse*, the first of the **hotels** that you come to, is basic, but clean and spacious and has a good café. The second, *Hôtel Sahara*, is marginally cheaper, but a bit dingy. Coming from Bouarfa, it is just before you get to the *gendarmerie* and the bus station, near a Shell station. A third, the *Hôtel-Camping Communal*, is at the top of the hill, to the right of the road as you leave town toward the Algerian border; it is signposted (just "Hotel") from the center. This has some pleasant rooms and rents **camping** space in its garden.

Exploring the Ksour

From the "center" of Figuig, **the ksour** spread out around the base of the hill—each enclosing its own palmery within high turreted walls. Although normally organized into a loose confederation, they were until this century fiercely independent—and their relations with each other were peppered with long and bitter blood feuds and, above all, disputes over the limited water supply. Their strange, archaic shape—with watchtowers rising above the snaking *feggaguir* (or irrigation channels)—evolved as much from this internal tension as from any need to protect themselves from the nomadic tribes of the desert. Likewise, within each of the *ksour,* the elaborate tunnel-like networks of alleys are deliberate (and successful) attempts to prevent any sudden or easy progress.

Your best chance of getting an overview of it all is to head for the **plat-forme**, poised above the *ksar* of Zenaga. The view from here spans a large

CROSSING INTO ALGERIA

Crossing into Algeria at Figuig is routine, with no restrictions on "pedestrian" passengers (as existed until recently at Oujda). However, there are a few formalities worth knowing before setting off.

First of all, before leaving the Figuig administrative center, you must get your passport stamped at the **gendarmerie**. This must be done on the same day you cross the border—effectively ruling out a really early start, since the police post opens at 8am (and closes at 3pm). Next, walk or hitch the 4km to the **border crossing**—a Beau Geste type of place with some palms and two tents—where you need to get more stamps on both the Moroccan and Algerian sides. There is a customs check, too, on the Algerian side—which can take a while, if the officers decide to do a search; they may well, as they don't have a lot to do. If you are driving, you will have to obtain (compulsory) insurance—currently 60 dinars for twenty days.

Beni Ounif

Finally, you can head for the Algerian frontier town of **BENI OUNIF**, another 3km. There are **banks** in Beni Ounif, and if you want to move on the same day, it's vital to get into town early enough to change money. The banks (closed, as are all in Algeria, on Fridays and Saturdays) are in the area to the right of the main road. There is just one, rather basic, **hotel**.

Buses going north stop by the yellow taxi stand; at around 1:30pm, there's a departure to Saïda, arriving in the evening (connections on from there to Algiers).There are also **trains** heading north, with early morning and evening departures.

part of the palmery and its pink-tinged *ksour,* and you can gaze at the weird, multicolored layers of the enclosing mountains. If you can find the energy—Figuig in summer feels a little like sitting inside a heater—head down into **Zenaga**, the largest of the seven villages. Going to your left, you should reach its center, more developed than most in this area, with a couple of cubicle shops and a café in addition to a mosque.

Of the other *ksour,* it is possible to loop to the right of the main administrative road, past **El Maiz** to **El Hammam el Foukanni**. El Maiz is the prettiest of the *ksour,* with small vaulted lanes and houses with broad verandas pointing south. In El Hammam, as the name suggests, there is a hot spring, used by the people for their ablutions. Anyone offering to guide you will take you to it. Back on the other side of the administrative road is the **Ksar El-Oudarhir**, which also has some natural springs (one hot, one salty), as well as terraces similar to the ones in El Maiz.

All of the *ksour* have exclusively Berber populations, though up until the 1950s and 1960s, there was also a considerable Jewish population. Until the beginning of the twentieth century, Figuig was also the final Moroccan staging point on the overland journey to Mecca.

Figuig to Oujda

Unless you have a strange fascination for (very) small town life, there is really nowhere else on this eastern plateau **between Figuig and Oujda** which offers very much temptation. **TENDRARA** (Tuesday market) and **Aït**

BENIMATHAR both have basic café-hotels, if you decide to stay overnight. Aït Benimather is the better choice—a quiet little **hot water oasis**, full of tortoises and snakes. Even if you don't want to stay, it's not a bad place to spend the middle of an afternoon, which you can do by taking the early morning bus from Figuig, and then catching one of the later ones for the final 50km to Oujda.

To the west of **BOUARFA**—where a mainly freight-carrying (and extremely slow) train begins the trip north to Oujda—the towns are all fairly bleak. If you're into *piste* driving, there are said to be troglodyte (cave) dwellings up in the hills behind BOUDENIB, toward GOUMARRA.

travel details

Buses

From Ouarzate Marrakesh (4 daily; 6 hr.); Zagora (3; 5 hr. 30 min.)*; Tailiouine/Taroudannt (2; 3 hr. 30 min./5 hr.); Tinerhir (3; 5 hr.).

From Zagora Ouarzazate (4 daily; 4–5 hr.)*; Marrakesh (2 daily; 9–11 hr.).*.

From Tinerhir Er Rachidia (2 daily; 3 hr.); Ouarzazate (3; 5 hr.).

From Er Rachidia Erfoud/Rissani (4 daily; 1 hr. 30 min./3 hr.); Tinerhir (2; 3 hr.); Figuig (1 daily via Bouarfa, currently at 5am; 10 hr.); Midelt (5; 3 hr. 30 min.); Fes (3; 8 hr. 30 min.) ; Meknes (1; 8 hr.).

From Erfoud Rissani (4 daily; 1 hr. 30 min.); Er Rachidia (4; 1 hr 30 min.); Fes (daily; 11 hr.).

From Rissani Tinejdad/Goulmina (daily; 3hr. 30 min./4 hr.).

From Figuig Oujda (4 daily; 7 hr.); Er Rachidia (via Bouarfa; 1 daily; 10 hr.).

*Most comfortable bus on the Marrakesh–Ourzazate–Zagora route is run by Ligne du Zagora

Grands Taxis

From Ouarzazate Regularly to Zagora (4 hr.). Negotiable for Skoura (1 hr.) and Aït Benhaddou (1 hr. 45 min., but expensive private trip).

From Boumalne Landrover taxi at least daily to Msemrir (3 hr.). Regular run to Tinerhir (50 min.).

From Tinerhir Regular runs to Boumalne (50 min.) and Tinejdad (1 hr.; from there on to Er Rachidia).

From Er Rachidia Fairly frequent runs to Erfoud (along the route you can negotiate a ticket to Meski) and to Tinejdad (2 hr.).

From Erfoud Fairly frequent runs to Rissani (1 hr. 30 min.) and Erfoud (2 hr.). Landrover trips direct to Merzouga (1 hr.; relatively expensive).

Trains

There is a line from Bouarfa to Oujda (8 hr.), but this is a night train, carries mainly freight, and is a distinctly eccentric alternative to the bus from Figuig.

TELEPHONE CODES

ER RACHIDIA ☎057   OUARZAZATE ☎088

CHAPTER SEVEN

AGADIR, THE ANTI-ATLAS, AND THE DEEP SOUTH

F lying to southern Morocco, your destination is most likely to be **Agadir**—built specifically as a resort following the earthquake in 1960, and something of a showpiece for the "new nation." It is unlikely, though, that you'll want to stay here for long. Agadir has been very carefully developed—its image is as a winter vacation spot for Europeans—and besides the beach and package tour hotels, there is not a lot of life to be found. There certainly isn't anything at all Moroccan: this is tourism at its most irrelevant and bland, straining hard to avoid contact with any local culture.

Fortunately, little of this applies to the rest of **the coast.** Just north of Agadir are a series of small fishing villages and beaches, many of them still without electricity or running water. **Tarhazoute**, a popular hippie center in the early 1970s, is the best known—though it is today a bit seedy, and not to everyone's taste. Inland from here, and part of the same mythology, is "Paradise Valley," a beautiful and exotic palm gorge, which culminates in the spring/winter waterfalls of **Immouzer des Ida Outanane**, a trip well worth making. To the south, the beaches are almost totally deserted in summer, ranging from solitary campgrounds at **Sidi Rbat** and **Sidi Moussa d'Aglou,** down to the old Spanish port of **Sidi Ifni**—only relinquished to Morocco in 1969, and full of bizarrely grandiose Art Deco colonial architecture.

Inland, the two main towns of the **Anti-Atlas**—and for outsiders, its major attractions—are Taroudannt and Tafraoute, provincial and somewhat genteel centers whose populations share the unusual distinction of having together cornered the country's grocery trade. *Tafraoutis*, in particular, can be found throughout Morocco (as well as in Paris and Marseilles) running corner grocery stores, but eventually returning home to retire. The physical difference between the two towns could hardly be greater, though. **Taroudannt** has massive walls and is the modern (and traditional) capital of the fertile **Souss plain**; it's an animated city, with good *souks* and hotels, and a natural place to stay on your way to Marrakesh or Ouarzazate. Farther south, and reached by bus via Tiznit, **Tafraoute** is essentially a collection of villages built of stone, absurdly picturesque in a startling natural landscape of pink granite and strange, vast rock formations. If you have time to visit only one place in the southwest, this should be it.

A more adventurous trip would take in the **Tata loop**, a little-traveled route across the southern Anti-Atlas to the pre-Sahara—a string of true desert oases. The route is most easily covered from Tiznit, but it is feasible—if you

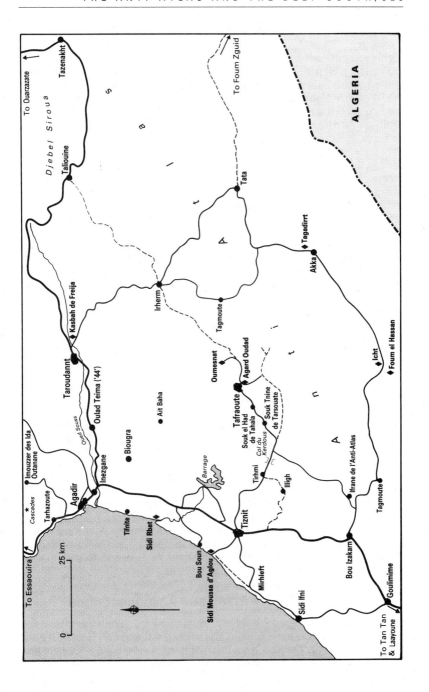

have the time to hang around waiting for buses—to do it east to west from Taroudannt. It's well off the usual (or even unusual) tourist trails and is highly recommended.

The **Deep South**, beyond Goulimine and down into the former territories of the Spanish Sahara, has become more stable in recent years, as the war in the **Western Sahara** has turned fairly quiet. There is now virtually no restriction on traveling down the coast through Tan Tan and Laayoune as far south as Ad Dakhla, on (for the most part) a well-paved road. At present, however, you cannot continue from Ad Dakhla into Mauritania.

For visitors, the Deep South's main appeal lies in the experience of travel itself in the desert, and in the great distances covered. **Goulimine**, the most accessible "desert town," is scarcely worth the trip for itself. Promoted for its camel market—the traditional meeting place of the "Blue Men" (Touareg tribesmen, whose faces are tinged blue by their masks and robes)—it is now more frequented by tourists than by anyone else. But it is quite a ride, all the same, and with your own vehicle you can explore true desert oases nearby.

Going even farther, you begin to need real commitment in order to travel to towns like **Tan Tan**, 125km farther down, or **Laayoune**, another 260km, both of which are essentially administrative centers. Again, however, you get a geniune taste of the desert, especially on the road between Tarfaya and Laayoune, with the dunes on one side, and the sands, dropping in sheer cliff to the ocean, on the other. Returning, if you don't fancy a repeat of the journey, there are flights from Ad Dakhla and Laayoune to Agadir.

Heading for the **Canary Islands**, there is now a regular car and passenger ferry from Agadir to Las Palmas. There are flights to the Canaries, too, from Agadir and Laayoune.

Agadir and Inezgane

Built up in organized sectors—one for tourist hotels, one for the port, and a third, some ways out, for industry and local residents—**AGADIR** doesn't really lend itself to excitement or spontaneity. It does, admittedly, have a magnificent beach and it has avoided the high rise architecture of its Spanish *costa* counterparts, but this is about as far as being positive will stretch. Unless you actually want a day or two's suspension from ordinary Moroccan life, it would be better to pass straight through. Rooms, in any case, can really be a problem to find at the height of the summer or winter/spring seasons.

If you are simply traveling through Agadir, as a means of getting south, you might well prefer to stay in the town of **Inezgane**—now almost a suburb of the city—13km southwest. It is at Inezgane (see section following) that almost all transport connections need to be made.

Orientation, Points of Arrival, and Accommodation

The basic layout of Agadir is pretty straightforward. The **beach** and the commercial zone (centered around Place Hassan II and Av. Hassan II) are marked on the map; the **port area** is to the north, below the old Kasbah; and the **industrial zone** spreads south toward **Inezgane**.

If you're coming in by **bus** from the south, you might actually be arriving in Inezgane. To get into Agadir from Inezgane, any number of local "city" buses (or *grands taxis*—correct fare 2dh) will drop you at the **Place Salam terminal** (bottom right on our map). All other buses—both *CTM* and private—use the **Talborjt bus station** behind Place Lahcen Tamri (top center-right on the map).

The **airport** is 4km outside of town on the Inezgane road; there's an occasional bus from here to Place Salam (much more regular ones if you walk 1km to the main road junction), or you can share a *grand taxi* (always available; about 50dh for up to six people).

Hotels

The hotels most likely to have space in Agadir are the cheaper, independently run places—too small or too basic for the package tour groups. Most of these are concentrated around and downhill from **Place Lahcen Tamri**, just below the main bus station. This quarter, known as Talborjt, is something of an "alternative Agadir," and frequented to an extent by young Moroccans on vacation. Good choices here, all keyed on our map, and in roughly ascending order of price, include:

Hôtel Massa (C), **Hôtel Canaria (D)**, both on Place Lahcen Tamri; no phone. No great claims to comfort or cleanliness, but generally the cheapest prices in Agadir. *Unclassified.*

Hôtel Diaf (G), **Hôtel Select (H)**, Rue Allal Ben Abdallah; no phones. Another pair of cheapies. *Unclassified.*

Hôtel de la Baie (I), Rue Allal ben Abdallah; ☎230.14. Good value choice, with some balconied rooms. *1*B.*

Hôtel Excelsior (A), Rue Yacoub el Mansour; ☎210.28. *1*B.*

Hôtel Tifawt (B), Rue Yacoub el Mansour; ☎243.54. *1*A.*

Hôtel Bahia (E), Rue Mehdi Ibn Toumert; ☎227.24. Unusually clean, tasteful, and good value. *1*A.*

Hôtel Sindibad (F), Place Lahcen Tamri; ☎234.77. Comfortable budget hotel. *2*A.*

Hôtel Paris (K), Av. Kennedy; ☎22694. Recently refurbished, with a pleasant courtyard set around a small fountain. *1*A.*

Hôtel Cinq Parties du Monde (L), Bd. Hassan II; ☎225.45. Modern, clean rooms in tiled courtyard, plus a set meal restaurant. *2*A.*

Hôtel Ayour, Rue de l'Entraide; ☎249.76. Another new, medium budget hotel—good for its class. A block north of Av. du Prince Moulay Abdallah. *2*A.*

There is no shortage of **more upscale hotels**, though rooms can be hard to come by, unless you book through one of the hotel chain's central reservation agencies. Among the more worthwhile places are:

Hôtel Cub Salam (M), Bd. Mohammed V; ☎221.20 (or reserve through *Societé Salam* in Casablanca, ☎0/36.79.22). Very tasteful hotel, with a fine pool. 4*A.

Hôtel El Oumnia, Chemin Oued Souss; ☎233.51. Sited at the edge of the beach—a big advantage—and with small apartment rooms scattered about the grounds. Reasonably priced for its class. *4*A.*

Campground

The city's **campground** (☎295.40) is reasonably well located, not far from the center or the beach, on Bd. Mohammed V. It is reasonably secure, and has a snack bar and other facilities. Prices are average to high.

Around the Town

Even more than most resorts, Agadir's life revolves around its beach. If you're not into sunbathing, you'll not want to stay long. If you're booked onto a package vacation here, take as many excursions as possible—Immouzer, Taroudannt, and Marrakesh are all in easy striking distance.

Few details are needed on the **beach** itself, which extends an impressive distance to the south of the town. There are a numnber of beach-cafés, which sell drinks and rent out sunbeds and umbrellas. The *Oasis Bar* is one of the nicest, very clean and with good service. These bars rent sunbeds and umbrellas as well as serving drinks. There's a municipal **swimming pool** at the north end of the beach if you don't care for the ocean.

As a break from the beach, the **city park**, several hundred yards long and wide, is a good place to get away. It's very green and shaded with eucalyptus trees. The **fishing port**, too, is worth a stroll. You can haggle for fish yourself, at very low prices, if you're doing your own cooking.

A little further afield, on the south side of town, Hassan II's **Palais Royale** is now nearing completion. It cannot, of course, be visited, but you can get a good view of it from the river estuary. Built in an imaginative blend of traditional and modern forms, it is very impressive, even when seen from outside the vast, encircling walls. If you're interested in **bird watching**, the estuary itself is also of interest—it's constantly filled with flocks of sea birds.

And finally, there is what remains of old Agadir—the **Kasbah** on the top of the hill to the north. This deserves a mention, though not perhaps a visit, unless you have a car for the eight-kilometer trip. Primarily, what you see when you get up there is a marvelous view of Agadir and the beach. The Kasbah, the main quarter of the pre-earthquake town, is little more than a bare outline of walls and an entrance arch with an inscription in Dutch recording that the Netherlands began trading here in 1746—capitalizing on the rich sugar plantations of the Souss plain.

It's not much, but it is one of the few reminders that Agadir has any past at all, so complete was the destruction of the 1960 earthquake. In fact, Agadir's history closely parallels that of the other Atlantic ports: colonized first by the Portuguese in the fifteenth century, then recaptured by the Saadians in the sixteenth, carrying on its trading with intermittent prosperity—overshadowed, more often than not, by the activities of Mogador/Essaouira. In 1911, then a relatively insignificant town, Agadir was the scene of a protest by the Germans against French and British plans to carve up North Africa. A German gunboat, the *Panther*, let loose a few rounds across the bay—an event, like the Fashoda crisis in Egypt, that very nearly set off World War I.

Restaurants, Bars, and Nightlife

Agadir's **restaurants** are less imaginative than you'd expect of a major resort—many of the package tourists seem to have meals included at their hotels. However, there are a few pleasantly located places along the oceanfront, as well as some worthwhile cheaper options scattered around town.

As with hotels, the most inexpensive places are **around Place Lahcen Tamri**, or streets running south from the square. At the most basic café-

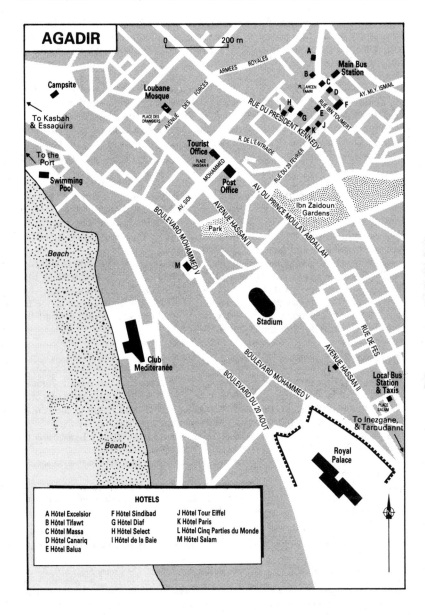

restaurants here, you can eat soup, tajine, and salads, at pretty much regular Moroccan prices; soup here goes for around 3dh, about one-fifth of the price at the touristy places by the sea.

Somewhat classier **prix fixé meals** are also available around Place Lahcen Tamri—try *Mille et Une Nuits* or the unnamed seafood restaurant around the corner from the bus station on Rue 29 Février. Other proimising locations are along Av. Hassan II (*Café Taverner*, here, is reliable), Av. Sidi Mohammed (*Pizzeria Annamunda* has decent food, and guitarists), and Place des Orangiers (off Av. Hassan II; *Le Tanalt* usually has a good menu). Near the Ibn Zaldoun gardens, *L'Etoile de Marrakech* serves generous portions of good food. For **late night** meals, try the *Jour et Nuit*, on the beachfront.

As for **drinking,** the clear winner is the *Corniche Restaurant Bar*, close by *the Jour et Nuit* on the beachfront, which hosts modern Moroccan bands—often excellent. This apart, things are a bit tame. The *Hôtel Sud Bahia* (the big hotel by the campground—not to be confused with the *Bahia*) has a "happy hour" between 5 and 6pm, and most of the other larger hotels have one or more bars, too, though none are especially exciting. If you want to buy your own booze, the cheapest spirits, beer and wine are sold by the *Uniprix* store at the corner of Av. Hassan II and Av. Sidi Mohammed. The *Uniprix* is also a useful store for pre-bargaining comparative shopping, since it sells a range of provisions and handicrafts at fixed prices.

Nightlife is otherwise limited to discos in the package tour hotels and the small area of seafront places on Bd. du 20 Août. Perhaps the best of the **discos** is the *Tan Tan* in the Hôtel Almohades; *Bylbos Disco* can also be pretty lively, though prices of admission and drinks are high; *Picnic* is one to avoid. Moroccan groups usually play, prior to the discos (from around 8–11pm) in the hotels, *Atlas* and *Sahara*.

Directory

If you're heading for the **Anti-Atlas** or cutting across to the **south,** Agadir offers the last facilities to speak of. Also, because it's very competitive, it's one of the cheapest places in the country to **rent a car**—and many of the rental companies will let you to return it in Marrakesh, Casablanca, or Fes.

Airlines *Royal Air Maroc* flies from Agadir to Laayoune and the Canary Islands, and to Tangier (via Casa). Its office is on Av. du General Kettani (☎321.45).

American Express c/o *Voyages Schwarz*, Bd. Hassan II; open Mon.–Fri. 9am–noon and 3–6pm; closed weekends .

Banks The *Banc Populaire* (open Mon.–Fri. 8am–noon and 2:30–5pm, Sat., Sun. 10am–noon) is the most helpful. *SGMB, Crédit du Maroc* and others can be found downtown, mainly along Av. des F.A.R. The *Hôtel Sahara* (Av. Mohammed V) exchanges currency at normal bank rates.

Bargaining If you do buy anything in Agadir—rugs, carpets, *babouches,* etc.—you shouldn't offer much more than a tenth of the asking price. For once, fixed-price shops are generally the better deal.

Books New and used English-language books are available at *The Crown English Bookshop* (by the tourist office on Av. Sidi Mohammed). Run by an American, this has one of the best stocks in the country, taking pride to maintain background books on Morocco, including Paul Bowles's translations of contemporary writers, as well as dictionaries, phrasebooks, and course books of Moroccan Arabic. You can sell or trade books, too. Strongly recommended.

Car Rental *Leasing Cars* (107 Av. Hassan II, ☎209.81; and at the airport) is one of the cheapest and most reliable. *L.V.S.* (52 Av. Hassan II), with branches in Marrakesh and Casablanca, is also worth trying; also *Afric Cars* (☎237.50) on Bd. Mohammed V. Others, including *Hertz,*

Avis, and *InterRent,* are grouped along Av. Hassan II and toward the campground on Bd. Mohammed V.

Car Repairs For Renaults try *Castano* (Av. El Moukaouama; ☎238.21); Citroëns, *Garage Citroën* (corner of Rue Bertholet/Rue Ampère); Fiats, *Auto-Hall* (Rue de la Foire; ☎224.86). And many others as well.

Medical Care *Hôpital Hassan II,* Route de Marrakesh (☎224.77). Most of the big hotels can also provide the addresses of English-speaking doctors.

Moped/Motorbike Rental *MotoRent,* near the beach, on Bd. du 20 Août, rents out Yamaha 125s at about 150dh a day (lower rates for the week), well worth considering for trips to Immouzer and beyond. It also rents cheaper mopeds, intended for local use but practical for shuttling to Banana Village and Tarhazoute (see "Around Agadir").

Post Office The main *PTT* is right in the middle of town at the end of Av. Sidi Mohammed; hours are Mon.–Fri. 9am–noon and 3–6pm, Sat. 9am–noon only; the efficient telephone section stays open 24 hr.

Tourist Offices *ONMT* (Block A, Av. Sidi Mohammed: along the raised walkway opposite the post office). *Syndicat d'Initiative* (Av. Mohammmd V; ☎226.95).

Leaving Agadir

Agadir has no train station, though the railroad company, ONCF, do operate a number of connecting **bus** services. These **express services** are the most comfortable public transportation out of the city. Departures are:

Marrakesh: 4:50am (arrive 8:50am); 2:26pm (arrive 6:26pm).

Goulemine/Tan Tan/Laayoune: 2:37am (arrive 6:02am/9:02am/1:52pm).

Regular CTM, SATAS, and other private line, buses cover a limited range of destinations from the main Talborjt terminal; more frequent departures (at least on private line services) run from Inezgane (see below). A bus to Immouzer, leaving Agadir daily at 2pm, arriving 6 hr. later, is operated by *Immouzer Transport,* from just around the corner from the Talborjt terminal. Buses to Inezgane and Tarhazoute go from the local Place Salam terminal.

Grands taxis from Agadir include a routine shuttle to Inezgane (2dh a place), from where you can make connections to Taroudannt, Taliouine, etc.

Domestic flights, operated by RAM, include most destinations in Morocco, including Laayoune, though most others are routed through Casablanca. There are direct flights to Las Palmas in the Canaries. See "Arriving" for details of getting to the airport.

Lastly, there is a new car/passenger **ferry service to Las Palmas**. This leaves weekly, at 7pm each Saturday, arriving at 5pm. One way fare in a four-berth cabin is from 400dh; small cars, 720dh. There is a ten percent discount if you book a return ticket (return crossings leave Las Palmas on Wednesdays at 5pm, arriving Agadir on Thursday at 11am). A novel feature is that you can stay on the ferry while in Las Palmas for 150dh a day, full board.

Inezgane

Thirteen kilometers south—and inland—of Agadir, **INEZGANE** makes for an attractive alternative base if you're not interested in resort life. It is also much more of a transportation hub than Agadir, with buses going to most southern destinations, including regular departures to Taroudannt, Essaouira, and Marrakesh.

Perhaps more importantly, the town sees very few tourists and so has a completely unaffected feel to it. There should always be room at the three or four **hotels** (all unclassified) along the main street, right near the bus terminals, and some of the **restaurants** here are excellent, too. Best of all, with superb French cooking, is *Les Pergolas* (☎307.05).

Around Agadir: Tarhazoute, "Paradise Valley," and Immouzer des Ida Outanane

Agadir may not be a prime destination in itself, but it is well situated for some very attractive excursions. **North of the town**, tourist development rapidly begins to fade and the beach at **Tarhazoute** belongs to an entirely different world—one of Morocco's last vestiges of its hippie past from the 1960s and 1970s. In a similar vein, just inland from here, is the aptly named "**Paradise Valley**," a beautiful, palm lined gorge.

Perhaps more compelling, and certainly less of a throwback to those days, is **Immouzer des Ida Outanane**, a wonderful mountain site, replete with sporadic waterfalls. **South of Agadir**, the lagoon near **Massa/Sidi Rbat** is a superb bird watching site, full of resident and migratory wading birds and other species.

Transportation to each of these destinations is pretty straightforward. From Agadir, city buses #12 and #14 run more or less on the hour up the coast to Tarhazoute. For Immouzer, there's a daily bus leaving Agadir at 2pm (from the street behind *Hôtel Sindibad* on Place Lahcen Tamri) which passes through the initial part of Paradise Valley; it returns each morning at 8am. Jitneys also make the trip to the Thursday market (reservations at any Agadir travel agent). For Sidi Rbat, there's a bus most of the way—it goes as far as Massa village.

Tarhazoute and "Banana Village"

A cluster of compact, color-washed houses, **TARHAZOUTE** (or TAGHAGANT, as it appears on some maps), lies 18km from Agadir and should be a delight. On either side of it—indeed, from way north of Cap Rhir down to Agadir—there's a great swathe of beach, interrupted here and there by headlands and for the most part deserted. Whether you are able to enjoy all this, however, depends a lot on your tastes. Tarhazoute, like Essaouira/ Diabat to the north, was Morocco's hippie resort *par excellence,* and the past is still surprisingly part of the present. The cafés here belt out rock music and local hustlers are a bit shocked if you're not interested in partaking of a little herbal indulgence to accompany the experience.

Until a couple of years ago, the village had no electricity, and it's still without running water—which, of course, is all part of the Tarhazoute "experience." **Accommodation** is mainly in private rooms, all pretty basic, and you're given buckets to fetch water from the spring beside the mosque. The rooms used to be very cheap but prices have gone up recently due to the increasing number of young and mostly affluent Moroccans who spend the summer here; expect to bargain for rates of 150–250dh a week. The alternative to renting a room is to camp out. There is an official **campground** on the beach just south of the village, with a café and cold showers. Unofficial camping also takes place—to the north, at *Anchor Point*—but it's not very secure and not to be recommended. For **meals,** everyone seems to head toward the street filled with cafés at the edge of the village or to the excellent *Taoui-Fik* restaurant down by the campground on the beach.

"Banana Village"

The road out to Tarhazoute (and the Agadir buses) passes through what has become known as **"Banana Village"**—12km from Agadir, 6km before Tarhazoute. Naturally enough, it's on the edge of a thriving banana grove, and all along the roadside stalls sell bunches of the fruit—at initially outrageous prices! In addition to bananas, the village has a couple of good café-restaurants and a **hammam** (women until 6pm; men afterwards), which is useful if you're staying in Tarhazoute.

In the center of Banana Village, the road to Immouzer des Ida Outanane leads off into the hills. If you're without transportation, it's usually a fairly simple route to hitch rides on, at least for the 10km to the start of **"Paradise Valley."**

"Paradise Valley" and Immouzer des Ida Outanane

Appropriately named, **"Paradise Valley"** begins as a deep, palm lined gorge—with a river snaking along the base (although by June, it's down to a mere trickle). Like Tarhazoute, it established a reputation in the 1960s and 1970s as a place to camp and hang out, and there are still sporadic groups of hippies to be seen in winter, as well as more "regular" travelers.

If you decide to **camp,** be aware of the possibility of flash floods (especially in spring) and pitch your tent well away from the riverbed. The best stretch of the valley starts just after the turnoff for Immouzer: get off the bus here (or park your car) and walk. If you have the time, it's possible to hire a mule to explore the valley's numerous Berber villages. The road is often closed in Spring, even to jeeps.

Immouzer des Ida Outanane

IMMOUZER DES IDA OUTANANE lies 61km from Agadir, a small village in a westerly outcrop of the Atlas mountains, and a minor regional and market center (of the Ida Outanane, as its full name suggests; there's a *souk* every Thursday). It is a beautiful day excursion from Agadir—better still, if you stay overnight, either camping out, or (assuming it is back in operation) at the wonderful Hôtel des Cascades.

In spring, if you're lucky, you will also get a chance to see the **waterfalls** for which the village is renowned. These roll down from the hills 4km below the village: follow the road down through the main square and off to the left. The falls used always to be spectacular in the spring—when the waters nearly reach flood levels and almond blossoms are everywhere—though tight control of irrigation has reduced the cascade on most occasions to a trickle. The villagers now "turn on" the falls for special events only—and for their own, not tourists' benefit. There's a second waterfall, though, which is still allowed to flow its natural course: ask locals to direct you, to "Le Deuxieme Cascade."

However, what is really appealing here is the overall feel of things. There's a small village just across the stream from the falls, and a **café** (*Café de Miel*), with basic food, near which you can camp out in the olive groves. The whole area is perfect for walkers. You can follow any of the paths with enjoyment. One of the most dramatic, near the village, cuts up across the cliffs to the *Hôtel Cascades*.

If you can afford it, and if it has opened again after renovation in progress in 1989, the **Hôtel des Cascades**, on the edge of Immouzer (and signposted from its main square) is a superb place to stay. Designated 3*B, and open to some bargaining on its "pension" rates, this must be one of the most beautiful hotels in Morocco—surrounded by gardens of vines, apple and olive trees, and hollyhocks, with a huge and placid panorama of the mountains rolling down to the coast. The food, too, is exquisite.

South of Agadir: Massa and Sidi Rbat

South of Agadir, toward Tiznit, there is almost no development at all beyond the three- to four-kilometer sprawl at the edge of town. Even the names on the map tend to be no more than fishing hamlets: TIFNITE, for instance, is a grim little collection of huts, despite its proximity to "international" Agadir.

If you want isolation, though, or are at all interested in birdlife, there is no better place to head than **MASSA**, or SIDI RBAT. The **lagoon** at Massa is one of the world's great **bird watching** areas, with a mixture of resident birds and migrants, desert visitors, and so on, and it's teeming with flamingos, avocets, and ducks. The best times to visit are March to April or October to November.

The lagoon itself is a restricted reserve, but you can catch a lot of birdlife, and enjoy some fine swimming, by staying a couple of kilometers north, along the coast road, at **SIDI RBAT**. Here, a small, Dutch-run **campground** (☎09) stands out on its own beside the sea, reached along a track that skirts the lagoon of the Massa river. At the campground there is a tea room and restaurant (serving dinner only), and there are also cabins for rent—more expensive than usual but very pleasant. The **beach** at Sidi Rbat can often be misty and overcast—even when Agadir is basking in the sun—but on a clear day, it's as good as anywhere else.

It is possible, though time consuming, **to get to Sidi Rbat** using a combination of buses and walking—there's no bus the whole way, since there's no village, only a *marabout's* tomb at the end of the track. From Agadir or Inezgane, take a bus to MASSA, just off the Tiznit road; ask directions there for the river (*oued*) and start walking—you might even get a ride along the way.

Taroudannt

With its majestic, red-ocher circuit of walls, **TAROUDANNT** is one of the more elegant towns in Morocco. Situated at the head of the fertile Souss Valley and its nearby plain, it has always been an important commercial and urban center, and often the first target and base of new imperial dynasties. It never became a "great city," however—even the Saadians (who made it their capital in the sixteenth century) moved on to Marrakesh. Its present status, a bustling but somewhat mundane market town of some 30,000 people, is probably much as it always has been—the usual historical pattern of wealth and construction, only to be followed by total destruction and obscurity. Taroudannt chanced this fate only once, at the end of its Saadian golden age, with a disastrous rebellion against Moulay Ismail, who contented himself with a mere massacre, later repopulating the town with equally troublesome Berbers from the Rif.

The walls, the *souks,* and the stark, often heat-hazed backdrop of the High Atlas to the north, are the town's chief attractions—though none of them are powerful enough to bring in the Agadir tour groups in any great number. Consequently, staying here is worth the effort, if only for a night, or for the privelege of getting up at 4am for the bus over Tizi n'Test to Marrakesh—the most dramatic regular road journey in Morocco (see *Chapter Six*).

Arrival and Hotels

On arrival, the town can seem highly confusing, with ramparts heading off for miles in every direction and large areas of open space. In fact, once you get your bearings, it's all pretty clear. There are two main squares—**Place Tamoklate** (aka Place de la Victoire) and **Place Assarag** (aka Place el Alouine)—and the town's main street (lined with shops) runs between them.

If you arrive by **bus**, you'll get off either in one of the squares (on a *CTM* or a *SATAS* bus) or outside the ramparts, by the Kasbah quarter (on the private-line buses). From the latter stop, it's a ten-minute walk to the squares—through the Kasbah quarter and along the main street. **Grands taxis**, like the buses, might let you off at either of these locations; they generally leave from Place Tamoklate.

Getting around the town, there are **petits taxis** (usually to be found in Place Tamoklate) and, with similar tariffs, a few **calèches**—horse drawn cabs.

Going **on from Taroudannt by bus** needs a little advance planning, as regards routes and terminals. The most reliable are operated by *SATAS*, which has an office in Place Assarag. They have departures three times a week for Tata (leaving Wednesday, Saturday, and Sunday), a daily express to Casablanca, and and also operate the service over the Tizi n'Test to Marrakesh. The *SATAS* **Tizi n'Test** bus (see *Chapter Six* for a description of the route) normally leaves from Place Assarag at 4am; however, it doesn't always run, in which case another bus leaves (again around 4am) from Place Tamoklate; it's essential to check times the night before. Buses to Ouarzazate, via Taliouine (see below), are run by private companies and leave from near the ramparts.

Hotels
Most of the cheaper **hotels** are grouped around Place Assarag, which, with its low, arcaded front and its many cafés, is very much the center of activity in Taroudannt. Among the basic, unrated places here, try either the *Hôtel Alouarda* or (the cheapest option), the *Hôtel de la Place*, or *Hôtel Roudani* (which generally has hot water—as well as good food).

For just a few dirhams more, however, you could stay at the 1*A *Hôtel Taroudannt* (again, in Place Assarag; ☎24.16)—well worth the extra money for its patio garden, cool air, and bar. The 2*A *Hôtel Saadien* (Borj el Mansour; ☎25.89) is a good modern hotel in the Medina. Or, going some way upscale, Taroudannt offers the opportunity to stay in a **palace**—albeit a fairly recent one—in the form of the 4*A *Hôtel Palais Salam* (☎23.12). Located just intside the ramparts, in the Kasbah quarter, this is a beautiful place, with its rooms either in the towers or garden pavilions. The Salam also has a small **swimming pool** (which, if you ask, may be open to nonresidents in the summer).

Restaurants
Basic but extremely inexpensive **café-restaurants** can be found just off the two main squares. *Café-Restaurant Dallas*, opposite the *Hôtel Taroudannt*, is a friendly place and fine value, or try one of the hole-in-the-wall stalls, with a couple of tables outside, on the street connecting the two main squares. The cafés at nos. 184 and 187 are excellent for soup or tajine.

For **more elaborate fare**, try the *Hôtel Taroudannt*, for solid French cooking, or, if you're prepared to pay fairly luxury prices, the Moroccan restaurant at the *Hôtel Palais Salam*.

The Town

Taroudannt's **souks** are not large by Moroccan city standards, but they are varied; there's a strong local crafts tradition, and much of the work you find here is of outstanding quality.

The best approach to the *souks* is to follow the road next to the *Banque Marocaine* in Place Assarag (you'll probably come out by the other square—it's that small an area), and look out especially for the "antique" **jewelry** and unusual, limestone **sculptures**. These are similar to the ones you find in the north at Chaouen, and are an obvious oddity—often figurative in design and much more African than Islamic. The jewelry comes mainly from the south (the town played its part in trans-Saharan trade) or was made by the many Jewish craftsmen who flourished here up to the 1960s. In April, the town is still host to a *handicrafts and folklore fair*.

The leather **tanneries**, as ever, are located some distance from the main *souks*—placed outside the town walls on account of their smell (leather is cured in cattle urine or pigeon droppings) and for the proximity to a ready supply of water. In comparison to Marrakesh, or particularly Fes, the ones here are small, but, sadly, they display a rare variety of skins for sale—not from just the ubiquitous sheep and cows, but silver foxes, racoons, and mountain cats as well. Many of these furs are illegal imports into the US and Canada, and we urge no participation in the process. If you want to visit the tanneries, all the same, follow the continuation of the main street past the *Hôtel Taroudannt* to the ramparts; turn left there and, after 100m, take the first right—they're to your right, and give off such a stench that they'd be impossible to miss.

The Walls—and Out to the Gazelle d'Or

The other feature of the town you can't avoid are the **walls and bastions**—best explored, if you have the energy, by renting a bike from either the *Hôtel Salam* or one of the stores on the main street.

On your way around, take a good look at the old **Kasbah quarter** around the *Salam*. Now a kind of ramshackle village within the town, this was once a winter palace complex for the Saadians and contains the ruins of a fortress built by Moulay Ismail.

You might also be interested in the palatial surroundings of a more recent past—if so, follow the signs to the **Hôtel Gazelle d'Or**, renowned as being the most exclusive in the country and situated within its own park. This was where the French colonials used to come in winter (and, to an extent, their successors are continuing the tradition); a mint tea on the terrace is just about affordable.

Hiking around Taroudannt

If you are interested in **hiking** in the Taroudannt area, Abdel Aziz Tali (BP132, Taroudannt) organizes trips staying in villages in the hills above the town. He can be contacted at the souvenir store between the two cafés on the east side of Place Assarag.

Among the more ambitious trips offered are hikes over the southern approaches to the **Tichka Plateau** (see Western High Atlas). These are, as yet, covered by no western hiking tour companies, so there is genuine sense of isolation and expedition. Strongly recommended for any walkers traveling in winter or spring.

Taliouine and the Djebel Siroua

Passing through a long stretch of scrubby *hammada*, the **P32 to Taliouine** lacks the drama of Tizi n'Test—the route most people take from Taroudannt. However, it is an efficient approach to the southern oases, and the scenery livens up on the Taliouine–Ouarzazate stretch, changing gradually to semi-desert, and offering views of the weirdly shaped mountains of the Anti-Atlas.

For hikers, once again, there are additional attractions. The **Djebel Siroua**, north of Taliouine, is one of the finest mountain sections of the Anti-Atlas. It is scarcely less impressive than the more established High Atlas trekking areas, and a great deal less frequented.

Taliouine

TALIOUINE lies at a pass, its land gathered into a bowl, with a scattering of buildings on or above the roadside. More village than town, it is dominated by a magnificent Glaoui Kasbah (see Telouet for details on the Glaoui).

Now largely in ruins, much of the **Kasbah** is used to house farm animals, but the best preserved section is still inhabited (as the TV antenna indicates) and you can look around the outside of it. The Kasbah's decoration is very different from those farther south: the walls are intricately patterned, the windows molded with palm fronds (still showing their original paint), and the towers (some of which, though derelict, you can climb) built around squat, downward-tapering pillars.

With your own vehicle, you can set out from Taroudannt, visit the Kasbah and move on easily enough to Ouarzazate the same day. Relying on public transportation, you should reckon on staying. Although it's theoretically possible to get a morning bus in to Taliouine (from Taroudannt or Ouarzazate) and a late afternoon bus out, beware that most buses arrive in Taliouine already full. You may strike lucky with a *grand taxi* (one normally passes through, en route to to Ouarzazate at about 11am), but as likely as not getting out will mean hitching. Rides, fortunately, are fairly easy to arrange.

Staying here, however, is an attractive proposition. Few tourists do, despite the presence of two **hotels**: the *Grand Hôtel du Sud—Ibn Toumert* (☎30; 4*B), right next to the Kasbah, and, on the main road below, the small *Auberge Souktana*. The latter is moderately priced and very atmospheric, with a swimming pool, great meals, and candles instead of electricity. In summer you can sleep out on their roof terrace. Other times it's too cold and since the hotel has just four rooms you should try to turn up early in the day.Traveling by bus, ask to be dropped at either the *Souktana* or the Kasbah.

Jadid Ahmed, co-manager of the *Auberge Souktana*, arranges **hiking trips into the Djebel Siroua**. They can be negotiated on arrival, or, with a group, in advance—around $150 for a week-long excursion, including travel to and from Agadir airport. However, it's obviously a lot cheaper to go by yourself, and Ahmed dispenses advice with or without hiring.

There is a Monday **souk** in Taliouine and a Friday *souk* in TAZENAKHT (at the junction of the Ourzazate and Foum Zguid roads, 84km east) on Fridays. The Tazenakht *souk* is usually helpful for getting rides with locals.

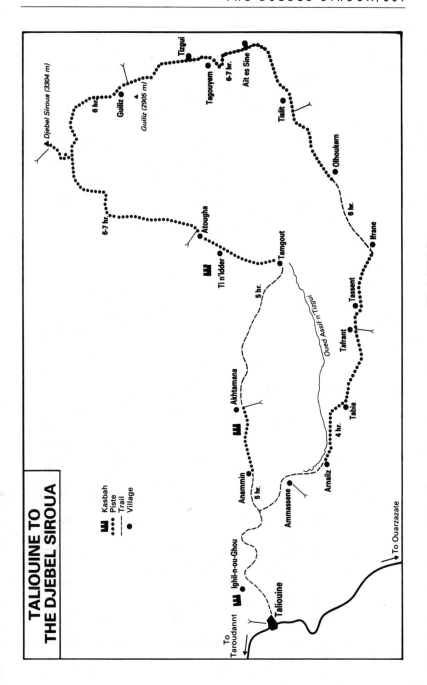

TALIOUINE TO THE DJEBEL SIROUA

Kasbah
••• **Piste**
— — **Trail**
● **Village**

Djebel Siroua (3304 m)

Guiliz

Guiliz (2905 m)

Tizgui

Tagouyem

6-7 hr.

Ait es Sine

6 hr.

Tislit

Olhoukem

6 hr.

6-7 hr.

Atougha

Ifrane

Ti n'Idder

Tamgout

Tassent

5 hr.

Oued Assif n'Tizgui

Tafrant

Akhtamana

Tabia

Amaliz

4 hr.

Anammin

5 hr.

Ammassene

5 hr.

Ighil-n-ou-Ghou

To Taroudannt

Taliouine

To Ouarzazate

Into the Djebel Siroua

The most straightforward route to the *djebel* is to follow the track east from Taliouine—combining rides with walking—to **AKHFAMANE**, where there are rooms and a Kasbah. A hike of another 5km, via TAMGOUT, will bring you to **ATOUGHA**, where, again, rooms should be no problem; from here, the **route to the summit of Siroua** is a direct (if tiring) hike lasting six or seven hours.

Coming down, you can follow the same trail to the base and then head south and east to complete a circuit. Six hours walk, from the summit, should take you to the tiny village of **GUILIZ**. The best bet is to take it slow (altitudes here are over 3000m) and bed down in a shelter or a camp; a tent isn't really necessary in the summer—just a thick blanket. From Guiliz you can head for **TISLIT** (again, about six hours) where rooms are available; from here it's another 6 hr. trek to **TAFRANT** (again, rooms available); then 4 hr. farther, via TABIA, to **AMMASSENE**. From Amassene it's possible to get a lift to Taliouine.

Toward Djebel Toubkal

Hikers might also consider an **alternative approach from Taliouine to Toubkal**. From AOULOUZ, between Taliouine and Taroudannt, there are fairly frequent, shared taxis to ASSARAG (where you'll find rooms). A few hours' walk north from here takes you to AMSOUZERTE, where you can stay at Omar's (see "Toubkal National Park," in *Chapter Six*), and from there you can reach Lac d'Ifni.

The Tata Circuit and Beyond

Heading **south across the Anti-Atlas** from Taroudannt, or east from Tiznit, you can travel by bus (or your own vehicle) to **the desert oases of Tata, Aka, and Foum El Hassan**. This is one of the great Moroccan routes, not much traveled by foreigners, and with the feel, still, of a desert world very much apart. The scenery is wild and impressive, with occasional camel herds, and lonely, weatherbeaten villages. It is poor country, though; in 1988, Tata and its region had their first decent spring rains in five years—only to be followed by swarms of locusts.

The route can be taken in either direction, from Taroudannt (as described below) or from Agadir/Tiznit.

From Taroudannt there are four departures a week to Tata; check the days (they should be Monday, Wednesday, and Saturday; returning from Tata to Taroudannt on Tuesday, Thursday, and Sunday; about 8–10 hr.) at the *SATAS* terminal, and the times, too—they used to leave at 4am, but now it's closer to 8am, following improvements on what used to be a very bad *piste* between Igherm and Tata.

From Tiznit, buses leave for Tata daily at 4:30am and at 11am. The 11am bus starts at Agadir, however, and may well be full by the time it reaches Tiznit. If it is, you could probably catch it at BOU IZAKARN (where it lets off some passengers), by taking a *grand taxi* there from Tiznit. On weekdays, the buses run through Ifrane de l'Anti Atlas (see overpage), to collect the mail.

Traveling by **car** is feasible—though, as with all these routes, take along essential spare parts (and extra gas).

The Circuit: Taroudannt to Tiznit

Leaving Taroudannt, the road is at first flat and straight, passing through FREIJA (4–5km)—a small oasis and crumbling Kasbah—and the turnoff for TIOUTE (15km), similar to Freija, but on a slightly larger scale. It then begins to wind and climb into the stark **Anti-Atlas mountains**.

At **IGHERM** (93km) there's a Wednesday *souk,* where the bus will stop for a long break. Said to be known for its silver daggers and inlaid rifle butts, more than likely you'll just find an assortment of handmade copper pots and water urns. Igherm, now an administrative center with some new buildings to prove it, was a copper center for centuries, carrying on its long distance trade with the Saharan caravans. After the *souk* is over, it settles back to being a very hot and sluggish town. For the dedicated driver, *pistes* lead from here **to Tafraoute and Taliouine**, but both are in terrible condition. If you need a place to stay, there are **rooms** of a kind at the *Café de la Jeunesse* on the main street.

Tleta n'Tagmoute

TLETA N' TAGMOUTE, 30km past Igherm, is the most interesting village on the way to Tata. It springs out of the barren surroundings with a flash of life and disappears almost as suddenly a couple of bends down the road. There's a high, fortresslike **agadir** that's quite impressive, with clusters of palm trees below it. The village itself seems to climb right up the hillside.

Beyond Tleta n' Tagmoute the road continues paved for about 6km, then it becomes dirt *piste* (not too difficult for passenger cars). This is a long, slow stretch, but is made enjoyable by the amazing contours of the mountains, which twirl and twist from pink to gray-green, the sharply defined bands of rock varying from horizontal to vertical.

You eventually come out on the Tata–Bou Izakarn road and must turn left for Tata (5km). The last 20km of this road is newly paved.

Tata Oasis

TATA itself is a large, rambling oasis. Here, as in other southern oases, you notice the desert influence of black turbans and the darker complexion of the people. The women, who dress in black throughout the Anti-Atlas, here wear colorful, sari-like coverings.

On the long main street you'll find two **hotels**. Near the middle of it are the *Sahara* and the *Salam*. The latter, though a little dirty, is cheap and is located above a café that has a small kitchen—if you buy your own food, they will happily cook it for you for a few dirhams. There is also a 2*B hotel, the *Renaissance* (☎42), on the edge of town, on your left as you come in; they serve meals in the café-restaurant underneath. Another (unnamed and unrecommended) hotel is by the bus station. For anything else to eat, there's not much except for one small fried-fish stall. There is, however, a **bank** and a **post office**.

The **Tata oasis** is enticing enough, though frustrating in that its flatness means you can never get a true sense of its extent. You can wander around just for a look at it. Oases are all pretty much similar in some respects, yet each retains its own special character. In some of them people live in separate houses, enclosed by private plots, while others have clusters of dwellings with open, unwalled groves, crisscrossed by paths and irrigation ditches. Dates from the oasis here are sold at the **Thursday and Sunday souks** in Tata.

Buses from Tata run daily to Bou Izakarn and on to Tiznit and Agadir.

Akka, Some Rock Carvings, and Foum El Hassan

Continuing toward Tiznit, you pass through another large oasis, **AKKA**, which has a couple of cafés and a police checkpoint. It's said to have been one of the northern depots of the ancient caravan routes, but you wouldn't guess that by looking at it today. Some guidebooks speak of nearby prehistoric rock carvings (in the hills opposite Oum el Aoloine village); you would need a car and a lot of luck to find them, though.

However, there are more accessible **rock carvings** near Foum El Hassan, 80km farther. If you have a car, stop 23km before Foum and look for a break in the wall of rocks running parallel to the road, on your left (the south side). Walk through the break, turn left, and you'll find several carvings on the far side of this hill of rocks. Most are of antelopes or sheeplike animals, 15–30cm high, and dating roughly from 2000–500 B.C.

There are more carvings in **FOUM EL HASSAN** itself. The bus will pull up near a large traffic circle set in a wide open square. In the middle of the circle is a black, concrete structure meant to resemble a nomad's tent, and in front of it are a couple of carved rocks; the irony is that there used to be many more of them, but now they're encased forever in tons of black concrete.

Foum is basically a military post on the edge of an oasis. Some fighting with Polisario took place here several years ago, but everything's quiet now; there is, however, passport control. If you need a **room,** the only possibility is at the café on the right side of the square. Besides a couple of shops, there's very little else.

To see more **rock carvings**, in situ, head for the huge V in the mountains that rise up behind the town. A dirt road follows the valley and, after 4–5km, you should find some carvings. The best require a little climbing to get to, but are reputed to be the finest in Morocco. Pictures of elephants and rhinoceroses have been discovered, dating back thousands of years to the time when the Sahara was full of lakes and swamps. You can hire a guide if you wish. **Camping** is possible here in the valley and preferable to staying in the town.

Amtoudi/Id Aïssa

West from Foum El Hassan, in addition to the daily Tiznit bus, you may find some extra traffic for hitching on Wednesday, the **souk** day.

With your own transportation, it's worth taking **an excursion to Amtoudi** (or Id Aïssa, as it appears on most maps), reached by turning right 55km from Foum el Hassan and about 18km before TARHJIJT. Without a car, Amtoudi is hard to reach: in Tarhjijt, a small oasis village, you might find a *grand taxi* willing to take you; alternatively, try hitching on a Monday, when there is a market at SOUK TNINE D'ADAÏ, on the way to Amtoudi. If you do hitch, be sure to have enough provisions, since Amtoudi has just one very small shop and a lunch-only restaurant for visiting tour groups from Agadir.

The sight that brings tour groups to **AMTOUDI** is its **agadir**, one of the most spectacular and best preserved in North Africa. *Agadirs* are collective, fortified storehouses, where grain, dates, gunpowder, and other valuables were kept safe from marauding tribes. This one is built impressively on a pinnacle of rock. You can climb a long mule trail and walk around in the site, providing the *gardien* is there. Unfortunately, you're unlikely to be alone, despite the remoteness, because the *agadir* is firmly on the excursion route from Agadir (the city). You can avoid the midmorning rush of tourists easily enough, though. A walk up the palm filled gorge (where yet another imposing but decaying *agadir* is perched on top of the cliff) will bring you, after about 3km, to a spring and a waterfall. It is possible to **camp** near the riverbed.

Back on the main road, TARHJLJT signals a return to regular communications: there are fairly routine *grands taxis* toward Tiznit, and a couple of roadside cafés. In TIMOULAY, 26km farther, you should be able to pick up a *grand taxi* coming from Bou Izakarn and going to Ifrane de l'Anti-Atlas.

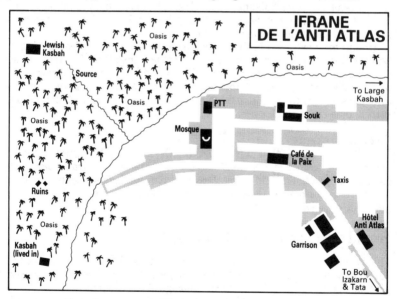

Ifrane de l'Anti-Atlas

Undoubtedly one of the most beautiful oases in the south, **IFRANE DE L'ANTI ATLAS** is a small Berber town, with three surrounding *douar* (each with its own Kasbah and endless walls) together with an administrative center containing a pink, fortlike barracks. The place is really out of the way and sees very few tourists—expect to be the object of attention and followed everywhere by the kids. However, if you can handle the isolation, Ifrane is a great place to stay, offering beautiful walks among the *douars,* springs, and ingenious water channels. There is a small, clean **hotel**, the *Anti-Atlas,* and a few cafés, one of which, *Café de la Paix,* has very nice rooms on the roof, with a balcony view looking out across the valley and distant oases. This café is perhaps also the best place to eat. A **Sunday souk** serves the surrounding villages and oases.

The town is the center of one of the oldest settled regions in Morocco. It was also among the last places in the south to convert to Islam—there were still Jewish and Christian Berber communities here in the twelfth century. Beyond the oasis of Ifrane and across the dry riverbed stand the ruins of the **old Jewish quarter**, the Mellah, which was supposedly settled in the sixth century B.C. by Jews fleeing persecution from King Nebuchadnezzar of Babylon. This particular history has yet to be substantiated, but it is certain that the Jewish community here goes back to pre-Islamic days. It endured up until the 1950s, when, as elsewhere in the south, there was a mass exodus to Israel and, to an extent, Morocco's northern cities, leaving the Mellah abandoned. A Berber family has since moved into one of the inhabitable houses, and a few of the other buildings remain partially intact; the rest, though, is a mass of crumbling walls. Local people recall their former Jewish neighbors as "good people" who kept mainly to themselves.

Around the next bend in the stony riverbed, and up the hill on the right, lies the Jewish **cemetery**. Broken tombstones, inscribed in Hebrew, lie strewn about. It's said that relatives still come here to visit the graves and burn candles in memory of the deceased. The Muslim past of Ifrane is evident as well, with white-domed tombs of saints and *marabouts* dotting the surrounding countryside.

On to Bou Izakarn

From Ifrane, it's just 14km to **BOU IZAKARN**, another administrative center and roadside town (several small hotels). Here, buses and *grands taxis* run routinely to Goulimine and Tiznit. Leaving from Bou Izakarn is also the best way to reach Tafraoute. (It is also possible—though unlikely to be easy—to get a ride on a truck from Ifrane to Tafraoute).

From Tata to Foum Zguid and Zagora

This is an even more remote journey than the "Tata loop," and strictly for the committed. At the time of writing, the route was open and could be traveled without a permit (a situation that could change at any moment).

From Tata, there are occasional trucks traveling over the 150km of rough *piste* to Foum Zguid. This is a rocky ride, not really practicable with anything less than four-wheel drive. The route runs through a wide valley, following the course of a seasonal river, amid some extremely bleak landscape, which is now and then punctuated by the occasional oasis and *ksour.* There are passport controls at TISSINT (halfway) and again as you approach **FOUM ZGUID**, a tiny place with a café (rooms, but not much to eat) opposite a welcome palmery and some *ksour.*

From Foum Zguid, there are *SATAS* **buses** three times a week (Tuesday, Thursday, and Saturday at 7am) to Ouarzazate—and on to Marrakesh. On the whole, we'd advise you to take these. However, a ride with a truck along some more very rough *piste* will get you to **Zagora** in seven or eight hours. This, again, is not suitable for light vehicles and the transportation here is a bit haphazard. The route also lacks most of the redeeming features of Tata–Foum, with no oases or villages to break the tedium of the trip.

Tiznit

Founded as late as 1882, when Sultan Moulay Hassan was undertaking a *harka*—a subjugation or (literally) "burning" raid—in the Souss and Anti-Atlas, **TIZNIT** still seems to signal a shift toward a desert, frontier-town mentality. To the west in the Anti-Atlas, the Chleuh Berbers suffered their first true occupation only with the bitter French "pacification" of the 1930s. To the south—admittedly quite some way to the south—the Moroccan government continues its traditional struggle to bring the Reguibat Touaregs under the control and administration of the state. The town bears the stamp of all this—huge *pisé* walls (over 5km in total), neat administrative streets, and a considerable garrison—but it's not such a bad staging point if (as is likely) you arrive here too late in the day to continue on to Tafraoute, Sidi Ifni, or Tata. There is, too, an exhilarating beach nearby at Sidi Moussa, where the surf and the fierce Atlantic currents have warded off all but the most limited development.

Practicalities

Arriving, buses or *grands taxis* will drop you in the **Mechouar**—the old parade ground, and now the main square—just inside the town walls. It's here that you'll find most of the facilities (bank, post office, bus offices) and all of the **cheap hotels**. The best one is the *Hôtel d'Atlas*, with a roof terrace overlooking the town; if that doesn't appeal to you, the *Hôtel Tiznit* (Rue de Tafoukt) is a slightly classier—2*A—alternative.

There are any number of **cafés** in and around the Mechouar, though things are slightly more animated (which isn't saying much) outside of the main gates, on Av. Mohammed V.

Around the Town

Tiznit is an important market center and holds a large **Thursday souk** (on the road to Tafraoute), but, otherwise, the promise of its walls turns out to be a little empty. There is, however, a certain fascination in realizing just how recent it all is—a traditional walled town built only a century ago—and it's interesting to see how the builders simply enclosed a number of existing *ksour* within their new street grid. Taking a brief loop through the town, start out at the **jewelry souk** (*Souk des Bijoutiers*), still an active crafts industry here despite the loss to Israel of the town's once large number of Jewish craftsmen. The jewelers are at the end of the main *souk* area: leaving the Mechouar on the side near the main gates, turn right one block before you reach the walls.

Going in the other direction from the Mechouar—to the right at the far end of the square—Rue de l'Hôpital winds around (past the hospital, over a stream, and up beside a cemetery) to the **Grand Mosque** and, next to it, the **Source Bleu de Lalla Tiznit.** The mosque has an unusual minaret, punctuated by a series of waterspouts, or perches, said to be an aid to the dead in climbing up to paradise. The *source,* resplendent on old postcards of the town, is dedicated to the town's patroness, a saint and former prostitute martyred on this spot (whereupon a spring miraculously appeared). In the summer at least, it is now profoundly unflattering to her.

Following the street on from here, you reach the north gate, **Bab Targua,** and the walls—take a right here and you can get up onto them, but it's a somewhat mournful vantage point, looking out as it does over decaying olive groves and an abandoned palmery.

Sidi Moussa d'Aglou

To get out to the beach at **SIDI MOUSSA D'AGLOU,** you'll have to negotiate a *grand taxi* from just outside the Mechouar (toward Av. Mohammed V). There is supposed to be a bus as well, but don't count on it. Hitching back into Tiznit isn't usually a problem.

The **beach,** 14km from Tiznit, along a barren, scrub lined road, is well worth the effort, though—it's an isolated expanse of sand, with a wild, body-breaking Atlantic surf (and with a dangerous undertow, too, so, be careful). There's no village as such at the beach itself, but walking around the headland to the right (as you face the sea), you come to a tiny **troglodyte fishing village**, its huts dug right into the rocks and surreal in its primitive austerity.

On a more practical level, there are a dozen or so ramshackle **cabins** for rent just to the left of the road as you come down to the beach, and, about 1500m farther down (along a track away from the beach), a **campground** with a **café** and a handful of rooms. To the right of the road, still under construction, is a new and larger campground, though this seems like a wildly optimistic gesture. Except in the middle of summer and around Christmas (when Moroccan families and migrant workers back from France come out here to camp), you're likely to be the only people around.

Moving On From Tiznit

A few details about **Tiznit's transportation.** All the private-line **buses** (three a day to Tafraoute—first and most direct at 6:30am; two to Sidi Ifni; four or five down toward Goulimine) leave from the Mechouar, as do the *SATAS* buses to Tata (at 4:30am and 7:30am) described in the previous section. *CTM* buses generally run from a gate called Bab Oulad Jarrar—200m away from the Mechouar, along the Agadir road (and just off the rotary and junction of the roads to Goulimine, Tafraoute, and Sidi Ifni).

Grands taxis toward Goulimine can be negotiated from outside the Mechouar, or by the road just past the rotary. For Tafraoute, there are **land-rover taxis** (it isn't always possible to get a seat, and the last one leaves at 4pm; about 35dh a place) which leave from a stop located between the new *Hôtel Tiznit* and the Thursday marketplace on the Tafraoute road (again, about 50m past the rotary).

Tafraoute

Approached by beautiful scenic roads through the Anti Atlas—from Tiznit or Agadir—**TAFRAOUTE** is worth all the effort and time it takes to reach. The town and its circle of villages built of stone are situated on the strange, wind eroded slopes of the Ameln Valley, shot through with pink and mauve-tinged bulbous fingers of granite, and enclosed by a jagged panorama of mountains—"like the badlands of South Dakota," as Paul Bowles put it, "writ on a grand scale." An alternative approach to Tafraoute (see below) is from Agadir, via Aït Baha.

The best time of all for a visit to Tafraoute is mid-February, in order to see the almond trees here in full blossom and to enjoy the accompanying **festival**. At any time of the year, though, a couple of days spent wandering around the Ameln is a rewarding experience, both in terms of the extraordinary physical features of the land, and in the interest its unique social system holds.

Among the Tafraouti villages, **emigration** to work in the successful grocery trade is a determining aspect of life. The men always return home to retire, building European looking villas amid the rocks, and most of the younger ones manage to come back for a month's vacation each year— whether it be from Casa, Tangier, Paris, or Belgium. But for much of the year, it is the women who run things in the valley, and the only men to be found are the old, the family supported, or the affluent. It is a system that seems to work well enough: enormously industrious, and very community minded, the *Tafraoutis* have managed to maintain their villages in spite of adverse economic conditions, importing all their foodstuffs except for a little barley, the famed Tafraouti almonds, and the bitter oil of the argan tree. Oddly enough, this way of life has exact parallels in Tunisia, with the people of Djerba; less surprisingly, both social structures developed through crisis and necessity. Between 1880 and 1882, this whole region was devastated by famine.

The Routes from Tiznit and Agadir

Both approaches to Tafraoute are rewarding, and you may well want to take advantage by coming in from Tiznit and leaving for Agadir, or vice versa. If you're doing just one, the Tiznit approach has a distinct edge, passing through a succession of gorges, and a grand mountain valley.

Tiznit to Tafraoute

The **road to Tafraoute from Tiznit** passes a succession of oasis-like villages, almost all of them named after the *souk* that they are host to (see *Basics* for explantion of the days). Most have cafés with the odd room— tempting bases for hiking.

Traveling along this road, hitching is unusually rewarding, as there are always Tafraouti emigrants returning in cars to visit their families.

Agadir/Inezgane to Tafraoute

The bus service along this route has been resumed, after being halted for a number of years. It runs from/to Inezgane (Agadir connections). The road is a bit drab between Agadir and Aït Baha, but the section from there to Tafraoute is a very scenic mountain ride, past a series of fortified villages. There is a confusing junction not far before you arrive at Tafraoute, with signs only in Arabic. Coming from Aït Baha, the road off to the left is to Ireherm, the right to Tafraoute.

AÏT BAHA, the largest village en route, is no great shakes: a characterless roadside halt, with a small hostel, two cafés, and very little shade. The buses generally make a stop here, for a tea.

Tafraoute: Some Practicalities

Tafraoute itself stands at the edge of a rambling palmery—quite unexpected after the approach of the last few kilometers. It is a small place, the administrative creation of the French; *Tafraoutis* generally prefer to stick to their villages or leave.

Arriving on the Tiznit road, you pass signs advertising the town's **campground**, a small and secure enclosure with good facilities; even if you decide not to stay, it can be worth a visit to arrange a ride when you come to leave the town.

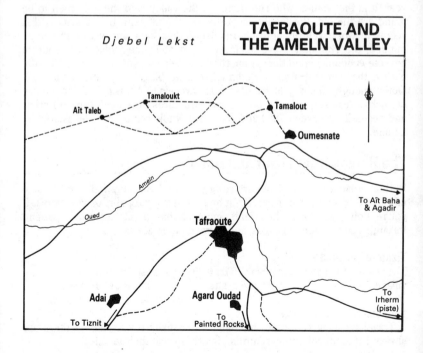

TAFRAOUTE AND THE AMELN VALLEY

Djebel Lekst

Tamaloukt

Aït Taleb

Tamalout

Oumesnate

Ameln

Oued

Tafraoute

To Aït Baha & Agadir

Adai

Agard Oudad

To Irherm (piste)

To Tiznit

To Painted Rocks

There are two modest, though unclassified, **hotels** near the bus station, close to the main square. There's little to choose between them. Most people seem to prefer staying at the *Hôtel Redouane* (☎66; clean rooms, hot showers, very relaxed and a friendly family), but eating at the *Hôtel Tanger*. There used to be a third hotel in the town, the *Salem*, but this disappeared when its gas refrigerator exploded; it's currently being rebuilt and will probably charge 2* prices when it reopens. The only alternative to these is the 4*B *Hôtel Les Amandiers* (☎8), ten minutes' walk up the hill above the center of town; built in mock-Kasbah style, it's a little unexciting (and its pool is rarely filled) but a good source for information on the nearby villages and festivals.

The best meals are, predictably enough, at *Les Amandiers*. In the town proper, and more suited to limited budgets, choose between the hotels *Redouane* and *Tanger*, the *Café Atlas*, and the *Restaurant l'Etoile du Sud*. The latter is a bit pretentious, with a tent done up for tourists, and a rather embarassing cabaret of music and belly dancing, but the food is excellent and reasonably priced.

Other facilities include a **hammam** (at the far end of town, in the direction of Tiznit: turn left where the bus stops); a PTT (8:30–noon and 2–6:30pm); and two **banks**. The *Banque Populaire* is open only on Wednesdays for the town's *souk*, but there's an inconspicuous branch of the *BMCE* on the road behind the PTT, with standard opening hours. Phone calls can be made from the Amandiers, when the PTT is closed; they charge 30 percent commission.

The Ameln Valley

You could spend days, if not weeks, wandering around the twenty-six villages of the **Ameln Valley**. Set against the backdrop of the rocks, they are all beautiful both from afar and closer up—with springs, irrigation systems, brightly painted houses, and mosques.

Oumesnat and a Northern Circuit

OUMESNAT, 7½km from Tafraoute town, is a good first objective. You can usually get a ride there (walking isn't advised: Tafraoute in the summer is *very* hot) or there's the occasional bus, since it's right off the road to Aït Baha and Agadir.

Like most Ameln settlements, the village emerges out of a startling green and purple rockscape, crouched against the rock walls of the valley, away from the arable land. It is accessible from the road only by crossing an intricate network of irrigation canals and market-vegetable plots. The houses, perched on the rocks above, from a distance seem to have sort of a bourgeois solidity to them—sensible blocks of stone, often three stories high, with parallel sets of windows. Close up, though, they seem bizarre, many of them built on top of older houses which have simply been deserted when they became too small or decrepit. Some of the houses, their rooms jutting out over the cliffs, are held up by enormous stilts and have raised doorways entered by short (and retractable) ladders.

From Oumesnat, you can walk through or above a series of villages all the way to **AÏT TALEB**, a meandering hike taking three to four hours. In the

---

THE BLUE ROCKS

In 1986 a French artist, **Alain Derain**, obtained permission from the Moroccan authorities to paint the rocks around Tafraoute. He had previously executed a similar project in Sinaï, so this was the development of a concept. Over the period since, the painted rocks have lost some of their sharpness of color, but they remain weird and wonderful, and should on all accounts be seen.

To reach Derain's canvas, you can ask anyone at Agard Oudad and a kid will be found to guide you to "Les Pierres Bleux." Alternatively, follow the road out to Agard Oudad until you reach the sign indicating the village. Here, turn onto a flat sandy piste, close to the base of the Chapeau de Napoleon (on your right). Follow this path for 4–5km, into a barren, flat land (a riverbed in winter), with rocky hills on either side. You pass a small house on your left, continue walking, and there they are—blue and red mountains, clusters of black and purple boulders, even some large technicolor rocks—all on a vast scale, and mesmerizing in effect.

Derain stayed in Tafraoute at the *Hôtel Redouane* and the family there will show you a coffee table book, detailing the project in its newly painted glory.

---

summer, though, this might prove to be more than enough—you can usually hitch back to town. To extend the circuit, you could keep on going to **ADAÏ**, looping back to Tafraoute along the Tiznit road.

Agard Oudad

A shorter but equally rewarding walk is to head south to **AGARD OUDAD** (3km from Tafraoute), a dramatic looking village built under a particularly bizarre outcrop of granite.

Like many of the rocks in this region, it has been given a name. Most of the others are of animals—people will point out their shapes to you—but this one is known (in good French-colonial tradition) as **Le Chapeau de Napoléon**. As if the rocks weren't weird enough, an even stranger sight awaits you to the south—in the form of Alain Derain's painted rocks (see box).

Elsewhere in the Valley and Beyond

Other possible excursions in the valley include **TAZAGHA**, about 2km past the Hôtel Amandiers, where there are some prehistoric paintings of gazelles—proof of the theory that the desert was once a fertile plain and home to many animals now no longer found. **AHEMUR** is also said to be beautiful, with its own *source bleu* (natural springwater pool).

With a car, a beautiful day's outing would be to drive southeast toward **SOUK EL HAD ARFALLAH IRHIR** (Sunday *Souk*), a route leading past a series of small oases that produce all kinds of fruit. Just taking in a part of this route is worth your while—follow the road past Agard Oudad for about 15km, then bear left when the *piste* comes to an end.

South Along the Coast: Sidi Ifni

SIDI IFNI is not the most obvious of tourist spots—empty, prone to lingering sea mist, and, all in all, extraordinarily wistful and melancholic. The town itself was relinquished by Spain only in 1969, after the Moroccan government closed off all landward access to the colonial enclave. The Spanish claim to Ifni dated from the Treaty of Tetouan (1860)—the culmination of Morocco's first military defeat by a European power in 200 years, and the start of its being carved up by the major colonial powers.

The harbor, once a thriving duty-free zone, is now more or less abandoned, and many of the old Spanish houses locked and left to decay. However, if the mood takes you, the town is rather wonderful. Built in 1934, on a site above the top of a cliff, it is full of sweeping Deco lines and elaborate ironwork: all in all, a unique memorial to colonialism and surely the only Art Deco military town ever built.

Approaching From Tiznit

The route down the coast from Tiznit passes, midway to Sidi Ifni, the roadside village of **MIRHLEFT**. There is a basic **hotel** here, the *Atlas*, and a couple of cafés, catering to the few groups of travelers who arrive for a stay by the sea—most often in the winter months. The beach is a kilometer from the village: a beautiful curve of sand, with crashing waves and (beware) strong currents. There are buses and *grands taxis* from Tiznit along this road.

Nearing Sidi Ifni, the road passes first through an extended Moroccan village, built across the valley from Ifni as a kind of rival garrison post. The Spanish town begins at the base of the hill beyond.

Sidi Ifni

Entering Sidi Ifni, a road leads off to the right, down to the sea and a reasonable **beach**; straight ahead, you wind around to the two main streets and **Place Hassan II** (the street signs here only partially reflect the change from its previous incarnation as *Plaza de España*).

The *plaza* is the heart of the town and immediately sets a tone for the place. An Andalusian garden and tiled fountain, perfect for the evening *paseo*, flank its center, while at one end stands a Spanish consulate—a building straight out of García Márquez, still open for business—and at the other, manically confused in its mixture of ideology and architecure, a church in Moorish-Deco style. More fine deco is to be seen in the post office, CTT in its Spanish form, and now severely underused; and in the monumental stairways, rambling down toward the port and beach.

Following these steps, below the square, you emerge at the main classified **hotel**, the 1*A *Hôtel Aït Ba Hamram* (☎51.73). Along the way, near the bottom of the steps, is the cheaper and steadily decaying *Hôtel Suerte Loca* ("Crazy Luck"), every bit a small-town Spanish fonda, with its bodega bar (no alcohol, though) and table soccer game.

The **best places to stay**, however, are either the *Hôtel Beau Rivage* (on the hill above—follow the signs) or the *Hôtel Bellevue* (1*A; ☎50.72), just off Place Hassan II. The latter is an amazing building, with loads of 1930s neon lights on the walls, welcoming, and good value. The *Beau Rivage*, friendly and cheap, is about the only place you'll find a meal, and it has a **bar**, too, which is pretty much the zenith of Ifni nightlife.

On Sundays, Sidi Ifni is host to a huge **souk**, complete with storytellers, musicians, and hundreds of donkeys.

Goulimine

GOULIMINE sounds great in the tourist brochures (and indeed in most other guides): the "Gateway to the Sahara," with its nomadic "blue men" and traditional camel market. The truth, though, is rather more mundane. True, the scenery is impressively bleak (liberal doses of it featured in both *Lawrence of Arabia* and *Mohammed, Messenger of God*), but the camel market is a sham, you're still far short of the Saharan dunes, and there are so many tourists bussed down from Agadir that the locals have begun to indulge in theatrical con games, bringing people out to see "genuine *hommes bleus*" in tents outside of town.

The one time that a visit to the town would be worthwhile in itself is if you could plan to coincide with one of Goulimine's annual **moussems**—when you really are likely to see Touareg nomads. It's difficult to get information about the exact dates of the *moussems*—they vary considerably from year to year—but, in general, there is usually one held in June at Asrir, 10km southeast of Goulimine; another, according to the local people, takes place in August, though the tourist board in Agadir do not seem to have any knowledge of it.

These apart, it is **the route down** that is the main attraction—best taken, at least in one direction, with a detour to Sidi Ifni (see above). Traveling on the inland route, the only place of any size that you pass is BOU IZAKARN, where the road to Ifrane and the Tata oases (see p.339) heads off east into the Anti-Atlas.

The Town, Accommodation, and Practicalities

The phoney camel market aside, Goulimine is a fairly standard administrative town—drawn out and somewhat shapeless, though with a distinctly desert feel to it, and with a couple of small, fairly animated *souks*.

The main street, **Av. Mohammed V**, is flanked at its top end by **Place Bir Nazarene**, where there is a **bank,** a **post office,** and (tucked in between this and the Grand Mosque) an excellent **hammam**. A five-minute walk down the hill takes you to the other—and livelier—square, **Place Hassan II**, the main commercial center of the town and the best place to eat. If you arrive by **bus**, you'll be let off just below this square; coming by **grand taxi**, you'll probably get out at the Nazarene.

Accommodation is limited in Goulimine, and prices at most of the hotels are hiked up every Friday night as tourists come into town for the camel market. The unclassified hotels are particularly bad offenders in this respect, and for this reason—as well as the fact that the most basic hotels are too small and crowded to cope with the summer heat—you might decide it's worth paying the extra money for a room at the 2*B *Hôtel Salam* (Route de Tan Tan, near Place Nazare; ☎20.57). This is the town's finest, and maintains a small bar.

Among the others, all on the Route de Tan Tan, or around the Nazarene, *Hôtel l'Ere Nouvelle* and *Hôtel de la Jeunesse* are marginally the best. Alternatively, for terrace space (without any water), you could try the *Café Alag* in Place Hassan II.

The **campground** is not much of an option—stony, exposed, and a walk of about 1200m from Place Hassan II (follow the signs; it's just below the military garrison).

The "Camel Market"

The most enduring impression of a trip to Goulimine's **Saturday "camel" market** are the lengths the local people have gone to in order to hide the fact that there hasn't been a real camel market here for years. What few camels there are have either been brought in just for show or to be sold off for meat. The market is held about a kilometer outside the town on the road to Tan Tan; it starts around 6am and a couple of hours later the first tourist buses arrive from Agadir, which to be honest makes the whole thing considerably more interesting.

Out to Some Oases

There's not much to do in Goulimine, but, to while away an afternoon, you might want to take a trip out to one of the **oases southeast of town**. This is easiest accomplished by car, though if you can get a group together, it's feasible to hire a grand taxi for the day. Be a little wary, though, of locals offering to drive you out on their mopeds. Stories circulate of some fairly unpleasant exploitation.

The largest and most spectacular oasis in the region is at **AÏT BOUKHA**, 17km from Goulimine (the final 7km on a *piste* from Asrir, where the oasis becomes visible). An opulent looking palmery, Boukha is a thriving agricultural community, little bothered by tourists or anything else. It has an especially lush strip along a canal, irrigated from the old riverbed and emerging from a flat expanse of sand; you might even see the odd herd of camels being grazed out here. To reach it, head for the thicket of palms about 2km behind the oasis (or pick up a guide on the way).

There are much smaller oases, closer to Goulimine, at **ABBAYNOU** and **IGUISSEL**, but these are both very much hustler territory, full of imitation "blue men" selling costume jewelry to tourists. In Abbaynou, there's a hot spring where you can have a swim, and a small *hôtel-camping*.

Into the Deep South

Few travelers venture south of Goulimine and on the surface there is little enough to commend the trip. The towns—**Tan Tan, Tarfaya, Laayoune**— are modern administrative centers, with no great intrinsic interest. The route, however, across vast tracts of *hammada*—bleak, stony desert—is another matter. The odd line of dunes unfolds on the horizon to the east, the ocean parallels much of the road to the west, and there is no mistaking that you have reached **the Sahara** proper.

An additional point of interest, now that the war with *Polisario* seems to be on the wane, is the attention being lavished on the region by the Moroccan authorities. The old Spanish Saharan colonial zone, reclaimed with the Green March in 1967, begins just to the north of Laayoune. **Laayoune** itself, never greatly regarded by the Spanish, is being transformed into a showcase capital for the new provinces, and there are major industrial plans, too, at **Tarfaya**. The region's current economic importance centers on the phosphate mines at **Boukra**, southeast of Laayoune, though these have not been greatly productive in recent years.

Note that throughout the former Spanish Saharan region, **Spanish** remains the dominant **second language**. Younger people and administrators, however, will generally speak good French.

SOUTH OF LAAYOUNE: The Saharan Provinces

Until 1987-88, any trip **south of Laayoune**, into the **former Spanish Sahara**, involved getting permission from the military authorities. The routes are today open quite routinely—indeed the Moroccan authorities are actively encouraging tourists to explore the region. There is a hotel complex under construction at Tan Tan, and a French *Club Med* vacation village already established at Laayoune.

The politics of the area are a highly sensitive matter in Morocco: so much so, that all maps and guides of the country must have the territory included as part of the Moroccan kingdom. Some background to the area is included in *Contexts*. The essential facts are that the old Spanish Southern Colonial Zone, sometimes referred to as the Western Sahara, was claimed and occupied by Morocco in 1976. The occupation was an enormously successful public relations exercise for King Hassan, who masterminded a **Green March** (*La Marche Verte*) into the territory by some 300,000 unarmed civilians. Territorial counterclaims, however, came almost immediately from Mauritania and from various groups among the indigenous Sahrawis. For the last decade, a war has raged on and off in the desert between the Moroccan army and authorities (who occupy and administer the entire former Spanish colony) and Algerian-backed *Polisario* guerrilla fighters, operating from bases around Tindouf, across the border in Algeria.

The war, which for a time affected areas within Morocco's "former" boundaries, has over the past few years largely been contained through the creation of an extraordinary "desert wall" (see *Contexts*), while in the meantime *Polisario* has increasingly turned to diplomacy to gather support. At present, there is only very sporadic fighting, around the wall, miles from any of the major routes. And with the rapprochement between Morocco and Algeria, there is genuine hope of a settlement. The UN are sponsoring talks about a long-discussed referendum amongst the population to choose between Moroccan or independent government. There seems little doubt, given the huge resources that the Moroccans have committed to their **Saharan Provinces**, that the territory will remain in the kingdom.

Given these somewhat uncertain factors, however, all travelers should check the most **up-to-date information** before attempting anything too ambitious in the region, and certainly before trying to take any road route into Mauritania (impossible at the time of writing). All the main road signs south of Agadir, however, now give the distances to Laayoune, Dakhla, and even Dakar.

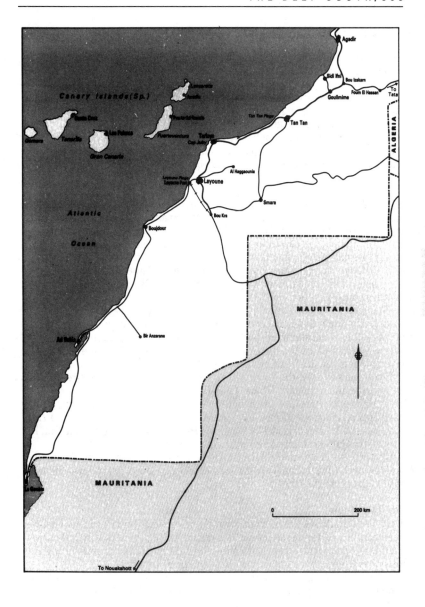

Goulimine to Tan Tan

The **approach from Goulimine to Tan Tan** runs along 125km of straight desert road, across a totally bleak area of *hammada*. By public transportation, you have a choice of either a **grand taxi** (leaving Goulimine from out on the Tan Tan road, toward the camel marketplace) or a **bus** (several daily, including express buses from Agadir).

There are no longer any military checkpoints north of Tan Tan, though when you arrive in town, you'll have to stop at the local *gendarmerie* to fill out a questionnaire, stating the purpose of your visit. This is a good place to inquire about the state of the roads south to Laayoune and beyond.

Tan Tan

Arriving at **TAN TAN**, you might find yourself wondering why you made the journey. Once the border crossing with the Spanish Sahara, it's now simply an administrative center, boosted in a very low-key way by its status as a duty-free zone (the stores are full of radios and electric razors) and by a string of small hotels, maintained for the families of troops on leave, and for long distance truck drivers. Tan Tan's one claim to fame is that it was a departure point for the famous **Green March** (*La Marche Verte)*, an event commemorated on postcards throughout the south.

The town has a population of around 50,000, many of them former nomads, who retain their distinctive pale blue robes. These are in evidence in the **souks**—the most animated part of a hot, sleepy town—as are a variety of *lithams*, strips of cotton to wrap around your head. The latter are a wise investment if you are heading farther south.

If you want to stay, there are five or six **hotels** and several café-restaurants around the main square, **Place Laayoune**, and several others nearby. The price differences are not great between one and another. The best, if they have space, are *Hôtel l'Etoile du Sahara* (17 Rue El Fida; ☎70.85) and *Hôtel Amgala*—both categorised 1*A—and the *Hôtel Dhakla* on Place Tan Tan. For a meal, try Café-Restaurant Le Jardin on Av. Mohammed V.

Grands taxis (possible to arrange to Laayoune, as well as Goulimine) operate out of Place Tan Tan; the **bus station** is about 200m down the main street, just off to the right.

Tan Tan Plage

TAN TAN PLAGE, 25km from town on the coastal route to Laayoune, has been earmarked for development as a resort. As yet, there is very little to see, even less to do, and nowhere to stay—but, if the weather hasn't brought in tons of seaweed, there's at least a chance to go swimming.

A four-star hotel, with tennis courts and swimming pool, and conference center, is **under construction**. Current facilities are limited to a pair of cafés.

A Loop Through Smara

Reports have come in of travelers making a loop **from Tan Tan along the new road to Smara,** returning by way of the P44 to LAAYOUNE, and from there over to Tan Tan via Tarfaya—a circuit of some 1000km.

There are gas stations in Tan Tan, Smara, and Laayoune—gas, incidentally, is subsidized throughout the Western Sahara—so if you embark on the trip be sure to fill up, and to carry good suplies of water. Between Tan Tan and Smara there is just one roadside hamlet, ABBTIH, with no facilities.

SMARA itself is basically a military garrison town, with scant remains of an earlier past as the base of Ma El Ainin, the "Blue Sultan", who controlled the region at the turn of the last century. There are two small and basic **hotels**, the *Erraha* and *Sakia El Houria*, on the main street, and a scattering of cafés. The **road east from the town**, towards the Algerian town of TINDOUF (where the *Polisario* have their main base), is firmly closed.

West from Smara, heading to Laayoune, you pass through one of the more fertile strips of the Western Sahara, along the vague oasis strip of the Seguiat Al Hamra. There are occasional nomadic tents to be seen. The road eventually joins with that from Laayoune to Boukra, 20km northwest of the latter.

BOUKRA is not really worth the detour: a mining town, with a large military garrison. South of Boukra is a militarily restricted zone. It is unlikely, though just feasible, that you will be allowed to continue to GUELTA ZEMMOUR and beyond, into Mauritania.

Completing the loop, **north to Laayoune**, the road from Boukra/Smara passes by the old Spanish fort of DCHIRA (off limits to all but the military) and the tiny oasis of LEMSEYED.

Tan Tan to Laayoune

The route between Tan Tan Plage and Laayoune is the most memorable stretch of the journey into the Deep South, cutting as it does between desert and ocean. The coast, somewhat defying expectations, is mainly cliff—the desert dropping directly away to the sea, with only the occasional stretch of beach.

Tarfaya

TARFAYA is a small roadside settlement, with a prominent monument to the Green March. It may, however, be in line for greater things if an oil shale development, currently under consideration by Shell, goes ahead.

For the moment it's a quiet place, probably not far different from its years as a staging post for the *Aeropostale Service*—when aviators such as Antoine St-Exupery used to rest up on their way down to West Africa. Oddly enough, the town was actually founded, at the end of the last century, by a British trader, and was originally known as Port Victoria. During the Spanish occupation, it was called VILLA BENS and served as very low-key capital for the "Southern Protectorate." Today it has been passed over by Laayoune, and has not even a hotel.

If you've got an interest in birdlife, you might find the Tarfaya area rewarding. The nearby **Khmiss Lagoon** is an important migratory site, maintained as a **bird sanctuary**. For most travelers, though, it is the sand desert south of Tarfaya, the **Erg Lakhbayta**, that is the most memorable feature. The drive to Laayoune takes about an hour by car or *grand taxi*.

Laayoune

With a population of 100,000, **LAAYOUNE** (AL AYOUN) is the largest and the most interesting town of the former Spanish Sahara. Its development as a provincial capital is almost immediately obvious—and impressive, as you survey the new 30,000-seat stadium, complete with real grass, maintained for the area's handful of soccer teams. There is in fact much new building throughout the town, and a few pleasant corners, like the landscaped gardens of the **Colline aux Oiseaux**, with their cages of exotic birds. Most striking of all, though, is the **Place du Mechouar**, beside the new Grand Mosque, with its exhibition hall devoted to photographs of the Green march.

There are two luxurious **hotels** in Laayoune, managed by the *Club Med* and on most occasions pretty much empty. The *Hôtel Parador* (Rue Okba Ben Nafia; ☎38.29) is the old Spanish state inn, and as good a place as any to hide away from the sun, if you can afford the rates. On a more budget level, try the 2*A *Hôtel Residencia* (Rue Prince Moulay Abdallah; ☎38.29) or 1*A *Hôtel Marhaba* (Avenue Hassan II). For food, choose between the café-restaurants or those in the two flash hotels.

On the practical front, Laayoune, rather incredibly, boasts an **ONMT** office (opposite the Parador), which can be a good source of information on the routes south from here; they can also arrange car rental (with or without driver). There are two **banks**: the *BMCE* (Rue Mohammed Zerktouni) and *Banque Populaire* (Av. Mohammed V). **RAM**, on Place Bir Anzarene (☎224.077), operates flights from the town airport (a short taxi ride east) to Agadir, the Canary Islands, and Ad Dakhla (3 a week).

LAAYOUNE PLAGE, 20km away, on the main road south, is a port for the region's phosphates, with a freight conveyor link to Boukra.

South from Laayoune

Depending on the military situation, you might be able to obtain permission to continue **south of Laayoune** down to Ad Dakhla. There are no buses, but if you're without a vehicle, it shouldn't be too hard to arrange a lift with a truck. The road is reputedly quite good, though take care of occasional sand-drifts, and camels grazing by or on the road. The sea is guarded by cliffs for most of the way to Boujdor.

The first stop along the road is at **LEMSID**, 110km, which, if you're not truly committed to travel for travel's sake, is perhaps the place to turn around. There is a small café at the settlement, providing basic meals to the route's truck drivers.

If you are determined, however, the route offers a brief stop at **BOUJDOR**, where you should expect to pass through a number of military checks. The landscape here is a little more mellow, with the village set by a lighthouse and fishing harbor. There is a gas station, and various cafés, though no official accommodation.

Finally, after another 322km drive south, you reach the town of **AD DAKHLA**, on a long spit of land. This was a Spanish outpost, Villa Cisneros, in the colonial days, and a minor administrative center for the Rio de Oro. It remains military in character, and once you have explained your presence, you should be prepared to mix largely with soldiers on leave. There are half a dozen basic **hotels**, cleanest of which is the *Hôtel Imlil* (in the center of town), a couple of **hammams**, and even a **bar**, *Bar Juan*, with real beers.

At present, **the road south of Ad Dakhla is closed** to all but military traffic. In theory, it might be possible to drive to LAGOURIA, the Moroccan frontier post with Mauritanian NOUADHIBOU.

t r a v e l   d e t a i l s

Buses

From Agadir Essaouira (6 daily; 3½ hr.); Taroudannt (4; 2½ hr.); Tiznit (4; 2 hr.); Goulimine (2; 4½ hr.); Marrakesh (5; Satas/*CTM* direct; 4 hr.); Tata (4am and 7am daily; 9 hr.); Casablanca (7:30pm; 5 hr.).

From Inezgane Marrakesh (4 daily; 3½ hr.); Goulimine (5; 4½ hr.); Taroudannt (4; 2 hr.); Taliouine/Ouarzazate (4; 3½ hr./5 hr.).

From Taroudannt Marrakesh via Tizi n'Test, (daily at 4am; 8½ hr.); Marrakesh, via Inezgane/Imi n'Tanoute (daily at 5am; 6 hr.); Taliouine/Ouarzazate (5 daily; 1½ hr./3 hr.); Tata (3 a week; 8–10 hr.).

From Tiznit Tafraoute (4 daily; 3½–6½ hr.); Goulimine (6; 2½ hr.); Sidi Ifni (2; 2½ hr.); Tata (2; 7 hr.).

From Tafraoute Agadir (4 daily; 5 hr.); Tiznit (3; 3 hr.).

From Goulimine Tan Tan (3 daily; 3 hr.).

Grands Taxis

From Agadir Shuttle to Inezgane (15 min.; 2dh); regularly to Oulad Teima* (1 hr.; connection to Taroudannt).

From Inezgane Regularly to Oulad Teima* (40 min.; connection to Taroudannt) and Tiznit (1½ hr.).

From Oulad Teima* Regularly to Taroudannt (1 hr.).

From Taroudannt Linked service, with changes, to Ouled Behril, Aoulouz and Taliouine.

From Tiznit Landrover taxis to Tafraoute (regular departures, but not always easy to get on; they stop running around 4pm; 2½ hr.) Regularly to Goulimine (2 hr.; sometimes with a connection at Bou Izarkan).

From Goulimine Regularly to Tan Tan (2¼ hr.).

**Oulad Teima* is also known as Quarante-Quatre—"44"—as it is 44km from Agadir.*

Ferries

From Agadir Weekly car/passenger ferry (Saturday, 7pm) to Las Palmas, Canary Islands (arrives Sunday, 5pm).

Flights

From Agadir Daily to Casablanca (and from there to Tangier, etc.); several times a week to Tan Tan, Laayoune, and Las Palmas (Canary Islands); 3 times a week to Ad Dakhla. International flights to London, etc., though not especially cheap if bought at this end.

From Tan Tan Most days to Laayoune.

From Laayoune Most days to Las Palmas (Canary Islands), Tan Tan, and Agadir.

From Ad Dhakla 3 times a week to Agadir.

TELEPHONE CODES

AGADIR ☎08	INEZGANE ☎08
GOULIMINE ☎087	TAN TAN ☎087

PART THREE

THE

CONTEXTS

THE HISTORICAL FRAMEWORK

Morocco's emergence as a "modern" nation-state is astonishingly recent, dating from the occupation of the country by the French and Spanish at the beginning of this century, and its subsequent independence in 1956. Prior to this, it is best seen as a kind of patchwork of tribes, whose shifting alliances and sporadic bids for power defined both the government and its extent.

With a handful of exceptions, the country's ruling sultans controlled only the plains, the coastal ports, and the regions around the imperial capitals of Fes, Marrakesh, Rabat, and Meknes. These were known as *Bled el Makhzen*—the governed lands, or, literally, "the Lands of the Storehouse." The rest of the Moroccan territories—the Rif, the three Atlas ranges, and the outlying deserts—comprised *Bled es Siba*, "the Lands of the Dissidents." Populated almost exclusively by Berbers, the original (pre-Arab) inhabitants, they were rarely recognized as being anything more than coming under local tribal authority.

The balance between government control and tribal independence is one of the two enduring themes of Moroccan history. The other is the emergence, expansion, and eventual replacement of the various **sultanate dynasties**. These at first seem dauntingly complicated—a succession of short-lived tribal movements and confusingly similar-named sultans—but there are actually just seven main groups.

The first of them, the **Idrissids**, became the model by founding the city of Fes toward the end of the eighth century and bringing a coalition of Berber and Arab forces under a central *makhzen* (government) authority. The last, the **Alaouites**, emerged in the mid-seventeenth century from the great palm oasis of Tafilalt and, continuing with the current king, Hassan II, still hold constitutional power. It is around these groups—together with the medieval dynasties of the **Almoravids, Almohads, Merenids, Wattasids** and **Saadians**—that the bulk of the following sections are organized.

PREHISTORY

The first inhabitants of the **Maghreb**—the Arab term for the countries of North Africa—probably occupied the **Sahara**, for thousands of years a great savanna fertile enough to support elephants, zebras, and a whole range of other game and wildlife. Little is known about these ancestors of the human species, although it seems likely that there were groups of hunter-and-gatherer hominids here as early as 1,000,000 B.C.

Around 15,000 B.C. there seem to have been **Paleolithic** settlements, and before the Sahara went into decline (from 3000 B.C.), primitive pastoral and agricultural systems had begun to develop. It is possible, too, to trace the arrival of two independent Stone-Age cultures in the Maghreb: the Neolithic **Capsian Man** (circa 10,000–5000 B.C.), probably emerging from Egypt, and slightly later, **Mouillian Man**. From these people, fair-skinned and speaking a remote "Libyan" language, stem the cave and rock drawings of the pre-Sahara and High Atlas, the earliest archaeological sites in Morocco.

PHOENICIANS AND CARTHAGINIANS

The recorded history of the area begins about 1100 B.C. with a series of trading settlements established by the **Phoenicians**. These were small, isolated colonies, usually built on defensible headlands around the coast, and there was probably little initial contact between them and the inhabitants of the interior, whom they knew as Libyans and Ethiopians—or collectively as *Barbaroi*, or **Berbers**.

As the emphasis shifted away from the Phoenicians themselves, and their African trading routes were taken over by the former colony of **Carthage** (modern Tunis), some of the ports grew into considerable cities, exporting grain and grapes, and minting their own coinage. On the "Moroccan" coast, the most important colonies were at Lixus (near Larache), Tingis (Tangier), and Chellah (near Rabat), but they spread as far east as Melilla; in the south a flourishing dye factory was also maintained on an island off Essaouira.

Officially, the Carthaginian empire collapsed with its defeat in the **Punic Wars** (196 B.C.) against Rome, but in these provincial outposts, life seems to have been little affected. If anything, the colonies grew in stature and prosperity, absorbing hundreds of Punic refugees after the Roman sacking of Carthage. It was a first sign of Morocco's intrinsic historic and geographic isolation in what was to become known as *Maghreb el-Aska* (The Land of the Farthest West). Even after the Romans had annexed and then abandoned the country, Punic was still widely spoken along the coast.

BERBER KINGDOMS AND ROMAN RULE

Prior to total Roman annexation, and the imposition of direct imperial rule in A.D. 24, the "civilized" Moroccan territories for a while formed the **Berber kingdom of Mauretania**. This was probably little more than a confederation of local tribes, centered around Volubilis (near Meknes) and Tangier, but it gained a certain influence through alliance, and occasional joint rule, with the adjoining Berber state of Numidia (essentially modern Algeria). The most important of the Berber rulers, and the only ones of which any substantial records survive, were **Juba II** (25 B.C.–A.D. 23) and his son **Ptolemy**. Both were heavily Romanized: Juba, an Algerian Berber by birth, was brought up and educated in Rome, where he married the daughter of Antony and Cleopatra. His reign, if limited in its extent, seems to have been orderly and prosperous, and under his son the pattern might well have continued. In A.D. 42, however, Emperor Caligula summoned Ptolemy to an audience in Lyons and had him assassinated—so the story goes—for appearing in a more brilliant cloak than his own. Whatever the truth, and it may just have been that Rome was eager for direct rule, it proved an inauspicious beginning.

ROMAN RULE

The early years of Rome's new imperial province were taken up with near constant **rebellions**—the first one alone needing three years and over 20,000 troops to subdue.

Perhaps discouraged by this unexpected resistance, the **Romans** never attempted to colonize Morocco-Mauretania beyond its old limits. The Rif and Atlas mountains were left

unpenetrated, and, of the interior, it was only **Volubilis**—already a city of sorts, and at the heart of the north's fertile vineyards and grain fields—that was in any way exploited. In this the Romans were establishing an enduring precedent: not just in their failure to subdue *Bled es Siba*, which also defied the later sultans, but also in their treatment of Morocco as a useful "corridor" to the greater agricultural wealth of Algeria, Tunisia, and Spain.

When the Roman legions were withdrawn in A.D. 253, and the **Vandals** took power in southern Spain, the latter were interested only in taking Tangier and Ceuta for use as staging posts en route to northern Tunisia. Similarly, the **Byzantine General Belisarius,** who defeated the Vandals and laid claim to the Maghreb for Justinian's Eastern Empire, did little more than replace the Ceuta garrison.

It was understandable, of course. Any attempt to control Morocco would need manpower far in excess of these armies, and the only overland route through the country—across the Taza gap—was scarcely practicable even in peacetime. Not until the tenth century, and the great northward expansion of the desert nomads, was Morocco to become a land worthy of substantial exploitation in its own right, and even then only through the unifying and evangelizing impetus of Islam.

THE COMING OF ISLAM

The irruption of **Islam** into the world began in A.D. 622, when the Prophet Muhammad moved with his followers from Mecca to Medina. Within thirty years they had reached the borders of India, to the east; were threatening Byzantine Constantinople, to the north; and had established themselves in the Maghreb at Kairouan in present-day Tunisia.

After this initial thrust, however, sweeping across the old provinces of the Roman world, the progress of the new religion was temporarily slowed. The Berbers of Algeria—mainly pagan but including communities of Christians and Jews—put up a strong and unusually unified resistance to Arab control. It was only in 680 that the governor of Kairouan, **Oqba Ibn Nafi**, made an initial foray into Morocco, taking in the process the last Byzantine stronghold at Ceuta.

What happened afterwards remains uncertain. There is a story, perhaps apocryphal, that

Oqba embarked on a 5000-kilometer **march through Morocco**, raiding and subjugating all in his path, and preaching Islam all the way to the west—the Atlantic Ocean. But whether this expedition had any real Islamizing influence on the Moroccan Berbers is unlikely. Oqba left no garrison forces and was himself killed in Algeria on his return to Kairouan.

Islam may have taken root among some of the tribes. In the early part of the eighth century, the new Arab governor of the West, **Moussa Ibn Nasr**, returned to Morocco and managed to establish Arab control (and carry out mass conversions to Islam) in both the northern plains and the pre-Sahara. Like the Romans and Byzantines before him, though, his main thrust was toward **Spain**. In 711, the first Muslim forces crossed over from Tangier to Tarifa and defeated the Visigoths in a single battle; within a decade the Moors had taken control of all but the remote Spanish mountains in northern Asturias; and their advance was only halted at the Pyrenees by the victory of Charles Martel at Poitiers in 732.

The bulk of this invading and occupying force were almost certainly **Berber converts** to Islam, and the sheer scale of their military success must have had enormous influence in turning Morocco itself into a largely Muslim nation. It was not at this stage, however, in any way an Arab one. The extent of the Islamic empire—from Persia to Morocco, and Ghana to Spain—was simply too great for Arab numbers. Early attempts to impose taxes on the Moroccan Berbers led to a rebellion and, once again outside the political mainstream, the Maghreb fragmented into a series of small, independent **principalities**.

THE IDRISSIDS (8TH–11TH c.)

This drift found an echo in the wider events of the Muslim world, which was undergoing its first—and most drastic—dissension, with the split into **Sunni** and **Shia** sects. In Damascus the Sunni Abbasid dynasty took power, the Shiites dispersing and seeking refuge both to the east and west.

One of them, arriving in Morocco around 787, was **Moulay Idriss**, an evidently charismatic leader and a direct descendant (great-grandson, in fact) of the Prophet Muhammad. He seems to have been adopted almost at once by the citizens of Volubilis—then still a vaguely Romanized city—and by the Aouraba Berber tribe. He was to survive for three more years, before being poisoned by order of the Sunni caliph, but in this time he managed to set up the infrastructure of an essentially Arab court and kingdom—the basis of what was to become the Moroccan nation. Its most important feature, enduring to the present with Hassan II, was his being recognized as *Imam*. To the Moroccans this meant that he was both spiritual and political leader, "Commander of the Faithful" in every aspect of their lives.

Despite the brevity of Moulay Idriss's reign, and his sudden death in 791 or 792, his successors, the **Idrissids**, were to become the first recognizable Moroccan dynasty. Moulay Idriss himself left a son, born posthumously to a Berber woman, and in 807, after a period of an apparently orderly regency, **Moulay Idriss II** was declared sultan and *imam*. He ruled for a little over twenty years—something of a golden age for the emerging Moroccan state, with the extension of a central, Arabized authority throughout the north and even to the oases beyond the Atlas.

Idriss's most important achievement, however, was the establishment (if perhaps not the foundation) of the city of **Fes**. Here, he set up the apparatus of court government, and here he also welcomed large contingents of Shiite **refugees**. Most prominent among these were groups from Córdoba and Kairouan, then the two great cities of western Islam. In incorporating them, Fes (and, by extension, Morocco) became increasingly Arabized, and was suddenly projected into being a major center in its own right. The **Kairaouine University** was established, becoming one of the three most important in Islam (and far ahead of those in Europe); a strong crafts tradition took root; and Fes became a vital link in the trade between Spain and the East, and between the Maghreb and Africa south of the Sahara.

Fes was to remain the major Moroccan city, and the country's Arab spiritual heart, right up until the present century. The Idrissid state, however, fragmented again into **principalities**, most of which returned to their old isolation, until, at the turn of the tenth century, the context began to change. In al-Andalus—the Muslim territories of Spain—the Western Caliphate collapsed and itself splintered into small rival states. In Tunisia, the well-established Fatimid dynasty moved their capital to Egypt, clashed with their nominated governors, the Zirids, and unleashed on them the hostile nomadic tribe of the Banu Hilal.

It was a move which was to have devastating effects on the Maghreb's entire lifestyle and ecological balance, as the **Hilali** nomads swept westwards, destroying all in their path, bringing to ruin the irrigation systems, and devastating the agricultural lands with their goats and other flocks. The medieval Maghrebi historian, Ibn Khaldun, described their progress as being like a swarm of locusts: "the very earth seems to have changed its nature," he wrote, "all the lands that the Arabs have conquered in the last few centuries, civilization and population have departed from them."

THE ALMORAVIDS (1062–1145)

Morocco was to some extent cushioned from the Hilali, and by the time they reached its southern oases (where they settled), the worst was probably over. But with the shattered social order of the Maghreb, and shifting power struggles in Spain, came an obvious vacuum of power.

It was this which created the opportunity for the two great Berber dynasties of the Middle Ages—the **Almoravids** and the **Almohads**. Both were to emerge from the south, and in each case their motivating force was religious, a purifying zeal to **reform** or destroy the decadent ways which had reached Morocco from the wealthy Andalusian Muslims of Spain. The two dynasties together lasted only a century and a half, but in this period Morocco was preeminent in all of western Islam, maintaining an empire that at its peak stretched right across the Maghreb to Libya, south to Senegal and Ghana, and north into Spain. Subsequent history and achievements never matched up to this imperial dream, though even today its memories are part of the Moroccan concept of nation. **"Greater Morocco,"** the nationalist goal of the late 1950s, sketched out areas that took in Mauritania, Algeria, Tunisia, and Libya, while even the present war in the Sahara looks back to the reality of the medieval empires.

The **Almoravids**, the first of these dynasties, began as a reforming movement among the Sanhaja Berbers in what is now Mauritania. A nomadic desert tribe—similar to the Touaregs who occupy the area today—they had been converted to Islam in the ninth century, but perhaps only to nominal effect. The founders of the movement, a local sheikh who had returned from the pilgrimage to Mecca and a *fakir* from the Souss plain, found widespread abuse of orthodox practice. In particular, they preached against drinking palm wine, playing licentious music, and taking more than four wives. It seemed like a message unlikely to captivate an already ascetic, tent-living people, but it rapidly took hold.

Founding a *ribat*—a kind of warrior monastery similar to the European Templar castles, and from which the movement takes its name—they soon gained a following and considerable military force. In 1054, they set out from the *ribat* to spread the message through a *jihad* (holy war), and within four years they had gained control of Ghana to the south. Turning toward Morocco, they established themselves in Marrakesh by 1062, and, under the leadership of **Youssef bin Tachfine**, went on to extend their rule throughout the north of Morocco and, to the east, as far as Algiers.

At no time before had any one leader exercised such strong control over these territories, uniting the tribes for the first time under a single religious doctrine—a simple, rigorous, and puritanical form of Sunni orthodoxy. And so it remained, at least as long as the impetus of *jihad* was sustained. In 1085, Youssef undertook his first, and possibly reluctant, expedition to **Spain**, invited by the Muslim princes of **al-Andalus** after the fall of Toledo to the Christians. He crossed over the straits again in 1090, this time to take control of Spain himself. In this he was successful, and before his death in 1107, he had restored Muslim control to Valencia and other territories lost in the first wave of the Christian Reconquest.

The new Spanish territories had two decisive effects. The first was to reorient Moroccan culture toward the far more sophisticated and affluent Andalusian civilization; the second to stretch the Almoravid forces too thin. Both were to contribute to the dynasty's decline. Youssef, disgusted by Andalusian decadence, had ruled largely from **Marrakesh**, leaving his governors in Seville and other cities. After his death, the Andalusians proved disinclined to accept these foreign overlords, while the Moroccans themselves became vulnerable to charges of being corrupt and departing from their puritan ideals.

Youssef's son **Ali** was, in fact, extraordinarily pious, but, unprepared for (and disinterested in) ceaseless military activity, he was forced to use Christian mercenaries to maintain control. His reign, and that of the Almoravids, was effectively finished by the early 1140s, as a new movement, the Almohads, seized control of the main Moroccan cities one after another.

THE ALMOHADS (1145-1248)

Ironically, the **Almohads** shared much in common with their predecessors. Again, they were forged from the Berber tribes—this time in the High Atlas—and again, they based their bid for power on an intense puritanism. Their founder **Ibn Toumert,** attacked the Almoravids for allowing their women to ride horses (a tradition in the desert), for wearing extravagant clothes, and for being subject to what may have been Andalusian corruptions—the revived use of music and wine.

He also provoked a **theological crisis**, claiming that the Almoravids did not recognize the essential unitary and unknowable nature of God: the basis of Almohad belief, and the source of their name—the "unitarians." Banished from Marrakesh by Ali, Ibn Toumert set up a *ribat* in the Atlas at **Tin Mal**. Here he waged war on local tribes until they would accept his authority, and eventually revealed himself to them as the Mahdi—"the chosen one" and the final prophet promised in the Koran.

Charismatic, and brutal in his methods, Toumert was aided by a shrewd assistant and brilliant military leader, **Abd el Moumen**, who took over the movement after his death and extended the radius of their raids. In 1145, he was strong enough to displace the Almoravids from Fes, and two years later he drove them from their stronghold in Marrakesh. With the two cities subdued, he was now effectively sultan.

Resistance subsided and once again a Moroccan dynasty moved **toward Spain**—this time finally secured by the third Almohad sultan, **Yacoub el Mansour** (The Victorious),

who in 1195 defeated the Christians at Alarcos. El Mansour also pushed the frontiers of the empire east to Tripoli, and for the first time, there was one single rule across the entire Maghreb. With the ensuing wealth and prestige, he launched a new building program—the first and most ambitious in Moroccan history—which included a new capital in Rabat and the magnificent gateways and minarets of Marrakesh and Seville.

Once more, however, imperial expansion precipitated disintegration. In 1212, Yacoub's successor, **Mohammed en Nasr,** attempted to drive the Spanish Christians as far back as the Pyrenees and met with decisive defeat at the battle of **Las Navas de Tolosa**. The balance was changing, and within four decades, only the Kingdom of Granada remained in Spanish Muslim hands. In the Maghreb, meanwhile, the eastern provinces had declared independence from Almohad rule and Morocco itself was returning to the authority of local tribes. In 1248, one of these, the **Merenids** (or Beni Merin), took the northern capital of Fes and turned toward Marrakesh.

THE MERENIDS AND WATTASIDS (1248-1554)

This last (300-year) period of Berber rule in Morocco is very much a tailpiece to the Almoravid and Almohad empires—marked by increasing domestic **instability** and economic stagnation, and signaling also the beginning of Morocco's **isolation** from both the European and Muslim worlds. The Spanish territories were not regained, and Granada, the last Moorish city, fell to Ferdinand and Isabella in 1492. Portuguese sea power saw to it that foreign seaports were established on the Atlantic and Mediterranean coasts. To the east, the rest of the Maghreb fell under Turkish domination, as part of the Ottoman Empire.

In Morocco itself, the main development was a centralized administrative system—the **Makhzen**—which was maintained without tribal support by standing armies of Arab and Christian mercenaries. It is to this age that the real distinction of *Bled el Makhzen* and *Bled es Siba* belongs—the latter coming to mean everything outside the immediate vicinities of the imperial cities.

THE MERENIDS

Perhaps with this background it is not surprising that few of the twenty-one **Merenid sultans**—or their cousins and successors, the Wattasids—made any great impression. The early sultans were occupied mainly with Spain, at first in trying to regain a foothold on the coast, later with shoring up the Kingdom of Granada. There were minor successes in the fourteenth century under the "Black Sultan," **Abou el Hassan**, who for a time occupied Tunis, but he was to die before being able to launch a planned major invasion of al-Andalus, and his son, **Abou Inan**, himself fell victim to the power struggles within the mercenary army.

The thirteenth and fourteenth centuries, however, did leave a considerable **legacy of building**, perhaps in defiance of the lack of political progress (and certainly a product of the move toward government by forced taxation). In 1279, the garrison town of Fes el Djedid was established, to be followed by a series of brilliantly endowed colleges, or *medersas*, which are among the finest surviving Moorish monuments. Culture, too, saw a final flourishing. The historians Ibn Khaldun and Leo Africanus and the traveling chronicler Ibn Battuta all studied in Fes under Merenid patronage.

THE WATTASIDS

The **Wattasids**, who usurped Merenid power in 1465, had ruled in effect for 45 years previously as a line of hereditary viziers. They maintained a semblance of control for a little under a century, though the extent of the *Makhzen* lands was by now minimal.

The Portuguese had annexed and colonized the seaports of Tetouan, Ceuta, Tangier, Asilah, Agadir, and Safi, while large tracts of the interior lay in the hands of religious warrior brotherhoods, or *marabouts*, on whose alliances the sultans had increasingly to depend.

THE SAADIANS AND CIVIL WAR (1554–1669)

The rise and fall of the **Saadians** was in some respects an abridged version of all of the dynasties that had come before them. They were the most important of the *marabouts* to emerge in the early years of the sixteenth century, rising to power on the strength of their religious positions (they were *Shereefs*—descendants of the Prophet), climaxing in a single, particularly distinguished reign, and declining amid a chaos of political assassinations, bitter factional strife, and, in the end, civil war.

As the first Arab dynasty since the Idrissids, they mark the end (to date) of Moroccan Berber rule, though this was probably less significant at the time than the fact that theirs was a government with no tribal basis. The *Makhzen* had to be even further extended than under the Merenids, and Turkish guards—a new point of intrigue—were added to the imperial armies.

Slower to establish themselves than the preceding dynasties, the Saadians began by setting up a small principality in the **Souss**, where they established their first capital in Taroudannt. Normally, this would have formed a regular part of *Bled el Makhzen*, but the absence of government in the south allowed them to extend their power to **Marrakesh** around 1520, with the Wattasids for a time retaining Fes and ruling the north.

In the following decades the Saadians made breakthroughs along the coast, capturing Agadir in 1540, and driving the Portuguese from Safi and Essaouira. When the Wattasids fell into bankruptcy and invited the Turks into Fes, the Saadians were ready to consolidate their power. This proved harder, and more confusing, than anyone might have expected. **Mohammed esh Sheikh**, the first Saadian sultan to control both the southern and northern kingdoms, was himself soon using Turkish troops, and was, in fact, assassinated by a group of them in 1557. His death unleashed an incredibly convoluted sequence of factional murder and power politics, which was only resolved, somewhat fortuitously, by a battle with the Portuguese twenty years later.

THE BATTLE OF THE THREE KINGS

This event, **The Battle of the Three Kings,** was essentially a Portuguese crusade, led by the youthful King Sebastião on the nominal behalf of a deposed Saadian king against his uncle and rival. At the end of the day, all three were to perish on the battlefield, the Portuguese having suffered a crushing defeat, and a little-known Saadian prince emerged as the sole acknowledged ruler of Morocco.

His name was **Ahmed "el Mansour"** (The Victorious), following this momentous victory, and he was easily the most impressive sultan of the dynasty. Not only did he begin his reign clear of the intrigue and rivalry that had dogged his predecessors, but he was immensely wealthy as well. Portuguese ransoms paid for the remnants of their nobility after the battle had been enormous, causing Portugal to go bankrupt—the country, with its remaining Moroccan enclaves, then passed under the control of Habsburg Spain.

Breaking with tradition, Ahmed himself became actively involved in European politics, generally supporting the Protestant north against the Spanish, and encouraging Dutch and British trade. Within Morocco he was able to maintain a reasonable level of order and peace, and diverted criticism of his use of Turkish troops (and his own Turkish-educated ways) by embarking on an **invasion of Timbuktu** and the south. This secured control of the Saharan salt mines and the gold and slave routes from Senegal, each sources of phenomenal wealth, which won him the additional epithet of *El Dhahabi* (The Golden One). It also reduced his need to tax Moroccans, which made him a popular man.

CIVIL WAR

Ahmed's death in 1603 caused abrupt and lasting chaos. He left three sons, none of whom could gain authority, and, split by **civil war**, the country once again broke into a number of principalities. A succession of **Saadian rulers** retained power in the Souss and in Marrakesh (where their tombs remain testimony to the opulence and turbulence of the age); another *marabout* force, the **Djila**, gained control of Fes; while around Salé and Rabat arose the bizarre **Republic of the Bou Regreg**.

The Bou Regreg depended almost entirely on **piracy**, a new development in Morocco, though well established along the Mediterranean coasts of Algeria and Tunisia. Its practitioners were the last Moors to be expelled from Spain—mainly from Granada and Badajoz—and they conducted a looting war against primarily Spanish shipping. For a time they met with astounding success, raiding as far away as the Irish coast, dealing in arms with the British and the French, and even accrediting foreign consuls.

MOULAY ISMAIL AND THE EARLY ALAOUITES (1665–1822)

Like the Saadians, the **Alaouites** were *shereefs*, first establishing themselves as religious leaders—this time in Rissani in the **Tafilalt**. The struggle to establish their power also followed a similar pattern, spreading first to Taza and Fes, and finally, under Sultan **Moulay Rashid**, reaching Marrakesh in 1669. Rashid, however, was unable to enjoy the fruits of his labor, since he was assassinated in a particularly bloody palace coup in 1672. It was only with Moulay Ismail, the ablest of his rival sons, that an Alaouite leader gained real control over the country.

MOULAY ISMAIL

The reign of **Moulay Ismail**, perhaps the most notorious in all of Morocco's history, stretched over 55 years (1672–1727) and was to be the country's last stab at imperial glory. In Morocco, where his shrine in Meknes is still an object of pilgrimage, he is remembered as a great and just, if unusually ruthless, ruler; to contemporary Europeans—and in subsequent historical accounts—he is noted more for his extravagant cruelty. His rule certainly was tyrannical, with arbitrary killings and an appalling treatment of his slaves, but perhaps it was not much worse than that of the European nations of the day. The seventeenth century was the age of the witch trials in Protestant Europe, and of the Catholic Inquisition.

Nevertheless, Moulay Ismail stands out among the Alaouites because of the grandness of the scale on which he acted. At **Meknes**, which he made his new imperial capital, he garrisoned a permanent army of some 140,000 black troops, a legendary guard he had built up personally through slaving expeditions in Mauretania and the south, as well as by starting a human breeding program. The army kept order throughout the kingdom—Morocco is today still littered with their Kasbahs—and were able to raise taxes as required. The Bou Regreg pirates, too (the so-called Sallee Rovers), were brought under the control of the state, along with their increasingly lucrative revenues.

With all this, Ismail was able to build a palace in Meknes that was the rival of its contemporary, Versailles, and he negotiated on equal terms with the **Europeans**. Indeed, it was probably the reputation he established for Morocco that allowed the country to remain free for another century and a half before the European colonial powers began carving it up.

SIDI MOHAMMED AND MOULAY SLIMANE

Like all the great, long-reigning Moroccan sultans, Moulay Ismail left innumerable sons and a terminal dispute for the throne, with the powerful standing army supporting and dropping heirs at will.

Remarkably, a capable ruler did emerge fairly soon—Sultan **Sidi Mohammed**—and for a while it appeared that the Shereefian empire was moving back into the mainstream of European and world events. Mohammed retook El Jadida from the Portuguese, founded the port of Essaouira, traded and conducted treaties with the Europeans, and even recognized the **United States of America**—one of the first rulers to do so.

At his death in 1790, however, the state collapsed into civil war, the two capitals of Fes and Marrakesh in turn promoting claimants to the throne. When this period drew to some kind of a close, with **Moulay Slimane** (1792–1822) asserting his authority in both cities, there was little left to govern. The army had dispersed; the *Bled es Siba* reasserted its old limits; and in Europe, with the ending of the Napoleonic wars, Britain, France, Spain, and Germany were all looking to establish themselves in Africa.

Moualy Slimane's rule was increasingly isolated from the new realities outside Morocco. An intensely orthodox Muslim, he concentrated the efforts of government on eliminating the power and influence of the Sufi brotherhoods—a power he underestimated. In 1818 the Berber tribes loyal to the Derakaoui brotherhood rebelled and, temporarily, captured the Sultan. Subsequently, the sultans had no choice but to govern with the cooperation of local sheiks and brotherhood leaders.

Even more serious, at least in its long term effects, was Moulay Slimane's attitude towards **Europe**, and in particular to Napoleonic France. Exports were banned; European consuls banished to Tangier; and contacts which might have helped maintain Moroccan independence were lost.

MOULAY HASSAN AND EUROPEAN DOMINATION

Once started, the European domination of Moroccan affairs took on an inevitable course—with an outdated, medieval form of government, virtual bankruptcy, and armies press-ganged from the tribes to secure taxes, there was little that could be done to resist it.

The first pressures came from the **French**, who defeated the Ottomans in 1830 and occupied Algiers. Called to defend his fellow Muslims, Sultan **Abd er Rahman** (1822–59) mustered a force but was severely defeated at Isly. In the following reign of **Mohammed III** (1859–73), **Spanish** aspirations were also established with the occupation of Tetouan—regained by the Moroccans only after the offer to pay the Spanish massive indemnities and provide them with an Atlantic port (which Spain later claimed in Sidi Ifni).

MOULAY HASSAN

Outright occupation and colonization were by the end of the nineteenth century proving more difficult to justify, but both the French and the Spanish had learned to use every opportunity to step in and "protect" their own nationals. Complaints by Moulay Hassan, the last pre-Colonial sultan to have any real power, actually led to a debate on this issue at the 1880 **Madrid Conference**, but the effect was only to regularize the practice on a wider scale, beginning with the setting up of an "international administration" in Tangier.

Moulay Hassan could, in other circumstances, have proved an effective and possibly inspired sultan. Acceding to the throne in 1873, he embarked on an ambitious series of modernizing **reforms**, including attempts to stabilize the currency by minting the *rial* in Paris, to bring in more rational forms of taxation, and to retrain the army under the instruction of Turkish and Egyptian officers. The times, however, were against him. He found the social and monetary reforms obstructed by foreign merchants and local *caids*, while the European powers forced him to abandon the plans for other Muslim states' involvement in the army.

He played off the Europeans as best he could, employing a British military chief of staff, Caid MacClean, a French military mission, and German arms manufacturers. On the frontiers, he built kasbahs to strengthen the defences at Tiznit, Saïdia, and Selouane. But the government had few modern means of raising money to pay for these developments. Moulay Hassan was thrown back on the traditional means of taxation, the *harka*, setting out across the country to subdue the tribes and to collect tribute. In 1894, returning across the Atlas on just such a campaign, he died.

THE LAST SULTANS

The last years of independent rule under Moulay Hassan's sons, Moulay Abd el Aziz and Moulay Hafid, were increasingly dominated by Europe.

The reign of **Abd el Aziz** (1894–1907), in particular, signaled an end to the possibilities of a modern, independent state raised by his reforming father. The sultan was just a boy of ten at his accession, but for the first six years of his rule the country was kept in at least a semblance of order by his father's vizier, Bou Ahmed. In 1900, however, Bou Ahmed died, and Abd el Aziz was left to govern alone—surrounded by an assembly of Europeans, preying on the remaining wealth of the court.

The first years of Morocco's twentieth-century history were marked by a return to the old ways. In the Atlas mountains, the tribal chiefs established ever-increasing powers, outside of the government domain. In the Rif, a pretender to the throne, **Bou Hamra**, led a five-year revolt, coming close to taking control of Fes and the northern seat of government.

European manipulation during this period was remorselessly cynical. In 1904, the French negotiated agreements on "spheres of influence" with the British (who were to hold Egypt and Cyprus), and with the Italians (who got Tripolitana, or Libya). The following year saw the German Kaiser Wilhelm visiting Tangier and swearing to protect Morocco's integrity, but he was later bought off with the chance to "develop" the Congo. France and Spain, meanwhile, had reached a secret arrangement on how they were going to divide Morocco and were simply waiting for the critical moment.

In 1907, the French moved troops into **Oujda**, on the Algerian border, and, after a mob attack on French construction workers, into Casablanca. Abd el Aziz was eventually deposed by his brother, Moulay Hafid (1907–12), in a last attempt to resist the European advance. His reign began with a coalition with the principal Atlas chieftain, Madani el Glaoui,

and intentions to take military action against the French. The new sultan, however, was at first preoccupied with putting down the revolt of Bou Hamra—whom he succeeded in capturing in 1909. By this time the moment for defense against European entrenchment, if indeed it had ever been possible, had passed. Claiming to protect their nationals—this time in the mineral mines of the Rif—the Spanish brought over 90,000 men to garrison their established port in Melilla. Colonial occupation, in effect, had begun.

THE TREATY OF FES

Finally, in 1910, the two strands of Moroccan dissidence and European aggression came together. Moulay Hafid was driven into the hands of the French by the appearance of a new pretender in Meknes—one of a number during that period—and, with Berber tribesmen under the walls of his capital in Fes, was forced to accept their terms.

These were ratified and signed as the **Treaty of Fes** in 1912, and gave the French the right to defend Morocco, represent it abroad, and conquer the *Bled es Siba*. A similar document was also signed by the Spanish, who were to take control of a strip of territory along the northern coast, with its capital in Tetouan and another thinner strip of land in the south, running eastwards from Tarfaya. In between, with the exception of a small Spanish enclave in Sidi Ifni, was to be French Morocco. A separate agreement gave Spain colonial rights to the Sahara, stretching south from Tarfaya to the borders of French Mauritania. The arbitrary way in which these boundaries were drawn was to have a profound effect on modern Moroccan history. When Moroccan nationalists laid claim to the Sahara in the 1950s—and to large stretches of Mauritania, Algeria, and even Mali—they based their case on the obvious artificiality of colonial divisions.

THE FRENCH AND SPANISH PROTECTORATES (1912–56)

The fates of **Spanish and French Morocco** under colonial rule were to be very different. When **France** signed its protectorate agreement with the sultan in 1912, its sense of **colonial mission** was running high. The colonial lobby in France argued that the colonies were vital not only as markets for French goods and as symbols of France's greatness, but also because they fulfilled France's *"mission civilisatrice"*—to bring the benefits of French culture and language to all corners of the globe.

There may have been Spaniards who had similar conceptions of their role in North Africa, but reality was very different. **Spain** showed no interest in developing the Sahara until the 1960s; in the north the Spanish saw themselves as conquerors, more than colonists. Its government there, described by one contemporary as a mixture of "battlefield, tavern, and brothel," did much to provoke the Rif rebellions of the 1920s.

LYAUTEY AND "PACIFICATION"

France's first resident general in Morocco was **General Hubert Lyautey**, often held up as the ideal of French colonialism with his stated policy: "Do not offend a single tradition, do not change a single habit." Lyautey recommended respect for the terms of the protectorate agreement, which placed strict limits on French interference in Moroccan affairs. He recognized the existence of a functioning Moroccan bureaucracy based on the sultan's court with which the French could cooperate—a hierarchy of officials, with diplomatic representation abroad, and with its own social institutions.

But there were other forces at work: French soldiers were busy unifying the country, ending tribal rebellion; in their wake came a system of roads and railroads that opened the country to further colonial exploitation. For the first time in Moroccan history, the central government exerted permanent control over the mountain regions. The **"pacification"** of the country brought a flood of French settlers and administrators.

In France these developments were presented as echoing the history of the opening up of the American Wild West. Innumerable articles celebrated "the transformation taking place, the stupendous development of Casablanca port, the birth of new towns, the construction of roads and dams . . . The image of the virgin lands in Morocco is contrasted often with metropolitan France, wrapped up in its history and its routines. . . ."

Naturally, the interests of the natives were submerged in this rapid economic development, and the restrictions of the protectorate agreement were increasingly ignored.

SPAIN AND THE REVOLT IN THE RIF

The early history of the **Spanish zone** was strikingly different. Before 1920 Spanish influence outside the main cities of Ceuta, Melilla, and Tetouan was minimal. When the Spanish tried to extend their control into the Rif mountains of the interior, they ran into the fiercely independent Berber tribes of the region.

Normally, the various tribes remained divided, but faced with the Spanish troops they united under the leadership of **Abd el-Krim**, later to become a hero of the Moroccan nationalists. In the summer of 1921, he inflicted a series of crushing defeats on the Spanish army, culminating in the massacre of at least 13,000 soldiers at Anual. The scale of the defeat, at the hands of tribal fighters armed only with rifles, outraged the Spanish public and worried the French, who had their own Berber tribes to deal with in the Atlas mountains. As the war began to spread into the French zone, the two colonial powers combined to crush the rebellion. It took a combined force of around 360,000 colonial troops to do so.

It was the last of the great tribal rebellions. Abd el-Krim had fought for an independent **Rifian state.** An educated man, he had seen the potential wealth that could result from exploiting the mineral deposits of the Rif. After the rebellion was crushed, the route to Moroccan independence changed from armed revolt to the evolving middle-class resistance to the colonial rulers.

NATIONALISM AND INDEPENDENCE

The French had hoped that by educating a middle-class elite they would find native allies in the task of binding Morocco permanently to France. It had the opposite effect. The educated classes of Rabat and Fes were the first to demand reforms from the French that would give greater rights to the Moroccans. When the government failed to respond, the demand for reforms escalated into demands for total independence.

Religion also played an important part in the development of a nationalist movement. France's first inkling of the depth of nationalist feeling came in 1930, when the colonial government tried to bring in a **Berber dahir**—a law setting up a separate legal system for the Berber areas. This was an obvious breach of the protectorate agreement, which prevented the French from changing the Islamic nature of government. Popular agitation forced the French to back down.

It was a classic attempt to "divide and rule," and as the nationalists gained strength, the French resorted more and more to threatening to "unleash" the Berber hill tribes against the Arab city dwellers. They hoped that by spreading Christianity and setting up French schools in Berber areas, the tribes would become more "Europeanized," and, as such, useful allies against the Muslim Arabs.

Before World War II, the nationalists were weak and their demands aimed at reforming the existing system, not independence. After riots in 1937, the government was able to round up the entire executive committee of the small nationalist party. In 1943, the party took the name of **Istiqlal** (Independence); the call for complete separation from France grew more insistent. The loyal performance of Moroccan troops during the war had raised hopes of a fairer treatment for nationalist demands, but France continued to ignore Istiqlal, exiling its leaders and banning its publications. But during the postwar period, it was at last developing into a mass party—growing from 10,000 members in 1947 to 100,000 by 1951.

The developments of the 1950s, culminating in Moroccan independence in 1956, bear a striking resemblance to the events in Algeria and Tunisia. The French first underestimated the strength of these independence movements, tried then to resist them, and finally had to concede defeat. In Algeria and Tunisia, the independence parties gained power and consolidated their positions once the French had left. In Morocco, on the other hand, Istiqlal was never uncontested after 1956 and the party soon began to fragment—becoming by the 1970s a marginal force in politics.

The decline and fall of Istiqlal was due mainly to the astute way in which Sultan (later King) **Mohammed V**, associated himself with the independence movement. Despite threats from the French government, Mohammed became more and more outspoken in his support for independence, paralyzing government operations by refusing to sign legislation. Serious rioting in 1951 persuaded the French to act: after a period of house arrest, the sultan was sent into exile in 1953.

This only increased his popularity. After a brief attempt to rule in alliance with **Thami el-Glaoui**, the Berber pasha of Marrakesh who saw the sultan's absence as an opportunity to expand his power base in the south, the French capitulated in 1955, allowing the sultan to return.

The government in Paris could see no way out of the spiraling violence of the nationalist guerillas and the counterviolence of the French settlers. Also, perhaps equally significant, they could not sustain a simultaneous defence of the three North African colonies—and economic interests dictated that they concentrate on holding Algeria. Finally, in 1956, Morocco was given full **independence** by France and Spain.

On independence, Sultan Mohammed V changed his title to that of king—reflecting a move toward a modern constitutional monarchy.

MOHAMMED V

Unlike his ancestors, the sultans, **Mohammed V** had inherited a united country with a well-developed industrial sector, an extensive system of irrigation, and a network of roads and railroads. But years of French administration had left little legacy of trained Moroccan administrators. Nor was there an obvious party base or bureaucracy for the king to operate within.

In 1956, Istiqlal party members held key posts in the first **government**. The regime instituted a series of reforms across the range of social issues. Schools and universities were created, a level of regional government was introduced, and ambitious public works schemes launched. There were moves, also, against European "decadence," with a wholesale clean-up of Tangier, and against the unorthodox religious brotherhoods—both long-time targets of the Istiqlal.

Mohammed V, as leader of the Muslim faith in Morocco, and the figurehead of independence, controlled huge support and influence in Morocco as a whole. In government, however, he did not perceive the Istiqlal as natural allies. The king bided his time, building links with the army—with the help of Crown Prince Hassan as commander-in-chief—and with the police.

Mohammed's influence upon the army would prove a decisive factor in the Moroccan state withstanding a series of **rebellions** against its authority. The most serious of these were in the Rif, in 1958-59, but there were challenges, too, in the Middle Atlas and Sahara. The king's standing, and the army's efficiency, stood the test. Crown Prince Hassan, meanwhile, as the army commander, helped to deflect internal pressures into renewed nationalism. The army began a quasi-siege in the south, exerting pressure on the Spanish to give up their claims to the port of Sidi Ifni.

In party politics, Mohammed's principal act was to lend his support to the **Mouvement Populaire** (MP), a moderate party set up to represent the Berbers, and for the king a useful counterweight to Istiqlal. In 1959, the strategy paid its first dividend. Istiqlal was seriously weakened by a split which hived off the more left-wing members into a separate party, the **Union Nationale des Forces Populaires** (UNFP) under Mehdi Ben Barka. There had always been a certain tension within Istiqlal between the moderates and those favouring a more radical policy, in association with the unions.

MODERN MOROCCO: HASSAN II (1956–)

The death of Mohammed V in 1961 led to the accession of **King Hassan II**, the current ruling monarch. Today, almost thirty years later, his reign represents the longest period of stability—albeit with a few uncertain periods—in the country's history.

For a colonized nation, with sparse government structure of its own at Independence, the nation's modern development has been remarkable.

CONSTITUTION AND ELECTIONS

Even before independence, in a 1955 speech, Mohammed V had promised to set up "democratic institutions resulting from the holding of free elections." The country's first **constitution** was not ready until after his death, however. It was only in 1962, under Hassan II, that it was put to, and approved by, a popular referendum.

The constitution was drafted in such a way as to favor the pro-monarchy parties of the center. In the **1963 elections** that followed, Mouvement Populaire was absorbed into a special alliance, the FDIC (*Front pour la Défense des Institutions Constitutionelles*), on a ticket giving total support to the king's policy. The FDIC, accordingly, won a majority of seats, though with a strong showing still by the Istiqlal, whose powerbase was (and remains) in Fes and the agricultural belt of the north, and by the UNFP, who held much support in the Souss and in Casablanca.

There followed regional elections, in which the FDIC won much more conclusive support— amid allegations of vote fixing. The socialist UNFP became increasingly radical and outspoken against the government, and in particular against the king, looking for inspiration to the republican models of Egypt and neighboring Algeria. In 1963, a plot against Hassan's life was "discovered," leading to the arrest of UNFP leaders and the exile of Ben Barka. After student riots in Casablanca in 1965, Hassan declared a **state of emergency** and took over the government directly.

The relative ease with which Hassan was able to rule without democratic institutions underlined the weakness of the parties. The Istiqlal was never able to recover from the 1959 split, and as an opposition party its power dwindled even further. The UNFP and the unions were weakened by the arrests of their leaders and by internal divisions over policy. Despite the increasingly strident attacks on what it called a "feudal" and "paternalistic" regime, the UNFP never managed to develop a coherent platform from which it could oppose the king and build real popular support.

The weakness of the parties was further revealed in 1970, when Hassan announced a **new constitution**, to bring an end to emergency rule. Its terms gave the king greater control over parliament than in 1962. As a sign more of their weakness in the face of royal power than of any new-found unity, the UNFP and Istiqlal came together in a "national front" to oppose it.

The events of 1971–72, however, were to show the real nature of the threat to the monarchy. In July 1971, a group of soldiers led by an army general broke into the royal palace in Skhirat in an attempt to stage a **coup**; more than 100 people were killed, but in the confusion Hassan escaped. The following year another attempt was launched, as the king's private jet was attacked by fighters of the Moroccan air force. Again, he had a very narrow escape—his pilot was able to convince the attacking aircraft by radio that the king had already died. The former interior minister, General Oufkir, seems to have been behind the 1972 coup attempt and it was followed by a major shake-up in the armed forces.

THE GREEN MARCH AND SAHARAN WAR

The king's real problem was to give a sense of destiny to the country, especially to the increasingly disillusioned Moroccan youth, for whom employment opportunities had conspicuously failed to appear. The game of the political parties had proved sterile. What Hassan needed was a cause similar to the struggle for independence that had brought such prestige to his father.

That cause was provided in 1975, when the Spanish finally decided to pull out of their colony in the **Western Sahara**. In the 1950s Istiqlal had laid claim to the Sahara, as well as parts of Mauritania, Algeria, and Mali, as part of its quest for a "greater Morocco." By 1975, Hassan had patched up the border dispute with Algeria and recognized the independent government in Mauritania; it turned out that this was only a prelude to a more realistic design—Moroccan control of the Western Sahara.

The discovery of phosphate reserves in the Sahara during the 1960s brought about Spain's first real attempt to develop its Saharan colony. Before then it had been content merely to garrison the small coastal forts in Ad Dakhla and La Guera, with occasional forays into the interior to pacify the tribes. With increased investment in the region during the 1960s, the nomads began to settle in the newly created towns along the coast, particularly the new capital in Laayoune. As education became more widespread, the Spanish were confronted with the same problem the French had faced in Morocco thirty years earlier—the rise of nationalism.

Pressure began to mount on General Franco's government to decolonize one of the last colonies in Africa. In 1966, he promised the UN that Spain would hold a referendum "as soon as the country was ready for it." Economic interests kept Spain from fulfilling its promise, and in 1969 work began on opening the phosphate mines in Bou Craa. Meanwhile, the Saharans began to press the case for independence themselves. In 1973, they formed the

Frente Popular para la Liberación de Saguia el-Hamra y Rio de Oro, or **Polisario**, which began guerrilla operations against the Spanish. Polisario gained in strength as Spain began to signal it would pull out of the Sahara and as the threat to Saharan independence from Morocco and Mauritania grew more obvious.

Spanish withdrawal in 1975 coincided with General Franco's final illness. King Hassan timed his move perfectly, sending some 350,000 Moroccan civilians southward on the "Green March"—*La Marche Verte*—to the Sahara. Spain could either go to war with Morocco by attacking the advancing Moroccans or take the easy way out and withdraw without holding the promised referendum. Hassan's bluff worked and in November 1975 a secret agreement was reached in Madrid to divide the Spanish Sahara between Morocco and Mauritania as soon as Spanish troops withdrew.

The popular unrest of the 1960s and the coup attempts of 1971–72 were forgotten under a wave of patriotism. Without shedding any blood, Morocco had "recaptured" part of its former empire. But the king had underestimated the native Sahrawis' determination to fight for an independent Sahara, their Saharan Arab Democratic Republic (SADR). Nearly 40,000 of them fled the Moroccan advance, taking refuge in Mauritania and Algeria. There, Polisario established a government in exile, together with refugee camps, schools, and hospitals.

In the following years, they mounted a hit-and-run campaign into Morocco, pinning down the Moroccan garrisons in the major Saharan towns and forcing the region's mines to shut down. Sahrawi resistance would soon have crumbled, though, if it hadn't enjoyed the security of bases in Algeria and Algerian military aid. **Algeria**, Morocco's rival for Maghrebi dominance, felt threatened by Hassan's expansionist policy and, short of committing Algerian troops, did everything it could to make the occupation impossible.

SOCIAL PROBLEMS

At home, the attention and budget demanded by the Saharan war compounded the problems of the economy. By 1981, an estimated 60 percent of the population were living below the poverty level, unemployment ran at approximately 20 percent (40 percent among the young), and perhaps 20 percent of the urban population lived in shantytowns, or *bidonvilles*.

The government, occupied by the war, seemed to neglect these pressing **social problems**; indeed, an austerity campaign to please its international creditors, including a wage freeze and a cut in subsidies for basic foodstuffs, appeared to increase the problems even more for the poor. In June 1981 the socialists of the UNFP mounted a challenge by organizing a one-day protest strike in June 1981, unfortunately with sad and dramatic effects. In Casablanca, the demonstrations led to a running battle with the police and at least 100 deaths. Demonstrators were brought to trial and given stiff sentences, as were the leader of the UNFP, Abderrahim Bouabid, and fourteen socialist members of parliament.

Local **elections** were held in June 1983, and appeared to be a resounding royalist victory, providing the government with a mandate to continue with its austerity measures. But the opposition parties, including Istiqlal, complained of electoral fraud, and the failure to proceed with parliamentary elections in October showed that all was not well. Using Article 19 of the constitution, Hassan assumed all executive and legislative power, **governing by decree** in the absence of an elected government. He managed to coax support from the parliamentary parties, including the socialists, by handing out ministerial posts to them, but he kept real power firmly in his hands.

It was a brave move on his part. The government was facing bankruptcy and if the IMF was to reschedule Morocco's massive debts, the austerity campaign would have to become even harsher. Hassan announced a 12.5 percent cut in government expenditures and massive cuts in subsidies, and then stood alone to face the backlash. Demonstrations against the cuts began in Marrakesh in early January 1984, and within a week had spread north to Nador and Al Hoceima. Later, **riots** broke out in Oudja and Tetouan. Clashes with the authorities were inevitable, and by the end of the month, between 100 and 600 people had died. Hassan announced on television that further cuts in subsidies would be postponed, but at the same time he condemned extremists on the left and right as being the instigators of the riots and promised the restoration of order. A massive campaign of arrests followed. Over 700 rioters were put in prison and, over the following months, sentenced to long prison terms.

NORTH AFRICAN UNITY MOVES

If the riots represented an expression of popular unrest, however, it was substantially defused by Hassan's surprise announcement of a **"Treaty of Union" with Libya** in August 1984. To the outside world, it seemed a bizarre act for Morocco to associate itself with Colonel Qaddafi, the arch enemy of the United States, which had for a decade been providing aid and military assistance to Morocco. But Hassan had correctly judged the mood of his people (in a referendum, the treaty was endorsed almost unanimously) and with attention drawn back to foreign affairs and Morocco's now-leading role in the popular move toward **Maghreb unity**, domestic troubles faded into the background. Feeling secure once more, Hassan went to the polls and was rewarded with the reelection of a centrist-royalist coalition. After six months of suspension, **democratic government** had been restored.

The Libyan union proved to be short-lived, but it left the legacy of an idea that seems set to be the major factor in Morocco's foreign relations at the turn of the 1980s. This is the necessity for some kind of **economic cooperation and unity in North Africa**. As Spain and Portugal entered the European Community, the North African economic ties—with France long the major trading partner—became under threat. Quotas for imports to EC nations are due for renegotiation, and a strong, unified North Africa is seen by most of the region's leaders as of vital importance.

In June 1988, a **Maghreb Summit** was held in Algiers. Hassan attended with a Moroccan delegation—his first visit to Algeria for two decades—and there was an immediate result in the resumption of full diplomatic ties between Morocco and Algeria, and the opening of the Oujda-Maghnia border to all traffic. In the longer term, plans were formulated for closer Maghreb links to counter the EC single market in 1992.

The summit, and resumption of relations, has also promoted hopes for a negotiated **settlement to the dispute in the Sahara**. With riots of their own at home in 1987-88, which included an attack on Polisario's office in

Algiers, the Algerian government is showing signs of wanting to pull out from the conflict. In any case, over the decade, Morocco had gradually been winning the war. Beginning in 1981, they have built a series of heavily defended **desert walls** that exclude the Polisario from successively larger areas of the desert; by 1985, the phosphate mines were back in use and by 1987, the sixth wall had effectively blocked off Polisario from Mauritania and left only 15 percent of the land area outside Moroccan control. Meanwhile the government was making concerted attempts to win the approval of the Saharan residents, injecting vast sums into creating a model city and capital in Laayoune.

Under United Nations auspices, a **cease-fire** was agreed in the spring of 1989. Although it has been somewhat sporadically observed, there has subsequently been no major military conflict. And in the UN negotiations continue for a referendum to be held among the Sahrawis to determine their future state. King Hassan has met with a Polisario deputation in Marrakesh, and has promised that if the Sharawis vote for independence, Morocco will be the first nation to open an embassy in Laayoune. Such talk reflects a new confidence in the situation, and a conviction, seemingly shared among all parties, that the conflict has burned itself out.

It must be hoped that the next months, or years, will bring a resolution to the conflict. Freed from the budgetary expenditure on the war, Morocco will be able to devote its attentions toward the equally pressing need for **economic growth** at home. There is some evidence that the economy is on a mild upswing, and initiatives, certainly, are in progress. Massive irrigation projects are planned, oil shale is being exploited to provide an alternative to imported oil, preferential tax laws have been enacted to encourage investment in manufacturing industry, and there have been increases in phosphate production. Sadly, the fruits of this labor have been slow to materialize, more due to the worldwide recession and the slump in commodity prices than to any fault of Morocco. In the meantime, government investment has thrown Morocco into the the the hands of its creditors. Further loans are necessary if Morocco is to carry out its development plan, a fact that Hassan, who has appointed as the last two prime ministers economists able to mediate with international financial institutions, has not been slow to realize.

CHRONOLOGY

10,000–5000 B.C.	**Capsian** and **Mouillian Man** spread across the Maghreb Neolithic cultures	**Rock carvings** in Oukaïmeden, Foum el Hassan, and other inaccessible sites
1100 B.C.	**Phoenician** settlements	Bronze Age. First trading port in **Lixus** (near Larache)
500 B.C.	**Carthaginians** take over Phoenician settlements and greatly expand them	Remains in Lixus, and in Rabat Archaeological Museum
146 B.C.	Fall of Carthage at end of the Third Punic War; Roman influence spreads into **Berber kingdoms** of Mauretania-Numidia	Bust of Juba II (Rabat)
27 B.C.	Direct **Roman** rule under Emperor Caligula	**Volubilis** developed as provincial capital; other minor sites in Lixus and Tangier. Mosaics in Tetouan and Rabat museums
A.D. 253	Roman legions withdrawn	
429	**Vandals** pass through	
535	**Byzantines** occupy Ceuta	

ISLAM

622	Muhammad and followers move from Mecca to Medina and start spread of Islam	
ca. 705	**Moussa Ibn Nasr** establishes Arab rule in north and pre-Sahara, and in 711 leads Berber invasion of Spain	

IDRISSID DYNASTY (788–923)

788	**Moulay Idriss** establishes first Moroccan Arab dynasty	Founding of Moulay Idriss and Fes
807	Moulay Idriss II (807–836)	**Fes** developed with Kairouan and Andalusian refugee quarters, and establishment of Kairaouine Mosque
10th–11th c.	Hilali tribes wreak havoc on Maghrebi infrastructure	

ALMORAVID DYNASTY (1062–1145)

1062	**Youssef bin Tachfine** establishes capital in Marrakesh; first great Berber dynasty	**Koubba** in Marrakesh is only surviving monument, except for walls and possibly a minaret in Tit (near El Jadida)
1090	Almoravid invasion of **Spain**	

ALMOHAD DYNASTY (1147–1248)

1120s	**Ibn Toumert** sets up a *ribat* in Tin Mal in the High Atlas	Ruined mosque of Tin Mal
1145–1147	**Abd el Moumen** takes first Fes, and then Marrakesh	Extensive building of walls, gates, and **minarets**, including the Koutoubia in Marrakesh
1195	**Yacoub el Mansour** (1184–99) extends rule to Spain, and east to Tripoli	New capital begun in **Rabat**: Hassan Tower, Oudaia Gate
1212	Defeat in Spain at Las Navas de Tolosa	

MERENID DYNASTY (1248–1465)

1250s	**Abou Youssef Yacoub** (1258–86) establishes effective power	*Zaouia* and mausoleum in **Chellah** (Rabat); new city (El Djedid) built in **Fes**
1330s–50s	**Abou el Hassan** (1331–51) and **Abou Inan** (1351–58), two of the most successful Merenids, extend rule briefly to Tunis	**Medersas** in Fes (Bou Inania, Attarin, etc.), Meknes, and Salé
1415	**Portuguese** begin attacks on Moroccan coast, taking Ceuta and later other cities	**Portuguese** cistern in El Jadida; walls and remains in Azzemour, Asilah, and Safi

WATTASID DYNASTY (1465–1554)

1465	Wattasids—Merenid viziers—usurp power	**Chaouen** built and **Tetouan** founded again by refugees
1492	Fall of **Granada**, last Muslim kingdom in Spain; Jewish and Muslim refugees settle in Morocco over next 100 years or so	
15th–16th c.	**Marabouts** establish *zaouias*, controlling parts of the country	

SAADIAN DYNASTY (1554–1669)

1550s	**Mohammed esh Sheikh** (d. 1557) founds dynasty in Marrakesh	**Saadian Tombs** and Ben Youssef *medersa* (Marrakesh); pavilion extensions to Kairaouine Mosque (Fes)
1578	Battle of Three Kings leads to accession of **Ahmed el Mansour** (1578–1603), who goes on to conquer Timbuktu and the gold and slave routes to the south	**El Badi** palace (Marrakesh)
1627	Pirate **Republic of Bou Regreg** set up by Andalusian refugees	**Rabat** Medina

ALAOUITE DYNASTY (1669–)

1672–1727	**Moulay Ismail** imposes the Alaouite dynasty on Morocco	New imperial capital in **Meknes** (Ismail's mausoleum, etc.); **Kasbahs** and **forts** built; **palaces** in Tangier and Rabat
18th c.	**Sidi Mohammed** (1757–90)	Ismail and his successors rebuild **grand mosques**, etc., especially in **Marrakesh**, where many later Alaouites make their capital—many of the city's **pavilions** and **gardens** date from the early 18th century
	Moulay Suleiman (1792–1822)	Final burst of **palace** building—El Badi (Marrakesh), Palais Jamai (Fes)
1912	**Treaty of Fes** brings into being French and Spanish **"protectorates" (1912–56)**	European **Villes Nouvelles** built outside the Moroccan Medinas; **"Mauresque"** architecture developed for administrative buildings (best in Casa, Rabat, Tetouan, and Sidi Ifni]
1921–27	Riffian revolt under Abd el Krim	
1920s–1956	**T'Hami el Glaoui** becomes Pasha of Marrakesh and rules south for French	**Glaoui palaces** in Telouet and Marrakesh; **Kasbah** fortresses throughout the south
1943	Nationalist **Istiqlal** party formed in Fes	
1956	**Independence**	
1961	Accession of **Hassan II**	New royal **palaces** in all major cities—most recently and spectacularly in Agadir
1975	**Green March into Western Sahara**	Hassan II Mosque in Casablanca

ISLAM IN MOROCCO

It's difficult to get any grasp of Morocco, and even more so of Moroccan history, without first knowing something of Islam. What follows is a very basic background: some theory, some history, and an idea of Morocco's place in the modern Islamic world. For more depth on each of these subjects, see the book listings in the section that follows.

BEGINNINGS: PRACTICE AND BELIEF

Islam was a new religion born of the wreckage of the Greco-Roman world around the south of the Mediterranean. Its founder, a merchant named **Muhammad*** from the wealthy city of Mecca (now in Saudi Arabia), was chosen as God's Prophet: in about A.D. 609, he began to hear divine messages which he transcribed directly into the **Koran**, Islam's Bible. This was the same God worshiped by Jews and Christians—Jesus is one of the minor prophets in Islam—but Muslims claim He had been misunderstood by both earlier religions.

The distinctive feature of this new faith was directness—a reaction to the increasing complexity of established religions and an obvious attraction. In Islam there is no intermediary between man and God in the form of an institutionalized priesthood or complicated liturgy; and worship, in the form of prayer, is a direct and personal communication with God. Believers face five essential requirements, the so-called **"Pillars of faith"**: prayer five times daily; the pilgrimage (*hadj*) to Mecca; the Ramadan fast; a religious levy; and, most fundamental of all, the acceptance that "There is no God but God and Muhammad is His Prophet."

---

*"Muhammad" is the standard spelling today of the Prophet's name—and a more accurate transcription from the Arabic. In Morocco there is some cause for confusion in that the name of the former king, *Mohammed* V, is still spelled that way on maps and street signs and in most Western histories.

THE PILLARS OF FAITH

The Pillars of Faith are still central to Muslim life, articulating and informing daily existence. Ritual **prayers** are the most visible. Bearing in mind that the Islamic day begins at sunset, the five daily times are sunset, after dark, dawn, noon, and afternoon. Prayers can be performed anywhere, but preferably in a mosque, or in Arabic, a *djemaa*. In the past, and even today in some places, a *muezzin* would climb his minaret each time and summon the faithful.

Nowadays, the call is likely to be less frequent, and prerecorded; even so, this most distinctive of Islamic sounds has a beauty all its own, especially when neighboring *muezzins* are audible simultaneously. Their message is simplicity itself: "God is most great (*Allah Akhbar*). I testify that there is no God but Allah. I testify that Muhammad is His Prophet. Come to prayer, come to security. God is great." Another phrase is added in the morning: "Prayer is better than sleep."

Prayers are preceded by ritual washing, and are spoken with the feet bare. Facing Mecca (the direction indicated in a mosque by the *mihrab*), the worshiper recites the Fatina, the first chapter of the Koran: "Praise be to God, Lord of the worlds, the Compassionate, the Merciful, King of the Day of Judgment. Thee do we worship and Thine aid do we seek. Guide us on the straight path, the path of those on whom Thou hast bestowed Thy Grace, not the path of those who incur Thine anger nor of those who go astray." The same words are then repeated twice in the prostrate position, with some interjections of *Allah Akhbar*. It is a highly ritualized procedure, the prostrate position symbolic of the worshipper's role as servant (Islam literally means "obedience"), and the sight of thousands of people going through the same motions simultaneously in a mosque is a powerful one. On Islam's holy day, Friday, all believers are expected to attend prayers in their local grand mosque. Here the whole community comes together in worship led by an *imam*, who may also deliver the *khutba*, or sermon.

Ramadan is the name of the ninth month in the lunar Islamic calendar, the month in which the Koran was revealed to Muhammad. For the whole of the month, believers must obey a rigorous fast (the custom was originally modeled on Jewish and Christian practice), forsaking all forms of consumption between sunrise and sundown; this includes food, drink, cigarettes, and any form of sexual contact. Only a few categories of people are exempted: travelers, children, pregnant women, and warriors engaged in a *jihad*, or holy war. Given the climates in which many Muslims live, the fast is a formidable undertaking, but in practice it becomes a time of intense celebration.

The pilgrimage, or **hadj**, to Mecca is an annual event, with millions flocking to Muhammad's birthplace from all over the world. Here they go through several days of rituals, the central one being a sevenfold circumambulation of the Kaba, before kissing a black stone set in its wall. Islam requires that all believers go on a *hadj* as often as is practically possible, but for the poor it may well be a once-in-a-lifetime occasion, and is sometimes replaced by a series of visits to lesser, local shrines—in Morocco, for instance, to Fes and Moulay Idriss.

Based on these central articles, the new Islamic faith proved to be inspirational. Muhammad's own Arab nation was soon converted, and the Arabs then proceeded to carry their religion far and wide in an extraordinarily rapid territorial expansion. Many peoples of the Middle East and North Africa, who for centuries had only grudgingly accepted Roman paganism or Christianity, embraced Islam almost immediately.

DEVELOPMENT IN MOROCCO

Islam made a particularly spectacular arrival in Morocco. **Oqba Ibn Nafi**, the crusading general who had already expelled the Byzantines from Tunisia, marked his subjugation of the far west by riding fully armed into the waves of the Atlantic. "O God," he is said to have exclaimed, "I call you to witness that there is no ford here. If there was, I would cross it."

This compulsory appreciation of Morocco's remoteness was prophetic in a way, because over the succeeding centuries Moroccan Islam was to acquire and retain a highly distinctive character. Where mainstream Islamic history is concerned, its development has been relatively straightforward—it was virtually untouched, for instance, by the Sunni-Shia conflict that

split the Muslim world—but the country's unusual geographical and social circumstances have conspired to tip the balance away from official orthodoxy.

Orthodoxy, by its very nature, has to be an urban-based tradition. Learned men—lawyers, Koranic scholars, and others—could only congregate in the cities where, gathered together and known collectively as the *ulema*, they regulated the faith. In Islam, this included both law and education. Teaching was at first based entirely in the mosques; later, it was conducted through a system of colleges, or *medersas*, in which students would live while studying at the often adjoining mosque. In most parts of the Islamic world, this very learned and sophisticated urban hierarchy was dominant. But Morocco also developed a powerful tradition of **popular religion**, first manifested in the eighth-century Kharijite rebellion—which effectively divided the country into separate Berber kingdoms—and endures to this day in the mountains and countryside.

MARABOUTS

There are three main strands of this popular religion, all of them deriving from the worship of saints. Everywhere in Morocco, as well as elsewhere in North Africa, the countryside is dotted with small domed **marabouts**: the tombs of holy men, which became centers of worship and pilgrimage. This elevation of individuals goes against strict Islamic teaching, but probably derives from the Berbers' pre-Islamic tendency to focus worship around individual holy men. At its simplest, local level, these saint cults attracted the loyalty of the Moroccan villages and the more remote regions.

More prosperous cults would also endow educational institutions attached to the *marabout*, known as **zaouias**, which provided an alternative to the official education given in urban *medersas*. These inevitably posed a threat to the authority of the urban hierarchy, and as rural cults extended their influence, some became so popular that they endowed their saints with genealogies traced back to the Prophet. The title accorded to these men and their descendents was *shereef*, and many grew into strong political forces. The classic example in Morocco is the tomb of Moulay Idriss, in the eighth century just a local *marabout*, but eventually, as the base of the Idrissid clan, a center of enormous influence that reached far beyond its rural origins.

Loyalty to a particular family—religiously sanctified, but essentially political—was at the center of the shereefian movements. In the third strand of popular devotion, the focus was more narrowly religious. Again, the origins lay in small, localized cults of individuals, but these were individuals worshipped for their magical and mystical powers. Taken up and developed by subsequent followers, their rituals became the focal point of **brotherhoods** of initiates.

THE AISSAOUA

Perhaps the most famous Moroccan brotherhood is that of Sidi Mohammed Bin Aissa. Born in Souss in the fifteenth century, he traveled in northern Morocco before settling down as a teacher in Meknes and founding a *zaouia*. His powers of mystical healing became famous there, and he provoked enough official suspicion to be exiled briefly to the desert—where he again revealed his exceptional powers by proving himself immune to scorpions, snakes, live flames, and other hostile manifestations. His followers tried to achieve the same state of grace. Six hundred were said to have attained perfection—and during the saint's lifetime, *zaouias* devoted to his teachings were founded in Figuig and elsewhere in the Maghreb.

Bound by its practice of a common source of ritual, the Aissaoua brotherhood made itself notorious with displays of eating scorpions, walking on hot coals, and other ecstatic customs designed to bring union with God. It was perhaps the most flamboyant of these brotherhoods, but most at any rate used some kind of dancing or music, and indeed continued to do so well into this century. The more extreme and fanatical of these rites are now outlawed, though the attainment of trance is still an important part of the *moussems*, or festivals, of the various confraternities.

TOWARD CRISIS

With all its different forms, Islam permeated every aspect of the country's pre-twentieth-century life. Unlike Christianity, at least Protestant Christianity, which to some extent has accepted the separation of church and state, Islam sees no such distinction. **Civil law** was provided by the *sharia*, the religious law contained in the Koran, and **intellectual life** by the *msids* (Koranic primary schools where the 6200 verses were learned by heart) and by the great medieval mosque universities, of which the Kairaouine in Fes (together with the Zitoura in Tunis and the Al Azhar in Cairo) was the most important in the Arab world.

The religious basis of Arab study and intellectual life did not prevent its scholars and scientists from producing work that was hundreds of years ahead of contemporary "Dark Age" Europe. The remains of a monumental water clock in Fes, and the work of the historian Ibn Khaldun, are just two Moroccan examples. Arab work in developing and transmitting Greco-Roman culture was also vital to the whole development of the European Renaissance. By this time, however, the Islamic world—and isolated Morocco in particular—was beginning to move away from the West. The crusades had been one enduring influence toward division. Another was the Islamic authorities themselves, increasingly suspicious (like the Western church) of any challenge, and actively discouraging of innovation. At first it did not matter in political terms that Islamic culture became static. But by the end of the eighteenth century, Europe was ready to take advantage. Napoleon's expedition to Egypt in 1798 marked the beginning of a century in which virtually every Islamic country came under the control of a **European power**.

Islam cannot, of course, be held solely responsible for the Muslim world's material decline. But because it influences every part of its believers' lives, and because East-West rivalry had always been viewed in primarily religious terms, the nineteenth and twentieth centuries saw something of a **crisis in religious confidence**. Why had Islam's former power now passed to infidel foreigners?

REACTIONS

Reactions and answers veered between two extremes. There were those who felt that Islam should try to incorporate some of the West's materialism; on the other side, there were movements holding that Islam should turn its back on the West, purify itself of all corrupt additions, and thus rediscover its former power. While they were colonies of European powers, however, Muslim nations had little chance of putting any such ideas into effective practice. These could only emerge in the form of cooperation with, or rebellion against, the ruling power. But the postwar era of **decolonization**, and the simultaneous acquisition through oil of relative economic independence, brought the Islamic world suddenly face to face with the question of its own spiritual identity. How should it deal with Western values and influence, now that it could afford—both politically and economically—almost total rejection? A return to the totality of Islam—**fundamentalism**—is a conscious choice of one consistent spiritual identity, one that is deeply embedded in the consciousness of a culture already unusually aware of tradition. It is also a rejection of the West and its colonial and exploitative values. Traditional Islam, at least in some interpretations, offers a positivist brand of freedom that is clearly opposed to the negative freedoms of Western materialism. The most vehement Islamic fundamentalists are not passive reactionaries thinking of the past, but young radicals—often students—eager to assert their new-found independence. Islam has in a sense become the "anti-imperialist" religion—think, for example, of the Black Muslim movement in America—and there is frequent confusion and even conflict between secular, left-wing ideals and more purely religious ones.

MODERN MOROCCO

There are two basic reasons why only a few Islamic countries have embraced a rigidly traditional or fundamentalist stance. The first is an ethical one: however undesirable Western materialism may appear, the rejection of all Western values involves rejecting also what the West sees as the "benefits" of development. Perhaps it is begging the question in strictly Islamic terms to say that the emancipation of women, for example, is a "benefit." But the leaders of many countries feel that such steps are both desirable and reconcilable with a more liberal brand of Islam, which will retain its place in the national identity. The other argument against militant Islam is a more prag-matic, economic one. Morocco is only one of many countries which would suffer severe economic hardship if they cut themselves off from the West: they have to tread a narrow line that allows them to maintain good relations both with the West and with the Islamic world.

ISLAM AND THE STATE

In Morocco today, Islam is the official state religion, and King Hassan's secular status is interwoven with his role as "Commander of the Faithful." Internationally, too, he plays a leading role. Meetings of the Islamic Conference Organization are frequently held in Morocco and, in one of the most unlikely exchanges, students from Tashkent in the USSR have come to study at Fes University. For all these indications of Islamic solidarity, though, **state policy** remains distinctly moderate—sometimes in the face of extremist pressure.

RURAL RELIGION

Not surprisingly, all of this has had more effect on urban than on rural life—a difference accentuated by the gap between them that has always existed in Morocco. Polarization in religious attitudes is far greater in the **cities**, where there is inevitably tension between those for and against secularization. Islamic fundamentalism offers a convenient scapegoat to many Western-oriented governments in the Muslim world, but if its actual strength is sometimes open to doubt, its existence is probably not.

Away from the cities, religious attitudes have changed less over the past two generations. Religious brotherhoods such as the Aissaoua have declined since the beginning of the century, when they were still very powerful, and the influence of mystics generally has fallen. As the official histories put it, popular credulity in Morocco provided an ideal setting for charlatans as well as saviors, and much of this has now passed. All the same, the rhythms of **rural life** still revolve around local *marabouts,* and the annual *moussems,* or festivals-cum-pilgrimages, are still vital and impressive displays.

Peter Morris

MUSIC

Wherever you go in Moroco you are likely to hear music. It is the basic expression of the country's folk culture—indeed to many of the illiterate countrypeople it is the sole expression—and in its traditions it covers the whole history of the country. There are long and ancient pieces designed for participation by the entire communities of Berber villages; songs and instrumental music brought by the Arabs from the east and from Andalusian Spain; and in more recent times, the struggle for independence, too, found celebration in song.

Although the most common musical phenomenon that you will hear is the *muezzin* calling the faithful to prayer, amplified from minarets or from doorways, most Moroccan music is performed for the sake of entertainment rather than religion. At every weekly *souk*, or market, you will find a band playing somewhere in a patch of shade, or a stall blasting out the cassettes they have on sale. In the evenings many cafés feature musicians, particularly during the long nights of Ramadan. Television also plays its part, with two weekly programs devoted to music—one dealing with traditional forms, the other a sort of cabaret of popular artists from the Maghreb and Middle East—and the radio stations broadcast a variety of sounds, from classical Andaluse music to contemporary electric pop.

BERBER MUSIC

Berber music is quite distinct from Arab influenced forms in its rhythms, tunings, and sounds. It is an extremely ancient tradition, probably long predating even the arrival of Arabs in Morocco, and has been passed on orally from generation to generation. There are three main categories: village music, ritual music, and the music of professional musicians.

Village music may have regional forms but it is always essentially a collective performance. Men and women of the entire village will assemble on festive occasions to dance and sing together. The best known dances are the ***ahouach***, in the western High Atlas, and the ***ahidus***, performed by the Chleuh Berbers in the eastern High Atlas. In each, drums (*bendirs*) and flutes are the only instruments used. The dance begins with a chanted prayer, to which the dancers respond in chorus, the men and women gathered in a large ring in the open air, around the musicians. The *ahouach* is normally performed at night in the patio of the Kasbah; the dance is so complicated that the musicians meet to prepare for it in a group called a *laamt* set up specially for the purpose. In the *bumzdi*, a variation on the *ahouach*, one or more soloists perform a series of poetic improvisations.

Ritual music is rarely absent from any rites connected with the agricultural calendar—such as *moussems* (see *Basics*)—or major events in the life of individuals, such as marriage. It may also be called upon to help deal with *djinn*, or evil spirits, or to encourage rainfall. Flutes and drums are usually the sole instruments, along with much rhythmic handclapping, although a community may have engaged professional musicians for certain events.

Professional musicans, or ***imdyazn***, of the Atlas mountains are itinerant, traveling during the summer, usually in groups of four. The leader of the group is called the *amydaz* or poet. He presents his poems, which are usually improvised and give news of national or world affairs, in the village square. The poet may be accompanied by one or two members of the group on drums and rabab, a single-string fiddle, and by a fourth player, known as the *bou oughanim*. This latter is the reed player, throwing out melodies on a double clarinet, and also acts as the group's clown. *Imdyazn* are found in many weekly souks in the Atlas.

Chleuh professional musicians are known as *rwais*. A *rwais* worthy of the name will not only know all the music for any particular celebration, but also have its own repetoire of songs—again commenting on current events—and be able to improvise. A *rwais* is made up of a single-stringed *rabab*, one or two *lotars*, and sometimes a *naquous*. Once the *lotar* has been tuned to the *rabab*, a piece begins with an improvisation on the *rabab* before the main tune, and quickens in pace as it builds towards an abrupt end. One of the most famous *rwais* performers is **Lhaj Aomar Ouahrouch** who has made numerous records, some of them available in the West.

ANDALUSE MUSIC

Morocco's classical music comes from the **Arab-Andalusian tradition** and is to be found, with variations, throughout the Maghreb. It is thought to have been invented, around a thousand years ago, in Córdoba, in then Moorish Spain, by an outstanding musician called Ziryab, from Baghdad. He founded the traditional form of the classical suite called *nawba*.

The original 24 **nawba** were directly linked with the hours in the day; only four full and seven fragmentary *nawba* have been preserved in the Moroccan tradition. Complete *nawbat*, which can last several hours, are rarely performed in one sitting. Pieces are usually chosen according to the hour of the day or the circumstances.

The movements are made up of poems, or *can'a*, set to music, with instrumental introductions. The monodies are usually sung by a choir, except the *baytayny muwwal*, which are sung by soloists in the interludes between movements of the *nawba*. The lyrics usually deal with love, though they are sometimes religious, glorifying the Prophet and divine laws.

When the Arabs were driven out of Spain, which they had known as Al Andalus, the different musical schools were dispersed over the Maghreb. The Valencian school continued in Fes, the Granadan in Tetouan and Chaouen. All have to an extent been influenced by Berber folk music. In fact many groups in northern Morocco play both Andaluse music and Berber

folk. The three most important **orchestras** are that of Fes, led by Abdelkrim Rais; that of Tetouan, led by Abdesadak Chekara; and that of Rabat, led by Loukili; Chaouen has also produced many great Andalucian musicians.

Orchestras are made up of rababs (fiddles), *ouds* (eleven string fretless lutes), *kamanjehs* (violins) of various pitches, *derbukas* (pottery drums), *tars*, and sometimes a *kanum* (zither).

FASSI MUSIC

Modern **Fassi**, the music of Fes, is a mixture of Andaluse music and Chaabi (see overpage). It takes the melodies of Andaluse music and puts them into popular song form. The leading exponent of this style is L'Hadj l'Hocine Toulali (or Toulali for short). He is also one of the leaders of the Andaluse orchestra of Fes.

RELIGIOUS MUSIC

As well as the chants of the Koran, which are improvised on a uniform beat, the *adhan*, or call to prayer, and the songs about the life of the prophet Mohammed, there is a whole other range of prayers and ceremonies belonging to the Sufi **brotherhoods**, or *tarikas*, in which music is seen as a means of getting closer to Allah. These include the music used in processions to the tombs of saints during moussems (see *Basics*).

The aim is for those present to reach a state of mystic ecstasy. In a private, nocturnal ceremony called the *hadra*, the Sufi brothers attain a trance by chanting the name of Allah (*dker*) or dancing in a ring holding hands. The songs and music are irregular in rhythm, quickening towards an abrupt end. Some brotherhoods play for alms in households who want to gain the favor of their patron saint.

GNAOUA

The **Gnaouas** are a religious brotherhood (see "Islam in Morocco") whose members are descendants of slaves brought from the Sudan by the Arabs. They have devotees all over Morocco, though the strongest concentrations are in the south, particularly in Marrakesh.

The brotherhood claim spiritual descent from Bilal, an Ethiopian who was the prophet's first muezzin. Most Gnaoua ceremonies, or *deiceba*, are held to placate spirits, good and evil, which have inhabited a person or place. These rites have their origins in sub-Saharan Africa, and an

African influence is evident in the music itself. The principal instrument, the *gimbri*, is a long-necked flute almost identical to instruments found in Mali, Senegal, and elsewhere in West Africa, among the Wolof and Mandinka peoples. The other characteristic sound of Gnaoua music is the *garagab*, a pair of metal castinets, which beat out a trance-like rhythm.

Nowadays, Gnaoua music can be heard at festivals and in the entertainment squares in Marrakesh and elsewhere.

THE ARAB TRADITION

The effect of constant wars and changes of ruler has been to prevent **Middle Eastern Arab music** from having as strong an influence as might be expected in this Moslem country. One kind of song with close Arab links is the classical *malhum*, which is accompanied on lute, *kamanjeh*, and percussion, always obeying the rules of the Eastern mode system, or *makam*.

The songs are classified according to the structure and meter of their verses, which are reflected in the music. One of the most famous contributors to this genre was the seventeenth century poet Abdelaziz al Maghrawi. More recently radio and television have brought *asri*, in which classical and popular, Eastern and European influences are mixed within the basic framework of the Middle Eastern *makam*, with plenty of instrumental improvization thrown in for good measure.

The popular Arab music known as *sh'sha'abi* follows the same mode system but has a different verse structure. *L'aita*, a variation on this from the plains between the Casablanca coast and the High Atlas mountains, relies for its effect on the interplay of free singing over a rhythmic accompaniment. One star of all these genres is **Abdeslam Cherkaoui** of Fes, who has made several records.

CHAABI: POPULAR MUSIC

Chaabi means popular and the music that takes this name started out as street music performed in the squares and souks. It can now be heard in cafés, at festivals, and at weddings, especially in the summer. At its more basic level, it is played by itinerant musicians, who will turn up at a café (some cafés keep their own instruments for musicans) and play some songs. Songs are usually finished with a *leseb*, which is often twice the speed of the song itself and forms a background for syncopated clapping, shouting, and dancing. Early evening during Ramadan is the best time to find music cafés of this kind in full swing.

During the 1970s a more sophisticated version of *chaabi* began to emerge, with groups setting themselves up in competition with the commercial Egyptian and Libyan music which dominated the market (and the radio) at the time. These groups were usually made up of two stringed instruments—a *sentir* (bass *guimbri*) and a lute—and a *bendir* and *darabuka* or *tan-tan* as percussion. As soon as they could afford to they updated their sound and image with the addition of congas, bouzoukis, banjos, and even electric guitars. The *sentir* and *bendir*, however, remain indispensable.

Their music is a fusion of Arab, African, and modern Western influences, combining Berber music with elements taken from the Arab *malhum* and Sufi rituals, Gnaoua rhythms, and the image of European groups. Voices play an important part. The whole groups sings, either in chorus or backing a lead soloist. The lyrics deal with both love and social issues, sometimes carrying messages which have got their authors into trouble with the authorities. Sometimes there are breaks for speeches.

The three most popular groups of this kind are Jil Jilala, Lem Chaheb, and Nass el Ghiwane, all from Casablanca. **Jil Jilala** was formed in 1972 as part of a Sufi theater group. Their music is based on a Milhun style, using poetry as a reference (and starting) point. More recently they have worked with Gnaoua rhythms. They use a *ghaita* and—rare in these lineups—some Western wind instruments. **Nass el Ghiwane**, the most politicized of the three (and frequently in trouble with the authorities), lays great emphasis on the words of its recitatives and anthems/verses and choruses. Its music again combines Sufi and Gnaoua influences.

Lem Chaheb is probably the Moroccan group best known abroad, through its work with the German group Dissidenten. Two of its members play and record with this group. It has an excellent lead singer, and the substitution of an electric guitar and congas for the *sentir* and *tan-tan* has enabled it to develop its music more than other groups.

In the 1980s another generation of groups has emerged which combines traditional with modern influences, this time based in Marrakesh but again concentrating on Gnaoua rhythms. The most successful of these is **Muluk el Hwa**, a group of Berbers who used to play in the Djemaa el Fna square. The line-up is entirely acoustic: *bendir, tan-tan, sentir, bouzouki, karkabat,* and hands.

Nass el Hal, formed in 1986, offers two shows, one using a traditional accoustic line-up with bouzouki and violin, the other with drum kit and electric guitar. Its repetoire includes peasant harvest and hunting dances, and religious dances.

Other groups with records to their name include **Izanzaren**, of the Casablanca school, and **Shuka**, who do everything from Andalucian to Gnaoua. Capitalizing on the success of all these groups and the demand for cassettes, several *sentir* players have also made recordings, with percussion accompaniment. These include Hassan el Gnaoui, L'Gnaoui Mahmoud, and company.

FUSION

Morocco is an ideal place for experiment with fusion of all kinds. Such disparate figures as Brian Jones, Robin Williamson, and John Renbourn have been attracted by its rhythms, and in 1989 the Rolling Stones returned to record an album, using the **Pan Pipers of Jajouka** (whom Brian Jones had originally recorded).

The most successful group has been the Berlin-based **Dissidenten**. Before their collaboration with Lem Chaheb, they had also worked with Mohammed Zain, a star *nai* (flute) player from Tangiers who belongs to a Sufi sect, and the Gnaoua *gimri* players Abdellah el Gourd, Abdelkader Zefzaf, and Abdalla Haroch, producing several records. The remarkable *oud* player **Hassan Erraji** has been working in Britain, and recently Belgium, with his groups Belcikal and Arabesque Music.

The **Spaniards** have concentrated mainly on Arab-Andalucian music. There have been several notable collaborations between flamenco musicians and Andalucian orchestras, such as that of José Heredia Maya and Enrique

Morente with the **Tetouan Orchestra**, and Juan Peña Lebrijano with the **Tangier Orchestra**. Muluk el Hwa has also done interesting work with the Spanish group Al Tall on the medieval Valencian music known as "Xarq Al Andalus."

RAÏ

Raï—the word means "opinion"—originated in the western Algerian region around the port of Oran, and in the last years of the 1980s it has been toppling the Egyptian and Libyan stars who once ruled the cassette stores.

It has traditional roots in Bedouin music, with its distinctive refrain (ha-ya-raï), but as a modern phenomenon has more in common with western music. The backing is now solidly electric, with rhythm guitars, synthesizers, and usually a rock drum kit as well as traditional drums. Its lyrics reflect highly contemporary concerns—cars, sex, sometimes alcohol—which have created some friction with the authorities. However, Moroccans have taken easily to the music and there are now up-and-coming Moroccan raï stars such as **Cheb Khader** and the mysterious **Chaba Zahouania**. The latter is said to be forbidden by her family from being photographed on her records.

Raï influence is also to be heard in the folk music of the **Oujda** area, the closest Moroccan town to Oran, in artists like **Rachid Briha** and **Hamid M'Rabati**.

Algerian raï stars who are popular in Morocco include Cheb Khaled, Cheb Mami, and Chaba Fadhela. Cassettes of all these artists are available in the cities.

SEPHARDIC MUSIC

Moroccan Jews, many of whom have now emigrated to Israel, left an important legacy in the north of the country. Their songs and ballads are still in the medieval Spanish, spoken at the time of their expulsion from Spain five centuries ago.

Apart from the narrative ballads, these are mainly songs of courtly love, as well as lullabies and some on biblical themes. They are usually accompanied on a *tar*. The marriage ceremony has also been carefully preserved.

FOLK INSTRUMENTS

Folk instruments are very rudimentary and fairly easy to make, and this, combined with the fact that many music cafés keep their own, allows for a genuinely amateur development. Many of the instruments mentioned below are also to be found under the same or similar names (and with slight variations) in Algeria, Tunisia, Libya, and even Egypt.

Morocco has a great many string and percussion instruments, mostly fairly basic in design. There are also a few **wind instruments**. The **Arab flute**, known by different tribes as the *nai*, *talawat*, *nira*, or *gasba*, is made of a straight piece of cane open at both ends, with no mouthpiece and between five and seven holes, one at the back. It requires a great deal of skill to play it properly, by blowing at a slight angle. The **ghaita** or *rhita*, a type of oboe popular under various names throughout the Muslim world, is a conical pipe made of hard wood, ending in a bell often made of metal. Its double-reeded mouthpiece is encircled by a broad ring on which the player rests his lips in order to produce the circular breathing needed to obtain a continuous note. It has between seven and nine holes, one at the back. The **aghanin** is a double clarinet, identical to the Arab *arghoul*. It consists of two parallel pipes of wood or cane, each with a single-reed mouthpiece, five holes, and a horn at the end for amplification. One pipe provides the tune while the other is used for adornments.

The most common **string instrument** is the **gimbri**. This is an African lute whose sound box is covered in front by a piece of hide. The rounded, fretless stem has two or three strings. The body of the smaller treble *gimbri* is pear-shaped, that of the bass *gimbri* (*hadjouj* or *sentir*) rectangular. The Gnaouas often put a resonator at the end of the stem to produce the buzz typical of Black African music. The **lotar** is another type of lute, used exclusively by the Chleuh Berbers. It has a circular body, also closed with a piece of skin, and three or four strings which are plucked with a plectrum.

The classic Arab lute, the **oud**, is used in classical orchestras and the traditional Arab orchestras known as *takhts*. Its pear-shaped body is covered by a piece of wood with two or three rosette shaped openings. It has a short, fretless stem and six strings, five double and one single. The most popular string instruments played with a bow are the **kamanjeh** and the **rabab**. The former is an Iranian violin which was adopted by the Arabs. Its present Moroccan character owes a lot to the Western violin, though it is held vertically, supported on the knees. The *rabab* is a spike fiddle, rather like a viol. The bottom half of its long, curved body is covered in hide, the top in wood with a rosette shaped opening. It has two strings.

The Chleuh Berbers use an archaic single-stringed *rabab* with a square stem and sound-box covered entirely in skin. Lastly, there is the **kanum**, a trapezoidal Arab zither with over seventy strings, grouped in threes, which are plucked with plectra attatched to the finger-nails. It is used almost exclusively in classical music.

Rapid hand-clapping and the clashes of bells and cymbals are only part of the vast repetoire of Moroccan **percussion**. Like most Moroccan drums the **darbuka** is made of clay, shaped into a cylinder swelling out slightly at the top. The single skin is beaten with both hands. It is used for both folk and classical music. The **taarija**, a smaller version of the *darbuka*, is held in one hand and beaten with the other. Then there are treble and bass **tan-tan** bongos, and the Moorish **guedra**, a large drum which rests on the ground. There is also a round wooden drum with skins on both sides called a **tabl**, which is beaten with a stick on one side and by hand on the other. This is used only in folk music.

As for **tambourines**, the ever-popular **bendir** is round and wooden, 40 or 50 cm across, with two strings stretched under its single skin to produce a buzzing sound. The **tar** is smaller, with two rings of metal discs around the frame and no strings under its skin. The **duff** is a double-sided tambourine, often square in shape, which has to be supported so that it can be beaten with both hands.

Only two percussion instruments are made of metal: **karkabat**, double castanets used by the Gnaouas, and the **nakous**, a small cymbal played with two rods.

WHERE TO BUY INSTRUMENTS

MEKNES

Musical instruments *souk* under the archway connecting Souk Bezzarin and Rue des Sarraria, on the edge of the Medina—just past Bab el Djedid, if coming from Place El Hedim. Stalls here are good value and there is much choice in a small area.

TETOUAN

A couple of stores in and around the Rue Terrafin and Rue Ahmed Torres areas.

FES

Both Talaa Kebira and Talaa Seghira, close to Bab Boujeloud have stor15 15 t intervals. Try also the ceramic drum stall detailed in the guide (p.142) in Kasbah Boujeloud.

AVERAGE PRICES

Oud ($5–10); *Ghaita* ($16–30); *Nai* ($5–10); *Bendir* ($5–10); *Tara* ($6–10); *Hadjouj* ($50–70); *Darabouka* ($14–16); *Qasba* ($1.50); *Garagab* ($3–4); *Tan-Tan* ($7–25); *Gimbri* ($25–50).

RECORDS

In Morocco, **cassettes** of all kinds are readily available—folk, traditional, modern, and especially those made by the better known groups, Jil Jilala, Nass el Ghiwane, Lem Chaheb, Muluk el Hwa, Nass el Hal, etc. They cost around 14–17dh ($1.50–2) for a 60- or 90-minute tape.

Records are much harder to find and better bought in Europe, though there they are limited to ethnic, folk, and Andalusian music, or fusion with European groups. In the listings below, those with an asterisk are highly recommended; with two asterisks, you'd be cheating yourself not to enjoy . . .

GENERAL COMPILATIONS

Music of Morocco (Library of Congress). A rare but wonderful compilation by Paul Bowles— available in some record libraries.*

Music of Morocco (Folkways). Another Library of Congress Project, more easily available.

BERBER MUSIC

Maroc/1, Musique Tachelhit: Rais Lhaj Aomar Ouahrouch (Ocora).*

Maroc/2, Moyen Atlas, Musique Sacrée et Profane (Ocora).*

Orchestre de Fes, *Maroc: Musique Classique Andalou-Maghrebine* (Ocora).**

Maroc: Chants et Danses (Le Chant du Monde).

Berberes du Maroc, Ahwach (Le Chant du Monde).*

Maroc Eternel (Arion).

Hmaoui Abd El Hamid, *La flûte orientale* (Arion).**

The Rwais, Moroccan Berber Musicians from the High Atlas (Lyrichord).*

Songs and Rhythms of Marocco (Albatros).

Muluk el Hwa, *Cançons de Jma-el-Fna* (Di-fussió Mediterrania).

Master Musicians of Jajouka (Adelphi).

RELIGIOUS MUSIC

Morocco, Music of Islam & Sufism (BM).

ARABIC TRADITIONS

Abdeslam Cherkaoui, *Morocco: Arabic Traditional Music* (Unesco collection - Auvidis).*

Hassan Erraji, *Moroccan Folk Song, Vol. 1* (ME).*

Arabic Songs And Dances (Request).

ANDALUSE MUSIC (AND CROSSOVERS)

Chekara con la Orquesta de Tetuan (Ariola).*

José Heredia Maya y Orquesta Andalusi de Tetuan, *Macama Jonda* (Ariola).*

Juan Peña "El Lebrijano" and the Orquesta de Tanger, *Encuentros* (Globestyle).**

FUSION

Kwaku Baah and Ganoua (Island).

Dissidenten, *Sahara Electrik* (Globestyle)*, *Arab Shadows* (Nuevos Medios).

SEPHARDIC MUSIC

Judeo-Español Songs from Morocco (Saga).

Sephardic Jews—Ballads, Wedding Songs, Songs, and Dances (Folkways).

MOROCCO IN LITERATURE

As any glimpse at the book listings, following, will show, there's a long tradition of British and American writing on Morocco. The pieces that follow—from Budgett Meakin, Walter Harris, Elias Canetti, and Paul Bowles—represent the best of this and much of its range.

BUDGETT MEAKIN: IN MOORISH GUISE

To those who have not themselves experienced what the attempt to see an eastern country in native guise entails, a few stray notes of what it has been my lot to encounter in seeking for knowledge in this style, will no doubt be of interest. Such an undertaking, like every other style of adventure, has both its advantages and disadvantages. To the student of the people the former are immense, and if he can put up with whatever comes, he will be well repaid for all the trials by the way. In no other manner can a European mix with any freedom with the natives of this country. When once he has discarded the outward distinguishing features of what they consider a hostile infidelity, and has as far as possible adopted their dress and their mode of life, he has spanned one of the great gulfs which have hitherto yawned between them.

Squatted on the floor, one of a circle round a low table on which is a steaming dish into which each plunges his fist in search of dainty morsels, the once distant Moor thaws to an astonishing extent, becoming really friendly and communicative, in a manner totally impossible towards the starchy European who sits uneasily on a chair, conversing with his host at ease on the floor. And when the third cup of tea syrup comes, and each lolls contentedly on the cushions, there is manifested a brotherly feeling not unknown in Western circles under analogous circumstances, here fortunately without a suggestion of anything stronger than "gunpowder."

Yes, this style of thing decidedly has its delights—of which the above must not be taken as the most elevating specimen and many are the pleasant memories which come before me as I mentally review my life "as a Moor." In doing so I seem to be again transported to another world, to live another life, as was my continual feeling at the time. Everything around me was so different, my very actions and thoughts so complete a change from what they were under civilization, that when the courier brought the periodical budget of letters and papers I felt as one in a dream, even my mother tongue sounding strange after not having heard it so long.

Often I have had to "put up" in strange quarters; sometimes without any quarters at all. I have slept in the mansions of Moorish merchants, and rolled up in my cloak in the street. I have occupied the guest chambers of country governors and sheikhs, and I have passed the night on the wheat in a granary, wondering whether fleas or grains were more numerous. I have been accommodated in the house of a Jewish Rabbi, making a somewhat similar observation and I have been the guest of a Jewish Consular Agent of a Foreign Power, where the awful stench from the drains was not exceeded by that of the worst hovel I ever entered. I have even succeeded in wooing Morpheus out on the sea-shore, under the lea of a rock, and I have found the debris by the side of a straw rick an excellent couch till it came on to rain. Yet again, I have been one of half a dozen on the floor of a windowless and doorless summer-house in the middle of the rainy season. The tent of the wandering Arab has afforded me shelter, along with calves and chickens and legions of fleas, and I have actually passed the night in a village mosque.

When I set out on my travels in Moorish guise, it was with no thought of penetrating spots so venerated by the Moors that all non-Muslims are excluded, but the idea grew upon me as I journeyed, and the Moors themselves were the cause. This is how it came about. Having become acquainted to some extent with the language and customs of the people during a residence of several years among them as a European, when I travelled—with the view of rendering myself less conspicuous, and mixing more easily with the natives—I adopted their dress and followed their style of life, making, however, no attempt to conceal my nationality. After a while I found that when I went where I was not known, all took me for a Moor till they heard my speech, and recognised the foreign accent and the blunders which no native could make. My Moorish friends would often remark that were it not for this I could enter mosques and saint-houses with impunity.

For convenience' sake I had instructed the one faithful attendant who accompanied me to call me by a Muslim name resembling my own, and I afterwards added a corruption of my surname which sounded well, and soon began to seem quite natural. This prevented the attention of the bystanders being arrested when I was addressed by my man, who was careful also always to refer to me as "Seyyid," Master, a term never applied to Europeans or Jews.

Having got so far, a plan occurred to me to account for my way of speaking. I had seen a lad from Manchester, born there of an English mother, but the son of a Moor, who knew not a word of Arabic when sent to Morocco by his father. Why could I not pass as such a one, who had not yet perfected himself in the Arabic tongue? Happy thought! Was I not born in Europe, and educated there? Of course I was, and here was the whole affair complete. I remember, too, that on one or two occasions I had had quite a difficulty to persuade natives that I was *not* similarly situated to this lad. On the first occasion I was taken by surprise, as one among a party of English people, the only one dressed in Moorish costume, which I thought under those circumstances would deceive no one. When asked whence I came, I replied "England," and was then asked, "Is there a mosque there?" I answered that I was not aware that there was one, but that I knew a project had been set on foot to build one near London. Other questions followed, as to my family and what my father's occupation was, till I was astonished at the enquiry, "Has your father been to Mekka yet?"

"Why, no," I answered, as it dawned upon me what had been my interrogator's idea— "he's not a Muslim!"

"Don't say that!" said the man.

"But we are not," I reiterated, "we are Christians."

It was not as difficult to persuade him that I was not at least a convert to Christianity from Islam, as I should have thought it would have been to persuade him that I was a Muslim. Bearing this in mind, I had no doubt that by simply telling the strict truth about myself, and allowing them to draw their own conclusions, I should generally pass for the son of a Moorish

merchant settled in England, and thus it proved. Once, during a day's ride in Moorish dress, I counted the number of people who saluted by the way, and was gratified to find that although on a European saddle this suggested to the thoughtful that my mother must have been a European, and I heard one or two ask my man whether she was a legal wife or a slave! In conversation, however, I was proud and grateful to proclaim myself a Christian and an Englishman. My native dress meant after all no more than European dress does on an Oriental in England: it brought me in touch with the Moors, and it enabled me to pass among them unobserved.

Another striking instance of this occurred in Fez, where, before entering any house, I paid an unintentional visit to the very shrine I wished to see. Outside the gates I had stopped to change my costume, and passing in apart from my faithful Mohammed, after a stroll to about the centre of the city, I asked at a shop the way to a certain house. The owner called a lad who knew the neighbourhood, to whom I explained what I wanted, and off we started. In a few minutes I paused on the threshold of a finely ornamented building, different from any other I had seen. All unsuspicious, I inquired what it was, and learned that we were in a street as sacred as a mosque, and that my guide was taking me a short cut through the sanctuary of Mulai Idrees!

Some days later, lantern and slippers in one hand, and rosary in the other, I entered with the crowd for sunset prayers. Perspiring freely within, but outwardly with the calmest appearance I could muster, I spread my prayer-cloth and went through the motions prescribed by law, making my observations in the pauses, and concluding by a guarded survey of the place. I need hardly say that I breathed with a feeling of relief when I found myself in the pure air again, and felt better after I had had my supper and sat down to commit my notes to paper. In the Karûeeïn I once caught a suspicious stare at my glasses, so, pausing, I returned the stare with a contemptuous indignation that made my critic slink off abashed. There was nothing to do but to "face it out."

From *The Land of the Moors: A Comprehensive Description*, by Budgett Meakin (London, 1901).

WALTER HARRIS: *THE DEATH OF A SULTAN*

In 1893 Mulai Hassen determined to visit the desert regions of Morocco, including far-off Tafilet, the great oasis from which his dynasty had originally sprung, and where, before becoming the ruling branch of the royal family, they had resided ever since their founder, the great-grandson of the Prophet, had settled there, an exile from the East.

Leaving Fez in the summer, the Sultan proceeded south, crossing the Atlas above Kasba-el-Maghzen, and descended to the upper waters of the Wad Ziz. An expedition such as this would have required a system of organisation far in excess of the capabilities of the Moors, great though their resources were. Food was lacking; the desert regions could provide little. The water was bad, the heat very great. Every kind of delay, including rebellion and the consequent punishment of the tribes, hampered the Sultan's movements; and it was only toward winter that he arrived in Tafilet with a fever-stricken army and greatly diminished transport.

Mulai Hassen returned from Tafilet a dying man. The internal complaint from which he was suffering had become acute from the hardships he had undergone, and he was unable to obtain the rest that his state of health required, nor would he place himself under a régime. For a few months he remained in the southern capital, and in the late spring 1894 set out to suppress a rebellion that had broken out in the Tadla region.

While camping in the enemy country he died. Now, the death of the Sultan under such circumstances was fraught with danger to the State. He was an absolute monarch, and with his disappearance all authority and government lapsed until his successor should have taken up the reigns. Again, the expedition was in hostile country, and any inkling of the Sultan's death would have brought the tribes down to pillage and loot the Imperial camp. As long as the Sultan lived, and was present with his expedition, his prestige was sufficient to prevent an attack of the tribes, though even this was not unknown on one or two occasions, and to hold his forces together as a sort of concrete body. But his death, if known, would have meant speedy disorganisation, nor could the troops themselves be trusted not to seize this opportunity to murder and loot.

It was therefore necessary that the Sultan's demise should be kept an absolute secret. He had died in the recesses of his tents, themselves enclosed in a great canvas wall, inside which, except on very special occasions, no one was permitted to penetrate. The knowledge of his death was therefore limited to the personal slaves and to his Chamberlain, Bou Ahmed.

Orders were given that the Sultan would start on his journey at dawn, and before daylight the State palanquin was carried into the Imperial enclosure, the corpse laid within it, and its doors closed and the curtains drawn. At the first pale break of dawn the palanquin was brought out, supported by sturdy mules. Bugles were blown, the band played, and the bowing courtiers and officials poured forth their stentorian cry, "May God protect the life of our Lord." The procession formed up, and, led by flying banners, the dead Sultan set out on his march.

A great distance was covered that day. Only once did the procession stop, when the palanquin was carried into a tent by the roadside, that the Sultan might breakfast. Food was borne in and out; tea, with all the paraphernalia of its brewing, was served: but none but the slaves who knew the secret were permitted to enter. The Chamberlain remained with the corpse, and when a certain time had passed, he emerged to state that His Majesty was rested and had breakfasted, and would proceed on his journey—and once more the procession moved on. Another long march was made to where the great camp was pitched for the night.

The Sultan was tired, the Chamberlain said. He would not come out of his enclosure to transact business as usual in the "Diwan" tent, where he granted audiences. Documents were taken in to the royal quarters by the Chamberlain himself, and, when necessary, they emerged bearing the seal of State, and verbal replies were given to a host of questions.

Then another day of forced marches, for the expedition was still in dangerous country; but Mulai Hassen's death could no longer be concealed. It was summer, and the state of the Sultan's body told its own secret.

Bou Ahmed announced that His Majesty had died two days before, and that by this time his young son, Mulai Abdul Aziz, chosen and nominated by his father, had been proclaimed at Rabat, whither the fleetest of runners had been sent with the news immediately after the death had occurred.

It was a *fait accompli.* The army was now free of the danger of being attacked by the tribes; and the knowledge that the new Sultan was already reigning, and that tranquillity existed elsewhere, deterred the troops from any excesses. Many took the occasion of a certain disorganisation to desert, but so customary was this practice that it attracted little or no attention.

Two days later the body of the dead Sultan, now in a terrible state of decomposition, arrived at Rabat. It must have been a gruesome procession from the description his son Mulai Abdul Aziz gave me: the hurried arrival of the swaying palanquin bearing its terrible burden, five days dead in the great heat of summer; the escort, who had bound scarves over their faces—but even this precaution could not keep them from constant sickness—and even the mules that bore the palanquin seemed affected by the horrible atmosphere, and tried from time to time to break loose.

No corpse is, by tradition, allowed to enter through the gates into a Moorish city, and even in the case of the Sovereign no exception was made. A hole was excavated in the town wall, through which the procession passed direct into the precincts of the palace, where the burial took place. Immediately after, the wall was restored.

From *Morocco That Was,* by Walter Harris (1921). Reprinted in a paperback edition by Greenwood Press.

ELIAS CANETTI: THE UNSEEN

At twilight I went to the great square in the middle of the city, and what I sought there were not its colour and bustle, those I was familiar with, I sought a small, brown bundle on the ground consisting not even of a voice but of a single sound. This was a deep, long-drawn-out, buzzing "e-e-e-e-e-e-e-e." It did not diminish, it did not increase, it just went on and on; beneath all the thousands of calls and cries in the square it was always audible. It was the most unchanging sound in the Djemaa el Fna, remaining the same all evening and from evening to evening.

While still a long way off I was already listening for it. A restlessness drove me there that I cannot satisfactorily explain. I would have gone to the square in any case, there was so much there to attract me; nor did I ever doubt I would find it each time, with all that went with it. Only for this voice, reduced to a single sound, did I feel something akin to fear. It was at the very edge of the living; the life that engendered it consisted of nothing but that sound. Listening greedily, anxiously, I invariably reached a point in my walk, in exactly the same place, where I suddenly became aware of it like the buzzing of an insect: "e-e-e-e-e-e-e-e."

I felt a mysterious calm spread through my body, and whereas my steps had been hesitant and uncertain hitherto I now, all of a sudden, made determinedly for the sound. I knew where it came from. I knew the small, brown bundle on the ground, of which I had never seen anything more than a piece of dark, coarse cloth. I had never seen the mouth from which the "e-e-e-e" issued; nor the eye; nor the cheek; nor any part of the face. I could not have said whether it was the face of a blind man or whether it could see. The brown, soiled cloth was pulled right down over the head like a hood, concealing everything. The creature—as it must have been—squatted on the ground, its back arched under the material. There was not much of the creature there, it seemed slight and feeble, that was all one could conjecture. I had no idea how tall it was because I had never seen it standing. What there was of it on the ground kept so low that one would have stumbled over it quite unsuspectingly, had the sound ever stopped. I never saw it come, I never saw it go; I do not know whether it was brought and put down there or whether it walked there by itself.

The place it had chosen was by no means sheltered. It was the most open part of the square and there was an incessant coming and going on all sides of the little brown heap. On busy evenings it disappeared completely behind people's legs, and although I knew exactly where it was and could always hear the voice I had difficulty in finding it. But then the people dispersed, and it was still in its place when all around it, far and wide, the square was empty. Then it lay there in the darkness like an old and very dirty garment that someone had wanted to get rid of and had surreptitiously dropped in the midst of all the people where no one would notice. Now, however, the people had dispersed and only the bundle lay there. I never waited until it got up or was fetched. I slunk away in the darkness with a choking feeling of helplessness and pride.

The helplessness was in regard to myself. I sensed that I would never do anything to discover the bundle's secret. I had a dread of its shape; and since I could give it no other I left it lying there on the ground. When I was getting close I took care not to bump into it, as if I might hurt or endanger it. It was there every evening, and every evening my heart stood still when I first distinguished the sound, and it stood still again when I caught sight of the bundle. How it got there and how it got away again were matters more sacred to me than my own movements. I never spied on it and I do not know where it disappeared to for the rest of the night and the following day. It was something apart, and perhaps it saw itself as such. I was sometimes tempted to touch the brown hood very lightly with one finger—the creature was bound to notice, and perhaps it had a second sound with which it would have responded. But this temptation always succumbed swiftly to my helplessness.

I have said that another feeling choked me as I slunk away: pride. I was proud of the bundle because it was alive. What it thought to itself as it breathed down there, far below other people, I shall never know. The meaning of its call remained as obscure to me as its whole existence: but it was alive, and every day at the same time, there it was. I never saw it pick up the coins that people threw it; they did not throw many, there were never more than two or three coins lying there. Perhaps it had no arms with which to reach for the coins. Perhaps it had no tongue with which to form the "*l*" of "Allah" and to it the name of God was abbreviated to "e-e-e-e-e." But it was alive, and with a diligence and persistence that were unparalleled it uttered its one sound, uttered it hour after hour, until it was the only sound in the whole enormous square, the sound that outlived all others.

From *The Voices of Marrakesh*, by Elias Canetti (Farrar Straus and Giroux, New York, 1988); first published in German in 1967.

PAUL BOWLES: POINTS IN TIME, X

The country of the Anjra is almost devoid of paved roads. It is a region of high jagged mountains and wooded valleys, and does not contain a town of any size. During the rainy season there are landslides. Then, until the government sends men to repair the damage, the roads cannot be used. All this is very much on the minds of the people who live in the Anjra, particularly when they are waiting for the highways to be rebuilt so that trucks can move again between the villages. Four or five soldiers had been sent several months earlier to repair the potholes along the road between Ksar es Seghir and Melloussa. Their tent was beside the road, near a curve in the river.

A peasant named Hattash, whose village lay a few miles up the valley, constantly passed by the place on his way to and from Ksar es Seghir. Hattash had no fixed work of any sort, but he kept very busy looking for a chance to pick up a little money one way or another in the market and the cafés. He was the kind of man who prided himself on his cleverness in swindling foreigners, by which he meant men from outside the Anjra. Since his friends shared his dislike of outsiders, they found his exploits amusing, although they were careful to have no dealings with him.

Over the months Hattash had become friendly with the soldiers living in the tent, often stopping to smoke a pipe of kif with them, perhaps squatting down to play a few games of ronda. Thus, when one day the soldiers decided to give a party, it was natural that they should mention it to Hattash, who knew everyone for miles around, and therefore might be able to help them. The soldiers came from the south, and their isolation there by the river kept them from meeting anyone who did not regularly pass their tent.

I can get you whatever you want, Hattash told them. The hens, the vegetables, oil, spices, salad, whatever.

Fine. And we want some girls or boys, they added.

Don't worry about that. You'll have plenty to choose from. What you don't want you can send back.

They discussed the cost of the party for an hour or so, after which the soldiers handed Hattash twenty-five thousand francs. He set off, ostensibly for the market.

Instead of going there, he went to the house of a nearby farmer and bought five of his best hens, with the understanding that if the person for whom he was buying them should not want them, he could return the hens and get his money back.

Soon Hattash was outside the soldiers' tent with the hens. How are they? he said. The men squeezed them and examined them, and pronounced them excellent. Good, said Hattash. I'll take them home now and cook them.

He went back to the farmer with the hens and told him that the buyer had refused them. The farmer shrugged and gave Hattash his money.

This seemed to be the moment to leave Ksar es Seghir, Hattash decided. He stopped at a café and invited everyone there to the soldiers' tent that evening, telling them there would be food, wine and girls. Then he bought bread, cheese and fruit, and began to walk along the trails that would lead him over the mountains to Khemiss dl Anjra.

With the twenty-five thousand francs he was able to live for several weeks there in Khemmiss el Anjra. When he had come to the end of them, he began to think of leaving.

In the market one morning he met Hadj Abdallah, a rich farmer from Farsioua, which was a village only a few miles from his own. Hadj Abdallah, a burly, truculent man, always had eyed Hattash with distrust.

Ah, Hattash! What are you doing up here? It's a while since I've seen you.

And you? said Hattash.

Me? I'm on my way to Tetuan. I'm leaving my mule here and taking the bus.

That's where I'm going, said Hattash.

Well, see you in Tetuan, said Hadj Abdallah, and he turned, unhitched his mule, and rode off.

Khemiss dl Anjra is a very small town, so that it was not difficult for Hattash to follow along at some distance, and see the house where Hadj Abdallah tethered his mule and into which he then disappeared. He walked to the bus station and sat under a tree.

An hour or so later, when the bus was filling up with people, Hadj Abdallah arrived and bought his ticket. Hattash approached him.

Can you lend me a thousand francs? I haven't got enough to buy the ticket.

Hadj Abdallah looked at him. No. I can't, he said. Why don't you stay here? And he went and got into the bus.

Hattash, his eyes very narrow, sat down again under the tree. When the bus had left, and the cloud of smoke and dust had drifted off over the meadows, he walked back to the house where the Hadj had left his mule. She still stood there, so he quietly unhitched her, got astride her, and rode her in the direction of Mgas Tleta. He was still smarting under Hadj Abdallah's insult, and he vowed to give him as much trouble as he could.

Mgas Tleta was a small tchar. He took the mule to the fondaq and left it in charge of the guardian. Being ravenously hungry, he searched in his clothing for a coin or two to buy a piece of bread, and found nothing.

In the road outside the fondaq he caught sight of a peasant carrying a loaf in the hood of his djellaba. Unable to take his eyes from the bread, he walked towards the man and greeted him. Then he asked him if he had work, and was not surprised when the man answered no.

He went on, still looking at the bread: If you want to earn a thousand francs, you can take my mule to Mdiq. My father's waiting for her and he'll pay you. Just ask for Si Mohammed Tsuli. Everybody in Mdiq knows him. He always has a lot of men working for him. He'll give you work there too if you want it.

The peasant's eyes lit up. He agreed immediately.

Hattash sighed. It's a long time since I've seen good country bread like that, he said, pointing at the loaf that emerged from the hood of the djellaba. The man took it out and handed it to him. Here. Take it.

In return Hattash presented him with the receipt for the mule. You'll have to pay a hundred francs to get her out of the fondaq, he told him. My father will give it back to you.

That's all right. The man was eager to start out for Mdiq.

Si Mohammed Tsuli. Don't forget.

No, no! Bslemah.

Hattash, well satisfied, watched the man ride off. Then he sat down on a rock and ate the whole loaf of bread. He had no intention of returning home to risk meeting the soldiers or Hadj Abdallah, so he decided to hide himself for a while in Tetuan, where he had friends.

When the peasant arrived at Mdiq the following day, he found that no one could tell him where Si Mohammed Tsuli lived. He wandered back and forth through every street in the town, searching and inquiring. When evening came, he went to the gendarmerie and asked if he might leave the mule there. But they questioned him and accused him of having stolen the animal. His story was ridiculous, they said, and they locked him into a cell.

Not many days later Hadj Abdallah, having finished his business in Tetuan, went back to Khemiss dl Anjra to get his mule and ride her home. When he heard that she had disappeared directly after he had taken the bus home, he remembered Hattash, and was certain that he was the culprit. The theft had to be reported in Tetuan, and much against his will he returned there.

Your mule is in Mdiq, the police told him.

Hadj Abdallah took another bus up to Mdiq.

Papers, said the gendarmes. Proof of ownership.

The Hadj had no documents of that sort. They told him to go to Tetuan and apply for the forms.

During the days while he waited for the papers to be drawn up, signed and stamped, Hadj Abdallah grew constantly angrier. He went twice a day to talk with the police. I know who took her! he would shout. I know the son of a whore.

If you ever catch sight of him, hold on to him, they told him. We'll take care of him.

Although Tetuan is a big place with many crowded quarters, the unlikely occurred. In a narrow passageway near the Souq el Fouqi late one evening Hadj Abdallah and Hattash came face to face.

The surprise was so great that Hattash remained frozen to the spot, merely staring into Hadj Abdallah's eyes. Then he heard a grunt of rage, and felt himself seized by the other man's strong arm.

Police! Police! roared Hadj Abdallah. Hattash squirmed, but was unable to free himself.

One policeman arrived, and then another. Hadj Abdallah did not release his grip of Hattash for an instant while he delivered his denunciation. Then with an oath he struck his prisoner, knocking him flat on the sidewalk. Hattash lay there in the dark without moving.

Why did you do that? the policemen cried. Now you're the one who's going to be in trouble.

Hadj Abdallah was already frightened. I know. I ought not to have hit him.

It's very bad, said one policeman, bending over Hattash, who lay completely still. You see, there's blood coming out of his head.

A small crowd was collecting in the passageway.

There were only a few drops of blood, but the policeman had seen Hattash open one eye and had heard him whisper: Listen.

He bent over still farther, so that his ear was close to Hattash's lips.

He's got money, Hattash whispered.

The policeman rose and went over to Hadj Abdallah. We'll have to call an ambulance, he said, and you'll have to come to the police station. You had no right to hit him.

At that moment Hattash began to groan.

He's alive, at least! cried Hadj Abdallah. Hamdul'lah!

Then the policemen began to speak with him in low tones, advising him to settle the affair immediately by paying cash to the injured man.

Hadj Abdallah was willing. How much do you think? he whispered.

It's a bad cut he has on his head, the same policeman said, going back to Hattash. Come and look.

Hadj Abdallah remained where he was, and Hattash groaned as the man bent over him again. Then he murmured: Twenty thousand. Five for each of you.

When the policeman rejoined Hadj Abdallah, he told him the amount. You're lucky to be out of it.

Hadj Abdallah gave the money to the policeman, who took it over to Hattash and prodded him. Can you hear me? he shouted.

Ouakha, groaned Hattash.

Here. Take this. He held out the banknotes in such a way that Hadj Abdallah and the crowd watching could see them clearly. Hattash stretched up his hand and took them, slipping them into his pocket.

Hadj Abdallah glared at the crowd and pushed his way through, eager to get away from the spot.

After he had gone, Hattash slowly sat up and rubbed his head. The onlookers still stood there watching. This bothered the two policemen, who were intent on getting their share of the money. The recent disclosures of corruption, however, had made the public all too attentive at such moments. The crowd was waiting to see them speak to Hattash or, if he should move, follow him.

Hattash saw the situation and understood. He rose to his feet and quickly walked up the alley.

The policemen looked at each other, waited for a few seconds, and then began to saunter casually in the same direction. Once they were out of sight of the group of onlookers they hurried along, flashing their lights up each alley in their search. But Hattash knew the quarter as well as they, and got safely to the house of his friends.

He decided, however, that with the two policemen on the lookout for him, Tetuan was no longer the right place for him, and that his own tchar in the Anjra would be preferable.

Once he was back there, he made discreet inquiries about the state of the road to Ksar es Seghir. The repairs were finished, his neighbors told him, and the soldiers had been sent to some other part of the country.

From *Points in Time,* by Paul Bowles (Ecco Press, New York, 1982).

ONWARD FROM MOROCCO

Going on from Morocco there are two basic options. The most obvious is to take in something of **Spain** and, if you've developed any interest in Moorish art, to visit the three great Andalusian cities of the south—Granada, Córdoba, and Seville. Each of these boast superb Islamic monuments, which, to be honest are more spectacular than any in Morocco. Granada has the fabulous fifteenth-century Alhambra palace, home of the last Moorish rulers in al-Andalus; Córdoba has a tenth-century mosque, now the city's cathedral; and Seville has one of Yacoub el Mansour's magnificent Almohad towers, again adapted for Christian use as the local bell tower, or Giralda. For all of this—and a great deal more—*The Real Guide Spain* (Prentice Hall, $12.95) is helpful.

The second option, and one that is considerably more ambitious, is to travel **"the Maghreb Circuit"** east from Morocco into Algeria and Tunisia, where, if you still have the time and energy, you can cross over by ferry to Italy and either loop back to northern Europe (Italian trains are cheap) or take another ferry on from Bari or Brindisi to Greece. Don't be put off by the distances involved in any of this, nor by travelers' tales of Algerian bureaucracy at the border (though these are true enough); it's an exciting, feasible, and immensely satisfying trip, and there's an added fascination in that all of this region—from Spain and Morocco up as far as Sicily—comprised the western Arab empire in the early Middle Ages.

Mosques, incidentally, may be visited freely in Algeria and, to an extent, in Tunisia.

ALGERIA

Algeria is much less well known in the West than either Morocco or Tunisia and it has always been the most adventurous part of North Africa to travel through. This it still remains—a vast expanse of often very extraordinary routes.

Algerians themselves are extremely hospitable, and there is none of the hustling that you find in Morocco. If you can speak French, you will be able to communicate with ease—the language of colonial years (150 years here, as opposed to just 50 in Morocco) endures, along with many facets of French culture. Indeed, all European travelers are initially assumed to be French. It tends to be an advantage if you can make it clear that you're not.

Red Tape

Visas are essential for all North Americans and Australasians; most Europeans are exempt. Visas can be acquired, within the day, at the Algerian consulate in Rabat (see Rabat "Directory"), or (a much longer process) in Oujda.

While in Algeria you are required to change $150 into Algerian currency at the official rate; it is sometimes obligatory to do this at the border. This restriction is no longer waived for students, as in the past, and money cannot be changed back again. The black market is widely used, and if you're staying longer than your $150 dollars (approximately 1050 dinars) will last, you will find rates offered up to three times better. The best currency for black market exchange is French francs.

Borders

There are two **borders** open between Morocco and Algeria—at OUJDA and, 300km to the south, at the desert oasis of FIGUIG. The former used to be closed to "pedestrian traffic" but it is now fully open, following the improvement in Moroccan-Algerian relations after the 1988 Maghreb Summit.

Routes

The fastest route through Algeria cuts across the big **northern cities** of ORAN, ALGIERS, and CONSTANTINE. This is not in itself the most interesting part of the country, though the mountain scenery is often spectacular.

Making relatively short detours the rewards are greater. TIMGAD, almost completely preserved, is one of the most extraordinary Roman towns anywhere; any one of the roads between BATNA and the immense oasis of BISKRA will take you through dramatic canyons; the TURQUOISE COAST, west of Algiers, is a long series of mountainous and isolated coves; and in the mountains by the Moroccan border, TLEMCEN's Islamic architecture is among the most important and beautiful in North Africa.

If you have time to spare, though, even as little as a week, try to take in at least something of **the south**. The sheer size of the desert regions here is hard to grasp: TAMANRASSET, near the Niger border, for instance, is farther from Algiers than London is. Closer, and easily accessible from the north, there are also some of the most spectacular Saharan dunes—stretching between EL OUED, the so-called "City of a Thousand Domes," and the fantastic architecture of GHARDAIA.

Going through the deep south really does feel more like travel than tourism and time and energy are needed to explore the desert *pistes*. The two really compelling attractions are both mountain ranges: the HOGGAR, rising over 3000m to the north of Tamanrasset, and the TASSILI, some ways to the east, with its exceptional prehistoric cave paintings.

Guidebooks

The trip across the Algerian Sahara to West Africa is covered in the *Real Guide West Africa* (forthcoming Fall 1990). Simon and Jan Glen's *Sahara Handbook* (Lascelles, UK) is also useful for this route. The only guides to Algeria itself are in French: try a combination of the *Guide Bleu: Algerie* and, for budget practicalities, the *Guide Routarde: Algerie-Tunisie* (both published by Hachette).

TUNISIA

Crossing from Algeria to Tunisia is normally straightforward, though the number of border posts that are open vary according to the state of relations between the two countries. The most regular are in the north at ANNABA-BABOUCH and SOUK AHRAS-GHARDIMAO (the train crossing), but at the time of this writing you can cross in the south, too, at EL OUED-HAZOUA.

Much more Westernized than either Morocco or Algeria, Tunisia is recognizably Mediterranean in character and a relaxed place to end up after a week or so of desert traveling. Its best-known attraction are the long white-sand **beaches** and easygoing resorts, and in a

North African context these are perhaps its greatest novelty. But there is considerably more to the country than this—not least its highly individual **desert architecture**, and the Maghreb's most important **Roman sites**—and the accessibility of everything (you can comfortably travel its length in a couple of days) makes it a satisfying place to visit and get to know.

Red Tape

North Americans need a **visa** to visit Tunisia. This can be obtained in a couple of hours from the Tunisian Consulate in Rabat (see Rabat "Directory").

On to Sicily or Beyond

Continuing on from Tunisia, there are regular, year-round **ferries** to the Sicilian ports of PALERMO and TRAPANI, and links from there to Naples, Genoa, Sardinia, and Malta. Apart from the last two weeks of August (when all ferries from Tunis are packed with returning migrant workers) it is usually possible to get tickets on these; if you have a car, however, it's essential to make your reservations in advance for travel between July and September.

Tunis, incidentally, is also a major link on international airline routes, so you can often pick up **bargain flights** to Cairo, Nairobi, Casablanca, and Algiers, as well as to Madrid, Rome, Athens, and most points in Europe.

Guidebook

For a full treatment of the country, *The Rough Guide to Tunisia* (Harrap-Columbus, UK) seems an obvious choice. The *Rough Guides* are the British equivalent of the *Real Guides*.

THE CANARY ISLANDS

A last alternative, onward from Morocco, is to head for the **CANARY ISLANDS**, just a few miles offshore from the disputed territory of the former Spanish Sahara. There is a weekly car and passenger ferry from Agadir to Las Palmas (see Agadir "Practicalities") between September and May. Alternatively, you can fly to Las Palmas from Agadir or Laayoune.

BOOKS

GENERAL/TRAVEL

Paul Bowles, *Points in Time* (Ecco Press, $11.95), *Their Heads Are Green & Their Hands Are Blue* (Ecco Press, $8.50)). Novelist, poet, and composer, Paul Bowles has lived in Tangier most of his life and more or less singlehandedly brought translations of local writers (see "Fiction") to western attention. *Points* is a remarkable series of tales and short pieces inspired by episodes and sources from earliest times to the present day—the final piece is excerpted in the "Morocco in Literature" section. *Heads* includes a couple of travel essays on Morocco and a terrific piece on the psychology of desert travel. Bowles's autobiography, *Without Stopping* (Ecco Press, $9.50) is also of interest for its Moroccan episodes.

Peter Mayne, *A Year in Marrakesh* (Hippocrene Books, $9.95). Mayne went to Marrakesh in the early 1950s, found a house in an ordinary district of the Medina, and tried to live like a Moroccan. He couldn't, but wrote an unusually perceptive account explaining why.

Elias Canetti, *The Voices of Marrakesh* (Farrar Straus and Giroux, $6.95). Impressions of Marrakesh in the last years of French rule, by the Nobel prizewinning author. The atmosphere of many pieces still holds—see the excerpt printed under "Morocco in Literature."

Walter Harris, *Morocco That Was* (Greenwood, $35.00). Harris, Times correspondent in Tangier from the 1890s until his death in 1933, saw the country at probably the strangest ever stage in its history—the last years of "Old Morocco" in its feudal isolation and the first of French occupation. This book,

originally published in 1921, is brilliant: alternately sharp, melodramatic, and very funny. *Land of an African Sultan* (1889) and *Tafilet* (1895), Harris's earlier travel books, are incorporated to some extent in *Morocco That Was.*

Gavin Maxwell, *Lords of the Atlas* (David and Charles, $13.95). Drawing heavily on Harris's accounts of the Moorish court, this is the story of the extraordinary Glaoui family—literally the "Lords" of the High Atlas, where they exercized almost complete control from the turn of the nineteenth century right through to Moroccan Independence in 1956. Not an attractive tale but a compelling one, and again superbly written. (Note: This book is technically banned from Morocco, due to its view of historical events).

Budgett Meakin, *The Land of the Moors* (State Mutual Book, $350), *The Moors: A Comprehensive Description* (1902, OOP). Long out of print, *The Land of the Moors* is now available in this costly edition. Best to pay a visit to the library for a browse through these wonderful encyclopedic volumes—the first really detailed books on Morocco and Moroccan life. Many of Meakin's descriptions remain accurate , and the sheer breadth of his knowledge (from "Berber Feuds" to "Specimen Recipes" and musical notations of "Calls to Prayer") is fascinating in itself.

Leo Africanus, *History and Description of Africa* (no recent edition, available in some libraries). Written in the mid-sixteenth century, this was the book Meakin himself followed, "astounded at the confirmation [of its accuracy] received from natives of remote and almost inaccessible districts." Leo, Moroccan by birth, was captured as a young man by Christian pirates, subsequently converting and living in Italy; the book was suggested to him by the Pope, so there's more than a hint of propaganda about some of the accounts. (See also Amin Malouf, under "Fiction").

OF LESSER INTEREST

Wyndham Lewis, *Journey into Barbary* (Black Sparrow, $12.50). Terrific drawings, but an obscure, eccentric, and very rambling text.

Edith Wharton, *In Morocco* (David & Charles, $13.95). First published in 1920 and dedicated to the Lyauteys. By no means a classic, it is nonetheless worth reading for its glimpses of harem life in the early part of the century.

Shirley Kay, *Morocco* (Charles River Books, $30.00). Glossy picture book introduction to the country and—as such—pretty good.

Rom Landau, *Morocco: Marrakesh, Fez, Rabat* (Putnam, OOP but is available in libraries). Landau has written numerous books on Morocco, none of them very inspiring. This one's redeeming feature is an excellent series of photographs—including mosque interiors.

HISTORY

Neville Barbour, *Morocco* (Walker, OOP, available in some libraries). A lucid, straightforward account of Morocco from the Phoenicians to "the present day" (1965).

Douglas Porch, *The Conquest of Morocco* (Fromm International Publishers, $11.95). Highly readable account of the extraordinary maneuverings and characters of Morocco's turn of the century history.

David Woolman, *Rebels in the Rif* (Stanford University Press, $25.00). Excellent, accessible account of the Riffian war in the 1920s and of the tribes' uprising against the Moroccan government in 1956.

Roger Le Tourneau, *Fez in the Age of the Marinides* (University of Oklahoma Press, $8.95). Interesting if slightly specialist study of the Merenid capital of Morocco. Tourneau's *The Almohad Movement* (out of print) is also worth looking out for in libraries.

Bernard Lewis, *The Jews of Islam* (Princeton University Press, $45.00). Morocco had over 30,000 Jews until the mass emigrations to Israel in the 1940s and 1950s. Lewis discusses their position (which was perhaps the most oppressed within the Arab world) and their political and cultural contributions. In this it's an excellent book, though disappointingly he doesn't attempt to cover the period of emigration itself.

Peter Mansfield, *The Arabs* (Penguin, $7.95). Best general introduction to the Arab world, from its beginnings through to the 1970s. Short final sections deal with each individual country.

J.M Abun-Nasr, *History of the Maghreb in the Islamic Period* (Cambridge University Press, $24.95). Morocco in the wider context of North Africa by a distinguished Arab historian.

R. Oliver and J. D. Fage, *A History of Africa* (Knopf, $29.45). Morocco within the context of its continent.

E. W. Bovill and **Robin Hallet**, *The Golden Trade of the Moors* (Oxford University Press, $9.95). Wide-ranging book about the trans-Saharan trade, including the old routes down from Morocco to Timbuctou and Niger.

Ibn Khaldun, *The Muqaddimah: An Introduction to History* (Princeton University Press, $28.00). Edited translation of the greatest work of the fourteenth-century Moorish scholar – a fascinating mix of history, sociology, and anthropology, centuries ahead of its time.

SOCIETY/POLITICS

Fatima Mernissi, *Beyond the Veil: Male-Female Dynamics in Modern Muslim Society* (Indiana University Press, $7.95). Seminal book by a feminist Moroccan sociologist from the Mohammed V University in Rabat.

Fatima Mernissi, *Doing Daily Battle: Interviews with Moroccan Women* (Rutgers University Press, $12.00). Eleven women— carpet weavers, rural and factory workers, teachers—talk about all aspects of their lives, from work and housing to marriage. A fascinating insight into a resolutely private world.

Elizabeth Fernea, *A Street in Marrakesh* (Doubleday, out of print). Highly readable account of a woman anthropologist's period of study and experiences in Marrakesh.

Elizabeth Fernea and Basima Q.Bezirgan, *Middle Eastern Muslim Women Speak Out* (Universijty of Texas Press, $13.95). Straightforward and accessible social anthropology, including interesting transcriptions of Berber women's songs from the High Atlas.

Ernest Gellner and **Charles Micaud** (eds.), *Arabs and Berbers* (Lexington books, OOP but available in some libraries). An authortiative collection of anthropological articles on Berbers and tribalism in Morocco. Interesting, if on a rather selective basis.

Ernest Gellner, *Saints of the Atlas* (University of Chicago Press, $20.00). The bulk of this book is an in-depth study of a group of *zaouia*-villages in the High Atlas, but there are excellent introductory chapters on Morocco's recent past and the concept and origins of Berbers.

Kevin Dwyer, *Moroccan Dialogues: Anthropology in Question* (Waveland Press, $9.95). Fascinating series of recorded conversations with a farmer from a village near Taroudannt, ranging through attitudes to women, religion, and village life to popular Moroccan perceptions of the Jews, the French, and even the hippies. Well worth a look.

Tony Hodges, *Western Sahara: the Roots of a Desert War* (Chicago Review, $14.95). The former Spanish colony of Western Sahara-Rio d'Oro is the most contentious issue of modern Moroccan politics: this is the latest, fullest, and most interesting book on the subject.

ISLAM

The Koran (Penguin, $4.95). The Word of God as handed down to the Prophet is the basis of all Islam, so essential reading for anyone interested. If you can find it, the Oxford University Press (UK) edition is a much clearer and livelier translation.

S.H.Nasr, *Ideas and Realities of Islam* (Unwin Hyman, $9.95). Probably the clearest and most useful general introduction.

Maxime Rodinson, *Muhammad* (Pantheon, $9.95). Challenging account of the Prophet's life and the immediate impact of his ideology.

ART/ARCHITECTURE

Richard Parker, *A Practical Guide to Islamic Monuments in Morocco* (Baraka Press, Charlottesville, Virginia). Exactly what it claims to be – a very helpful and well informed, with introductory sections on architectural forms and motifs, and craft traditions. Available in Rabat.

Titus Burckhardt, *Moorish Culture in Spain* (OOP but available in libraries). Spain is a superb study of architecture, history, Islamic city-design and the mystical significance of its art—as such its entirely relevant to medieval Morocco.

Leslie Frederick Brett, *The Moors* (OOP but available in libraries). A beautifully illustrated survey of the Moorish Empire, extremely well thought out with an understanding text. Worth a trip to the library.

David Talbot Rice, *Islamic Art* (Thames & Hudson, $11.95). Clear, interesting, and well-illustrated survey—though only two chapters directly concern Morocco.

Andre Paccard, *Traditional Islamic Craft in Moroccan Architecture* (Editions Artelier, France, 2 vols). French coffee table tome beyond all possible rival. The text is forgettable, but it is massively illustrated and—uniquely—includes photographs of Moroccan Royal Palaces currently in use: this alone makes it worth a look.

MOROCCAN FICTION

PAUL BOWLES TRANSLATIONS
Mohammed Mrabet

Love with a Few Hairs; The Boy Who Set the Fire & Other Stories; The Lemon; M'Hashish (published by City Lights, $6.95 each, except *M'Hashish* which is $3.95).

The Chest; Marriage With Papers (both Tombouctou, $7.95/$6.00)

The Big Mirror, Harmless Poisons, Blameless Sins, Look and Move On: An Autobiography (Black Sparrow Press; some titles out of print).

Mohammed Choukri, *For Bread Alone: An Autobiography* (City Lights, $6.95).

Larbi Layachi, *A Life Full of Holes* (Published under name Driss ben Hamed Charhadi; Grove Press, $3.50).

Five Eyes, stories by **Mohammed Mrabet**, **Larbi Layachi**, **Mohammed Choukri**, **Ahmed Yacoubi** and **Abdesiam Boulaich** (Black Sparrow, oop).

All of the above are taped and translated from the Moghrebi, sometimes edited too, by **Paul Bowles**. It is hard to generalize about them, except to say that they are for the most part 'tales' (even the autobiographies, which seem little different from the fiction), share a common fixation with intrigue and unexpected twists in the narrative, and are often punctuated by episodes of extreme violence. None have particular characterization, though this hardly seems relevant since they have such a strong, vigorous narrative style – brilliantly matched by Bowles's sharp, economic language.

The **Mrabet** stories—*The Beach Cafe* is perhaps his best—are often kif-inspired, and this gives them a slightly paranoid quality, as Mrabet himself explained; "Give me twenty or thirty pipes . . . and an empty room can fill up with wonderful things, or terrible things. And the stories come from these things."

OTHER MOROCCAN FICTION

Tahar Ben Jalloun, *The Sand Child* (Harcourt Brace, $17.95). Ben Jalloun, resident in Paris, is Morocco's most acclaimed writer – and in the case of this novel the reputation is just. An unusually 'fictional' tale, its subject, the Sand Child, is a girl whose father brought her up as a boy. Very readable.

Larbi Layachi, *Yesterday and Today* (Black Sparrow, $8.50), *The Jealous Lover* (Tombouctou, $7.50). The former is a kind of sequel to *Life Full of Holes* (see above), describing in semi-fictionalized form Layachi's time with Paul and Jane Bowles; the latter is more of a story and rather less successful.

Abdelhak Serhane, *Messaouda* (Carcanet, $15.95). Adventurous; semi-autobiographical novel about growing up in Azrou during the 1950s. The narrator's development parallels that of his country, with his attempts to free himself from the patriarchy and authoritarianism of his father used as an allegory for the struggle against French colonialism and its aftermath.

Driss Chraibi, *Heirs to the Past* (Heinemann Editions, $6.00). Again concerned with the crisis of Moroccans' postcolonial identity, and again semiautobiographical as the author-narrator (who has lived in France since the war) returns to Morocco for the funeral of his father. Also available—though in rather over-literal and unspirited translation—are two further novels, *The Butts* and *Mother Comes of Age* (Three Continents, both $8.00).

WESTERN FICTION

PAUL BOWLES

NOVELS: *The Sheltering Sky* (Ecco Press, $9.50); *Let It Come Down* (Black Sparrow, $10.95); *The Spider's House* (Black Sparrow, $12.50). (A fourth novel, *Up Above the World*, is set in Latin America.)

STORIES: *Collected Stories of Paul Bowles 1939–76* (Black Sparrow, $12.50); *A Distant Episode: Selected Stories* (Ecco Press, 1989, $10.95); and other editions.

As with Moroccan literature, Bowles stands out as the most interesting (and the most prolific) writer using North African themes. Many of his stories are in fact quite close to Mrabet's: with the same sparse forms, bizarre twists and interjections of violence. The novels

are something different, exploring both Morocco (or, in *The Sheltering Sky*, Algeria) and the ways in which Europeans and Americans react to and are affected by it.

If you read nothing else on the country, at least get hold of **The Spider's House** —one of the best political novels ever written, its backdrop the traditional daily life of Fes, its theme conflicts and transformation at the last stages of the French occupation of the country.

OTHER FICTION SET IN MOROCCO

Amin Malouf, *Leo the African* (Quartet, UK). Superb historical novel, recreating the life of Leo Africanus, the fifteenth century Moorish geographer, in Granada and Fes, and on his later travels.

Arturo Barea, *The Forging of a Rebel* (Flamingo, UK; 3 volumes). Translation of a Spanish autobiographical novel of the 1930s. The second volume, *The Track*, concerns the war and colonization of the Rif, the Spanish entry into Chaouen, and life in Tetouan. Highly recommended.

Richard Hughes, *In the Lap of Atlas* (Chatto, UK). Traditional Moroccan stories – cunning, humorous, and ironical – reworked by the author of *A High Wind In Jamaica*. Also includes a narrative of Hughes's visit to Telouet and the Atlas in 1928.

Elisa Chimenti, *Tales and Legends of Morocco* (Astor-Honor, $10.95). Traveling in the 1930s and 1940s with her father, personal physician to Sultan Mailay Hassan, Chimenti learned many of these simple, fable-like tales from Berber tribesmen whose guest she was.

Anthony Burgess, *Earthly Powers* (Penguin, UK; oop in the USA), *Enderby* (Norton, $5.95), *Enderby Outside* and *Enderby's Dark Lady* (McGraw, $5.95/$4.95). Sporadic scenes in 1950s-decadent Tangier.

Brion Gysin, *The Process* (Overlook Press, $18.95). Beat novel by ex-Tangier resident and friend of William Burroughs. Fun, if a little caught in its (zany 1960s) age.

Robin Maugham, *The Wrong People* (GMP, UK). Gay classic, set in Tangier.

Elspeth Davie (ed.), *Original Prints Volume II* (Polygon, UK). New writing by Scottish women—includes an excllent account of a Moroccan wedding ("Jamila's Wedding") by Gillean Somerville.

LANGUAGE

Very few people who come to Morocco learn to speak a word of Arabic, let alone anything of the country's three individual Berber dialects. This is a pity—you'll be treated in a very different way if you make even a small effort to master basic phrases—though not really surprising. Moroccans are superb linguists: much of the country is bilingual in French, and anyone who has significant dealings with tourists will know some English and maybe half a dozen other languages, too.

If you can speak **French,** you'll be able to get by almost anywhere you care to go; it is worth refreshing your knowledge before coming—and, if you're not too confident, bringing a good English–French phrasebook. **Spanish** is also useful, and widely understood in the old Spanish colonial zones around Tetouan and the Rif, and in the Deep South.

MOROCCAN ARABIC

Moroccan Arabic, the country's "official" language, is substantially different from "classical" Arabic, or from the modern Arabic spoken in Egypt and the Gulf States. If you speak any form of Arabic, however, you will be able to make yourself understood. Egyptian Arabic, in particular, is familiar to most Moroccans, through soap operas on TV, and many will adapt their speech accordingly.

Pronunciation

There are no silent letters—you pronounce everything that's written. Letters and syllables in italics should be stressed.
Here are some keys to follow in pronouncing:

kh	like the "ch" in Scottish lo*ch*	ay	as in "say"
gh	like the French "r" (a slight gargling sound)	q	like "k" but farther back in throat
ai	as in "eye"	j	like "s" in pleasure

Basics

Yes	*Naham, Ee*yeh	(Very) good	Mizee*yen* (b*zef*)
No	La	Bad	*Me*shee mizee*yen*
Please	Min*fad*lik/ *A*fek	Today	Ly*oom*/ lee*oom*
Thank you	*Sho*kran/ Baraka*lay*fik	Tomorrow	*Gh*edda
(polite response—*Ble*jmeel)			

Greetings and Farewells

Hello	La *bes*	What's yours?	S*mee*tik?
(informal, to one person)		See you later.	N'*shoo*fik min bad
Hello	Sal*am* Wa*lay*koom	... God willing	... In*shall*ah
(formal, to a group; response—Wa*lay*koom sal*am*)		(response to "In*shall*ah" is In*shall*ah)	
Good morning	Sbah l'*khir*	Good night	*Lee*la sa*ee*eda
Good afternoon	Msa l'*khir*	Good-bye	B*sle*mah
My name is	Ismee...	Bon voyage	Treq sa*lama*

Directions, Traveling, and Accommodation

Where is . . . ?	Fayn kayn . . . ?	Here, there	Hnna, Temma
. . . a (good) hotel?	. . . Otel (mizeeyen)	When is the bus/train?	Waqtash l'kar/tren?
. . . a campground?	. . . Mookhaiyem	First/last/next	Loowel/L'akher/Lee minbad
. . . a restaurant?	. . . Restaurant	Write it (please).	Ktib ha (Afek)
. . . a bank?	. . . Bank	Do you have a room?	Wesh andik wahid beet?
. . . the bus station?	. . . Mahatat d'Ikeeran	Can I see it?	Wesh yimkin nshoof?
. . . the train station?	. . . Mahatat d'Itren	Is there. . . ?	Wesh kayn . . . ?
. . . a toilet?	. . . Vaysay/ W.C.	. . . a (hot) shower?	. . . Doosh (skhoon)
Straight	Neesham/ tol	. . . a window?	. . . Serjem
(To the) left, right	(Al) Leeser, Leemin	. . . a key?	. . . Saroot
Near, far	Qreeb, Baieed	Can we camp here?	Wesh yimkin nkhaimoo
Intersection	Rompwa		hanna

Buying and Numbers

How much (is that)?	Bsh hal (hadeek)	I want something. . .	Bgheet shihaja . . .
This isn't good	Hadee meshee mizeeyen	. . . else	. . . okhra
Too expensive	Ghalee bzef	. . . better than this	. . . khir min hadee
. . . (for me)	(aliya)	. . . like this	. . . bhal hadee
Still too expensive	Mazal ghalee bzef	(but)	(walakeen)
Do you have. . . ?	wesh andik. . . ?	. . . larger, smaller	. . . kbeera, sgjeera
Okay	Wakha	. . . cheaper	. . . rkhaysa

1	wahed	12	etnach	50	khamsin
2	tnin (Classical)	13	tlatach	60	settin
	joob (everyday)	14	arbatach	70	seba'in
3	tlata	15	khamstach	80	tmanin
4	arba	16	settach	90	tsa'in
5	khamsa	17	sebatach	100	mia
6	setta	18	tmentach	200	mitin
7	seba	19	tsatach	300	tlata mia
8	tmenia	20	achrin	400	arba mia
9	tse'ud	21	wahed u achrin	1000	alef
10	achra	30	tlatin		
11	hadach	40	arbain		

Reactions, etc.

I've seen it already.	Shift ha badas	Help!	Ateqq/ Ownee!
I don't want any.	Mabgheet shee	How do you say?	Keef tkooloo?
I don't understand.	Mafhemsh	Excuse me	Smeh lee
Do you understand?	Wesh fhemtee?	Sorry, I apologize	Asif
Get lost!	Seer!	Never mind, so it goes	Maalesh
Everything's fine.	Koolshee mizeeyen	No problem	Mush mushkillah
Let's go!	Halla!	Respect yourself	Ihtarim nafsak
Watch out!	Andak/ Balek!	(a term of admonition)	
I've lost . . .	Msha leeya . . .	Calm down	Tawil balak
. . . passport	. . . passeport	(literally, "lengthen your	
. . . ticket	. . . beeyay/ warqa	mind")	
. . . key	. . . saroot	You honor us	Too-shah-rif-na
. . . baggage	. . . baggai/howayj	Patience is a virtue	As-sobrmin Allah

BERBER WORDS AND PHRASES IN TASHELHAÏT

There are three **Berber dialects** which encompass roughly geographical areas. They are known by several names, of which these are the most common:

Riffi—The Rif Mountains and Northern Morocco
Zaian, Tamazight—The Middle Atlas and Central Morocco
Tashelhaït, Soussi, Chleuh—The High and Anti Atlas and the South

As the most popular Berber areas for visitors are the High Atlas and South, the following is a very brief guide to **Tashelhaït words and phrases.**

Basics

Yes, no	Eyeh, Oho	Today	Zig sbah
Thank you, please	Barakalaufik	Tomorrow	Ghasad
Good	Eefulkee/Eeshwa	Yesterday	Eegdam
Bad	Khaib	Excuse me	Semhee
		Berbers	Shleuh

Greetings and Farewells (All Arabic greetings understood)

Hello	La bes darik (man)	See you later	Akrawes dah inshallah
(response—*la bes*)	La bes darim (woman)	Goodbye	Akayaoon Arbee
How are you?	Meneek antgeet?	Say hello to your	Sellum flfamilenik
(response—*la bes Imamdulah*)		family	

Directions and Names on Maps

Where is. . . ?	Mani heela . . . ?	I want to go to . . .	Reeh . . .
. . . the road to . . .	. . . aghares s . . .	(literally, "I want")	
. . . the village . . .	. . . doowar . . .	**On survey maps you'll find these names:**	
. . . the river . . .	. . . aseet . . .	Mountain	Adrar, Jbel
. . . the mountain . . .	. . . adrar . . .	River	Assif, Oued
. . . the pass . . .	. . . tizee . . .	Pass (of)	Tizi (n.)
. . . your house	. . . teegimeenik	Shepherd's hut	Azib
Is it far/close?	Ees yagoog/eeqareb?	Hill, small mountain	Aourir
Straight	Neeshan	Ravine	Talat
To the right/left	Fofaseenik/fozelmad	Rock	Azrou
Where are you going?	Manee treet? (s.)	("n" between words indicates the	
	Manee drem? (pl.)	possessive, "of")	

Buying and Numbers

1	yen	21	Ashreent d yen d mrawet	A lot/little	Bzef/eemeek
2	seen	22	Ashreent d seen d mrawet	Do you have . . . ?	Ees daroon . . . ?
3	krad	30	Ashreent d mrawet	Is there . . . ?	Ees eela . . . ?
4	koz	40	Snet id ashreent	. . . food	. . . teeremt
5	smoos	50	Snet id ashreent d mrawet	. . . a mule	. . . aserdon
6	sddes	100	Smoost id ashreent/meeya	. . . a place to sleep	. . . kra lblast
7	sa				mahengwen
8	tem	How much is it?	Minshk aysker?	. . . water	. . . amen
9	tza	No good	oor eefulkee		
10	mrawet	Too expensive	Eeghula bzef	**Imperatives you may hear**	
11	yen d mrawet	Come down a	Nuqs emeek	Sit	Gawer, Skoos
12	seen d mrawet	little (in price)		Drink	Soo
20	Ashreent	Give me . . .	Feeyee . . .	Eat	Shta
		I want . . .	Reeh . . .	Here	Omz
		Big/Small	Mqorn/Eemzee	(when handing something to someone)	

FRENCH ESSENTIALS

Basics and Greetings

Yes/no	Oui/non	Could you?	Voulez-vous?
Hello, good day	Bonjour	Why?	Pourquoi?
Sorry, excuse me	Pardon	What?	Quoi?
How are you?	Ça va?	Open	Ouvert
Goodbye	Au revoir	Closed	Fermé
Please	S'il vous plait	Go away!	Va-t-en
Thank you	Merci	Stop messing me about!	Arrête de m'emmerder!
I/you	Je/tu	No confidence!	Pas de confiance

Directions

Where is the road for . . . ?	Quelle est la route pour . . . ?	Far	Loin
Where is . . . ?	Où est . . . ?	When?	Quand?
Do you have . . . ?	Avez vous . . . ?	At what time?	A quelle heure?
. . . a room?	. . . une chambre?	Write it down, please	L'écrivez, s'il vous plait
Here, there	Ici, la	Now	Maintenant
Right	A droite	Later	Plus tard
Left	A gauche	Never	Jamais
Straight on	Tout droit	Today	Aujourd'hui
Near	Proche, près	Tomorrow	Demain
		Yesterday	Hier

Things

Bus	Car, autobus	Key	Clef
Bus station	Gare routière	Roof	Terrasse
Railroad	Chemin de fer	Passport	Passeport
Airport	Aeroport	Exchange	Change
Railroad station	Gare	Post office	Poste
Ferry	Ferry	Stamps	Timbres
Truck	Camion	Luggage consignment	Consigne
Ticket (return)	Billet (de retour)	Visa	Visa
Bank	Banque	Money	Argent

Buying

How much/many?	Combien?	Like this/that	Comme ceci/cela
How much does that cost?	Combien ça coute?	What is it?	Qu'est-ce que c'est?
Too expensive	Trop cher	Enough	Assez
More/less	Plus/moin	Big	Grand
Cheap	Bon marché	Little	Petit

ARABIC NUMERALS

١	1	١٠	10	١٩	19	٨٠	80
٢	2	١١	11	٢٠	20	٩٠	90
٣	3	١٢	12	٢١	21	١٠٠	100
٤	4	١٣	13	٢٢	22	٢٠٠	200
٥	5	١٤	14	٣٠	30	٣٠٠	300
٦	6	١٥	15	٤٠	40	٤٠٠	400
٧	7	١٦	16	٥٠	50	١٠٠٠	1000
٨	8	١٧	17	٦٠	60		
٩	9	١٨	18	٧٠	70		

ARABIC/BERBER PHRASEBOOKS AND LEARNING MATERIALS

Arabic Phrasebooks

Lamzoudi, *Guide de Conversation* (Editions El-Atlassi, Casablanca). French–Moroccan Arabic. Not very functional, but the only widely available Moroccan Arabic phrasebook.

(There is no English–Moroccan Arabic phrasebook).

Arabic Coursebooks

Ernest T. Abdel Massih, *An Introduction to Moroccan Arabic* ($18; 3 accompanying tapes, $20); *Advanced Moroccan Arabic* ($15; 4 tapes $32). Both published by University of Michigan Press.

Richard S. Harris and Mohammed Abn Tald, *Basic Course in Moroccan Arabic* (Georgetown Univ. Press, 1980).

Berber Coursebooks

Ernest T. Abdel Massih, *A Course in Spoken Tamazightt: Berber Dialects of the Middle Atlas* ($15; 7 tapes $49); *A Reference Grammer of Tamazight, Plus An Introduction to the Berber Language* ($15). University of Michigan Press.

Arabic Lessons in Morocco

Contact the *American Language Center* (head office: 1 Place de la Fraternité, Casablanca).

University of Michigan Publications.

For **books** write to The Publications Secretary, Center for Near Eastern and North African Studies, 144 Lane Hall, University of Michigan, Ann Arbor, Michigan 48109. For **tapes** write to: Michigan Media Resource Center (Tape Duplication Service), University of Michigan, 400 S. Fourth Street, Ann Arbor, Michigan 48103.

Bookstores

The following bookstores usually have language reference material:

Librairie des Colonnes, Bd. Pasteur, Tangier.

American Language Center Bookstore, Bd. Moulay Youssef, Casablanca.

American Bookstore, Rue Tanja, Rabat.

Crown English Bookstore, Av. Sidi Mohammed, Agadir.

GLOSSARY OF MOROCCAN TERMS

ADHAN the call to prayer

AGADIR fortified granary

AGDAL garden or park containing a pool

AGUELMANE lake

AÏN spring

AÏT tribe (literally, "sons of"); also BENI

ALAOUITE ruling Moroccan dynasty from the seventeenth century to the present king, Hassan II

ALMOHAD the greatest of the medieval dynasties, ruled Morocco (and much of Spain) from ca.1147 until the rise to power of the Merenids ca.1224

ALMORAVIDS dynasty that preceded the Almohads, from ca. 1060 to ca. 1147

ANDALOUS Muslim Spain (a territory that centered on modern Andalucía)

ARABESQUE geometrical decoration or calligraphy

ASIF river that flows throughout the year

BAB gate

BABOUCHES slippers (usually yellow)

BALI (or **QDIM**) old

BARAKA sancity or blessing, obtained through saints or *marabouts*

BARBARY European term for North Africa in the sixteenth–nineteenth centuries

BENI tribe (as Aït)

BERBERS native inhabitants of Morocco, and still the majority of the population

BLED countryside, or, literally "land"; **BLED ES MAKHZEN**—governed lands; **BLED ES SIBA**—land outside government control

BORDJ fort

CAID district administrator; **CADI** is an Islamic judge

CHLEUH southern Berber from the High or Anti-Atlas or plains

COL mountain pass (French)

DAR house or palace; **DAR EL MAKHZEN**, royal palace

DAYA, DEYET lake

DJEBEL mountain; hence **DJEBALI**, someone from the mountains; the **DJEBALA** are the main tribe of the Western Rif

DJEDID, JDID new

DJELLABA wool or cotton hooded outer garment

DJEMAA, JAMAA mosque, or Friday (the main day of worship)

DJINN nature spirits (genies)

ERG sand dune

FAKIR, FKIH Koranic schoolteacher or lawyer, or just an educated man

FANTASIA display of horsemanship performed at larger festivals or *moussems*

FASSI inhabitant of Fes

FILALI alternative name for the Alaouite dynasty—from the southern Tafilalt region

FOKKARA underground irrigation canal

FONDOUK inn and storehouse, known as a *caravanserai* in the eastern part of the Arab world

GANDOURA man's cotton garment (male equivalent of a kaftan)

GHARB coastal plain between Larache and Kenitra

GNAOUA Moroccan black person, originally from Guinea; also a sect, or brotherhood, which plays drum-based trance music

HABBOUS religious foundation or bequest of property for religious charities

HADJ pilgrimage to Mecca

HAMMADA stony desert of the sub-Sahara

HAMMAM Turkish-style steam bath

HARKA "burning" raid undertaken by sultans in order to raise taxes and assert authority

IDRISSID first Arab dynasty of Morocco—named after its founder, Moulay Idriss

IMAM Prayer leader and elder of mosque

ISTIQLAL nationalist party founded during the struggle for independence

JOUTIA flea market

KASBAH palace center and/or fortress of an Arab town; also a feudal family castle in the south. Like the Spanish *alcazar*

KIF hashish, cannabis

KOUBBA dome; small *marabout* tomb

KSAR, KSOUR (pl.) village or tribal stronghold in the south

LALLA "madam"

LITHAM veil

MAGHREB "West" in Arabic, used for Morocco and the North African countries

MAKHZEN government

MARABOUT holy man, and by extension his place of burial. These tombs, usually white-washed domes, play an important (and unorthodox) role in the religion of country Berber areas.

MECHOUAR assembly place, court of judgment

MEDINA literally, "city," now used for the original Arab part of any Moroccan town. The Kasbah is usually a quarter of the Medina.

MELLAH Jewish quarter

MEDERSA student residence and, in part, a teaching annex, for the old mosque universities

MERENIDS dynasty from eastern plains who ruled from the thirteenth to fifteenth centuries

MIHRAB niche indicating the direction of Mecca (and for prayer)

MINARET tower attached to a mosque, used for call to prayer

MINZAH pavilion in a (usually palace) garden

MOULAY descendant of the Prophet Muhammad, a claim and title adopted by most Moroccan sultans

MOULOUD festival and birthday of the Prophet

MOUSSEM pilgrimage-festival

MSALLA prayer area

MUEZZIN, MUEDDIN singer who calls the faithful to prayer

NAZARENE, NSRANI Christian

OUED river; also **ASRIR**

PISÉ mud and rubble building material

PISTE rough road

PROTECTORATE period of French and Spanish colonial occupation (1912–56)

QAHOUAJI café patron

RAMADAN month of fasting

RAS source

RAS EL MA water source

RIBAT monastic fortress

SAADIAN southern dynasty from Drâa valley, who ruled Morocco during the fifteenth century

SEBGHA lake or lagoon

SEGUIA irrigation canal

SHEIKH leader of religius brotherhood

SHEREEF descendant of the Prophet

SIDI, SI respectful title used for any man, like "Sir" or "Mister"

SOUK market, or market quarter

SUFI religious mystic; philosophy behind most of the religious brotherhoods

TABIA mud building material, as *pisé*

TIGHREMT similar to an *agadir*—fortified Berber home and storage place

TOUAREG nomadic Berber tribesmen of the disputed Western Sahara, fancifully known as "Blue Men" because of the blue dye of their cloaks (which gives a slight tinge to their skin)

TIZI mountain pass; as COL in French

WATTASID fifteenth century dynasty who replaced their cousins, the Merenids

ZAOUIA sanctuary established around a *marabout*'s tomb; seminary-type base for religious brotherhood

ZELLIJ geometrical mosaic tilework

INDEX

Abbtih 355
Abbaynou 351
Abd el Krim 90–91, 370
Accommodation 22–23
Adai 348
Ad Dakhla 356-7
Addresses 38
Afensou 286, 287
Agadir 324–329
Agard Oudad 348
Agdz 296–7, 301
Agoudal 310
Agoundis valley 273, 276–7
Aguelmane Azigza 168
Aguelmane Sidi Ali 169
Aguensioual 272
Aguersaffen 286
Ahemur 348
Aïd el Kebir 29
Aïd es Seghir 29
Aïn Leuh 168
Aït Arbi 304
Aït Baha 346
Aït Benhaddou 282, 295–6
Aït Benimathar 321
Aït Boukha 351
Aït Driss valley 287
Aït Hani 308–309, 310
Aït Kherrou 177
Aït Mehammed 175
Aït Menad 266
Aït Messaoud 171
Aït Oudinar 304
Aït Saoun 296
Aït Taleb 347–8
Aït Youb 277
Ajmou n'Aït Ali ou Hasso 266
Akhfamane 338
Akka 340
Aknoul 93
Alaouite dynasty 367–375
Algeria, entry to 107–108, 320, 396–7
Al Hoceima 98–99
Al Hoceima–Ketama/Chaouen 90–93
Al Hoceima–Oujda 99–104
Almohad dynasty 277–278, 364–365
Almoravid dynasty 364–365
Alnif 301

Amassene 298
Amazrou 264
Ameln valley 347–348
American Express agencies 12
Amizmiz 261
Ammassene 338
Amsouzerte 270, 338
Amtoudi 341
Amemiter 283
Anemour 307
Anti Atlas 322–349
Aoufouss 315
Aoulouz 338
Architectural chronology 376–377
Aremd 268
Arg 272, 277
Argan trees 330
Arhbala 172, 311
Arhbalou 259
Arhbar 301
Around (see Aremd)
Asilah 64–66
   International Festival 32
Asni 266
Assarag 338
Atougha 338
Azilal 174
Azrou 166–167
Azrou–Midelt/Er Rachidia 169–171
Azrou–Fes 165–166
Azrou–Marrakesh 171–176
Azzemour 215

Bab Berred 91
Bab Taza 90
Baggage 38
Banana village 331
Banks 12
Bargaining 34
Bars 18
BBC World Service 18
Beer 26
Beni Mellal 172–173
Beni Ounif (Algeria) 320
Beni Snassen mountains 103
Berber language 404
Berkane 104
Bin el Ouidane 174
Books on Morocco 398–401
Boudenib 321
Bou Goumez valley 175
Bou Izakarn 342
Boujdor 356

Boukra 355
Boumalne du Dades 303–304
Bouarfa 321
Bouzmou 274
Bowles, Paul 392–395, 398, 400–401
Brotherhoods 379–380
Buses 19

Cabo Negro 79
Campgrounds 23
Canary Islands 397
Canetti, Elias 391–392, 398
Cannabis 27–28
Cap Malabata 64
Cap Sim 222
Cap Spartel 63
Car rental 20
Carpets 33
CASABLANCA (Dar el Baida) 202–211
  Aïn Diab 209
  Arriving 203, 206
  Beach 209
  Directory 211
  Eating and Nightlife 210
  Habbous 208
  Hassan II Mosque 207–208
  History 202–203
  Hotels 206–207
  New Medina 208
  Old Medina 209
  Ville Nouvelle 207–209
Casablanca–Rabat 201–202
Cascades d'Ouzoud 173–174
Cascades de Ras el Oued 97
Ceuta 70–72
  Border 70–71
Ceuta–Tangier (coast) 64
Ceuta–Tetouan (coast) 78–79
Chichaoua 285
Chaouen 80–84
Chaouen–Ketama/Al Hoceima 90–93
Chefchaouen (See Chaouen)
Cherket 311
Chiker lake 97
Cirque Jaffar 175
Chronology 376–377
City transit 21
Climate, see Introduction
Clothes, Moroccan 33
Consulates in Morocco 38, 196
Consulates, Moroccan Overseas 10
Contraceptives 38
Costs 11

Cotta (Roman site) 64
Crafts 33–34
Credit cards 12
CTM buses 19
Currency 11
Customs regulations 38

Dades gorge 304–305, 309–310
Dades valley 302–312
Dar Caid Hadji 218
Dar Caid Ouriki 218, 259
Dar Tahar Ben Abbou 249
Dayet Aouwa 165
Dchira 355
Deep South 324, 351–357
Demnate 175
Diabat 222
Djebel Anngour 272
Djebel Awlim 287
Djebel Erdouz 277
Djebel Igdat 277
Djebel Ougnat 266
Djebel Sahro 296
Djebel Siroua 337
Djebel Tazzeka 97–98
Djebel Tinerghwet 287
Djebel Toubkal 262–272
Djebel Yagour 260
Djebel Zagora 265
Drâa valley 291–301
Drinks 26
Drugs regulations 23
Driving to Morocco 8
Driving within Morocco 20

Ech Chiana 202
El Ayoun (see Laayoune)
Electrical voltage 38
El Jadida 211–214
El Jadida–Essaouira 215–218
El Jebha 93
El Kelâa des Mgouna 303
El Khemis 93
El Ksiba 172
El Makhzen 276
Enjil des Ikhatarn 98
Erfoud 315
Erfoud–Er Rachidia 314–315
Erfoud–Rissani/Merzouga 315–317
Erg Cherbi 317
Erg Lakhbayta 355
Er Rachidia 313–314
Er Rachidia–Erfoud 315–317

Er Rachidia–Figuig 318
Er Rachidia–Midelt/Azrou 170–171
Essaouira 218–222
Essaouira–El Jadida 215–218
Expedition vacations 7

Ferries to Morocco 9
FES 129–161
  Andalous mosque 154–155
  Andalous quarter 155
  Arriving 132
  Attarin medersa148–149
  Attarin souk 148–150
  Bab Boujeloud 139
  Bou Inania water-clock 144
  Bou Inania medersa 149
  Cherabliyyin mosque 145
  Cherratin medersa 151
  Dar Batha museum 139–142
  Dar el Makhzen 158
  Dar Saada 152
  Dyers' souk 151
  Eating and Drinking 159–160
  Fes el Bali 138–155
  Fes el Djedid 155–158
  History 130–131
  Hotels 135–137
  Kairaouine mosque 147–148, 149
  Kissaria 152
  Mechouar 157
  Mellah 157–158
  Merenid tombs 138–139, 157
  Misbahiya medersa 149
  Nejjarin souk 147
  Palais de Fes 149
  Palais Jamai hotel 137, 153
  Place des Alaouites 158
  Potters' quarter 155
  Seffarin medersa 150–151
  Talâa Kebira 144–146
  Tanneries 151–152
  Ville Nouvelle 158–161
  Zaouia Moulay Idriss 146
Fes–Azrou/Marrakesh 161–176
Fes–Ketama 93
Fes el Bali (village) 93
Festivals 28–32
Fiction, Moroccan 400–401
Figuig 318–320
Border 320
Figuig–Algeria 320
Figuig–Er Rachidia 318
Figuig–Oujda 107

Flights to Morocco
  From Canada 5
  From the USA 3–4
  Via Britain 6
Flights within Morocco 21
Folklore Festival of Marrakesh 32
Food 23–26
Foum El Hassan 340
Foum Zguid 301, 342
Foum Zguid–Tata 342
Foum Zguid–Zagora 301
Freija 339
French, Colonization and Protectorate 369–371
Friouato caves 97

Gays, attitudes/laws 38
Gendarmerie 38
Glaoui, T'Hami el 281–282, 371
Glossary of Moroccan terms 407–409
Goulimine 350–351
Goulimine–Sidi Ifni 348–349
Goulimine–Tan Tan/Laayoune 351–355
Goulmina 311
Goumarra 321
Goundafi kasbahs 279–280
Grands taxis 18
Green March 373
Grotte du Chameau 103
Guelta Zemmour 355
Guides 16–17
Guiliz 338

Hammams 23
Harris, Walter 390–391, 398
Hashish 22–23
Hassan II 372–375
Health 13
High Atlas 257–288
  Crossing 308–309
Hiking 20, 262–263
Hiking tours 7
Hiking maps 16
History of Morocco 361–375
Hitching to Morocco 8
Hitching within Morocco 19
Homosexuality 38
Hospitals 38
Hotels, categories 22–23
Hustlers 16–17

Ibn Toumert 277–278, 364
Id Aïssa (see Amtoudi)

Idni 275
Idrissid dynasty 363–364
Ifouriren 277
Ifrane (Middle Atlas) 165–166
Ifrane de l'Anti Atlas 341–342
Igherm (Anti Atlas) 339
Iguissel 351
Ijoukak 275, 276–277
Ikiss 272
Imi n'Tanoute 285
Imilchil 310, 311
Imlil (Imi n'Tanoute) 242
Imlil (Toubkal) 267
Immouzer des Ida Outanane 332
Immouzer du Kandar 165
Independence struggle 370–371
   Riffian revolt 90–91
Inezgane 329–330
Inoculations 13
Insurance, Health/Travel 14
Irherm (Tizi n'Tishka) 282
Islam 378–81
   Origins 362–363
Itzer 169

Jardins Exotiques 200
Jewelry 33

Kalah Iris 92
Kariet Arkmane 100
Kâaseras 79
Kasba Hamidouch 218
Kasba Tadla 172
Kenitra 201
Kenitra–Rabat 200–201
Ketama 91–92
Ketama–Al Hoceima 90–93
Ketama–Chaouen 90–91
Ketama–Fes 93
Khenifra 171–172
Khenifra–Tinerhir 307–311
Kif 27–28, 91–92
Khmiss lagoon 355
Kik plateau 275
Ksar el Kebir 69
Ksar es Seghir 64
Ksour 297

Laayoune 356
Lac d'Ifni 269–270
Lac Ouiouane 168
Lalla Fatma 218

Languages 402–406
   Arabic 402–403
   Berber 404
   French 406
Larache 66–67
Laundromats 38
Layoune, see Laayoune
Lepiney refuge 273
Lixus (Ancient Site) 67–68

Majoun 28
Maps 15–16
Marabouts 379–380
Markets 33–34
MARRAKESH (Marrakech) 226–257
   Agdal gardens 252
   Almoravid koubba 242
   Arriving 231
   Ben Youssef medersa 240–241
   Dar el Glaoui 244
   Dar Si-Said 251
   Directory 256–257
   Djemaa el Fna 234–235
   Eating and Drinking 254–255
   El Badi palace 247–249
   El Bahia palace 250–251
   Folklore Festival 256
   History 227–230
   Hotels 231–233
   Koutoubia mosque 236
   Majorelle gardens 253
   Mamounia Hôtel 233, 253–254
   Mellah 249–250
   Menara gardens 253
   Palmery 253
   Saadian tombs 244–247
   Sidi Bel Abbes Zaouia 243
   Souks 236–240
   Tanneries 242
   Transit 257
Marrakesh–Agadir 171–173
Marrakesh–Azrou 175–176
Marrakesh–Ouzarzate 279–284
Marrakesh–Taroudannt 273–279
Martil 78–79
Massa 332–333
Massif du Kandar 164
Mazagan (see El Jadida)
Mdiq 79
Meakin, Budgett 388–389, 398
Medersas, Development in Fes 143
Meghraoua 97
Mehdiya Plage 201

MEKNES 112–123
Arriving 112
Bab Mansour 117
Bou Inania medersa 117
Dar Jamai 120
Dar el Kebira 119
Dar el Makhzen 119
Directory 116
Eating and Drinking 113–114
Heri as-Souani 119
History 116
Hotels 113
Imperial City 116–120
Medina 120–123
Moulay Ismail mausoleum 118
Rouah 120
Sidi Ben Aissa Moussem 31
Souks 121–122
Ville Nouvelle 116
Melilla 101–103
Border 102–103
Mellab 312
Merenid dynasty 365–366
Merzouga 317–318
Meski 314
M'Hamid 299–300
Midelt 169
Midelt–Er Rachidia 170–171
Middle Atlas 109–175
Mirhleft 349
Mischliffen 166
Mogador (see Essaouira)
Mohammed V 370–372
Mohammedia 202
Money 11
Mont Araoui 100
Monuments 34–35
Moroccan Tourist Board (ONMT) 15
Mosques 34
Moulay Abdallah 214
Moulay Bousselham 69–70
Moulay Idriss 123, 128–129
Moulay Idriss 128, 363
Moulay Ismail 116, 367–368
Moulay Yacoub 162
Mouloud 30
Moussems 30–32
Msemrir 305
Music 382–387
Mzouzite 277, 286

Nador 99–100
Nador–Oujda 103–104

Neltner refuge 269
Nfis river 275, 276–277, 286

ONMT (tourist board) 15
Oualidia 216
Ouaouizarnt 175
Ouarzazate 293–295
Ouarzazate–Tinerhir 302–305
Ouarzazate–Zagora 296–297
Oued Laou 79
Ouezzane 84–85
Ougdemt valley 277
Ouirgane 274–275
Oujda 104–108
Border 107–108
Oujda–Algeria 107–108
Oujda–Nador 103–104
Oukaïmeden 260
Oum er Rbia, Sources 168
Oumesnat 347
Ourika valley 258–261

Paradise valley 331–332
Petits taxis 21
Pharmacies 13
Phonecalls 27
Plage des Nations 200–201
Plage Sidi Ouafi 214
Plateau des Lacs 310, 311
Police 21, 38
Poste restante 27
Postal services 27
Public holidays 29

RABAT 180–196
Archaeological Museum 193
Arriving 181
Buses 181
Bab er Rouah 192
Chellah 192–194
Consulates 196
Eating and Drinking 195
Hassan Mosque and Tower 190–191
History 180–181
Hotels 184–185
Kasbah des Oudaias 187–189
Medina 185–187
Mohammed V Mausoleum 191
Mellah 186
Museum of Moroccan Arts 190
Souks 186
Ville Nouvelle 99

Rabat–Casablanca 201–202
Rabat–Kenitra 200–201
Rafsaï 93
Ramadan 29–30
Ras el Ma (Nador: see Ras-ka-Bona)
Ras-ka-Bona 100
Relationships with Moroccans 38
Restinga–Smir 79
Rich 171
Rif, The 87–103
Rissani 316–317
Rissani–Erfoud 315–317
Rissani–Merzouga 317
Rissani–Zagora 317
Roman Morocco 362
Route de l'Unité 93

Saadian dynasty 366–367
Safi 216–218
Saïdia 104
Salé 196–200
Sebta (see Ceuta)
Sefrou 162–164
Setti Fatma 259–260
Sexual harassment 35–38
Sidi Abdallah des Rhiata 98
Sidi Bouchta 216
Sidi Bouknadel 200–210
Sidi Bouzid 218
Sidi Chamharouch 268, 270
Sidi Harazem 162
Sidi Ifni 348–350
Sidi Moussa d'Aglou 344
Sidi Rahhal 175
Sidi Rbat 332–333
Sidi Yahia 106–107
Sijilmassa 316–317
Skhirat 202
Skhirat Plage 202
Skiing 39, 261
Smara 355
Skoura 302–303
Souira Kedima 218
Souk El Arba du Rharb 69
Souk El Had Arfallah Irhir 348
Souk El Khemis (W. High Atlas) 286
Souk Sebt Talmakent 287
Souk Sebt Tamammert 286
Souk Tnine d'Adad 341
Souks 33–34
Spanish Colonization and Protectorate 369–370
Sûreté Nationale 38
Swimming pools 39

Tabia 338
Tachedirrt 260, 261, 270–271
Taddert 282
Tafilalt 312–318
Taforalt 103
Tafrant 338
Tafraoute 345–348
Tafraoute–Agadir 346
Tafraoute–Tiznit 345
Taghagant (see Tarhazoute)
Taghbart 276
Talâat n'Yacoub 279–280
Taliouine 336
Taliouine–Taroudannt 336
Talzemt 97
Tamda 175
Tamegroute 300
Tamgout 338
Tamguememt 282
Tamjlocht 287
Tamnalt 304
Tamnougalt 297
Tampons 39
Tamtatouchte 309
TANGIER (Tangiers) 45–64
   Arriving 46
   Beach 52, 63
   Caves of Hercules 63
   Directory 60–62
   Eating and Drinking 58–59
   Ferries 46, 62
   Hotels 50–51
   Kasbah 56–57
   Leaving 61
   Medina 54–56
   Mountain, The 63
   Palace 56
   Petit Socco 54
   Shopping 59–60
   Ville Nouvelle 52–53
Tangier–Ceuta (coast) 45
Tansikht 301
Tan Tan 354
Tan Tan Plage 354
Tan Tan–Goulimine 351–354
Tan Tan–Laayoune 355–356
Taounate 93
Taourirt 97
Tarfaya 355
Targuist 92
Tarhazoute 330–331
Tarhijt 341
Taroudannt 333–335

Taroudannt–Taliouine 336
Taroudannt–Tata 338–343
Tashelhaïtt (language) 404
Tata 339–340
Tata–Foum Zguid 302–303
Tata–Taroudannt 338–343
Tata–Tiznit 338–343
Taxis 18, 21
Taza 94–97
Tazaghârrt 273
Tazenakht 301
Tazzarine 301
Tazzerte 175
Telouet 280–282
Temara 201
Temara Plage 201
Tendrara 320
Tetouan 73–79
　Arriving 73
　Beaches 78–79
　Eating 76
　Hotels 75–76
　Medina 76–78
　Museum of Moroccan Arts 77
　Ville Nouvelle 78
Tetouan–Ceuta (coast) 78–79
Tichka plateau 286–288
Tifnite 352
Tifoultoutte 295
Tijrhicht 276
Timichi 271
Timiderte 297
Time 39
Timersgadiouine 286
Timoulay 341
Tinejdad 312
Tinerhir 305–306
Tinerhir–Imilchil/Khenifra 307–311
Tinerhir–Ouazarzate 302–305
Tinerhourine 272
Tinfou 299, 300
Tin Mal mosue 277–279
Tinzouline 297
Tioute 339
Tissaldai 270
Tislit 338
Tit 214
Tizi n'Aguensioual 272
Tizi n'Likemt 270

Tozi Mâachou 284–285
Tizi n'Ouanoumss 269
Tizi Oussem 273
Tizi Ouzla 275
Tizi n'Tabghourt 286
Tizi n'Talrhment 170
Tizi n'Test 273–280
Tizi n'Tichka 280–284
Tizi n'Tierherhouzine 310
Tizi n'Timirout 287
Tizi n'Tinififft 296
Tizi n'Wannas 287
Tiznit 343–344
Tiznit–Tafraoute 345
Tiznit–Tata 338–343
Tizza 287
Tleta Ketama 92
Tleta n'Tagmoute 339
Todra gorge 306–311
Torres de Alcala 92
Toubkal national park 263–276
Trains to Morocco 6–7
Trains within Morocco 18
Travelers' checks 12
Trucks 19
Tunisia, Entry to 397

Volubilis 123–127
Visas, renewals 10

Xaouen (See Chaouen)

Water 13
Wattasid dynasty 366
Western High Atlas 284–287
Western Sahara 324, 351–357
Woman's perspective 35–37
Work 39
Workcamps 39

Zagora 297–299
Zagora–Foum Zguid 301
Zagora–Ouarzazate 296–297
Zagora–Rissani 317
Zaouia Ahanesal 175
Zaouia Temga 175
Zegzel gorge 103
Ziz gorge 171, 314

MAP INDEX

General maps of Morocco
The Country iv
Road/Rail Networks vi–vii
The Chapter Regions 41

Chapter Regions
Tangier, Tetouan, and the Northwest 44
The Rif Mountains and Mediterranean
  Coast 88-89
Rabat to Essaouira: the West Coast 179–179
Fes, Meknes, and the Middle Atlas 110–111
Marrakesh and the High Atlas 224–225
The Southern Oasis Routes 290–291
Agadir and the Anti Atlas 323
The Deep South 353

Cities or Individual Regions
Agadir 327
Casablanca 204–205
Cascades d'Ouzoud 173
Ceuta 71
Chaouen 81
Djebel Siroua 337
Djebel Toubkal National Park 264–265
El Jadida 213
Essaouira 219

Fes
  Fes El Bali 140–141
  Fes Djedid and Ville Nouvelle 132–133
  Bab Boujeloud area 136
Figuig Oasis 319
Ifrane de l'Anti Atlas 341
Marrakesh
  General map 228–229
  Souks 238
  Lower medina 245
Meknes
  General map 114–115
  Medina 121
Melilla 101
Oujda 105
Rabat
  General map 182–183
  Kasbah des Oudaias 188
  Chellah 193
Safi 217
Salé 197
Sefrou 163
Tafraoute and the Ameln Valley 346
Tangier
  General map 48–49
  Medina and Kasbah 55
Taza 95
Tetouan 74
Todra Gorge—and Over the High Atlas 307
Volubilis 125
Western High Atlas 284–285

HELP US UPDATE

We've gone to great lengths to ensure that this first edition of *The Real Guide: Morocco* is completely up-to-date and accurate. But Moroccan information changes fast; hotels and restaurants open and close, standards rise and fall, roads get washed away, buses change their terminals, all with chaotic frequency.

If you feel there are places we've overrated or underpraised, or find we've missed something or covered something which no longer exists, then please write and tell us about it. Letters about obscure routes through the mountains and desert are as interesting as the low-down on your favorite nightclub, hotel or restaurant.

We'll acknowledge all information used in the next edition (already being compiled) and will send a **free copy**, or any other *Real Guide* if you prefer, to the most useful (and legible!) letters. Send them along to:

Mark Ellingham, The Real Guides, Prentice Hall Trade Division, A Division of Simon and Schuster Inc., 15 Columbus Circle, New York, NY 10023.